Those

Roving

Rittgers

VOLUME ONE

Joyce Rorabaugh

HERITAGE BOOKS

2015

HERITAGE BOOKS

AN IMPRINT OF HERITAGE BOOKS, INC.

Books, CDs, and more—Worldwide

For our listing of thousands of titles see our website
at
www.HeritageBooks.com

Published 2015 by
HERITAGE BOOKS, INC.
Publishing Division
5810 Ruatan Street
Berwyn Heights, Md. 20740

International Standard Book Numbers
Paperbound: 978-0-7884-0977-6
Clothbound: 978-0-7884-6129-3

TABLE OF CONTENTS

Reading This Book

If, while reading the following pages of this book, the reader will keep these few facts in mind, a much clearer understanding of the contents will result. The format or style used in this book is known as the **Modified Register System,** which has been refined by the National Genealogical Society.

Two types of numbers are used: one to uniquely identify the individual, and one to indicate the generation into which that person falls. The identification numbering system used in this book is called **The Henry System**. The starting person is .X, his first child is .X1. A digit or letter is added for each generation that a person represents, with his numerical value reflecting birth-order within the nuclear family. In large families, the numerical value of 10, 11, 12, etc., is replaced with the letter A, B, C, etc.

When an individual is introduced in his/her separate sketch, the name appears in boldface letters with the surnames in all capital letters. The name is preceded by the identification number. The last given name is followed immediately by a superscript number indicating the number of generations from the starting individual in this book. In parentheses following the name is a list of direct ancestors back to the starting individual. Only the given name is listed, followed by the generation number in superscript.

When the list of children is presented, the plus (+) sign indicates that more about this child will be presented in his/her separate sketch. The ID number is printed, followed by the name is followed by the birth and death dates.

The term "Spouse" may have several different meanings: husband, wife, partner, mate, parent, or significant other. The couple involved may not be legally married. The term "stepchild" may have several different meanings: the child may be a stepchild, adopted child, foster child, or just raised in the home. If there are any other children of the spouse, they will be designated as stepchildren.

The index is arranged alphabetically by surname. Under each surname, the given names are alphabetically arranged. The number to the right indicates the page where this name appears. The wife appears under her maiden name and under her married names with her maiden name in parentheses.

Acknowledgments

We were strangers to this family, having descended from a "Roving" line, but now we have walked on the land and felt the soil. Our eyes have been dazzled by the shades of green on corn stalks taller than our heads. We have dined on produce from the land owned by the family for 150 years. We have visited the ancestors as they lay at their final rest in a shaded field on that land, and talked to the descendants who knew them. We have listened to stories of triumphs and failures, long days of manual labor, family gatherings, births and deaths, stories told with love and pride. Now we are not strangers, we are family.

In calling this Vol. I, it is our hope that "roving" cousins will submit their family information to be included in a Vol. II. If you are a Rittgers descendant, even if your name isn't Rittgers but you are descended from a female line, please submit your information to this author. Include names, dates, places, and a few lines about yourself and your family such as interests, occupations, past times, anything that you would like to share with the family. Please do not send original documents. If you have any old obituaries, pictures, or family papers you would like to submit, please send a photocopy. Make sure we have your current address if you would like to be put on a family mailing list. This will not be released to outside solicitors, but will be used to inform you of family reunions and data updates.

Send submissions to : Joyce Rorabaugh
3562 Manatee Rd.
Tavares, Fla. 32778-4884

Many family members have submitted research to this project. It would be a dull tome, indeed, without the stories and data others have taken the time to pursue.

Anna Lou (Peacock) Arnett has researched the Chillicothe Land records, and has sent in innumerable "tidbits"of information she has located in Ohio and Missouri.

Laura (Rittgers)(Peitzman) Emmert submitted two handwritten spiral-bound notebooks full of names and dates, apparently gathered at various family reunions over the years. Several entries had her notations and "remembrances" of her personal family stories.

The late Charles Roberts and wife Mary Ann (Rittgers)(Bowen) Roberts have submitted data base information, as well as Rittgers Family Cemetery information.

Jon Findley has furnished much of the information on the Findley branches, as well as several family stories on these lines.

A very special THANK YOU goes out to the family of Clarence Rittgers. They live on part of the original Rittgers purchase in Johnston, Ia., and continue to farm it. He has maintained the family cemetery for several years. Wife Mary (Noonan) and daughter Mary Esther are referred to in this volume as the "Rittgers super-sleuths." They trekked into the Shenandoah Valley and located a lot of information about the Comer family and our ancestral grand-mother, Catherine. The family not only work on the ancestral lines, but have been active in maintaining the family reunions. Son Parker is hard at work trying to locate "roving" cousins and bring them back into the fold by way of a newsletter and a more expanded format for the family reunions. On a research trip to Iowa this author was a guest in their home, an experience that will long be warmly remembered. They are true experts in "Family."

Introduction to Sources

Those enemies of us all, Time, Distance, and Money, have conspired to make this genealogy no more than a stepping stone for you to research your Rittgers family. It is impossible for one person to check every reference and every vital record in all the areas the family has migrated from and to. When you read information given without source, it was taken from the submitted family records. Keep in mind that the information was mostly gathered first hand, probably told to the compiler by the person himself. But also keep in mind that the information was recopied unknown times before being submitted to this author. It is easy for errors, such as transposed numbers, to have happened. Each researcher needs to accept this information only as a guide to finding the original record. Any record this author has viewed personally will be followed by a notation containing a key to the source, followed by individual book or page number in brackets [ ]. To find out more about that source, refer to the following list.

Our largest source of information has been the United States Census. This is taken every ten years and shows different information each census. From 1790 to 1840, only heads of household were listed, with others in the home listed only by age and gender. Starting in 1850, everyone in the home was listed, including servants and "laborers." The 1890 census was almost totally lost in a fire in Washington, but there are projects underway in many areas to try to compile listings of residents based on tax records and other sources. The last census released for public use is the 1920 census. There is a 72 year privacy law that prohibits release of later U.S. Federal census reports. The 1930 census is due to be released in 2002. A word of caution about census records: they are notoriously full of errors! Often the census taker was chosen because they had some reading and writing skill. They dutifully reported what was told to them by whomever was answering the questions, so the record is only as it was reported. Another problem is that many people speaking to the recorder had foreign accents and poor English language skills, so their name was recorded phonetically. Ages were confused and numbers mis-quoted, so these records are by no means a primary source. It was not unusual for a family to get overlooked on a census. They may have been migrating or living in a remote area. Their entry could have been missed when the record was copied. When you do find your family, it will give you enough information to pursue the vital records. Microfilmed copies of the census are located in regional or state archives, in most large libraries, or can be rented from several genealogical suppliers or from the LDS Family History Center. To locate an ancestor on the census reels, first find the year, then the state, then the county. In the bracketed reference the page and other locator data will be given.

In the Iowa State Genealogical Soc., Des Moines, Ia., we find three state census'.
1856: 1856 State Census, transcribed by the Iowa Pioneer Sons and Daughters, published by the Ia. Gen. Soc., 1994. A copy also in the State Historical Library, Des Moines.
1885: On microfilm in the Ia. Gen. Soc., Des Moines, reel #71. Several townships missing, including Valley Twp., where many of our family lived.
1895: 1895 State Census, Webster Twp., Pok Co., Ia. Transcribed by Laura Olmstead Jennings, transcript also in the Iowa Historical Library, Des Moines.
The following sources are listed alphabetically by the bracketed source tag following the entry quoted:

ABST 62638: AMERICAN ABSTRACT CO.; Des Moines, Ia.; abstract of land included in "Estate of J[acob] Rittgers (#1.2); being Lot 9, sect. 6, Twp. 79 N., Range 24 West;" entries submitted from 30 Oct 1848 to 20 Jan 1964.

ABST 76811: PEOPLES ABSTRACT CO.; Des Moines, Ia.; abstract of land known as "Rittgers Acres", lots 1,2,3,4,5,6, and lots A, B, C, section 6, Twp. 79 N., Range 24 West., entries from 30 Oct 1848 to 26 may 1939. This property settled by Daniel Rittgers (#1.6)

Arnett: Information and family group sheets submitted by Anna Lou (Peacock) Arnett.

Berens: Family group sheets, descendency of Susanna Rittgers, #1.9, with documentation from the church records of [St. James] and from St. Trinity (Sponagle) Church in Fairfield Co., Oh., submitted 1997.

Bigham: Family group sheets on the Grove family line from Robert Bigham., submitted 1997.

BPTx: BOONE CO., IA., POLL TAX LIST; compiled by Boone Co. Gen. Soc., typed manuscript in the Iowa State Historical Society, Des Moines, Ia.

Bright: Bright, Rev. Dean, W.; FAMILY OF GEORGE & LANNIE BRIGHT and RELATED FAMILIES; 1978; Manuscript in the Hocking Co., Public Library, Logan, Oh.

DalCem: DALLAS CO. CEMETERIES, VOL VI; Sugar Grove Twp.; pub. By Iowa Gen. Soc.; copy in the State Historical Society, Des Moines, Ia.

DDBible: Gorenson, Rita, and Burgess, JoAnn; MISC. IOWA RECORDS, VOL I; Denny- Dunn Bible, p. 1.

DKCoM1: DARKE CO., OHIO, MARRIAGES, 1851-1898; compiled by the Darke Co. Gen. Soc., a chapter of the Ohio Genealogical Society; a printed copy located in the Sherman room of the Mansfield Public Library, Mansfield, Oh.

DKCoM2: DARKE CO., OH., MARRIAGES, 1899-1911; excerpts extracted by Anna Lou Arnett.

DVRB: Dallas Co., Ia., Birth Records, located in the Dallas Co. Courthouse, Adel, Ia.

DVRM: Dallas Co., Ia., Marriage Records, Dallas Co. Courthouse, Adel, Ia.

Dunn: Bunz, Doris; OBITUARY NAME & DATE ABSTRACTS FROM THE DORIS B. DUNN COLLECTION, POLK CO., IA.; Ankeny, Ia., 1976. Bound manuscript in Ia. Historical Society, Des Moines, Ia.

EmEv: CHURCHBOOK OF THE EMMANUEL EVANGELICAL LUTHERAN CONGREGATION; Marion Twp. Hocking Co., Oh., transcribed by Fairfield co. Chapter of the Ohio Gen. Soc; copy found in the Ohio Genealogical society, Mansfield, Oh.

FCoD: CEMETERIES OF RUSH CREEK TWP., FAIRFIELD CO., OH; transcribed by the Fairfield Co., a copy of transcript in the Ohio Gen. Soc., Mansfield, Oh.

FCoM: FAIRFIELD CO. BOOK OF MARRIAGES, 1803-1865; a typed transcript photocopied and in the Ohio Gen. Soc., Mansfield, Oh.

FDeeds: Fairfield Co. Book of Deeds, Fairfield Co. Courthouse, Lancaster, Oh.

FOFH: FISHER-OLIVER FUNERAL HOME RECORDS, ANSONIA, OH., 1908-1939; transcribed by Darke Co., Oh., Genealogical Soc.,a copy found in the Ohio Gen. Soc., Mansfield, Oh.

FVRM: Fairfield Co., Oh., Vital Records, Marriages, Fairfield Co. Courthouse, Lancaster, Oh.,

GPCem: SUNNY HILL CEMETERY; Grimes, Webster Twp., Polk Co., Ia.; from a list compiled by the Iowa Gen. Soc.; manuscript found in the Iowa Historical Soc., Des Moines, Ia.

Hartman: Hartman, Karen (Peacock); HISTORY OF RANDOLPH CO., IND., 1818-1990; page 626, photocopy of article submitted with no further information on the book.

HVRD: Book 1 of Deaths; Hocking Co., Oh.; located in the Hocking Co. Courthouse, Logan, Oh.

HVRM: Hocking Co., Marriage Records, Hocking Co. Courthouse, Logan, Oh.

HCoCem: HOCKING COUNTY, OHIO, CEMETERIES, transcript in the Hocking Co. Library, Logan, Oh., transcribed by the Hocking Co. Genealogical Soc.

Kocher: Kocher, L. Richard; SECTION MAPS WITH ENTRYMAN ON LANDS IN HOCKING CO., OH.; Ohio Gen. Soc., 1992; copy in Ohio Gen. Soc., Mansfield, Oh.

LDS-IGI: Latter Day Saints Church (Mormon) Family History Center records; information needs to be researched, as no documentation on the microfiche. This information is often submitted by researchers, and is known to contain many errors.

MPCem: MCDIVITT CEMETERY RECORDS, Johnston, Polk Co., Ia.; transcribed by Polk Co. Gen. Soc.; manuscript in the Iowa Historical Soc., Des Moines, Ia.

PCC: POLK CO., IA., CEMETERIES; transcribed by Polk Co. Gen. Soc., Des Moines, Ia.

PDeed: Polk Co., Books of Deeds, Polk Co. Courthouse, Des Moines, Ia.

Polk Co: HISTORY OF POLK CO., IA.; Union Historical Co.; Birdsall, Williams & Co.; Des Moines, Ia; 1880. Copy found in the Public Library, Des Moines, Ia.

PVRB: POLK CO., IA., BIRTH REGISTRY; transcribed by and located in Iowa Historical Soc., Des Moines., Ia.

CHAPTER 1

Those Roving Rittgers

Listing 1977 descendants for 9 generations.

GENERATION NO. 1

1 John Augustin¹ RITTGERS was born 2 Dec 1767 in Prussia, now Germany.

Our research starts with a letter written 11 Nov 1914 to Judge Harry E. Rittgers, Jamestown, N. Dakota, from Sarah (Rittgers) Good(12.A), San Diego, Calif., the original is possibly lost, but in a copy widely circulated in the family we find:

"My Grandfather Rittgers came from Germany when he was young to escape having to go to war. He had but one brother and this brother did not come to America. My grandfather settled in Virginia (Shenandoah?) and married there a German Girl named Sarah Comer and raised his family to speak the German Language. While they were young he moved to Fairfield Co., Ohio, now Hocking Co., Ohio. I think he took up Government land. He had four sons - John, Joseph, Jacob B. (who was my father) and Daniel - and five daughters. Of the girls, one married an Amspaugh, another married Daubenmeier, another Root or Roat, and another John Strohl. All settled in Hocking Co. and all in close visiting distance. My grandfather's name was John A. Rittgers. I well remember him and his visits to our home and of our visits to his home - my father and us. I often heard my father say that his father said that he had but one brother and that he and his brother were the only men living by the name of Rittgers. My father, Jacob B., moved from Ohio in 1853 to the farm he lived on and now lies on, NE of Johnston, Iowa. Uncle Daniel came from Ohio to Iowa in 1854 or 1855 to the farm on the Des Moines River where he died. It is now owned by James Denney. (one mi. east of Merle Hay and NW 67th Ave, and ½ mi. So. was their home. Some of this land lies between the Des Moines River and Beaver Drive and other of it lies on the west side of NW Beaver Dr.[This was inserted in the copy submitted]) Uncle John and Uncle Joseph stayed in Ohio."

This letter has been widely shared within the family and the copy submitted to this researcher was handwritten off a copy, but this appears to form the base from which all the families have carried on their histories. While presenting the family history, this author hopes to correct errors in the early renditions.

EARLY HISTORY

In his naturalization papers, John A. Rittgers is listed as being "of the Kingdom of Prussia." The area is now along the Rhine Valley in north and central Germany, and is credited with being the "seat of German Militarism."[Allee, John Gage, Ph.D.; Webster's Encyclopedia of Dictionaries, New American Edition; 1983; p. 297.] The constant turmoil of war in Germany drove many thousands from their homeland, including, in about 1795, John A. Rittgers. We must use our imagination to put ourselves in his place - making the decision to leave everything familiar behind, including his brother who, according to Sarah (Rittgers) Good, was the only other man named Rittgers, to cross an ocean to a land he had only heard of. He most probably made his way down the Rhine to the coast of the North Sea. Then he had to find a ship's captain who would take a bond for his passage. It was common practice for someone to sign a contract with the captain for passage, then to have the contract sold (at a profit, of course,) at the arrival

KNOW all men by thefe Prefents, That *John Augustine Richards, & John Comre* are held and firmly bound unto his Excellency *James Wood* Efq. Governor of Virginia, in the juft and full fum of one hundred and fifty dollars, to which payment well and truly to be made, to the faid Governor, or his fucceffors, we bind ourfelves, our heirs, executors, and adminiftrators, jointly and feverally, firmly by thefe Prefents, Sealed with our feal , and dated this *9th* day of *May* 1797

THE condition of the above obligation is fuch, that, whereas there is a marriage fuddenly intended to be folemnized between the above bound *John Augustine Richards* and *Catharine Richards Comre* now if there be no lawful caufe to obftruct the faid Marriage, then the above obligation to be void and of no effect, otherwife to remain in full force and virtue.

Sealed and delivered
in prefence of

David Smith

John Augustin Rittgers (feal)

Lazarus (feal)

Jammer

point. Along the way, the determined traveler had to face thieves; "press gangs," those who roamed the waterfront knocking out unwary travelers and selling their unconscious bodies to sea captains for crew; price gougers at every stop; and the possibility that no one would buy the bond upon arrival.

It was shared with family researcher Wanda Iverson that there is a family using the name "RITGER" that immigrated to New Jersey and Va. To confuse the names further, there is one John Ritger, b. about 1812 who married a Katherine Vogel. They, too, have Jacobs, Michaels, Johns, and other names we see in our early generations. To date, no connection has been made between our John and this family from Bavaria, an area now in Germany, also. There are "Ritger"'s in Wisconsin who are researching possible links to this family.

MARRIAGE

John married (1) **Catharine COMER** 9 May 1797 in Shenandoah, Va.[Shenandoah Co. Marr., 1772-1850, microfilm in Shenandoah Co. Library, Edinburg, Va. The original bond record is on file in the state archives, we were told] She was born 29 Apr 1775[tombstone] in Shenandoah County, Va., the daughter of John COMER and Mary Ann KIBLER.(see Comer Appendix) That John Comer bought John Rittgers' bond is shown in the marriage record of John to Catharine Comer. It is here we also encounter the first of many misspellings of the Rittgers name!

We might draw several conclusions from this record:

1. John Rittgers married **Catherine**, not Sarah, Comer as so many family records report.
2. that John has probably already married Catharine because of the crossed out signature.
3. since the above document was printed, with the names written in, the rate of passage at that time must have been the equivalent of one hundred fifty dollars of the current currency, as that is stated in the preprinted form. Note that this entry doesn't specify how long the bond had been in effect. John Comer probably just "held the paper" until the marriage changed the relationship between the two men. This custom of bonded foreigners marrying "the farmer's daughter" must have been common, as this part also printed.
4. the pronunciation of Rittgers must have been with the soft "ch" sound as the misspelling is "Richards." (Today more of the family uses the "hard T" sound when pronouncing their names.)
5. John Rittgers probably spoke very little English and read none, as the misspellings are consistent and uncorrected.
6. based on the clarity and style of John Rittgers' signature, it appears he had some education. Note that he spells it "Ruttgers". Compare it to John Comer's signature which is barely legible.

To date, no deeds for John Rittgers have been found in Shenandoah or Page Co., Va. He most probably continued to work on his father-in-law's farm. In the will of John Comer, dated 6 Oct 1804, he gives to daughter Catharine "Richards the sum of six pounds in addition to what she has received." He left eighteen pounds to the other daughters, so this difference might have been the bond.

It appears that John and Catharine stayed in this area, now known as Luray, Page Co., Va., until about 1816. He probably cared for the Comer lands until John Comer's minor sons could take over their inheritance. With the influx of more settlers to Shenandoah Valley, the land prices had probably climbed to the point that John couldn't afford his own farm. As more people moved into the area, slavery was introduced. When asked by our family super-sleuths, Mary and Mary Esther Rittgers, why the Rittgers would chose to leave such a beautiful area, they were told by a Comer historian in Page Co., Va., that the Germans in that area were Calvinists and did not believe in slavery.(See Comer Appendix)

At about this time there was a fairly large local migration to the mid-Ohio area, as "government lands" opened up. For any of the above reasons, or a combination of reasons, John packed up his wife and eight children and joined the migration. There is some confusion in the family data submitted by descendants as to birthplaces - including statements that some were born in Pennsylvania! There is no indication that John ever lived there, and it appears all but the youngest, Susanna, were born in what is now Luray, Page Co. Va. Susanna was born in Fairfield Co., Oh.

OHIO LANDS - CHILLICOTHE LAND OFFICE

"Congress Lands" were lands for sale to the general public by the government. The Chillicothe Office in south-central Ohio covered the lands in what is now Fairfield and Hocking Counties, as well as abutting portions of the surrounding counties. It was surveyed by the "rectangular system of land survey" - using longitudinal and latitudinal parallels as base lines to form six mile square townships. A range was one township wide and several townships tall. Each township was then further divided into one mile square lots, with lot number 16 in each township set aside for a school. If you study a map, it is easy to see the results. Most of the "American Heartland" was surveyed thus and continues to have square boundaries for counties and towns, with the few irregularities being fairly good sized rivers. From the start of surveying in 1785 until 1787 there were few purchasers. There was a constant threat of Indian attack, as well as the gouging practices of unscrupulous land speculators. Complaints to Congress brought about the formation of the Northwest Territory on 13 July 1787. A governor and officers were established, the Greenville Treaty with the Indians removed the threat of attack, and soon small towns were forming.

Fairfield Co., Northwest Territory, was created in 1800, the state of Ohio created in 1803, and Hocking Co. was created in 1818 from parts of Fairfield and other counties. Initially, one had to buy an entire one-mile square lot, 640 acres, priced at $1 per acre - cash. Several people would go in together to purchase these lots and subdivide them. Later prices were $2 per lot, with half down in cash and half on credit for one year. In 1800, one could buy one-half lots, one-fourth down and pay in installments. By 1804, one-quarter lots were available for $2 per acre.

In the land record certificate #4770, we find J.A. Rittgers at Fairfield County bought the "northeast quarter section of section no. 31 in township no. 16 of range no. 17 containing 160 acres for two dollars per acre. In his receipt #14656, dated 5 Mar 1816 we find he paid $16 on deposit, and on the same day receipt #14657 for $64 was his first payment for this land located in Rush Creek Twp., Fairfield Co., Oh. He is left with a mortgage of $240, first installment of $80 on 5 Mar 1818, and subsequent payments due March 1819, and March 1820. He is to pay 6% interest, but at the bottom of the contract it states that if payment is made on or before the due date, "no interest will be demanded."

We see John A. "Richard" on the Rush Creek, Fairfield Co., Oh., 1820 census. He has 3 females under age 10, 2 males and 1 female ages 10-15, 1 male and 1 female ages 16-25, one male "45 and over"(himself) and one female "45 and over.(Catharine)"[p. 104A] This accounts for all the children known to have been born to John and Catherine.

Apparently the entire area had a problem meeting their payments, as we find in the land records a printed form "Certificate of Further Credit". Congress passed "An Act for the Relief of the Purchasers of the Public Lands, prior to the 1st day of July, 1821." In this certificate, numbered 866, we see where John relinquishes the eastern half of his quarter section. His mortgage on the remaining 80 acres is $80, to be paid in six annual installments of $13.33, due on or before 31 Dec of each year starting in Dec. 1821. Certificate #20450, dated 28 Mar 1825, indicates that "John A. Ruttgers" paid a total of $57.00. on the mortgage. This reflects the "discount allowed at the rate of 37 ½ per annum" of $34.19." A computation on the bottom of the page indicates he paid "52. in Ohio paper and 5. Silver." On 4 Apr 1825, we find that "John Augustus Ruttgers" assigned all his right, title, and claim to the North East quarter of section 31, to James McFadden for value received. We see recorded in Vol 51, p. 84, a preprinted page from John Quincy Adams, President, stating that this property has been paid for on 23 May 1825 by "James McFadden assignee of John A. Rittgers."(This form was issued for all government lands as they were paid off.) These records must have been kept in the Chillicothe land office, as it is entered into Fairfield Co. Book 1 or 7 (handwriting questionable) of Deeds, p. 84, until 20 Apr 1897. We note that his name has been consistently spelled Ruttgers with two dots over the "u".

On 8 Oct 1821 it is recorded that J.A. Rittgers bought subdivision 6 NE, Range 17, Township 15 - 1/2-158.94 acre plot, Marion Twp., Hocking Co., Oh. This was in Fairfield Co., at the time of purchase, but an adjustment of the county lines in 1850 place this property now in Hocking Co. This plot was mortgaged to Jacob B. Rittgers 19 July 1844, for $900. In the margin of the deed entry, it is reported that "for value received" Jacob declares the mortgage repaid on 27 Jan 1848. This is witnessed by John and Joseph Rittgers. [Book 10 of Deeds, p. 262, Fairfield Co., Oh.] (This area now the resort called "Hide-Away Hills" and is a restricted community in northern Hocking and southern Fairfield Co's.)

The 1830 census for Rush Creek, Fairfield Co., Oh., gives John "Richey", one male and one female 50-59; one daughter age 10 -14, two daughters 15-19, and one son 20-29.[p 133]

CATHARINE RITTGERS' DEATH

Catharine (Comer) Rittgers died 9 May 1834, most probably at home. She is buried in a small and very old cemetery in front of a lovely old country church - St. Paul's Evangelical Lutheran Church. This can be located by going southwest out of North Berne, Oh. It is off Bauman Hill Road on Lutheran Church Road. Catharine's stone reads: IN MEMORY - of Catharine - Rittgers Dau - ghter of John - Comer who was - born April 29 - 1775 and died - May 9 1834 - age 59 years.[From photo of tombstone, dashes indicate new lines on the stone.]

SECOND MARRIAGE

Another piece of unexpected information to surface was that John married (2) **Elizabeth HOCKE** 1 Jan 1836 in Fairfield County, Oh. [FVRM, Bk 1]   In his probate records, we find that he left spouse Elizabeth.[Probate Book 1, p.19, rec #219] On the 1840 census, we see John "Richey", in "Swan Twp.", Hocking Co., Oh., with one male 50-59, and one female 50-59.[p. 168]

NATURALIZATION

Many family researchers were using the family story that John A. Rittgers died in 1842, but we find on record in the Fairfield Co. Common Pleas Court Journal #17, page 202, that one John A (looks like H. in the original record) Rittgers of the Kingdom of Prussia, took the Oath of Citizenship at the October 1844 Term of Common Pleas Court, Fairfield Co., Ohio. Since all of his sons were born in Virginia, there was no need for them to take the oath, therefore, this is John the Elder (#1). [Fairfield Co., Oh., Common Pleas Court Journal #17, p. 202-204.] We don't know what motivated him to become naturalized at this time.

DEATH

John is buried beside Catharine in the cemetery of St. Paul's Evangelical Church, rural North Berne, Oh. His stone reads: In memory of - JOHN A. RITTGERS - Died - Feby 27th - 1848 - Aged - 80 yrs., 2 - mo. 27 dy. On the very bottom of the stone it appears that the stonecutter signed it J. Strickler. This is a rare find, but in the estate papers there is a notation that $6 was paid to "John Strickler for making and putting tombstones at the grave of said decd'."

In searching the estate records in the Fairfield Co. Courthouse, Lancaster, Oh., this writer found that there was no will. Among the estate papers we found the inventory and sale of personal belongings, [Fairfield Co. Courthouse, Lancaster, Oh., Estate No. 2367.] There were scraps of paper indicating billing against the estate and the inventory. On 24 Feb 1848: "Rec'd of JOHN AMSPACKER (JOHN AMSPAUGH) $5.50 being for coffen for John A. Rittgers, dec'd in full - Christian Good." Also on 24 Feb: "Mr. Richey (Rittgers? JR) Bot of Wm C. Davy 6 yds bleached muslin 11 2/3 (poss. the price per yd. but doesn't come to $1.00 as indicated in a column to the side) 1 yd. cambric muslin 44 (with 44 extended into the column at the side) Total 1.44 Feb'y 24.48 Rec'd Payment Wm. Davy" 10 Mar 1848 "$6 received of John A. Collins, Administrator of the estate of John A. Rittgers, Dec'd six dollars for making & putting tombstone at the grave of said dec'd. John Strickler."   24 Mar 1848 the notice of estate appeared in the Lancaster Gazette, and was published for 4 weeks. On 3 Apr 1848, Samuel Jackson was appointed to appraise the estate. On the 4th of Apr, Samuel Jackson, J.P. took the oath of Christian Geil and George Strohl to appraise the estate. Among the usual items of bedding and furniture, we find "One family Bible and two German books." He had tools and casks of food items, as well as 16 acres in wheat and 6 acres of rye, of which he owned one third.(Possibly two sons shared the fields.) He also held notes from sons-in-law that are "supposed to be good for ballance and interest." There were three notes held on non-relatives which were believed to be no good. The inventory concluded with the following statements. "The deceased left neither widow or minor children that we know of. April 4th A.D. 1848." What happened to widow Elizabeth? On 5 Apr 1848 there was a sale of personal property. The family had to buy his furniture and possessions! We find that son John bought the Family Bible for $4.12½ (of current money-not to be confused with current values) Son-in-law Peter Daubenmeyer bought "History of Martyrs" for $.50. There was also a hymnal and a set of almanacs. This collection of books, and the hand writing on the marriage paper, gives us an indication of John's educational level.   On a small scrap of paper folded into the estate papers, we find "Received of John A. Collins, Administrator of the estate of John A. Rittgers, Dec'd one dollar for washing & cleaning up the clothers beds room & etc of said deceased after his death. Catharine Amspaugher" She signed it with her mark.

On 6 June 1848, John Rittgers, Jr., filed a suit in the Court of Common Pleas, Fairfield Co., Oh., seeking the Partition and Assignment of Dower.[Partition Record, Bk#6, 1848-1851, pps.90-96] In the following account of the estate, we will capitalize the names of the children and sons-in-law of John A. Rittgers to show proof of lines of descent.   "John A. Rittgers, deceased. Widow Elizabeth Rittgers of Cincinnati, Hamilton Co., Oh. Children: JOHN RITTGERS; JOSEPH RITTGERS; JACOB RITTGERS: MAGDALENE, wife of JOHN ROOT; ELIZABETH, wife of JOHN STROHL; all residents of Hocking Co., CATHARINE, widow of JOHN AMSPAUGH; DANIEL RITTGERS; MARY, wife of ELI DEEL; SUSAN, wife of PETER DOBERMYER, all residents of Fairfield Co."

The property is referred to as "the East half of the NorthEast quadrant of section 6, Twp. 15, range 17, and also the East half of the West half of the North East quarter of section 6, Twp. 15, range 17...containing 120 acres of land" in "Auburn Twp., Fairfield Co., Oh." This strip of four miles high and the width of one township was taken from Rush Creek Twp. in 1840. In 1850, in an effort to balance the total square miles of Hocking, Fairfield, and Vinton Co's, the lower 2 miles were given to Marion Twp., Hocking Co., and the upper two miles were returned to

Rush Creek Twp., Fairfield Co. Auburn Twp. is given as location for the property through this suit, but now is in Marion Twp., Hocking Co., abutting the Fairfield Co. line.

In the division of property, Elizabeth is awarded the north 1/3 of the property. It cost $10.50 to have the crew survey out the line, as they needed "chainbearers, markers, flagman and a surveyor" to do it. The property was given a value of $6 per acre. Since it was determined by the assessors that the other 2/3 could not be divided without "manifest injury to the whole," it would have to be sold as one piece. It appears that none of the siblings wanted to buy the entire piece, as it went to a sheriff's sale on 16 Dec. 1948. The sheriff was required to accept no bid lower than 2/3 of the assessed value. At the "public outcry", the highest bidder, at $4.51 per acre was Samuel S. Rittgers(#12.1). His total purchase price was $549.04 1/3cent, indicating he bought the entire piece, including the dower. The deed wasn't to be delivered until the entire amount was paid - one third on purchase, one third in one year and the last in two years. It appears that Samuel worked out the purchase price, as we see him receiving a deed from the sheriff for this property on 25 July 1849. This deed was entered into Book 16 of Fairfield Co. Deeds, p. 402, and is immediately followed by a deed showing Samuel selling the same piece to Nicholas Wagner for $600 on the same day.[Book of Deeds 16, p. 403] The first deed mentions "subject to right of Dower" but the second records that the piece sold is 120 acres, with no mention of Dower.

This land is now part of "Hide-Away Hills", an exclusive and gated community in northern Hocking Co., and southern Fairfield Co. Most of John's piece of land is under the lake, called Lake of Four Seasons, that was formed when the developers blocked a valley and allowed it to fill with water from mountain run-off. It can be located from Rt. 33 (Logan-Lancaster Rd) near the Hocking-Fairfield county line. Follow the "Lake of Four Seasons" and the "Hide-Away Hills" signs. Entry to the community can only be gained by authorization of a realtor at the Real Estate office across the road from the main entrance.

The final accounting of his estate was not done until 17 Apr 1852, when the Administrator, John A. Collins, filed his report of accounts, noting that the final cash in the administrators hands is $67.60. There was no accompanying record of the actual disbursement of the money. We need to note that there is no real estate mentioned in the accounting, and we don't know how the family kept the property out of the estate. Nor did we locate the Sheriff's final accounting, showing he disbursed the money from the land sale.

ISSUE:

+ .1.1   Joseph RITTGERS, born 1799, died 1860/1870.
+ .1.2   Jacob B. RITTGERS, born 9 Feb 1800, died 17 Dec 1879.
+ .1.3   John Augustin RITTGERS, Jr., born 1 Jan 1802, died 6 Apr 1880.
+ .1.4   Magdalene RITTGERS, born 8 Jun 1804, died 12 Jun 1862.
+ .1.5   Katherine RITTGERS, born 22 Nov 1807, died 13 Apr 1871.
+ .1.6   Daniel R. RITTGERS, born 10 Sep 1810, died 9 Jun 1859.
+ .1.7   Elizabeth RITTGERS, born 1815.
  .1.8   Mary B. RITTGERS, born abt.1816 in Shenandoah Co.,Va., or Fairfield Co., Oh. Family stories give us a "Molly" born abt. 1805/6, Shenandoah Co., Va., to John and Sarah (Comer) Rittgers. It was thought "Molly" died in infancy, as nothing more known about her. In the 1830 census, we find children of John Rittgers broken down by ages. There are nine children indicated (the 1850 census is the first where children were listed by name) which fits our family record. It lists THREE daughters after the last son, which is Daniel. It further breaks down their ages to "10-14, and 15-20" [reel 130, p 104A] Thus, based on ages of the other daughters

as found on the 1850 census, we must place Mary here, and as the middle of these three girls. In the accounting of her father's estate, we see that the children all appear to be listed in birth order, with Mary next to last, which supports this assumption. In a petition to divide the estate of John A., of Fairfield Co., Oh., 1849, Journal #6 of the Court of Common Pleas, p. 90, is the listing of the heirs of John Rittgers. This includes one daughter "Mary, wife of Eli DEEL." She is listed as living in Fairfield Co. at this time. This researcher has failed to find "Eli" and/or Mary Deel on the 1850 census. In the records of the Pleasant Twp., Fairfield Co., Lutheran Church Cemetery records, we see that "Mary Magdalina, daughter of Elias and Mary Deal, died 15 Sept 1842, age 2 years, 7 mo., 20 days." We may speculate that either they moved out of state, or Mary died and Eli is one "Elias Deal" found in Fairfield Co. on 1850 census. The census lists in this order: Jacob Deal, 70, b. Pa., Wagon Maker; Mary M., 66, b. Va.; Sarah 29, b. Va.; Samuel Pugh, 18, laborer, b. Oh.; Israel Heller, 17, shoe maker, b. Oh; Sarah Deal, 13, b. Oh; George W., 3, b. Oh.; Elias, 40, Carpenter, b. Va. [p 364 fam #59/59] One Elias Deal purchased 45.18 acres in Falls Twp., Hocking Co., Oh., range #17, Twp. #14, Sect. #1, on 12 Nov 1835. His residence at that time was listed as Fairfield Co., Oh. [Kocher, p. "Falls 01"] There were "quadrennial enumerations" done in Fairfield Co. In 1831, 1839, 1847, 1851 and 1859. On these, we see in Pleasant, Rush Creek Twp., Jacob Deal in 1831 and 39, and Eli and Jacob Deal listed in 1847. By 1851, we see Eli in Greenfield Twp., and no Jacob. The only other information to date, is that there are some later deeds listing one Elias and Rebecca. It is possible that Eli remarried. There is a family group sheet submitted to the Logan, Oh., public Library which report lineage of Sarah Deal, daughter of Elias and Mary (Rickel) Deal. We shall need a Rittgers Super Sleuth to "dig up" Mary's family.

+ .1.9   Susanna RITTGERS, born 10 Oct 1818, died 27 Oct 1884.

CHAPTER 2

GENERATION NO. 2

1.1 Joseph² RITTGERS (John¹) was born 1799 in Shenandoah Co., Va., the son of John Augustin RITTGERS and Catharine COMER. He married **Anna** _____ about 1819 in Hocking Co., Oh. She was born about 1799 in Md.[census] His marriage to Anna _____ not found in the Hocking or Fairfield Co., Oh., marriage books to date. On the 1830 census, Rush Creek Twp., Fairfield Co., Oh., we see Joseph "Richey". His household includes one male 30-39(himself), one female age 20-29, one female 5-9, one male 0-4, and one female 0-4.[p 133] Entryman maps show that he purchased 9 Jan 1836, the NE Quarter of the NE quarter of section 19, Twp. 15, Range 17, Marion Twp., Hocking Co., Oh. The 1850 census, Marion Twp., Hocking Co., Oh., gives name as "Rittchers", age 52, farmer, $1000 real estate value, b. Va. Wife Anna, age 51, b. Md., last five children listed. [p. 855, fam. #212/218.] On the 1860 census, Marion Twp., Hocking Co., Oh., his name is correctly spelled. Joseph is age 62, farmer, $2000 Real Estate value and $500 in personal property, b. Va., Wife Anna, 61, b. Md. No children at home. [p. 158, fam. 1036/1024.] They have apparently both died by 2 Nov 1864, as we see son Abraham buying from sisters Julia "Giger" and Anne Grove their undivided 2/6 interest in Section 19, Twp., 15, Range 17, the NW quarter of the NW quarter.

ISSUE:

+ .11.1   Julia A. RITTGERS, born about 1823.
+ .11.2   Abraham RITTGERS, born 11 Nov 1829, died 13 Aug 1897.
+ .11.3   Lucinda RITTGERS, born 11 Jan 1830, died 27 Mar 1878.
+ .11.4   Catherine RITTGERS, born about 1832, died before 1900.
+ .11.5   Mary RITTGERS, born 1834.
+ .11.6   Anna RITTGERS, born 6 May 1839, died 26 Apr 1904.

1.2 Jacob B.² RITTGERS (John¹) was born 9 Feb 1800 in Shenandoah Co., Va., the son of John Augustin RITTGERS and Catharine COMER. There is a photocopy of an ornate "Certificate of Birth and Baptism" in the family that states "John A. Rittgers and his wife Catharine, a daughter of J. Comer, was born a son on the ninth day of February in the year of our Lord 1800. This child was born in [left blank] in [blank] County, in the state of Virginian in North America: was baptized by the Rev. [blank] and received the name of Jacob B. Rittgers. Witness present at the Act of Baptism: Peter Nail and his wife Elisabeth." The names were all filled in by the same hand, and the form has no printing date visible, thus we have no idea how much later than the baptism the form was filled out. It must have been done before the family lost touch with the Comer family, as Elisabeth Nail (nee Comer) is a sister of Catharine (Comer) Rittgers. We are told that the original Certificate is in the possession of Bobbie (Rittgers) Lonker of Medicine Lodge, Ks.

"Jacob Richards" married 16 Dec 1822 (1) **Hester PATTERSON** in Fairfield Co., Oh. She was born 1803 in Md. In 1830, we find Jacob Rittgers in Hocking Co., Oh. He has in his house one male and one female between 20-29; one each between 5-9; and one each between 0-5.[reel 132] On the Ohio River Survey Map, Congressional Lands, we see Jacob Rittgers bought 39.50 acres in Range #17, Twp #15, section #20, Marion Twp, Hocking Co., Oh., on 16 Sept 1834. His residence at that time was listed as Fairfield Co., Oh. [Kocher, p. "Marion 20".] "Jacob and Easter his wife" sell for $1 to the Directors of School District 3, Marion Twp., 1/4 acre from the

SW corner of his property. The directors receiving the property were Jacob Rittgers, Joseph Rittgers and John Wagner. Jacob signed the deed, but Esther made her mark.[Hocking Co. Deed Bk D, p.37]

On the 1840 census, Marion Twp., Hocking Co., Oh., we find Jacob "Ritgers", age 30-39, with one female in home age 30-39, and another age 40-49. Also in home are 2 males and one female 0-4, one male and one female 5-9, and one male 15-19. [p 138] On 22 Feb 1843, we see Adam Strohl mortgaging his property to Jacob "Ritgers" and Joseph "Ritgers".[Bk G, p.106] On 19 July 1844, Jacob took a mortgage on his father's farm in Fairfield Co., Oh. [Fairfield Co, Oh., Book 10 of deeds, p. 260, Lancaster, Oh.]

The 1850 census, Marion Twp., Hocking Co., Oh., shows us Jacob, age 50 with wife "Easter", 47, and 10 children. Missing are the three oldest. Of them, son Samuel is next door, daughter Isabelle is married and nearby, and daughter Nancy died young. All ages correspond with family information. [p. 855, fam. #213/219] We see that Jacob and Esther sold their farm on section 20, Twp.15, Range 17, 120 acres, to Gottleib Jurgenmeier for $1500.

In the widely quoted letter of 1914 from Sarah (Rittgers) Good we see he: "Came to Iowa in 1852 or 1853 and purchased a large tract of land on Beaver Prairie, a few miles north of what is now the city of Des Moines, but which at that time was a small town. The following year (1854?) he moved his family by wagon train from Ohio to this Iowa Prairie. (It can be seen today by driving east of Johnston [Polk Co., Ia.] on NW 67th Ave, turning north on NW Beaver Dr. As you approach the stop sign 1/2 mi. north, you will see a large white house in the yard in front of you.) (This house has since been moved, and homes going in on this spot. JR.) This was the home spot. The land lay in all directions around this point but mainly to the north and to the west. NW Beaver Drive intersects what was once Johnston Rittgers' farm, the same land as Jacob B. purchased. The Rittgers Cemetery is on the south side of NW Beaver Dr. about 1/4 mile west (and north) of the home.]" This believed added by a later transcriber. In the copy received by this author, as it was transcribed the following was inserted "A great granddaughter of Jacob B., Mary Ann Roberts, lives in the brick home across NW Beaver Dr. from the old home place. Many descendants of Jacob B. live in Iowa now, many in the N.W. part -in the West Bend area and some near Paton in Central Iowa. They are descendants of Ben and George." [Shared with us by Laura (Rittgers)(Pietzman) Emmert.]

In the warranty deeds of Polk Co., Ia., we find that William P. Koger and Elizabeth, his wife, sold 7 Apr 1853, to Jacob B. Rittgers "the SE 1/4 of section 6-79-24, West 5th P.M., excepting three acres...and other property." [Deeds Book F., p. 4., Polk Co., Ia.] On 5 Apr 1856, he sold 40 acres to Joseph H. Hamilton, husband of his daughter, Margaret (#12.6). [Book H, p. 493] These taken from a photocopy of land abstract No. 76811, p. 19, Polk Co., Ia.

Hester died 19 Jan 1856 and is buried in Rittgers Cemetery, Johnston, Ia. On the 1856 State census, we find that Jacob Rittgers, 56, is a widower. He is a farmer and has been in Ia. for 3 years. With him is Eli, 18, through Henry, 9. Also in the home is son Samuel, also a widower, and his two children. [1856,p.274,fam #26.]

Hartman tells us that "After Esther died, Jacob sent to Germany for a bride, Anna "Catherine" Schleigh (1827-1913)." We find contradictory evidence on later census records. Jacob married (2) **Catherine Anne SCHLEIGH** 17 July 1856.[PVRM, Bk 1, p.180] She was born 30 Mar 1827 in Germany.

On the 1860 census, Jefferson Twp., Polk Co., Ia., [p. 95, fam. #765/700] we find Jacob, age 60, a farmer, with real estate valued at $10,000 and personal property at $500. With him is wife Catharine, b. Wutenburg, age 33. Also in the home, besides the Rittgers' children, is one Guttip

Bates, listed as "son". He is age 5 and born in Indiana. This must be Christina's son. On the 1900 census, she reports she immigrated in 1851.

Guttip is found on the 1870 census with Perry C. Rittgers, name spelled Golleib Botz, 15, in Walnut Grove, Saline Co., Ks. In a newspaper article, submitted with no news banner or date, we see that "Brothers Meet for the First Time in Sixty-Five Years. Three brothers met at Bakersfield, Calif, who had not met for 65 years. G.W. Betts, a half-brother, Bakersfield, went to California during the gold rush; threw his anchor out in the wheat fields south of Bakersfield, where they have lived ever since. On Feb. 1 they celebrated their 60th wedding anniversary." No wife given, and no date in the article. The others present were sister Mrs. J.J. Stewart, (Catherine, #12.F), G.M. Rittgers, Jefferson, Ia., and B.F. Rittgers, Rolfe, Ia.

On the 1870 census, Valley, Polk Co., Ia.[p. 406, fam. # 97/107] Jacob age 70, with wife Catherine, age 43, and children as reported in family records with the exception of Mary, who was not yet born. Ages correspond to our information.

We can be sure that by 1871, Jacob is well aware of the passing years. He deeds to nephew Reuben Rittgers (#16.2) for "one dollar in hand....as trustee.. " premises situated in Polk County, Iowa, for the express use of the Rittgers family and their connections for the burial of the dead of their respective families.." dated 21 Jan 1871, filed 6 May 1874. [Photocopy had no book number, but appears to be from the original as transcribed into a book of deeds.] Jacob died 17 Dec 1879 in Jefferson Twp., Polk, Ia., and was buried in Rittgers Cemetery, Johnston, Ia.[RitCem]

By the 1880 census, Catherine, age 53 is head of house in Valley Twp., Polk Co., Ia. [ED 172, p. 541, fam #131/134] With her are Benjamin, age 17, through Mary age 8. In a rare find, Jacob's name is listed last, age 79, with the notation that he died Dec 1879 and a single line drawn through the entry. Jacob's death started quite a public family discord. In his will, Jacob included a passage stating that he bequeaths to Catherine all property and money "for the purpose of raising, clothing, and educating the children born to us until such time that Mary our youngest child shall attain the age of fifteen." Then he adds that "at that time or as soon thereafter as can be conveniently done" everything was to be sold and the "proceeds thereof be equally divided between my wife Catherine Rittgers and my children who shall survive me and of any children who shall have died between the time of my decease and the time of such division or distribution to be entitled to such share of shares as their respective ancestors would have been entitled to receive...and the share of my real and personal estate bequeathed to my wife to be in lieu of her dower." His will was written 15 Dec 1877 and filed 27 Dec 1879. [Abst #62638; Probate 2, #916; Will Rec. 3-198, Polk Co.,Ia.]

What follows is a landmark court case that upheld the widow's right to her dower - in spite of what the will specified. On 6 Mar 1880, Catherine filed a "Petition for Assignment of Dower", or the right of a surviving spouse to have one-third of the estate left by a deceased spouse. She wants a referee to be appointed to "assign and set apart to her one third in value of all the said Real Estate as and for her share and interest..." The adult children, coincidentally being the children of Jacob and first wife, Hester and being the children that we are told Catherine alienated and drove from the home, petitioned to have the will upheld, that Catherine should only get one/twenty-third of the estate at the time the youngest child is fifteen. Despite protests, "under Iowa Law" Catherine won her right to dower. She was given 70 acres that contained the homestead "exclusive of the family burying ground situated thereon." This case is in law books and is required reading for law students. [This author received a photocopy of the entries relating to this case, but no bibliography. The page is titled "Supreme Court of Iowa, June Term 1881, p. 218. Much of this is supported in the land abstract, also.] Her dower, one third of the property, was set aside on 20 Feb 1882. She was allowed to maintain the entire estate until the youngest, Mary, was 15. At that time, she gave a report to the court - citing much hardship in raising the younger children, "that the income from the estate has been insufficient to raise the family and only by the personal exertions and earnings of the Executrix and by the use of the income from her separate estate has she been able to raise the family and keep the Estate out of debt." This estate is marked "Closed" on the face of the docket following this entry. The last entry in the abstract is a deed from Johnson Rittgers to his mother, buying most of the land from her, dated 21 Oct 1901, and mortgage satisfied acknowledged 4 Mar 1902. The corner Johnson didn't buy may have been taken by heirs living in the area.

On the 1895 state census, Polk Co., Webster Twp., we see Catherine, 68 and Lutheran, with three of her adult children, Priscilla, Andrew and Mary.[#123]

The 1900 census finds Katherine, age 73 and b. May 1827 in Germany, with son Johnson as head of household in Grimes, Polk Co., Ia.[p.290, fam. #151/158] With them are also two of Jacob and Katherine's daughters; Priscilla, age 36 (b. Jan 1864) and Mary, 29 (b. Sept 1871). On the 1910 census we find Catherine, age 83, living with youngest child, Mary, and her husband, Herschel Rhoad in Rippey, Greene Co., Ia. [ED 106, p 9A, fam. #188/190] Catherine died 5 Apr 1913, and was buried in Rittgers Cemetery, in Johnston, Polk Co., Ia. Her stone in the Rittgers Family Cemetery reads "Anna Catharine.".

ISSUE of Jacob and Hester:

+ .12.1   Samuel S. RITTGERS, born 21 Feb 1823, died 20 Dec 1909.

+ .12.2   Isabelle RITTGERS, born 7 Mar 1825, died 1855.

.12.3   Nancy RITTGERS, born 25 Mar 1826 in Hocking Co., Oh., died 1827 in Hocking Co., Oh.

.12.4   John A. RITTGERS, born 21 Feb 1829 in Marion Twp., Hocking Co., Oh., died 1898 in Calif. In the 1850 census we find John A., age 21, b. Oh., with parents there.[p 855 fam #213/219] He was not seen on the 1856 state census with his family or on another farm in that area. Family Record states he never married. It also states that "with his brother, Israel (#12.5) he crossed the plains to California in 1850." The 1870 census gives us John, 38, in Lone Pine, Inyo Co., Calif. living with his brother, Israel. They declare they each have $1000 in real estate and $150 in personal estate. They are farming. [p 331 fam #27/26] In 1880 we see John, now 51, living with brother Israel and Israel's wife Amelia in Lone Pine, Ca. He "works on farm". [p 503 fam #150/198] On his father's estate, he is listed as living in "Five Point, Calif." in Mar, 1880. Family stories tell us he "was a farmer and rancher throughout life," and died prob. Calif.

+ .12.5   Israel P. RITTGERS, born 25 Apr 1831, died 1912.

+ .12.6   Margaret RITTGERS, born 2 Feb 1833, died 1916.

+ .12.7   Jacob R. RITTGERS, born 13 Oct 1834, died 11 Sep 1920.

+ .12.8   Eli D. RITTGERS, born 22 Aug 1836, died 14 Oct 1909.

+ .12.9   Perry C. RITTGERS, born 16 Mar 1838, died 30 Jun 1903.

.12.A   Sarah RITTGERS, born 11 Feb 1840 in Marion Twp., Hocking Co., Oh. It is Sarah's letter that gives us so much information on her grandparents, John A. and Catharine (Comer) Rittgers, as well as much Iowa information - especially of her father, Jacob. (#1.2) We first see her on the 1850 census, age 10, with parents in Marion Twp.[p 855 fam #213/219] She is seen on the 1856 state census, age 15, with her father in Polk Co., Ia.[p.274, fam#26] We are told that Sarah was thrown out of the house by stepmother, Catherine, at age 15. "Her older brother, Eli, left with her." She worked in a bakery in Des Moines prior to her marriage to Samuel M. GOOD, 3 Nov 1856.[PVRM, Bk 1,p.182] He was born about 1824 in Ohio. On the 1860 census we see her in Des Moines, Polk Co., Ia., with her husband, Samuel M. Good, "Pedler." [p 8, fam #66/59] Newspapers of the late 1800's carry small ads for various supplies available from the store of "S.M.Good, Des Moines." [Newspapers microfilmed and on file in Iowa Hist. Soc., Des Moines.] In her father's estate, 1880, she is listed as "wife of S.M. Good residing in Des Moines, Ia." A letter she wrote to "Mrs. Rittgers"(Abigail (Findley) Rittgers) on 27 Nov 1893 to console her on the death of her husband Reuben(#16.2) has been shared with us by Barbara (Fisher) Abrams. Sarah was living in San Diego when she wrote the letter, and reported that they planned to visit Iowa the next summer. She mentioned that she "only got two short letters from brother Jacob in the past four years.." so probably moved to San Diego about 1889. The letter is full of religious reference We are told they had one child who died in infancy. Samuel died in San Diego, Calif. Sarah died 1919 in San Diego, San Diego Co., Calif.

.12.B   Peter M. RITTGERS, born 21 Feb 1842 in Marion Twp., Hocking Co., Oh., died 1924 in Gypsum Creek, McPherson Co., Ks. On the 1850 census, age 8, b. Oh., with parents there.[p 855 fam #213/219] In 1856, the Ia. State census shows Peter, 13, with his father in Polk Co. On 1860 census, age 18, with father and stepmother, Jefferson Twp., Polk Co., Ia., farm laborer. [p. 95 fam #765/700] Peter never married. He moved to Kansas and farmed most of his life. We are told he enlisted in the Civil War at the beginning and served four years. During the War, William Nosler (who later married Peter's sister Esther) was one of his "buddies". "He saw service in Tennessee and along the Red River of the South. Was never wounded." The only enlistment we find for Peter M. Rittgers is 12 May 1864. It appears he, Reuben and John Henry all signed up at the same time. He is described as being 22, blue eyes, light hair, and light complexion, and is 5 ft. 7 ½ inches tall. He reports on his enlistment that he was born in Fairfield Co., Oh. He went in for 100 days, and served in the 44th Ia. Vols, Co. "H", mustering out in Davenport, Ia., 15 Sept 1864. In 1870, at age 26, he was in Walnut Grove, Saline Co., Ks., working on the farm of his brother, Perry, (#12.9)[p 50 fam #144/141] In father's estate in 1880, he was listed as being of "Silada, Ks." On 1900 census, "P.M." Rittgers is found as a boarder with one J.S. Cummins in Gypsum, McPherson Co., Ks. His age is given as "53 - b. Feb 1847." The 1910 census shows Peter, 65, in Gypsum Creek Twp, McPherson Co., Ks. With him is nephew Jacob (#129.B), age 20, son of Perry, and Jacob's wife, Nina, age 21. They have been married "0" years. Peter states he owns the farm free and clear. Jacob is a farm laborer, "working out".[p. 3B, ED 54, Fam #53/53] Peter is found yet again on the 1920 census, age 77, where he is with his nephew, Sanford Rittgers (#121.9) in Gypsum Creek Twp., Roxbury, McPherson Co., Ks. [ED 67, p 6A, fam 76/76]

+ .12.C   Esther May RITTGERS, born 28 May 1844, died 1892.
+ .12.D   Henry C. RITTGERS, born 6 May 1849, died 8 Mar 1933.
                           ISSUE of Jacob and Catherine:
+ .12.E   Daniel R. RITTGERS, born 26 Apr 1857, died 4 Apr 1916.
+ .12.F   Catherine Anne RITTGERS, born 3 Aug 1858.
.12.G   Salina RITTGERS, born 2 Oct 1860 in Jefferson Twp, Polk, Ia., died 1862 in Jefferson Twp., Polk Co., Ia., and was buried in Rittgers Cemetery, Polk Co., Ia.

+ .12.H   Benjamin Franklin RITTGERS, born 2 Aug 1862, died 1944.
  .12.I   Priscilla RITTGERS, born 29 Jan 1864 in Jefferson Twp., Polk Co., Ia. She is on
             the 1870 census, age 5, with parents in Valley Twp., Polk Co., Ia. [p 406 fam
             #97/107] On 1880 census there, age 16, with mother.[ED 172, p 541, fam
             #131/134] Never married. On the 1900 census, age 36, in home with brother,
             Johnson, sister Mary, and mother, in Grimes, Polk Co., Ia.[p 290A fam #151/158]
             She lived for many years with her sister, Mary (Rittgers) Rhoad, near Rippey, Ia. In
             1910, she is listed as age 40!, in home of Herschel and Mary (Rittgers) Rhoad,
             Washington Twp., Greene Co., Ia.[fam #188/190] In 1920, at age 52, she continues
             in home of Herschel and Mary Rhoad in Washington, Greene Co., Ia.[ED 118, p 4B,
             fam #87/87] In a newspaper article without banner, but dated 1953, we see that she
             had a party for her 89th birthday on "Thursday, January 29th..". She was a resident
             of the Edith Crandell Home. "Her dinner guests were her sister, Mr. & Mrs.
             Herschel Rhoad, with whom she had always made her home previous to her illness."
             We are told "the day was spent reading the cards, greetings and letters received as
             a shower in her honor. Among other gifts she also received cut flowers from
             California relatives." We are also told that "Priscilla has been in failing health for the
             past year and a half. When health permits she enjoys radio and television, including
             the inauguration of President Eisenhower. Her favorite radio program is Rev. R.R.
             Brown Gospel Tabernacle each Sunday morning." Priscilla died 12 Feb 1953 in
             Rippey, Greene Co., Ia., and is buried in Rippey Cemetery, Block 12, lot 41, with
             sister Mary and Herschel Rhoad.[RGrCem, p.51]
+ .12.J   George McClellan RITTGERS, born 8 May 1865, died 1956.
+ .12.K   Andrew Johnson RITTGERS, born 23 Jun 1867, died 26 Jul 1941.
+ .12.L   Lily RITTGERS, born 3 Mar 1869.
+ .12.M   Mary RITTGERS, born 26 Sep 1871, died 1959.

1.3 John Augustin² RITTGERS, Jr. (John¹) was born 1 Jan 1802 in Shenandoah Co., Va.,
the son of John Augustin RITTGERS and Catharine COMER. Many family papers state he was
born in Pennsylvania, but there is no evidence that the family ever resided in Pa. He states on
later census records that he was born in Virginia.
    John married about 1824, **Catherine _____**. The early records of the area are sparse, and
with the many spellings attributed to Rittgers in those records, the marriage may be uncovered
with diligent search of those misspellings. In records of the Ruff Cemetery we find that one
Savilla, daughter of John & Catherine Rittgers died 2 Sept 1856.[FCoD] John bought 84.11
acres, the E ½ of the SE quarter of section 10, Twp. 15, range 10, on 5 July 1856.[Kocher] At
the time of purchase, this was in Fairfield Co., but in 1850, this section was transferred into
Hocking Co.
    We find on the 1830 census Hocking Co., Oh., John Rittgers, with one male and one female,
20-29; one female 5-9; and one each between 0-4. This supports the report of the three older
children. [reel 132] He married (2) **Lydia _____** about 1831 in Oh. She was born 12 Jun 1812
in Pa. John and Lydia bought for $300 the NE quarter of Section 14, Twp. 16, Range 17. Also
in this deed and part of the transaction was part of a 33 acre tract in the SW quarter of Section
11, Twp 16, Section 17, on 8 Feb 1834.[Hocking Co. Deed book W, p.328-329]
    In 1840, we see 9 children in the home, one male and 2 females 10-14; two males and one
female 5-9; and three females 0-4. This conforms to our information on the children.[reel 132]

In 1848, John filed a suit against his siblings to force them to partition their parent's property.[Fairfield Co.Court of Common Pleas, book 17, p.90] There are several deeds in John's name. He takes mortgages on various properties as well as buying and selling them. In one, dated 17 Nov 1831, he accepts a mortgage of $150 from the widow on the property of the Estate of Abraham Miller.[Fairfield Co. Deed bk 1, p. 263] Then on 21 Jan 1838, he filed a Petit Suit against Daniel Shaw and other heirs of Abraham Miller.[Bk 10, p.353] He is still owed $88.89 by the widow and he forecloses on the property. The sheriff finally deeded the land to John on 24 Oct 1844[Bk 10, p.430]

On the 1850 census of Marion Twp., Hocking Co., Oh, John is age 48, farmer, $1200 value of Real Estate, b. Va. Has wife Lydia, age 37, b. Pa. and 10 children. [p. 841, fam. #118/120] Lydia died 5 July 1853, age 45 yr., 22 days, in Marion Twp., Hocking Co., Oh., and is buried in Ruff Cemetery.[HCoCem.] This gives us a birth date of 19 June 1808 for Lydia. John, Jr. married (3) **Catherine HOCKMAN** 21 Apr 1859 in Hocking Co., Oh.[HVRM, Bk B., p. 302] She was born about 1814 in Va. He is still in Marion Twp. on the 1860 census, where John, age 57, b. Va., farmer, has $1000 value in Real Estate & $350 worth of personal property. Wife Catherine, age 46, b. Va., is caring for the three children still in the home, including one Leah, age 14. Since she was not on 1850 census, we must assume that she is really "Leah Hockman".[p 150, fam # 936/924] Missing from the census, that we would have expected to find in the home are John A. III who would be 18, Margaret who would be 15, and Jacob who would be 13. We haven't found John III or Margaret as yet, but found Jacob living with older sister Elizabeth (#13.9).[Marion Twp., p. 158, fam 1040/1028] The 1870 census shows us John, age 69, a farmer with real estate valued at $2000. Wife Katherine, 66, and youngest daughter, Rosan - here stated age is 15, but on the 1860 census, she was 10! A common error on census'. [p. 510, fam #269/272] Over the past several years he has sold off much of his land in several pieces. John died 6 Apr 1880 at the age of 78yrs, 2 mo., and 6 days. He "resided in Marion Twp. - farmer - died of palsy."[HVRD, Bk 1, 1867-1883, p. 128, record #2043] He had very little in his estate to tell us about his life.[Hocking Co. Estate #1190]

ISSUE of John and Catharine:

.13.1   Sophia RITTGERS, born 27 Jul 1825 in Hocking Co., Oh.. Not on 1850 census with family

.13.2   Mathias RITTGERS, born 26 Jul 1827 in Hocking Co., Oh.. Not on 1850 census with family

.13.3   Savillah RITTGERS, born 13 Feb 1829 in Hocking Co., Oh.. Not on 1850 census with family. Died 2 Sept 1856, age 27 years, and is buried in Ruff Cemetery, Marion Twp., Hocking Co., Oh., row 3, #4. [HCoCem]

ISSUE of John and Lydia:

+ .13.4   Tobias RITTGERS, born 13 Mar 1832, died 8 Feb 1882.

.13.5   Barbery RITTGERS, born 13 Mar 1832 in Marion Twp., Hocking Co., Oh. On the 1850 census, age 18, with twin, parents, and siblings there. [p 841 fam #118/120]

+ .13.6   Noah RITTGERS, born 7 Jan 1834.

+ .13.7   Mary RITTGERS, born 8 Oct 1835.

+ .13.8   Anna RITTGERS, born 15 Oct 1837, died before 1900.

+ .13.9   Elizabeth RITTGERS, born 30 Nov 1839.

.13.A   John A. RITTGERS, III, born 27 Mar 1842 in Marion Twp, Hocking Co., Oh. Census - 1850 - age 8, with parents there.[p 841 fam #118/120] Not found with family on the 1860 census.

.13.B   Margaret RITTGERS, born 29 Oct 1845 in Marion Twp., Hocking Co., Oh.. She is on the 1850 census, age 5, with parents there.[p 841 fam #118/120] Not present with parents on 1860 census.

+ .13.C   Jacob M. RITTGERS, born 7 Feb 1847, died 1904.

+ .13.D   William F. RITTGERS, born 8 Aug 1849, died before 1910.

.13.E   Rosan RITTGERS, born about 1850 in Marion, Hocking Co., Oh. She is on 1860 census, age 10, with father and step-mother there.[p 150 fam #936/924] On the 1870 census, she is the only child at home with father and step-mother in Marion Twp., but her age is given as 15! Only five years difference![p 510 fam #269/272]

.13.F   Catherine RITTGERS, born 30 Nov 1851 in Hocking County, Oh. Not on census.

1.4 Magdalene[2] RITTGERS (John[1]) was born 8 Jun 1804 in Shenandoah Co., Va., the daughter of John Augustin RITTGERS and Catharine COMER. Family records call her Mary Magdalene, but in her father's estate papers she is referred to as "Magdalene, wife of John Root of Hocking Co." There is also a "Mary, wife of Eli Deel." listed in the same paragraph.

    She married **John ROOT** 21 Dec 1825 in Fairfield Co., Oh. He was born 19 Jan 1793 in N.Y. She is called "Molly" on her marriage record. [FCoM, Bk 1, p. 28] We see John Root on the 1840 census in Laurel Twp., Hocking Co., Oh. In his home are one male 40- 49, one female 30-39, 2 males and one female 10-14, one male and one female age 5-9, and one male 0-4.[p 182] These ages correspond to the known children of John and Magdalene.

    On Maps of the Ohio River Survey, Congressional Lands, we see that John Root purchased 42.18 acres on 26 Dec 1836, and an additional 42.18 acres - separated from the original purchase by two farms - on 25 Apr 1837. These are in Range #18, Twp. #12, Section #24, Laurel Twp., Hocking Co., Oh. [Kocher, p. "Laurel 24".]

    The 1850 census gives us John, 57, born in N.Y., a farmer with $300 in real estate in Marion Twp, Hocking Co.. With him is wife Magdalene, age 45. The eldest child that is listed in the family record, Ephriam, is not in the home, but the rest are shown on the census.[p 57, fam #411/420] We are told Magdalene died 12 June 1862, Marion, Hocking, Oh. In Hocking Co. Book "C" of Marriages, p. 510, one John Root married 25 Feb 1869, Catharine Steele. We are told he died in the 1860's, so this might be son John, or another John Root altogether, as the Root family was large.

ISSUE:

+ .14.1   Isaac ROOT, born about 1826.

+ .14.2   Ephriam ROOT, born about 1827.

+ .14.3   Sarah ROOT, born about 1829.

+ .14.4   Daniel ROOT, born 12 Apr 1830.

+ .14.5   Katherine ROOT, born about 1834.

.14.6   John Root, JR., born about 1838 in Marion Twp., Hocking Co., Oh. Seen on 1850 census, age 12, with parents there.[p 57 fam #411/420]

.14.7   Sophrona ROOT, born about 1840 in Marion Twp., Hocking Co., Ohio. She married Henry MELCHER 14 Feb 1858.[HVRM Bk B,p.277] On 1850 census, age 10, with parents there.[P 57, fam #411/420]

.14.8   Balinda ROOT, born about 1845 in Marion Twp., Hocking Co., Oh. Seen on 1850 census, age 5, with parents there.[p 57 fam #411/420]

.14.9   Mary ROOT, born about 1848 in Marion Twp., Hocking, Ohio. On 1850 census, age 2, with parents there.[P 57, fam #411/420]

1.5 **Katherine**[2] **RITTGERS** (John[1]) was born 22 Nov 1807 in Shenandoah Co., Va., the daughter of John Augustin RITTGERS and Catharine COMER. Her name is spelled both with a "K" and a "C" in public records and family documents. She married (1) **John AMSPAUGH** 29 Dec 1825[FCoM,Bk 1] in Fairfield Co., Oh. He was born 18 Dec 1799 in York Co., Pa., the son of Conrad and Susana (__) "Amspacher". [Bates, Marlene S.; York Co. Church Records of 18th Cent., 1991.] Conrad b. Nov 1775 in Pa., d. 13 Sept 1864, Fairfield Co., Oh. Susana b. 15 May 1778, d. 22 July 1825, Fairfield Co., Oh. [deaths from Cemeteries of "Liberty Twp., Fairfield Co., Oh." Fairfield Chapter, Oh. Gen. Soc.] Susanna is in the St. Paul's Cemetery in the same row as John and Catherine Rittgers, with only Elizabeth, daughter of Conrad & Susannah Amspaugh, d. 28 Sept 1845, age 34, and two infant stones, marked "Durr", between them.

John "Amspacker" paid for his father-in-law's coffin, 24 Feb 1848. In records of St. Jacobus Evangelical Lutheran, Rushcreek, Fairfield Co., Oh., we find a notation that "Johan Amspach died 10 Mar 1848, 47 yrs, 3 mo." [EmEv, p. 81.] (This gives us a birth on 10 Dec 1800. JR) John is buried next to his mother, and in the same row as John A. and Catharine (Comer) Rittgers in the Cemetery at St. Paul's Evangelical Lutheran Church, rural North Berne, Fairfield Co., Oh. Katherine is listed in her father's estate papers, 1848, as "Catherine, widow of John Amspaugh." This was a very difficult time for Katherine, as she lost both father and husband within a few months. There is a scrap of paper in the estate file for her father that she was paid one dollar for "washing & cleaning up the clothes beds, room, and [some sort of mark] of the said deceased after his death."

On the 1850 census, Marion Twp, Hocking Co., Katherine Amspaugh, age 41, with no husband listed. The eight children listed on census agree with family record.[p 6, fam #182/187]

Katherine married (2) **Peter Wagoner, SR.** 16 Feb 1854 in Hocking Co., Ohio.[HVRM, Bk B, p. 202] He was born 1793 in Germany. Peter died 10 Dec 1876 in Marion, Hocking Co., Oh. [St. Jacobus, p. 81.] The 1860 census shows us that Peter Wagoner, age 67 and born in Germany, a farmer, has wife Catherine, age 52, born in Germany. (we will see how many times the census is in error, and this is one.JR) Four children in the home. [p.156, fam #1006/994] George has brought one son, George, to the home. The rest of his children are grown, including son Peter, who married Elizabeth, daughter of John Rittgers, Jr. (#13.6)

On the 1870 census, Marion Twp., Hocking Co., Oh., we see Peter, 76, farming land he values at $1800. He and wife Katherine, 70!?!, value their personal possessions at $400. Amspaugh daughters Elizabeth, 27, and Lydia, 23, are still in the home.[p 493 fam #25/26] In records of the St. Jacobus Evangelical Lutheran Church, Rush Creek Twp., Fairfield Co., Oh., we find on page 81; "Katharina Wagner previously Amspach, daughter of Johann Augustinus Richers, b. 22 Nov 1807, Bpt. in her youth. Confirmed by Pastor Johannes Wagenhals. In year 1825 married Johann Amspach who died in 1848. They had 11 children. [We have found 9 children, the others may have died in infancy.] In 1854 she married for the second time 18 Feb (1854) Peter Wagner. (Katherine) D. 13 Apr 1871, age 63 yr., 4 mon., and 22 da." Another entry tells us "Peter Wagner d. 10 Dec 1876, age 83 yr., 7 mo., 2 da." In his will, made 8 Dec 1876, Peter leaves the "home place" in Marion Twp. to son George, providing he pays his brother's, Peter and Philip, and sister Catherine Miller, a total of $600 in installments over 5 years. He requires George to erect a stone over his grave, and that of wife Catherine, but no cemetery given. We also don't know if "Catherine" means his first wife or our Katherine. His will has been entered into probate 15 Dec 1876.[Hocking Co. Probate Bk "B", p.240] Amspaugh has been interpreted on the records as "Amsbaugh", Amspacher", "Amspach", to name a few known spellings.

ISSUE:

.15.1   Conrad AMSPAUGH, born about 1827 in Hocking Co., Oh. On the 1850 census, we find Conrad, age 23, working his father's farm there. He is taking care of his widowed mother and seven younger siblings.[p 6 fam #182/187] He married Lovina ____. She was born about 1835 in Ohio. The 1870 census of Marion Twp., Hocking Co., Oh., has "Coonrad", age 40, with wife Lovina, age 35, and Harry Grim, age 19, farm hand. No children listed.[p 507 fam #227/230]

+ .15.2   Noah AMSPAUGH, born about 1829.

+ .15.3   Susan AMSPAUGH, born 19 Jul 1830, died 7 Mar 1896.

+ .15.4   Jonas AMSPAUGH, born Dec 1831, died 6 Jan 1911.

+ .15.5   Lovina AMSPAUGH, born about 1834.

+ .15.6   Daniel AMSPAUGH, born about 1837.

.15.7   Elizabeth AMSPAUGH, born 30 Sep 1839 in Hocking Co., Oh.[EmEv,p.62] 1850 census with mother there in Marion Twp., age 11.[p 6 fam 192.187] 1860 census with mother and step-father, Peter Wagoner, Sr., in Hocking Co., Oh., She is now 22.[p 156 fam #1006/994]

+ .15.8   Leah AMSPAUGH, born 11 Feb 1842.

+ .15.9   Lydia AMSPAUGH, born 7 Aug 1845, Christened 2 Mar 1846.[St.James]

1.6 Daniel R.[2] RITTGERS (John[1]) was born 10 Sep 1810 in Shenandoah Co., Va., the son of John Augustin RITTGERS and Catharine COMER. He married (1) **Eve FOGHT** 11 Feb 1836 in Fairfield Co., Oh.[FCoM, Bk 1, p. 22, Record #259, by David Young, J.P.] She was born 2 Mar 1819. We have no proof of parentage of Eve, but Daniel's father, John, is one farm away from that of one John Foght. Daniel bought the NE quarter of the NW quarter of sect 26, Twp., 15, range 17, Hocking Co., for $175.[Hocking Co. Deeds Bk 5] Daniel and "Eave" sell this for $500, 12 Apr 1844[Hocking Co. Bk G, p.616] Eve died 8 Jan 1848, and is buried in Pleasant Hill Cemetery, Fairfield Co., Oh.[FCoCem]

Daniel married (2) **Christina Magdalene SMITH** 1 Aug 1848 in Fairfield Co., Oh. She was born 10 Aug 1830 in Wurttemberg, Germany. [FCoM, Bk 1A, p. 354, Record 4111, by John Sammott, J.P.] On 12 Mar 1849, Daniel bought part of the NW quarter of the NW quarter of section 24, Twp. 14, range 18, containing18 acres. [Fairfield Co. Deed Bk 15,p.708] He bought for $385, 38 acres in sect 13, Twp. 14, range 18, in Berne Twp., Fairfield Co., on 23 Feb 1850.[Fairfield Bk 17, p.329.]

The 1850 census shows us Daniel, age 39, with wife Christina, age 20, born in Oh. With them are David, 13, through Michael, 1/12 (or one month old). Daniel is a farmer with $3000 worth of property in Berne Twp., Fairfield Co., Oh. We know that Christina was not born in Ohio. This is a common error in census. In later census' she is listed as from Germany. [p 442 fam #147/160] Family record gives her birth, but age on stone calculates to 30 Aug 1830.

Daniel and Christina sold the above pieces of land for $2500 on 24 Sept 1853.[Fairfield Bk 21, p.12]

In her letter of 1914, Sarah (Rittgers) Good, (#12.A) tells us "Uncle Daniel came from Ohio to Iowa in 1854 or 1855 to the farm on the Des Moines River. He MAY also have owned land on the west side of Beaver or perhaps not. James Denny of the next generation owned on the west side."

In the land records of Polk Co., Ia., we find that Daniel Rittgers purchased from Stephen Y. Gose, a "fractional quarter" of land for $1400 dated October 29, 1853 and filed Nov. 3. The area is now listed as Rittgers Acres. [Abst #76811]

Iowa state census was done in 1856. Here we find Daniel, 45, farmer in Polk Co., who has been in Iowa 2 yrs. With him was wife Christina, 25, and eight children.[1856, p.285, #63] Descendent Jon Findley reports that he owns an old mantle clock that has been passed on to him through his family. In an attempt to restore the clock, he opened the back panel and found stuck in the casework a note: "Clock bot second hand from a family going west by the name Wright who were overloaded and wanted to sell about 1856 to 1858 bot by Danial Rittgers."

Daniel died 9 June 1859, and is buried in the Rittgers Cemetery, Johnston, Iowa. The estate was opened 17 June 1859. At that time only David and Reuben were of age. The others are listed as "minor child". Reuben was appointed administrator. Christina kept the children together and all the family stories tell us she was a wonderful mother to Eve's children as well as her own.[Probate Journal "O", p. 541. Reported in Abst 76811.] Reuben(#16.2) kept a journal over several years. In it he mentions "Mother" many times, mentioning the things he does for her. Daughter Mary Ann filed an "Oral Will" regarding her father's property dated 16 July 1859. In it she states that he bequeathed her $300 as a legacy over and above the share she would be entitled to as a legal heir. The court apparently asked the other heirs, as there is an "Order Establishing Oral Will" filed reporting that this was a true statement. She was paid $300 on an administrators report dated 28 June 1862. It is quite probable that this legacy was made as Mary Ann was blind.

The widow was assigned her dower - the homestead - and the remainder of the property was divided among the children. Over several years the lands were purchased from the others by Reuben. He had in his ownership most of this land at his death in 1893.[Abst.76811]

Christina, 29, is head of house in Jefferson Twp., Polk Co., Ia., on the 1860 census and has Reuben, at 22 the oldest child in the home, with her - apparently farming the land - and all the rest of the children, both hers and Eve's, down to one year old Nancy J. [fam #742/697] By the 1870 census, George, Christina's first, is the oldest at home, age 21, with the younger children. [p 406 fam #96/106]   Reuben (#16.2) married in 1865 and brought his bride, Abigail Findley to the Rittgers home until he could build their house. In a diary kept the first year of their marriage, Abigail speaks several times of "Mother Rittgers". In a carefully kept accounting, Reuben and Abigail kept track of what they "borrowed" from Christina, items such as "August 31st both ate two meals" "Sept 8 Myself two Reuben one [meal]", "Borrowed of Mother Rittgers sugar .50; Lining for shirt cuffs." "All accounts between Mother and us being ballanced up to July 27, 1866, I find myself in debt to Mother $35.45 being in full of all accounts. R.R. Rittgers."

In the records of Fairfield Co., Oh., we found a deed by one John M. Smith and others, selling property there in Twp. 14, range 18. Among the signers was Christina Rittgers. The others were John M. and Christina Smith; Henry & maria Zeingmeister, Frederick and Doretta Dowler, and Christina Smith, widow of Michael, deceased. Could this be her father and mother?

Christina married Moses Lawson on 30 Sept 1874,[PVRM,Bk1, p.166] and the family tells us she married a lot of hard work, as he was not a good provider. In "History of Polk Co.", [p. 986] we find an article on Moses Lawson that reports he married as his second wife "Miss Christina Rittgers." Moses was born in York Co., Pa., Aug 1827. He moved to Indiana about 1837, where he "learned the trades of carpenter and millwright." In 1855 he came to Polk Co., Ia. By 1857 he was "engaged in the saw-mill business, and in the spring of 1864 commenced farming. He married first in Indiana, 6 Sept 1854, Miss Abigail Finnick, who died 3 Oct 1872." At the time of his marriage to Christina, 30 Sept 1874, Moses had seven children, and Christina still had two or three daughters at home.

In 1868 one Moses Lawson purchased property that had originally belonged to Jacob Rittgers. In 1870 we find Moses with his wife Abigail and seven children in Valley Twp. Another mortgage in the name of Moses Lawson "and wife" is on file in 1872. Yet another in 1876 lists Moses and "wife Christina." By 1979 all three mortgages were declared free and clear with no taxes or liens. The 1880 census, Valley Twp., Polk Co., Ia., shows Moses and Christina with children, surnamed Lawson, Elizabeth A, 18; Henry E., 14; Marilda E., 11; and Minnie, 7. [ED 3 fam 122/125] She raised Eva's, then hers, and now is raising yet another family!! The Iowa state census of 1895 shows Moses, 66, a laborer, and wife Christina, 64, win Webster Twp., Polk Co.[1895, #100] In 1900, Webster, Polk Co., we find Christina, age 69 and giving a birth date of Aug 1838. She declares they have been married 25 years and she has born 5 children, all alive at this time. Moses H. is 72, b. Aug 1838, declares he is a farmer, retired. They are boarding an 11 year old boy, John Krupka, in their home. [ED 112, p 5, fam #164/171]

Christina died 1 Apr 1905 in Polk County, Ia., and was buried with Daniel in the Rittgers Cemetery, Johnston, Ia. Her stone reads "Christina - Wife of - Daniel Rittgers". Moses Lawson died 2 Sept 1906, and is buried with his first wife, Abigail, in the Kinsey Cemetery, Johnston, Polk Co., Ia.[Tombstone]

ISSUE of Daniel and Eve:

+ .16.1   David Foght RITTGERS, born 14 Feb 1837, died 16 Apr 1926.
+ .16.2   Reuben R. RITTGERS, born 19 Apr 1838, died 18 Nov 1893.
  .16.3   Mary Ann RITTGERS, born 23 Apr 1841 in Berne Twp., Fairfield Co., Oh. We find her on records also called "Anna Mary" She is on 1850 census, age 11, with father and step-mother there.[p 442 fam #147/160] After her father's death, June 1859, she petitioned the Polk Co., Ia., Court on 18 July 1859, stating that her father made a verbal will bequeathing her "$300 as a legacy over and above and in addition to her share of the estate..." Mary is seen on the 1860 census, age 19, with step-mother and siblings, Jefferson Twp., Polk Co., Ia.[p fam #742/697] That she received $300 before June 1862 is shown in abstract #76811 of her father's property, as taken from Probate Journal 1, p. 353. She married George W. SNYDER 31 Mar 1868 in Polk County, Ia.[Family Bible of Rosannah (Rittgers) Findley, now in possession of Jon Findley of Tempe, Az.] George was the widower of sister Malinda RITTGERS (See number 16.5) They had no children. Family history tells us Mary was blind and taught at a school for the blind. On the 1870 census we find George "Snider", 30, born in Pa., with $4637 in Real Estate and $1585 in personal estate in Valley Twp., Polk Co., Ia., with wife Mary, age 29. It is noted on the census record that she is blind. [p 108 fam #115/124] "Anna Mary" died 13 Oct 1884 and is buried in the Rittgers Cemetery.[RitCem]
+ .16.4   Sarah RITTGERS, born 10 Sep 1842, died 13 Jul 1925.
  .16.5   Malinda RITTGERS, born 3 Jul 1844 in Berne Twp., Fairfield Co., Oh. She is age 7 on 1850 census there, with father and step-mother.[P. 442, fam #147/160], and on the 1860 census, age 15, with family in Jefferson Twp, Polk Co., Ia. She married George W. SNYDER in Polk Co., Ia. He was born about 1840 in Pa. George also married (2) Mary Ann RITTGERS (See number 16.3) Malinda died 31 Oct 1866, and was buried in Rittger's Cem., Polk, Ia.[RitCem]
  .16.6   John Henry RITTGERS, born 21 Jun 1846 in Berne Twp., Fairfield Co., Oh. He is on the 1850 census, age 4, with father and step-mother there.[p 442 fam #147/160] On 1860 census, age 13, now in Jefferson Twp., Polk Co., Oh.[p fam #742/697] John enlisted in the 44th Iowa Vols, Co. H., at the same time as brother

Reuben and cousin Peter, on 12 May 1864. Because he was a minor, age 18, Reuben as his guardian had to sign for him to go. In his enlistment, John is described as having hazel eyes, Auburn hair and dark complexion. He was 5'6" tall. At the time of the expiration of their enlistment, 100 days later, the two brothers and their cousin were sent to Davenport, Ia. Peter and Reuben mustered out on the 15th of Sept, 1864, the same day John Henry died. We were told he died of Measles, but in the "Inventory of the effects" it is reported that he died at General Hospital, Davenport, Ia., on 15 Sept 1864 of "chronick direah." Here we see he had in his possession one blouse, one cap, one neck tie. We are told that he had "drawn clothing to the amount of $18.29." Probably not knowing how ill John was, Reuben went home. Reuben writes in his diary of driving a team of horses as far as Kellogg, Ia., as far west as the train tracks came, then boarding a train to Davenport [Ia.] where he received the body of his young brother." We are told the Army paid him to come get the body, but in "Roster Iowa Volunteers, p. 1264, we are told that John is buried in the National Cemetery, Rock Island, Ill. John Henry was returned to the family fold and is buried in the Rittgers Cemetery.

ISSUE of Daniel and Christina:

+ .16.7   George RITTGERS, born 28 Jan 1849, died 21 Mar 1914.
+ .16.8   Michael RITTGERS, born 1 Sep 1850, died 2 Mar 1919.
+ .16.9   Caroline "Nina" RITTGERS, born 10 Mar 1853, died 18 Mar 1929.
+ .16.A   Rosannah RITTGERS, born 4 Jan 1856, died 21 May 1929.
+ .16.B   Nancy Jane RITTGERS, born 6 Sep 1858, died 28 Feb 1922.

1.7 Elizabeth^2 RITTGERS (John^1) was born 1815 in Shenandoah Co., Va., the daughter of John Augustin RITTGERS and Catharine COMER. "Elizabeth Richard" married **John STROHL** 14 Aug 1831, Fairfield Co., Oh.[FVRM, Bk R,p.15] On the 1840 census, we see a John Strohl listed as head of household in Laurel Twp., Hocking Co., Oh. There are one male 30-39, one female 20-29, one male age 5-9, one male 0-4, and three females 0-4.[p 182] On the 1850 census in Laurel Twp., John is a farmer, age 40, thus born about 1803, in Pa. Wife Elizabeth is 35. The first ten children, as listed below are on the census.[p 28, fam #405/414] On the 1860 census we find John Strohl, age 57 (?) He has $400 worth of real estate and $400 in personal estate. Wife Elizabeth is 46 and born in Ohio[?]. Eight children still in the home.[p. 156 fam #983/971] In 1870 John, now listed as 67, values his property at $2600 and personal property at $100. Elizabeth is 53 and with them is George W., 17; Lucinda, 16; and Rosa age 14.[p 489, fam #212/212] They have lived in Laurel Twp., Hocking Co., Oh., on all the census records. On Plat maps of the Ohio River Survey, Congressional Lands, we find that John Strohl purchased two adjacent plots of 34.89 and 34.78 acres each. On 30 Nov 1836, at the time of the first purchase, he is listed as living in Fairfield Co. On 26 Dec 1836 he purchased the second and was listed as being of Hocking Co.[Kocher] John's death is recorded in the Ohio Gen. Soc., THE REPORT, Spring 1990, Vol 30, #1, p. 26, Early Hocking Co., Undertakers Records, where we see one - John "Stroll" 9 Apr 1872, $15.00.(probably amount paid to the undertaker) No death date for Elizabeth has been found to date.

ISSUE:

+ .17.1   Noah STROHL, born about 1834.
  .17.2   William STROHL, born about 1835 in Laurel Twp., Hocking Co., Oh.   On 1850 census, age 15, with parents there.[p 28, fam #405/414] He married Susan PRIMMER 22 Nov 1857 in Hocking Co., Oh.[HVRM, Book "B", p. 273.]

+ .17.3   Caroline H. STROHL, born about 1836.
  .17.4   Mary STROHL, born about 1837. We see her on the 1850 census, age 13, with her
               parents [p 28 fam #405/414], but she is not on the 1860 census.
+ .17.5   Eve STROHL, born about 1839.
  .17.6   Elizabeth STROHL, born about 1840 in Laurel Twp., Hocking Co., Oh. On 1850
               census with parents there, age 10.[p 28 fam #405/414] On 1860 census there with
               parents, age 17.[p 156 fam #983/971] Hocking Co. Book "C" of Marriages., p. 56
               gives us marriage of Christian Berry to Elizabeth Strohl, 4 Apr 1861, Hocking Co.,
               Oh. It also reports on page 71, the marriage of Joseph Primmer and Elizabeth
               Strohl 1 Sept 1861. Further research needed to determine which is our Elizabeth.
  .17.7   John STROHL, born about 1841 in Laurel Twp., Hocking Co., Oh. On 1850 census
               with parents there, age 9.[p 28 fam #405/414] On 1860 census there with parents,
               age 19.[156 fam #983/971] No marriage found for him in Hocking Co., Oh.
  .17.8   Joseph STROHL, born about 1846 in Laurel Twp., Hocking Co., Oh. On 1850
               census with parents there, age 7.[p 28 fam #405/414] On 1860 census there with
               parents, age 14.[p 156 fam #983/971] No marriage found for him in Hocking Co.
+ .17.9   Jacob STROHL, born about 1848.
  .17.A   Daniel STROHL, born May 1850 in Laurel Twp., Hocking Co., Oh. With parents
               there on the 1850 census, age 1/12.[p 28 fam #405/414] On the 1860 census, we are
               told he is 10.[p 156 fam #983/971] He married Susan NIHISER 4 Mar 1875 in
               Hocking County, Oh.[HVRM, Bk.D,p.218] She was born about 1850.
  .17.B   George Westley STROHL, born about 1852 in Laurel Twp., Hocking, Oh. On the
               1860 census there with parents, age 8, called Westley.[p 156 fam #983/971] On the
               1870 census, age 17, called George W. Working on father's farm.[p 489 fam
               212/212]
  .17.C   Lucinda STROHL, born about 1853 in Laurel Twp., Hocking, Oh. On the 1860
               census there with parents, age 7.[p 156 fam #983/917], and on the 1870 census, age
               16, "helps mother", still with parents.[p 489 fam 212/212] She married John D.
               BOWERS 20 Jul 1871 in Hocking County, Oh. [HVRM, Book "D", p. 2]
  .17.D   Rosanna STROHL, born about 1856 in Laurel Twp., Hocking, Oh. On 1860 census
               there with parents, age 4.[p 156 fam #983/917] and on 1870 census, "Rosa" age 14,
               with parents.[p 489 fam 212/212] She married Adam NIBLING 3 Dec 1875 in
               Hocking County, Oh.[HVRM, Book "D", p. 266]

1.9 Susanna[2] RITTGERS (John[1]) was born 10 Oct 1818 in Rush Creek Twp., Fairfield Co,
Oh., the daughter of John Augustin RITTGERS and Catharine COMER.[EmEv, p. 38.] "Susan
Richie" married **Peter DAUBENMIRE** 24 Jan 1836 in Fairfield County, Oh.[FVRM Bk R,p.15]
He was born 11 Oct 1805 in Steinbach, Dtechl, Germany. On the 1850 census we find Peter,
45, a farmer in Marion Twp., Hocking Co., Oh., b. Germany. They have $600 in Real Estate.
Susanna is 34, born in Ohio, and they have with them seven children.[p 853 fam #191/196] On
the 1860 census, still in Marion Twp. with a Logan Post Office, Hocking Co., Oh., Peter is now
55 and still farming. Susannah is 42. Still seven children, the older ones have left and she has
born more. [p 157 fam #1027/1015] By 1870, Peter at 65 is still farming in Marion. "Susan" is
52 and there are still seven children home.[p 506 fam #212/215] In 1880, 75 year old Peter is still
farming. Susanna, now 63, has a notation by her name "Rheumatitis." In the home are also
Barbara, 19; and Daniel, 17. [ED 63 fam #129/131] In Records from the Emmanuel Evangelical
Lutheran Congregation, Marion Twp., Hocking Co., Oh., we find her death as 27 Oct 1884.

There are several errors in the record, but we see she had suffered from rheumatism, and was survived by husband & 12 children. It states she was born in Rushcreek Twp., Fairfield Co., 10 Oct 1818, baptized 24 Jan 1826. It also reports that she was survived by 6 aunts and 2 uncles! These MUST be from the Comer side of the family, as we have yet to find any other Rittgers Elders. In the same records we find that Peter, b. 11 Oct 1805, Steinbach, Deutchland, married 24 Jan 1836, to Susanna "Ritche". They had 14 children - 3 sons and 11 daughters. He died 27 Aug 1888, age 82 yrs., 10 mo., 18 days. He may have remarried, as we see he is survived by an unnamed wife and 2 children. We question the "wife and children" statement, and there is no entry in the Hocking Co. Marriages for a Peter Daubenmire between 1884 & 1888, and the entry has many other errors..

ISSUE:

.19.1	Eva DAUBENMIRE, born in Marion Twp., Hocking, Oh.
+ .19.2	Rosana DAUBENMIRE, born 16 Oct 1836.
+ .19.3	Susana DAUBENMIRE, born 20 Sep 1837.
+ .19.4	Elizabeth DAUBENMIRE, born 1 Mar 1839.
.19.5	Unnamed DAUBENMIRE, born 10 Feb 1841 in Marion Twp., Hocking Co., Oh.
.19.6	Eve DAUBENMIRE, born about 1842 in Hocking Co., Oh. On 1850 census, age 8, with parents, Marion Twp., Hocking Co., Oh.[p 853 fam #191/196.] She married William PIFER 1858 in Hocking Co., Oh. Husband's name spelled "Pheifer" in St. James records.[HVRM, Book "B", p. 298]
.19.7	Catherine DAUBENMIRE, born about 1843 in Hocking Co., Oh.. On the 1850 census age 7, with parents, Marion Twp., Hocking Co., Oh.[p 853 fam #191/196] Still with parents on 1860 census in Marion Twp, age 17. Oldest child in home at this time.[p 157 fam #1027/1015] On 1870 census, age 26, continues in parent's home.[p 506 fam #212/215]
+ .19.8	Peter B. DAUBENMIRE, born 18 Dec 1846, died 30 Jan 1934.
+ .19.9	Christina DAUBENMIRE, born 6 May 1849, died 8 Apr 1912.
+ .19.A	Maria Magdalena DAUBENMIRE, born 18 Mar 1851.
+ .19.B	Sarah Elizabeth DAUBENMIRE, born 5 Mar 1853, died 15 Jun 1937.
+ .19.C	Caroline DAUBENMIRE, born 7 Jan 1856.
+ .19.D	Jacob A. DAUBENMIRE, born 1 Aug 1858, died 25 Jan 1936.
+ .19.E	George DAUBENMIRE, born 13 May 1860, died 1942.
.19.F	Barbara DAUBENMIRE, born 28 Apr 1861 in Marion Twp., Hocking Co., Oh. She is on the 1870 census, age 10, with parents in Marion, Hocking Co., Oh.[p 156 fam #212/215] and on the 1880 census, age 19, with them there.[ED 63, p 195B, fam #129/131]

CHAPTER 3

GENERATION NO. 3

11.1 Julia A.[3] RITTGERS (Joseph[2], John[1]) was born about 1823 in Hocking Co., Oh., the daughter of Joseph RITTGERS and Anna ____. She married **Joseph GUISER** 29 Mar 1840 in Hocking Co., Oh.[HVRM, Bk A, p. 8.] He was born about 1818 "on the ocean", he reports in census record. On their marriage record, Joseph's name is spelled "Guiser", and on the 1850 census, we find it under "Geiser". The census shows us that Joseph, 32, is a laborer and Julia, 27 is caring for the children. They live in the home of a farmer named Snider in Bern Twp., Fairfield Co., Oh.[p 460 fam #511/404] We find that following her father's death before Nov 1864, Julia "Giger" sells her share of their father's lands to brother Abraham on 2 Nov 1864. There is no mention of a husband. Julia "Geiger" married (2) Jacob Kreashbaum on 3 Nov 1870 in Hocking Co., Oh.[HVRM Bk C., p605]

ISSUE:
.111.1　Louisa GUISER, born about 1842 in Bern Twp., Fairfield Co., Oh. She is on the 1850 census, age 8, with parents there.[p 460 fam #511/404]
.111.2　Abraham GUISER, born about 1844 in Bern Twp., Fairfield Co., Oh. He is on the 1850 census, age 6, with parents there.[p 460 fam #511/404]
.111.3　Ann GUISER, born about 1846 in Bern Twp., Fairfield Co., Oh. She is on the 1850 census, age 4, with parents there.[p 460 fam #511/404]
.111.4　George GUISER, born about 1849 in Bern Twp., Fairfield Co., Oh. He is on the 1850 census, age 1, with parents there.[p 460 fam #511/404] One George Geiger married on 2 May 1869, Elizabeth White, Hocking Co., Oh.[HVRM Bk C, p.523]

11.2 Abraham[3] RITTGERS (Joseph[2], John[1]) was born 11 Nov 1829 in Hocking Co., Oh., the son of Joseph RITTGERS and Anna. On the 1850 census, Marion Twp., Hocking Co., Oh., Abraham, 21, is listed with his parents.[p 855 fam # 212/218] He married **Catherine LEFLER** 9 Sep 1853 in Marion Twp.[HVRM, Book "B", p. 173] She was born about 1834 in Hocking Co., Oh. "Abram" sells the SE part of the SW quarter of Section 8,Twp. 15, Range 17, 50 acres, for $32. It reports Catherine also on deed, but deed dated 11 Feb 1853![Hocking Co. Bk M, p.147] He purchases on 25 Nov 1858 the SW quarter of the NW quarter of section 19, from his father for $400.[Hocking Co. Bk Q, p.548] On the 1860 census, "Abram", age 30, is a farmer in Marion Twp. Wife Catherine, 26, is caring for their 2 children.[p 158 fam #1037/1025] On 4 Aug 1860, Abraham and Catherine sell their SW section of the NW quarter to John Ruff.[Hocking Co. Bk V, p.299] In Book Y of Hocking Co. Deeds, we see that Abraham purchased from his sisters, Julia "Geiger" and Anna Grove, their undivided 2/6 interest in their father's land, 4 Aug 1860.[P.208] On 4 Nov 1864, he buys from Henry and Catherine Hufford, their 1/6 interest in her father's property.[p.209] On 4 Aug 1860 he buys out David and Mary Lefler's portion.[p.210] On the same day he sells the entire piece to Daniel Ruff.[p.211] We don't see sister Lucinda being bought out - it is possible that the deed didn't get recorded. By 1870 "Abram" is in Brown Twp, Darke Co., Oh. (West and a bit north of Hocking Co. on the Indiana border.) He is 41 and a farmer with $1600 real estate and $500 worth of personal property. Catherine, 35, is caring for their 3 children.[p 3, fam # 41/40] They continue in Brown Twp. in 1880, where Abram, 51, is a farmer. Catherine, 45, continues to care for the home, and two sons, Joseph, age 24, is a farmer; and Samuel, 13, "works on farm".[ED 56 p

46D, fam #74/74]   Family history tells us he died 13 Aug 1897, Darke Co., Oh., and is buried
in the "Old Brick Cemetery, north of Union City, [Darke Co.,] Oh." We are told the Old Brick
Cemetery is actually in Randolph Co., Ind., but possibly straddles the state line. On older maps,
it appears that Union, Oh., possibly crossed the state line.

ISSUE:

+ .112.1   Daniel RITTGERS, born 14 Jun 1853, died 15 May 1928.
+ .112.2   Joseph RITTGERS, born Dec 1855, died 1910/1920.
+ .112.3   Samuel RITTGERS, born Nov 1865.

11.3 Lucinda[3] RITTGERS (Joseph[2], John[1]) was born 11 Jan 1830 in Hocking Co., Oh., the
daughter of Joseph RITTGERS and Anna____. On the census 1850 age 20, b. Oh., at home
with parents in Marion Twp., Hocking Co., Oh. [p 855 fam #212/218] She married **David C.
CONRAD** 24 Jun 1852 in Marion Twp., Hocking Co., Oh. [HVRM, Bk B, p. 170] He was born
21 Dec 1815. It appears that David's parents were Christopher and Barbary A. (__) Conrad,
"who came from Wirt Co., W.Va. in 1827." (then W.Va. was part of Va.) [OGS, THE
REPORT, Vol 23, #4, Winter, 1983, p. 217.] The 1860 census shows us David "Coonrod", age
45, b. Va., a farmer with $400 in real estate and $353 in personal belongings. Lucinda is age 30,
and taking care of her four children in Goodhope Twp., Hocking Co., Oh. [p 37 fam #522/515]
By 1870 David "Coonrad", age 54, values his farm in Goodhope at $3000. Lucinda, now 40, is
taking care of their six children.[p 453 fam #168/168]   David died 4 Feb 1875 in Hocking Co.,
Oh., and was buried in the Conrad Cemetery, Good Hope Twp., Hocking, Oh. The Cemetery
appears to be in a poorly accessible area, as a notation reads "this family cemetery was found
only with the help of historian...." [from THE REPORT, Ohio Gen. Soc. Newsletter, Vol 23, #2,
Summer 1983, p. 73.] Just why Lucinda went to Brown Twp., Darke Co., Oh., is not known.
Lucinda died 27 Mar 1878 in Darke County, Oh., and was buried in Old Brick Cemetery,
Randolph Co., Ind.

ISSUE:

+ .113.1   Emanuel J. CONRAD, born Apr 1853, died May 1937.
  .113.2   Mary E. CONRAD, born May 1855 in Hocking Co., Oh. She is age 5, on 1860
              census with parents, Good Hope Twp. (S. Bloomingville) Hocking Co., Oh.[p 37
              fam # 522/515] and age 15 with parents there on the 1870 census.[p 453 fam
              #168/168] The 1880 census shows Mary, 25, sister of Emanuel Conrad, in his home
              in East Precinct, Jackson Twp., Darke Co., Oh.[p 220B fam #50/51] She married
              Simeon BEERY 28 Dec 1884 in Darke County, Oh.[DkCoM, p. 22] In 1900 we
              find Mary E. Beery, 45, a widow in the home of her sister, Emma. Mary declares
              she has born one child, that child died. She is listed as "servant, private family."[ED
              60, p 27A, fam #262/279]
+ .113.3   Emma CONRAD, born about 1858.
+ .113.4   Lafayette Fountaine CONRAD, born 6 May 1860, died 5 Jun 1934.
  .113.5   Effie A. CONRAD, born about 1864 in Good Hope Twp., Hocking Co., Oh. She
              is on 1870 census, Good Hope Twp., (Gibsonville P.O.) Hocking Co., Oh., age 6,
              with parents.[p 453 fam #168/168] She is not on 1880 census with siblings in
              Jackson, Darke Co., Oh., where we would have expected to find her at age 16.[p
              22B fam #50/51]
+ .113.6   Jesse CONRAD, born Aug 1869.
  .113.7   William CONRAD, born 1872 in Oh. He is on the 1880 census, age 8, with siblings
              in home of oldest brother Emanuel Conrad, E. Precinct, Jackson, Darke Co., Oh.[p

220B fam #50/51] He married Florence HART 15 Oct 1893 in Darke Co., Oh. [DkCoM, p 57.]

11.4 Catherine³ RITTGERS (Joseph², John¹) was born about 1832 in Hocking Co., Oh., the daughter of Joseph RITTGERS and Anna ____. On the 1850 census age 18, b. Oh., at home with parents, Marion Twp., Hocking Co., Oh.[p 855 fam # 212/218] She married **Henry HUFFORD** 5 Feb 1860 in Hocking Co., Oh. He was born Dec 1836 in Oh. On her marriage record she is listed as Catherine "Richey."[HVRM, Bk C, p.6] In 1860, we see Henry 23, and Catherine 23, on the farm of A.G. Jackson, Good Hope Twp., Hocking Co., Oh., where Henry is a Laborer. They have $50 in personal possessions.[p 36 fam #507/499] On the 1880 census, Henry, 45, is farming in Brown Twp., Darke Co., Oh. Catherine, 44, is caring for their four children.[p 4 fam #78/84] Catherine died before 1900 in Brown Twp., Darke, Oh., as we see on the 1900 census, Henry is a widower living with son Theodore and family in Brown Twp., Darke Co., Oh.[E.D. 50, p 98, fam #196/199]

ISSUE:

+ .114.1   Theodore HUFFORD, born Nov 1860.
  .114.2   William HUFFORD, born about 1862 in Good Hope Twp., Hocking Co., Oh. Age 18 on 1880 census, with parents, Brown Twp., Darke Co.,Oh.[ED 56, p 4, fam #78/84]
+ .114.3   Ida HUFFORD, born Aug 1867.
+ .114.4   Abraham HUFFORD, born Jul 1872.

11.5 Mary³ RITTGERS (Joseph², John¹) was born 1834 in Marion Twp., Hocking Co., Oh., the daughter of Joseph RITTGERS and Anna ____. She is on the 1850 census, age 16, b. Oh., with parents there.[p 841 fam #118/120] She married **David LEFLER** 2 Oct 1859 in Marion Twp., Hocking Co., Oh. [HVRM, Bk B, p. 310] The LDS-GedCom, Ver. 1.0, 1993, Ancestral File CD; shows us one David Lefler, [#JXVG-FB, this no. is the individual #on this file] b. abt 1840, to Peter and Barbara (Springer) Lefler (no place given), married Mary Rittgers. [#JSVG-8G] On 1860 census, Marion Twp., Hocking Co., Oh., we find David, age 23, a "Sawyer" (one who cuts wood) and Mary, age 25. On 4 Aug 1866, David and Mary Lefler sell her share of their father's property to her brother, Abraham.[Hocking Co. Bk Y,p.210] They have $1200 in real estate and $300 in personal property. One David Lefler married 20 Sept 1866, Hocking Co., Oh., Lucinda Peters.

ISSUE:

+ .115.1   Malinda LEFLER, born 27 Apr 1862, died 13 Jan 1933.

11.6 Anna³ RITTGERS (Joseph², John¹) was born 6 May 1839 [Bigham] in Marion Twp., Hocking, Oh., the daughter of Joseph RITTGERS and Anna____. On the 1850 Census, age 11, with parents there.(p 855 fam #212/218) Anna "Richards" married **Samuel GROVE** 27 Mar 1859 in Hocking Co., Oh.[HVRM, Bk B, p.300] He was born 31 Mar 1834 in Hocking County, Oh. On the 1860 census, Samuel is alone as a farm laborer, age 23, in Bern Twp., Fairfield Co., Oh. Mary is listed with her sister, Julia "Giger", on a deed selling their share of their father's property to brother Abraham, 2 Nov 1864.[Hocking Co. Deed Bk Y,p.208] Her husband is not mentioned in the deed. We are told Samuel enlisted in Co. H, 58th Regiment, Ohio infantry Vols on 5 Oct 1861, and is discharged 11 Jan 1865. While stationed at Fort Donaldson, Tenn., on 1 Mar 1863, he contracted diarrhea "and some morbid affection of the liver, the source of which he cannot designate, that said disease is the result of exposure and the water he had to use and that said diseases have resulted in the general and constant weakness." He is described as being 5'11" tall, dark complexion and blue eyes. Samuel's cause of death, 12 Mar 1897 in Hocking Co., Oh., is given as "diarrhea." as a result of the infection contracted during the Civil War. Anna died of Smallpox 26 Apr 1904 in Marion Twp., Hocking Co., Oh. [Berens]

ISSUE:

+.116.1   George GROVE, born 12 Mar 1860, died 28 Feb 1892.

.116.2   Effie Jane GROVE, born 20 Apr 1860 in Millville, Hocking Co., Oh. She married Wilas M. McCONNELL 1884 in Hocking Co., Oh. Millville now called Rockbridge.

.116.3   Mary GROVE, born 30 Mar 1867 in Millville, Hocking Co., Oh. She married James F. POLING 26 Jan 1888 in Hocking Co., Oh.[HVRM,BkE,p.447] Millville now called Rockbridge.

.116.4   Elizabeth GROVE, born 24 Jun 1869 in Millville, Hocking Co., Oh, died 22 May 1871 in Millville, Hocking Co., Oh. Millville now called Rockbridge.

.116.5   William GROVE, born 1 Mar 1871 in Millville, Hocking Co., Oh, died 14 Jul 1871 in Millville, Hocking Co., Oh. Millville now called Rockbridge.

.116.6   Francis GROVE, born 24 Aug 1872 in Millville, Hocking Co., Oh. Millville now called Rockbridge.

.116.7   James GROVE, born 7 May 1875 in Hocking Co., Oh.

.116.8   Edward Theodore GROVE, born 20 Apr 1878 in Good Hope Twp., Hocking Co., Oh. He married Ada____.

+.116.9   Rosetta GROVE, born 2 Mar 1881, died 14 Oct 1954.

.116.A   Joseph Ellsworth GROVE, born 18 Jun 1885 in Rockbridge, Hocking Co., Oh.

12.1 Samuel S.[3] RITTGERS (Jacob[2], John[1]) was born 21 Feb 1823 in Hocking Co., Oh., the son of Jacob B. RITTGERS and Hester PATTERSON. In Dec 1848, he bid $4.51 per acre on his grandfather's property, 3/4 of Sect 6, Twp. 15, Range 17, when it went to Sheriff's auction. It was deeded to him for a total price of $549.04 1/3(cent) on 25 July 1849. He sold it the same day for $600, to Nicholas Wagner. On an 1876 Hocking Co. Plat map, we can see Nicholas as owner. He married (1) **Rosannah SHERBROWN** (Sherbaum, Sherburn) 7 Mar 1850 in Marion Twp., Hocking, Oh.[MVRM, Bk B, p. 131.] She was born about 1833 in Ohio. We find Samuel on the 1850 census next door to his father, Jacob, in Marion Twp., Hocking Co., Ohio. He is 26, a farmer, with wife Rosanna, age 17.[p 855 fam #214/220] Samuel bought 93.5 acres from his father 3 Dec 1855 [Polk Co. Book of Deeds H, p. 404.] This deed corrected 31 Oct 1874 to show that land was actually in different part of the section than originally specified.[Abstract #62638, p 3] Rosanna died in Polk Co., Ia., 29 Mar 1856, age 22 yrs., 10 mo., 23days.[RitCem] On the 1856 state census, we find Samuel, 30, in his father's home. With him is Emmaline, 4, and Ellen, 2. He declares he has been 0 years in Ia.(not there a full year) [p 274,fam #26] Samuel married (2) **Christina EDGELL** 28 Dec 1856 in Polk Co., Ia. She was born about 1830 in Germany. By the 1860 census, he is listed next door to his father, Jacob (#1.2) in Jefferson Twp., Polk Co., Ia. With him is Christina and his children by Rosannah. Also in the home is one Mary E. "Edzell," 6. [p 93, fam #747/682] Christina died 27 Sep 1875 in Mercer Co., Mo. Samuel married (3) **Marinda (Boston) HURST** 5 Nov 1876. She was born about 1841 in Mo. The 1880 census shows Samuel, age 56, a farmer, in Washington Twp.("West half" stated on census record), Mercer Co., Mo. He has wife Merinda C., age 39 born in Missouri. She declares her father born in New York. Record too faint to read where mother born. [p 152A fam #1/1] In his father's estate, 1880, he is called "S.S.Rittgers a son of full age residing in Princeton, Mo." [Abstract #62638] Marinda died 6 Jan 1892 in

Mercer Co., Mo. The 1900 Census gives Samuel, age 76, b. Sept. 1823 in Ohio. He is still farming. With him are his two youngest children, Sanford, age 18, b. June 1881 and Maggie, age 16, b. May 1884. They are in Harrison, Mercer Co., Mo.[ED 113, p 6B, fam #117/119] Samuel died 20 Dec 1909 in Mercer Co., Mo., and was buried there in Union Cemetery. Hartman's article tells us that Samuel moved to Mo. to "raise fruit trees. He was very self conscious of his heavy German accent - he had been raised with German as his first language - and never allowed his children to learn that language. He was united with the Methodist Evangelical Church."

ISSUE of Samuel and Rosannah:

.121.1   Emmaline RITTGERS, born 6 Jan 1851 in Marion Twp., Hocking Co., Oh, died 8 Feb 1866. On 1856 special census, Polk Co., Ia., she is age 4, with father and grandfather on 1860 census, age 9, with parents Jefferson Twp., Polk Co., Ia.[p 33, fam #747/682]
+ .121.2   Martha "Elly" RITTGERS, born 6 Feb 1853, died 20 Jul 1935.
.121.3   George RITTGERS, born 10 Jan 1855 in Polk Co., Ia., died 3 Aug 1855 in Jefferson Twp, Polk Co., Ia.

ISSUE of Samuel and Christina:

+ .121.4   Alice RITTGERS, born 18 Dec 1858.
+ .121.5   Albert Clarence RITTGERS, born 9 Apr 1861, died 1 May 1935.
+ .121.6   Perry RITTGERS, born 10 Sep 1863.
+ .121.7   Sarah Isabel RITTGERS, born 18 Oct 1866, died 12 Apr 1906.

ISSUE of Samuel and Marinda:

.121.8   Birty C. RITTGERS, born 13 Mar 1878 in Mercer Co., Mo., died there 30 Mar 1884
+ .121.9   Sanford S. RITTGERS, born 7 Jun 1881.
+ .121.A   Margaret RITTGERS, born 22 May 1884, died 1922.

12.2 Isabelle[3] RITTGERS (Jacob[2], John[1]) was born 7 Mar 1825 in Hocking Co., Oh., the daughter of Jacob B. RITTGERS and Hester PATTERSON. She married **Samuel ILES,** 22 Oct 1846, in Hocking Co., Oh.. [HVRM, Book "B", p. 80.] He was born about 1812 in Oh. On the 1850 census we see Samuel, age 38, a farmer in Marion Twp., Hocking Co., Oh. Wife Isabelle is caring for their child, John H., age 2 [p 861 fam #248/256] "Isabelle Iles" d. 27 June 1858, at age 33 yrs., 3 mo., 20 days. She is buried in the "Iles-Vine" Cemetery, Marion Twp., Hocking Co., Oh.[HCoCem] Samuel married (2) Mary Ann Webb 17 Mar 1859.[LDS-IGI] The 1860 census shows Samuel Illes, age 47, a farmer in Falls Twp, Hocking Co., Oh., with wife Mary Ann, age 34. With him are John H., 12; Hester Ann, 10; Isabel, 7; Jeremiah, 6/12; and Daniel, 7. Because Daniel is listed last, and out of birth order, it is this author's conclusion he is probably Mary Ann's son from a previous marriage, and most probably John, Hester, and Isabel, are Isabelle's children.[p 113 fam #423/425] LDS-IGI also gives a marriage for Samuel Iles to Susan Griffin, 10 Sept 1865. Children of these last two marriages are NOT Rittgers Descendants. Record of the Iles-Vine Cemetery lists Samuel Iles, d. 12 Dec 1865, age 50 yrs, 5 mo., 17 days, which gives us a birth date of 25 June 1815. In the estate of Jacob Rittgers, 1880, we see named John H. Iles and Esther Mason, "children of Isabella Iles a deceased daughter, and the only surviving heirs of the deceased daughter residing in Polk Co. [Ia.]"

ISSUE:

.122.1   John Henry ILES, born about 1848 in Marion Twp., Hocking Co., Oh. On 1850 census, age 2, with parents there.[p 861, fam #248/256] On 1860 census, age 12 with father and step-mother, Falls Twp, Hocking Co., Oh.[p 113 fam #423/425] In 1880 he is named on grandfather's estate as "surviving heir of deceased daughter Isabella." States he is of Polk Co., Ia. at this time. [entry #10, p 5] He is listed with the heirs living out of state in November 1880 when the court attempted to notify all heirs about the filing of the court action against Catharine Rittgers, widow of Jacob. He apparently traveled to Iowa to acknowledge this action as it is stated that he was in Polk Co., Ia., then. [Abst. 62638] We find no evidence he ever lived here.

+ .122.2   Hester Ann ILES, born about 1850.

.122.3   Isabel ILES, born about 1853 in Marion Twp., Hocking Co., Oh. On 1860 census with father and step-mother, age 7, in Falls Twp., Hocking Co., Oh.[p 113 fam #423/425] In grandfather's estate, 1880, it states that Isabel's brother and sister are the only living heirs of Isabelle (Rittgers) Illes.

12.5 Israel P.³ RITTGERS (Jacob², John¹) was born 25 Apr 1831 in Marion Twp., Hocking Co., Oh., the son of Jacob B. RITTGERS and Hester PATTERSON. He is on the 1850 census, age 18, with parents there. [p 855 fam #213/219] On the 1870 census, we find him, age 40, with no wife, living with brother John in Lone Pine, Inyo Co., Calif. They are farming and each declare $1000 worth of real estate and $150 in personal estate.[p 331 fam #27/26] Israel married **Amelia SHERICK**. She was born about 1845 in Ohio. By 1880 we find Israel, 49, now has wife Amelia B., 35, with him. Also, Della, age 10. Della was born in Iowa and her parents both born in Ohio. This must be the adopted daughter reported in family records. Brother John is still living with them.[p 503 fam #150/189] In Mar 1880, in his father's estate papers, we are told that he is living in "Five Point, Calif." Israel died 1912, most probably in Calif.

ISSUE:

.125.1   Della RITTGERS, born about 1870 in Ia. She is on the 1880 census, age 10, on the Lone Pine, Inyo Co., Calif.[p 503, fam #150/189] Family story tells us she was adopted, and lived later in Oregon.

12.6 Margaret³ RITTGERS (Jacob², John¹) was born 2 Feb 1833 in Hocking Co., Oh., the daughter of Jacob B. RITTGERS and Hester PATTERSON. On the 1850 census, age 17, with parents, Marion Twp., Hocking Co., Oh.[p 855 fam #213/219] She married (1) **Joseph H. HAMILTON** 10 Apr 1851 in Hocking Co., Oh.[HVRM, Bk B., p. 149] He was born 21 Oct 1826. On 5 Apr 1855, Jacob sold to Joseph H. Hamilton 40 acres of land. [Book H. of Deeds, p. 493, abst. #76811] They must have gone to Iowa with her father, as we see on the 1856 state census, in Polk Co., J.H. Hamilton, 26, carpenter, born in Ohio, 3 years in Ia. With him is wife Margaret, 22, and three children. Joseph died 5 Jun 1856 in Polk Co., Ia. He was buried in Rittgers Cemetery, Polk Co., Ia.[PCC, Extracted from DAR records, 1933, no page number] Margaret married (2) **Paul C. MANTZ** 1857. He was born Feb 1833 in Oh. We find Paul C. Mantz on the 1860 census in Alton, Union Twp., Boone Co., Ia. He is 28, a farmer with $800 in real estate and $350 in personal estate. With him is Margaret, age 28, and four children, three of them surnamed Hamilton.[p 322 fam #723/569] She sold the Polk Co. property on 4 Feb 1861 to Charles Snodgrass. He later sold it to Moses Lawson who married Christina (Smith) Rittgers, widow of Daniel (#1.6)[Family record] By 1870, we find this family in Dallas Twp., Dallas Co., Ia. Paul and Margaret are now both 38. Paul is a farmer with $1400 in real estate and $837 in personal property. There are three children with them, only one, Catherine, surnamed Hamilton. [p 548 fam #25/25] On father's estate papers, 1880, Margaret is listed as being in "Perry, Dallas Co., Ia." They lived the later part of their life on a small farm near Rippey, Greene Co., Ia. We see she and Paul on the 1900 census alone on their farm in Rippey. It states that they were both born Feb 1833 and are now 67 years old. They have been married 43 years (thus married in 1857). She reports she has born seven children, four are alive in 1900. [ED 97, p 11A, fam #221/221] We are told that Margaret died on that farm about 1916.

ISSUE of Joseph and Margaret:

.126.1   Reuben HAMILTON, born 31 Aug 1851[RitCem] in Hocking Co., Oh. Seen with parents on the 1856 Polk Co., Ia., state census, age 4. On 1860 census with mother and step-father, Paul Mantz, in Union Twp., Alton P.O., Boone Co., Ia.[p 322, fam #723/569] Died 21 Sept 1868, buried in Rittgers Cem., Polk Co., Ia. [RitCem]

.126.2   Catherine HAMILTON, born about 1854 in Polk Co., Ia. Seen with parents on the 1856 Polk Co., Ia., state census, age 2. On 1860 census, age 6, with mother and stepfather, Union, Boone Co., Ia. [p 322 fam #723/569] On 1870, age 18, with them in Dallas, Dallas Co., Ia.[p 548 fam #25/25]

.126.3   Jacob HAMILTON, born about 1856 in Polk Co., Ia. Seen with parents on the 1856 Polk Co., Ia., state census, age 1. On the 1860 census, age 4, with mother and step-father, Paul Mantz, in Union Twp., Boone Co., Ia.[p 322 fam #723/569] On the 1870 census in Valley, Polk Co., Ia., with mother's cousin, David Foght Rittgers (#18.1) Jacob is 14, born in Oh. It doesn't state if he is working on David's farm or going to school.[p 407 fam #108/118]

ISSUE of Paul and Margaret:

.126.4   Philip MANTZ, born about 1858 in Polk or Boone Co., Ia. On 1860 census, age 2, called "D.S.", with parents in Union Twp., Boone Co., Ia.[p 322 fam #723/569] With them in Dallas Twp., Dallas Co., Ia., age 11, on 1870 census.[p 548, fam #25/25]

.126.5   Mary M. MANTZ, born about 1865 in Boone or Dallas Co., Ia. On 1870 census, age 5, with parents, Dallas, Dallas Co., Ia.[p 548 fam #25/25]

12.7 Jacob R.[3] RITTGERS (Jacob[2], John[1]) was born 13 Oct 1834[RitCem] in Marion Twp., Hocking Co., Oh., the son of Jacob B. RITTGERS and Hester PATTERSON. Often called "Jake" in family records. We find him on the 1850 census, age 15, b. Oh., with parents in Marion Twp, Hocking Co., Oh. [p 855 fam #213/219] On the 1856 state census, he is 20,and in his father's home in Polk Co.,Ia. In 1860 he is age 24, single, farm laborer on census with family of J. D. Snyder., Jefferson Twp, Polk Co, Ia.[p 92, fam #676] He married **Mary F. WHIPPS** (Whipple on marr. record, also Whippo in some records)18 Jul 1853 in Jefferson Twp., Polk Co., Ia.[PVRM, Bk B., p.352] She was born 29 Nov 1846 in Pa. [Polk Co., p. 983] On the 1870 census, he is age 34, with wife Mary, 23, and 2 month old child, Martin L., in Valley Twp., Post Office-Des Moines, Polk Co., Ia. No profession listed. (assume he farming)[p 406 fam #100/110] In 1880 at age 44, he is farming in Jefferson Twp., Polk Co., Ia. Wife Mary F., 33, and son, Martin L., 10. They also have a servant, John Hammond, age 15, b. in Ia.[p 592 fam #12/12] The 1885 Ia. state census show Jacob, 49, a farmer in Jefferson Twp., Polk Co., Ia. Mary is 38 and son Martin S., 15. Their address is "Range 80, Twp., 25, section 36".[1885, #78] Mary died 8 Mar 1890 in Polk Co., Ia., and was buried in Rittgers Cemetery, Johnston, Ia.[RitCem] In 1910, Grimes, Jefferson Twp., Polk Co., Ia., Jake, 76, a retired farmer, is a widower with son "Leaut", and his wife Mattie.[ED 176, p 1A, fam #7/7] The 1920 census, taken Jan, 1920, shows Martin L., 49, as head of household with his father, Jacob R., age 85. Martin states he is divorced and Jacob is a widower. They are renting on Pleasant St., in Des

Moines, Ia. Neither one is working.[ED 113, p. 9A, fam. #158/269] Jacob died 11 Sep 1920 in Des Moines, Polk, Ia., and was buried in Rittgers Cem., Johnston, Ia.[RitCem]

ISSUE:

+ .127.1   Martin Luther "Luke" RITTGERS, born 30 Apr 1870, died after 1932.

12.8 Eli D.[3] **RITTGERS** (Jacob[2], John[1]) was born 22 Aug 1836 in Marion Twp., Hocking Co., Oh., the son of Jacob B. RITTGERS and Hester PATTERSON. On the 1850 census, age, 13, with parents there.[p 855 fam #213/219] On the 1856 state census, Eli is 18 and in the home with his widower father in Polk Co., Ia.[1856, p.274,fam#26] He married **Virginia Weis MYERS** 1880 in Salina, Ks. In a letter written by Dorothy R.(?) we get the descendancy, marriage, and death date. Extracted from "Hist. of State of Kansas", A.T. Andreas, Vol. 1, p. 705: (retyped transcript submitted, no author cited.): "E.D. Rittgers, miller, firm C.R. Underwood & Co., etc. Mr. Rittgers came to Morris Co., Kansas, in 1858, where he engaged in farming for four years, then followed teaming from Leavenworth west for two years, then carried on the saw mill business for two years in Morris Co., Kansas. In 1866 he moved to Salina, erected a saw mill and ran the same for four years, then with C.R. Underwood, erected a steam grist mill, three stories; capacity, 100 barrels per day. He ran this for three years, then in company with C.R. Underwood & Co., erected the Western Star Mills; three high; capacity 200 barrels, which he has run ever since. E.D. Rittgers was born in Hocking Co., Ohio, August 22, 1836. Moved to Polk Co., Ia, in 1853, where he obtained a common school education, and farmed till he came to Kansas. He was married in Salina, Kansas, in 1880, to Miss Jennie Myers, a native of Iowa. He is a member of I.O.O.F."[submitted transcript from Andreas, A.T.; HISTORY OF STATE OF KANSAS; Vol I, p.705] Following this, the unnamed transcriptionist stated that "Information was probably written by Eli so I figure dates, places and names pretty accurate. Probably written between 1880-1890 since daughter not mentioned." In father's estate, 1880, he is listed as being of "Silada, Ks." The 1900 census shows Eli in Smokey Hill Twp., Saline Co., Kansas. He declares he is 63, b. Aug 1836 in Oh. He is a widower, farming. With him is Etta G., niece, b. June 1873 in Kansas, age 26. She is probably in the home to care for Eli's daughter, Edith H., b. Aug 1891, age 8. Even though the birth dates don't quite coincide, this is probably daughter of Perry, #129.5.[fam #256/256] Eli died 14 Oct 1909 in Salina, Saline, Ks.

ISSUE:

+ .128.1   Edith Helen RITTGERS, born Aug 1891, died 11 Jun 1984.

12.9 Perry C.[3] **RITTGERS** (Jacob[2], John[1]) was born 16 Mar 1838 in Marion Twp., Hocking Co., Oh., the son of Jacob B. RITTGERS and Hester PATTERSON. On the 1850 census, age 12, with parents, Marion Twp., Hocking Co., Oh. [p 855 fam #213/219] The 1856 state census shows us Perry, 16, in his father's home in Polk Co., Ia.[p.274,fam#26] Family record contained the following: "obtained at the Hutchinson, Ks., Library, printed in "The Tree Climber," a local genealogical publication, he is on the voter's registration for 1863, age 25, a miller living at 112 Front St., Salina, Saline Co., Ks." He married **Myra Jane MORRISON** 24 Apr 1870 in Salina, Saline Co., Ks. She was born 3 Sep 1854[Funeral Card] in Oh., the daughter of Rev. A.A. and Nancy C. (Beaty) Morrison. From her Obituary, dated 2 Dec 1931 (no paper given), we find that she was born in Ohio, and came to Kansas as a small child. She was a member of the Presbyterian Church and lived at 110 South Ohio St., Salina, Ks. On the census she declares her father is from North Carolina and her mother born in Indiana. In son William's (#129.B) obituary, A.A. Morrison is called "first Presbyterian minister in Salina." The 1870 census shows us Perry, age 32, a farmer in Walnut Grove, Salina post office, Saline Co., Ks. He has with him wife "Meysa" (Myra, poor writing) age 15, b. Ohio. Also brother Peter Rittgers (#12.B), age 26; Melissa Merlmes (sp. ?), domestic servant, and Gulleib Botz, age 15. (This is the Guttip Bates, age 5, on the 1860 census with step-father Jacob in Polk Co., Ia.)[p 50 fam #144/141] In 1880, Perry, 42, and Myra, 25, are in Liberty Twp., Saline Co., Ks. They have five children with them.[fam #93/99] In his father's estate, 1880, he is "of Silada, Ks." On the 1900 census he is in Liberty Twp., Saline Co., Ks., age 62 with wife "Mira", age 45, b. Sept 1854. They have been married 29 years and Myra has born 13 children, 12 still alive. Perry is a farmer, with two sons and his son-in-law, Archie Koplin, working for him. It appears that Archie and wife Daisy, with their children, are also living in the household. [ED 118, p 195B, fam #32/32] A copy of an old photo, showing Perry and the next three brothers, has been shared with us. Perry has a full white beard and quite a receded hairline. Perry died 30 Jun 1903 in Assaria, Saline Co., Ks. Typical of the older obituaries, his is a treasure of information. "Perry Ritger who lives three miles from Assaria died at his home at 8 o'clock this morning of paralysis. He had been sick for a couple of weeks but was thought to have passed the crisis of the disease until yesterday, when he was taken much worse and continued declining until death came this morning. The deceased was an old settler and was well known in the city and county."[date and paper not supplied with the photocopy of the obituary] The 1910 census shows Myra, 55, as head of household. Listed with her in Ward 3, Salina, Saline Co., Ks., are sons Hugh G., 25, Arthur, 16, and William, age 12; sister Mary E. Morrison, 61; and grand-daughter LaVera A. Whelchel. Myra tells us she bore 13 children and 11 are alive - she has lost another child (LaVera's mother Etta (#129.5)) since the last census.[p 304 fam #47/47] Myra died 2 Dec 1931 in Colorado Springs, Colo., and was buried in Gypsum Hill Cemetery, Salina, Ks. [Funeral Card] From her obituary, 2 Dec 1931[newspaper not cited,] she died of "heart disease" while visiting daughter Bertha Guy. Her sister, Mary Etta Morrison is the only surviving sibling, and she is in Goldendale, Wash.

ISSUE:

.129.1   Infant RITTGERS, born 6 Jan 1871 in Bridgeport, Saline Co., Ks., died 6 Jan 1871 in Bridgeport, Saline Co., Ks.. In family records called "Our Baby Girl".

+ .129.2   Esther RITTGERS, born 27 Feb 1872, died 1 May 1926.

.129.3   Selena Sarah RITTGERS, born 14 Nov 1873 in Bridgeport, Saline Co., Ks. She is on the 1880 census, age 6, with parents in Liberty Twp., Saline Co., Ks.[ED 299, p 24, fam #93/99] She married George BOLTON about 1898 in Saline Co., Ks. He was born 27 Jun 1867. States his parents born in Ohio. On the 1900 census, we find George L. Bolton, age 32, with wife Sarah, 26. His occupation is not recorded. They live at 340 7th St., Salina, Saline Co., Ks., and have been married 2 years with no children.[ED 121, p 29, fam #212/218] In 1910, Selena, 36, is on the census with husband George Bolton, 42. They have been married 12 years with no children. George is listed as a "trader - livestock."[ED 137, p 13B, fam #36/327] By 1920, George L., 52, is a "laborer - common." "Sarah S.", 46, is tending the home.[ED 148, p 6B, fam #138/167] George died 1940, and was buried in Gypsum Hill Cem., Salina, Ks. Selena died Jan 1944 in Salina, Saline Co., Ks., and was buried in Gypsum Hill Cem., Salina, Ks. Salina's death was newsworthy. When she failed to respond to a tenant's knock for the second day in a row, the tenant went in and found her sitting in a rocking chair - dead apparently of a heart attack. At this time her address was given as 112 South Ohio. The article was a photocopy with no newspaper information. What the article didn't mention was a single date!

+ .129.4   Evelyn RITTGERS, born 19 Nov 1875, died 1938.

+ .129.5   Etta RITTGERS, born 7 Jul 1877, died 6 Dec 1903.
+ .129.6   Daisy RITTGERS, born 6 Aug 1879, died 1932.
  .129.7   Mabel RITTGERS, born 1 Oct 1881 in Bridgeport, Saline Co., Ks. She is on the
                1900 census, age 18, with parents, Liberty Twp., Ks.[ED 118, p.195B, fam #32/32]
                She married Leuthon HANSEN. We are told they had no children. In her mother's
                obituary, 1931, in sister Salina's Obituary, 1944, and in brother John's obituary in
                1945, and Perry's obituary, 1947, Mabel is said to be living in Goldendale, Wash.
                Mabel died 19 Jun 1951 in Goldendale, Klickitat Co., Wash.
+ .129.8   John Andrew RITTGERS, born 7 Aug 1883, died 19 Sep 1945.
  .129.9   Hugh RITTGERS, born 7 Mar 1885 in Bridgeport, Saline Co., Ks.. He is on the
                1900 census, age 15, with parents in Liberty Twp., Saline, Ks.[ED 118, p 195B, fam
                #32/32] The 1910 census shows us Hugh, 25, listed in Ward 3, Salina, Saline Co.,
                Ks., with his mother, Myra. He is listed as farmer, "working out."[ED 135, p 2B,
                fam #47/47] On 1920 census, age 34, a farm laborer on the farm of Harry Freetly,
                in Manning, Warren Twp., Carroll Co., Ia. No indication he is married at this time.
                He married Loretta (Simpson) BROWNING. She was a widow with three
                daughters. We are told they never had any children. Hugh died 10 Aug 1926, and
                was buried in Gypsum Hill Cemetery, Salina, Ks.
+ .129.A   Bertha RITTGERS, born 19 Dec 1886.
+ .129.B   Jacob RITTGERS, born 11 Jun 1889, died 7 Dec 1954.
+ .129.C   Perry Arthur RITTGERS, born 23 Jul 1893, died 17 Jan 1947.
+ .129.D   William Henry RITTGERS, born 18 Aug 1897, died 8 Nov 1962.

12.C Esther May[3] RITTGERS (Jacob[2], John[1]) was born 28 May 1844 in Marion Twp.,
Hocking Co., Oh., the daughter of Jacob B. RITTGERS and Hester PATTERSON. Seen on
the 1850 census, age 6, with parents there. [p 855 fam #213/219] On the 1856 state census, she
is age 11, and in her father's home in Polk Co., Ia.[p.274,#26] Not with father on 1860 census
- she would be 16 - but not supposed to have married until during or after the Civil War. She
married **William Henry Harrison NOSLER**. He was born Jan 1840 in Ind. We are told he
was a best "buddie" to her brother, Peter (#12.B), during the civil war. We find in the Civil War
papers in the Iowa Historical Soc. that William H. Nosler age 21, a resident of Des Moines, Ia.,
enlisted in Co "D" of the Second Cavalry, 2 Aug 1861. He was taken prisoner 28 May 1863,
but is shown as re-enlisting at Memphis, Tenn., 28 Mar 1864. He was promoted to Second
Corporal 1 Nov 1864,and mustered out 19 Sept 1865, Selma, Ala. We find in War of the
Rebellion Official Records, Series I, Vol 24, that the 2nd Iowa Cavalry was in almost constant
action through the entire war. They were assigned to the District of West Tenn., and fought
"skirmishes" in Tenn. and Miss. This reference doesn't give us any clue as to his capture or
release, but occasionally mentions men captured and rescued by this unit. LDS gives us the
births of her first two sons in Des Moines, Polk Co., Ia. [IGI, 1992, Iowa, p. 6,725] On the 1870
census, William, 30, is teaching school in Perry, Dallas Twp., Dallas Co., Ia. With him is wife,
Esther, 25, and first three children, the youngest 8 months old.[p 549 fam 31/31] LDS gives us
birth of Samuel and Israel in Coos Co., Ore. [IGI, 1992, Oregon, p. 1,480] From the census
records and stated birthplaces of the children, we can follow their travels between Oregon and
California. They were in Oregon by Aug, 1872; then in Healdsburg, Calif, by Feb 1880. The
1880 census records them in Healdsburg, Mendocino Twp., Sonoma Co., Calif. Wm. H., 40,
is a carpenter. He declares he b. Ind, parents b. Ky. Esther, 36, caring for seven children. [p
190C, ED 128, fam #169/169] In her father's estate, 1880, her residence is left blank -

apparently the family didn't know just where she was. Family story told us she was "somewhere out around Washington State.", but we have no evidence she ever lived there. Family story tells us Esther died abt. 1892. (Calif or Oregon?) On the 1900 census William, 60, is back in Coquille, Coos Co., Ore.., where he is a house carpenter. With him is second wife, Amanda L. _____, 40. She declares they have been married 5 years and she has born one child, that child is son William M., age 4. He is NOT a Rittgers descendant.[ED 12, p. 40, fam #148/149] William, 24, "nephew", is found in 1920 in the Coquille Precinct, Coos Co., Or., home of Louis G. Simmons, 62, and wife, Elizabeth, 57. Also in home is Joseph Abel, 15, "step-son." It is believed that Louis is probably a brother to Amanda, as they were both born in Kansas. William CANNOT read or write, and he is a "wagon driver, general hauling."[ED 126 p. 95, fam # 25/25] William Henry not found on 1910 or 1920 census in Coos Co., Ore.

ISSUE:

+ .12C.1   Alva Asbury NOSLER, born 8 Jan 1867.
  .12C.2   Oscar Lawrance NOSLER, born 27 Feb 1869 in Des Moines, Polk Co., Ia. [LDS-IGI, 1992, page 6,725] He is seen on the 1870 census, age 2, with parents, Perry, Dallas Twp., Dallas Co., Ia.(p 549, fam #31/31) and on the 1880 census, Healdsburg, Mendocino Twp., Sonoma Co. Calif., age 12, with parents.[ED 128, p 190C, fam #169/169] He married Birdie _____ about 1895, most probably in Coquille, Coos Co., Ore. She was born Oct 1875 in Ks. On the 1900 census, Coquille, Coos Co., Ore., age 31, (states b. Ill.) day laborer. With him is wife Birdie, age 24. She declares they have been married 5 years and she has born no children. They are next door to his father, William.[ED 12, p 38, fam #147/148] Here she declares her parents both b. in Ill., but on the next census it gives Iowa as their birth place. On the 1910 census, Coquille, Coos Co., Ore, gives Oscar, age 43, b. Ia., laborer in a steam laundry. (His brother Samuel owns a "laundry and ice co.") Birdie, 34, declares they have been married 15 years and she has born no children.[Ed 55, p.48A, fam #201/205]
  .12C.3   Sarah A. NOSLER, born about 1870. She is seen on the 1870 census, age 8/12, with parents, Perry, Dallas Twp., Dallas Co., Ia.[p 549, fam #31/31] and on the 1880 census, Healdsburg, Mendocino Twp., Sonoma Co. Calif., age 10, with parents.[ED 128, p 190C, fam #169/169] It states on this census that she was born in Missouri.
  .12C.4   Samuel Manford NOSLER, born 19 Aug 1872 in Cogville, Coos Co., Ore. [LDS IGI, 1992, Ore., fiche #1297, p 1,480.] He is on the 1880 census, age 7, with parents, Healdsburg, Mendocino Twp., Sonoma Co., Calif. [ED 128, p 14, fam #169/169] He married Lula M. MOULTON about 1896 in Coquille, Coos Co., Ore. She was born Apr 1876 in Ore. On the 1900 census, Coquille, Coos Co., Ore., age 27, farmer. Wife Lula, age 24, declares they have been married 3 years and she has born no children.[ED 12, p 1, fam #4/4] In 1910, Coquille, Coos Co., Ore., Samuel is now 38, and proprietor of a laundry and ice co. Lulu M., is 34, and declares they have been married 14 years with no children. In the home is her brother, George T. Moulton, age 44, with no occupation is listed.[ED 55, p 4B, fam #148/152] In 1920, continuing in Coquille, Samuel is 47, "merchant-groceries." Lulu is 43 and has still not born any children. Continuing in home is George Moulton, 53, "merchant, commission".[ED 126, p 13, fam #264/288]

.12C.5   Mary NOSLER, born about 1875 in Coos Co., Ore. On the 1880 census, age 5, with
           parents, Healdsburg, Mendocino Twp., Sonoma Co., Calif.[ED 128, p 14, fam
           #169/169]

.12C.6   Israel Rittgers NOSLER, born 10 Sep 1876 in Coquille, Coos Co., Ore. [LDS-IGI;
           1992, Ore, fiche #1297, page 1,480] He is on the 1880 census, age 3, with parents
           in Healdsburg, Mendocino Twp., Sonoma Co., Calif.[ED 128, p 14, fam #169/169]
           He married Alice N. ____ about 1907, probably in Coquille, Coos Co., Ore. She
           was born about 1883 in Ore. Alice declares that her father was born in Kansas and
           her mother in Ohio. The 1900 census shows us Israel, age 23, with father and
           step-mother, in Coquille, Coos Co., Ore. He is listed as a "day laborer".[ED 12, p
           7, fam #148/149] On the 1910 census, Coquille, Coos Co., Ore., Israel is 33 and the
           manager of a theater. Wife Alice, 27, is keeping house. She declares they have been
           married 3 years and she has born no children. [ED 55, p 26, fam #160/164] By 1920
           census, San Diego, San Diego Co., Calif., Israel, age 43, is the proprietor of
           apartments. Wife Alice N., 37, has no children listed with her. They live at 1336,
           Union St.[ED 314, p 1, fam 4/7]

+ .12C.7   Alberta Evalene NOSLER, born Feb 1880.

.12C.8   Minnie Etta NOSLER, born 10 Jan 1883 in Sonoma, Healdsburg Co., Ca.[LDS-IGI;
           Calif, 1992, fiche #0067, page 3,651] Not with family on 1900 census.

+ .12C.9   Eugene Elmer NOSLER, born 12 Oct 1886.

12.D Henry C.[3] RITTGERS (Jacob[2], John[1]) was born 6 May 1849 in Marion Twp., Hocking
Co., Oh., the son of Jacob B. RITTGERS and Hester PATTERSON. On the 1850 census, age
2, with parents, Marion Twp., Hocking Co., Oh.[p. 855 fam #213/219] In 1856, the state census
records Henry, 9, in his father's home in Polk Co., Ia.[p.274, fam#26] On the 1860 census he
is age 12, with father and step-mother, Jefferson Twp., Polk Co., Ia.[p 95 fam #765/700] After
attending "common schools", Western College (now abandoned) and a term at what is now
Drake University in Des Moines, Henry taught country schools a total of 142 months. He and
his wife met while attending the "normal school" at Jefferson, Ia., we are told. He married
Luesia Jennette EDWARDS 25 Dec 1872. She was born 29 Mar 1853 in Lockport, N.Y.
Louisa was the only living child of James Edwards (b. Surrey, Eng., 6 Nov 1819; d. 3 Feb 1896,
Angus, Ia.) and his wife Emma S. (b. 6 July 1830, Eng.; d. 27 Sept 1901, Angus, Ia.) Her father
was a stonemason and arrived in this country about 1848. He worked for a while on the locks
on the Erie Canal. Later he farmed in "Savannah, Illinois, near the Mississippi River, and cleared
the farm of heavy timber." After the Civil War, they moved to Angus, Greene Co., Ia. We are
told the Edwards' lie in Rippey Cemetery, Greene Co., Ia. After the birth of Henry and Louisa's
first child, they went to Lone Pine, Calif., where brothers Israel and John were. Henry farmed
or ranched and taught school. He also worked some months for a mining company which
operated a gold quarts (quartz?) crusher and mine in the Panamint Mts. We find them here on
the 1880 census. Henry, now 32, gives his occupation as "laborer". With him is Louisa, 27,
William H., 6; Emma I., 4; and John A., 3. Emma and John both born in California. They live
next door to brothers Israel and John.[p 503 fam #148/188] In father's estate, 1880, they are
listed as being of Five Point, Calif. We are told that after about ten years in California, the
family moved back to Rippey, Ia. We find in records of Rippey Cemetery, Rippey, Ia., that they
buried twins, Perry and Percy, there in Lot 45, Block 2, in 1886.[RGrCem, p 8] We find them
in Emmetsburg, Palo Alto Co., Ia., in 1900. Henry, farmer, is 51 and Louise is 46. With them
are Lily, 19; Harry, 16; and Joe Ross, 12.[ED 151, p 12A, fam #22/22] They continued moving

about, renting farms in Iowa until 1902, when they moved to a farm near Glenwood, Pope Co. Minn. They lived here until retirement in 1917, when they moved into the city of Glenwood. Here we see them on the 1920 census. Henry is 70 and Louisa is 66.[p 2B, ED136, fam #35/37] Henry died 8 Mar 1933 in Glenwood, Minn.

ISSUE:

+ .12D.1   William Henry RITTGERS, born 30 Nov 1873, died 6 Feb 1936.
+ .12D.2   Emma Irene RITTGERS, born 16 Sep 1875, died 22 Apr 1943.
+ .12D.3   John Arthur RITTGERS, born 4 Feb 1877, died 23 Jan 1941.
+ .12D.4   Lily Magdalene RITTGERS, born 5 Apr 1881.
+ .12D.5   Harry Edwards RITTGERS, born 13 Jan 1884, died Dec 1971.
  .12D.6   Perceival RITTGERS, born 30 Mar 1886 in Rippey, Greene Co., Ia., died 11 Aug 1886 in Rippey, Greene, Ia, and was buried in Rippey Cem., Greene Co., Ia. He and twin, Perry, lie in Block Two, lot 45. Family was living in Surrey, Greene Co., Ia., at the time of his birth and death. [RGrCem, p 8]
  .12D.7   Perry RITTGERS, born 30 Mar 1886 in Rippey, Greene Co., Ia., died 24 Aug 1886 in Rippey, Greene, Ia, and was buried in Rippey Cem., Greene Co., Ia. He and twin, Percy, lie in Block Two, lot 45. Family was living in Surrey, Greene Co., Ia., at the time of his birth and death.[RGrCem, p 8]
+ .12D.8   Joe Ross RITTGERS, born 11 May 1888.

12.E Daniel R.[3] **RITTGERS** (Jacob[2], John[1]) was born 26 Apr 1857[tombstone] in Jefferson Twp., Polk Co., Ia., the son of Jacob B. RITTGERS and Catherine Anne SCHLEIGH. On the 1860 census, age 3, with parents in Jefferson Twp., Polk Co., Ia. [p 95 fam #765/700] In 1870, age 13, Valley, Polk Co., Ia. [p406 fam #97/107] He married (1) **Mary Ann FRY** 6 Apr 1880, in Washington Twp., Greene Co., Ia., according to family reports. We find in Polk Co. Book 1 of Marriage, p. 237, that they married 3 Dec 1875. She was born 19 Jan 1860 in Mo.[tombstone] On the 1880 census we see Daniel, age 23, a farmer in Washington Twp., Greene Co., Ia. With him is wife Mary, age 20, and a farm hand, Nelson Adkins, age 27.[ED 99 fam #13/13] On the 1910 census there, Daniel is 52, a farmer on a "general" farm he owns free and clear, with wife Mary, age 50. With them are Burton, 26 and Grover, 19.[ED 106, p 5B, fam #116/118] Mary died 30 Oct 1912 in Rippey, Greene, Ia., and is buried in Block 8, Lot 22, Rippey Cem., Rippey, Ia.[RGrCem] Daniel married (2) **Ethel HUNT** 10 Aug 1913 in Greene Co., Ia. She was born 1887 in Mo. We are told he "Was an active and well-known farmer and stock raiser in vicinity of Rippey, Greene Co., Ia., for many years. He was a physically powerful man, very energetic and hard working. His sturdiness physically, as well as a citizen of the community, is well represented by the monument over his grave in Rippey Cemetery: 'Bluff, Outspoken, but Kindly Uncle Dan.'" Daniel died 4 Apr 1916 in Rippey, Greene Co., Ia., and was buried in Rippey Cemetery, Greene Co., Ia. On the 1920 census, we find Ethel, a widow, age 32, born in Ia. - as was her parents - with Wesley, age 5. She indicates no form of employment. Ethel died 1971, and was buried in Rippey, Greene Co., Ia. In the Rippey Cemetery, we find under "Wilson" one Ethel Rittgers, d. 1971. She is in Block 7, lot 35, along with Homer O. (1861-1958) and Ida L. (1864-1938) Hunt. (RGrCem)

ISSUE of Daniel and Mary:

+ .12E.1   Almeda Catharine RITTGERS, born 9 Aug 1881.
+ .12E.2   Burton A. RITTGERS, born 10 Feb 1884, died Aug 1966.
+ .12E.3   Grover C. RITTGERS, born 9 May 1890, died 1945.

ISSUE of Daniel and Ethel:

.12E.4   Wesley D. RITTGERS, born 25 Sep 1914 [RGrCem, p 54; also SS] in Rippey, Greene Co., Ia. He is on the 1920 census, age 5, with widowed mother, Ethel, in Rippey, Washington Twp., Greene Co., Ia.[ED 118, p 172, fam #10/10] He married Lois Mae ____. She was born 1917. Lois' birth date is etched on their tombstone. At the time the Rippey Cemetery book was compiled, there was no death date on her stone. Wesley died Nov 1966[SS] in Greene County, Ia., and was buried in Rippey Cemetery, Greene Co., Ia. In records of Rippey Cemetery, we find Wesley D, 1914-1966, in Block 12, Lot 74. With him is Lois Mae, 1917- ____.

12.F Catherine Anne³ RITTGERS (Jacob², John¹) was born 3 Aug 1858 in Jefferson Twp., Polk Co., Ia., the daughter of Jacob B. RITTGERS and Catherine Anne SCHLEIGH. On the 1860 census, age 1, with parents in Jefferson Twp., Polk Co., Ia.[p 95 fam #765/700] In 1870, age 11, in Valley with her parents.[p 406 fam #97/107] We don't know when, how or why she went to California but we find Catherine in Lone Pine, Inyo Co., on the 1880 census with her husband. She married **James J. STEWART** about 1878. There is a reference to their marriage in the 1878 "San Francisco Call" newspaper. Full article not on internet where this found. [http://feefhs.org/ethnic.html] He was born Apr 1843 in Mich[1900 census]. In one family record, we find the following story: "James J. Stewart was born in Cuba, and then moved with his family to Michigan. When the Civil War broke out, he joined the 5th Michigan Cavalry, and shortly after the close of the war went to Ca., died there Feb 1929 shortly before his 87th birthday at the home of his son Fred in Paradise Valley, and was buried at Paradise Valley on Feb 5, 1929." He consistently states on his census return that he was born in Michigan to a father born in Pa. and a mother born in Scotland. The 1880 census has Catherine and John in the home of Anna B. Stewart, in Lone Pine, Inyo Co., Calif. Anna is 58 and listed as head of the house, born in Scotland, as were her parents. In the same house is John J. Stewart, son, age 32, Post Master. His wife Catherine is 22, born in Ia. With them is Frederick B., b. July 1879 in California.[p. 505 fam #219/262] The 1900 census shows the family still in Inyo Co., Calif. John, age 57, b. Apr 1843 in Michigan, has with him wife Catherine, 41. Fred, 21 and "John E." 16, are in the home as well as John's mother, Anna, age 79.[ED 32, p 49A fam # 51/51] The 1910 census gives us John, 66, with "own income" in occupation. His wife, Katherine, 51, declares they have been married 32 years and she has born 2 children, one alive at this time. In the home is son Fred, so we must assume that son John has died. They are listed in "4th Twp. (Lone Pine)", Inyo Co., Calif.[ED 18, p 1A, fam #10/10] We do not see them in Lone Pine in 1920. James died Feb 1929 in Paradise Valley, Humbolt Co., Nev., and was buried there 5 Feb 1929. In a photocopied newspaper article, with no news banner or date, we see that Mrs. J.J. Stewart was in Bakersfielf, Calif., with brothers B.F. Rittgers of Rolfe, Ia., and G.M.Rittgers, Jefferson, Ia., and a half brother G.W.Betts, of Bakersfield, Ca. It reports that the brothers had not met for sixty- five years. It reports that "Mrs. J.J. Stewart, Paradise Valley, Nev." hadn't seen her brothers for 25 years. "She went to California when a young girl and made her home with her brother until she married J.J. Stewart, postmaster of Lone Pine. After he passed away she moved to Paradise Valley, Nev., where she could be near her son who runs a large cattle ranch."

ISSUE:

.12F.1   Frederick B. STEWART, born Jul 1879 in Lone Pine, Inyo Co., Calif. He is on the 1880 census, age 11 months, with parents and paternal grandmother there.[p 505 fam #219/262] On the 1900 census, age 21, he is still with parents in Inyo Co., Calif. States he a school teacher.[ED 32, p 49A, fam #51/51] On the 1910 census, he is still with his parents in Lone Pine. Fred is 30 and a "Civil Engineer, Mine." He isn't in Lone Pine in 1920, and family story reports that his father died at his home in Paradise Valley, Nev., in 1929, but we don't know just when they moved there.

.12F.2   John Ernest STEWART, born Apr 1884 in Ca., died before 1910. He is on the 1900 census, age 16, with parents in Lone Pine, Inyo Co., Calif.[ED 32, p 49A, fam #51/51] He apparently died before the 1910 census, as we find his mother has declared she bore 2 children, one living at that time, and brother Fred is seen in the home. [ED 18, p 1A, fam #10/10]

12.H Benjamin Franklin[3] **RITTGERS** (Jacob[2], John[1]) was born 2 Aug 1862 in Jefferson Twp. Polk Co., Ia., the son of Jacob B. RITTGERS and Catherine Anne SCHLEIGH. He is on 1870 census, age 7, with parents in Valley Twp., Polk Co., Ia.[p 406 fam # 97/107] In 1880 he is 17, and the oldest child home with mother.[p 541, fam #131/134] He married **Iora McCLUNE** 13 Apr 1890,[GVRM, p. 5] in Rippy, Ia.[obit] She was born 25 Nov 1874 in Deep River, Ia.[obituary] On their marriage record, it is states she is the daughter of Hugh McClune & Martha Lowe. She was 16 at the time of their marriage, and Benjamin was 28. We are told that he "took his bride to their farm home...six miles northwest of Rolfe, Iowa, where the tall corn really grows." On the 1900 census, he is age 37, in Des Moines Twp., Pocahontas Co., Ia., a farmer. Wife Iora, 25, declares they have been married 10 years. She has born 5 children, four alive at this time. These four with them.[p 56, ED 167, fam #184/187] In 1910 Benjamin, 47, is in Rolfe, Des Moines Twp., Pocahontas Co., Ia., where he is a farmer. Wife Iora M., 35, declares they have been married 20 years and she has born 9 children, all alive at this time. All are in the home.[ED 192; p 8A; fam #89/89] In 1920, we see Ben F., age 58, farming in Des Moines Twp., Pocahontas Co., Ia. With him are wife, Iora, age 45, and ALL children listed below.[p 1A, ED 208, fam #3/3] In an article submitted without news banner or date, it reports he was in Bakersfield, Ca., to see his sister, Mrs. J.J. Stewart, of Paradise Valley, Nev., brother G.W. Rittgers, and half brother, G.W. Betts. This meeting was after James Stewart died in 1929. He farmed in Rolfe, Pocahontas Co., Ia., and was very successful in raising stock and in business matters. He and his wife, Iora, celebrated their 50th Wedding Anniversary on 13 Apr 1940. A newspaper article on the occasion of their 50th was submitted without date or news banner. It tells us that 10 of their 11 children and 15 grand children were present, as well as over 100 guests. Daughter Mary Barron of Phoenix, Arizona, telegraphed her congratulations. Benjamin died in the Lutheran Hospital, at Fort Dodge, Ia., 11 Dec 1944, at the age of 82 years, 4 months, and 9 days. In his obituary, also submitted with no banner, it reports that he left 11 children and 19 grand-children, and a wife who was ill. We are told here that Ben came to "his present farm site 62 years ago in a covered wagon." Iora died 11 July 1946, in Rolfe, Pocahontas Co., Ia. They are buried in the Powatan Cemetery, Rolfe, Ia.

ISSUE:

+ .12H.1   Horace B. RITTGERS, born 1 Aug 1892, died Jul 1976.
+ .12H.2   Clara Catherine RITTGERS, born 14 Aug 1894, died 1987.
+ .12H.3   Hattie Lovina RITTGERS, born 22 Oct 1897, died 11 May 1995.
+ .12H.4   Coral Martha RITTGERS, born 15 Jul 1899, died 1995.
+ .12H.5   Frank Elmer RITTGERS, born 24 Jul 1901, died 19 Oct 1991.
+ .12H.6   Ernest J. RITTGERS, born 26 Feb 1903, died 13 Sep 1994.
  .12H.7   Blanche Alta RITTGERS, born 27 Feb 1906 in Rolfe, Pocahontas Co., Ia. She is age 14, with parents in Des Moines Twp., Pocahontas Co., Ia. on 1920 census.[ED 208, p 1A, fam #3/3] She married (1) Elwyn HANSON 3 Feb 1927. Elwyn died

29 Dec 1939. In his obituary, submitted with no news banner or date, we find that he was 39 when he died at home after an illness of seven weeks, following an operation. There was a long list of those from out of town that attended his funeral. He was the "eldest son of Julius A. and Jennie Hansen, b. in Herscher, Ill, 25 Mar 1900..." Blanche married (2) Dr. W. F. JONES in Pocahontas Co., Ia. She died 1979, and was buried in Pocahontas Co., Ia. Her obituary, submitted without news banner or date, doesn't tell us her date of death, but reports her to be 74 years old.

+ .12H.8   Ruth Iora RITTGERS, born 6 Jun 1907.

.12H.9   Mary Merle RITTGERS, born 7 Apr 1909 in Rolfe, Pocahontas Co., Ia. She is age 10, with parents in Des Moines Twp., Pocahontas Co., Ia. on 1920 census.[ED 208, p 1A, fam #3/3]. She married (1) Robert BARRON 1939. Mary married (2) Louis POPE. Mary died 1992. Last known residence was Phoenix, Az.

+ .12H.A   Jacob B. RITTGERS, born 10 Apr 1911.

+ .12H.B   Robert Woodrow RITTGERS, born 15 Mar 1913.

12.J George McClellan[3] RITTGERS (Jacob[2], John[1]) was born 8 May 1865 in Jefferson Twp., Polk Co., Ia., the son of Jacob B. RITTGERS and Catherine Anne SCHLEIGH. He is on 1870 census, age 4, with parents in Valley Twp., Polk Co., Ia. [p 406 fam #97/107] and there in 1880, age 15, with mother.[p 541 fam #131/134] He married **Julia LAMB** 19 Jun 1892. She was born 27 Jul 1865 in Ill. On the 1900 census we see George, age 35, a farmer in Rippey, Ia. Julia is 34, they have been married 8 years and she has born 4 children at this time. We also learn that her parents were born in Ill. With them also is Lavon Carlisle, b. Feb 1881, Ill., a nephew and farm laborer.[ED 97, p 7A, fam #187/187] In 1910 George, now 44, is farming in Dawson Twp., Greene Co., Ia. Wife Julia is 44, also. She declares they have been married 19 years, that she bore 8 children, all still alive. With them are children Glen, 16 thru Homer, 1 yr. and five mo. [ED 93, p 6A, fam #75/75] They are still farming in Dawson in 1920. George is 55 and Julia, 54. With them are children Gertrude, 20, thru Homer, 11.[ED 103, p 1A, fam 4/3] He was a farmer and stock raiser near Rippey, Greene Co., Ia. In his later years he made his home with his daughter, Marvel (Rittgers) Wilbur at Jefferson, Polk Co., Ia. He made a trip to Bakersfield, Ca. to see his half brother, G.W.Betts, and sister Catherine, after 1929. (See article under #12.F, Catherine Rittgers) Julia died 11 Jun 1935 in Paton, Greene Co., Ia., and George died 1956 in Rippey, Greene Co., Ia. They are buried in Rippey Cemetery, Block 8, Lot 22, with his brother Daniel. [RgrCem, p. 36]

ISSUE:

+ .12J.1   Glen Edwin RITTGERS, born 7 Feb 1894, died 1959.

.12J.2   Guy Lamb RITTGERS, born 28 Oct 1895 in Rippey, Greene Co., Ia. He is on the 1900 census, age 3, with parents there.[ED 97, p 7A, fam #187/187] In 1910 he is 14, and a farmer with his father in Dawson Twp., Greene Co., Ia.[ED 93, p 6A,fam #75/75] We are told he died in Rocky Ford, Colo. He is buried in Block 8, lot 27., Rippey Cemetery, with his brother Floyd. [RGrCem, p 36]

+ .12J.3   Bessie Elizabeth RITTGERS, born 8 Jan 1897.

+ .12J.4   Gertrude Mary Bernice RITTGERS, born 17 Jul 1899.

.12J.5   Floyd Allison RITTGERS, born 12 Apr 1901 in Rippey, Greene Co., Ia. A twin to Lloyd, he is on the 1910 census, age 9, in Dawson Twp., Greene Co., Ia.[ED 93, p 6A, fam #75/75] Still with parents in Dawson on 1920 census, age 18.[ED 103, p 1A, fam #4/3] Floyd died 1 Oct 1921, and was buried in Rippey Cem., Greene Co., Ia.

+ .12J.6   Lloyd Ellison RITTGERS, born 12 Apr 1901, died 20 Jan 1988.
  .12J.7   Marvel Margaret RITTGERS, born 1 Mar 1907 in Rippey, Greene Co., Ia. With
            parents in Dawson, Greene Co., on 1910 census, age 3.[ED 93, p 6A, fam #75/75]
            On 1920 census, continues with parents in Dawson, age 14.[ED 103, p 1A, fam
            #4/3]   She married Roy WILBUR 19 Jun 1936.   Marvel died 16 Jun 1954 in
            Bellflower, L.A. Co., Ca. She was a professional nurse. We are told they had no
            issue.
  .12J.8   Homer George RITTGERS, born 4 Dec 1909[SS] in Rippey, Greene Co., Ia. Seen
            on the1910 census age 1 5/12, with parents in Dawson, Greene Co., Ia.[ED 93, p
            6A, fam #75/75] and continues with them on 1920 census, age 11.[ED 103, p 1A,
            fam #4/3] They probably resided for a time in Minn., as this is where they were
            issued their social security cards. He married Myrtle FRANZ 4 Dec 1928. She was
            born 12 Aug 1907.[SS] Myrtle died Aug 1983 in Montgomery Co., Pa.[SS] Homer
            died Jul 1980 in Flourtown, Montgomery Co., Pa.[SS]

12.K Andrew Johnson[3] RITTGERS (Jacob[2], John[1]) was born 23 Jun 1867 in Jefferson Twp.,
Polk Co., Ia., the son of Jacob B. RITTGERS and Catherine Anne SCHLEIGH. He is on the
1870 census, age 3, with parents in Valley, Polk Co., Ia. [p 406 fam #97/107] and there ,age 13,
with mother on the 1880 census.[p 541 fam #131/134] By 1900, "Johnson" is 33 and head of
household, farming in what is now Grimes in Webster Twp., Polk Co., Oh. He has with him his
mother, Catherine, now 73; and sisters Priscilla and Mary.[p 290A fam #151/158] On 21 Oct
1901, Catherine sold him 219 acres - all but a small portion of Jacob's original holding. She
charged him "$12,000 of the purchase money yet unpaid." Several months later he paid it off.
He married **Virginia "Jennie" BEER** about 1902 in Polk Co., Ia.[abst. #62638.] In 1940 she
wrote a letter, apparently in response to questions about her parentage: "My Grandfather Beer
was an Englishman, so that 'Beer' don't mean Dutch! Grandfather Philip Snyder was
Pennsylvania Dutch and his wife was Scotch-Irish. My father died when I was 14 months old and
my brother Anthony was 3 years old. Our mother moved to Iowa from Ohio when I was eight
years old as her two brothers were in Jones Co., Ia. When I was eleven years old, she married
Dad Philips, and if anybody had a good daddy, we did in him." In 1910 we see them in Precinct
#1, Webster, Polk Co., Ia. Andrew, a farmer, is 43. Wife Virginia is 41. They have been
married 8 years and she states she has born 4 children, all living. Also in the home are his in-laws
Luther Phillips, 75, born in Conn., and his wife Lucinda, 72, born in Pa. The Phillips have been
married 33 years and Lucinda states she has born 4 children - one alive now.[p 8A, ED 184, fam
#87/87] On the 1920 census, A. Johnson Rittgers, 52, is listed in Webster, Polk Co., as a general
farmer. Wife Virginia, is 50.[ED 187, p 12B, fam #196/198] Johnson lived on the homestead
on Ridgedale Rd. until his death, at age 74, 26 Jul 1941. In his will, copied in land abstract
#62638, and filed 29 Aug 1941, he leaves everything to his wife Virginia in her lifetime. Upon
her death, the lands are to be divided among his four children. The division of land is specified.
Andrew owned Lots 1,2,6,7,8,and 9 in section 6, and lot 10 in section 5, all in Township 79,
Range 24 of the partition plat of the estate of Jacob B. Rittgers. Virginia died 26 Mar 1943 in
Johnston, Polk Co., Ia. They are buried in the Rittgers Cemetery, Johnston, Ia. Virginia is
listed on the family cemetery list with no dates.

ISSUE:

+ .12K.1   Raymond RITTGERS, born 12 Mar 1903, died Jan 1971.
+ .12K.2   Anthony Theodore RITTGERS, born 13 Feb 1905, died 23 Oct 1995.
+ .12K.3   Robert Johnson RITTGERS, born 10 Oct 1907, died Jul 1975.

+ .12K.4   Pauline Elfreda RITTGERS, born 26 Feb 1910, died 2 Feb 1994.
  .12K.5   Andrew Johnson RITTGERS, born 18 Jan 1912 in Grimes, Polk Co., Ia., died there
             22 Jan 1912 and was buried in Rittgers Cem., Johnston, Ia. Stone states "Baby
             Andrew".

12.L Lily³ RITTGERS (Jacob², John¹) was born 3 Mar 1869 in Jefferson Twp., Polk Co., Ia.,
the daughter of Jacob B. RITTGERS and Catherine Anne SCHLEIGH. On the 1870 census,
age 1, Valley Twp., Polk Co., Ia., with parents.[p 406 fam #97/107] and there on the 1880
census, age 11, with mother and siblings.[p 541 fam #131/134] She married **William TIARA**
3 Feb 1892 in Polk Co., Ia.[PVRM, book 5, p. 261] On the 1900 census, Saylor Twp., Polk
Co., Ia., William is age 35, b. Jan 1865, Ia., a farmer. His father b. Alabama and mother b. Ohio.
Wife Lily, age 31, b. Mar 1869, declares they have been married 8 years and she has born one
child, seen with them.[ED 109, p 3A, fam #33/34]
                                      ISSUE:
  .12L.1   Lester TIARA, born Feb 1893 in Polk Co., Ia. On 1900 census, age 7 with parents
             in Saylor Twp., Polk Co., Ia.[ED 109, p 3A, fam #33/34]
+ .12L.2   Olah Irene TIARA, born 15 Aug 1900, died 9 Nov 1990.

12.M Mary³ RITTGERS (Jacob², John¹) was born 26 Sep 1871[Abst #62638] in Jefferson
Twp., Polk Co., Ia., the daughter of Jacob B. RITTGERS and Catherine Anne SCHLEIGH. She
is on the 1880 census, age 8, with mother and siblings in Valley Twp., Polk Co., Ia.[p 541 fam.
#131/134] She is the youngest child mentioned in her father's estate, 1880. On the 1900 census,
age 29, Mary is living with brother Johnson in Grimes, Polk Co., Ia. In the home is her mother,
Katherine, age 73, and sister Priscilla, age 36. Mary states she is 29, b. Sept "1868", and single.
[p 290 fam #151/158] She married **Hershel RHOAD** 2 Jan 1901, Polk Co., Ia. [PVRM, bk 10,
p 223] "She went as a bride to a farm near Rippey, (Greene Co., Ia.) where the hollyhocks
grow," the family record tells us. We find them on their farm in Rippey on the 1910 census.
Herschel is 39 and born in Ia. He states his parents were born in "U.S." Mary is 38 and declares
they have been married nine years. She has had no children. With them we see "Percilla"
Rittgers age 40, and listed as "sister in law", and Katherine Rittgers, 83, mother-in-law, who
immigrated from Germany in 1851. Also listed is Herman Rhoad, 11 months, an adopted son
born in Iowa. His parents birthplace not known.[ED 106, p. 9A; fam #188/190] On a map of
Washington Twp., Greene Co., Ia., 1917, showing landowners, we see H.V. & Mary R. Rhoad
own 160 acres. It is designated as the S.W. quarter of section 16, Twp. 83, Range 29. This is
about 2 miles southwest of the town of Rippey. On the 1920 census, age 48, Mary continues
with husband Hershel, age 49, a farmer. Also listed are Herman, age 10, and Priscilla Rittgers,
sis-in-law, age 52.[ED 188, p 4B, fam #87/87] Hershel died 1954 in Rippey, Greene Co., Ia.
Mary died in 1959, and is buried with Herschel in Block Twelve, lot 41, Rippey Cem., Rippey,
Greene Co., Ia.[Tombstone, RgrCem, p. 51]
                                      ISSUE:
  .12M.1   Herman RHOAD, born Jul 1909 in Greene Co., Ia., died 1951, and was buried in
             Rippey Cem., Greene Co., Ia. On 1910 census with adoptive parents, age 11
             months, in Rippey, Greene Co., Ia.[ED 106, p 9A, fam #188/190] In 1920, age 10,
             with parents in Rippey, Greene Co., Ia.[ED 188, p. 4B, fam #87/87] We are told
             he was "a doctor of Medicine and Surgery, and was for some time in the service of
             the U.S. Govt." "Lt.Col. Dr. Herman H. Rhoad, 1909-1951, WW II" on his stone
             in Block 12, Lot 41, Rippey Cemetery.[RGrCem., p 51]

13.4 Tobias[3] RITTGERS (John, Jr.[2], John[1]) was born 13 Mar 1832 in Marion Twp., Hocking Co., Oh., the son of John Augustin RITTGERS, Jr. and Lydia____. On the 1850 census, age 18, with parents there.[p 841, fam #118/120] He married **Phebe WILLIAMS** 3 May 1855 in Hocking Co., Oh.[HVRM, Book B, p. 225] She was born about 1835 in Oh., the daughter of Isaac and Isabella (Martin) Williams. Found on the 1860 census, age 26, farmer, with wife Phebe, age 25, and first four children, Marion Twp., Hocking Co., Oh.[p 149 fam #913/901] We continue to see Tobias, now 38, and Phebe, 36, in Marion Twp. in 1870. They have $800 in real property value and $200 in personal property. With them are children Anna through Lydia.[p 511, fam #277/280] On the 1880 census for Marion Twp., Tobias, 48, and wife Phebe, age 48, have eight children.[p 109C fam #244/247] Tobias died 8 Feb 1882 in Marion, Hocking, Oh. of consumption.[HVRD, book 1, record #2218.]. His death record states he "lived and died in Marion Twp., Hocking Co., Oh." Phebe died 6 Feb 1888 in Hocking Co., Oh.[HVRD, book 2] There was no estate until Phebe died. We find that her estate, #1428, Hocking Co., Oh., was opened 22 Feb 1888. In her list of heirs are William, Isaac, John, Albert, Theron and Abraham. William also signed off for the children of deceased daughter Anna (Rittgers) Wolf, Cora, Oscar, and Rosa. In Hocking Co. Guardianship Book, entry #921 - 23 may 1888, Isaac is guardian for Abraham, age 14, "Therew", 17, and Albert with no age given. Isaac noted in his guardianship accounting "that Albert J. became of age shortly after appointment (of guardian) and nothing ever came into my hands." Among the personal estate due the minors mentioned in the accounting was "pension from U.S. Govt. Due Abram L." This possibly a Civil War Pension. Theron's accounting ended 26 May 1890 and Abraham's ended 13 Aug 1893. Phebe left such "goods and chattels" as fruit cans and jars, tools, half barrel of salt, a keg of soap grease, a 2-horse wagon, a buggy, 103 pounds of meat, greenware and glassware. Also mentioned were furnishings such as "parlor stove and pipe". Livestock listed - 3 hogs, 1 calf, 1 white cow, 1 spotted cow, 1 black mare. Also 6 acres of wheat in the ground. Her possessions were sold at auction, with her sons buying much of the goods. One expense mentioned is to "Dr. Blosser-$2." By the time the estate was balanced, 30 Mar 1889, there was $127.66 to be divided among the heirs. In Hocking Co. Deed Book 17, p. 372-376, we find deeds where the heirs sell their share in Tobias's land, the S.W. quarter of the S.E. quarter of Section 13, Twp. 15, Range 17, to Isaac Blosser. Isaac sells the shares of Abraham and "Therew" for $142.85.[p.372] William F. et al (and others) sell their share for $285.72. [p.374] Noah Wolfe sold the share his children entitled to for $71.43.[p.376] All these deeds dated 20 may 1890. Note that NOWHERE in the estate or sales of property are James (#134.B) or his wife or son Elmer mentioned.[*Dates from family group sheet submitted by James F. Rittgers*]

ISSUE:

+ .134.1   Anna "Jane" RITTGERS, born 6 Mar 1856, died 9 Apr 1882.
+ .134.2   William Franklin RITTGERS, born 2 Jul 1857, died 24 Aug 1930.
  .134.3   Sarah Isabella RITTGERS, born 7 Mar 1859 in Marion Twp., Hocking Co., Oh. She is on the 1860 census, age 1, with parents there.[p 149, fam # 913/901] She is age 11 with parents in Marion, 1870 census, and age 20, with parents in 1880.[p 109C, fam #244/247] We are told she died 22 Oct 1881 in Marion Twp., Hocking Co., Oh., of consumption, "age 22 yrs, 6 mo, 14 days." [HVRD, book 1, pages not numbered. Recorded 27 June 1882]
+ .134.4   Isaac W. RITTGERS, born 14 Apr 1860, died 26 Feb 1934.
+ .134.5   John B. RITTGERS, born 21 Mar 1863, died 21 Jun 1921.

.134.6   Charles E. RITTGERS, born 29 Mar 1864 in Marion Twp., Hocking Co., Oh., died
            17 May 1886. He is there on the 1870 census with parents, age 6., and on the 1880
            census, age 16,[ED 63, p 109C, fam # 244/247]

+ .134.7   Albert J. RITTGERS, born 28 Mar 1868, died 2 Feb 1934.

.134.8   Lydia RITTGERS, born 18 Nov 1869 in Marion Twp., Hocking Co., Oh. She is on
            the 1870 census, age 2; with her parents there, and continues with them there on the
            1880 census, age 10.[ED 63, p 109C, fam #244/247.] She died there 25 Nov 1883.

.134.9   Theron RITTGERS, born 18 Nov 1872 in Marion Twp., Hocking Co., Oh. He is
            on the 1880 census, age 8, with parents there.[ED 63, p 109C, fam 244/247] Under
            guardianship of his older brother, Isaac, during the probate and sale of his parents'
            property. Among the accounting are such items as "overalls & boots - $2.00.
            Theron's accounting ended 26 May 1890. He died there 2 May 1891.

.134.A   Abraham Lincoln RITTGERS, born 23 May 1873 in Marion Twp., Hocking Co.,
            Oh. With parents there on the 1880 census, age 6, Listed as "Abraham W.",but
            name given as "A. Lincoln Rittgers" on other submitted information.[ED 63, p
            109C, fam #244/2447] In his parents' estate we find him called Abraham L. His
            brother, Isaac, was guardian with a careful accounting submitted. It reports that
            "Abram L." was entitled to a pension from the U.S. Government. His guardianship
            ended 13 Aug 1893. We are told he lived in Philadelphia, Pa., but later family story
            reports he "lived to ripe old age and retired to St. Petersburg, Fla."

+ .134.B   James R. RITTGERS, died 26 Dec 1890.

13.6 Noah³ RITTGERS (John, Jr.², John¹) was born 7 Jan 1834 in Marion Twp., Hocking Co.,
Oh., the son of John Augustin RITTGERS, Jr. and Lydia____. On the census in 1850, age 16,
with parents there. [p841 fam # 118/120] He married **Alcinda HINESMAN** 3 Jul 1856 in
Hocking Co., Oh.[HVRM, Book B, p. 245] In 1860 we find Noah, 25, a day laborer with $20
in personal possessions, in Rush Creek, Bremen P.O., Fairfield Co. Wife Alcinda, 24, is caring
for their son.[p 297 fam #85/85] Family story tells us he lived in Decatur, Macon Co., Ill., and
names one son.

ISSUE:

.136.1   John RITTGERS, born about 1857 in Fairfield Co., Oh.. On 1860 census, age 3,
            with parents in Rush Creek, Fairfield Co., Oh.[p 297 fam # 85/58]

13.7 Mary³ RITTGERS (John, Jr.², John¹) was born 8 Oct 1835 in Hocking Co., Oh., the
daughter of John Augustin RITTGERS, Jr. and Lydia____. On the 1850 census there, age 14,
with parents.[p 855 fam #212/218] She married **George MOWREY** 11 Oct 1853 in Hocking
Co., Oh.[HVRM, Bk B, p.194] He was born Oct 1834 in Ohio. The 1860 census shows George,
age 32, born in Ohio, a farmer with $100 in real estate and $60 in personal property. He declares
his parents were born in Pa. Mary, age 25 and born in Ohio is caring for their two children.[p
153 fam #966/954] In 1900 we find them in Greenfield Twp., Fairfield Co., Oh. George, 65,
is still farming. Mary, 62, declares they have been married 44 years and she has born 8 children,
2 alive at that time.[ED 8, p 101A, fam #203/203] On the 1900 census, it is stated she b. Oct
1837, but the family record date given above appears more accurate based on her age on 1850
census.

ISSUE:

.137.1   Amandy MOWREY, born about 1854 in Marion Twp., Hocking Co., Oh. Amandy
            is age 6 on 1860 census with parents there. [p 151, fam #942/930]

.137.2   Jacob MOWREY, born about 1858 in Marion Twp., Hocking Co., Oh. Jacob is age 2 on 1860 census with parents there.[p 151, fam #942/930]

13.8 Anna³ RITTGERS (John, Jr.², John¹) was born 15 Oct 1837 in Marion Twp., Hocking Co., Oh., the daughter of John Augustin RITTGERS, Jr. and Lydia____. She is on 1850 census, age 11, with parents there.[p 841 fam #118/1120] She married (1) **William WOLF** 5 Apr 1859 in Hocking Co., Oh.[HVRM, Bk B, p.222] William was probably deceased by 1867, when we find Anna Wolf buying a piece of property from brother Jacob on 16 Mar 1867, for $1000. [Hocking Co. Deed Bk 2, p.535] She sells the piece back to him on 5 Mar 1870 for $100.[Bk 2, p.537] These 2 deeds, plus the deed where Jacob buys the property for $1000, dated 11 Aug 1866, were all recorded together in 1875. It is not clear just what the purpose of these deeds was. Anna Wolf married (2) **Abraham HOCKMAN,** 22 Mar 1870.[HVRM, Bk C., p.575] On the 1870 census we find Abraham, 17, a farmer, married to Anna, 30, in Marion Twp., Hocking Co., Oh. She is caring for her three children surnamed Wolfe.[p 510, fam #271/274] At some point they may have resided in Pickaway Co., Oh., as we see the birth of son Sylvester there in 1872 on LDS-IGI. In 1880, Abe, 27, is farming in Marion, Hocking Co, Oh. Anna, 42, is caring for six children.[ED 63, p 27, fam #249/249] Anna died 1 Nov 1899 and us buried row 4, #4, South Harvey Chapel Cemetery, Marion Twp., Hocking Co., Oh. On her stone is "Gates Ajar - Anna Rittgers Wife of Abraham Hockman born 19 Oct 1837 died 1 Nov 1988 - She Believed and Sleeps in Jesus". On the 1900 census, Abraham, 48, farming in Marion Twp. He states he is married and has been for 30 years! In the home is son John, 29, and his wife and family.[ED 32, p 110A, fam # 48/48] On the 1910 census we find Abraham Hockman, 58, and a farmer, still in Marion Twp., Hocking Co., Oh., married to Nancy J., 37. They have been married 9 years and Nancy has born 3 children - the three are on the census with them. James Cotterman, 13; Franklin Hockman, 7 and Samuel Hockman, 6.[ED 88, p. 4B, fam #72/72] These are NOT Rittgers descendants.

ISSUE of Anna and William:

+ .138.1   Mary WOLF, born Feb 1859.
+ .138.2   Isaac WOLF, born about 1862.
+ .138.3   William WOLF, born Feb 1863.

ISSUE of Anna and Abe:

+ .138.4   John HOCKMAN, born Feb 1871.
+ .138.5   Sylvester HOCKMAN, born 10 Sep 1872.
  .138.6   Ida HOCKMAN, born about 1879 in Marion Twp., Hocking Co., Oh. She is on the 1880 census, age 1, with parents there.[ED 63, p 27, fam #249/249]
  .138.7   James HOCKMAN. Born to Abe and Anna (Rittgers) Hockman, according to family story. Not on 1880 census with family, nor on the 1900 census with father. May have been born after 1880 census and died young.

13.9 Elizabeth³ RITTGERS (John, Jr.², John¹) was born 30 Nov 1839 in Marion Twp., Hocking Co., Oh., the daughter of John Augustin RITTGERS, Jr. and Lydia____. She is on the 1850 Census, age 10, with parents there.[p 841 fam #118/120] She married **Peter WAGONER** 10 Sep 1857 in Hocking County, Oh.[HVRM, Book "B", p. 267] He was born about 1832 in Oh. On the 1860 census we find Elizabeth, age 20, married to Peter Wagoner, age 28, a farm hand. They have son Jacob, age 2, with them. It appears they are living in the home of, and working for, Daniel Leffler and his wife and children. Also in the house with Peter and Elizabeth is Jacob Rittgers, age 13.[p 158 Fam #1040/1028] On the 1850 census we find

Peter Wagoner at home with his father Peter, in Marion Twp., Hocking Co., Oh. Father Peter later married Catherine (Rittgers) Amspaugh (#1.7).

ISSUE:

.139.1   Jacob WAGONER, born about 1858 in Marion Twp., Hocking Co., Oh. On the 1860 census, age 2, with parents there.[158, fam #1040/1028]

13.C Jacob M.³ RITTGERS (John, Jr.², John¹) was born 7 Feb 1847 in Marion Twp., Hocking, Oh., the son of John Augustin RITTGERS, Jr. and Lydia____. He is on the 1850 census there, age 3. with parents, [p 841 fam #118/120] and there on the 1860 census, age 13, with sister Elizabeth and her husband, Peter Wagoner, on farm of Daniel Lefler.[p 158 fam #1040/1028] He married **Frances RED** 20 Aug 1868 in Hocking Co., Oh.[HVRM, Book "C", p. 474] She was born about 1846 in Oh., the daughter of Isaac and Sarah (__) Red. She is seen on 1860 census, age 16, with parents in Marion Twp., Hocking Co., Oh. Isaac, 63, farmer, b. Va., and Sarah, 57. [fam #1077/1065] The 1870 census shows us Jacob, 23, with wife Frances, 25, and son "Ugene" age 1. They are still in Marion Twp., Hocking Co.[p 510 fam #270/273] In 1880 he is 33, and still farming in Marion Twp. With him is wife Frances, age 34, 34, and seven children.[ED 63, p. 109C, fam #244/247] We see his name on several deed transactions in Hocking Co. The Family Story tells us that he was a "veteran of the Civil War, and in the late eighties did an extensive timber business in Ohio, owning and operating several saw mills and a coal mine. Later he entered the Ministry, in which Profession he remained until his death about 1904. He was an able man in business and quite successful in the Ministry." The family story also reports that the information for this family was collected in 1914! Three of his children are said to have died prior to that.

ISSUE:

.13C.1   Eugene RITTGERS, born 3 Aug 1869 in Marion Twp., Hocking Co., Oh.[HVRB, book B, p. 42.], died before 1914. He is on the 1870 census with parents in Marion Twp. Named spelled "Ugene".[p 510, fam #270/273] Shown on the 1880 census there, age 11, with parents.[ED 63, p 109C, fam #244/247]

.13C.2   Cleophas RITTGERS, born 1871 in Marion Twp., Hocking Co., Oh. He is there on the 1880 census, age 9, with parents.[ED 63, p 109C, fam #244/247] Referred to in family records as "Clee." We are told he later lived in Huntington, Ind.

.13C.3   Franklin RITTGERS, born 7 Jan 1872 in Marion Twp., Hocking Co., Oh. He is there on the 1880 census, age 8, with parents.[ED 63, p 109C, fam #244/247] We are told he was later a farmer at New Paris, Ind.

.13C.4   Samuel RITTGERS, born 5 Apr 1873 in Marion Twp., Hocking Co., Oh.[HVRB, book B, p 142], died before 1914. He is there on the 1880 census, age 7, with parents. [ED 63, p 109C, fam #244/247]

.13C.5   Maud RITTGERS, born about 1874 in Marion Twp., Hocking Co., Oh. She is there on the 1880 census, age 6, with parents.[ED 63, p 109C, fam #244/247] We are told she married a "Mr. Morrow of Kearney, Neb."

.13C.6   John RITTGERS, born 1 Jan 1876 in Marion Twp., Hocking Co., Oh.[HVRB, book B, p 176] He is there on the 1880 census, age 4, with parents. [ED 63, p 109C, fam #244/247]

.13C.7   Harley E. RITTGERS, born about 1878 in Marion Twp., Hocking Co., Oh. He is on the 1880 census there, age 2, with parents   Name spelled "Carley" on census.[ED 63, p 109C, fam #244/247] We are told he lived in Huntington, Ind.

13.D William F.[3] RITTGERS (John, Jr.[2], John[1]) was born 8 Aug 1849 in Marion Twp., Hocking Co., Oh., the son of John Augustin RITTGERS, Jr. and Lydia_____. There on the 1850 census, 10/12ths of a year old, with parents.[p 841 fam #118/120], and on the 1860 census, age 12, with father and step-mother.[p 150 fam #936/924] He married **Lydia WILLIAMS** 15 Apr 1869 in Hocking County, Oh.[HVRM, Book "C", p. 519] She was born about 1844 in Oh., the daughter of Isaac and Isabella (Martin) Williams, and sister of Phebe Williams who married Tobias.(#13.4) We find on the 1870 census that William is 20 and a farm hand in Marion Twp., P.O. Haydonville, Hocking Co., Oh. Wife Lydia is 26.[p 511 fam #273/276] On the 1880 census, though, William is declared to be 38! (We see that error often) At this time he is a "steam engineer" in Monday Creek Twp., Perry Co., Oh. Lydia is 33, and caring for their three children.[ED 212, p 210D, fam #312/312] On the 1900 census we find William, 50, a "clerk", in Falls Twp., Hocking Co., Oh. Wife, Liddie, 55, declares they have been married 31 years and she bore 3 children, all alive at this time.[ED 28, fam #351/371] Besides 2 adult children in the home, they also have 2 boarders, Harley Thomas, 23, a conductor; and William Fox, 22, a laborer on a brick yard.[ED 28, p 66B, fam #351/371] William died in 1901[tombstone] We find on the 1910 census Lydia is living with daughter Rose and her husband George Krickbaum in Logan, Hocking Co Oh. Here she is 66, has born 3 children, all living at this time.[ED 83, p 9A, fam #201/210] On 1920 census, Lydia continues in home of daughter, Rose, in Logan, Hocking Co., Oh. She is 75.[ED 40, p. 71, fam #304/330] Lydia died in 193?(apparently the stone unreadable). They are buried in Mt. Zion Cemetery, Marion Twp., Hocking Co., Oh.[HCoCem]

ISSUE:

.13D.1   Minerva Bell RITTGERS, born 9 May 1872 in Oh.. On the 1880 census "Bell" is 8, with parents in Monday Creek, Perry Co., Oh. [ED 212, p 210D, fam #312/312]

.13D.2   Ellis RITTGERS, born 16 Apr 1874 in Oh. On the 1880 census Ellis is 6, with parents in Monday Creek, Perry Co., Oh.[ED 212, p 210D, fam #312/312] We are told in family story that he died young, yet we find him on the 1900 census, Falls Twp, Hocking Co., Oh. Ellis (name spelled "Allice" on census) declares his birth to be Aug 1873, age 26, a day laborer. He is in the home of his parents.[ED 28, p 66B, fam #351/371] Ellis, a butcher, married 9 Dec 1909 in Hocking Co., Ida Liff (Luff) of Logan, a waitress. She was born Nov 1871, the daughter of John and Ella (Heston) Liff.[HVRM Bk K, p.526] In 1910 Ellis is 35, and a meat cutter in Logan, Hocking Co., Oh. Wife Ida, 37, reports they have been married "0" years and she has born 0 children. This is the first marriage for both. They reside at 260 Wood St.[ED 83, p. 7A, fam #154/158] We find Ellis Rittgers died 10 Nov 1916 in Hocking Co., Oh.[HVRD, Vol 2095, cert #68789, Code 37] Ida is seen on the 1920 census, age 47, with her mother, Margaret "Luff," age 77, in Logan, Hocking Co., Oh. Ida made her will 22 Dec 1932, and administration was granted 27 Dec 1932. Her heirs are mother, Margaret Ellen Liff; sister Minnie Groves, brothers John and Charley; and nieces and nephews. She leaves all her possessions to her mother.[Hocking Co. Probate]

+ .13D.3   Rose Alma RITTGERS, born 25 Jan 1878.

14.1 Isaac[3] ROOT (Magdalene[2], John[1]) was born about 1826 in Marion Twp., Hocking Co., Oh., the son of John ROOT and Magdalene RITTGERS. He is on the 1850 census, age 24, with parents, in Marion, Hocking Co., Oh. [p 57 fam #411/420] He married **Jemima SHOAF** 26 Sep 1850 in Hocking Co., Oh.[HVRM, Book "B", p. 138] She was born about 1833 in Oh.

The 1860 census finds Isaac Root, age 35, a cabinet maker, with wife Jemima, age 27, in Falls Twp, Logan P.O., Hocking Co., Oh. They have with them four children, and Jemima's sister Mary Ann Shoaf, 19.[p.113, fam #411/413]

ISSUE:

.141.1 Zelda ROOT, born about 1852 in Falls Twp., Hocking Co., Oh. She is there on the 1860 census, age 8, with parents.[p 113, fam #411/413]

.141.2 Martha ROOT, born about 1854 in Falls Twp., Hocking Co., Oh, She is there on the 1860 census, age 6, with parents. [p 113, fam #411/413]

.141.3 John ROOT, born about 1857 in Falls Twp., Hocking Co., Oh. He is there on the 1860 census, age 3, with parents.[p 113, fam #411/413]

.141.4 Nancy ROOT, born about 1859 in Falls Twp., Hocking Co., Oh. She is there on the 1860 census, age 1, with parents. [p 113, fam #411/413]

14.2 Ephriam³ ROOT (Magdalene², John¹) was born about 1827 in Marion Twp., Hocking Co., Oh., the son of John ROOT and Magdalene RITTGERS. Family history gives us this name as being the eldest child of John and Magdalene (Rittgers) Root. He married **Amanda** _____ about 1851 in Oh. She was born about 1831 in Pa. We find on the 1860 census, Ephriam Root, 33, Master Carpenter, in Rush Creek, Fairfield Co., Oh. With him is wife Amanda, 29, b. Pa. and four children.[p 306]

ISSUE:

.142.1 Levina E. J. ROOT, born about 1852 in Rush Creek, Fairfield Co., Oh. There on 1860 census, age 8, with parents. [p 306]

.142.2 Sarah ROOT, born about 1854 in Rush Creek, Fairfield Co., Oh. There on 1860 census, age 6, with parents.[p 306]

.142.3 Clara ROOT, born about 1854 in Rush Creek, Fairfield Co., Oh. There on 1860 census, age 4, with parents.[p 306]

.142.4 George Albert ROOT, born about 1858 in Rush Creek, Fairfield Co., Oh. There on 1860 census, age 2, with parents.[p 306]

14.3 Sarah³ ROOT (Magdalene², John¹) was born about 1829 in Marion Twp, Hocking Co., Ohio., the daughter of John ROOT and Magdalene RITTGERS. She is there on the 1850 census, age 21, with parents [p 57 fam #411/420] In Marriage Book B, p.197, the intention of Sarah Root and **John BROWN** is entered on 20 Nov 1853. The side where the marriage date is to be entered is blank. He was born about 1820 in Oh. The 1860 census shows John, age 40, a laborer, and Sarah, age 30, with $50 in personal possessions and no property in Goodhope Twp., Hocking Co., Oh. They have with them three children, Isaac, 7; Henrietta, 11; and Mary, 2. It is probable that John was married before and Isaac and Mary are Sarah's, Henrietta born by first wife.[p 43 fam #601/600]

ISSUE:

.143.1 Isaac BROWN, born about 1854. On 1860 census, age 6, with parents in Goodhope Twp., Hocking Co., Oh.[p 43, fam #601/600]

.143.2 Mary BROWN, born about 1858. On 1860 census, age 2, with parents in Goodhope Twp., Hocking Co., Oh.[p 43, fam #601/600]

14.4 Daniel³ ROOT (Magdalene², John¹) was born 12 Apr 1830 in Marion Twp., Hocking Co., Ohio., the son of John ROOT and Magdalene RITTGERS. On the 1850 census there with parents. Listed as "David" from the handwriting.[p 57 fam #411/420] He married **Margaret Ann**

ZELLER 7 Oct 1852 in Hocking County, Oh.[HVRM, Book "B", p.174] She was born about 1839 in Oh. We find Daniel on the 1870 Census, in Valley Twp, Polk Co., Ia. He is age 39, a farmer with $500 in personal estate. Wife Margaret is 31 and with them are 7 children; Sarah, 17; thru Margaret, 2.[p 107 fam #110/12)] By studying the children's births, we see that the family moved to Iowa between July 1868 and June 1870 when census places them in Polk Co., Ia. The 1880 census for Webster Twp., Grimes, Polk Co., Ia. shows us Daniel, 42, a farmer. His wife is Margaret, also 42, caring for the six children at home. This erroneously states that all children born in Ohio. [p 589 fam #262/266] The Iowa state census for 1885 reports Daniel Root, age 53, a farmer, living in Webster Twp., Polk Co., Ia. Wife Margaret A., 52, is caring for their five children. We are told that the family later moved to Marshaltown, near Ames, Ia. The family story tells us that when early family reunions were formed, some of the Rittgers were upset when Roots showed up. They had lost contact and didn't know they had Roots cousins!

ISSUE:

+ .144.1   Sarah ROOT, born 16 Jul 1853, died 1946.
+ .144.2   Jacob M. ROOT, born 12 Feb 1857, died 1926.
  .144.3   Anna Katherine ROOT, born 22 Jul 1858 in Oh. She is age 12 on 1870 census, with parents in Valley Twp., Polk Co., Ia.[p 107 fam #110/120]
  .144.4   Mary Magdalene ROOT, born 13 Oct 1860 in Oh. She is age 10 on 1870 census, with parents in Valley Twp., Polk Co., Ia.[p 107 fam #110/120]
  .144.5   Daniel ROOT, born 25 Jul 1863 in Van Wert County, Oh. He is age 7 on 1870 census, with parents in Valley Twp., Polk Co., Ia.[p 107 fam #110/120] and on 1880 is age 17, with parents in Webster, Polk Co., Ia. [p 589 fam # 262/266] On the 1885 Iowa state census, we see "David", age 21, in his father's home in Webster Twp., Polk Co.[fam #8] He married Emma R. FRY 2 Jul 1898 in Polk Co., Ia.[PVRM, book 9, p 227 (transcript p 41)] She was born 1868. Emma died 1941 [RPCem, p 8] in Polk Co., Ia. Daniel died 1952[RPCem, p 8] in Polk Co., Ia. They are buried in Section "S", row 5, Ridgedale Cemetery. Jefferson Twp., Polk Co., Ia.[RPCem,p.8]
+ .144.6   Elmer Ellsworth ROOT, born 13 Jul 1866.
  .144.7   Margaret Almeda ROOT, born 23 Jun 1868 in Oh. She is age 2 on 1870 census, with parents in Valley, Polk Co., Ia.[p 107 fam #110/120] and on 1880 is age 12, with parents in Webster, Polk Co., Ia.[p 589 fam # 262/266] On the 1885 Iowa state census, we see "Margeretia", age 16, in her father's home in Webster Twp., Polk Co.[fam#8]
  .144.8   Cyrus Kenneth ROOT, born 15 Apr 1871 in Polk Co., Ia.[LDS-IGI, 1992; fiche #1255, p 7738] He is on the 1880 age 9, with parents in Webster, Polk Co., Ia.[p 589, fam #262/266] On the 1885 Iowa state census, we see Cyrus, age 13, in his father's home in Webster Twp., Polk Co.[fam#8]
  .144.9   John Wesley ROOT, born 20 Sep 1875 in Polk Co., Ia, [LDS-IGI, Iowa, 1992; fiche #1255, p. 7,739], died 10 Dec 1876 in Polk Co., Ia., and was buried in Rittgers Cemetery, Johnston, Ia.[RitCem]
  .144.A   Emma Violet ROOT, born 26 Apr 1873 in Polk Co., Ia.[LDS-IGI, 1992; fiche #1255, p. 7738] She is on the 1880 age 7, with parents in Webster, Polk Co., Ia.[p 589, fam #262/266] On the 1885 Iowa state census, we see Emma V., age 11, in her father's home in Webster Twp., Polk Co.[fam#8]
  .144.B   Clara Alice ROOT, born 20 Nov 1876 in Polk Co., Ia. Family record records her birth, but may have died young, as not on 1880 or 1885 state census.

14.5 Katherine³ ROOT (Magdalene², John¹) was born about 1834 in Marion Twp., Hocking, Ohio., the daughter of John ROOT and Magdalene RITTGERS. She is there on the 1850 census, age 16, with parents. [p 57 fam #411/420] She married **John COOK** 18 Nov 1852 in Hocking Co., Oh.[HVRM, Book "B", p. 176] He was born about 1835 in Oh. The 1860 census shows in Laurel Twp., Hocking Co., John Cook, age 25 a "Laborer" with a personal property value of $90. Catherine is age 24, and caring for their children.[P. 78, fam #1072/1059]

ISSUE:

.145.1   Malinda COOK, born about 1853 in Laurel Twp., Hocking Co., Oh. On 1860 census, age 7, with parents there.[p 78, fam #1072/1059]

.145.2   Daniel COOK, born about 1855 in Laurel, Hocking Co., Oh. On 1860 census, age 5, with parents there.[p 78, fam #1072/1059]

.145.3   Samuel COOK, born about 1857 in Laurel, Hocking Co., Oh. On 1860 census, age 3, with parents there.[p 78, fam #1072/1059]

.145.4   Amanda A. COOK, born about 1859 in Laurel, Hocking Co., Oh. On 1860 census, age 1, with parents there.[p 78, fam #1072/1059]

15.2 Noah³ AMSPAUGH (Katherine², John¹) was born about 1829 in Hocking Co., Oh., the son of John AMSPAUGH and Katherine RITTGERS. He is on 1850 census, age 21, with widowed mother.[p 6 fam #182/187] He married **Elizabeth _____** about 1855 in Oh. She was born about 1836 in Oh.

ISSUE:

.152.1   Mary C. AMSPAUGH, born about 1856 in Washington Twp., Adams Co., In.

.152.2   Rachel S. AMSPAUGH, born in Washington Twp., Adams Co., In.

.152.3   John AMSPAUGH, born about 1867 in Washington Twp., Adams Co., In.

.152.4   Ketty AMSPAUGH, born about 1869 in Washington Twp., Adams Co., In.

15.3 Susan³ AMSPAUGH (Katherine², John¹) was born 19 Jul 1830 in Hocking Co., Oh., the daughter of John AMSPAUGH and Katherine RITTGERS. She married **Jacob Frederick BODAMER** 20 Jun 1848. He was born 26 Nov 1824 in Dobel, Ger. Susan died 07 Mar 1896, and Jacob died 30 Sept 1901, Marion Twp., Hocking Co., Oh. In Jacob's estate#1932 in Hocking Co., Oh., we find that "Susan, wife of Frank Blosser, declines administration in favor of Noah Bodamer." Susan is listed as "grand daughter" on the estate, but we don't know who her parents were. Among the assets in the estate, is the Bodamer property, S.W. quarter of N.W. quarter of Section 17, Twp. 15, range 17, 40 acres. Household items were listed, as well as on clock and one "express wagon."

ISSUE:

.153.1   Noah BODAMER. He married Demarius. Named in his father's estate, as being of Bremen, Oh.[HockProb, est. #1932]

.153.2   John BODAMER. Named in his father's estate, as being of Corning, Oh.[HockProb, est. #1932]

.153.3   Jacob BODAMER. He married Phebe A.. Named in his father's estate, as being of Willmine, Ill.[HockProb, est. #1932]

.153.4   Daniel BODAMER. He married Gertrude. Named in his father's estate, as being of Lintner, Ill.[HockProb, est. #1932]

.153.5   Elizabeth BODAMER. She married John MARLEY. Named in her father's estate, as being of Pickinville, Ill.[HockProb, est. #1932]

.153.6   Lanie BODAMER. She married Stephen KUSTERMAN.   Named in her father's
           estate, as being of Highland, Ill.[HockProb, est. #1932]
.153.7   Catherine BODAMER. She married Charles MANSKER.   Named in her father's
           estate, as being of Early Sack City,Ia.[HockProb, est. #1932]
+ .153.8   Susan BODAMER, born 7 May 1857.
.153.9   Matilda BODAMER. She married Lewis LAUGHLIN.   Named in her father's
           estate, as being of Flagdale, Oh.[HockProb, est. #1932]
.153.A   Lavina BODAMER. She married_____ TIPPLE.   Named in her father's estate, as
           being of Lancaster, Oh.[HockProb, est. #1932]

15.4 Jonas[3] AMSPAUGH (Katherine[2], John[1]) was born Dec 1831 in Hocking Co., Oh., the
son of John AMSPAUGH and Katherine RITTGERS. On 1850 Census, age 18, with widowed
mother Marion Twp., Hocking Co., Oh.[p 6 fam #182/187] He married **Barbara
DOUBENMIRE** 3 Dec 1854 in Hocking Co., Oh.[HVRM, Bk "B", p. 215, Jonas "Ambaugher"
& Barbara "Doubenmire] She was born Jan 1836 in Ohio. The 1860 census shows Jonas
"Omspaugh", age 26, in Lancaster, Fairfield Co. He is a day laberor with $50 in personal estate
and no property. With him is wife Barbary, 24, and three children.[p 28 fam #397/389] On 1870
census, age 39, farmer in Marion Twp, Hocking Co., Oh., with $700 in Real Estate and $300
in personal property. Wife Barbary, age 34, and six children are also in the home.[p 507 fam
#230/233] In 1880, this family is in Greenfield Twp., Fairfield Co., Oh. Jonas, 48, and Barbara
44, have with them 8 children and one grandchild, son of daughter, Barbara Ellen.[p 142 fam
#110/115] On the 1900 census, Jackson Twp., Darke Co., Oh., Jonas, 68, and Barbara, 64, have
been married 45 years. Barbara has born 11 children, 8 alive at this time. They live with
daughter Sarah, 32, and her husband, George Weiss.[ED 59, p 4B, fam #75/75] In 1910, Jonas,
78, and Barbara, 73, are shown in their own home 107 Chestnut St., Union, Jackson Twp.,
Darke Co., Oh.[ED 93, p 5A, fam # 122/126] In 1920, Barbara is a widow, living there with her
widowed daughter, Louisa RITTGERS, widow of Joseph Rittgers, (#112.2)[ED 108, p 13, fam
#303/303] Jonas died 6 Jan 1911. Barbara died after 1920.
                                   ISSUE:
.154.1   Mary M. AMSPAUGH, born 2 Jul 1855 [EmEv,p66] in Marion Twp., Hocking Co.,
           Oh. The 1860 census gives us Mary, age 4, with parents in Lancaster, Fairfield Co.,
           Oh.[p 28, fam #397/389] On 1870 census, age 15, with parents, Marion, Hocking,
           Oh.[p 507 fam #230/233] She married John WILSON.
+ .154.2   John D. AMSPAUGH, born 13 Apr 1857.
+ .154.3   Barbarey Ellen AMSPAUGH, born about 1860.
+ .154.4   Louisa Jane AMSPAUGH, born 17 Aug 1862.
.154.5   Susanna D. AMSPAUGH, born about 1864 in Marion Twp., Hocking Co., Oh. On
           1870 census, age 6, with parents there.[p 507 fam #230/233], and age 16, in 1880
           with her parents in Greenfield Twp., Fairfield Co., Oh. [p 142, fam #110/115] She
           married Charles LIVINGSTON.
.154.6   Jonas Franke AMSPAUGH, born 18 Apr 1866 [EmEv, p.33] in Marion Twp.,
           Hocking Co., Oh. He is on the 1870 census, age 4, with parents there.[p 507 fam
           #230/233), and age 14, in 1880 with her parents in Greenfield Twp., Fairfield Co.,
           Oh. [p 142, fam #110/115]
+ .154.7   Sarah Katherina AMSPAUGH, born 9 Feb 1868.
.154.8   Wilhem Karl AMSPAUGH, born 28 Jun 1870 in Hocking Co., Oh., died 13 May
           1871 in Hocking Co., Oh.

.154.9   George AMSPAUGH, born 9 Aug 1872 [EmEv, p.36] in Hocking Co., Oh. On
         1880 census, age 7, with parents in Greenfield Twp., Fairfield Co., Oh.[p 142, fam
         #110/115]
.154.A   Almeda R. AMSPAUGH, born about 1875 in Oh. On 1880 census, age 5, with
         parents in Greenfield Twp., Fairfield Co., Oh. [p 142 fam #75/75]
.154.B   Margaret E. AMSPAUGH, born about 1877 in Oh. On 1880 census, age 3, with
         parents in Greenfield Twp., Fairfield Co., Oh.[p 142 fam #75/75]

15.5 Lovina[3] AMSPAUGH (Katherine[2], John[1]) was born about 1834 in Hocking Co., Oh., the
daughter of John AMSPAUGH and Katherine RITTGERS. 1850 census, age 16, with widowed
mother in Marion Twp., Hocking Co., Oh. She married **Frederick DOUBENMIER** 1854 in
Fairfield County, Oh.[LDS-IGI, 1992, fiche #187, p 14, 510] (Marriage date not given, but
names given together as parents of several of their children.)

ISSUE:

.155.1   Emma DOUBENMIER, born 1 Nov 1855 in Fairfield Co., Oh.[LDS]
.155.2   Jacob Frederick DOUBENMIER, born 11 Jul 1857 in Fairfield Co., Oh.[LDS] On
         1880 census, we see one Jacob F. Doubenmire, 23, a hired man-laborer, on the farm
         of George Oohs, in Fairfield Co., Oh.[p 219B, fam #10/10]
.155.3   Lewis L. DOUBENMIER, born 9 Feb 1859 in Fairfield Co., Oh.[LDS]
.155.4   Daniel DOUBENMIER, born 15 Dec 1861 in Fairfield Co., Oh.[LDS]
.155.5   Elmer DOUBENMIER, born 15 Jan 1863 in Fairfield Co., Oh.[LDS]
.155.6   William S. DOUBENMIER, born 9 Jul 1865 in Fairfield Co., Oh.[LDS]
.155.7   Albert C. DOUBENMIER, born 28 May 1867 in Fairfield Co., Oh.[LDS]
.155.8   John W. DOUBENMIER. Family history gives his name as the only child of
         Frederick and Lovina (Amspaugh) Doubenmier. LDS-IGI shows us seven children
         and he is not among them.

15.6 Daniel[3] AMSPAUGH (Katherine[2], John[1]) was born about 1837 in Hocking Co., Oh., the
son of John AMSPAUGH and Katherine RITTGERS. On 1850 census with mother, Catherine
(Rittgers) Amspaugh, in Marion Twp., Hocking Co., Oh, age 13. [p 6 fam #182/187]   He
married **Margaret (__) DEFENBAUGHER** 29 Jan 1856 in Hocking Co., Oh.[HVRM, Book
"B", p. 237] She was born about 1833 in Ohio. Name also given in records as "Daubenmire."
The 1860 census shows Daniel, 23, a farmer with $1800 in real estate and $500 in personal
estate. Wife Margaret is 29. It shows them with two children, Barbary, age 10, and Rosann, age
7, both born in Ohio. Margaret must have been married previously, as these children born prior
to this marriage. We also see three children born within this marriage.[p 166 fam #1133/1128]
1870 census shows Daniel Amspaugh, age 33, a farmer, with wife Margaret, age 32. (Note there
is a seven year discrepancy in the two census records) They have six children with them.
Barbary and Rosann aren't on the 1870 census.[p 503 fam #166/169] .

ISSUE:

+ .156.1   John AMSPAUGH, born Apr 1855.
  .156.2   Christina AMSPAUGH, born about 1859 in Marion Twp., Hocking Co., Ohio She
           is on the 1860 census, age 2,[p 166 fam #1133/1128] and there on 1870 census, age
           11, with parents.[p 503, fam #166/169]
+ .156.3   Daniel Frederick AMSPAUGH, born 29 Mar 1860.
  .156.4   Elly AMSPAUGH, born about 1861 in Marion Twp., Hocking Co., Ohio. She is on
           the 1870 census, age 9, with parents there.[p 503, fam #166/169]

.156.5   Edward AMSPAUGH, born about 1866 in Marion Twp., Hocking Co., Ohio. He
              is on the 1870 census, age 4, with parents there.[p 503, fam #166/169]

15.8 Leah³ AMSPAUGH (Katherine², John¹) was born 11 Feb 1842 [EmEv] in Hocking Co.,
Oh., the daughter of John AMSPAUGH and Katherine RITTGERS. On the 1850 census with
mother Catherine (Rittgers) Amspaugh, Marion Twp., Hocking Co., Oh., age 8.[p 6 fam
192.187] and on the 1860 census with mother and step-father, Peter Wagoner, Sr., in Hocking
Co., Oh., She is now 18.[p 156 fam #1006/994] She married **Jacob DITTMAR** 17 Apr 1866.
                                          ISSUE:
.158.1   Elizabeth DITTMAR, born 19 May 1867.
.158.2   Mary Catherine DITTMAR, born 21 Jul 1868.
.158.3   Justin Luther DITTMAR, born 31 Oct 1870.

15.9 Lydia³ AMSPAUGH (Katherine², John¹) was born about 1846 in Hocking Co., Oh., the
daughter of John AMSPAUGH and Katherine RITTGERS. On the 1850 census with mother
Catherine (Rittgers) Amspaugh, Marion Twp., Hocking Co., Oh., age 4.[p 6 fam 192.187]and
1860 census with mother and step-father, Peter Wagoner, Sr., in Hocking Co., Oh., She is now
16.[p 156 fam #1006/994]   Family story tells us she married one _____ **MASON** and had
a daughter, Myrtle.
                                          ISSUE:
.159.1   Myrtle MASON. She married _____ TINKHAM.   We are told she lived in
              Milwaukee, Wis.

16.1 David Foght³ RITTGERS (Daniel², John¹) was born 14 Feb 1837 in Marion Twp.,
Hocking Co., Oh., the son of Daniel R. RITTGERS and Eve FOGHT. On the 1850 census, he
is age 13, with father and step-mother in Berne Twp., Fairfield Co., Oh.[p 442 fam #147/160]
We see him with his family, age 19, on the 1856 Polk Co., Iowa State census.[p.285,fam363]
He married **Sarah Elizabeth DENNY** 20 Mar 1859 in Polk Co., Ia. She was born Jan 1843 in
Wilmington, Del. On the 1860 census, they were in Jefferson Twp., Polk Co., Ia. David is 23,
a farmer with property worth $1000 and personal property worth $300. Wife Sarah E. is age 17.
[p 104 fam #830/764] They live next door to his sister Sarah, who just married James Denney,
brother of his wife. In 1870 we find David, 33, a farmer in Valley, Polk Co., Ia. His property
is valued at $5000 and personal property is $2050. Wife Sarah, age 27, who was born in
Delaware, has two children. They also have in their home 4 others. Jacob Hamilton is 14. (Son
of David's cousin, Margaret (#12.6 daughter of Jacob Rittgers), and Joseph Hamilton.) David
also has Anna Wooley, age 10, born in Ohio; George Curl, 21, b. in Indiana; and Sarah Root,
17, born in Ohio. (David's aunt Mary (#1.4) married John Root. Their son Daniel Root has a
daughter, Sarah, b. 1853.) We have found no connection to the Wooley child or George Curl,
but they could be kin to Sarah.[p 407 fam #108/118] On the 1880 census, we see David
continues to do well. He is now 43, and a farmer in Valley, Polk Co., Ia. With him are wife
Sarah, 37; six children, and four servants listed: Wilbur Gray, 25, b. Ohio, a farm laborer; Annie
Wobry, 19 (Wooley on 1870 census?) "died Oct 1879", b. Ohio; Job Truman, 56, b. Ohio; and
William Ogden, 28, b. N.J.[ED 172, p 545, fam #214/219] In 1900, David 63, and Sarah E., 57.,
still have four children in the home, as well as grand-daughter, Mina May Wilson, age 4.
(#1618.1) On the 1920 census we see "D.F." age 82, a retired farmer, in Des Moines, Polk Co.,
Ia. With him are wife Sarah, 76, and son Carl C., 31. It notes Carl is farming father's farm. Also
with them is Mary Holmquist, 67, "roomer", a seamstress from Germany, who arrived in

1875.[ED 84, p 4A, fam #97/84] We are told David died 16 Apr 1926 "from pleural pneumonia from getting hot in the garden and cooling off too fast." It is reported that in 1929, Sarah had 18 grandchildren and 6 great-grandchildren. Sarah died 18 Dec 1931. They are buried in the Rittgers Cemetery Johnston, Ia.[RitCem] They were members of Grace Methodist Church, Des Moines, Ia.

ISSUE:

.161.1   Francis Daniel RITTGERS, born 31 Oct 1860 in Jefferson Twp., Polk Co., Ia. Died of Cholera and "fantum" there 29 Apr 1862 and was buried in Rittgers Cemetery, Johnston, Ia.[RitCem]

.161.2   Charles Sanford RITTGERS, born 8 Sep 1862 in Jefferson Twp., Polk Co., Ia. Died there of "fly blister poultice" 29 Feb 1863 and was buried in Rittgers Cemetery, Johnston, Ia.[RitCem] The event of his death is noted in Reuben Rittgers' diary, "died of diptheria." On Sunday, March 1, "Funeral Services of Charles Sanford by H. Badley from suffer little children to prayer." H. Badley was the minister at their local church.

.161.3   Ira Wesley RITTGERS, born 20 Jan 1864 in Jefferson Twp., Polk Co., Ia. Died there of "fly blister" and diphtheria 16 Oct 1864 and was buried in Rittgers Cemetery, Johnston, Ia.[RitCem]

+ .161.4   Timothy Denny RITTGERS, born 8 Sep 1866, died 7 May 1944.

+ .161.5   Edmund Grant "Eddy" RITTGERS, born 24 Jan 1869, died 3 Feb 1900.

+ .161.6   Kitty Klyde RITTGERS, born 18 Dec 1871, died 9 Feb 1944.

+ .161.7   George Eugene "Gene" RITTGERS, born 28 Jan 1873, died 22 Jan 1928.

+ .161.8   Flora May RITTGERS, born 17 Feb 1875, died 14 Jan 1897.

.161.9   Sarah O'Dessa RITTGERS, born 6 Apr 1877 in Valley, Polk Co., Ia. She is there on the 1880 census, age 3, with parents.[ED 172, p 545, fam #214/219] She married George Washington HAY 20 Mar 1901. We are told she had no issue. She died 14 Sep 1903, at home suddenly from a blood clot to her heart, and is buried in Mingo, Jasper Co., Ia.

+ .161.A   James Albert "Jim" RITTGERS, born 9 Jan 1882, died 3 Jul 1953.

+ .161.B   Cora Nina RITTGERS, born 11 Sep 1886, died 1 Apr 1970.

.161.C   Carl Clinton RITTGERS, born 17 Aug 1888 [SS] in Valley, Polk Co., Ia., died 4 Aug 1975[SS; funeral memorial card], and was buried in Rittgers Cemetery, Polk Co., Ia. He is on the 1920 census, in Des Moines, Polk Co., Ia., age 31, "farming father's farm". In the home are also his parents, "D.F." and Sarah E. Rittgers. They have a boarder, Mary Holmquist, 67, a seamstress from Germany, who immigrated in 1875.[ED 84, p 4A, fam #97/84] He was a farmer and a veteran of WW I, a member of the Grace United Methodist Church and the Johnston Lions Club. We are told he never married. He owned a large farm that is now being developed into a housing development in Johnston, Polk Co., Ia.

16.2 Reuben R.³ RITTGERS (Daniel², John¹) was born 19 Apr 1838 in Fairfield Co., Oh., the son of Daniel R. RITTGERS and Eve FOGHT. On the 1850 census, age 12, with his father and step-mother, Berne Twp., Fairfield Co., Oh.[p 442 fam #147/160] He moved west with his family in 1853. We see him there, age 17, with his family on the Polk Co., Ia., 1856 state census. He is age 22, and the oldest child home with his stepmother, Christina, on the 1860 census in Jefferson Twp., Polk Co., Ia.[fam #742/697] The family story is told to us in a journal supplied by Laura (Rittgers)(Peitzman) Emmert:

"Reuben was a carpenter and a farmer, Johnston, Ia. He built a house at `Appledoor' 1/2 mile E. of Merle Hay Rd. on NW 62nd Ave. North side of road. Reuben was a devout Christian and his diaries tell of his attendance at worship services. Perhaps he went to Methodist Meetings in a bldg. on the SE corner of the intersection (now) of Merle Hay and NW Beaver Dr. I think this church had disbanded by the time a Presbyterian Church was built in the yard just south of Ridgedale Cemetery, across the road from Hyperion Club House. Reuben wrote in his diaries of attending "meeting" at McDevett's Grove (70th and Meredith Dr.) and at Prairie Home, a school house located 2 mi. west & so. of Grimes.(It wasn't until many years later that the area was called Johnston, but it identifies the area where the land is.)

"Probably the Findleys worshiped at Prairie Home and I suspect it was not altogether the service there that attracted him." Reuben writes of helping Abel, his future father-in-law, build a log house. He wrote several comments in his diaries about Abigail, so we are told.

Other entries in his early diaries reflect his religious beliefs. "Worked on the Beaver Bridge as road work. Thought much on and of the impressions L. had concerbing my duty to God and toward man." He notes the weather, such as "Cold", "snowed", "thawed"; notes his daily work projects. "Repared my shop. Filed my saws." "Butchered for Mother." He also writes of going to "spelling." Apparently it was a class, as he writes of being at the school. He kept meticulous financial records in his journals, including how many meals he eats "at mothers".

Civil War erupted. In the manuscript collection of the Iowa Historical Society in Des Moines, Ia., we find Civil War information. Among their papers is the "Volunteer Enlistment" paper of Reuben R. Rittgers, dated 11 May 1864. He is described as age 26, 5'9", with hazel eyes, dark hair and light complexion. Reuben was mustered into the U.S. Army on 1 June 1864, in the 44th Iowa Volunteers, Co. "H", for a term of 100 days.

A letter has been shared with us by descendant Barbara Ann (Fisher) Abrams(#162113.4) from Reuben, stationed at "Picket Station one mile from camp," dated 1 July 1864. In it he speaks of not getting letters from home, then talks about camp life. He is upset through much of it as he hasn't received any mail in several days. He refers to several family members in it. He drew a map at the end, showing he is in on Picket duty around Memphis, Tenn. In the same file located in the Ia. Historical Archives, is Reuben's "President's Thanks and Certificate of Honorable Service." It is a form thanking the "Volunteers of 100 days from the States of Indiana, Illinois, Iowa and Wisconsin".

A story related in Emmert's Journal tells us that Reuben had barely gotten home in Sept 1864 when word reached the family that brother John Henry had succumbed to measles on the way home from his military service. Reuben hitched up the team and drove the wagon into Kellogg, Ia., which is as far as the train came at that time. He stabled the horses and took the train to Davenport, Ia., to receive John's body. Back in Kellogg, he again hitched the horses and brought John home to be buried in the Rittgers family cemetery. We are told by other family members that Reuben was paid by the Army to transport John's body home.

Reuben soon was again active in his community. Shared with us by Barbara (Fisher) Abrams is an accounting dated 7 Oct 1864, compiled by Reuben, "Names of those who subscribe to the Mount Pleasant Church and the amounts paid and the amounts yet unpaid attached to each name." Among the names are several family members.

He married **Abigail Ann FINDLEY** 29 Aug 1865 in Dallas Co., Ia.[Dallas Co., Ia., Marr. Bk 1A, p.128] She was born 1 Feb 1845 in Westmoreland Co., Pa., the daughter of Abel FINDLEY, Jr. and Mary Jane KERR. In a diary owned by descendant Gail (Rorabaugh) Cox of Mount Dora, Fla., Abigail documented their first year of marriage. She speaks respectfully of "Mother Rittgers." Among the brief entries of her domestic chores, and visits with friends and family, she notes "Election Day. Went over with Reuben but didn't go to the Lecter was afraid they would object to my voting." On 31 Oct 1865, we learn that "Reuben came home today very sick, had a high fever..." The next day "..better today but far from well. He thinks it is a very severe turn of Ague..." He continued ill until 4 Oct, when Abigail "sent to Des Moines for Dr. Beach...He said that the fever was bordering on Typhoid, left some medicine which (thanks be to God) works like a charm and he is better already." Reuben didn't get back on his feet until 15 Oct. Then on 28 Dec, Reuben hurt his back. It appears Reuben had been thinking about going into the ministry, as she writes "Promised Reuben to go with him through all the trials he may have to encounter in his new calling. I know we shall have to bear many hardships in many different ways, but God is good...I thank Him that I have been enabled to give up all my worldly anticipations with as light a struggle as I have." This is the only mention of this "calling", and we know he remained on his farm. They also kept a careful accounting of what they cost "Mother Rittgers" and noted she was paid in full. It is interesting to note that she mentions "being ill" in one of the last entries in the diary, but never once mentions she is pregnant! The diaries were discovered in the attic at Appledoor by Gretchen Rittgers in the 1920's and are now all in the possession of Laura (Rittgers) (Peitzman) Emmert and Thomas E. Rittgers, with the exception of the one mentioned above. Another note in Emmert's Journal points out "Reuben and Abbie were very devout Christians and raised their children in a 'religious emphasis' atmosphere."

Reuben's name appears over several years in the estate of his father, Daniel. It appears that Reuben purchased back most of the land that had been divided between he and his brothers and sisters. He was appointed administrator of the estate 21 Nov 1865, when the former administrator resigned. At this time he was also made guardian of his minor brothers & sisters. He was discharged as administrator 16 Jan 1867, upon declaration that all debts were paid, and he is ordered to pay all heirs their share of the estate. His guardianship ended 14 July 1877, when the youngest became 18. [Abst. #76811]

A handwritten paper, handwriting verified by Florida descendants as being Abigail's handwriting, is now in the possession of Vivian Adelaid (Rittgers) Rorabaugh's son Philip Rorabaugh (#162A.4). It is entitled FAMILY RECORD and gives birth of Abigail's parents, their marriage date, and verifies her birth and marriage to Reuben Rittgers.

A story passed down in the family reports that, with her parents, Abigail rafted down the Allegheny and Ohio Rivers to the Mississippi. The family story gives her age as 16, but when we look at the births of her siblings, we see that the trip was made in 1852 or 1853, when she was seven or eight. The family moved to Polk Co., Ia., after July 1860 (as that is the date the census was taken in Van Buren Co., showing the family there at that time) and before July 1863, when her youngest sister was born.

In a story told by the family of U.S. and Rosa (Rittgers) Findley we learn that shortly after the family first settled in Iowa, an Indian boy was seen by their fence several days. Over a period of time he became bolder and was soon looking in the cabin windows. The family tried to ignore him until one day the boy and his father came to the yard. The Indian father approached Abel Findley about buying his 11 year old daughter as a bride for his son. Abel was shocked and ordered them away. A few days later, the Indian father returned. He asked Abel to step outside to talk. No one could hear what was said, but after the Indian left, Abel secured the house and ordered everyone to stay inside. He enlisted the help of a few neighboring farmers to watch his family and he left for two days. When he returned, he had sold his farm and his mill, and the family moved "to the next county." The family was never told what the Indian father had said to Abel. The way the story was reported, it is said that the family moved from Polk to Dallas Co., when this happened, but at the time Abigail was 11, the family lived in Lee Co., Ia. When they left in a hurry, they went just north to Van Buren Co., where they are seen on the 1860 census. We are told that Abel had a wagon and hauled freight from the Mississippi River to Des Moines.

On the 1870 census, Reuben listed as living near Christine and family. He is 30, married to Abigail and they have Ambrose, age 3. Reuben is a farmer and claims his land is worth $7500, with $1395 worth of personal property. [p 407 fam #109/119] 1880 finds our family growing rapidly. Reuben, 42, continues farming in Valley Twp., Polk Co., Ia. Abigail, 36, is caring for their six children. The youngest, Walberg age 2, has a notation, not often seen in the records, that states "Paralized, Dr. Carter". He died shortly after the census was taken.[ED 172, p 545, fam #213/218]

In 1890 the United States Government passed a bill enabling disabled Civil War Soldiers to have a pension. Reuben applied on 12 Sept 1890. He states he is now 52 years old, was honorably discharged and "unable to earn a support by manual labor, by reason of Rupture on right side; partial deafness; diseased condition of eyes; general debility; catarrh of head" (Catarrh is an old fashioned term for chronic congestion of mucous membranes, such as in sinus conditions. Also was sometimes used for emphysema or asthma in the elderly.) Death was caused by Bronchitis. The pension records contain an Affidavit of Death filed by Abigail giving the date of death as 18 Nov 1893. In a rare find, a copy of his will is in his pension file, as well as a transcript from Dallas Co. of their marriage. The land abstracts and pension file follow Reuben's estate over the next several years. At his death in 1893, Reuben left nine minor children. The next entry in his pension file tells us that Abigail is filing for widow's benefits. She states Reuben was receiving $12 per month. His will reports that property, including "land situated in Colorado & six and one half acres of timber land situated in Jefferson Twp., Polk Co., may be sold" He speaks of children under age 21, but none are listed by name. Reuben died 18 Nov 1893 in Webster, Polk, Ia, and was buried in Rittger's Cem., Johnston, Ia.[RitCem]

There was a state census conducted in 1895. Here we see "Mrs. R.R. Rittgers" 50 and a widow, farming. She is called a Presbyterian on the record. With her are children, "Finley", age 20, down to Eva, age 8. Also in the house is Bessie Jennings, 21, teacher. This is the daughter of Abigail's sister, Elizabeth.

The 1900 census finds Abigail as head of household in Grimes, Polk Co., Ia. As we have found many times, the record is wrong in that it states Abigail was born in 1855 and is 45 years old. The record taker transposed the numbers. She states that she bore 13 children, 10 are alive at this time. (Vision, Branch, and Walberg died as infants.) Four minor children in the home at this time. [ED 112, p. 8B, fam #152/159] Abigail had to apply twice for widow's pension. The first time she was declined as she had property that brought in "in excess of $250 per year." As she got older and the law changed, she got $12 per month by 1908. On the 1910 census Abigail is with son John and his wife Gretchen in Precinct #1, Webster Twp., Polk Co., Ia. She is 65 and a widow.[ED184,p.8A,fam #89/89] By 1916 she was receiving $20 per month from her husband's pension. We see Abigail one more time on the 1920 census. She is now 74 and in the home of son John and his wife Gretchen in Walnut Twp., Dallas, Ia.[ED 21, p 8B, fam #192/194]

From a journal shared with us by Josephine Rorabaugh,(#162A.2) daughter of Vivian (Rittgers) Rorabaugh,(#162.A), we learn that Abigail traveled to Clermont, Lake Co., Florida to see Vivian on more than one occasion. In a letter shared with us by Barbara (Fisher) Abrams, we see that she was in Florida on 20 Feb - unfortunately, she didn't put a year date on it. In it she mentions that William and Vivian and the children are at church, that Mabel and John Genso have been in Clermont and are now gone again. She comments on how nice John is. She notes that it has been cool and "the children go to school barefoot and you can hardly get them to wear their shoes the coldest days." Abigail also describes a strange and wonderful fruit, the tangerine, describing how they can be peeled and broken into sections.

Abigail died 22 Jun 1920 in Johnston, Polk Co., Ia. On 4 July 1920, The postmaster at Grimes, Ia., had the sad duty to return a pension check to the government in the amount of $85.50 (quarterly payment) because the pensioner, Abigail A. Rittgers died 22 June 1920. Her cause of death is listed as "Hypostatic Pneumonia, Myocarditis." or heart failure. She is buried in Rittgers Cemetery with Reuben.[RitCem] Vivian's oldest child, John Rorabaugh, told the story of Vivian receiving word that Abigail was quite ill. She had to take her youngest, Abigail, as she was still nursing, but the other children were in school. It was up to John to take care of the other children while their father worked. Vivian rode the train to Iowa, and stayed until after Abigail had passed away and was buried. The children reported it was a great relief to see their mother getting off the train when she returned. They tell us John was too strict and not a good cook!

The estate of Abigail was handled by son Jasper Rittgers, and in a Petition for Administration, it is stated that "since that time [Abigail's death] by agreement of a majority of the heirs, Jasper C. Rittgers has been managing the real estate belonging to the estate." In a final report, 3 June 1936, it lists that at her death, Abigail "was seized of" several pieces of real estate, including about 160 acres locally, and 6 acres of timber, as well as "160 acres preemption claim in Kiowa Co., Colo." It appears that Jasper bought much of the land from his siblings. In the records of Abstract #76811, we can follow the next generation for several years.

ISSUE:

+ .162.1   Ambrose Robert RITTGERS, born 7 Oct 1866, died 14 Apr 1938.
 .162.2   Vision RITTGERS, born 9 Mar 1868 in Polk Co., Ia, died 12 Mar 1868 in Polk Co., Ia, and was buried in Rittgers Cemetery, Polk Co., Ia. On her tombstone it gives name as "Little Vision" Rittgers, age is "3 Days".[RitCem]
 .162.3   Branch RITTGERS, born 9 Mar 1868 in Grimes, Polk Co., Ia., died Jun 1870 in Grimes, Polk co., Ia., and was buried in Rittgers Cemetery, Polk Co., Ia. [RitCem]
+ .162.4   Daisy Marie RITTGERS, born 25 Jan 1871, died 5 Jan 1901.
 .162.5   Reuben RITTGERS, born and died 31 Dec 1872 in Polk Co., Ia.
+ .162.6   Maxwell M. RITTGERS, born 4 Jan 1873, died 20 Dec 1943.
+ .162.7   Abel Findley RITTGERS, born 19 Jul 1874/1875, died Sep 1921.
+ .162.8   Jasper C. "Jass" RITTGERS, born 8 Jun 1876, died 1 Oct 1965.
 .162.9   Walberg RITTGERS, born 6 Apr 1878 in Valley, Polk Co., Ia., died 15 Sep 1880 in Valley, Polk Co., Ia., and was buried in Rittgers Cemetery, Polk Co., Ia.[RitCem] On the 1880 census, states "Walberg, age 2, Paralized, Dr. Carter." [p 545, fam #213/218]
+ .162.A   Vivian Adelaid RITTGERS, born 25 Jul 1880, died 12 Mar 1959.
+ .162.B   Carrie Mabel RITTGERS, born 5 Apr 1882, died 8 Sep 1957.
+ .162.C   Chester Daniel RITTGERS, born 7 Jun 1883.
+ .162.D   John Henry RITTGERS, born 14 Nov 1884, died 8 Sep 1957.
+ .162.E   Mary Eve RITTGERS, born 2 Sep 1886, died 16 Dec 1974.

16.4 Sarah³ RITTGERS (Daniel², John¹) was born 10 Sep 1842 in Berne Twp., Fairfield Co., Oh., the daughter of Daniel R. RITTGERS and Eve FOGHT. Sarah is there, age 9 on the 1850 census in Ohio with her father and step-mother.[p 442 fam #147/160] She is age 13 when seen on the 1856 Iowa State census in Polk Co.[p.285,fam#63] with h She married **James DENNY**

14 Sep 1859.[PVRM, Bk 1, p.200] He was born 16 Jan 1837 [DD Bible, p 1.] in New Castle Co., Del., the son of Timothy and Ann (__) Denny. He is seen, age 19, with his parents in Polk Co., Ia. On the 1860 census we find James, 23, a farm laborer, and wife Sarah, 17, in Jefferson Twp., Polk Co., Oh. They live next door to her brother David, who married James' sister, Sarah.[p 104 fam #829/769] In 1870 they are in Walnut Twp., Polk Co., where we see James, 32, a farmer with $2800 worth of Real Estate and $1665 in personal property. Sarah, 27, is caring for John 9, and Ida, 3. In the home is also Lizzie Findley, 23, a teacher. (Abigail Findley, who married Reuben Rittgers (#16.2), had a sister Elizabeth called Lizzie.)[p 421 fam #163/112] On the 1880 census, in Grimes, Polk Co., Ia., James is 43, and a farmer. Sarah is now 37, and caring for four children in the home. Joseph Crisper age 19 works on the farm.[ED 175, p 586C, fam #219/223] In "History of Polk Co.", [no author listed; Union Hist. Co., Des Moines., Ia., 1880 p. 91,] we find that James is "Farmer, section 9, P.O. Des Moines. Was born in New Castle Co., Del...When 15 years of age he moved with his parents to this county...now owns a fine farm of 200 acres." Marriage date and children listed. In 1900 we find James, 63, still farming in Bloomfield, Polk Co., Ia. With him is wife Sarah, 57, and A.R. (Albert), 29. Also in the home, and working as a farm laborer, is nephew James Rittgers, 18. [ED 91, p 5A, fam #58/59] In 1910, Webster Twp., Polk Co., Ia., James, 73, is farming. With him is wife Sarah, 68. She declares they have been married 50 years and she has born 4 children, three alive at this time. They are next door to son Albert.[ED 184 p 8 fam #106/106] James died Apr 1918 in Polk County, Ia.[DD Bible, p. 1] In 1920, we find Sarah, age 76, with son John T. Denny in Waukee, Polk Co., Ia.[ED 21, p 8] Sarah died 13 Jul 1925 in Polk County, Ia.[DD Bible, p 1] Sarah and James both are buried in Rittgers Cemetery, Johnston, Polk Co., Ia.

ISSUE:

+ .164.1   John Timothy DENNEY, born 14 Aug 1860.
  .164.2   Infant DENNEY, born 18 Mar 1865, died 4 Apr 1865.[DDBible]
+ .164.3   Ida DENNEY, born 23 Jun 1867.
+ .164.4   Albert R. DENNEY, born 31 Mar 1871.

16.7 George³ RITTGERS (Daniel², John¹) was born 28 Jan 1849 [Abst 76811 gives year as 1848, but all other records support his birth as 1849] in Berne Twp., Fairfield Co., Oh., the son of Daniel R. RITTGERS and Christina Magdalene SMITH. The 1850 census shows George, age 2, with his parents there.[p 442 fam #147/160] He is age 7 in his father's home in Polk Co., Ia., on the 1856 state census.[p.285,fam#63] In 1860 he is with his widowed mother, age 11, in Jefferson Twp., Polk Co., Ia.[fam #742/697] 1870 shows him as the oldest at home with his mother, age 21, in Valley, Polk Co., Ia.[p 406 fam #96/106] He married **Mary Alice RHOADS** 20 Mar 1872 in Polk Co., Ia.[PVRM, Bk 1, p.230] She was born 12 Oct 1852 in Highland Co., Oh. Mary had been a school teacher. From a family group sheet, we see her parents are Charles W. (1820-1878) and Elizabeth (Hill) (1822-1911) Rhodes. Elizabeth lived with George and Mary in her later years. On the 1880 census, we find George, age 30, a farmer. Wife Mary, 27, is caring for their two children. (p 546 fam #215/220) We find George, 46, on the 1895 Iowa state census in Webster Twp., Polk Co. Wife Mary A., 43, and two children. Also in the home is Elizabeth Rhoads, 73.[1895, fam #104] By 1900 census, George, now 51, continues farming in Grimes, Polk Co., Ia. He and Mary, 47, are alone except for Mary's mother, Elizabeth Rhodes, age 78, who declares she has born 5 children, 4 alive at this time. She reports her parents b. Oh. Mary declares she and George have been married 28 years and she has born 2 children, both alive at this time.[p 290 fam #155/162] On the 1910 census, in Webster, Polk Co., Ia., George is now 61 and Mary is 58. She declares they have been married 38 years and that she bore two children, both living. Mary's mother, Elizabeth, now 89, is still with them. [ED 184, p 7B, fam #78/78.] George died 21 Mar 1914. We are told that George "was carried to the cemetery in a car." That HAS to be an interesting story! Mary died 24 Feb 1920 in Grimes, Polk, Ia, They are in Sec 2, lot 221, of Sunny Hill Cemetery, Grimes, Ia.[GPCem]

ISSUE:

+.167.1   Harry RITTGERS, born about 1874, died 1945.
+.167.2   Grace RITTGERS, born 20 Feb 1877, died 15 May 1948.

16.8 Michael[3] RITTGERS (Daniel[2], John[1]) was born 1 Sep 1850 [PVRB, p 209; Abst 76811] in Berne Twp., Fairfield Co., Oh., the son of Daniel R. RITTGERS and Christina Magdalene SMITH. On the 1860 census, age 9, with his mother in Polk Co., Iowa.[p 442 fam #147/160] In 1870 he is still in his mother's home, age 19.[p 406 fam #96/106] He married **Mary Ellen "Nell" BARTON** 8 Dec 1875.[PVRM, Bk 1] She was born about 1847 in Me. (The 1880 census reports her parents b. Maine, also, but 1900 gives her mother as being born in New Brunswick, Canada.) On the 1880 census, Grimes, Webster Twp., Polk Co., Ia., Michael is now 29, a farmer, married to Mary E, age 33, born in Maine as were her parents. They have in their home one Addie Lawson. Addie is 18, born in Ia., and states that her father was born in Pa. and her mother in Connecticut. She is listed as a servant. (Could she be daughter of Moses Lawson, who was by this time married to Michael's mother? He has a daughter, Elizabeth, who would be 18 at this this time.)[ED 175, p 587A, fam #282/232] In 1900 we find Michael still farming in Webster (Grimes) Polk Co., Ia. He is 49 and Mary E. is 53. She declares they have been married 24 years and she has born 3 children, 2 alive at this time. Also listed is one Lizzie Close, boarder, age 10, born July 1889 in Ia., as were her parents. Family history tells us that Michael and Mary Ellen took in a "Florence" and raised her. [p 290B fam #154/162] Florence later married their son Anson. The 1910 census shows them in Webster, Polk Co., Ia. Michael is 59 and still farming. Mary E. is 63. With them is Florence Close, 20, a servant. She states she born in Ia., but doesn't know where parents born.[ED 84, p 7B, fam #77/77] Michael died of pernicious anemia 2 Mar 1919.[PVRD, p. 278] In 1920 we find Mary, now 73 and a widow, with son Charles, a widower, and seven of Charles' children in Webster, Polk Co., Ia. We may assume he is farming his father's property.[ED 187, p 12B, fam #125/126] Mary died 1933 in Grimes, Polk Co., Ia, and was buried with Michael in Rittgers Cemetery, Johnston, Ia.[RitCem]

ISSUE:

+.168.1   Charles R. RITTGERS, born 26 Dec 1872, died 5 Dec 1957.
.168.2   Elizabeth Gretchen RITTGERS, born 19 May 1878 in Webster Twp., Polk Co., Ia. "Lizzie" is age 2 on 1880 census with her parents there.[ED 175, p 587A, fam #282/236] and 22 on the 1900 census.[ED 112, p 290, fam #154/162] Called Gretchen in the family record. Her obituary reads: "Elizabeth Rittgers, daughter of Mr. and Mrs. M.D. Rittgers, was born May 19, 1878 and died May 25, 1917, aged thirty-nine years and six days. She leaves besides her parents, two brothers, Charles R. of Brooklyn, New York, and Anson B. of Ankeny, Iowa. She was converted in early childhood and united with her home church. Believing that the teacher's profession afforded greater opportunity for doing good, she chose that for her life work and followed it until failing health compelled her to cease. A successful teacher, a devoted daughter and sister and loving friend, she had gone from our midst, leaving only tender memories and kindly deeds. With truth it can be said of her: "She hath done what she could." She died 23 May 1917 of diabetes and chronic

kidney infection from the diabetes., and was buried in Rittgers Cemetery, Johnston, Ia.

.168.3   Walter RITTGERS, born 1880, died 1881, and was buried in Rittgers Cemetery, Johnston, Ia. He is not shown on the 1880 census, so born after 1 June 1880.

+ .168.4   Anson RITTGERS, born 22 Sep 1885, died 30 Mar 1950.

16.9 Caroline "Nina"[3] RITTGERS (Daniel[2], John[1]) was born 10 Mar 1853 in Berne Twp., Fairfield Co., Oh., the daughter of Daniel R. RITTGERS and Christina Magdalene SMITH. On the 1860 census records we find Nina, age 7, with widowed mother in Jefferson Twp., Polk Co., Ia.,[p 442 fam #147/160] and 17 on the 1870 census.[p fam #742/697] She married **Palmer McDOWELL** 30 Apr 1871, in Polk Co., Ia. [PVRM, p. 64; recorded in Book 1, p 180] He was born about 1844 in Ind. We found him on the 1856 state census and on the 1860 census in Jefferson Twp. Co., Ia., with his parents, Dale and Susan McDowell, both born in Kentucky. He declares he born in Indiana.[p 105 fam #826/761] On 1870 census, Palmer is with his older brother, William, as a farm laborer in Union Twp., Perry P.O., Boone Co., Ia. He is 27 and declares he has $800 in real estate and $410 in personal property. [p 158] On the 1910 census, she is age 57, with husband in Cass Twp., Guthrie Co., Ia. She declares they have been married 39 years, and she has born 8 children, all alive at this time. Peter, 67, is farming a general farm.[ED 52; p. 6A; fam #116/119] Also in the home is Claude Devilbis, 25, hired man. Palmer died before 1920, as we see Nina on the 1920 census, age 66, a widow, listed as head of house in Panora, Guthrie Co., Ia. In home are daughters Pearl and Jessie.[ED56, p 228, fam 38/40] Caroline died 18 Mar 1929. She and Palmer are buried in Brethren Cemetery, Panora, Guthrie Co., Ia.

ISSUE:

+ .169.1   Nellie Josephine McDOWELL, born 24 Feb 1872, died 22 Jan 1966.

.169.2   Myrtle McDOWELL, born 19 Feb 1874.

+ .169.3   Jennie McDOWELL, born 13 Aug 1877.

.169.4   Fred V. McDOWELL, born 13 Jun 1883.

.169.5   Walter McDOWELL, born 4 Dec 1885. We are told he married Belle _____ .

.169.6   May L. McDOWELL, born 25 May 1887. She married _____ SHEELY. We are told she married _____ Sheely.

.169.7   Pearl N. McDOWELL, born 2 Nov 1890. On the 1920 census, age 29, single, a "teacher, Rural School.", in home with mother in Panora, Guthrie Co., Ia.[ED 56, p 2A, fam #38/40] She married John DAVIS. John also married (1) Jessie V. McDOWELL **(See number 169.8)**.

.169.8   Jessie V. McDOWELL, born 21 Apr 1895. On the 1910 census, age 15, in parents home in Cass Twp., Guthrie Co., Ia. [ED 52; p. 6A; fam 116/119]   On 1920 census, age 24, single, a "teacher, Rural School.", in home with mother in Panora, Guthrie Co., Ia.[ED 56, p 2A, fam #38/40] She married John DAVIS. John also married (2) Pearl N. McDOWELL **(See number 169.7)**.   We are given the same name for her husband as for sister Pearl's husband in the family records. Did she marry her sister's husband?

16.A Rosannah[3] RITTGERS (Daniel[2], John[1]) was born 4 Jan 1856 [Abst. 76811] in Jefferson Twp., Polk Co., Ia., the daughter of Daniel R. RITTGERS and Christina Magdalene SMITH. We first see her on the 1856 Iowa State Census, age 1, with her parents in Polk Co. [1856,p.285,#63.] She is age 4 on 1860 census, with mother and siblings there.[p 94, fam

#742/697] and on 1870 census, age 14.[p 406 fam #96/106] She married **Ulcestes S. FINDLEY** 29 Mar 1875 in Polk County, Ia.[Abst #76811, entry #25, p 17 of abstract]. He was born 27 Mar 1849 in Allegheney Co., Pa., the son of Abel FINDLEY, JR. and Mary Jane KERR, and brother of Abigail Findley who married Reuben Rittgers.(#16.2) He was about three when the family made their journey west, rafting down the Ohio River. In 1880 Ulcestes, 31, is farming in Walnut Twp., Dallas Co., Ia. Wife RoseAnn, 23, is caring for their children. [p 38 fam #311/313] By 1900 Ulcestes, 51, and Roseanne, 44, own their own farm in Walnut Twp., Dallas Co., Ia. They have been married 25 years and she has born 6 children, five alive at this time. These five are with them, as well as servant, Ella Wendell, "cook."[ED 19, p 8B, fam #158/161] On the 1910 census they continue in Walnut Twp. He is 61 and a farmer. Rosan is 54 and declares they have been married 34 years and she has born six children, five are still alive. With them are Wendal, age 24; and Fern C., age 17.[ED 20, p 7a, fam #139/143] In 1920 they are still in Walnut Twp. Ulcestes is 70 and Rosa A. is 63. Fern, now 26, is still in the home.[ED 21, P 8A, fam #184/186] Ulcestes died 3 Jan 1924 in Grimes, Polk Co., Ia. Rosannah died 21 May 1929 and had an extensive obituary written about her. It outlines her religious convictions and the moral character of her children. A copy of her "Memorial Record" is in the possession of Jon Findley, and is a roster of the Rittgers and Findley families of that time. They are buried in Sunny Hill Cem., Grimes, Polk Co., Ia. Wandah M. (Findley) Diehl (#16A3.3) shares with us some memories of her grand-parents.

She reports Ulcestes was often called "Uncle Bub." When about three, Wandah remembers him holding her on his lap in a big rocking chair. She doesn't remember if she was tired or sick, but shares how safe and loved she felt as she looked up into his beard. Wandah has that rocking chair now and loves it. "Aunt Fern" had a doll she would allow the girl cousins to play with only when seated on the window box in her room. Wandah also has that doll, as well as a large bowl her grandmother used on special occasions. She remembers playing in front of the fireplace, and "Grandma" giving the grandchildren big sugar cookies. Times were hard, growing up during the depression, but Wandah remembers the love and good times with the family; the bags of candy, nuts and fruit Santa would pass out at church on Christmas Eve, dinners at one or another of the many families. Ulcestes had several pear trees, and the children would pick the pears and wrap them in newspaper to ripen slowly. She sadly remembers when Rose was ill. They let her go into the room where she was and told her that Grandma had a sleeping sickness. Later, the children saw the men sliding the casket out of the bedroom window, as the house had too many turns and twists to get it out through the house.

ISSUE:

+ .16A.1   George Abel FINDLEY, born 24 Jan 1877, died 13 Feb 1961.

.16A.2   Rose May FINDLEY, born 12 May 1878 in Grimes, Polk Co., Ia., died 1881, and was buried in Rittgers Cem., Johnston, Ia.[RitCem] Seen on the 1880 census, age 2, with parents in Walnut Twp., Dallas Co., Ia.[38, fam #311/313]

+ .16A.3   Ray Ulcestes FINDLEY, born 13 May 1880, died 1956.

+ .16A.4   Charles Daniel FINDLEY, born 13 Jan 1883, died 1950.

+ .16A.5   Wendell Ivan FINDLEY, born 9 Oct 1885[DVRB, Bk 1, p.156] d. 1975.

.16A.6   Fern Christina FINDLEY, born 30 Jul 1892 in Dallas Co., Ia, died 31 Jul 1982, and was buried in Sunny Hill Cemetery, Grimes, Ia. She is seen on the 1900 census, age 7, with parents, Walnut Twp., Dallas Co., Ia.[ED 19, p. 8B, fam #158/161] and on the 1910 census, age 17, there with them.[ED 20, p 7A, fam #139/143] In 1920, at age 27, she is still with her parents.[ED 21, p 8A, fam #184/186] It is said that she stayed and cared for her parents until their death.

16.B Nancy Jane³ RITTGERS (Daniel², John¹) was born 6 Sep 1858 [Abst. #76811] in Jefferson Twp., Polk Co., Ia., the daughter of Daniel R. RITTGERS and Christina Magdalene SMITH. On 1860 census, age 1, with widowed mother and siblings in Jefferson Twp, Polk Co., Ia.[p fam #742/697], and in Valley Twp., Polk Co., Ia., on the 1870, age 11.[p 406, fam #96/106] She married **William PICKENBROCK** 15 Sep 1871 in Polk Co., Ia.[PVRM, Book 1, p. 220. She listed as "Jennie N."] He was born Sep 1856 in Ia. On the 1880 census we find William, 23 and Nancy, 21, in Valley, Polk Co., Ia. William's father was born in Germany and his mother was born in Poland. He was born in Ia. With them is Clarence, age 2. They are listed next to her father, Reuben, on the census record, so probably lived next door.[ED 3, p 545, fam #212/217] On the state census, 1895, we see William A., 38, a farmer and a Lutheran, living in Webster Twp., Polk Co, Ia. Wife Jennie, 36, declares she a Methodist. Three children in the home. In 1900 we see William and Nancy in Des Moines, Polk Co., Ia. where he is 43 and a stock dealer. Nancy, 41, declares they have been married 22 years and have 3 children, all alive at that time. Carrie and Victor are with them.[ED 68 p. 34, fam #255/264] William died 6 Dec 1905. Nancy died 28 Feb 1922. They are buried in McDivitt Cemetery, Sec. C, lot 24, row 3.[MPCem, p 9]

ISSUE:

+ .16B.1   Clarence PICKENBROCK, born about 1878, died 1959.
  .16B.2   Carrie PICKENBROCK, born Jan 1881 in Polk Co., Ia. She is on the 1900 census, age 19, with her parents in Des Moines, Polk Co., Ia., living at 839 19th St. [ED 68, p 14A, fam #255/264]
  .16B.3   Victor PICKENBROCK, born Nov 1883 in Polk Co., Ia., He is on the 1900 census, age 16, with his parents in Des Moines, Polk Co., Ia., living at 839 19th St. [ED 68, p 14A, fam #255/264] Victor died 25 Jan 1916 in Polk Co., Ia., and was buried in McDivitt Cem., Polk, Ia., in Sec. C, lot 24, row 6.[MPCem, p 9]
  .16B.4   Jennie PICKENBROCK. Family history gives us her name. She most probably born after 1900, as on this census, mother declares she has born 3 children and we have those three accounted for.

17.1 Noah³ STROHL (Elizabeth², John¹) was born about 1834 in Laurel Twp., Hocking Co., Oh., the son of John STROHL and Elizabeth RITTGERS. On 1850 census, age 16, with parents there.[p 28 fam #405/414] He married **Mary C. HOOPER** 18 Mar 1858 in Hocking Co., Oh.[HVRM, book B, p. 58] She was born about 1839 in Oh.. The 1860 census shows Noah, 26, a farmer in Laurel Twp., Hocking Co., Oh., with wife Mary, age 22, and daughter Eve, age 1.[p 72 fam # 986/974] On the 1870 census, he is in Jefferson Twp., Polk Co., Ia., with wife and family. Noah is now 39, a farmer with $460 in personal property. Mary is 31, and they have five children with them. The census tells us that the youngest child, the unnamed infant, age 4 months, was born in Iowa, but the three year old Noah was born in Ohio, so we see they moved between 1867 and 1869.[p 334 fam #31/31] Also in the home is William and wife Eve (Strohl) Hooper with their children. There is a James Hooper buried in the Rittgers Cemetery, Johnston, Ia., 6 June 1867, age 26 yrs, 9 mo, 12 days. This may be brother of Mary and William.

ISSUE:

  .171.1   Eve STROHL, born about 1859 in Hocking Co., Oh. She is on the 1860 census, age 1, with parents, Laurel Twp., Hocking Co., Oh. [p 72, fam #986/974] and on the 1870 census, age 11, with parents, Jefferson Twp., Polk Co., Ia.[p 334, fam #31/31]
  .171.2   William T. STROHL, born about 1861 in Hocking Co., Oh. He is on the 1870 census, age 9, with parents Jefferson Twp, Polk Co., Ia.[p 334, fam #31/31]

.171.3   John M. STROHL, born about 1863 in Hocking Co., Oh. He is on the 1870 census, age 7, with parents Jefferson Twp, Polk Co., Ia.[p 334, fam #31/31]

.171.4   Noah STROHL, born about 1867 in Hocking Co., Oh. He is on the 1870 census, age 3, with parents Jefferson Twp, Polk Co., Ia. [p 334, fam #31/31]

.171.5   Unnamed infant, b. abt. Feb., 1870, Polk Co., Ia. On the 1870 census, age 4 mo. with parents there.[p 334, fam #31/31]

17.3 Caroline H.[3] **STROHL** (Elizabeth[2], John[1]) was born about 1836 in Laurel Twp., Hocking Co., Oh., the daughter of John STROHL and Elizabeth RITTGERS. On the 1850 census, age 14, with parents there.[p. 28 fam #405/414] She married **David UNKLE** 16 Mar 1856 in Hocking Co., Oh.[HVRM, Book "B", p. 239] He was born about 1837 in Oh. The 1860 census shows David "Uncle", 23, farmer with no dollar value on property or personal estate, Marion Twp., Hocking Co., Oh. Wife Caroline H., 21, is caring for their 2 children. Also listed is Barbara "Uncle", widow, age 59, and born in Germany.[p 72 fam #995/983] On the 1870 census, they are in Laurel Twp.. David is 34, a farmer with $1400 in real estate and 800 in personal property. Caroline is 33 and cares for the children, Elizabeth through Daniel. We find also, Barbarey Unkle, 69, "on farm", b. Wutenburg. [p. 490, fam 232/232] The 1880 census for Laurel Twp. gives us David, 44, farmer, born in Ohio, but parents born in Wutenberg. Wife Caroline, 42, has her hands full with the children, Elizabeth through Cara. Barbara Unkle is not listed with the family. [p 95B fam #233/244]

ISSUE:

.173.1   William UNCLE, born about 1857 in Marion Twp., Hocking Co., Oh.. He is on the 1860 census, age 3, with parents in Laurel Twp., Bloomingville P.O., Hocking Co., Oh. [p 72 fam #995/983] May have died as he is not with parents in 1870.

.173.2   Elizabeth A. UNKLE, born about 1859 in Marion Twp., Hocking Co., Oh.. She is on the 1860 census, age 1, with parents in Laurel Twp., Bloomingville P.O., Hocking Co., Oh.[p 72, fam #995/983], on the 1870 census, age 11, there with parents,[p 490, fam #232/232] and on the 1880 census, age 21, with her parents there.[p 95B, fam #233/244]

+ .173.3   Solomon F. UNKLE, born Oct 1861.

+ .173.4   John J. UNKLE, born Sep 1862.

.173.5   Barbary Ellen UNKLE, born about 1864 in Hocking Co., Oh. The 1870 census shows Barbary E., age 6, with parents in Laurel Twp., Hocking Co., Oh.[p 490, fam #232/232] On the 1880 census, called Ellen, age 16, with parents there, occupation listed as "school".[p 95B fam #233/244]

.173.6   Mary J. UNKLE, born about 1865 in Hocking Co., Oh. The 1870 census shows Mary J., age 5, with parents in Laurel Twp., Hocking Co., Oh.[p 490, fam #232/232] She is on the 1880 census, 15, with parents there, occupation listed as "school".[p 95B fam #233/244] She married Lewis M. PHILLIPS 29 Dec 1883 in Hocking Co., Oh.[HVRM, Bk E., p.220]

+ .173.7   Daniel UNKLE, born about 1869.

.173.8   Emma UNKLE, born about 1870 in Hocking Co., Oh. On the 1880 census, age 10, with parents, Laurel Twp., Hocking Co., Oh.[p 95B, fam #233/244]

.173.9   Essa A. UNKLE, born about 1873 in Hocking Co., Oh. On the 1880 census, age 8, with parents, Laurel Twp., Hocking Co., Oh.[p 95B, fam #233/244] She married Andrew PRION, 16 June 1889.[HVRM, Bk F., p.1]

.173.A   Cora UNKLE, born about 1877 in Hocking Co., Oh. On the 1880 census, age 3, with parents, Laurel Twp., Hocking Co., Oh.[p 95B, fam #233/244]

17.4 Mary³ STROHL (Elizabeth², John¹) was born about 1837 in Laurel, Hocking Co., Oh., the daughter of John STROHL and Elizabeth RITTGERS. On the 1850 census, age 13, with parents, Hocking Co., Oh.[p 28 fam #405/414] She married **George W. HIGHLY** 5 Oct 1854 in Hocking Co., Oh. [HVRM, book B, p. 212] He was born about 1834 in Oh. On the 1860 census, we find George, age 26, a farmer, born in Ohio, with wife Mary, 23. They are in Falls Twp., Hocking Co., Oh.[p 14 fam #383/382]

ISSUE:

.174.1   Martha HIGHLY, born 1857 in Hocking Co., Oh. On 1860 census, age 3, with parents, Falls Twp., Hocking Co., Oh.[p 14, fam #383/382]
.174.2   John HIGHLY, born 1859 in Hocking, Oh.. On 1860 census, age 1, with parents, Falls Twp., Hocking Co., Oh.[p 14, fam #383/382]

17.5 Eve³ STROHL (Elizabeth², John¹) was born about 1839 in Laurel Twp., Hocking Co., Oh., the daughter of John STROHL and Elizabeth RITTGERS. On the 1850 census, age 11, with parents, Hocking Co., Oh.[p 28 fam #405/414] She married **William T. HOOPER** 16 Mar 1859 in Hocking Co., Oh.[HVRM, Book "C", p. 299] He was born about 1833 in Oh. On the 1860 census, we find William, 27,a farmer in Laurel Twp., Hocking Co., Oh. Wife Eve, 20, is caring for their daughter, Caroline.[p 72 fam #984/972] In 1870 we find William T., 36, farmer with $1400 in Real Estate and $500 in personal property in Jefferson, Polk Co., Ia. They are in the home of Eve's brother Noah and his wife, Mary (Hooper), and very near the other Rittgers relatives.[p 334 fam #31/32] Also in the home is Crystal Hooper, 21. Eve's youngest child, Sarah, age 2, was born in Iowa and the next oldest, Mary age 5, born in Ohio. Thus, they moved to Iowa between 1865 & 1868. In 1880 they are on their own farm in Grant Twp., Dallas Co., Ia. William, 46, is a farmer, wife Eve, age 40, is caring for the four children in the home.[ED 49, p 219, fam #82/84]

ISSUE:

.175.1   Caroline HOOPER, born about Jul 1859 in Laurel Twp., Hocking Co., Ohio. She on 1860 census, age 11/12, with parents there.[p 72 fam #984/972] In the 1870 census, she is not with her parents in Jefferson, Polk Co., Ia.[p 334 fam #31/32]
.175.2   Malinda HOOPER, born about 1860 in Hocking Co., Oh. On the 1870 census, age 10, with her parents in Jefferson Twp., Polk Co., Ia.[p 334 fam #31/32]
.175.3   Catherine Elizabeth HOOPER, born about 1862 in Hocking Co., Oh. On the 1870 census, age 8, with her parents in Jefferson Twp., Polk Co., Ia.[p 334 fam #31/32] On 1880 census, called Elizabeth, age 18, with parents in Grant Twp., Dallas Co., Ia.[ED 49, p 219, fam #82/84]
.175.4   Mary A. HOOPER, born about 1865 in Hocking Co., Oh. On the 1870 census, age 5, with her parents in Jefferson Twp., Polk Co., Ia.[p 334 fam #31/32] On 1880 census, age 15, with parents in Grant Twp., Dallas Co., Ia.[ED 49, p 219, fam #82/84] Married 1 Apr 1884, Benjamin Moreland, Dallas Co., Ia.[DVRM, Bk 1]
.175.5   Sarah E. HOOPER, born about 1868 in Polk Co., Ia. On the 1870 census, age 2, with her parents in Jefferson Twp., Polk Co., Ia.[p 334 fam #31/32] On 1880 census, age 13, with parents in Grant Twp., Dallas Co., Ia.[ED 49, p 219, fam #82/84]

.175.6   Jennie E. HOOPER, born 2 Mar 1876, Van Meter Twp., Dallas Co., Ia. She is on
          the 1880 census, age 4, with parents in Grant Twp., Dallas Co., Ia.[ED 49, p 219,
          fam #82/84] Jennie died 4 Jan 1881, Van Meter Twp., age 3 yrs., 10 mo., 2 days.
          [DVRD, Bk 1, p.7]

17.9 Jacob³ STROHL (Elizabeth², John¹) was born about 1848 in Laurel, Hocking Co., Oh.,
the son of John STROHL and Elizabeth RITTGERS. With his parents on 1850 census, Laurel
Twp., Hocking Co., Oh, age "5".[p 28 fam #405/414] On 1860 census, we are told he is 12.[p
156 fam #983/971] He married **Mary A. KNEICKBAUM** (possibly Krickbaum) 30 May 1867
in Hocking Co., Oh.[HVRM, Book "C", p. 393] She was born about 1849 in Oh. 1870 census
tells us Jacob is a farmer in Valley Twp., Polk Co., Ia. He and his wife, Mary, are both 21. They
have with them Ellen, age 3, born in Ohio; and Elmer, 1, born in Iowa.[p 406 fam #95/105] He
also has in his home John Krickbaum, 39. We later find one George Krickbaum, b. 1873,
married to a descendant of John Rittgers #1.3.
                                        ISSUE:
.179.1   Ellen STROHL, born about 1867 in Hocking Co., Oh. On 1870 census with parents,
          Valley Twp., Polk Co., Ia.[p 406, fam #95/105]
.179.2   Elmer STROHL, born about 1869 in Ia. On 1870 census, age 1, with parents, Valley
          Twp., Polk Co., Ia.[p 406, fam #95/105]

19.2 Rosana³ DAUBENMIRE (Susanna²˒ John ¹) was born 16 Oct 1836 [Berens-St.James] in
Marion Twp., Hocking Co., Oh., the daughter of Peter DAUBENMIRE and Susanna
RITTGERS. On 1850 census, age 14, with parents there.[p 853 fam #191/196] She married
August MEILY 3 Dec 1863 in Hocking Co., Oh. His name spelled "Maile" in St. James
Records. [HVRM, Book "C", p. 170]
                                        ISSUE:
.192.1   Wilhelm Fredrich MEILY, born 22 Jan 1867 in Marion Twp., Hocking Co., Oh.

19.3 Susana³ DAUBENMIRE (Susanna²˒ John ¹) was born 20 Sep 1837 [Berens-St.James] in
Marion Twp., Hocking Co., Oh., the daughter of Peter DAUBENMIRE and Susanna
RITTGERS. On 1850 census, age 12, with parents there.[p 853 fam #191/196] She married
Philip KULL 7 Mar 1867 in Hocking Co., Oh.. He was born 20 Sep 1845 in Marion Twp.,
Hocking Co., Oh., the son of Gottfried and Margaretha (Duerr) Kull (Cull)[HVRM, Book "C",
p. 376.] Philip died 7 Mar 1877 in Carroll Twp., Fairfield Co., Oh, and was buried in Forest Rose
Cem., Lancaster, Oh.[Berens]
                                        ISSUE:
.193.1   Wilhelm Thomas KULL, born 3 Aug 1870 in Marion Twp., Hocking Co., Oh.
.193.2   Emma Barbara KULL, born 3 Aug 1872 in Marion Twp., Hocking Co., Oh.

19.4 Elizabeth³ DAUBENMIRE (Susanna², John¹) was born Mar 1840 in Hocking Co., Oh.,
the daughter of Peter DAUBENMIRE and Susanna RITTGERS. On the 1850 census, age 10,
with parents, Marion Twp., Hocking Co., Oh.[p 853 fam #191/196] She married **Daniel RUFF**
11 Feb 1858 in Hocking Co., Oh.[EmEv, p. 30] He was born Aug 1836 in Oh., the son of
Johann and Elizabeth (__) Ruff. The 1860 census, Marion Twp., shows Daniel Ruff, age 24,
as a farm hand with no real estate, but they have $300 in personal estate. Wife Elizabeth, 21;
and child John, age 1, are with him. Also in home is a Solomon Ready, age 8.[p 152 fam
#958/946] In 1870, Daniel 30 and a farmer with $1600 in real estate and $300 in personal

property continues in Marion Twp., with a Haydonville Post Office. Wife Elizabeth is 31 and caring for their children.[p 506 fam #216/219] The 1880 census show us they are still in Marion Twp. Daniel, age 44, b. Oh., but father born Wutenburg, Ger., and mother b. Pa. He is farming. Elizabeth, 42, is caring for their six children.[ED 63,p 101D, fam #106/107] In 1900 in Marion Twp. we see Daniel, b. Aug 1836, is 63. Elizabeth, b. Mar 1840, is now 60. They have been married 41 years and she has born 8 children, 6 alive at this time.[ED 32, p 115B, fam #163/163] In 1910 we see them continue to live there by themselves. Daniel, 74, is still listed as a farmer in Marion Twp. Elizabeth, 71, declares they have been married 52 years.[ED 88, p. 7A, fam #125/128] On 1920 census, age 84, Daniel is retired. He and wife Elizabeth, 80, are in the home with son Jacob, Marion Twp., Hocking Co., Oh.[ED 45, p 10A, fam #182/182] According th their tombstones, located in the Ruff Cemetery, Marion Twp., Hocking Co., Oh., they both died in 1922.[HCoCem]

ISSUE:

+ .194.1   John RUFF, born Dec 1859.
.194.2   Emanuel RUFF, born Aug 1862 in Marion Twp., Hocking Co., Oh. The 1870 census shows Emanuel, 10, with parents there[p506, fam #216/219] and continues there on the 1880 census, age 19, with parents. Listed as "laborer".[ED 63, p 101D, fam #106/107] He married Ella____ 1896 in Fairfield Co., Oh. She was born Sep 1870 in Oh.. She declares her parents born in Ohio, also. In 1900 we see Emanuel, age 37, farming in Greenfield Twp., Fairfield Co., Oh. With him is wife Ella, age 29, who declares they have been married four years and she has born no children. With them is Harmon Webb, "man servant, day laborer"[ED 8, p 2A, fam #30/30]
+ .194.3   William RUFF, born Jun 1863.
+ .194.4   Frederic RUFF, born Jun 1864.
.194.5   Margaret RUFF, born about 1866 in Marion Twp., Hocking Co., Oh. The 1870 census shows "Mary A.", age 4, with parents there.[p506, fam #216/219] and continues there on the 1880 census, age 14, with parents.[ED 63, p 101D, fam #106/107]
.194.6   Caroline RUFF, born 4 Sept 1869 in Marion Twp., Hocking Co., Oh.[HVRB, Bk 1, p.42] The 1870 census shows Caroline, age 1, with parents in Marion Twp., Hocking Co., Oh. [p506, fam #216/219] Not on the 1880 census, so probably died young.[ED 63, p 101D, fam #106/107]
+ .194.7   Jacob RUFF, born Jun 1873.

19.8 Peter B.[3] DAUBENMIRE (Susanna[2,] John [1]) was born 18 Dec 1846 [Berens-St.James] in Marion Twp., Hocking Co., Oh., son of Peter DAUBENMIRE and Susanna RITTGERS. On the 1850 census, age 3, with parents there.[p 853 fam # 191/196] On the 1860 census, age 14, with parents there.[p 157 1027/1015] He married **Anna Mary ELLINGER** 23 Jun 1868 in Hocking Co., Oh. [HVRM, book C, p 466.] She was born 17 Oct 1846 in Hocking Co., Oh., the daughter of Jacob F., and Helene (__) Ellinger. She is named in father's estate, 1871. On the 1900 census, Marion Twp., Hocking Co., Oh., we find Peter, 52, a farmer. Wife Mary, 53, is caring for niece Minnie, 13, b. Dec 1886. Since no name given, probably Minnie Daubenmire. Mary declares they have been married 32 years and she has born no children.[ED 32, p 115B, fam #165/165] In 1910 Peter, 63, is still farming in Marion Twp. Wife Mary, 63, declares they have been married 41 years and she has born no children.(Was Jacob adopted, or did the transcriber make a mistake?)[ED 88, p 7B/8A, fam #138/137] Anna died 9 Jul 1919, and Peter died 30 Jan 1934. They are buried in Sponagle Cemetery, Berne Twp., Fairfield Co., Oh.

ISSUE:

.198.1   Jacob W. DAUBENMIRE, born 15 Feb 1873 [Berens-St.James] in Marion Twp.,
          Hocking Co., Oh., died 19 Jan 1920, and was buried in Sponagle Cemetery, Berne
          Twp., Fairfield Co., Oh.[Berens-St. Trinity]

19.9 Christina³ DAUBENMIRE (Susanna²˙ John ¹) was born 6 May 1849 [Berens-St.James]
in Marion Twp., Hocking Co., Oh., the daughter of Peter DAUBENMIRE and Susanna
RITTGERS. On the 1850 census, age 1, with parents there.[p 853 fam #191/196] On the 1860
census she continues there, age 10.[p 157 fam #1027/1015] She married (1) **Johann Friedrich
KULL** 27 Feb 1868 in Hocking Co., Oh.[HVRM, book C, p 443] He was born 1 Oct 1835 in
Neusatz, Wuerttemburg, Ger., the son of Gottfried and Margaretha (Duerr) Kull. Johann died
5 Jan 1874 in Berne Twp., Fairfield Co., Oh. Christina married (2) **Jacob F. ELLINGER**
22 Feb 1876 [Berens-St.Trinity] in Berne Twp., Fairfield Co., Oh. He was born 7 Feb 1845 in
Oh., the son of Jacob F. and Helene (Ulmar) Ellinger. Christina died 8 Apr 1912, and was buried
in Sponagle Cem., Berne Twp., Fairfield Co., Oh.[Berens-St.Trinity] Jacob died 1 May 1917,
and was buried in Sponagle Cem., Berne Twp., Fairfield Co., Oh.
                              ISSUE of Johann and Christina:
.199.1   Gottfried KULL, born 19 Nov 1868 in Berne Twp., Fairfield Co., Oh, died 1 Dec
          1873 in Berne Twp., Fairfield Co., Oh.. [Berens]
.199.2   Ara Semi Susanna KULL, born 4 Apr 1870 in Marion Twp., Hocking Co., Oh.
          [Berens]
.199.3   Daniel KULL, born 9 Sep 1871 in Marion Twp., Hocking Co., Oh. [Berens]
.199.4   Johann KULL, born 9 Jan 1873 in Marion Twp., Hocking Co., Oh. [Berens]

19.A Maria Magdalene³ DAUBENMIRE (Susanna², John¹) was born about 1852 in Marion
Twp., Hocking, Oh., the daughter of Peter DAUBENMIRE and Susanna RITTGERS. She is
on 1860 census, age 8, with parents there.[p 157 fam #1027/1015] The 1870 census gives her
as 20 and still with parents.[p 506 fam #212/215] She married **William ELLINGER** 20 Apr
1876 in Hocking Co., Ohio. [HVRM, Book D, p. 76.] He was born about 1852 in Oh., the son
of Jacob and Helene (Ulmar) Ellinger. He is named in his mother's estate, 1901. On the 1880
census William, 28, a Laborer on Farm, with wife Magdalene, 29, and daughter, Elizabeth, 2,
in Falls Twp., Hocking Co., Oh.[p 1A fam 2/2]
                                       ISSUE:
.19A.1   Elizabeth ELLINGER, born Sep 1878 in Falls Twp., Hocking, Oh. She is on the
          1880 census, age 2, with parents in Falls Twp., Hocking Co., Oh.[p 18A, fam #2/2]
          On 1900 census, age 21, b. Sept 1878, servant in the home of Charles Jurgensmeier,
          Falls Twp., Hocking Co., Oh.[ED 26, p 10A, fam #202/208]

19.B Sarah Elizabeth³ DAUBENMIRE (Susanna², John¹) was born 5 Mar 1853 in Marion
Twp., Hocking Co., Oh., the daughter of Peter DAUBENMIRE and Susanna RITTGERS. She
is on the 1860 census, age 7, with parents there.[p 157 fam #1027/1015] and on the 1870 census,
age 17 with parents.[p 506 fam #212/215] She married **John Philip ELLINGER** 9 Feb 1871
in Hocking Co., Oh.[HVRM, book C, p. 627] He was born 24 Feb 1849 in Fairfield Co., Oh.
On a family group sheet submitted to the Fairfield Co, Oh., Historical Soc., we find John Ellinger
son of Jacob Frederick and Heleniah (Ulmar) Ellinger. We see this family on the 1850 census,
Marion Twp., Hocking Co., Oh. Father Jacob is 45, and a farmer from Germany. Hellenah, 25,
is caring for their children. John is age 1.[fam #211/217] On 1860 census, John, 11, is with his

parents in Marion Twp.[p 855 fam #428/428] In 1880 John, 31, a farmer and wife Sarah D., 27, are in Walnut Twp., Fairfield Co., Oh. With them are first four children.[p 259B fam #255/270] On 1900 census there, John P., 51, continues farming. Wife Sarah, 47, declares they have been married 29 years and she has born 11 children, 9 alive at this time. Six in the home.[ED 24, p 351A, fam #117/121] In 1910, John is 61 and still farming in Walnut Twp.. Sarah, 57, has in the home "daughter, Tina, 24." She may be widow of one of the sons, as Sarah says here she lost another child since 1900. Son Elmer, 17, is also in the home.[ED 80, p 1A, fam #4/4]John died 13 Apr 1919 in Fairfield Co., Oh. Sarah died 15 Jun 1937 in Fairfield Co., Oh.

ISSUE:

.19B.1   Daniel E. ELLINGER, born about 1872 in Fairfield Co., Oh. He is on the 1880 census, age 8, with parents in Walnut Twp., Fairfield Co., Oh.[P 259B, fam #255/270]

.19B.2   Sarah ELLINGER, born about 1875 in Fairfield Co., Oh. She is on the 1880 census, age 5, with parents in Walnut Twp., Fairfield Co., Oh.[P 259B, fam #255/270]

+ .19B.3   Charles ELLINGER, born Sep 1877.

.19B.4   Clara ELLINGER, born Jul 1879 in Fairfield Co., Oh. On 1880 census, age 11/12, with parents in Walnut Twp., Fairfield Co., Oh. [p 259B, fam #255/270] Not on the 1900 census with family, and since mother states has lost 2 children, possibly she died young.

.19B.5   Emma ELLINGER, born Feb 1881 in Oh. On 1900 census, age 19, with parents in Walnut Twp., Fairfield Co., Oh.[ED 24, p 35A, fam #117/121]

.19B.6   John Henry ELLINGER, born Sep 1882 in Fairfield Co., Oh. On 1900 census, age 17, with parents in Walnut Twp., Fairfield Co., Oh.[ED 24, p 351A, fam #117/121]

+ .19B.7   Bertha ELLINGER, born 23 Sep 1887, died 30 Mar 1975.

.19B.8   Andrew ELLINGER, born Jul 1890 in Fairfield Co., Oh. On 1900 census, age 9, with parents in Walnut Twp., Fairfield Co., Oh.[ED 24, p 351A, fam #117/121]

.19B.9   Elmer ELLINGER, born Aug 1892 in Fairfield Co., Oh. On 1900 census, age 7, with parents in Walnut Twp., Fairfield Co., Oh.[ED 24, p 351A, fam #117/121] Continues with parents, age 17, in 1910.[ED 80, p 1A, fam #4/4]

19.C Caroline[3] DAUBENMIRE (Susanna[2], John[1]) was born Jan 1856 in Marion Twp., Hocking Co., Oh., the daughter of Peter DAUBENMIRE and Susanna RITTGERS. She is on 1860 census, age 4, with parents there.[p 157 fam #1057/1015] The 1870 census gives us Caroline, age 11!, with her parents there.[p 506 fam #212/215] Caroline "Disbonnet" married **Jacob ELLINGER** 17 Oct 1872 in Hocking Co., Oh.[HVRM, Bk D, p.76] He was born about 1845 in Oh. We see Jacob, brother of John, who married Sarah Daubenmire (#19.9) in this family on the 1850 census, Marion Twp., Hocking Co., Oh. Their father Jacob is 45, and a farmer from Germany. Hellenah, 25, is caring for their children. Jacob is age 5. [fam #211/217] On 1860 census, Jacob, 15, is with his parents in Marion Twp.[p 855 fam #428/428] On the 1880 census we find them in Falls Twp., Hocking Co., Oh. Jacob, 30, is a farmer, born in Oh. of German parents. Wife Caroline, 25, cares for the children.[p 22B fam #88/89] 1900 census shows them in Marion Twp., Hocking Co., Oh., Jacob's date of birth and age have been printed over, making the figures unreadable, but birth month given as July. It almost looks like 1845 and age 55, but this not clear. Caroline states she born Jan 1856, is now 44, they have been married 27 years and she has born 15 children, 13 alive at this time! The children at home on this census plus those listed on the 1880 census total 13 children.[ED 32, p 13A & B, fam #114/114] In 1910, Jacob

65, still lists himself as a farmer. Caroline, 56, states they have been married 35 years and she has born 15 children, 12 alive at this time.[ED 88, p. 9B, fam #182/183]

ISSUE:

.19C.1   George ELLINGER, born May 1875 in Falls Twp., Hocking Co., Oh. He is on 1880 census, age 6, with parents there.[p 22B, fam #88/89] On 1900 census, age 25, a roomer with M. Banholzer, Springfield, Clark Co., Oh. Occupation listed as "brewer".[ED 15, p 12B, fam #226/168]

.19C.2   Sarah ELLINGER, born about 1875 in Falls Twp., Hocking Co., Oh. On 1880 census, she is age 5, with parents there.[p 22B, fam #88/89]

.19C.3   Jacob ELLINGER, born Sep 1876 in Falls Twp., Hocking Co., Oh. He is on 1880 census, age 4, with parents there.[p 22B, fam #88/89] On 1900 census, age 23, a roomer with M. Banholzer, Springfield, Clark Co., Oh. Occupation listed as "brewer".[ED 15, p 12B, fam #226/168]

.19C.4   John ELLINGER, born Jan 1878 in Falls Twp., Hocking, Oh. He is on 1880 census, age 3, with parents there.[p 22B, fam #88/89] On 1900 census, age 22, a roomer with M. Banholzer, Springfield, Clark Co., Oh. Occupation listed as "laborer, shop".[ED 15, p 12B, fam #226/168]

.19C.5   Caroline ELLINGER, born about 1878 in Falls Twp., Hocking Co., Oh. On 1880 census, she is age 2, with parents there.[p 22B, fam #88/89]

.19C.6   Mary B. ELLINGER, born Oct 1879 in Falls Twp, Hocking Co., Oh. On 1880 census, she is age 7 months, with parents there.[p 22B, fam #88/89]

+ .19C.7   Frank ELLINGER, born Aug 1882.

+ .19C.8   Frederic ELLINGER, born Mar 1884.

.19C.9   Michael ELLINGER, born Aug 1886 in Marion Twp., Hocking Co., Oh. He is age 13, with parents on 1900 census [ED 32, p 113A, fam #114/114] and with them in 1910, age 23, farm laborer-working out.[ED 88, p 9B, fam #182/183]

.19C.A   Minnie ELLINGER, born Sep 1887 in Marion Twp, Hocking Co., Oh. She is age 12, with parents on 1900 census there. [ED 32, p 113A, fam #114/114]

.19C.B   Solomon ELLINGER, born Oct 1890 in Marion Twp., Hocking Co., Oh. He is age 9, with parents on 1900 census there.[ED 32, p 113A, fam #114/114] and with them in 1910, age 20, farm laborer-home farm.[ED 88, p 9B, fam #182/183] On 1920 census, age 28, in the home of brother Fredrick, called "Samuel". He is single and a grocer.[ED 41, p 5B, fam #101/104]

.19C.C   Christine E. ELLINGER, born Oct 1892 in Marion, Hocking, Oh. She is age 7, with parents on 1900 census there. [ED 32, p 113A, fam #114/114] and age 17, with parents there in 1910.[ED 88, p 9B, fam #182/183]

.19C.D   Teresa ELLINGER, born Mar 1897 in Marion Twp., Hocking Co., Oh. She is age 3, with parents on 1900 census there [ED 32, p 113A, fam #114/114] and age 12, with parents there in 1910.[ED 88, p 9B, fam #182/183]

19.D Jacob A.[3] DAUBENMIRE (Susanna[2], John[1]) was born Aug 1859 in Marion Twp, Hocking Co., Oh., the son of Peter DAUBENMIRE and Susanna RITTGERS. He is on the 1860 census, age 2, with parents there.[p 157 fam #1027/1015] and on the 1870 census, age 12, with parents there.[p 156 fam #212/215] He married **Sophia ELLINGER** 25 Jan 1883 in Hocking Co., Oh.[HVRM, Book E., p.166] She was the daughter of Jacob and Helene (Ulmar) Ellinger. In 1900, Jacob, 40, a farmer, and wife Sophia, 38, b. Mar 1862, in Ohio, live in Marion Twp., Hocking Co., Oh. She declares they have been married 18 years; she has born six children, all alive at this time.[ED 32, p 117A, fam #210/210] On 1910 census, Marion Twp., age 51 and a farmer. He owns his farm free and clear. With him is wife Sophia, age 47, b. Oh., but parents born in Germany. She declares they have been married 28 years, she has born 8 children, all alive. There are five with them on this census.[ED 88, p 7A, fam # 120/121] In 1920 Jacob, 61, owns his own farm on Schwartz Mill and Sugar Grove Rd., Marion Twp. Wife Sophia, 57, is caring for the three children still in the home.[ED 45, p. 10A, fam # 185/186] On the 1920 census, they continue in Marion Twp., Jacob, now 61, still farms. Sophia, 57, declares that she can read and write, but that Jacob cannot. They still have 3 children in the home.[ED45, p.910A, fam#185/186] Sophia died 26 Jan 1929, and Jacob died 25 Jan 1938. They are buried in Sponagle Cemetery, Bern Twp., Fairfield Co., Oh.[Berens]

ISSUE:

.19D.1   Sophia Maria DAUBENMIRE, born 20 Oct 1883 [Berens] in Marion Twp., Hocking Co., Oh. On 1900 census, Mary, age 16, with parents there.[ED 32, p 117A, fam #210/210]

.19D.2   Wilhelm Emanuel DAUBENMIRE, born 23 May 1885 [Berens] in Marion Twp., Hocking Co., Oh. On 1900 census, William, age 15, with parents there.[ED 32, p 117A, fam #210/210]

.19D.3   Miene Katharine DAUBENMIRE, born 12 Dec 1886 [Berens] in Marion Twp., Hocking Co., Oh. On 1900 census, Minnie, age 13, with parents there.[ED 32, p 117A, fam #210/210]

.19D.4   Cora Helena DAUBENMIRE, born 9 Feb 1892 [Berens] in Marion Twp., Hocking Co., Oh. On 1900 census, Cora, age 9, with parents there.[ED 32, p 117A, fam #210/210] and there with parents, age 18, on the 1910 census.[ED 88, p 7A, fam #120/121]

.19D.5   Anna S. DAUBENMIRE, born Apr 1897 in Marion Twp., Hocking Co., Oh. On 1900 census, age 3, with parents Marion Twp., Hocking Co., Oh.[ED 32, p 117A, fam #210/210] and there with parents, age 12, on the 1910 census.[ED 88, p 7A, fam #120/121] She and Loda are twins. On 1920 census, age 21, still in home with parents in Marion Twp. Twin Loda not in home.[ED 45, p. 10A, fam #185/186]

.19D.6   Loda M. DAUBENMIRE, born Apr 1897 in Marion Twp., Hocking, Oh. On 1900 census, age 3, with parents there,[ED 32, p 117A, fam #210/210] and there with parents, age 12, on the 1910 census.[ED 88, p 7A, fam #120/121] She and Anna are twins.

.19D.7   Levi A. DAUBENMIRE, born about 1903 in Marion, Hocking, Oh. On 1910 census, age 7, with parents there.[ED 88, p 7A, fam #120/121] On 1920 census, age 17, continues there in parent's home. [ED 45, p. 10A, fam #186/186]

.19D.8   Homer E. DAUBENMIRE, born about 1907 in Marion, Hocking, Oh. On 1910 census, age 3, with parents there,[ED 88, p 7A, fam #120/121] and there on 1920 census, age 13. [ED 45, p. 10A, fam #186/186]

19.E George³ DAUBENMIRE (Susanna², John¹) was born May 1864 in Marion Twp., Hocking Co., Ohio., the son of Peter DAUBENMIRE and Susanna RITTGERS. He is on the 1870 census, age 7, with parents there,[p 156 fam #212/215] and on the 1880 census, age 17, with them there.[ED 63, p 195B, fam #129/131] He married **Sophia SENIG** 27 May 1888 in Hocking Co., Oh.[HVRM, Book E, p. 504] She was born Jan 1871 in Oh. In 1900 we see George, 36, a farm laborer. Wife Sophia, age 29, and three children, are with him in Berne Twp., Fairfield Co., Oh. Sophia declares she has born 3 children, all alive at this time.[ED 3, p 25B, fam #116/131]Sophia died 1942, and George died 1959. They are buried in Stukey Cemetery, Berne Twp., Fairfield Co., Oh.[Berens]

ISSUE:

.19E.1   Dora Carolina DAUBENMIRE, born 21 Jul 1889 in Marion Twp., Hocking Co., Oh. On 1900 census, age 10, with parents in Berne Twp., Fairfield Co., Oh.[ED 3, p 25B, fam #116/131]

.19E.2   Johann Eduard DAUBENMIRE, born 28 Jan 1891 in Marion Twp., Hocking Co., Oh. On 1900 census, John, age 9, with parents in Berne Twp., Fairfield Co., Oh.]ED 3, p 25B, fam #116/131]

.19E.3   Renetta DAUBENMIRE, born Aug 1895 in Oh. On 1900 census, age 4, with parents in Berne Twp., Fairfield Co., Oh.[ED 3, p 25B, fam #116/131]

CHAPTER 4

GENERATION NO. 4

112.1 Daniel[4] RITTGERS (Abraham[3], Joseph[2], John[1]) was born 14 Jun 1853 in Marion Twp., Hocking Co., Oh., the son of Abraham RITTGERS and Catherine LEFLER. He is on the 1860 census, age 7, with parents there [p 158 fam #1037/1025], and on the 1870 census, age 16, with parents in Brown Twp., Darke Co., Oh.[p 3 fam #41/40] He married **Mary Ann WAGNER** 28 Oct 1877 in Darke Co., Oh. She was born 15 Apr 1858 in Darke Co., Oh. Family group sheet tells us she was daughter of John and Mary (__) Wagner. By 1880, we see Daniel, age 26, now married to Mary, age 22, and farming in Brown Twp, Darke Co., Oh. They have with them daughter, Jennie, age 1.[ED 56, p 46D, fam #70/75] The 1900 census shows this family still in Brown Twp. Daniel is now 46, married 23 yrs., still farming on his own farm. Wife Mary L., 42, reports she has born six children. The six children, as listed below, appear on the census. Also, grand-daughter, Beatrice J. Porter, age 1, is listed. Beside oldest daughter, Virginia's, name is the indication she is married, but last name not specified on record.[ED 50, p 57B, fam #193/196] In 1910, Daniel, now 56, is still farming. Mary, 51, declares they have been married 32 years and she has born 7 children, 6 alive at this time. [ED 76, p 1A, fam #13/13] The 1920 census shows Daniel, 66, and wife Mary A., 61, in Brown Twp., where he continues to farm on the Jackson Twp.-Brown Twp. Rd. Son Ira, a widower, 39, is in the home with his son Everett A. [ED 93, p. 1B, fam #24/24] Mary died 17 Jan 1922 in Greenville, Darke Co., Oh., and was buried 20 Jan 1922 in Teegarden Cemetery, Darke Co., Oh. Her death record tells us she died "1 mile west of Greenville." [FOFH, p. 91] Daniel died 15 May 1928 in Darke County, Oh., and was buried 18 May 1928 in Teegarden Cemetery. Daniel's death record reports he died "1 mile south of Elroy, Oh." It further states he was born in Fairfield Co., Oh. Even though we see his parents in Hocking Co., in 1850 and 1860, his mother may have gone to Fairfield Co. to family for the birth.[FOFH, p. 91]

ISSUE:

+ .1121.1   Virginia RITTGERS, born 30 Jun 1879, died 9 Jan 1963.
+ .1121.2   Ira RITTGERS, born 18 Dec 1880, died 15 Sep 1963.
+ .1111.3   Minnie RITTGERS, born 20 Sep 1883, died 28 May 1955.
+ .1121.4   Perry RITTGERS, born 30 Jan 1887, died 22 Oct 1918.
+ .1121.5   Eli (Pete) RITTGERS, born 3 Mar 1893, died 28 Oct 1968.
  .1121.6   Esta Opal RITTGERS, born 16 Sep 1895 in Brown Twp., Darke Co., Oh. She is on the 1900 census, age 4, with parents there.[ED 50, p 57B, fam #193/196] Esta died 6 Aug 1908 in Darke County, Oh., and was buried in Teegarden Cem., Darke Co., Oh.
  .1121.7   Owen RITTGERS, born 19 Jan 1903 in Brown Twp., Darke Co., Oh., died 19 Oct 1962 in Oh, and was buried in Teegarden Cem, Ansonia, Oh. Owen is on the 1910 census, age 7, with his parents there.[ED 76, p 1A, fam #13/13] and age 16, there with his parents on the 1920 census.[ED 93, p 1B, fam #24/24] We are told he never married, He worked for Shell Oil Co.

112.2 Joseph[4] "Jose" RITTGERS (Abraham[3], Joseph[2], John[1]) was born Dec 1855 in Marion Twp., Hocking Co., Oh., the son of Abraham RITTGERS and Catherine LEFLER. He is on the 1860 census, age 4, with parents there.[p 158 fam #1037/1025] On the 1870 census, age 16, with parents in Brown Twp., Darke Co., Oh.[p 3 fam #41/40] Continues there in 1880, age 24, with parents, a farmer. He married **Louisa Jane AMSPAUGH (See number 154.4)** 23 July 1882, Darke Co., Oh.[DKCoM, p 237] She was born 17 Aug 1862 in Marion Twp., Hocking Co., Oh., the daughter of Jonas AMSPAUGH (#15.4) and Barbara DOUBENMIRE.(This makes them second cousins.) She is on the 1870 census, age 8, with parents, Marion Twp., Hocking Co., Oh.[p 507, fam #230/233] and continues with parents in 1880, age 17, Greenfield, Fairfield Co., Oh.[p 142, fam #110/115] The 1900 census shows Joseph, age 44, a farmer in Brown Twp., Darke Co., Oh., with his wife, Lydia (?), age 37. She declares they have been married 18 years and she has born one child. Sylvester, age 16 is listed with them, as is one David Lefler, Uncle, age 63. He is a widower, born Oct 1836. This probably is his mother's brother, and widower of Mary Rittgers (#11.5)[ED 50, p 57B, fam #194/197] 1910 census finds Joseph still a resident of Brown Twp. He is 54 and living on "own income." Louisa, 47, declares they have been married 28 years and she has born 1 child. Sylvester is still in the home, age 26 and farmer, general farm.[ED 76, p 8A, fam #172/176] On the 1920 census in Brown Twp., Louisa, age 57, widow, is caring for mother, Barbara Amspaugh.[ED 108, p 13, fam #303/303] Joseph died 10 Nov 1910, and Louisa died 3 Jan 1952. We are told they are buried in Teegarden Cemetery, Darke Co., Oh.

ISSUE:

.1122.1   Sylvester RITTGERS, born Nov 1884 on one record and 25 Mar 1884 in another in Darke Co., Oh. He is seen on the 1900 census, age 16, with his parents there.[ED 50, p 57B. fam #194/197] Continues in his parents' home in 1910, where, age 26, he is listed as a farmer.[ED 76, p 8A, fam #172/176] We are told he died 8 Jan 1912.

112.3 Samuel[4] RITTGERS (Abraham[3], Joseph[2], John[1]) was born 22 Nov 1865 in Hocking Co., Oh., the son of Abraham RITTGERS and Catherine LEFLER. He is there on the 1870 census, age 3, with parents.[p 3 fam #41/40], and there on the 1880 census, age 13, with parents, where he works on farm. [ED 56, p.46D, fam #74/74] We are told he married (1) Lizzie Jane Hufford, born 16, Aug 1871, died 7 July 1897. He married (2) **Hulda S. STONEROCK** 9 Feb 1899 in Brown Twp., Darke Co., Oh.[DkCoM-2, p 210] She was born Nov 1879 in Oh. The entry in "Darke Co. Marriages" gives parents as "Jonathan Stonerock and _____ Hassinger." On the 1900 census, Samuel is age 34 and a farmer, in Brown Twp., Darke Co., Oh. Wife Hulda S., 21, declares they have been married one year and she has born one child, seen in the home. She reports that her father was born in Ohio, but her mother born in Virginia. [ED 50, p 58A, fam #203/206] In 1910, Samuel, 44, and Hulda 31, continue on their farm in Brown Twp. Hulda declares they have been married 11 years and she has born 3 children, seen in the home. They live next door to brother Joseph. [ED 76, p 8A, fam #173/177] The 1920 census finds Samuel, 54 and still farming in Brown Twp. Hulda is 40. Their three sons are still in the home.[ED 93, p 2] We are told Samuel died 23 Feb 1927, and Hulda died 1957. They are buried in Teegarden Cemetery, Darke Co., Oh.

ISSUE:

.1123.1   Floyd A. RITTGERS, born 25 Aug 1899[SS] in Brown Twp., Darke Co., Oh. He is seen there with his parents on the 1900 census, age 9/12,[ED 50, p 58A. fam #203/206] Continues in his parents' home in 1910, where he is 10.[ED 76, p 8A, fam #173/177] In 1920, age 20, he is still with them, listed as a carpenter.[ED 93, p 2] He died Aug 1983.[SS] He married Clara FLATTER 19 Apr 1924. She was born 19 Apr 1924. Floyd died 12 Aug 1983.

+ .1123.2   Vernon RITTGERS, born 21 Oct 1901, died 15 Mar 1986.
+ .1123.3   Elva Stanton RITTGERS, born 1904, died 1956.
+ .1123.4   Velda E. RITTGERS, born 7 Sep 1921.

113.1 Emanuel J.[4] CONRAD (Lucinda[3], Joseph[2], John[1]) was born Apr 1853 in Hocking Co.,
Oh., the son of David C. CONRAD and Lucinda RITTGERS. Seen, age 7, on 1860 census with
parents, Good Hope Twp., S. Bloomingville P.O., Hocking Co., Oh.[p 37 fam #522/515]   In
1870 he is 17, with parents there.[p 453 fam #168/168] Emanuel married Margaret Lowrey, 27
Sept 1877, in Hocking Co., Oh.[HVRM, Bk D, p.364] The 1880, Brown Twp., Darke Co., Oh.,
census finds Emanuel as head of house, age 27, a farmer, with no spouse. It is also noted that
he is "consumptive." This usually indicates tuberculosis, but could be a chronic bronchitis, as
we find he lived to a ripe old age![p 220B fam #50/51] He married (2) **Julia A. KERNS** 9 Apr
1882 in Brown Twp., Darke Co., Oh.[DkCoM, p 57] She was born 25 Feb 1851 in Fairfield Co.,
Oh.   On the 1900 census, Emanuel is 47, a farmer in Brown Twp. With him is wife Julia, 49.
They have been married 18 years and she has born 4 children three still alive. The three children
are listed with them.[ED 50,p. 63B, fam #321/328] In 1910, Emanuel is 56 and continues a
farmer in Brown Twp., on his own farm. With him is wife Julia A., 59. They have been married
28 years and she has born 4 children, three survive at this time.[ED 76, p 3A, fam #56/57]   On
the 1920 census, age 66, no occupation, in Jackson Twp., Darke Co., Oh. Wife Julia, 68, is with
him. They are living on a farm on "Jackson Twp.-Brown Twp. Road. [ED93, p. 1B, fam #14/14]
Julia died 26 Sept 1928, and was buried 29 Sep 1928 in Teegarden Cemetery, Ansonia, Oh. On
her death record we see Julia died "at home 1 mile north of Ansonia. [Darke Co., Oh] Father
Lewis Kerns, mother Sarah Cradlebaugh of Fairfield Co., Oh." Julia declares on the census that
her parents were born in Ohio.[FOFH, p. 21]   Emanuel died May 1937. He apparently remarried
after Julia died, as his death record tells us he died "5 mile northeast of Red Key, In[diana], and
left widow **Margaret PHILLIPPS** "[FOFH, p. 21] He is buried in Teegarden Cemetery.
ISSUE:
.1131.1   Mimi CONRAD, born Apr 1883 in Brown Twp., Darke Co., Oh. On 1900, census,
     age 17, with parents there.[ED 50, p 63B, fam #321/328]
.1131.2   Goldie I. CONRAD, born Mar 1888 in Brown Twp., Darke Co., Oh. On 1900,
     census, age 12, with parents there.[ED 50, p 63B, fam #321/328] Continues in home
     on 1910 census, age 22.[ED 76, p 3A, fam #56/57]
.1131.3   Sylvia B. CONRAD, born May 1894 in Brown Twp., Darke Co., Oh. On 1900,
     census, age 16, with parents there.[ED 50, p 63B, fam #321/328] Continues in home
     on 1910 census, age 15.[ED 76, p 3A, fam]

113.3 Emma[4] CONRAD (Lucinda[3], Joseph[2], John[1]) was born about 1858 in Hocking Co., Oh.,
the daughter of David C. CONRAD and Lucinda RITTGERS. She is on the 1860 census, age
2, with parents, Good Hope Twp., S. Bloomingville P.O., Hocking Co.,Oh.[p 37 fam #522/515],
and on the 1870, age 12, with parents there.[p 453, fam #168/168] She married (1) **Amos
TIPPLE** 23 Jan 1880 in Darke Co., Oh.[DkCoM, p. 291] Amos died before 1898. Emma
married (2) **Henry ARMSTRONG** about 1898 in Darke Co., Oh.. He was born Apr 1851 in
Ohio. On the 1900 census, we find Henry Armstrong, 49, is a day laborer in Jackson Twp., City
of Union, Darke Co., Oh. Wife Emma E., 39, caring for the home. Emma declares they have
been married 2 years. She has born 8 children, 7 living at this time. In the home we only see three
children. Also in home is her sister, Mary Beery, widow.[ED 60, p 27A, fam #262/279]
Known ISSUE of Emma and Amos:

.1133.1   Ross TIPPLE, born Jan 1892 in Oh.
.1133.2   Emmie TIPPLE, born Sep 1894 in Oh.
                  Known ISSUE of Emma and Henry:
.1133.3   Hugh ARMSTRONG, born Aug 1899 in Darke Co., Oh.

113.4 Lafayette Fountaine⁴ CONRAD (Lucinda³, Joseph², John¹) was born 6 May 1860 in
Hocking Co., Oh., the son of David C. CONRAD and Lucinda RITTGERS. On the 1860 census
he is age 2/12 (2 months) with parents in Good Hope Twp., S. Bloomfield Post Office, Hocking
Co., Oh.[p 37 fam #522/515] In 1870, age 10, he continues with parents there.[p 453 fam
#168/168] The 1800 census finds him, age 20, listed as in the home of Emanuel Conrad, his
brother, in E. Precinct, Jackson Twp., Darke Co., Oh.[p 220B fam #50/51] He married **Laura
Ellen SULLENBARGER** 28 Feb 1892 in Darke Co., Oh. [DkCoM-1, p. 57] She was born
12 Jul 1870 in Darke Co., Oh., the dau. of George M. and Kathryn (Hart) Sullenbarger. On the
1900 census, Lafayette, 40, and wife Ella L., 29, are in Jackson Twp., Darke Co., Oh. With
them is son Ray B, age 4. There is no occupation listed for him, but is most probably farming.
Ella declares they have been married 8 years and she has born 2 children, one living at this time.
[ED 59, p 60, fam #14/14] In 1910, "Lafe R.", a farmer, is 49, and Ella, 39, are in Jackson
Twp., Union, Darke Co., Oh. They have three children in their home on "Elry Pike."[ED 92, p
9A, fam #187] They are still in Jackson in 1920. Lafayette, 59 is still farming. Ella is now 49,
and caring for the two youngest, who are still in the home.[ED 108 p 6A, fam #119/119]
Lafayette died 15 Jun 1934, and Laura died 10 Feb 1959 both in Darke County, Oh.(*This lineage
submitted by Darlene Berens*)
ISSUE:
.1134.1   Purla Conrad, born 4 Sept 1893, died 19 Oct 1893
+ .1134.2   Ray Benson CONRAD, born 30 Sep 1895, died 7 May 1984.
.1134.3   George CONRAD, born about 1901 in Darke Co., Oh. With parents on 1910
                  census, age 9, Jackson Twp., Union, Darke Co., Oh.[ED 92, p 9A, fam # 187] On
                  1920 census, age 19, with parents there.[ED 108, p 6A, fam #119/119]
.1134.4   Ruth CONRAD, born about 1904 in Darke Co., Oh. With parents on 1910 census,
                  age 6, Jackson Twp., Union, Darke Co., Oh.[ED 92, p 9A, fam #187] On 1920
                  census, age 16, with parents there. [ED 108, p 6A, fam #119/119]

113.6 Jesse⁴ CONRAD (Lucinda³, Joseph², John¹) was born Aug 1869 in Good Hope Twp.,
Hocking Co., Oh., the son of David C. CONRAD and Lucinda RITTGERS. He is on the 1870
census, age 1, with parents in Good Hope Twp., Gibsonville P.O., Hocking Co., Oh.[p 453 fam
#168/168] On the 1880 census he is in the home with brother Emanuel Conrad as
head-of-household in Jackson Twp., Darke Co., Oh. Jessie is age 12 and listed as a farmer.[p
220B fam #50/51] He married **Martha ZEEK** 26 Apr 1891 in Brown Twp., Darke Co., Oh.
[DkCoM-1, p. 57] She was born Apr 1873 in Oh. In 1900, Jessie, is in Harrison, Paulding Co.,
Oh. No occupation listed. "Marthy", 27, declares they have been married nine years and she has
born 3 children, two living at this time.[ED 50, p 8, fam #156/157] In 1910, Jesse is 41, and a
"night police, city" in Union, Jackson Twp., Darke Co., Oh. With him is wife Martha, 37. She
states they have been married 19 years and she has born 4 children, two living at this time. Opal
and Dewey are listed with them. [ED 93, p 11A, fam #270/280] By 1920, Jesse is 51 and Martha
46, in Jackson, Darke Co., Oh. Jesse is a "painter, Railroad".[ED 109, p 3, fam #72/75]
ISSUE:

.1136.1   Opal CONRAD, born Apr 1895 in Jackson Twp., Darke Co., Oh. On 1900 census,
           age 5, with parents in Harrison, Paulding Co., Oh.[ED 50, p 8A, fam #156/157] On
           1910 census, age 15, with parents in Union Twp., Jackson Twp., Darke Co.,
           Oh.[ED 93, p 11A, fam #270/280]
.1136.2   Russell Dewey CONRAD, born Mar 1898 in Darke Co., Oh. Called "Russel D." on
           1900 census, age 2, with parents in Harrison, Paulding Co., Oh.[ED 50, p 8A, fam
           #156/157] On 1910 census, called "Dewey," age 12, with parents in Union, Jackson
           Twp., Darke Co., Oh.[ED 93, p 11A, fam #270/280]
.1136.3   LaVernon H. CONRAD, born about 1913 in Jackson Twp., Darke Co., Oh. On
           1920 census, age 6, with parents in Union, Jackson Twp., Darke Co., Oh.[ED 109,
           p 3, fam #72/75]

114.1 Theodore⁴ HUFFORD (Catherine³, Joseph², John¹) was born Nov 1860 in Good Hope
Twp., Hocking Co., Oh., the son of Henry HUFFORD and Catherine RITTGERS. He is on the
1880 census, age 19, with parents, Brown Twp., Darke Co., Oh.,[ED 56, p 4, fam #78/84] He
married **Amanda____** about 1882. She was born 1864 in Oh. We see them on the 1900 census
continuing in Brown Twp. Theodore is age 39, with wife Amanda, 35. She declares they have
been married 18 years and she has born 9 children six alive at this time. Also in the home is his
father, Henry, now 63, and a widower.[ED 50, p 57B, fam #196/199]
                                            ISSUE:
.1141.1   Pearly M. HUFFORD, born Jan 1884 in Brown Twp., Darke Co., Oh. On 1900
           census, age 16, with parents there.[ED 50, p 57B, fam #196/199]
.1141.2   Lurie HUFFORD, born Aug 1885 in Brown Twp., Darke Co., Oh. On 1900 census,
           age 14, with parents there.[ED 50, p 57B, fam #196/199]
+ .1141.3 William HUFFORD, born Oct 1887.
.1141.4   Henry HUFFORD, born Mar 1891 in Brown Twp., Darke Co., Oh. On 1900 census,
           age 9, with parents there.[ED 50, p 57B, fam #196/199]
.1141.5   Charles HUFFORD, born Aug 1895 in Brown Twp., Darke Co., Oh. On 1900
           census, age 4, with parents there.[ED 50, p 57B, fam #196/199]
.1141.6   Lizzie HUFFORD, born Nov 1899 in Brown, Darke, Oh. On 1900 census, age 7/12,
           with parents there.[ED 50, p 57B, fam #196/199]

114.3 Ida⁴ HUFFORD (Catherine³, Joseph², John¹) was born Aug 1867 in Oh., the daughter
of Henry HUFFORD and Catherine RITTGERS. Age 14 on 1880 census, with parents, Brown
Twp., Darke Co.,Oh.[ED 56, p 4, fam #78/84] She married **Thomas L. HART** in Hocking Co.,
Oh. He was born Mar 1861 in Oh. In 1900, we find Thomas, 39, a farmer in Jackson Twp.,
Union City, Darke Co., Oh. Wife Ida, 32, declares they have been married 14 years and she has
born 2 children, both alive. They are in the home with their parents.[ED 59, p 2A, fam #20/20]
                                            ISSUE:
.1143.1   Archie R. HART, born Jul 1891 in Darke County, Oh.
.1143.2   Ernest R. HART, born Mar 1896 in Darke County, Oh.

114.4 Abraham⁴ HUFFORD (Catherine³, Joseph², John¹) was born Jul 1872 in Oh., the son of
Henry HUFFORD and Catherine RITTGERS. He is on the 1880 census, age 7, with parents in
Brown Twp., Darke Co., Oh.[ED 56, p 4, fam #78/84] He married **Della M.____** 1890 in
Union, Darke Co., Oh. She was born May 1873. On the 1900 census, Abraham, 27, is a grocer
in Union. Della, 27, declares they have been married 9 years. She has born 3 children, all alive

at this time.[ED 59, p 5B, fam #107/107] The 1910 census finds them in Ansonia, Brown Twp., Darke Co., Oh. "Abram", 37, is in "sales - clothing."[ED 75, p 5A, fam #140/140] Della declares they have been married 19 years and she has born 3 children, shown with them. Abraham died before the 1920 census, as we find Della, age 47 and a widow, in the home of son Lawrence in Piqua, Miami Co., Oh. She reports she is an "operator, underwear mill."[ED 190, p. 8B. fam #211/199]

ISSUE:

+ .1144.1   Lawrence R. HUFFORD, born Aug 1891.
  .1144.2   Onda O. HUFFORD, born Dec 1893 in Union., Darke Co., Oh. On 1900 census, age 6, with parents there.[ED 59, p 5B, fam #107/107] Continues on 1910 census, age 16, with parents there.[ED 75, p 5B, fam #140/140] 1920 census, age 26, with brother Lawrence and his family in Piqua, Miami Co., Oh. She reports she is an "inspector, underwear mill." [ED 190, p 8B, fam #211/199]
  .1144.3   Ina O. HUFFORD, born Dec 1897 in Union, Darke Co., Oh.. On 1900 census, age 2, with parents there.[ED 59, p 5B, fam #107/107] and age 12, on the 1910 census.[ED 75, p 5B, fam 140/140]

115.1 Malinda[4] LEFLER (Mary[3], Joseph[2], John[1]) was born 27 Apr 1862 in Darke Co., Oh., the daughter of David LEFLER and Mary RITTGERS. [Found on the LDS-GedCom Ancestry File, Ver. 1.0, 1993 CD.(#JXVG-9M)] She married **Jeremiah LEFLER.** He was born 31 Oct 1856 in Mercer Co., Mo., the son of Simeon Lefler and Leah Beery. Malinda died 13 Jan 1933 in Canton, McPherson Co., Ks., and Jeremiah died 10 Nov 1945, Wichita, Sedgwick Co., Ks. They are buried in Canton Cemetery, Canton, McPherson Co., Ks.

ISSUE:

+ .1151.1   William Arthur LEFLER, born 7 May 1889, died 14 Jun 1962.

116.1 George[4] GROVES (Anna[3], Joseph[2], John[1]) was born 12 Mar 1860 in Millville, Hocking Co., Oh. He was the son of Samuel GROVE and Anna RITTGERS. He married **Lavina "Vine" HAMPTON** 25 Feb 1885 in Hocking County, Oh.[HVRM, Bk E., p.292] She was born about 1858 in Hocking County, Oh. Lavina's parents are John and Rachael (Kimble) Hampton. They lived in Jobes, Hocking Co., a coal mining town, where George was a laborer. George died 28 Feb 1892 in Jobes, of Typhoid Fever at age 31 yrs., 11 mo., 20 days. Lavina married (2) Sherman Septer in 1893. He was born abt. 1870, and so 12 years younger than Lavina. She died 1921 in Hocking County, Oh, and was buried in Centenary Cemetery, Hocking Co., Oh. Millville now called Rockbridge. [Bigham]

ISSUE:

  .1161.1   Rexie Freddonia GROVE, born 13 Jan 1886 in Rockbridge, Hocking Co., Oh. She married Samuel Dow SIMMONS. Rexie died 1959 in Franklin Co., Oh, and was buried in Centenary Cem., Hocking Co., Oh. [Bigham]
  .1161.2   Bertha Viola GROVE, born 16 Oct 1889 in Rockbridge, Hocking Co., Oh. She married Fred HARPER. Bertha died Dec 1981 in Columbus, Franklin Co., Oh. [Bigham]
+ .1161.3   Willard Elsworth GROVE, born 17 Jun 1891, died 19 Aug 1967.

116.9 Rosetta[4] GROVES (Anna[3], Joseph[2], John[1]) was born 2 Mar 1881 in Rockbridge, Hocking Co., Oh. She was the daughter of Samuel GROVE and Anna RITTGERS. She married **Edward Allison RITCHEY** 4 Aug 1899 in Logan, Hocking Co., Oh. He was born 24 Jul 1878 in Emlenton, Venango Co., Pa., the son of Francis Lemuel and Ellen Caroline (Shirey) Ritchey. His father came to Ohio from Venenago Co., Pa., to work in the oil fields. When oil was discovered in Southern California in 1923, Edward and Rosetta went to California with his father and two brothers and their families to work in the oil fields. Edward died 1 Dec 1949 in Long Beach, Los Angeles Co., Ca, and was buried 3 Dec 1949 in Sunnyside Memorial Cemetery, Long Beach, Ca. Rosetta died 14 Oct 1954 in Long Beach, Los Angeles Co., Ca, and was buried 16 Oct 1954 in Sunnyside Memorial Cemetery, Long Beach, Ca. [Bigham/Berens]

ISSUE:

.1169.1   Kenneth Allison RITCHEY, born 3 Dec 1899 in Lancaster, Fairfield Co., Oh, died 19 Jan 1965 in Long Beach, Los Angeles Co., Ca, and was buried 22 Jan 1965 in Sunnyside Memorial Cemetery, Long Beach, Ca. [Bigham/Berens]

+ .1169.2   Helen Leone RITCHEY, born 13 Dec 1901, died 13 Aug 1984.

.1169.3   Loren M. RITCHEY, born 6 Sep 1904 in Lancaster, Fairfield Co., Oh, died 5 Jun 1928 in Lone Pine, Inyo Co., Oh, and was buried in Ventura, Ventura Co., Ca.. We are told he drowned.[Berens/Bigham]

121.2 Martha "Elly"[4] RITTGERS (Samuel[3], Jacob[2], John[1]) was born 6 Feb 1853 in Marion Twp., Hocking, Oh., the daughter of Samuel S. RITTGERS and Rosannah SHERBROWN. On the 1860 census, age 7, with father, Samuel and step-mother, Christina (Edgell), Jefferson, Polk Co., Ia.[P 93, fam 747/682] On the 1870 census, we see Martha in the home of Jacob and Catherine Sherburn, in Jefferson, Polk Co., Ia. Jacob was born in Ohio and may possibly be a brother to Martha's deceased mother, Rosanna.[p 109 fam #105/110] She married **William F. "Willie" WOODS** before 1876. He was born 30 Aug 1850 in Tenn. William died 10 May 1900, and was buried in New Union Cemetery, Mercer Co., Mo. On the 1900 census for Milgrove Village, Washington Twp., Mercer Co., Mo., we see Martha Woods, head of house, widow, age 47. She reports she a farmer owning a mortgaged farm. Two children still in the home.[ED 122, p.15A, fam #305/305] Martha died 20 Jul 1935 in Mercer Co., Mo., and was buried in New Union Cem., Mercer Co., Mo. In transcript reporting death dates, it is noted that she was called Elly. [Mercer County, Mo., Cemetery Book, *extracted and submitted by Anna Lou Arnett. Information reported on tombstone*]

ISSUE:

+ .1212.1   Effie A. WOODS, born 1876, died 1960.

+ .1212.2   Lulu Belle WOODS, born 24 Jun 1886, died 11 Sep 1980.

+ .1212.3   Eldon D. WOODS, born Jan 1889.

121.4 Alice[4] RITTGERS (Samuel[3], Jacob[2], John[1]) was born 18 Dec 1858 in Jefferson Twp., Polk Co., Ia., the daughter of Samuel S. RITTGERS and Christina EDGELL. She is on the 1860 Census, age 1, with parents there.[p 93, fam #747/682] On the 1880, with father and step-mother at Dist 232, Mercer Co., Mo.[ED 232, p 152A, fam #1/1] She married **John SMITH** 1885 in Mercer Co., Mo. He was born Sep 1857 in Mo. On the 1900 census we find John Smith in Washington Twp., Mercer Co., Mo., farming. He is 42, and a farmer on his own general farm. Wife Alice, Age 41, was born Dec 1858. They have been married 14 yrs. and have had 3 children, two still living.[ED 122, p 14B, fam #296/298] In 1910, we find them still in Mill Grove. John is 53 and still farming. Alice, 52, states they have been married 24 years and that she has born 3 children, 2 alive at this time. Both sons still in the home, as is Scott's bride, Eunice.[ED 126, p 13A, fam #269/273]

ISSUE:

.1214.1   Scottie SMITH, born Jun 1886 in Washington Twp., Mercer Co., Mo. On the 1900
           census, age 13, with parents, Washington Twp., Mercer Co., Mo.[ED 122, p 14B,
           fam #296/298] He married Eunice____ abt. 1909 in Mercer Co., Mo. She was born
           about 1892 in Mo. On the 1910 census, Mill Grove, Mercer Co., he is age 24, in
           parent's home - probably working on the farm. Eunice, 18, declares they have been
           married 1 year and she has born no children.[ED 126, p 13A, fam #269/273]
.1214.2   Orville SMITH, born Jan 1888 in Washington Twp., Mercer Co., Mo. On 1900
           census, age 12, with parents there,[ED 122, p 14B, fam #296/298] and continues
           in the home in 1910, age 22.[(ED 126, p 13A, fam #269/273]

121.5 Albert Clarence⁴ RITTGERS (Samuel³, Jacob², John¹) was born 9 Apr 1861., the son
of Samuel S. RITTGERS and Christina EDGELL. He is on the 1880 census, 18, with parents
in Mercer Co., Mo.[ED 232, p 152A, fam #1/1] On the 1900 census, he is 34, and a single
farmer, boarding with William Brewer, in Kickapoo Twp., Lincoln Co., Okla.[ED 122, p 12, fam
#249/250]He married **Ann McCABE** 23 Feb 1902 in McLoud, Shawnee Co., Okla. She was
born 1885. On the 1910 census, Lincoln Co., Okla., he is 39, and wife, Annie is 25. His age is
off by 10 years, but this was a common transcription error on the census. [ED 99, p 16A, fam
#221/230] They lived in Oklahoma City, Okla., until his death in May 1935 in Oklahoma City,
Okla.
ISSUE:
.1215.1   Virden A. RITTGERS, born 7 Dec 1902[SS] in McLoud, Shawnee, Okla, died
           26 Nov 1989 in New Milford, Bergen Co,, NJ.[SS] On 1910 census, age 7, with
           parents in Lincoln Co., Okla.[ED 99, p 16A, fam #221/230] Family story tells us
           he lived in New Milford, N.J.

121.6 Perry⁴ RITTGERS (Samuel³, Jacob², John¹) was born 10 Sep 1863 in Mercer Co., Mo.,
the son of Samuel S. RITTGERS and Christina EDGELL. Age 15 on 1880 census, Washington
Twp., Mercer Co., Mo., with father.[ED 232, p 152A, fam #1/1] We are told he lived in
McLoud, Shawnee Co., Okla., and married **Belle HONEING** there.
ISSUE:
.1216.1   Mercedese RITTGERS. Lived in Oklahoma City, Okla.,
.1216.2   Serepta RITTGERS. Lived in Oklahoma City, Okla.,
.1216.3   Lafayette RITTGERS, born 15 Apr 1904, died Feb 1984[SS] in Oklahoma City,
           Oklahoma, Ok. Per family record, lived in Chicago, Ill. At time of death, Feb 1984,
           residence listed as Oklahoma City, Oklahoma Co., Okla. The family had a query
           regarding one Lafayette Rittgers, who used to sculpt baseball figurines. None of the
           family knew of this.   One Helen Rittgers is listed in SS death index with same data
           as Lafayette's. She b. 9 Dec 1906, died Nov 1988, Oklahoma City, Oklahoma Co.,
           Okla.
.1216.4   Neta RITTGERS, died young.

121.7 Sarah Isabel⁴ RITTGERS (Samuel³, Jacob², John¹) was born 18 Oct 1866 in Mercer
Co., Mo., the daughter of Samuel S. RITTGERS and Christina EDGELL. On the 1880 census,
age 13, with parents in Washington Twp., Mercer Co., Mo. [ED 232, p. 152A, fam #1/1] She
married **Andrew Jackson "Jack" VIRDEN** 18 Nov 1888 in Mercer Co., Mo. He was born
1 Dec 1857. The family group sheet reports his parents are William Thomas Virden(b. 1829,
Sussex Co., Del-d. 1896, Mercer Co., Mo.) and Margaret N. "Peggy" King (b.1837, Marion Co.,

Oh.-d. 28 Mar 1922, Mercer Co., Mo.) In 1900 we see Andrew J., 42, a farmer in Harrison Twp., Mercoer Co., Mo. Wife Sarah J., 33, declares they have been married 11 years and she has born 2 children, both alive at that time. [ED 113, p. 108B fam #68/60] Family record tells us that Jack, as he was called, was a stockman and an accomplished violinist. Sarah died 12 Apr 1906 in Mercer County, Mo., and was buried in Goshen Cemetery, Mercer Co., Mo. In 1910 Andrew is 52 and in his home in Harrison with his two daughters, and William Finney, husband of daughter Nellie . Andrew died 13 Oct 1924 in Mercer Co., Mo, and was buried in Goshen Cemetery, Mercer Co., Mo. [Family record, submitted by grand daughter Margaret (Finney) Thomas. Also family group sheet submitted to Ohio Gen. Soc., by Anna Lou (Peacock) Arnett.]

ISSUE:

+ .1217.1   Nellie Avis VIRDEN, born 10 Aug 1889, died Oct 1961.
+ .1217.2   Agnes Elizabeth VIRDEN, born Dec 1889.

121.9 Sanford S.[4] RITTGERS (Samuel[3], Jacob[2], John[1]) was born 7 Jun 1881 in Mercer Co., Mo., the son of Samuel S. RITTGERS and Marinda (Boston) HURST. He is on the 1900 census, age 18, with widowed father and younger sister in Harrison, Mercer Co., Mo.[ED 113, p 6B, fam #117/119] He married **Etta GAY** before 1904 in Mo. She was born 17 Jan 1882[SS] in Mo. Etta died 30 Apr 1968 in Ks.[SS] Her last reported residence in Peabody, Marion Co., Ks. 1920 census finds "Sanferd Rittiger", 38, in Roxbury, Gypsum Creek Twp., McPherson Co, Ks. He has with him wife Ettie, 37, and five children, plus his uncle Peter "Rittiger" (#12.B), age 77.[ED 67, p 6A, fam #76/76] Family story tells us he remained on Uncle Peter Rittgers' estate in McPherson Co., Ks.

ISSUE:

+ .1219.1   Freda RITTGERS, born 18 Mar 1904.
  .1219.2   Marie RITTGERS, born about 1906 in Ks. On 1920 census, age 14, with parents in Roxbury, McPherson Co., Ks.[ED 67, p 6A, fam #76/76]
  .1219.3   Lea RITTGERS, born about 1909 in Ks. On 1920 census, age 11, with parents in Roxbury, McPherson Co., Ks.[ED 67, p 6A, fam 76/76]
  .1219.4   Letha RITTGERS, born about 1911 in Ks. On 1920 census, age 9, with parents in Roxbury, McPherson Co., Ks.[ED 67, p 6A, fam #76/76]
  .1219.5   Lloyd RITTGERS, born Oct 1915 in Ks. On 1920 census, age 4 3/12, with parents in Roxbury, McPherson Co., Ks.[ED 67, p 6A, fam 76/76]

121.A Margaret[4] RITTGERS (Samuel[3], Jacob[2], John[1]) was born 22 May 1884 in Mercer Co., Mo., the daughter of Samuel S. RITTGERS and Marinda (Boston) HURST. She is on the 1900 census, age 16, with widowed father and brother, Sanford, in Harrison, Mercer Co., Mo.[ED 113, p 6B, fam # 117/119] She married **Joe HERIFORD**. He was born 1878. Margaret died 1922 in Mo., and was buried in Union Cem., Mercer, Mo. Joe died 1947, and was buried in Union Cemetery, Mercer Co., Mo. [Mercer Co. Cemetery Book, transcript submitted by Anna Lou Arnett.]

ISSUE:

+ .121A.1   Hollie HERIFORD.
  .121A.2   Keith HERIFORD.
  .121A.3   Kenneth HERIFORD, born 1910 in Mercer Co., Mo., died 1925.

122.2 Hester Ann[4] ILLES (Isabelle[3], Jacob[2], John[1]) was born about 1850 in Marion Twp., Hocking Co., Oh., the daughter of Samuel ILLES and Isabelle RITTGERS. On the 1860 census, age 10, with father and step-mother, Falls Twp., Hocking Co. Oh.[p 113 fam #423/425] She married **J. R. MASON** about 8 May 1873, in Hocking Co., Oh.[HVRM, bk D, p.113] He was born 12 May 1849 in Pa.[Birth date extrapolated from tombstone] In the estate of Jacob Rittgers (1.2) in 1880, we find listed "Esther Mason... surviving heir of the deceased daughter..." Isabella Iles.[Abst 62638] On the 1880 census, Valley Twp., Polk Co., Ia., we find next door to Christina Rittgers, "Annie E." Mason, 29, b. Oh., as were her parents. With her is John L., 4, son, b. Oh., but father b. Pa., mother b. Oh.[ED 172, p 34, fam #133/136] In Rittgers Cemetery Records, we find the name of "J.R.Mason, 8 Jan 1878, age 28 yrs, 7 mo., 27 days." There is a stone in the Rittgers Cemetery, Johnston, Polk Co., Ia., with no date on it that gives the name Esther Iles Mason.

ISSUE:

.1222.1   John L. MASON, born about 1876 in Oh. On 1880 census, Valley., Polk Co., Ia., with widowed mother, listed next door to his deceased grandfather's second wife, Catharine (Schleigh) Rittgers. [ED 172, p 34, fam]

127.1 Martin Luther "Luke"[4] RITTGERS (Jacob[3], Jacob[2], John[1]) was born 30 Apr 1870 in Valley Twp., Polk Co., Ia., the son of Jacob R. RITTGERS and Mary F. WHIPPS. He is on the 1870 census, age 2 months, with parents there.[p 406 fam #100/110] On the 1880 census we see him, age 10, still with parents and the only child listed.[p 592 fam #12/12] We are told by his nephew, Ted Rittgers, that he had new cars before anyone in the area. He married **Martha Leola MILLER** before 1910.[PVRB, book 6, gives her full maiden name, as mother of Martin's child] She was born about 1881 in Ia. On the 1910 census, Jefferson Twp., Grimes, Polk Co., Ia., "Leaut" Rittgers, 39, is farming, and wife Mattie, 29, is housekeeper. They have been married 1 year and she has born no children. Mattie declares her father born in Germany and her mother born in Michigan. With them is his father, Jake, age 76, retired. Also in home is V.F. Walker, 23; and Roolin Wood, 25, employees-farm labor.[ED 176, p 1A, fam #7/7] On the 1920 census we find Martin, 49, living at 1016 Pleasant St., Des Moines, Polk Co., Ia., as head of household. With him is his father, Jacob, 85. It states neither one has an occupation. Martin is divorced and Jacob is a widower.[ED 113, p 9A, fam #158/269] Martin died after 1932, and was buried in Rittgers Cemetery, Johnston, Ia. His death date never was etched onto his stone.

ISSUE:

.1271.1   Floyd Raymond RITTGERS, born 3 Jul 1910 in Grimes, Polk Co., Ia.[PVRB, book 6, p 97 of manuscript]

128.1 Edith Helen[4] RITTGERS (Eli[3], Jacob[2], John[1]) was born Aug 1891 in Salina, Saline Co., Ks., the daughter of Eli D. RITTGERS and Virginia Weis MYERS. Age 8 on 1900 census there with widowed father and cousin Etta G. Rittgers.[p fam #256\256] She married **Roland Blanchard CAYWOOD** 29 Jun 1915. Edith died 11 Jun 1984, and was buried in Kansas City, Mo.

ISSUE:

+ .1281.1   Ronald Wade CAYWOOD, born 24 Jun 1916.
+ .1281.2   Frank Rittgers CAYWOOD, born 28 Jun 1920, died before 1993.
  .1281.3   Donald Wilson CAYWOOD, born 25 May 1922 in Salina, Saline Co, Ks., died 1925.

129.2 Esther[4] RITTGERS (Perry[3], Jacob[2], John[1]) was born 27 Feb 1872 in Bridgeport, Saline Co., Ks., the daughter of Perry C. RITTGERS and Myra Jane MORRISON. She is on the 1880 census, age 8, with parents in Liberty Twp., Saline Co., Ks.[ED 299, p 24, fam #93/99] She married **Erma F. PATTEE** 27 Feb 1894. He was born Apr 1873 in Ind. Erma states his parents both born in Ind, also. We find Erma Pattee, 27, a farmer in Battle Hill Twp., McPherson Co., Ks. Esther is 28, married 6 years and has born 4 children, all alive at this time. There is one "not named - dau" b. Jan 1900, which must be Maud.[ED 127, p 66, fam #35/35] Esther died 1 May 1926. Erma died 1941.

ISSUE:

+ .1292.1   Myra A. PATTEE, born Jan 1895.
+ .1292.2   Perry B. PATTEE, born Nov 1896, died July 1965, last known residence, Or.[SS]
+ .1292.3   Peter F. PATTEE, born Aug 1897.
+ .1292.4   Maude PATTEE, born Jan 1900.
+ .1292.5   Patrick PATTEE, born 4 Sep 1914, died 9 Apr 1989, last known residence, Santa
             Ana, Orange Co., Ca.[SS]
  .1292.6   Mabel PATTEE. Not listed on the 1900 census with her parents

129.4 Evelyn[4] RITTGERS (Perry[3], Jacob[2], John[1]) was born 19 Nov 1875 in Bridgeport, Saline Co., Ks., the daughter of Perry C. RITTGERS and Myra Jane MORRISON. She is on the 1880 census, age 4, with parents in Liberty Twp., Saline Co., Ks.[ED 299, p 24, fam #93/99] She married **Frank DARLING**. He was born 1872 In her mother's obituary, 1931, "Mrs. Evelyn Darling" was living then in Vancouver, Washington. Evelyn died 1938. Frank died 1963.

ISSUE:

+ .12941   Roy DARLING, born 1901.

129.5 Etta[4] RITTGERS (Perry[3], Jacob[2], John[1]) was born 7 Jul 1877 in Bridgeport, Saline Co., Ks., the daughter of Perry C. RITTGERS and Myra Jane MORRISON. She is on the 1800 census, age 2, with parents in Liberty Twp., Saline Co., Ks.[ED 299, p 24, fam #93/99] On 1900 census with Uncle, Eli Rittgers, apparently taking care of Eli's 8 year old daughter, Edith. Eli is 63 and a widower in Smokey Hill Twp., Saline Co., Ks. She married **Cyrus Clinton WHELCHEL** about 1901. Etta died 6 Dec 1903, and was buried in Gypsum Hill Cemetery, Salina, Ks. After Etta died, daughter LaVera lived with grandmother, Myra Rittgers in Salina, Ks. On 1920 census, Saline, Salina Co., Ks., Cy, 55, has remarried and has a son Clinton by wife Edna D. (__) Miller. Clinton is NOT a Rittgers Descendant. In the home also is one Harry Miller, 16. Cy is an "engineer - tractor".[ED 148, p 6B, fam #138/166] They live next door to Etta's sister Sarah (Rittgers) Bolton.

ISSUE:

  .1295.1   LaVera WHELCHEL, born 2 Aug 1903, died 1983. She is on the 1910 census, age
             6, in Ward 3, Salina, Saline Co., Ks., with her maternal grandmother, Myra
             (Morrison) Rittgers.(ED 135, p 2B, fam #47/47)

129.6 Daisy[4] RITTGERS (Perry[3], Jacob[2], John[1]) was born 6 Aug 1879 in Bridgeport, Saline Co., Ks., the daughter of Perry C. RITTGERS and Myra Jane MORRISON. She is on the 1880 census, age 10/12, with Parents in Liberty Twp., Saline Co., Ks.[ED 299, p 24, fam #93/99] She married **Archie KOPLIN** about 1897. He was born Jul 1874 in Ind. On the 1900 census, he declares his father b. Wisconsin and mother in Ohio. He is age 25, a farm laborer, wife Daisy is 20. They are living in the home of her father, Perry, in Liberty Twp., Saline Co, Ks . Daisy declares they have been married 3 years and she has born 2 children, both also in the home.[ED 118, p 195B, fam #32/33] On the 1920 census, Vancouver, Clarke Co., Washington; Archie, 46, is farming. Daisy, 40, keeps house for him and four children.[ED 7, p 7A, fam #115/115] In her mother's obituary in 1931, Daisy is said to be living in Vancouver, Washington. Daisy died 1932. Archie died 1943.

ISSUE:

+ .1296.1	Lester KOPLIN, born Mar 1898.
+ .1296.2	Artie KOPLIN, born Sep 1899, died 1918.
+ .1296.3	Elmer Charles KOPLIN, born 1901.
  .1296.4	Bertha "Hazel" KOPLIN, born 1904 in Ore. On the 1920 census, Vancouver, Clark Co., Wash., we don't see a "Hazel" with the family. Based on the birth year given in family records, we place her as "Bertha", 15.[ED 7, p 7A, fam #115/115] She married _____ DOWNING. Bertha died 1947.
  .1296.5	Wilda Maretta KOPLIN, born 1907. She married Cecil HEMMINGER. Cecil died 1951/1952. On the 1920 census, Vancouver, Clark Co., Wash., we don't see a "Maretta" with the family. Based on the birth year given in family records, we place her as "Wilda M.", 13.[ED 7, p 7A, fam #115/115]
  .1296.6	Helen V. KOPLIN, born 1908 in Wa. She married _____ FIELDS. On the 1920 census, Vancouver, Clark Co., Wash., we see "Hellen V.", age 11, with her parents there. [ED 7, p 7A, fam #115/115]
+ .1296.7	Lois KOPLIN, born 1921.

129.8 John Andrew[4] RITTGERS (Perry[3], Jacob[2], John[1]) was born 7 Aug 1883 in Bridgeport, Saline Co., Ks., the son of Perry C. RITTGERS and Myra Jane MORRISON. He is on the 1900 census, age 16, with parents in Liberty Twp., Saline Co., Ks.[ED 118, p 195B, fam #32/32] He married **Lula Maude MONTGOMERY** Aug 1905 in Marion, Marion Co., Ks. She was born 28 Aug 1886 in Asseria, Saline Co., Ks., the daughter of William Thomas and Nancy Ellen (Fulton) Montgomery. She declares on the census that both parents born in Pa. On the 1910 census, age 26, a farmer in Walnut Twp., Saline Co., Ks. With him is wife Maud L., age 24, who declares they have been married 3 years and she has born 2 children, both alive at that time.[ED 124, p 61, fam #158/163] The 1920 census shows John, 35, a truck driver living on East __row (unreadable) Ave., Salina, Saline Co., Ks. With him is wife, Lula M., 33, caring for their two children.[ED 148, p 7B, fam #163/191] In his mother's obituary in 1931, and his sister Selena's in 1944, he is of Hutchinson, Ks. John died 19 Sep 1945 in Hutchinson, Reno Co., Ks. In his obituary it states he was "supervisor of the Cary Park." He was a member of the Methodist Church and the Odd Fellows Lodge.[obituary had no newspaper banner] Lula died 17 May 1962 in Hutchinson, Reno Co., Ks, and was buried in Gypsum Hills Cemetery, Salina, Ks. (Family record submitted by Anna C. (Attwater) Jones.)

ISSUE:

+ .1298.1	Dorothy Evelyn RITTGERS, born 4 Dec 1907, died 15 Dec 1985.
+ .1298.2	William Dale Arlington RITTGERS, born 14 Apr 1909, died 13 Jun 1950.

129.A Bertha[4] RITTGERS (Perry[3], Jacob[2], John[1]) was born 19 Dec 1886 in Bridgeport, Saline Co., Ks., the daughter of Perry C. RITTGERS and Myra Jane MORRISON. She is on the 1900 census, age 13, with parents in Liberty Twp., Saline Co., Ks.[ED 118, p 195B, fam #32/32] She married (1) **Grover PEASE** abt 1908. He was born about 1890. On the 1910 census, we find Grover Pease, age 20, farming in Glendale, Saline Co., Ks. With him is wife Bertha, age 23, who reports they have been married 2 years and have no children. They have with them her brother, "hired man" Arthur P. Rittgers, age 16.(#129.C)[ED 128, p 1A, fam #2/2] They moved to Colorado between 1915 and 1920 where we find them on the 1920, census there in Bland Precinct, Elbert Co. Grover, 29, is a farmer on a general farm. Bertha, 32, is caring for their children.[ED 127, p 3A, fam #54/55] Bertha married (2) **George GUY**. In her Mother's obituary, dated 1931, she is called Mrs. Bertha Guy of Colorado Springs, Colo. In sister Selena's obit, 1944, Mrs. George Guy; brother John's obituary, 1945, and Perry's in 1947 she is Mrs. Bertha Guy of Colorado Springs., Co.

ISSUE:

.129A.1   Orrin G. PEASE, born 1910 in Ks. On the 1920 census, he is in Bland Precinct, Elbert Co., Colo., age 9, with parents.[ED 127, p 3A, fam #54/55]

.129A.2   Mary Etta PEASE, born 1912 in Glendale, Saline Co., Ks. She is seen on the 1920 census, Bland Precinct, Elbert Co., Colo., age 6, with parents.[ED 127, p 3A, fam #54/55]

.129A.3   Agnes PEASE, born in Ks.

129.B Jacob⁴ RITTGERS (Perry³, Jacob², John¹) was born 11 Jun 1889 in Bridgeport, Saline Co., Ks., the son of Perry C. RITTGERS and Myra Jane MORRISON. He is on the 1900 census, age 10, with parents in Liberty Twp., Saline Co., Ks.[ED 118, p 195B, 32/32] He married **Nina SURAN** 1910 in Ks. She was born 13 Oct 1886. On the 1910 census, we find Jacob, 20, a farm laborer with his uncle, Peter Rittgers (#12.B). Jacob's wife, Nina, 21, declares they have been married 0 years and she has born 0 children.[ED 54, p 3B, fam #53/53] They are on the 1920 census in Glendale, Saline Co., Ks. He is 36 and a farmer. With him is wife Nina, 33, and two children. Also in the home are niece Katherine Conlin, 12, and nephew Robert Conlin, 9. We have not found this name in our records, so will assume they are from Nina's side of the family.[ED 138, p8A, fam #49/31] In his mother's obituary, dated 1931, he was living in Glendale, Ks. Sister Selena's obituary, 1944, and brother John's obituary, 1945, place him in Detroit, Ks. Brother Perry's obituary, 1947, placed him in Junction City, Ks. [obituary, photocopy submitted with no date or newspaper stated.]Jacob died 7 Dec 1954 in Ogden, Geary Co., Ks., and was buried in Abilene, Dickerson Co., Ks. Nina died 15 May 1965.

ISSUE:

+ .129B.1   Ruth RITTGERS, born 27 Feb 1911, died 18 Jul 1975.
+ .129B.2   Vernon LeRoy RITTGERS, born 29 Oct 1912.
+ .129B.3   Frances RITTGERS, born 16 Jan 1915.
+ .129B.4   Maxine RITTGERS, born 12 Feb 1920.
+ .129B.5   Arletta RITTGERS, born 11 Nov 1922.
+ .129B.6   Kathryn Jean RITTGERS, born 6 Jul 1924.
+ .129B.7   Jacob B. Rittgers, JR., born 30 Jul 1927, died 16 Dec 1974.
+ .129B.8   Darrell RITTGERS, born 28 Feb 1929.

129.C Perry Arthur⁴ RITTGERS (Perry³, Jacob², John¹) was born 23 Jul 1893[SS] in Bridgeport, Saline Co., Ks., the son of Perry C. RITTGERS and Myra Jane MORRISON. He is on the 1900 census, age 6, with parents in Liberty Twp Saline Co., Ks.[ED 118, p 195B, fam #32/32] In 1910 we find him listed twice. He is first found, age 16, with mother, Myra, in Ward 3, Salina, Saline Co., Ks., listed as a farm laborer, "working out."[ED 135, p 2B, fam #47/47] Then we find him with his sister, Bertha (#129.A) and her husband Grover Pease in Glendale, Saline Co., Ks. where he is a "hired hand."[ED 128, p 1A, fam #2/2] He married **Anna REINBOLD** 6 Jun 1915 in Salina, Saline Co., Ks.. She was born 15 Mar 1894. The 1920 census shows "P.A.", 26, a farmer, with wife Anna B., 25, and son Kenneth, 3, in Greely, Saline

Co., Ks.[ED 139, p 2D, fam #46/47] We are told he lived his entire life in Salina, Saline Co., Ks. and died there of a heart attack on 17 Jan 1947[SS] He was buried in Gypsum Hill Cemetery, Salina, Ks. His address is given as 1008 East Ash St.[obituary, photocopy submitted with no date or newspaper I.D] Anna died 18 Mar 1973 in Ks. [SS]

ISSUE:
+ .129C.1   Kenneth Arthur RITTGERS, born 28 Aug 1916, died 30 Apr 1966.
+ .129C.2   Bernard Edward RITTGERS, born 12 Jan 1921.
+ .129C.3   Robert Dean RITTGERS, born 9 Jul 1924.
+ .129C.4   Anna Lee RITTGERS, born 26 Sep 1932.
+ .129C.5   Marlene Rose RITTGERS, born 24 Oct 1935.

129.D William Henry[4] RITTGERS (Perry[3], Jacob[2], John[1]) was born 18 Aug 1897[SS] in Bridgeport, Saline Co., Ks., the son of Perry C. RITTGERS and Myra Jane MORRISON. On the 1910 census, William, age 12, was home with his mother, Myra, in Ward 3, Salina, Saline Co., Ks.[ED 135, p 2B, fam #47/47] He was apparently missed on the 1900 census where we would have expected to find him age 2! He married **Frances UNDERWOOD** about 1917. She was born 22 Jan 1894. We find William, 22, on the 1920 census in Salina, Saline Co., Ks. He is a "butcher - own shop." Frances is 25, and caring for their son. They live at 326 Center St., Saline, Ks.[ED149,p1, fam #4/4] In his mother's obituary, 1931; sister Selena's obituary, 1944, and brother John's obituary, 1945, it is noted that he resides in Wichita, Ks. From his obituary, we learn that William lived first in Hutchinson, Ks., then moved to Wichita in 1929. He was in the grocery business until he retired about 1952. He was a member of the Epworth Methodist Church, and lived at 842 S. Madison, Wichita, Ks. It is noted that he is a "descendant of a Salina Pioneer family."[Submitted with no banner or date] Frances died 11 Sep 1951. William died 8 Nov 1962 [SS] in Wichita, Sedgwick Co., Ks., and was buried in White Chapel Gardens., Wichita, Ks.

ISSUE:
+ .129D.1   William Glea RITTGERS, born 7 Sep 1917, died 19 May 1989.

12C.1 Alva Asbury[4] NOSLER (Esther[3], Jacob[2], John[1]) was born 8 Jan 1867 in Des Moines, Polk Co., Ia., the son of William Henry Harrison NOSLER and Esther May RITTGERS. [LDS-IGI; Ia., 1992, page 6,725] He is seen on the 1870 census, age 3, with parents, Perry, Dallas Twp., Dallas Co., Ia.[p 549, fam #31/31] and on the 1880 census, Healdsburg, Mendocino Twp., Sonoma Co. Calif., age 13, with parents.[ED 128, p 190C, fam #169/169] He married **Alice E. COLTON** 1890 in San Diego, San Diego Co., Calif.[LDS-IGI; Calif, fiche #0067, p 3,650] She was born Mar 1870 in Nev. On the 1900 census, San Diego, San Diego Co., Calif., Alva A., 34, is a "transferman." Wife Alice C., is caring for their three children. She declares her father was born in Nova Scotia, and her mother in England. Also in the home is niece Georgia Long, 4, b. Calif, father b. Mich., mother b. Nev. Assume this is Alice's sister's child.[ED 196, p 7, fam #160/229] Continuing in San Diego in 1910, Alva, 42, is now an Expressman for a lumber company. Alice E., 40, declares they have been married 20 years and she has born 3 children, all alive at this time, and in the home. Their address is given as 2031 "D" Street.[ED 159, p 236, fam #196/236] In 1920 they continue in San Diego. Alva, 52, is now manager of a transfer company. Alice 49, continues to care for family, now grown by presence of daughter-in-law Thelma, wife of Arthur, and granddaughter Betty. Their address is given as 358 21st St.[ED 336, p 8B, fam #186/252]

ISSUE:

.12C1.1   Harry W. NOSLER, born Aug 1890 in San Diego, San Diego Co., Calif. On the
           1900 census, age 9, with parents in San Diego, San Diego Co., Ca.[ED 196, p 11A,
           fam #160/229] and on the 1910 census, age 18, with parents there.[ED 159, p 236,
           fam #196/236] He married Osha ____. She was born about 1888 in Ill. On the 1920
           census, San Diego, Harry is age 28 and a bookkeeper, munitions plant. Wife Osha,
           32, with him. No children shown.[ED 336, p 8B, fam #186/252] She declares her
           father born in Ohio and mother born in Tenn.
+ .12C1.2   Arthur Morrison NOSLER, born Oct 1892.
.12C1.3   Alva Asbury NOSLER, Jr., born May 1896 in San Diego, San Diego Co., Calif.
           [LDS-IGI; Calif, 1992, fiche #0067, page #3,650] Seen on the 1900 census, age 4,
           with parents in San Diego, San Diego Co., Calif.[ED 196, p 11A, fam #160/229]
           On the 1910 census, age 13, with parents there.[ED 159, p 236, fam #196/236] On
           1920 census, age 23, and a "chauffeur, transfer co." in home with parents, San
           Diego.[ED 336, p 8B, fam #186/252]

12C.7 Alberta Evalene[4] NOSLER (Esther[3], Jacob[2], John[1]) was born Feb 1880 in Healdsburg,
Sonoma Co., Ca., the daughter of William Henry Harrison NOSLER and Esther May
RITTGERS. On the 1880 census, age 4/12, with parents, Healdsburg, Mendocino Twp.,
Sonoma Co., Calif.[ED 128, p 14, fam #169/169] She married **Charles T. SKEELS** 1900 in
Coquille, Coos Co., Ore. He was born May 1876 in Ind. On the 1900 census, Coquille, Coos
Co., Ore., Charles, 24, is a day laborer. Alberta, 20, declares they have been married 0 years and
she has born no children.[ED 12, p 9A, 190/192] By the 1910 census, East Coquille, Coos Co.,
Ore., Charles, 34, is a retail merchant, general store. Alberta E., 30, declares they have been
married 10 years and she has born 1 child, that child alive at this time. Also in the home, is
Eugene Nosler, 23, "brother in law" (to head of house, Charles)[ED 55, p 4B, fam #149/153]
On the 1920 census, Colquille, Charles is 43 and a manager of a grocery co. Alberta E., 39, is
caring for their two children. He declares his parents born in Ohio.[ED 126, p14, fam #279/305]
                                          ISSUE:
.12C7.1   Marvel E. SKEELS, born about 1902 in Coquille, Coos Co., Ore. On 1910 census,
           age 8, with parents there[ED 55, p 4B, fam #149/153], and on 1920 census, age 18,
           with parents there.[ED 126, p 14A, #14A, fam #279/305]
.12C7.2   Charles M. SKEELS, born about 1916 in Coquille, Coos Co., Ore. On 1920 census,
           age 4, with parents there.[ED 126, p 14A, #14A, fam #279/305]

12C.9 Eugene Elmer[4] NOSLER (Esther[3], Jacob[2], John[1]) was born 12 Oct 1886 in Healdsburg,
Sonoma Co., Ca., the son of William Henry Harrison NOSLER and Esther May RITTGERS.
[LDS-IGI; Calif., 1992, fiche #0067, page 3,651] He is on the 1900 census, age 13, with father
and stepmother, Coquille, Coos Co., Ore.[ED 12, p 7, fam #148/149] and on the 1910 census,
age 23, with sister Alberta and her husband, Charles Skeels, in Coquille, Coos Co., Ore. He is
a teamster, express wagon.[ED 55, p 4B, fam #149/153] He married **Nina C.** ____ about 1914
in Coos Co., Ore. She was born about 1894 in Minn. Nina reports that her father was born in
Ill., and her mother in New Hampshire. On the 1920 census, age not recorded, Eugene is a
farmer in Cunningham Precinct, Coos Co., Ore. With him is wife Nina C., 26, who is caring for
their son. They are listed on the enumeration last before the "county farm" begins. Everyone at
the "farm" is listed as "inmate"!![ED 116, p 4B, fam #64/65]
                                          ISSUE:

.12C9.1   Elwyn NOSLER, born about 1915 in Coos County, Ore.. On 1920 census, age 5, with his parents there. [ED 116, p 4B, fam # 65/66]

12D.1 William Henry[4] RITTGERS (Henry[3], Jacob[2], John[1]) was born 30 Nov 1873 in Rippey, Greene Co., Ia., the son of Henry C. RITTGERS and Luesia Jennette EDWARDS. He is on the 1880 census, age 6, with parents in Lone Pine, Inyo Co., Ca.[p 503 fam #148/188] He married **Melissa May MERRIAN** 19 Dec 1900 in Ia. She was born about 1889 in Ia. The family story tells us he married in "Robert, Ia." We are told he lived three years at Emmetsburg, Palo Alto Co., Ia, where their first child, Ross, was born. On the 1910 census, they are in Glenwood, Pope Co., Minn. Wm. H., 33, is a "fireman, locomotive". Melissa, 31, declares they have been married 9 years. She has born 4 children, three alive at this time. She states her father born in Ohio and her mother born in NY. [ED 99, p 7B, fam #91/106] We are told William entered the employ of the Soo Railroad as a fireman, later became an engineer, and operated out of Glenwood and Thief River Falls. Later lived at Anoka, Minn, then entered the employment of the Great Northern Railroad at Minneapolis, Minn. William died 6 Feb 1936 in Minneapolis, Minn.

ISSUE:

.12D1.1   Ross Henry RITTGERS, born 1 Oct 1901[SS] in Emmetsburg, Palo Alto Co., Ia. On 1910 census, age 8, with parents in Glenwood, Pope Co., Minn.[ED 99, p 7B, fam #91/106] Ross died 28 Oct 1988 in Altadina, Los Angeles Co., Ca.[SS]
.12D1.2   Charles Edgar RITTGERS, born 6 Feb 1903 in Emmetsburg, Palo Alto Co., Ia., died 19 Feb 1903.
+ .12D1.3   Odessa Fern RITTGERS, born 26 Jun 1904, died June 1942.
+ .12D1.4   Lester Norman RITTGERS, born 22 Jul 1907, died 17 Nov 1966.
+ .12D1.5   Eula Mae RITTGERS.
+ .12D1.6   Kenneth Herbert RITTGERS, born 15 Aug 1913.
.12D1.7   Bernadine RITTGERS, born in Minn.

12D.2 Emma Irene[4] RITTGERS (Henry[3], Jacob[2], John[1]) was born 16 Sep 1875 in Lone Pine, Inyo Co., Calif., the daughter of Henry C. RITTGERS and Luesia Jennette EDWARDS. She is on the 1880 census, age 4, with parents there.[(p 503, fam #148/188] Not seen with parents on 1900 census. She married **George W. THOMPSON** 16 Oct 1902 in Des Moines, Ia.[PVRM, Book 10, p. 262] She and George moved to Rancine, Washington. They also lived in Racine, Wisc., and finally settled in Waukesha, Wisc., a suberb of Milwaukee. Emma died 22 Apr 1943 in Waukesha, Waukesha Co., Wisc..

ISSUE:

.12D2.1   Dorothy Louise THOMPSON, born 7 Sep 1903 in Racine, Racine Co,, Wisc.
.12D2.2   Gladys Irene THOMPSON, born 7 May 1906 in LaCrosse, LaCrosse Co., Wisc.
.12D2.3   Beatrice Evelyn THOMPSON, born 1910 in Racine, Racine Co,, Wisc.

12D.3 John Arthur[4] RITTGERS (Henry[3], Jacob[2], John[1]) was born 4 Feb 1877 in Lone Pine, Inyo Co., Calif., the son of Henry C. RITTGERS and Luesia Jennette EDWARDS. He is on the 1880 Census, age 3, with parents there. [p 503, fam #148/188] In 1900, age 22, and a "fresh fish salesman," he appears with his maternal grandmother, Emma Edwards, in Angus, Union Twp., Boone Co., Ia. Emma Edwards, 69, widow, declares she has born 2 children, one alive at that time. She was born July 1830, in England and immigrated in 1851, being here 48 years.[ED 20, p 9A, fam 174/174] He married **Cora Elizabeth RANDALL** Oct 1904 in Edin Valley, Minn. She was born about 1887 in Minn. He worked for the Soo Rail Road in Minn. On 1910 census, age 32, "car repairer, railway", in Glenwood, Pope Co., Minn. Cora, age 23, b. Minn., states they have been married 5 years. She has born 1 child, living at that time. She states her parents both born in Minn. [ED 99, p 18A, fam #269/316] In 1920 they are still in Glenwood. John, 42, is "car inspector, railroad". Cora, 33, is caring for their 4 children. John died 23 Jan 1941 in Minn.

ISSUE:
.12D3.1   Agnes Emmeline RITTGERS, born 8 May 1907 in Edin Valley, Meeker Co., Minn. Found on the 1910 census, age 2, with parents in Glenwood, Pope Co., Minn.[ED 99, p 18A, fam #269/316] and there with parents in 1920, age 12.[ED 136, p 21A, fam #413/433]
.12D3.2   Lloyd Alvin RITTGERS, born 12 Aug 1911 in Glenwood, Pope Co., Minn. On the 1920 census, age 8, with his parents there.[ED 136, p 21A, fam #413/433]
.12D3.3   Claude Arthur RITTGERS, born 4 Feb 1914 in Glenwood, Pope Co., Minn. On the 1920 census, age 6, with his parents there.[ED 136, p 21A, fam #413/433]
.12D3.4   Donald Melvin RITTGERS, born 4 Aug 1916 in Glenwood, Pope Co., Minn. On the 1920 census, age 3 4/12, with his parents. [ED 136, p 21A, fam #413/433]

12D.4 Lily Magdalene[4] RITTGERS (Henry[3], Jacob[2], John[1]) was born 5 Apr 1881 in Lone Pine, Inyo Co., Calif., the daughter of Henry C. RITTGERS and Luesia Jennette EDWARDS. She is on the 1900 census, age 19, with her parents in Emmetsburg, Palo Alto Co., Ia. Her birth date given on census is Jan 1881.[ED 151, p 12A, fam #22/22] She married **George W. TRESLER** 25 Nov 1902. She and her husband lived in Glenwood, Minn., until 1915, when they moved to a farm near Walker, Minn. They were living there in the 1940's.

ISSUE:
.12D4.1   Walter Earl TRESLER, born 31 Aug 1903 in Glenwood, Pope Co., Minn.
.12D4.2   Edith Bernice TRESLER, born 12 Mar 1905 in Glenwood, Pope Co., Minn.
.12D4.3   Harry Edward TRESLER, born 16 Feb 1908 in Glenwood, Pope Co., Minn.
.12D4.4   Hazel Marie TRESLER, born 7 Mar 1909 in Glenwood, Pope Co., Minn.
.12D4.5   Glen Orville TRESLER, born in Glenwood, Pope Co., Minn.
.12D4.6   Floyd Alvin TRESLER, born in Glenwood, Pope Co., Minn.
.12D4.7   Ralph TRESLER, born in Glenwood, Pope Co., Minn.
.12D4.8   Harold TRESLER, born in Glenwood, Pope Co., Minn.
.12D4.9   Violet Irene TRESLER, born in Glenwood, Pope Co., Minn.
.12D4.A   George W. Tresler, JR., born in Glenwood, Pope Co., Minn.
.12D4.B   Roy Henry TRESLER, born in Glenwood, Pope Co., Minn.
.12D4.C   Clarence TRESLER, born in Glenwood, Pope Co., Minn.

12D.5 Harry Edwards[4] RITTGERS (Henry[3], Jacob[2], John[1]) was born 13 Jan 1884[SS] in Lone Pine, Inyo Co., Calif., the son of Henry C. RITTGERS and Luesia Jennette EDWARDS. He is on the 1900 census, age 16, with his parents in Emmetsburg, Palo Alto Co., Ia.[ED 151, p 12A, fam #22/22] Harry graduated 1903 from Glenwood, Minn., High School and attended the U. of Minn., taking business courses and shorthand. He married (1) **Ruth IWEN** 15 Dec 1907 in Minot, Ward, N.D. She died 28 Jun 1909. We are told "He worked for R.A. Neston in Minot, N.D., who later became governor of N.D. He was a court reporter then, but later studied law and was admitted to the bar June 1913. Harry practiced Law in Jamestown, Stutsman Co., and was District Court Reporter of the District Court, until April 1919. Since that time he solely engaged in Law." Harry married (2) **Ethel HEALY**. She was born 1888. On the 1920 census,

Jamestown, Stutsman Co., Minn., age 35, "Lawyer, office in city". With him is wife Ethel, 32, caring for the two children we are told they adopted, as well as Mrs. Bell Healey, Mother in Law., age 58, b. Canada. Bell declares her parents both born in Canada. Bell further states she immigrated in 1883 and is naturalized. Their address is given as 420 2nd Ave., N., in Jamestown.[ED 239, p 9, fam #168/188] "For about 10 years, 1922-1932, was in practice with John W. Garr, later Lt. Governor of N.D. During this time he was also assistant State's Attorney for the County of Stutsman, and then City Attorney for Jamestown, N.D. Ethel died 8 Jan 1935. Harry married (3) **Cytella DAHN** 27 Mar 1937. She was born 3 Oct 1900.[SS] She was an attorney, having attended law school in Minneapolis. We are told she "earned her own way being an efficient stenographer and accountant." She was admitted to the bar in June 1934, and has been the official court reporter of the district court. Her parents were of German descent, and farmers near Jamestown, having lived prior to that near Madison, Wisc. about 1909. He practiced alone until 1941, when he took in a new partner. Harry died Dec 1971 in ND.[SS] Cytella died May 1978 in Stutsman County, ND.[SS]

ISSUE of Harry and Ruth:

.12D5.1   Ruth RITTGERS, born 1 Oct 1908 in Larimore, Grand Forks Co., N.D.

ISSUE adopted by Harry and Ethel:

.12D5.2   Paul Ernest RITTGERS, born 19 Jul 1917 in Larrimore, Grand Forks Co., N.D.,
           died 25 Nov 1988 in Tillamook Co., Ore. On 1920 census, age 2 5/12, with parents
           in Jamestown, Stutsman Co., ND.[ED 239, p 9B, fam #168/188]   Believed to be
           the Paul Rittgers listed on Social Security Death Index, b. 9 Aug 1917. Obtained
           S.S. # in Oregon and death benefit sent to Oregon. D. 25 Nov 1988.

.12D5.3   Mildred RITTGERS, born 10 Aug 1919 in Larrimore, Grand Forks Co,, N.D., died
           14 Aug 1922 in Larrimore, Grand Forks Co., N.D. On 1920 census, age 4/12, with
           parents in Jamestown, Stutsman Co., N.D. [ED 239, p 9B, fam #168/188]

12D.8 Joe Ross[4] RITTGERS (Henry[3], Jacob[2], John[1]) was born 11 May 1888 in Rippey, Greene Co., Ia., the son of Henry C. RITTGERS and Luesia Jennette EDWARDS. On the 1900 census, age 12, with parents in Emmetsburg, Palo Alto Co., Ia.[ED 151, p 12A, fam #22/22] He married **Georgia Anna DOBBINS**. He and Georgia lived in Emmetsburg, Ia., and later in Glenwood, Minn. He was a farmer and stockman.

ISSUE:

.12D8.1   Clarice Louise RITTGERS, born 26 Jan 1916. She married Russell BUCHOLZ.
           Russell and Clarice live in Glenwood, Minn.

.12D8.2   Doris Ann RITTGERS, born 8 Aug 1924. She married _____ DUTCHAK.

.12D8.3   Bruce RITTGERS. He married Grace.

+ .12D8.4   Orville Thomas RITTGERS, born 7 Oct 1930.

12E.1 Almeda Catharine[4] RITTGERS (Daniel[3], Jacob[2], John[1]) was born 9 Aug 1881 in Greene Co, Ia., the daughter of Daniel R. RITTGERS and Mary Ann FRY.[GVRB, p 13; taken from p 29 of original book, entry #376] She married **Orsanus W. YOUNG** 18 Mar 1909. On the 1910 census, Orsanus, 27, is in Rippy, Greene Co., Ia., where he is a farmer. Wife Almeda, 28, declares they have been married 1 year and she has born no children. In the home is one Martin J. Kopf, 36, laborer, who was born in Iowa to German parents. Also in the home, with no designation, is George Reynolds, 10, born in S.D., but parents' birthplace not given.[ED 106, p. 11B; fam #240/243] On 1920 census, Washington Twp., Greene Co., Ia., Orsanus, 37, is a farmer on a general farm. Almeda, 39, is caring for their son.[ED 118, p 3B, fam #66/66] Family story reports she lived on the home farm near Rippey. Orsanus died 27 Dec 1955. Almeda died Mar 1971[SS]. Her last given address was Perry, Dallas Co., Ia.[SS]

ISSUE:
.12E1.1 Infant YOUNG, born 5 Oct 1913, died in in infancy.
.12E1.2 Orsanus Young, JR., born 30 Nov 1917, died 23 Apr 1919.
+ .12E1.3 Bryan O. YOUNG, born 10 Sep 1919.
+ .12E1.4 Wallace YOUNG, born 4 Mar 1922.
+ .12E1.5 Mary Ella YOUNG, born 6 May 1925.

12E.2 Burton A.[4] RITTGERS (Daniel[3], Jacob[2], John[1]) was born 10 Feb 1884[SS] in Rippey, Greene Co., Ia., the son of Daniel R. RITTGERS and Mary Ann FRY. He is on the 1910 census, age 26, with parents in Rippey, Greene Co., Ia.[ED 106, p 5B, Fam # 116/118] He married **Effie Mae FORD** 16 Mar 1911. She was born 1888 [RGrCem, p 39] in Ia. On the 1920 census, we see Burton, age 35, in Paton, Greene Co., Ia., farming. Wife Effie, 31, is caring for the home. We are told he was a stockman all his life. Effie died 1963 in Greene Co., Ia. On her tombstone we are told there is an Eastern Star Emblem.[RGrCem, p 39] Burton died Aug 1966 in Rippey, Greene Co., Ia. On his tombstone is a Mason emblem. He and Effie, with Baby Albert, are buried in Lot 6, Block Nine, Rippey Cemetery.[SS; RGrCem, p 39]

ISSUE:
+ .12E2.1 Alice Almeda RITTGERS, born 21 Dec 1911.
.12E2.2 Albert RITTGERS, born 7 Feb 1921, died 10 Feb 1921. Buried with his parents. Stone reads "Baby Albert."[RGrCem, p 39]

12E.3 Grover C.[4] RITTGERS (Daniel[3], Jacob[2], John[1]) was born 9 May 1890 in Rippey, Greene Co., Ia., the son of Daniel R. RITTGERS and Mary Ann FRY. He is on 1910 census, age 19, Rippey, Washington Twp., Greene Co., Ia., with parents.[ED 106, p 5B, fam #116/118] He married **Nellie GROVES** about 1913. She was born 26 Oct 1891.[SS] On the 1920 census, age 29, farming in Washington Twp., Greene Co., Ia. With him is wife Nellie, age 28, caring for their daughter.[ED 118, p 4B, fam #94/94] Grover was a farmer and a stockman. He died 1945 in Greene Co., and Nellie died 19 Jan 1991 in Greene Co., Ia. They are buried in Rippey Cem., Greene Co., Ia. On his tombstone in Lot 1, Block Nine, of Rippey Cemetery we are told there is a Masonic Emblem.[RGrCem, p. 38]

ISSUE:
+ .12E3.1 Mary Zetta RITTGERS, born 1 Oct 1914.

12H.1 Horace B.[4] RITTGERS (Benjamin[3], Jacob[2], John[1]) was born 1 Aug 1892[SS] in Rolfe, Pocahontas Co., Ia., the son of Benjamin Franklin RITTGERS and Iora McCLUNE. He is on the 1900 census, age 7 with parents in Des Moines Twp., Pocahontas Co., Ia.[ED 167, p 56, fam #184/187] He is age 26, with his parents in Des Moines Twp., Pocahontas Co., Ia. on 1920 census, farming at home. It is noted that he is divorced.[ED 208, p 1A, fam #3/3]We don't have the name of his first wife. He married **Phyllis Mildred TURNER** 1927. She was born 20 Jan 1895.[SS] He lived near Gilmore City, Pocahontas Co., Ia., but his residence at the time he died was in West Bend, Palo Alto Co., Ia. Horace died Jul 1976[SS], and was buried in Pocahontas County, Ia. Phyllis died 15 Jul 1990.[SS]

ISSUE:
+ .12H1.1 Benjamin Joseph RITTGERS, born 3 Apr 1933.

12H.2 Clara Catherine[4] RITTGERS (Benjamin[3], Jacob[2], John[1]) was born 14 Aug 1894 in Rolfe, Pocahontas Co., Ia., the daughter of Benjamin Franklin RITTGERS and Iora McCLUNE. She is on the 1900 census, age 6 with parents in Des Moines Twp., Pocahontas Co., Ia.[ED 167, p 56, fam #184/187], and age 25, with her parents in Des Moines Twp., Pocahontas Co., Ia. on 1920 census. She is a "teacher - public school."[ED 208, p 1A, fam #3/3] She married **Ora P. ALBERTS** 16 Jun 1920. They lived on a "fine farm" near Pocahontas, Ia., the family story tells us. Clara was active in the Rebecca Lodge and served as "Noble Grand". Ora died 1969. Clara died Sept 1987[SS], and was buried in Pocahontas Co., Ia.

ISSUE:
+ .12H2.1   Arlene LaVonne ALBERTS, born 16 Feb 1925.

12H.3 Hattie Lovina[4] RITTGERS (Benjamin[3], Jacob[2], John[1]) was born 22 Oct 1897 in Rolfe, Pocahontas Co., Ia., daughter of Benjamin Franklin RITTGERS and Iora McCLUNE. She is on the 1900 census, age 2 with parents in Des Moines Twp., Pocahontas Co., Ia.[ED 167, p 56, fam #184/187] She is age 22, with her parents there on 1920 census, listed as a "teacher - public school."[ED 208, p 1A, fam #3/3] In her obituary, submitted without a newsbanner, it is reported that she graduated from "Plover High School and taught rural schools in Pocahontas Co." She married **Otto John NAEVE** 1930 in Ft. Dodge, Ia. He was born 7 May 1899. Hattie and Otto had a farm near Humbolt, in Corinth Twp., Pocahontas Co., Ia. Otto died 23 Dec 1988 in Humbolt, Ia. Hattie died 11 May 1995 in Humbolt, Pocahontas Co., Ia., and was buried in Pocahontas Co., Ia.

ISSUE:
+ .12H3.1   Richard Allen NAEVE, born 24 Oct 1930.
+ .12H3.2   Philip Frederick NAEVE, born 12 Oct 1932.
+ .12H3.3   Keith Lowell NAEVE, born 28 May 1938.

12H.4 Coral Martha[4] RITTGERS (Benjamin[3], Jacob[2], John[1]) was born 15 Jul 1899[SS] in Rolfe, Pocahontas Co., Ia., the daughter of Benjamin Franklin RITTGERS and Iora McCLUNE. She is on the 1900 census, age 11/12 with parents in Des Moines Twp., Pocahontas Co., Ia.[ED 167, p 56, fam #184/187] She is age 20, with her parents there on the 1920 census, listed as a "teacher - public school."[ED 208, p 1A, fam #3/3] She married **Alfred J. BREIHOLZ** 4 Feb 1923. They lived on a farm in northern Iowa. Coral died 14 Feb 1995[SS], and was buried in Pocahontas County, Ia.

ISSUE:
+ .12H4.1   Delores Marie BREIHOLZ, born 12 Jul 1926.
+ .12H4.2   Robert Alfred BREIHOLZ, born 19 Apr 1931.

12H.5 Frank Elmer[4] RITTGERS (Benjamin[3], Jacob[2], John[1]) was born 24 Jul 1901[SS] in Rolfe, Pocahontas Co., Ia., the son of Benjamin Franklin RITTGERS and Iora McCLUNE. He is age 18, with parents in Des Moines Twp., Pocahontas Co., Ia. on 1920 census.[ED 208, p 1A, fam #3/3] He married **Lucy (Reyburn) HARTLEY** 23 Apr 1929. She was born 10 Sep 1904 in Pocahontas, Pocahontas Co., Ia., the daughter of Frank and Arcana Celestia (Pascal) Reyburn. She married (1) Myron L. Hartley, and had daughter Darlene Cecilia Hartley, b. 15 Sept 1924 in Dewitt, Clinton Co., Ia. Darlene married Donald G. Hudek, 27 July 1946. Frank and Lucy lived near Pocahontas, Ia., but may have spent time in Arizona, as his social security card was issued there. He was a farmer in Pocahontas Co., Ia. They were Methodists. Frank died 19 Oct

1991[SS], and was buried in Pocahontas, Pocahontas Co., Ia.[Family record submitted by Darlene (Hartley) Hudek.]
ISSUE:
+ .12H5.1 Laura Jean RITTGERS, born 11 Oct 1933.
+ .12H5.2 Iora Kay RITTGERS, born 2 Oct 1942.
+ .12H5.3 Mary Ann RITTGERS, born 1 Sep 1944.

12H.6 Ernest J.[4] RITTGERS (Benjamin[3], Jacob[2], John[1]) was born 26 Feb 1903[SS] in Rolfe, Pocahontas Co., Ia., the son of Benjamin Franklin RITTGERS and Iora McCLUNE. He is age 15, with parents in Des Moines Twp., Pocahontas Co., Ia. on 1920 census.[ED 208, p 1A, fam #3/3] He married **Leila Alice GILLELAND** 1926. He and Lila farmed near Havelock, Ia. Ernest died 13 Sep 1994[SS], and was buried in Pocahontas Co., Ia.
ISSUE:
+ .12H6.1 Roland Dale RITTGERS, born 26 Dec 1926.
+ .12H6.2 Wanda Lucerne RITTGERS, born 22 Jul 1928.

12H.8 Ruth Iora[4] RITTGERS (Benjamin[3], Jacob[2], John[1]) was born 6 Jun 1907 in Rolfe, Pocahontas Co., Ia., the daughter of Benjamin Franklin RITTGERS and Iora McCLUNE. She is age 12, with parents in Des Moines Twp., Pocahontas Co., Ia. on 1920 census.[ED 208, p 1A, fam #3/3] She married **Earl Jones COOKSEY** 1933. He was born 13 Aug 1906.[SS] Earl and Ruth had a farm near Pocahontas, Pocahontas Co., Ia. He died Nov 1987, with his last known address given as Spirit Lake, Dickinson Co., Ia.[SS] In sister Hattie's obituary, 1995, it is said that she is living in Arnolds Park, Ia., called "Ruth Reis."
ISSUE:
+ .12H8.1 Larry Lee COOKSEY, born 18 Jul 1940.

12H.A Jacob B.[4] RITTGERS (Benjamin[3], Jacob[2], John[1]) was born 10 Apr 1911 in Rolfe, Pocahontas Co., Ia., the son of Benjamin Franklin RITTGERS and Iora McCLUNE. He is age 8, with parents in Des Moines Twp., Pocahontas Co., Ia. on 1920 census.[ED 208, p 1A, fam #3/3] He married **Jeane SCHEFFERS** 1935. Jacob was a farmer and stockman and lived on the home farm in Rolfe, Pocahontas Co., Ia. We see "Jake B." listed in the 1969 Pocahontas Co. Farm and Ranch Directory. In sister Hattie's obituary, 1995, it is said he is living in Rolfe, Ia. A family story reports he traveled to the area north of Rolfe in a covered wagon. Jacob is buried in Pocahontas Co., Ia.
ISSUE:
+ .12HA.1 Donald Eugene RITTGERS, born 29 May 1936.
+ .12HA.2 Joan Kay RITTGERS, born 5 Jun 1938.
+ .12HA.3 Allen Lee RITTGERS, born 20 Feb 1940.

12H.B Robert Woodrow[4] RITTGERS (Benjamin[3], Jacob[2], John[1]) was born 15 Mar 1913 in Rolfe, Pocahontas Co., Ia., the son of Benjamin Franklin RITTGERS and Iora McCLUNE. He is age 6, with parents in Des Moines Twp., Pocahontas Co., Ia. on 1920 census.[ED 208, p 1A, fam #3/3] He married **Beulah Maureen CHRISTENSEN** Jun 1934 in Bridgegate, Ia. She was born 10 Jan 1915 in Bridgegate, Ia. Robert was a farmer and stockman and lived on the home farm in Rolfe. In sister Hattie's obituary, 1995, it is said he is living in Humbolt, Ia. Robert died, and was buried in Rolfe, Pocahontas, Ia.
ISSUE:

+ .12HB.1   Janet Katherine RITTGERS, born 19 Dec 1934.
+ .12HB.2   Barbara Jean RITTGERS, born 9 Dec 1936.
+ .12HB.3   Jon Curtis RITTGERS, born 9 May 1940.

12J.1 Glen Edwin⁴ RITTGERS (George³, Jacob², John¹) was born 7 Feb 1894 in Rippey, Greene Co., Ia., the son of George McClellan RITTGERS and Julia LAMB.[GrVRB, Vol 2, entry #3641] On the 1900 census, he is age 5, with parents there. [ED 97, p 7A, fam #187/187] Still with parents in 1910 in Dawson Twp., Greene Co., Ia. He is age 16, and a farmer.[ED 93, p 6A, fam #75/75] He married (1) **Laura N. SEXTON** 24 Dec 1915. She was born 1888 in Ia.[PGrCem, p 28] In 1920 we find him, age 26, farming in Paton, Greene Co., Ia. With him is wife "Nora", 29, caring for their children. She declares that her father was born in England and her mother born in NY.[ED 116, p 7A, fam #50/50] Laura died 1923 in Ia., and was buried in Paton Twp. Cemetery, Greene Co., Ia.[PGrCem, p 28] Glen married (2) **Hazel OWEN** 21 Aug 1930. She was born 1901. Hazel died 18 Jul 1936.[PGrCem, p 28] Glen died 1959 in Paton, Greene Co., Ia. Glen, Nora (called Laura M. on the tombstone) and Hazel E. are all buried in Lot 18 of Block Fourteen, Paton Twp. Cemetery. They resided in Mason City, Ia. [PGrCem, p 28]

ISSUE of Glen and Laura:
.12J1.1   Glendora Veda RITTGERS, born 2 Jan 1917 in Paton, Greene Co., Ia. On 1920 census, age 2 4/12, with parents there.[ED 116, p 7A, fam #50/50]
+ .12J1.2   Maynard LeRoy RITTGERS, born 5 Feb 1918.
.12J1.3   Marion RITTGERS, born 1920, died 1920, and was buried in Paton Twp. Cemetery, Greene Co., Ia.
.12J1.4   Beth Marie RITTGERS, born 30 Aug 1922 in Ankeney, Polk Co., Ia.
ISSUE of Glen and Hazel:
.12J1.5   Owen Arnett RITTGERS, born 1 Jul 1933 in Cerro Gordo County, Ia.

12J.3 Bessie Elizabeth⁴ RITTGERS (George³, Jacob², John¹) was born 8 Jan 1897 in Rippey, Greene Co., Ia., the daughter of George McClellan RITTGERS and Julia LAMB. She is on the 1900 census, age 2, with parents there.[ED 97, p 7A, fam 187/187] With parents on 1910 census, age 12, in Dawson, Twp., Greene Co., Ia.[ED 93, p 6A, fam #75/75] She married **Roy Dennison GAYLORD** 30 May 1918.

ISSUE:
+ .12J3.1   Joyce Georgette GAYLORD, born 3 Jan 1922.
+ .12J3.2   Roy Dennison GAYLORD, Jr., born 3 May 1924.

12J.4 Gertrude Mary Bernice⁴ RITTGERS (George³, Jacob², John¹) was born 17 Jul 1899 in Rippey, Greene Co., Ia., the daughter of George McClellan RITTGERS and Julia LAMB. On 1900 census, age 6/12 (6 months) with parents there.[ED 97, p 7A, fam 187/187] With parents on 1910 census, age 10, in Dawson, Greene Co., Ia.[ED 93, p 6A, fam #75/75] Still in Dawson with parents on 1920 census, age 20.[ED 102, p 1A, fam #4/3] She married **Ivil L. PORTER** 16 Oct 1920. Gertrude died Sept 1985, with her last known address, Owenton, Owen Co., Ky.[SS]

ISSUE:
.12J4.1   Ivil L. Porter, Jr., born 18 Jun 1922, died Nov 1973.[SS]
.12J4.2   Gerald Allison PORTER, born 23 Jan 1924 in Greene Co., Ia.
.12J4.3   Patricia Jane PORTER, born 17 Jul 1926 in Greene Co., Ia.

12J.6 Lloyd Ellison[4] RITTGERS (George[3], Jacob[2], John[1]) was born 12 Apr 1901[SS] in Rippey, Greene Co., Ia., the son of George McClellan RITTGERS and Julia LAMB. A twin to Floyd, he is on the 1910 census, age 9, in Dawson Twp., Greene Co., Ia.[ED 93, p 6A, fam #75/75] Still with parents in Dawson on 1920 census, age 18.[ED 103, p 1A, fam #4/3] He married **Margaret Ann TUCKER** 27 Oct 1927 in Mason City, Cerro Gordo Co., Ia. She was born 14 May 1907 in Grand Junction, Greene Co., Ia., the daughter of Frank and Ruth (Herrick) Tucker. Lloyd was a farmer in central Iowa. They were Methodists. Lloyd died 20 Jan 1988 in Jefferson, Greene Co., Ia., and Margaret died there 15 Feb 1992[SS]. [Family group sheet submitted by Maureen (Canavan) Rittgers]

ISSUE:

+ .12J6.1   Dick Duane RITTGERS, born 15 Jul 1933.

12K.1 Raymond[4] RITTGERS (Andrew[3], Jacob[2], John[1]) was born 12 Mar 1903[SS] in Polk Co., Ia., son of Andrew Johnson RITTGERS and Virginia "Jennie" BEER. He is with his parents on 1910 census, age 7, in Webster Twp., Polk Co. Ia.[ED 184, p 8A, fam #87/87] Continues with parents there, age 16, on 1920 census.[ED 187, p 12B, fam #196/198] He married **Dorothy Evelyn McCORMICK** 31 Jul 1929. She was born 4 Sep 1906 in Boone Co., Ia. Her parents were listed on the Boone Co. Tax lists, as George W. and Evelyn (Warren) McCormick. [BPTx, p 550] We see him on the poll tax list for Boone Co. residing in Union Twp., Boone Co. in 1934. Raymond died Jan 1971[SS] in Dallas Co., Ia.

ISSUE:

.12K1.1   Doris Jean RITTGERS, born 10 Feb 1936 in Polk Co., Ia.
.12K1.2   Marvin Eugene RITTGERS, born 10 Jan 1938 in Polk Co., Ia..
.12K1.3   Patricia Rae RITTGERS, born 16 Mar 1940 in Polk Co., Ia..
.12K1.4   Linda Lee RITTGERS, born 28 Dec 1944 in Des Moines, Polk Co., Ia.
.12K1.5   Eric Raymond RITTGERS, born 19 Dec 1947 in Des Moines, Polk Co., Ia.

12K.2 Anthony Theodore[4] RITTGERS (Andrew[3], Jacob[2], John[1]) was born 13 Feb 1905[SS] in Johnston, Polk Co., Ia., the son of Andrew Johnson RITTGERS and Virginia "Jennie" BEER. On the 1910 census, age 5, with parents in Webster, Polk Co., Ia.[ED 184, p 8A, fam #87/87] On 1920 census, age 14, with parents in Webster.[ED 187, p 12B, fam #196/198] He married **Florence THOMPSON** 1 Dec 1939.PVRM, book 30, p 258. She was born 13 Dec 1909. We find in the 1948 Polk Co. Farm Directory, p. 148, we see he owns "50 acres, (Rockaway Beach)" It also reports that he is a general farmer and owns a 1937 ford car. Lists children as "Ronald, 5 and Anthony, Jr. 3." Florence died, and was buried in Rittgers Cem., Johnston, Ia., no dates on her stone. Anthony died 23 Oct 1995 in Johnston, Polk Co., Ia, and was buried in Rittgers Cemetery, Johnston, Ia. After his death, the 37 acres that his home sat on was sold to developers. A young couple in the area had admired that house for years and when it was offered to them if they would move it, they jumped at the chance. It almost didn't come into their possession, as they couldn't find a suitable spot to move it to. Finally, with the deadline for demolition looming on the horizon, they located a piece of property on the other side of Beaver Creek, about a mile from its original location. The local newspaper, the Johnston News and Johnston Advance, have several articles about the home and its move, complete with pictures in the June 13, 1996 edition.

ISSUE:

.12K2.1   Ronald Roosevelt RITTGERS, born 14 Aug 1942.
+ .12K2.2   Anthony Johnson RITTGERS, born 2 Feb 1945.

12K.3 Robert Johnson[4] **RITTGERS** (Andrew[3], Jacob[2], John[1]) was born 10 Oct 1907[SS] in Johnston, Polk Co., Ia., the son of Andrew Johnson RITTGERS and Virginia "Jennie" BEER. [PVRB, book 6, p 97] On the 1910 census, age 2, with parents in Webster, Polk Co., Ia.[ED 184, p 8A, fam #87/87], and on the 1920 census, age 12, with parents there.[ED 187, p 12B, fam #196/198] He married (1) **Cecil "Marjorie" SNYDER** 12 Jun 1931; they divorced.[PVRM, p 52, from book 30 of marriages, p.258] Robert married (2) **Florence BANNING**. He was a farmer, and lived on the original land owned by Jacob Rittgers, Johnston, Ia. Robert died Jul 1975[SS] in Jacksonville, Duval Co., Fla., and was buried in Rittgers Cemetery, Johnston, Ia. Florence's name is also on the stone.

ISSUE of Robert and Marjorie:
+ .12K3.1   Mary Ann RITTGERS, born 8 Feb 1932.
+ .12K3.2   Carol Virginia RITTGERS, born 16 Apr 1933.

ISSUE of Robert and Florence:
.12K3.3   Robin Andrew RITTGERS, born in Johnston, Polk Co., Ia. He is a medical doctor.
+ .12K3.4   Rex Van RITTGERS.
.12K3.5   Dixie Lynn RITTGERS, born in Johnston, Polk Co,, Ia.
.12K3.6   R. John RITTGERS.

12K.4 Pauline Elfreda[4] **RITTGERS** (Andrew[3], Jacob[2], John[1]) was born 26 Feb 1910 in Johnston, Polk Co., Ia., the daughter of Andrew Johnson RITTGERS and Virginia "Jennie" BEER.[PVRB, book 6, p 97] On the 1910 census, age 2/12, with parents in Webster, Polk Co., Ia.[ED 184, p 8A, fam #87/87], and on 1920 census, age 9, with parents there.[ED 187, p 12B, fam #196/198] She married **Clifford Donald BLOOM** 7 Sep 1936. He was born 29 Aug 1908(SS gives birth of 27 Jan 1908). Pauline died 2 Feb 1994. Her last known address was Dunn Co., Wisc.[SS] Clifford died 1 Dec 1994.[SS]

ISSUE:
+ .12K4.1   Barry Clifford BLOOM, born 2 Nov 1942.
+ .12K4.2   Robert Jay BLOOM, born 17 Apr 1946.

12L.2 Olah Irene[4] **TIARA** (Lily[3], Jacob[2], John[1]) was born 15 Aug 1900, the daughter of William TIARA and Lily RITTGERS. She married **Lt. A. M. HARVEY** before 1928. At the time of their marriage, he was a Lieut. in the U.S. Navy. Anna Lou Arnett shares with us that Irene lived in Grass Valley, Ca. She died 9 Nov 1990 in Sacramento County, Ca. [Calif. Death Records, Reg. #6765, fil #177831; submitted by Anna Lou (Peacock) Arnett]

ISSUE:
.12L2.1   Hoover Revere HARVEY.

134.1 Anna "Jane"[4] **RITTGERS** (Tobias[3], John, Jr.[2], John[1]) was born 6 Mar 1856 in Marion Twp., Hocking Co,, Oh., the daughter of Tobias RITTGERS and Phebe WILLIAMS. She is on the 1860 census, age 4, with parents, Marion Twp., Logan Post Office, Hocking Co., Oh.[p 149, fam # 913/901] Age 14 with parents in Marion, 1870 census.[p. 54, fam #277/280] She married **Noah WOLFE** 23 Mar 1877 in Hocking County, Oh.[HVRM, book D, p 285] On 1880 census, Monday Creek, Perry Co., Oh., we see Noah Wolf, 26, a laborer, b. Ohio. With him is wife "Jane", 24, caring for the children. Three listed, but Rosa is not among them, as family records report. It could be she was born after the census.[ED 212, p 32, fam #303/303] Anna died 9 Apr 1882 in Hocking Co., Oh. [Family group sheet submitted by James F. Rittgers]

In her mother's estate, 1888, we find that Noah is guardian of Cora, Oscar, and Rosa. He signs off on the children's right to property due Anna and is paid for it.

ISSUE:

.1341.1 Cora B. WOLFE, born about 1877 in Monday Creek, Perry Co., Oh. On 1880 census, age 3, with parents there. [ED 212, p 32, fam 303/303]

.1341.2 Oscar D. WOLFE, born about 1878 in Monday Creek, Perry Co., Oh. On 1880 census, age 2, with parents there. [ED 212, p 32, fam 303/303]

.1341.3 Myrtle WOLFE, born Mar 1880 in Monday Creek, Perry Co., Oh. On 1880 census, age 2 mo, with parents there.[ED 212, p 32, fam 303/303] Not mentioned in grand mother's estate, 1888.

.1341.4 Rosa M. WOLFE, born after 1880, most probably in Monday Creek, Perry, Oh. She married _____ STARR. Named in grandmother's estate, 1888.

134.2 William Franklin[4] RITTGERS (Tobias[3], John, Jr.[2], John[1]) was born 2 Jul 1857 in Marion Twp., Hocking Co,, Oh., the son of Tobias RITTGERS and Phebe WILLIAMS. He is on the 1860 census, age 2, with parents there.(p 149, fam # 913/901) Age 13 with parents in Marion Twp. on the 1870 census.[p. 54, fam #277/280] He married **Melissa STIMMEL**, 1877, in Perry Co., Oh. In 1880, Franklin, 21, is a limestone miner, living in Monday Creek, Perry Co., Oh. Wife Melissa, 23, is caring for their daughter.[ED 212, p 207A, fam #233/233] We see he and Melissa signing off on the deed of sale of his father's property, following his mother's death in 1888. On the 1900 census, Frank, 42, a Blast Furnace Boss., with wife Melissa, 44. They have been married 22 years. She has born 2 children, one living. They live next door to daughter Emma, and her husband Charles Lanning, in Falls Twp., Hocking Co., Oh.[ED 26, p 1A, fam #12/12] He is listed in his mother's estate, 1901, Hocking Co., Oh. In 1910, Frank, 52, is a merchant, general store. "Malissa," 53, declares they have been married 32 years, and she has born 2 children, one living at this time. Daughter Emma and her husband and son are in the home with them.[ED 82, p 17A, fam #364/364] The 1920 census shows Frank, 62, and "Malissa", 63, living in Falls Twp., Hocking Co., Oh. With them are daughter Emma and husband Charles Lanning, and grandson, Franklin L., age 20. Both "Frank" and Charles Lanning declare they are miners in the coal mine. They live on the Logan-Straitsville Rd. [ED 37, p. 16B, fam #364/367] William died 24 Aug 1930 in Falls Twp., Hocking Co,, Oh.[Family group sheet submitted by James F. Rittgers] In his estate #3417, he names daughter Emma as administrator. In his estate, it reports he owned a house and 3 lots on Hunter and E. Main St., Logan, Oh., with a value of $3000. His estate amounts to $8200 after his house is sold. Emma was awarded $1500 to care for Melissa.

ISSUE:

+ .1342.1 Emma RITTGERS, born May 1878.

134.4 Isaac W.[4] RITTGERS (Tobias[3], John, Jr.[2], John[1]) was born 14 Apr 1860 in Marion Twp., Hocking Co., Oh., the son of Tobias RITTGERS and Phebe WILLIAMS. He is on the 1860 census, age 3/12, with parents, Marion Twp., Logan Post Office, Hocking Co., Oh.[p 149, fam # 913/901] Age 9 with parents in Marion, 1870 census [p. 54, fam #277/280], and age 18, with parents in 1880.[p 109C, fam #244/247] He married **Nancy Alice POLING** 30 Sep 1889 in Fairfield Co., Oh. She was born May 1865 in Oh., the daughter of John and Elizabeth Ann (Short) Poling. In 1890 he is named as guardian of his minor brothers, "Therew" and Abraham. He signs off their portion of the deed selling his father's property. Isaac and Alice signed off their own portion of the deed. The 1900 census shows Isaac, 40, a farmer in Rush Creek,

Fairfield Co., Oh. Wife Alice N., 35, declares they have been married 12 years and she has born 5 children, all alive at this time.[ED 12, p 308B, fam #256/257] In 1910, we find them still in Rush Creek, on Startsville and Hobbs Summit Rds. Isaac is "47" and still farming. "Mary Alice", 44, declares they have been married 21 years. She has born 10 children, 8 alive at this time.[ED 76, p 3B, fam # 68/69] The 1920 census shows Isaac, 59, and wife "N. Alice", 54, with the last four children. They are still on the farm in Rush Creek Twp., Fairfield Co., Oh. [ED 30, p 10B, fam #245/247] We are told by grandson Richard C. Rittgers, (#1344A.1) that Isaac lived on the farm of his father, Tobias, all his life. It was 80 acres of rich farmland in a "pie" shape that straddled the Fairfield-Hocking Counties line. Because we find them listed on the census as a family in Rush Creek, Fairfield Co., we will use this as their location. To confuse matters, when Isaac was a child, we find them, on the family farm, listed in Marion Twp., Hocking Co.! It could be determined by where their house was located on the property, too. Isaac died 26 Feb 1934 in Rush Creek, Fairfield Co., Oh., and was buried 1 Mar 1934 in S. Harvey Cemetery, Hocking Co, Oh.. *[Family group sheet submitted by grandson, Richard Rittgers]* "Alice N." died 1941, and is buried with Isaac.[HCoCem]

ISSUE:

.1344.1   Floyd RITTGERS, born 11 Mar 1890 [SS] in Rush Creek, Fairfield Co., Oh. On 1900 census, age 10, with parents in Rush Creek, Fairfield Co., Oh.[ED 12, p 308B, fam #256/257] On 1910 census, age 19, with parents there.[ED 76,p 3B, Fam #68/69] He married Myrtle RIGGLE about 1918 in Fairfield Co., Oh. She was born 16 Mar 1897[SS] in Oh. 1920 census finds Floyd, 28, employed in a glass factory. His wife, Myrtle, 22, works in a lingerie shop. They are residing with her parents, George, 72, and Quala H. (sp. questionable-poor quality census film), 51; as well as Catherine Lawrence, 74, "sister". Because of age, we will assume that this is George's sister. At this time, Floyd and Myrtle have no children. Their residence is in Lancaster, E. Precinct., Fairfield Co., Oh. [ED 15, p 1B, fam #20/17] Floyd died 13 Dec 1963[SS] in Lancaster, Fairfield Co., Oh, and was buried in Columbus, Franklin Co., Oh. Myrtle died May 1970 in Franklin County, Oh.[SS] [Family group sheet submitted by Richard Rittgers (#1344A.1)]

.1344.2   Raymond R. RITTGERS, born 28 Jun 1893[SS] in Rush Creek, Fairfield Co., Oh. On 1900 census, age 7, with parents in Rush Creek, Fairfield Co., Oh.[ED 12, p 308B, fam #256/257] and 1910 census, age 16, with parents there.[ED 76, p 3B, fam #68/69] He married Margaret ____. She was born 7 Aug 1890. After their marriage, Ray and Margaret lived in Syracuse, N.Y. Margaret died Mar 1966 in Onondaga County, NY. Raymond died Jul 1965[SS] in Syracuse, NY.

.1344.3   Glen E. RITTGERS, born 15 Jan 1896 in Rush Creek, Fairfield Co., Oh. On 1900 census, age 4, with parents in Rush Creek, Fairfield Co.,[ED 12, p 308B, fam #256/257] and 1910 census, age 14, with parents there.[ED 76, p 3B, fam #68/69] He married Ola D. SHEETS about 1920. She was born about 1898 in Oh. On 1920 census, Fairfield Co., Oh., age 23, with wife Ola D., age 22. Glen died 13 Feb 1958 in Lancaster, Fairfield Co., Oh., and was buried there 16 Feb 1958.[FCoD] Ola died 1972.

.1344.4   Wilbur F. RITTGERS, born Jan 1898[1900 census] in Rush Creek, Fairfield Co., Oh. On 1900 census, age 2, with parents in Rush Creek, Fairfield Co., Oh.[ED 12, p 308B, fam #256/257] and 1910 census, age 12, with parents there.[ED 76, p 3B, fam #68/69] On 1920 census, age 22, Franklin Co., Oh. He married Louise PATTERSON. She was born 29 Jul 1897. Louise died Apr 1973 in Oh. Wilbur died 5 May 1954 in Columbus, Franklin Co., Oh., and was buried 8 May 1954 in Columbus, Franklin Co., Oh.

+ .1344.5   Connel E. RITTGERS, born 16 Dec 1899, died Jul 1970.

.1344.6   Charles A. RITTGERS, born 1902 in Rush Creek, Fairfield Co., Oh. On 1910 census, age 8, with parents there (ED 76, p 3B, fam 368/69) and age 17, there with parents on 1920 census.[ED 30, p 10B, fam #245/247] He married Mary TAYLOR. Charles died 31 Oct 1976 in Lancaster, Fairfield Co., Oh., and was buried 3 Nov 1976.

.1344.7   Earl RITTGERS, born 9 Apr 1904 in Rush Creek, Fairfield Co, Oh., died 19 June 1904. He was buried in S. Harvey Cemetery, Hocking Co., Oh.[HCoCem]

.1344.8   Pearl RITTGERS, born 1906 in Rush Creek, Fairfield Co., Oh., died there 1906. He was buried in Harvey Cemetery, Hocking Co., Oh.

.1344.9   Wayne RITTGERS, born 1907 in Rush Creek, Fairfield Co., Oh., died there in 1963. He was buried in Harvey Cemetery, Hocking Co., Oh. On 1910 census, age 3, with his parents in Rush Creek, Fairfield Co., Oh.[ED 76, p 3B, fam #68/69] and there with them on 1920 census, age 13.[ED 30, p 10B, fam #245/247] We are told that he was born with a cleft palate and could not speak well enough to attend public school. He work on the family farm, and never married.

+ .1344.A   Walter Reed RITTGERS, born 17 May 1909, died 1 Jun 1993.

134.5 John B.[4] **RITTGERS** (Tobias[3], John, Jr.[2], John[1]) was born 21 Mar 1863 in Marion Twp., Hocking Co., Oh., the son of Tobias RITTGERS and Phebe WILLIAMS. He is on the 1870 census, age 7, with parents there [p. 54, fam #277/280], and continues there 1880, still with parents, age 17.[p. 109C, fam #244/247] He married **Zeuriah Edith DAVIS** 26 Apr 1888 in Hocking Co., Oh. [HVRM, book E] Zeuriah is called Edith in family records. Family story tells us he lived in Camden, N.J. John died 21 Jun 1921.

ISSUE:

+ .1345.1   Minnie B. RITTGERS.

.1345.2   Howard RITTGERS, died young.

134.7 Albert J.[4] **RITTGERS** (Tobias[3], John, Jr.[2], John[1]) was born 28 Mar 1868 in Marion Twp., Hocking Co., Oh., the son of Tobias RITTGERS and Phebe WILLIAMS. He is on the 1870 census, age 3 [p. 54, fam #277/280], and on the 1880 census, age 13, with parents [ED 63, p 109C, fam #244/247] He married **Mary L. "Mollie" McLIN** 5 Apr 1889 in Marion, Hocking Co, Oh.[HVRM, book E, p 557] She was born Jun 1871 in Oh., to parents born Ohio. On the 1900 census, we see Albert, 32, farming in Marion Twp. Wife Mary, 29, declares they have been married 11 years and she has born 5 children, four alive at this time. They are listed in the home.[ED 32, p 110A, fam #43/43] By 1910 Albert, 42, and Mary, 39, have been married 21 years. She declares she has born 7 children, all living.[ED 82, p 16A, fam #338/342] On 1920 census, age 51, a farmer owning his own mortgaged farm, in Marion Twp. Wife Mary, 48, is keeping house for the five children seen with them.[ED 45, p. 3A, fam 47/47] Albert died 2 Feb 1934. We find family info in his estate.[Hocking Co. Probate #3706]

ISSUE:

+ .1347.1   Virginia Grace RITTGERS, born Apr 1889.

+ .1347.2   Herbert McCullough RITTGERS, born Apr 1893, died Aug 1949.

+ .1347.3   James F. RITTGERS, born 24 Mar 1896, died Dec 1980.

.1347.4   John Franklin RITTGERS, born 24 Mar 1899 in Marion Twp., Hocking Co., Oh. [HVRB, book C, p. 164] On 1900 census, age 1, with parents there.[Ed 32, p 110A, fam #43/43]. With parents in Falls Twp., Hocking Co., Oh., in 1910, age 11.[ED 82, p 16A, fam #338/342] On the 1920 census, we see him, age 21, a miner in coal mine, living in parent's home on Webbs Summit Rd., Marion Twp., Hocking Co., Oh.[ED 45, p. 3A, fam #47/47] John is named in his father's estate #3706, Hocking Co., as living in Logan, Oh., in 1934. He married Helen Josephine (Wolfe) PRICE, the daughter of Eber and Jessie (Inboden) Wolfe. We are told in Helen's marriage record that they had no issue. We find her name and marital history in the record of her third marriage. She married (1) Carl Price, who died in 1933, and had four children by him. Her second marriage was to John Rittgers, who "died 1959." She married (3) 13 Apr 1964, Chester Gilbert Six.[HVRM, book CC, p 368-John's death noted in marriage record of his widow.]

.1347.5   Hugh William RITTGERS, born 8 Mar 1901 in Hocking Co., Oh.[HVRB-bk C, p. 165] On 1910 census, age 9, with parents in Falls Twp., Hocking Co., Oh.[ED 82, p 16A, fam #338/342] In 1920 we see him, age 18, a farm laborer on the home farm, with parents in Marion Twp., Hocking Co., Oh.[ED 45, p. 3A, fam #47/47] He married Edna M. KIENZLE 17 Nov 1921 in Hocking Co., Oh. [HVRM, book P, p 20] She was born 7 May 1902 in Fairfield Co., Oh., the daughter of William and Sarah (Seifort) Kienzle. We find in HVRB Bk 1, p.7, that "Hugh William Rittgers, 21 and a farmer, and Edna May Kienzle, 19, had their first child, Harley Maywood Rittgers, 7 Apr 1922, Hocking Co., Oh. We find no other reference to this child, and he may have died young. Reported in father's estate, 1934, to be living in Logan, Oh. Marriage Book "U", p. 92, tells us that Edna, "widow of Hugh Rittgers," married on 17 Oct 1938, John G. Byerly of Logan, Hocking Co., Oh. John is a "Clerk". This led us to believe Hugh died before Oct 1938, yet on the social security death record we find one Hugh Rittgers with the same birth date, but a death date of Aug 1975. It is possible that he hadn't died when his wife remarried, but that they divorced.

.1347.6   Edwin N. RITTGERS, born 21 Jan 1904 in Hocking Co., Oh,[HVRB, book C, p 165; SS] died Dec 1983 in Oh.[SS] On 1910 census with parents, age 5, in Falls Twp., Hocking Co., Oh.[ED 82, p 16A, fam #338/342] In 1920 seen age 14, in his parent's home, Marion Twp., Hocking Co., Oh.[ED 45, p. 3A, fam #47/47] Named in his father's estate as living in Logan, Oh., in 1934.

.1347.7   Lorenza Dow RITTGERS, born 23 Mar 1907 in Hocking Co., Oh.[HVRB, Book C, p. 166], died Sep 1982 in Oh.[SS] On 1910 census with parents, age 2, in Falls Twp., Hocking Co., Oh.[ED 82, p 16A, fam #338/342] Family paper calls him "L. Dow". In 1920 we see him, age 12, with parents in Marion, Hocking Co., Oh.[ED 45, p. 3A, fam #47/47] Named in his father's estate, 1934, as living in Toledo, Oh. We are told that the "Ruby Rittgers" found on the Social Security Death index, 1995, is spouse of "Dow Rittgers." She was born in Ohio 6 Sept 1904, and died Apr 1980, Toledo, Lucas Co., Oh.

.1347.8   Ivy Irene RITTGERS, born 30 Sep 1913 in Hocking Co, Oh. On 1920 census, age 6, with parents in Marion, Hocking Co., Oh.[ED 45, p 3A, fam #47/47] She married Daniel William RUFF 24 Mar 1934 in Hocking Co County, Oh. He was born 7 Jul 1911 in Fairfield County, Oh.[HVRM, Book "S", p. 425] He is the son of A.W. and

Anna (Grince) Ruff. She is named in her father's estate, 1934, as living in Logan, Oh.

134.B James R.⁴ RITTGERS (Tobias³, John, Jr.², John¹). He was given to this author as the son of Tobias RITTGERS and Phebe WILLIAMS, but has not been found on the census with the family, nor are there any other children who could be this person. No birth date given, but must be before about 1870 for him to marry and father a child before the death date given . He married **Laura ALLEN** in Perry Co., Oh., in 1883.[Ref: the Perry Co. Marriage Index, gives us Bk 6, p.426] We do find that James M. Rittgers buys 2 acres of the NW corner of the E. ½ of the S.E. quarter of section 13, Twp. 15, range 17 from Isaac and Isabella Williams - Phebe's parents - for $1.[Deed Bk 13, p.138] This almost abuts the property of Tobias and Phebe, and is located off Bear Run Road, Marion Twp., Hocking Co. The 1890 census is lost to us due to a fire in Washington before it could be copied, so we have no idea where James and Laura were at that time. James died 26 Dec 1890 in Oh. Laura applied for guardianship on 4 Mar 1892, of Elmer and Lettie.[Guardianship #982, Docket #C261, Hocking Co., Oh.] We find that Laura E. Rittgers, guardian of Elmer C. & Lettie M. Rittgers, sells the above 2 acre property for $180 on 15 Mar 1892. She gave a final accounting of her guardianship on 3 Apr 1894. [Bk 19, p.365] In 1900 we find Laura E. Rittgers, 35, b. June 1864, and widowed, a servant- house keeper to Patric (poor writing but appears to be) Ferrites and his family. They are in Rush Creek Twp., Fairfield Co., Oh. Laura declares that she has born 3 children, one alive at this time. She also reports her father born in Virginia and her mother in Oh.(ED 21, p 85, fam #94/94) Her son, Elmer is working on a nearby farm. Neither James, Laura nor Elmer are mentioned in Phebe's estate, nor did they sign off on the deed of sale when Tobias' property sold.

ISSUE:
+ .134B.1   Elmer C. RITTGERS, born 2 Jan 1885.
  .134B.2   Lettie M. RITTGERS, born 5 may 1887, died bef. 1900.

138.1 Mary⁴ WOLF (Anna³, John, Jr.², John¹) was born 5 Feb 1859 in Oh., the daughter of William WOLF and Anna RITTGERS. She is on the 1870 census, age 10, with mother and step-father, Abe Hockman, Laurel, Hocking Co., Oh.[p 510, fam #271/274] She is age 21 on the 1880 census with them in Marion Twp., Hocking Co., Oh.[ED 63, p 27, fam #249/249] She married **Peter Whitehead BRIGHT** 16 Sep 1880 in Hocking Co., Oh.[Bright,p.26] He was born 20 Dec 1847 in Elkhart Co., Ind. Bright tells us he was a school teacher at the "Bethany EUB Church." The 1900 census, Falls Twp., Hocking Co., Oh., finds Peter Bright, 52, farming. Wife Mary, 41, declares they have been married 19 years and she has born 6 children, all alive at that time. In the home with them is Elizabeth Bright, "mother", b. Dec 1818, age 81, a widow, who declares she and her mother born in Ohio. Her father born in Virginia.[ED 26, p. 8A, fam #150/155] On the 1910 census, Peter is still farming in Falls Twp. Mary, 51, declares they have been married 29 years and she has born 7 children, all alive at this time. Three children in the home.[ED 82, p 5B, fam #107/107] At this time we can only account for six of the seven children. Peter died 10 May 1934 in Hocking County, Oh. and Mary died 27 Mar 1938. They are buried in Oak Grove Cemetery, Logan, Hocking Co., Oh.

ISSUE:
+ .1381.1   Isaac Rolland BRIGHT, born 31 Aug 1881, died 17 Jan 1969.
+ .1381.2   Samuel Hamilton BRIGHT, born 13 Apr 1883, died 9 Sep 1963.
+ .1381.3   James Henry BRIGHT, born 29 Dec 1884, died 11 Mar 1968.
+ .1381.4   Bertha May BRIGHT, born 28 Apr 1887.

+ .1381.5   Charles M. BRIGHT, born 21 Mar 1890.
+ .1381.6   Lillie Maude BRIGHT, born 28 Jan 1892.
  .1381.7   Joseph Elburn BRIGHT, born 15 Jul 1905 in Hocking Co., Oh. We see him on the
               1910 census, age 4, with his parents in Falls Twp., Hocking Co., Oh.[ED82, p.5B,
               fam#107/107] He married Iola NOWBRAY. Iola died in died young, and was
               buried in Oak Grove Cemetery, Logan, Oh.. Joseph died 22 Jun 1937, and was
               buried there. No issue. He worked in the county surveyor's office.[Bright, p.60]

138.2 Isaac[4] WOLF (Anna[3], John, Jr.[2], John[1]) was born about 1862 in Oh., the son of William
WOLF and Anna RITTGERS. On 1870 census, age 8, with mother and step-father, Abe
Hockman, in Laurel, Hocking Co., Oh.[p 510, fam #271/274] In 1880, age 19, he continues in
the home, now listed in Marion Twp., Hocking Co., Oh.[ED 63, p 27, fam #249/249] He
married **Chloe____** about 1885 in Hocking County, Oh. She was born Sep 1862 in Oh. He is
on the 1900 census, age 39, a farmer in Rush Creek, Fairfield Co., Oh. With him is wife Chloe
____, age 37. She declares they have been married 15 years and she has born 7 children, three
alive at this time.[ED 21, p 13B, fam # 276/276] In 1910, Isaac, now 49, is still farming his land.
Choe, 47, declares they have been married 25 years and she has born 9 children, 5 alive at this
time.[ED 76, p 9A, fam #194/203] In 1920, Isaac, 58, continues to farm in Rush Creek. Wife
Chloe, 56, continues to care for the home.[ED 31, p 10B, fam #261/266]
                              ISSUE:
  .1382.1   Levi C. WOLF, born 10 Jan 1886 in Hocking County, Oh, died 2 Nov 1892 in
               Hocking County, Oh., and was buried in the Ruff Cemetery, Marion Twp., Hocking
               Co., Oh.. On tombstone, age given as 6 yrs., 9 mo., 23 days.[Ruff Cemetery,
               Marion Twp., Hocking Co., Oh. Transcript in Hocking Co. Public Library, Logan.]
+ .1382.2   Charles A. WOLF, born Aug 1887.
  .1382.3   Laura WOLF, born 22 May 1889 in Hocking County, Oh, died 28 Sep 1890 in
               Hocking County, Oh., and was buried in the Ruff Cemetery, Marion Twp., Hocking
               Co., Oh. On tombstone listed as being 1 yr., 4 mo., 6 days.[Ruff Cem. Record]
  .1382.4   Homer WOLF, born 7 May 1891 in Hocking County, Oh, died 11 Nov 1896 in
               Hocking County, Oh., and was buried in Ruff Cemetery, Marion Twp., Hocking
               Co., Oh.. On tombstone listed as being 5 yr., 6 mo., 4 days.[Ruff Cem. Record]
  .1382.5   Clara E. WOLF, born Mar 1894 in Rush Creek Twp., Fairfield Co., Oh. On 1900
               census, age 6, with parents there.[ED 21, p 13B, fam #276/276] In 1910 "Clair",
               age 16, continues in her parents' home.[ED 76, p 9A, fam #194/203] On 1920
               census, age 25, in home on Harriett St. with parents in Rush Creek Twp. No
               occupation listed.[ED 31, p 10B, fam #261/261]
  .1382.6   Louis WOLF, born 14 Jan 1897 in Hocking County, Oh., died 17 Feb 1897 in
               Hocking County, Oh., and was buried in Ruff Cemetery, Marion Twp., Hocking
               Co., Oh.. Age 1 mo., 3 days.[Ruff Cemetery, Marion Twp., Hocking Co., Oh.]
  .1382.7   Addie E. WOLF, born Sep 1898 in Rush Creek Twp., Fairfield Co., Oh. On 1900
               census, age 1, with parents there.[ED 21, p 13B, fam #276/276] In 1910 "Clair",
               age 11, continues in her parents' home.[ED 76, p 9A, fam #194/203] Not on the
               1920 census with parents.
  .1382.8   Mary J. WOLF, born about 1901 in Rush Creek Twp., Fairfield Co., Oh. In 1910
               she is seen, age 9, in her parents' home there.[ED 76, p 9A, fam #194/203] On 1920
               census, age 18, in home on Harriett St. with parents in Rush Creek Twp.[ED 31,
               p 10B, fam #261/261]

.1382.9   Roy WOLF, born about 1907 in Rush Creek Twp., Fairfield Co., Oh. In 1910 he is seen, age 3, in his parents' home there.[ED 76, p 9A, fam #194/203] On 1920 census, age 12, in home on Harriett St. with parents in Rush Creek Twp.[ED 31, p 10B, fam #261/261]

138.3 William⁴ WOLF (Anna³, John, Jr.², John¹) was born Feb 1863 in Oh., the son of William WOLF and Anna RITTGERS. On 1870 census age 7, with mother and step-father, Abe Hockman, Laurel Twp., Hocking Co., Oh.[p 27, fam #249/249] He married **Elizabeth FICKLE** 28 Aug 1884 in Hocking Co., Oh.[LDS-IGI] She was born in Oh. On the 1900 census, in Rush Creek Twp., Fairfield Co., Oh., William is 37 and a blacksmith. Elizabeth, 34, declares they have been married 16 years and she has 4 children, all living at this time. Four children listed with them.

ISSUE:

.1383.1   Carol A. WOLF, born Oct 1886 in Fairfield Co., Oh. On 1900 census, age 13, with her parents in Rush Creek Twp., Fairfield Co., Oh.

.1383.2   Clarence H. WOLF, born Mar 1888 in Fairfield Co., Oh. On 1900 census, age 12, with parents in Rush Creek Twp., Fairfield Co., Oh.

.1383.3   Anna I. WOLF, born Oct 1897 in Fairfield Co., Oh. On 1900 census, age 2, with parents in Rush Creek Twp., Fairfield Co., Oh.

.1383.4   Charles D. WOLF, born Dec 1899 in Fairfield Co., Oh. On 1900 census, age 5/12, with them in Rush Creek Twp., Fairfield Co., Oh.

138.4 John⁴ HOCKMAN (Anna³, John, Jr.², John¹) was born Feb 1871 in Hocking Co., Oh. He was the son of Abe HOCKMAN and Anna RITTGERS. He is on the 1880 census, age 8 with parents, Marion Twp., Hocking Co., Oh.[ED 63, p 27, fam #249/249] He married **Sarah E.____** about 1895 in Hocking Co., Oh. She was born Apr 1869 in Oh. On the 1900 census, John, age 29, is a farm laborer on his father's farm in Marion Twp., Hocking Co. Sarah states they have been married for five years. She has born 4 children, all living, but only three shown with parents.[ED 32, p 110A, fam #48/48] In 1910, John, 39, is a "laborer, odd jobs." "Sadie", 41, declares that they have been married 15 years and she has born 7 children, all shown in the home.[ED 76, p 9B, fam 191/200] The child not shown on 1900 census, was probably Bertha, who we see here as age 10. Some census takers didn't list unnamed infants. On 1920 census, John, 48, is a farm laborer, "working out." in Rush Creek Twp., Fairfield Co., Oh. Wife "Sadie E." 50, is caring for the two children still in the home.[ED 30, p. 10A, fam #230/231]

ISSUE:

.1384.1   Ethel M. HOCKMAN, born Oct 1895 in Marion Twp., Hocking Co., Oh. On 1900 census, age 4, with parents there.[ED 32, p 110A, fam #48/48] In 1910 she is age 14, with her parents in Rush Creek Twp., Fairfield Co., Oh.[Ed 76, p 9B, fam #191/200]

.1384.2   Anne F. HOCKMAN, born Feb 1897 in Marion Twp., Hocking Co., Oh. On 1900 census, age 3, with parents there.[ED 32, p 110A, fam #48/48] In 1910 she is age 13, with her parents in Rush Creek Twp., Fairfield Co., Oh.[Ed 76, p 9B, fam #191/200]

.1384.3   Mary E. HOCKMAN, born Jul 1898 in Marion Twp., Hocking Co., Oh. On 1900 census, age 1, with parents there.[ED 32, p 110A, fam #48/48) In 1910 she is age 11, with her parents in Rush Creek Twp., Fairfield Co., Oh.[Ed 76, p 9B, fam #191/200]

.1384.4   Bertha HOCKMAN, born about 1900 in Marion Twp., Hocking Co., Oh. On the 1900 census, her mother declares she has born 4 children, all alive at that time, yet only 3 were listed. This is probably that fourth child. In 1910 she is age 10, with her parents in Rush Creek Twp., Fairfield Co., Oh.[Ed 76, p 9B, fam #191/200]

.1384.5   John HOCKMAN, born 1902 in Oh. In 1910 he is age 8, with his parents in Rush Creek Twp., Fairfield Co., Oh. [Ed 76, p 9B, fam #191/200] On the 1920 census, age 18, a farm laborer, "working out", in home with parents in Rush Creek Twp.[ED 30, p. 10A, fam #230/231]

.1384.6   James HOCKMAN, born about 1904 in Oh. In 1910 he is age 6, with his parents in Rush Creek Twp., Fairfield Co., Oh.[Ed 76, p 9B, fam #191/200] On the 1920 census, age 16, a farm laborer, "working out", in home with parents there.[ED 30, p. 10A, fam #230/231]

.1384.7   Ida HOCKMAN, born about 1906. In 1910 she is age 4, with her parents in Rush Creek Twp., Fairfield Co., Oh.[Ed 76, p 9B, fam #191/200]

138.5 Sylvester[4] HOCKMAN (Anna[3], John, Jr.[2], John[1]) was born 10 Sep 1872 in Pickaway Co., Oh., the son of Abe HOCKMAN and Anna RITTGERS. He is on the 1880 census, AGE 6, Marion Twp., Hocking Co., Oh., with parents.[ED 63, p 27, fam #249/249] He married **Mary E.____** about 1896 in Hocking Co., Oh. She was born Jul 1877. On the 1900 census, Sylvester Hockman, 27, is a farmer in Marion Twp., Hocking Co., Oh. Wife Mary E., 22, declares they have been married 4 yrs. and she has born 3 children, all living and in the home.[ED 32, p 111B, fam #80/80] On 1910 census, Sylvester is now 37 and still farming in Marion Twp. With him, wife Mary E., 33, declares they have been married 14 years and she has born 5 children, all living at this time and in the home.[ED 88, p 4A, fam #58/58]

ISSUE:

.1385.1   Ella May HOCKMAN, born Jul 1896 in Marion Twp., Hocking Co., Oh. On 1900 census, age 3, with parents there.[ED 32, p 111B, fam #80/80] On 1910 census, age 13, with parents there, living at #9 Scotch Ridge Rd.[ED 88, p 4A, fam #58/58]

+ .1385.2   Earl HOCKMAN, born Nov 1897.

.1385.3   George N. HOCKMAN, born Feb 1899 in Marion Twp., Hocking Co., Oh. On 1900 census, age 1, with parents in Marion Twp., Hocking Co., Oh.[ED 32, p 111B, fam #80/80] On 1910 census, age 10, with parents there, living at #9 Scotch Ridge Rd.[ED 88, p 4A, fam #58/58]

.1385.4   Altee M. HOCKMAN, born about 1901 in Marion Twp., Hocking Co., Oh. On 1910 census, age 9, with parents there, living at #9 Scotch Ridge Rd.[ED 88, p 4A, fam #58/58]

.1385.5   Dorothy HOCKMAN, born about 1906 in Marion Twp., Hocking Co., Oh. On 1910 census, age 4, with parents there, living at #9 Scotch Ridge Rd.[ED 88, p 4A, fam #58/58]

13D.3 Rose Alma[4] RITTGERS (William[3], John, Jr.[2], John[1]) was born 25 Jan 1878., the daughter of William F. RITTGERS and Lydia WILLIAMS.[HVRB, book B, p 240] On the 1880 census, she is age 2, with parents in Monday Creek Twp., Perry Co., Oh. [ED 212, p 210D, fam #312/312] On the 1900 census, Falls Twp., Hocking Co., Oh., Rose is 21, and gives her birth as Sept 1878. She is in the home of her parents with no occupation listed.[ED 28, p 66B, fam #351/371] She married **George J. KRICKBAUM** about 1901 in Oh. He was born about 1873 in Oh. In 1910 George J., 37, is a "salesman, grocery". He and Rose, 30, live at

116 W. Hunter St., Logan, 1st ward, Hocking Co., Oh. With them is daughter Ruth, age 7, and Lydia Rittgers, Mother-in-law.[ED 83, p 9A, fam #201/210] They continue in Logan on the 1920 census. George, 46, is a salesman, retail grocer. Wife Rose A., 40, is caring for the home and her mother, Lydia, who continues with them.[ED 40, p 23B, fam #304/330]

ISSUE:

.13D3.1   Ruth KRICKBAUM, born 1903 in Hocking Co., Oh. On 1910 census, age 7, with parents in Logan, 1st Ward, Hocking Co., Oh.[ED 83, p9A, fam #201/210], and there, age 16, with parents in Ward 2, Logan., living at 160 Hunter St.[ED 40, p 23B, fam #304/334]

144.1 Sarah⁴ ROOT (Daniel³, Magdalene², John¹) was born 16 Jul 1853[Tombstone] in Oh., the daughter of Daniel ROOT and Margaret Ann ZELLER. Counted twice on the 1870 census. Shown with her parents, age 17, in Valley Twp., Polk Co., Ia.[p 107 fam #110/120] Sarah is also enumerated with her cousin, David Foght (#16.1) and his family, also in Valley Twp., Polk Co., Ia. Even though an occupation not listed, she is probably working in their home.[p 407 fam #108/118] She married **Benjamin F. SHORT** 22 Jul 1871.[PVRM, Bk 1, p.245] He was born 19 Aug 1852. We see in family records of other family members renting the "Short farm." On the 1885 Iowa state census, we find family #7, Sarah Short, 31, with children Clara and Charles. Benjamin not listed. Here it is reported that they owned the NE quarter of the NE quarter of section 13, Twp. 25, Range 19, Webster Twp., Polk Co., Ia.[185, #7] Benjamin died 9 Jun 1914, and Sarah died 1946. They are buried in Rittgers Cemetery, Johnston, Ia.[tombstone, RitCem]

ISSUE:

.1441.1   Orville SHORT, born 23 Aug 1872, died 8 May 1873 in Polk Co., Ia.
.1441.2   Clara Alice SHORT, born 20 Nov 1876 in Polk Co., Ia. She married L. L. HIXSON 12 Jun 1906. We are told she had no children.
+ .1441.3   Charles Vincent SHORT, born 22 Aug 1880.

144.2 Jacob⁴ M. ROOT (Daniel³, Magdalene², John¹) He was born 12 Feb 1857 in Oh., the son of Daniel ROOT and Margaret Ann ZELLER. We see him on the 1870 census, age 13, with parents in Valley Twp., Polk Co. Ia.[p 107 fam #110/120] and on the 1880 census, age 23, with parents in Webster Twp., Polk Co., Ia.(Valley Twp. changed to Webster Twp.)[p 589, fam #262/266] He married Sarah L. FRY, 26 Oct 1881.[PVRM, Bk 2, p.195] She was born 1862. We are told Jacob and Sarah had two infant sons who died shortly after birth. There is a W.D. Root in the Rittgers Cemetery, with no other information. On the 1910 census, Wells St., Des Moines Twp., Dallas Co., Ia., age 53, a house carpenter. Wife Sarah is 48, and caring for the six children in the home. Jacob died 1926 and Sarah died 1944. They are buried in Rittgers Cemetery, Johnston, Ia.

ISSUE:

.1442.1 Ada V. ROOT, born abt 1883.
.1442.1 Unknown son
.1442.3 Effie O. ROOT, born abt 1890
.1442.4 Lena E. ROOT, born abt 1892
.1442.5 Unknown son.
.1442.6 John M. ROOT, born abt 1896
.1442.7 Merton I. ROOT, born abt 1898
.1442.8 Ira M. ROOT, born abt 1901.

144.6 Elmer Ellsworth[4] ROOT (Daniel[3], Magdalene[2], John[1]) was born 13 Jul 1866 in Van Wert Co., Oh., the son of Daniel ROOT and Margaret Ann ZELLER. He is age 4 on 1870 census with parents in Webster Twp., Polk Co., Ia.[p 107 fam #110/120] and age 14 on the 1880 census with his parents there.[p 589, fam #262/266] On the 1885 Iowa state census, we see Elmer, age 18, in his father's home in Webster Twp., Polk Co.[fam#8] He married **Marilda** _____ about 1888. On the 1895 Iowa state census, Elmer, 28, a laborer in Webster Twp., Polk Co., Ia. "Rillia", 26, is caring for the children.[#103] Elmer is age 33, on the 1900 census, and farming in Grimes, Webster Twp., Polk Co., Ia. With him is wife Marilda, age 31, caring for their five children. She declares she was born Apr 1869 in Ia., to parents b. Indiana; she and Elmer have been married 12 years and she has born 5 children.[ED 112, p 8A, fam #150/154]

ISSUE:

.1446.1   Harry E. ROOT, born Jan 1889. On the 1895 Ia. State census, age 5, with parents in Webster Twp. it reports he born in Oregon. On 1900 census, age 11, with parents in Grimes, Webster Twp., Polk Co., Ia.[ED 112, p 8A, fam #150/154]

.1446.2   William A. ROOT, born Jul 1892. "Arthur", age 3, is on the 1895 Ia. State census with parents. It reports he born in Oregon. On 1900 census, age 7, with parents in Grimes, Webster Twp, Polk Co., Ia.[ED 112, p 8A, fam #150/154]

.1446.3   Clarence ROOT, born Jun 1894 in Grimes, Polk Co., Ia. On the 1895 Iowa state census, age 1, with parents. It reports he born in Polk Co. On 1900 census, age 6, with parents in Grimes, Webster Twp, Polk Co., Ia.[ED 112, p 8A, fam #150/154]

.1446.4   Eugene ROOT, born June 1896 in Grimes, Polk Co., Ia. On 1900 census, age 4, with parents in Grimes, Webster Twp, Polk Co., Ia.[ED 112, p 8A, fam #150/154]

.1446.5   Velma B. ROOT, born Feb 1899 in Grimes, Polk Co., Ia. On 1900 census, age 1, with parents in Grimes, Webster Twp, Polk Co., Ia.[ED 112, p 8A, fam #150/154]

153.8 Susan[4] BODAMER (Susan[3], Katherine[2], John[1]) was born 7 May 1857 in Hocking Co., Oh., the daughter of Jacob Frederick BODAMER and Susan AMSPAUGH. She married **John Casper RAAB** 12 Nov 1878 in Oh. He was born 3 Jun 1849 in Durrenmungenau, Ger. John died 23 May 1925 in Lancaster, Fairfield Co., Oh. Named in her father's estate, as being of Colfax, Ia.[HockProb, est. #1932]

ISSUE:

+ .1531.1   Eva Susanna RAAB, born 23 Jul 1884, died 15 Oct 1910.

154.2 John D.[4] AMSPAUGH (Jonas[3], Katherine[2], John[1]) was born 13 Apr 1857 in Marion Twp., Hocking Co., Oh., the son of Jonas AMSPAUGH and Barbara DOUBENMIRE. The 1860 census shows us John, age 3, with parents in Lancaster, Fairfield Co., Oh.[p 28, fam #397/389] On 1870 census, age 13, with parents, Marion Twp., Hocking Co., Oh.[p 507 fam #230/233] He married (1) **Mary Jane VOUGHT** about 1880 in Oh. She was born in Oh. In 1900, we see John, 43, farming in Greenfield Twp, Carroll Precinct, Fairfield Co., Oh. Wife Mary Jane, 42, declares she has been married 20 years and has born 9 children, 8 alive at this time. With them are 8 children.[ED 7, p 4A, fam #76/79] John married (2) **Elizabeth** _____. The 1920 census shows John D., 62, still in Carroll Precinct farming. Wife Elizabeth, 60, with two children in the home; Carl, 19; and Ada 35.[ED 9, p. 9A, fam #80/82]

ISSUE:

.1542.1   Ida AMSPAUGH, born Nov 1880 in Oh. She married Charles HUBER. On 1900 census, age 19, with parents in Greenfield Twp., Fairfield Co., Oh.[ED 7, p 4A, fam #76/79]

.1542.2   Effie Grace AMSPAUGH, born Oct 1882 in Oh. On 1900 census, age 17, with parents in Greenfield Twp., Fairfield Co., Oh.[ED 7, p 4A, fam #76/79] By her name it states she has born one child, not living at this time.

.1542.3   Charles Edward AMSPAUGH, born Oct 1884 in Oh. On 1900 census, age 15, with parents in Greenfield Twp., Fairfield Co., Oh.[ED 7, p 4A, fam #76/79]

.1542.4   Ada Bell AMSPAUGH, born Mar 1886 in Oh. On 1900 census, age 14, with parents in Greenfield Twp., Fairfield Co., Oh.[ED 7, p 4A, fam #76/79] Age 35, on 1920 census with father and step-mother in Greenfield, Fairfield Co., Oh.[ED 9, p. 9A, fam #80/82]

.1542.5   Harry H. AMSPAUGH, born Mar 1888 in Oh. On 1900 census, age 12, with parents in Greenfield Twp., Fairfield Co., Oh.[ED 7, p 4A, fam #76/79]

.1542.6   Emmett AMSPAUGH, born Feb 1891 in Oh. On 1900 census, age 9, with parents in Greenfield Twp., Fairfield Co., Oh.[ED 7, p 4A, fam #76/79]

+ .1542.7   James AMSPAUGH, born Mar 1893.

.1542.8   Howard AMSPAUGH, born Mar 1898 in Oh. On 1900 census, age 2, with parents in Greenfield Twp., Fairfield Co., Oh.[ED 7, p 4A, fam #76/79]

.1542.9   Carl AMSPAUGH, born 1901 in Oh. On 1920 census, age 19, with father and stepmother in Greenfield Twp., Fairfield Co., Oh.[ED 9, p. 9A, fam #80/82]

154.3 Barbarey Ellen[4] AMSPAUGH (Jonas[3], Katherine[2], John[1]) was born about 1860 in Marion Twp., Hocking Co., Oh., the daughter of Jonas AMSPAUGH and Barbara DOUBENMIRE. On 1870 census, age 10, with parents, Marion Twp., Hocking Co., Oh.[p 507 fam #230/233] She married _____ **WELLWOOD**. In 1880, she is listed as "Ellen B. Wellwood", age 20, in parents' home in Greenfield Twp, Fairfield Co., Oh. She has son Clarence, age 3/12, with her.[p 142, fam #110/115] We are told that she also married Joseph Ritchie.

ISSUE:

.1543.1   Clarence WELLWOOD, born Mar 1880 in Oh. With mother in home of maternal grandparents, Jonas and Barbara Amspaugh, age 3/12, on 1880 census, Greenfield Twp., Fairfield Co., Oh.[ED 201, p 142, fam #110/115]

154.4 Louisa Jane[4] AMSPAUGH (Jonas[3], Katherine[2], John[1]) was born 17 Aug 1862 in Marion Twp., Hocking Co., Oh. She was the daughter of Jonas AMSPAUGH and Barbara DOUBENMIRE. She is on the 1870 census, age 8, with parents there.[p 507, fam #230/233] Continues with parents in 1880, 17, Greenfield Twp., Fairfield Co., Oh.[p 142, fam #110/115] She married **Joseph RITTGERS(See number 112.2)** about 1882. He was born Dec 1855 in Marion Twp., Hocking Co., Oh., the son of Abraham RITTGERS and Catherine LEFLER. On 1920 census in Brown Twp., Darke Co., Oh, age 57, caring for mother, Barbara Amspaugh.[ED 108, p 13, fam #303/303]

154.7 Sarah Katherina[4] AMSPAUGH (Jonas[3], Katherine[2], John[1]) was born 9 Feb 1868 in Marion Twp., Hocking Co., Oh., the daughter of Jonas AMSPAUGH and Barbara DOUBENMIRE.[EmEv, p. 35]   On 1870 census, age 2, with parents there.[p 507 fam #230/233], and age 12, in 1880 with her parents in Greenfield Twp, Fairfield Co., Oh.[p 142, fam #110/115] She married **George WEISS** about 1897. He was born Sept 1869 in Oh. to parents b. in Germany. On the 1900 census, Sarah C., age 32, has been married three years to George, age 30. Sarah declares she has only born one child, and he alive at this time. They are living with her parents, Jonas and Barbara Amspaugh, in Jackson, Darke Co., Oh.[ED 59, p 4B, fam #75/75] In 1920, George, 50, is farming in Jackson Twp., Darke Co., Oh. Wife Sarah, 51, is caring for the home and three children. George's father, Philip, age 83, is in the home. He declares he born in Germany.[ED 108, p. 11A, fam #238/238]

ISSUE:

.1547.1   Carl R. WEISS, born Mar 1898 in Jackson Twp., Darke Co., Oh. On 1900 census, age 2, with parents there.[ED 59, p 4B, fam #75/75]

.1547.2   Pauline WEISS, born about 1902 in Jackson Twp., Darke Co., Oh. On 1920 census, age 18, with parents there.[ED 108, p. 11A, fam #238/238]

.1547.3   Alva H. WEISS, born about 1808 in Jackson Twp., Darke Co., Oh. On 1920 census, age 12, with parents there.[ED 108, p. 11A, fam #238/238]

156.1 John[4] AMSPAUGH (Daniel[3], Katherine[2], John[1]) was born Apr 1855 in Marion Twp., Hocking Co., Ohio., the son of Daniel AMSPAUGH and Margaret (__) DEFENBAUGHER. He is on the 1860 census, age 3,[p 166 fam #1133/1128] and on 1870 census, age 15, with parents there.[p 503, fam #166/169] He married **Mary E.____** about 1879 in Oh. She was born Jul 1863 in Oh. On the 1900 census, age 45, a farmer, with wife Mary E., 36, and 7 children in Rush Creek Twp., Fairfield Co., Oh. She declares they have been married 21 years and she has born 7 children, all alive at that time.[ED 21, p.45, fam #127/127]

ISSUE:

.1561.1   Irvin AMSPAUGH, born Apr 1882 in Fairfield Co., Oh. On 1900 census, age 18 with parents in Rush Creek Twp., Fairfield Co., Oh. Listed as a farm laborer - attended school 2 months this past year.[ED 21, p 6A, fam #127/127]

.1561.2   Iry AMSPAUGH, born Apr 1884 in Fairfield Co., Oh. On 1900 census, age 16 with parents in Rush Creek Twp., Fairfield Co., Oh.[ED 21, p 6A, fam #127/127]

.1561.3   Arthur AMSPAUGH, born May 1886 in Fairfield Co., Oh. On 1900 census, age 14 with parents in Rush Creek Twp., Fairfield Co., Oh.[ED 21, p 6A, fam #127/127]

.1561.4   Fanny AMSPAUGH, born Sep 1888 in Fairfield Co., Oh. On 1900 census, age 11, with parents in Rush Creek Twp., Fairfield Co., Oh.'ED 21, p 6A, fam #127/127]

+ .1561.5   Alta L. AMSPAUGH, born Oct 1891.

.1561.6   Delpha AMSPAUGH, born Oct 1894 in Fairfield Co., Oh. On 1900 census, age 5, with parents in Rush Creek Twp., Fairfield Co., Oh.[ED 21, p 6A, fam #127/127]

.1561.7   Ivy M. AMSPAUGH, born Sep 1899 in Fairfield Co., Oh. On 1900 census, age 5/12, with parents in Rush Creek Twp., Fairfield Co., Oh.[ED 21, p 6A, fam #127/127]

156.3 Daniel Frederick[4] AMSPAUGH (Daniel[3], Katherine[2], John[1]) was born 29 Mar 1860 in Logan, Hocking Co., Oh., the son of Daniel AMSPAUGH and Margaret (__) DEFENBAUGHER. He is on the 1860 census, age 3/12,[166 fam #1133/1128] and on 1870 census, age 13, with parents in Marion, Hocking, Oh.[p 503, fam #166/169] He married **Susan ZELLER** 16 Oct 1892 in Oh. She was born May 1870 in Oh. Susan is listed as "Susie C." Zeller on LDS-IGI; 1992, Oh., fiche #1157. On the 1900 census, Daniel, age 40, is farming in Brown Twp., Darke Co., Oh. Wife Susan, 30, declares they have been married 8 years and she has born 4 children, all alive at this time and seen in the home.[ED 50, p 13B, fam #136/141]

ISSUE:

.1563.1   Dallas L. AMSPAUGH, born Aug 1893 in Darke Co., Oh. On the 1900 census, age 6, with parents in Brown Twp., Darke Co., Oh.[ED 50, p 13B, fam #136/141]

.1563.2   Estelle M. AMSPAUGH, born Dec 1894 in Darke Co,, Oh. On the 1900 census, age 5, with parents in Brown Twp., Darke Co., Oh.[ED 50, p 13B, fam #136/141]

.1563.3   Josephine M. AMSPAUGH, born Dec 1896 in Darke Co., Oh. On the 1900 census, age 3, with parents in Brown Twp., Darke Co., Oh.[ED 50, p 13B, fam #136/141]

.1563.4   Zeller W. AMSPAUGH, born Dec 1898 in Darke Co., Oh. On the 1900 census, age 1, with parents in Brown Twp., Darke Co., Oh.[ED 50, p 13B, fam #136/141]

161.4 Timothy Denny[4] RITTGERS (David[3], Daniel[2], John[1]) was born 8 Sep 1866 [Tombstone, BDCem.] in Jefferson Twp., Polk Co., Ia., the son of David Foght RITTGERS and Sarah Elizabeth DENNY. He is on the 1870 census, age 3, with parents [p 407, fam #108/118] and on the 1880 census, age 13, with parents,[ED 172, p 545, fam #214/219] both in Valley Twp., Polk Co., Ia. He is single when seen on the 1895 Iowa State census, age 28, a farmer and a Presbyterian, in Webster Twp., Polk Co., Ia.[#117] He married (1)**Agnus WILSON** 6 Mar 1895.[PVRM, book 7, p 233(p 39 of transcript)] She was born 19 May 1866 in Banbridge, Co. Down, Ire., the daughter of Thomas WILSON and Jane B. FRYER., and immigrated with her parents in spring of 1880. On the 1880 census, age 14, with her parents in Grimes, Polk Co., Ia.[ED 175, p 588C, fam #252/252] On the 1900 census, we see Timothy, age 43, with wife Agnes, 34, who declares they have been married 5 yrs., she has born 2 children, both alive at this time. They are living in Grant Twp., Dallas Co., Ia., where Timothy is farming.[ED 9, p 5, fam #86/87] On the 1910 census, Granger, Grant Twp., Dallas Co., Ia., Timothy is 43 and farming. Agnes, 43, declares they have been married 15 years and she has born 4 children, all alive. They are listed with their parents.[ED 9, p 4B, fam # 76/77] In 1920 they are located in Granger, Dallas Co., Ia. and have at home Francis, age 20; Elizabeth, 16, and Robert, 13. Timothy and Agnes are both 53, and he is farming a general farm.[ED 10, p 7A, fam #138/143] We are told Timothy attended Drake University and was a farmer and stock raiser near Grimes, Ia. He was a member of the Presbyterian Church and member of the Farm Bureau. Agnus died 18 Sep 1935 in Grimes, Polk Co., Ia. We find in a transcript from the Dallas Center Newspaper that Timothy D. Rittgers married (2) Mrs. Anna Hamilton. Timothy died 7 May 1944 in Dallas Co., Ia., from a heart attack and is buried with Agnes in Sec E, lot 13, Brethren Cemetery, east of Dallas Center, Dallas Co., Ia.[Tombstone, BDCem]

ISSUE:

.1614.1   William Arthur RITTGERS, born 27 May 1897 [DalCCem, p 31] in Polk Co., Ia. On 1900 census, age 3, with parents Grant Twp., Dallas Co., Ia.[ED 9, p 5, fam #86/87] On 1910 census, age 12, called Arthur, with parents in Granger, Polk Co.[ED 9, p 4B, fam #76/77] Died 28 Sept 1918, at Great Lakes Naval Station, N. Chicago, Lake Co., Ill., during WW I from pneumonia. He was buried with his parents in Sec. E., Lot 13, in Brethren Cemetery, Dallas Co., Ia. Stone indicates "Co. G., 2 Reg." There is often confusion about William. Some family records give "William" and "Arthur" as two separate people. "Wm. Arthur" is on his stone. [DalCCem, p 31]

+ .1614.2   Francis "Frank" RITTGERS, born 24 Jun 1899, died 26 Sep 1976.

+ .1614.3   Elizabeth A. RITTGERS, born about 1904.

+ .1614.4   Robert RITTGERS, born 5 Aug 1907, died Nov 1983.

161.5 Edmund Grant "Eddy"[4] RITTGERS (David[3], Daniel[2], John[1]) was born 24 Jan 1869 in Valley Twp., Polk Co., Ia., the son of David Foght RITTGERS and Sarah Elizabeth DENNY.

On the 1870 census, age 1, with parents,[p 407 fam #108/118] and on the 1880 census, "Elly" Everett, age 11, with parents.[ED 172, p 545, fam #214/219] living in Valley Twp. He married **Della YOUTZ** 2 Apr 1893 in Polk County, Ia. She was born May 1869 in Ia.[PVRM, book 7, p 228.(p 39 of transcript)] We are told he died from the "creeping paralysis", 3 Feb 1900. On 1900 census, taken in June, we find Della, age 31, who declares she married 7 years and has born 2 children, both alive. They are with her on Valley Junction Rd., Des Moines, Polk Co., Ia., as is her mother, Jane D. Youtz. Jane b. Jan 1837, in Ind. Della declares her father b. Conn. She married (2) 2 Apr 1901, Walter Warren.[PVRM, book 10, p 276. (p 36 of transcript)]

ISSUE:

.1615.1   Ona Bella RITTGERS, born 16 Sep 1896 in Polk Co., Ia. She is on the 1900 census, age 3, with widowed mother, Des Moines, Polk Co., Ia.[ED 66, p 29B, fam #556/580] She married _____ DeVRIES. Ona died 20 Mar 1973.

.1615.2   Edna Mae RITTGERS, born 16 Aug 1899 in Polk Co., Ia. She is on the 1900 census, age 9/12, with widowed mother, Des Moines, Polk Co., Ia.[ED 66, p 29B, fam #556/580] She married _____ Vander LINDEN. Edna died 27 Mar 1968.

161.6 Kitty Klyde[4] RITTGERS (David[3], Daniel[2], John[1]) was born 18 Dec 1871 in Valley Twp., Polk Co., Ia., the daughter of David Foght RITTGERS and Sarah Elizabeth DENNY. She is on the 1880 census, age 9, with her parents there.[ED 172, p 545, fam #214/219] She married **William "Carl" GARTEN** 19 Feb 1896.[PVRM, book 8, p 89.(p 31 of transcript)] He was born Feb 1865 in Ger. The 1900 census, Webster Twp., Polk Co., Ia., shows us William C. Garten, 35, farming in Webster, Polk Co., Ia. Wife Kittie K., age 28, declares they have been married 4 yrs and she has born 1 child, shown with them.[ED 112, p 8B, fam #160/167] They lived in Boone, Boone Co., Ia., and later Woodward and Moulton, Ia. During WW I people had very little to with the family as Carl was from Germany and wore "the typical German mustache" we are told. In 1920, Boone, Boone Co., Ia., William C., 55, continues to farm. Wife Kittie is 49. Both children still in home. William died 14 Sep 1941. Kitty died 9 Feb 1944 of a heart attack, and was buried in Boone, Boone Co., Ia.

ISSUE:

+ .1616.1   Carl "Glenn" GARTEN, born 5 Feb 1897, died 12 Feb 1976.

+ .1616.2   Pearl Elizabeth GARTEN, born 29 Dec 1900.

161.7 George Eugene "Gene"[4] RITTGERS (David[3], Daniel[2], John[1]) was born 28 Jan 1873 in Valley Twp., Polk Co., Ia., the son of David Foght RITTGERS and Sarah Elizabeth DENNY. He is on the 1880 census, age 7 with parents in Valley Twp., Polk Co., Ia.[ED 172, p 545, fam #214/219] He married **Margaret "Maggie" CHRISPIN** 19 Feb 1896 in Polk Co., Ia.[PVRM, book 8, p 224. (p 32 of transcript)] She was born Jan 1874 in Oh. The Crispins are seen intermarried with the Wilson/Friar family that is also seen marrying into the Rittgers family. On the 1900 census we find in Grimes, Polk Co., Ia., Eugene, 27, a farmer, He and Maggie have been married 5 years and she has had one child, Harold D., age 1 on the census.[ED 112, p 290A, fam #151/151] In 1910, we see George, 37, farming in Precinct #1, Webster Twp., Polk Co., Ia. With him is wife Margaret, 36. They have been married 14 years and she has had 3 children, two still alive and in the home. Also in home are her parents and nephew, Byron C. Crispin, 18. Maggie's father, Benjamin, 82, declares he and his parents were born in Pa. Maggie's mother, Mary L., 71, declares they have been married 50 years and she has born 12 children, 11 alive at this time. Mary was born in Oh., but declares her father born in NJ and her mother b. in Oh. Maggie's sister, Sarah, married Robert Friar and we see her parents in their home in

Walnut Twp., Polk Co., Ia., on the 1900 census, ED 112, p 4, fam #74/77.[ED 184, p 6B, fam #48/48] The 1920 census finds George E., 46, farming in Indian Creek Twp., Story Co., Ia. With him is wife Margaret, 46. Both sons are still in the home and are laborers on their father's farm.[ED 193, p 10A, fam #13/13] George died of cancer 22 Jan 1928, and was buried in Maxwell, Story Co., Ia.

ISSUE:

+ .1617.1   Harold David RITTGERS, born 24 Jul 1898, died Apr 1978.
+ .1617.2   Dale Eugene RITTGERS, born 15 Mar 1903.

161.8 Flora May[4] RITTGERS (David[3], Daniel[2], John[1]) was born 17 Feb 1875 in Valley Twp., Polk Co., Ia., the daughter of David Foght RITTGERS and Sarah Elizabeth DENNY. She is on the 1880 census, given as "Laura May" age 5, with her parents there.[ED 172, pa 545, fam #214/219] She married **Alexander "Alec" WILSON** 13 Mar 1895.[PVRM, book 7, p 295.(p 40 of transcript)] He was born 5 Nov 1864 in Banbridge, Co. Down, Ire., the son of Thomas WILSON and Jane B. FRYER. He immigrated with his parents in the spring of 1880. On 1880 census, age 15, with parents in Grimes, Polk Co., Ia.[ED 175, p 588C, fam #252/252] Flora died 14 Jan 1897 in Polk Co., Ia., of measles or pneumonia and is buried in McDivitt Cemetery, Webster Twp., Polk Co., Ia., Section B, Lot 62., next to the Wilsons.[Tombstone, PCC, p 12] Alexander is living alone on a rented farm in Webster Twp., Polk Co., Ia. on the 1900 census.[ED 112, p 7B, fam #134/140] He married (2) 27 Feb 1901, Sierra Nevada Reid, b. 27 June 1871, Bullion, Nev., d. 25 May 1929. In 1910 Alexander, 45, is farming in Webster Twp., Precinct 1, Polk Co., Ia. Wife Sierra, 38, is caring for the children, including Flora's daughter, Mina M., 14. Sierra declares they have been married 9 years and she has born 5 children, four alive at this time.[p 6B, fam #59/59] On the 1920 census, Grimes, Polk Co., Ia., age 55, Alexander is farming. Wife Vada, 48, b. Nev., is caring for their children.[ED 187, p 10B, fam #78/78] He is referred to as "Alec", and "Alex" in various records. Alexander died 18 Jan 1940 in Des Moines, Polk Co., Ia. and was buried in McDivitt Cemetery, Webster Twp., Polk Co., Ia. Because these children of Alexander and Sierra Nevada, surnamed Wilson, often show up on family records, we will note them here. They are NOT Rittgers descendants.[Pledge]

1. Gerald Reid, b. 22 Feb 1903. Age 7 on 1910 census and 16 on 1920 census with parents.
2. Leland Alexander, b. 28 Mar 1905. Age 5 on 1910 census and 14 on 1920 census with parents.
3. Evelyn Emma, b. 2 Jan 1909. Age 1 3/12 on 1910 census and 11 on 1920 census with parents.
4. Alice Jane, b. 15 Jan 1910. "Baby" Age 3/12 on the 1910 census and 10 on 1920 census with parents.

ISSUE of Alexander and Flora:

+ .1618.1   Mina May WILSON, born 15 Dec 1895, died 19 Jul 1979.

161.A James Albert "Jim"[4] RITTGERS (David[3], Daniel[2], John[1]) was born 9 Jan 1882 in Valley Twp., Polk Co., Ia., the son of David Foght RITTGERS and Sarah Elizabeth DENNY. On the 1900 census, we see James, age 18, as a farm laborer with his uncle, James Denney(#16.4), in Bloomfield, Polk Co., Ia.[ED 91, p 5A, fam #58/59] He married **Daisy Porter BISHOP** 7 Mar 1907.[PVRM, book 13, p 224.(p 46 of transcript)] She was born 3 Jul 1881. In 1910 James and Daisy, both 28, have been married 3 years and are living in Webster, Polk Co., Ia. She has born one child, but it died. He is a farmer.[ED 184, p 7B, fam #81/81] On the 1920 census we find James A., 38, farming in Webster Twp.. Wife Daisy P., 38, is caring for the children.[ED 187, p 12B, fam #200/202] James died 3 Jul 1953, and was buried in Oakland Cemetery, Hutchinson, Minn. Daisy died 3 Nov 1967.

ISSUE:

.161A.1   Mary Elizabeth RITTGERS, born 1 Jun 1910, died 1 Jul 1910.
+ .161A.2   Gertrude Isabel RITTGERS, born 1 Mar 1912, died 14 Mar 1991.
+ .161A.3   William James RITTGERS, born 4 Oct 1914, died 9 Mar 1993.

161.B Cora Nina⁴ RITTGERS (David³, Daniel², John¹) was born 11 Sep 1886 in Valley Twp., Polk Co., Ia., the daughter of David Foght RITTGERS and Sarah Elizabeth DENNY. She married **William James "Will" WILSON** 21 Feb 1905.[PVRM, book 12, p 285. (p 43 of transcript)] He was born 15 Apr 1880 in Polk Co., Ia., the son of Thomas WILSON and Jane B. FRYER. William was the first of the Wilson children born in this country. We see him on the 1880 census, age 3 months, with parents in Grimes, Polk Co., Ia.[ED 175, p 588C, fam #252/252] On the 1910 census, William, 30, is a farmer in Webster Twp., Polk Co., Ia. Wife Cora, 23, is caring for their two daughters. She declares they have been married 5 years and she has born 2 children, both alive at that time.[ED 189, p 6B, fam #53/53] On the 1920 census, William, 40, a farmer in Peoples Twp., Boone Co., Ia., with wife Cora 33. Five children shown - the first six listed below, Edna had died.[ED 24, p 4B, fam #88/88] William died 6 Apr 1960 in Madrid, Boone Co., Ia. Cora died 1 Apr 1970, and was buried in Grimes Cemetery, Grimes, Ia.

ISSUE:

.161B.1   Dorothy Jane WILSON, born 12 Dec 1907 in Grimes, Polk Co., Ia. She is seen on the 1910 census, age 2, with her parents in Webster Twp., Polk Co., Ia.[ED 184, p 63A, fam #53/53], and with them in People's Twp., Boone Co., Ia., in 1920, age 12.[ED 24, p 4B, fam #88/88] She married Ernest BETZ in Woodward, Dallas Co., Ia. We are told her marriage was annulled.

.161B.2   Mildred Elizabeth WILSON, born 2 Aug 1909 in Grimes, Polk Co., Ia. She is seen on the 1910 census, age 9 mo., with her parents in Webster Twp., Polk Co., Ia.[ED 184, p 63A, fam #53/53], and with them in People's Twp., Boone Co., Ia., in 1920, age 10.[ED 24, p 4B, fam #88/88] died 22 Aug 1930 in Des Moines, Polk Co., Ia. We are told "She died when a new doctor touched her ulcer when removing her appendix." Having extensive medical background, this author finds this suspect. There are many other things that might have contributed to her death.

.161B.3   Edna Minnie WILSON, born 10 Sep 1911 in Grimes, Polk Co., Ia., died 28 Mar 1912 in Dallas County, Ia. We are told that she was born and died "near Grimes, Ia." Cause of death was pneumonia.

+ .161B.4   Hazel Pearl WILSON, born 4 Aug 1913.
+ .161B.5   Charles Woodrow WILSON, born 16 Mar 1915.
+ .161B.6   Cora Beth WILSON, born 6 Jan 1917.
+ .161B.7   William George WILSON, born 24 Oct 1920.
.161B.8   _____ WILSON, born 1923.

162.1 Ambrose Robert⁴ RITTGERS (Reuben³, Daniel², John¹) was born 7 Oct 1866 in Valley Twp., Polk Co., Ia., the son of Reuben R. RITTGERS and Abigail Ann FINDLEY. He is on the 1870 census, age 3, with parents there.[p 407 fam #109/119], and age 14 with parents there on the 1880 census.[p 545 fam #213/218] He married **Verta Alice SNIDER** 30 Jan 1891 in Polk Co., Ia.[PVRM, book 5, p 226. (p 49 of transcript)] His obituary reports they were married in

Towner, Co. on this same date. She was born 30 Jan 1872, Snyder Point, Polk Co., Ia., the daughter of Andrew J. and Margaret (Farnsworth) Snider.[Death Cert.] She is seen age 7, on the 1880 census, Valley Twp., Polk Co., Ia., with her parents. Andrew is 56 and a farmer, b. Ind. His parents were born in Kentucky. Wife Margaret, 37, is caring for the three children in the home. She was born in Ill., but her parents were born in Ind. Based on the age of the two sons, Oliver, 16, and Robert B., 13, and the age of Margaret, it is possible that Margaret is a second wife and not the mother of the two boys.[ED 172, p 34, fam #133/137] Shortly after marrying, Ambrose and Verta moved to Eads, Colo., where Ambrose held a position in the County Courthouse. On the 1900 census we find Ambrose, 32, working as a Printer in Waltentown, Precinct 3, Kiowa Co., Colo. Verta, 26, declares they have been married 9 years and she has born 4 children, all alive at this time.[ED 43, p 3A, fam #44/46] The 1910 census, shows Ambrose, 42, now a "deputy clerk, courthouse". Verta, 36, declares they have been married 18 years and she has born 9 children, all alive at this time. They are listed in "precinct 5" Kiowa co., Colo.[ED 88, p 5A, fam #106/108] In 1920 Ambrose, 52, is listed as "district clerk, court house". Verta, 47, is raising the last 5 children. In the home is also "Marie Coster, Mother-in-law", who is a 61 year old widow. Since Verta's mother, Margaret, would now be 77, she is possibly a step-mother who remarried following the death of Andrew Snyder. They are shown living on Burt St., Eads, Kiowa Co., Co.[ED 109, p 4A, fam #81/87] Two of Ambrose's children, Archie and Pearl, came to Iowa to attend High School, as there was none in Eads at that time. They made their home with their "Uncle Fin" (Abel Findley Rittgers, #162.4) Verta died 14 Apr 1936 in Eads, Kiowa Co., Colo., of cancer of the liver and stomach. Ambrose died 14 Apr 1938 in Eads, Kiowa Co., Colo.[Abst. #76811], from High blood pressure & paralysis following a stroke. They are buried in the Eads Cemetery. Among his many civic positions mentioned in his obituary (submitted with no banner or date) are mayor of Eads, Justice of the peace, School Board member and Clerk of the District Court. One family story told to us was that Ambrose knew the railroad was coming through the area of Eads. He felt this would be a more suitable county seat than the one chosen earlier. We are told that he and a few other men went by buggy to the other town during the night and stole the county records. By morning they were established in Eads and he was guarding them. When the track for the railroad was finally laid down, it proved to be withing feet of the spot he designated as the spot for the county courthouse.

ISSUE:

+ .1621.1   Mary Alice RITTGERS, born 30 Oct 1891, died 21 Sep 1945.
+ .1621.2   Reuben Burn RITTGERS, born 21 Sep 1893, died 11 Jan 1974.
+ .1621.3   Luetta Blanche RITTGERS, born 27 Dec 1896, died 6 Apr 1920.
+ .1621.4   Edith Pearl RITTGERS, born 25 Jan 1898, died 2 Sep 1947.
+ .1621.5   Sylvia Ann RITTGERS, born 6 Jul 1900, died 14 Aug 1955.
+ .1621.6   Archibald Maurice RITTGERS, born 8 Jul 1902, died 9 Sep 1989.
+ .1621.7   Abigail Violet RITTGERS, born 24 Aug 1905, died 10 Aug 1947.
+ .1621.8   Clara Sunshine RITTGERS, born 16 Nov 1907, died 12 Jul 1985.
+ .1621.9   Donald Howard RITTGERS, born 25 Feb 1910, died 10 Nov 1991.
+ .1621.A   Verta Faye RITTGERS, born 8 Mar 1912.
  .1621.B   Fern B. RITTGERS, born 8 Mar 1912, died 13 Mar 1912 in Eads, Kiowa Co., Co.
+ .1621.C   Roy Verlaine RITTGERS, born 2 Feb 1914, died 7 Oct 1958.

162.4 Daisy Marie[4] RITTGERS (Reuben[3], Daniel[2], John[1]) was born 25 Jan 1871 in Valley Twp., Polk Co., Ia., the daughter of Reuben R. RITTGERS and Abigail Ann FINDLEY. She is age 9 on 1880 census, with parents there.[p 545, fam # 213/218]   She married **Robert A. WILSON** 5 Apr 1894 in Polk Co., Ia.[PVRM, Bk 7, p.291(p 40 of transcript)] He was born 11 Apr 1872 in Banbridge, Co. Down, Ire., the son of Thomas WILSON and Jane B. FRYER. Robert immigrated with his parents in 1880 from Ireland. We see him on the 1880 census, age 9, with his parents, Thomas and Jane B. (Fryar) Wilson in Grimes, Polk Co., Ia.[ED 175, p 588C, fam #252/252] On the 1895 Iowa State census, Robert is 22 and a farmer in Webster Twp. Daisy, 24, is caring for the home. Also in the home is Alex F. Wilson, 30, farmer. [#95]   On the 1900 census we find Robert, age 29, farming in Grimes, Polk Co., Ia. Wife Daisy, 29, declares they have been married five years. She has born 4 children, with 4 alive. Also a cousin, Dolly (Wilson, we assume, as no other last name is given,) age 19, born Apr 1881.[ED 112, p 10, fam #201/208] There is much confusion about the death date of Daisy, frequently given as Jan of 1900. We have just seen that she was alive on the 1900 census, dated 19 June 1900, and had not had twins Daisy and Marie as yet. The twins were born Dec 28 1900 and Daisy died a week later, 5 Jan 1901. The 1900 death date is carried through in the land abstracts for "Rittgers Acres," showing Robert and the minor children - with the twins named - as heirs of the estate of Reuben Rittgers. She is buried in Ridgedale Cemetery, Sect. S, row 3. Daisy's stone reads "1871-1901." In the Ridgedale Cemetery records is a page labeled "Extracted from Polk Co., Ia, death records". Here it gives Daisy's date of death as 3 Jan 1901, age 29 yr, 11 mo, 22 days. Robert married (2) Elizabeth JENNINGS 28 May 1902 in Polk Co., Ia. Elizabeth was a first cousin of Daisy's, and daughter of her mother's sister, Elizabeth (Findley) Jennings of McPherson, Ks. Robert died 4 Dec 1950. Elizabeth died 22 Sep 1956. They are buried in Ridgedale Cemetery, Sect. S, row 3.

Children of Robert and Bessie, surnamed Wilson.(These are FINDLEY and WILSON descendants, not RITTGERS descendants.)

1 Jewell Jane, b. 4 June 1903
2 Thomas Blueford, b. 3 Aug 1905
3 Rodney George, b. 14 June 1917

ISSUE Of Robert and Daisy:

+ .1624.1	Lloyd Rittgers WILSON, born 16 Sep 1895, died 28 Apr 1984.
  .1624.2	Lester WILSON, born 28 Nov 1896 [RPCem, p 10] in Grimes, Polk Co., Ia., On 1900 census, age 3, with parents there.[ED 112, p 10, fam #201/208] He is named in his grandfather, Reuben Rittgers', estate as heir to a share of his deceased mother's share of her father's estate. Several references until it is noted in 1912 that he has died. (Apparently no action taken on estate from 1906 until next entry dated 1912.) Lester died 6 Aug 1908 in Grimes, Polk Co., Ia., and was buried in Ridgedale Cem., Polk Co., Ia., in Sec. S, row 3, with his parents. [RPCem, p 10]
+ .1624.3	Paul James WILSON, born 16 Jul 1898, died about 1980.
  .1624.4	Bethia WILSON, born 3 Oct 1899 in Grimes, Polk Co., Ia., Called Betty G. on the 1900 census, she was age 8 mo. in the home with her parents there.[ED 112, p 10, fam #201/208] Bethia died 30 Aug 1900 in Webster Twp., Polk Co., Ia., and was buried in Ridgedale Cemetery, Polk Co., Ia.[Tombstone, RPCem., p 1]
+ .1624.5	Daisy WILSON, born 8 Dec 1900.
+ .1624.6	Marie WILSON, born 8 Dec 1900.

162.6 Maxwell M.[4] RITTGERS (Reuben[3], Daniel[2], John[1]) was born 4 Jan 1873 in Valley Twp. Polk Co., Ia., the son of Reuben R. RITTGERS and Abigail Ann FINDLEY. He is on the 1880 census with parents there.[p 545, fam #213/218] He married (1) **Rebecca WILSON** 19 Mar

1895.[abst. 76811] She was born 13 Mar 1870 in Co. Down, Ire., the daughter of Thomas WILSON and Jane B. FRYER, and immigrated with them in 1880. On 1880 census, age 11, with parents in Grimes, Polk Co., Ia.[ED 175, p 588C, fam 252/252] A story submitted by descendant Mary Esther Rittgers tells us that Rebecca died 31 Dec 1899 of a heart condition caused by rheumatic fever. We are told that son Thomas felt responsible for her untimely death. Rebecca fell as she was running down stairs to see what he was up to, and died soon after that. Apparently the family lived in Oklahoma or Texas at the time, and brought her body back by train to be buried next to her parents in sec. C, lot 27, row 5, McDivitt Cemetery, Polk Co., Ia.[PVRD, book 5 of deaths, transcript p 52.; also MPCem, p 13] On the 1900 census, son Thomas, called "Park S." on census, age 4, is with his maternal grandparents, Thomas and Jane (Fryar) Wilson in Grimes, Webster Twp., Polk Co., Ia.[ED 112, p. 288B, fam #97/102] Max, age 27 and a farmer, is in Beaver Twp., Dallas Co., Ia., a boarder with William Ogden.[ED 4, p 7B, fam 135/137] Maxwell married (2) **Effie HELMS**. There is a picture shared with this author showing a small wood house with "wrap-around" porch. It sits in a very open Plaines area, with one other house seen far in the background. A man in bib overalls has a saw in his hand and appears to be talking to a lady in an ankle length dress. To one side is a lad in his early teens, swinging a hatchet. It appears that the small plot the house is on is fenced in with barbed wire strung on crude fence posts. It is labeled "Dad, Me, and Forest's mother, Effie, Lyford, Texas." In 1907,we see Max and "Effie his wife" deeding over his "right, title, and interests in the estate of Reuben R. Rittgers, including the west 40 acres...." to his mother, Abigail, for $600. In 1913 Max W. Rittgers and Effie Rittgers "Releases the mortgage..."[ABST. 76811, p. 34] Maxwell married (3) **Kate JOHNSON**.[abst. 76811] She was born 27 Sep 1859 in Monroe Co., Ia., the daughter of "hos. Johnson and M. Atwood."[Boone Co. poll tax list, 1934] On the 1920 census, age 46, Max states he is "commercial traveler, Medicine" With him are wife, Katheryn, 59, and son Forest (by Effie), age 17, residing in Boone City, Greene Co., Ia.[ED 12, p 1A, fam #5/5] He was called the "Watkins Man" for the products he sold. In the family, there are photos of Max posing beside a truck with "Red Ball Products" painted on the side. Another picture shows Max in front of one that has the word "Remedies" visible. On 1 Dec 1923, Max signs an "Assignment of Interest" to "Kate Johnston Rittgers, wife of grantor" in consideration of the sum of $800 in hand paid, and this assignment is to cover both real and personal property coming to me from said estates [of Reuben and Abigail] "being now unsettled and undivided." This filed at Boone, Ia. Filed June 19, 1935 is an entry where Max and "Kate Johnston Rittgers, his wife" convey to Jasper Rittgers all right, title and interest in the undivided share of the estate of R.R. Rittgers, now being probated. This deed was refiled 26 May 1939. Because Max had put the estate business in Kate's name, we see her name on the tax searches to clear the title that were done in 1938.[Abst 76811] In a transcript of Boone Co Poll tax, done by the Boone Co., Ia., Hist. Soc., and a copy located in the Iowa Historical Library, Des Moines, on p. 550 we see an entry for "Rittgers, M.W., Res. 1915 Story [St. or Ave.] Boone. We are told he put all his property in Kate's hands following a serious traffic accident where another person died. This would keep him from losing everything if he was sued. It backfired! We are told that at Kate's death, she left everything to her family, leaving Max almost penniless! Max spent his late years living with his sons and "visiting" his sisters and brothers. A picture in the family of Vivian (Rittgers) Rorabaugh (#162.A) shows she and Max in her yard in Clermont, Lake Co., Fla. Judging from their apparent ages, it was probably taken in abt. 1940-42. Maxwell died 20 Dec 1943 in Superior, Wisc., and was buried in Boone, Boone Co., Ia. In his obituary, we find he was "a deeply religious man, having united with the Ridgeland Presbyterian Church in 1889...a member of the board of Deacons of Baptist Church, Boone."(in Boone Co., Ia.) We are told that there were several glaring errors in the obituary.[Obituary, with no newspaper banner; Pledge] ISSUE of Maxwell and Rebecca:

+ .1626.1   Thomas Park Findley RITTGERS, born 20 Jan 1896, died 11 Mar 1986.
ISSUE of Maxwell and Effie:
+ .1626.2   Lt. Col. Forest Sheldon RITTGERS, born 2 Jul 1902, died 21 Mar 1980.

162.7 Abel Findley[4] RITTGERS (Reuben[3], Daniel[2], John[1]) was born 19 Jul 1874/1875 [Polk Co. Death Records, p 355, give 1875; fam records give 1874] in Grimes, Polk Co., Ia., the son of Reuben R. RITTGERS and Abigail Ann FINDLEY. Named for his maternal grandfather, we first see him age 6 on the 1880 census with his parents in Valley Twp., Polk Co., Ia.[p 545 fam #213/218] In 1900 we find "Findley" Rittgers, 24, in Stella Twp., Woods Co., Ok. He married **Mabel McCREIGHT** 23 May 1906 in Polk Co., Ia.[PVRM, book 12, p 225(p 43 of transcript] She was born 4 Feb 1877 in Aledo, Mercer Co., Ill.[Birth record of dau. Mildred, PVRB, book 7, p 127 of transcript.] On the 1910 census he is age "33" and a Dairy farmer. He and wife Mabel, age 32, have been married 3 years. She has born 2 children, one is living.[ED 184, p 9A, fam #119/119] In the family record he is called "Uncle Fin". He and brother John owned a grocery store in Polk Co., Ia., on the NW corner of Merle Hay and Rt. 62. In an ad from a "Farmer's Directory" (undated photocopy), is an ad for "Rittgers Bros. General Merchandise Coal and Grain Dealers, A.F. Rittgers - J.H. Rittgers, Herold, Ia." This place is Herold Station now the site of Camp Dodge, Polk Co., Ia. Findley and Mabel boarded two of Ambrose's (#162.1) children when they came from Eads, Colo., to go to High School. On the 1920 census we find A. Findley Rittgers, 45, a storekeeper-general merchandise in Webster, Polk Co., Ia. Wife Mabel, 42, is caring for the children. If any of Ambrose's children are here at this time, they are not listed on the census.[ED 187, p 11B, fam #106/106] In the estate of his parents, "A.F. Rittgers" purchases the land that had been left to his sister, Daisy's son, Paul Wilson, filed 24 June 1921.[Abst 76811] Family story tells us; "In September of 1921, Uncle Fin was digging a ditch for sewer line for their dwelling beside the grocery store building. The house was made by joining three `Camp Dodge houses', many of which were left at Camp Dodge after World War I. (We are told these were just 1 and 2 room wood cottages) The soil in the Johnston area is quite sandy and the ditch Fin was digging was probably 7-8 feet deep. He had quipped at noon, `It would be a joke if that ditch caved in on me.' Well, in mid afternoon when someone checked on him, they found that the ditch had caved in! Neighbors, friends, and relatives rushed to dig him out but he was not alive. He was standing with the shovel raised over his head as if he had just thrown sand - or possibly he sensed the cave-in and was going to throw the shovel out before he climbed out at the end. Mabel was left with three small daughters, a grocery store and a partially finished home. Fin's brothers, Jasper and John, came to aid what they could by `running the store' until she felt able to assume the responsibility. I think Pearl was living there and working in Des Moines and perhaps Archie helped with the store, altho it would seem he would have finished 12th grade. Later, school teachers roomed with kitchen privileges. It was very tough going for Mabel. She worked very hard and I remember she was always tired." Told by Laura (Rittgers)(Peitzman) Emmert. His death record tells us he "suffocated by cave in of tile ditch". Abel died 13 Sep 1921 in Johnston, Polk Co., Ia, and was buried in Rittgers Cemetery, Polk, Ia.[Polk Co. Death Records, p 355] Mabel Rittgers, wife of "A.F. Rittgers, deceased" petitioned for administration of his estate on 7 July 1922. She gives date of death as 13 Sept 1921 and lists the three daughters - Helen, 12; Mildred, 9; and Dorothy, 6 - as the sole heirs at law. It states he owned at his death "certain real estate in Minnesota, Indiana and

Texas." An inventory was filed 7 July 1922. Mabel applied for "Widow's allowance" on 14 May 1924, asking for $1200. In 1935, the court is petitioned to sell several pieces of property, which coincides with bits and pieces of Reuben's original holdings.[Abst 76811; gives probate docket #43-13190] "Some years after Dorothy and Kenneth (Webster) had married and were living in Chicago, Mabel had the courage to start a new life. She moved to an apartment near Dorothy and got work in a dress shop where she could use her very able talent of sewing. She relaxed and could enjoy her work." Laura Emmert also marvels at how brave she was to start traveling at age 75. "She was a woman with a small body but I shall always remember her as large with love." Mabel died 10 Feb 1969[SS] in Downers Grove, Du Page Co., Ill., and is buried in Rittgers Cemetery, Johnston, Ia.

ISSUE:

.1627.1   Baby Boy RITTGERS, born 19 Jul 1907, died 19 Jul 1907.[RitCem]
+.1627.2   Helen Lucille RITTGERS, born 22 Mar 1909, died 4 Feb 1985.
.1627.3   Mildred Louise RITTGERS, born 17 Aug 1913 in Johnston, Polk Co., Ia.[PVRB, book 7, p 127 of transcript] She is age 6, on 1920 census with parents, Webster, Polk Co., Ia.[ED 187, p 11B, fam #106/106] Listed as age 9 in 1922 when her mother filed estate administration for her father.[Abst 76811, p. 35] In Laura Emmert's Journal, she had some memories of Mildred: "Mildred had diabetes at an early age. Insulin was quite new and a real blessing. I remember how brave she was to stick herself with the insulin syringe and needle and how accurately she kept track of which area should next be stuck - She was a fun loving, plucky little girl. She and I were closer in companionship and in age than Helen or Dorothy and we played together more when I visited them at Johnston. Helen was older and had her neighbor friends to play with. Helen often had some mysterious secret going for her that Mildred and I tried desperately to guess. Dorothy was enough younger that we ignored her as much as we could. Mildred developed tuberculosis while in high school and made a valiant fight. I remember visiting her at the Broadlawns, Polk Co. Tuberculosis Hospital. She died there 11 Nov 1933 I well remember the day of the funeral which was held in the Johnston Community Church which had only basement rooms. I believe that Helen Findley and I sang and how hard that was for me. I vividly remember ascending the basement church step's and noticing how very dark all outdoors had become in mid-afternoon. It was the first of the many terrible dust storms which were to follow as dust seemed to blow freely NE from Okla. and Kansas. Mildred was buried in the Rittgers Cemetery, (NW Beaver Dr. in Johnston) beside her father."
+.1627.4   Dorothy Marguerite RITTGERS, born 12 Dec 1915.
.1627.5   _____ RITTGERS, born 22 Jul 1917, died 22 Jul 1917.[RitCem]

162.8 Jasper C. "Jass"[4] RITTGERS (Reuben[3], Daniel[2], John[1]) was born 8 Jun 1876 [Pledge] in Valley Twp., Polk Co., Ia., the son of Reuben R. RITTGERS and Abigail Ann FINDLEY. He is on the 1880 census, age 4, with parents there,[p 545 fam #213/218] and on 1900 census, age 24, with widowed mother in Grimes, Webster Twp., Polk Co., Ia.[ED 112, p 8B, fam #152/159] He married **Margaret "Maggie" WILSON** 10 Sep 1902. She was born 31 Jan 1878 in Banbridge, Co. Down, Ire., the daughter of Thomas WILSON and Jane B. FRYER. On the 1880 census, she is age 2, with parents in Grimes, Polk Co., Ia.[ED 175, p 588C, fam #252/252] She is seen on the 1900 census, age 22, in the home of her parents in Grimes, Webster Twp., Polk Co., Ia.[ED 112] and is listed as the last child in the family born in Ireland.

On the 1910 census, we see Jasper, 32, farmer, and Maggie, 32, in Webster, Polk Co., Ia. They have been married 7 years and she has born 2 children, both alive.[ED 184, p 7B, fam #80/80] We are told "In 1913 they moved to a larger farm near Ankeny (Polk Co., Ia.) They attended the Congregational Church, bobsledding to church in the winter and using a buggy the rest of the year." In 1920 they are in Crocker, Polk Co., Ia. Jasper, 43, is still farming. Maggie is 42. She declares she immigrated in 1880 and was naturalized in 1903. With them are children Lawrence, 16, thru Margaret, 2 7/12 yrs.[ED 232, p 2A, fam #32/32] Jasper was the administrator for his mother's estate and he bought back much of the original holdings from his brothers and sisters. "The family owned a 1918 Ford touring car with Snap-on curtains. They drove it around to visit the rest of the family." We are told also of his success as a farmer, growing a variety of crops. His farm, described in colorful detail in family stories, supplied timber for many uses, including as support posts in a nearby coal mine. There was a creek through the property with a fallen log as a foot bridge "for the children to cross the creek on their way to a country school about two miles distant." He raised corn, beans, oats, hay, and wheat, as well as raspberries, peanuts and a kitchen garden. They had chickens, cows, horses, hogs, and sheep. We are told Jasper enjoyed reading, and raised their children in "a home where God and the Bible were loved and respected." When his sister Mabel (172.B) and her husband were missionaries in Korea, he helped her "in many ways throughout her life." Margaret died 6 Aug 1958. In her obituary, we see she died in a nursing home, "after a long illness." She is listed as a member of the Gospel Missionary Church. Jasper died 1 Oct 1965[SS]. They are buried in Union Cem., Sect. W, Row 8, Ankeny, Polk Co., Ia.[UPCem] [obituary, submitted with no newspaper banner.]

ISSUE:

+ .1628.1   Lawrence RITTGERS, born 13 Jun 1904, died 11 Jun 1990.
+ .1628.2   Ruth Evelyn RITTGERS, born 19 Aug 1905.
  .1628.3   Lloyd Emerson RITTGERS, born 16 Sep 1910[PVRB, book 6, p 97 of transcript] in Webster Twp., Polk Co., Ia. On the 1920 census, age 9, with parents in Crocker, Polk Co., Ia.[ED 232, p 2A, fam #32/32] He married Neva ADAMSON 7 Nov 1942. [Pledge] She was born 26 Apr 1914 in Waynesburg, Pa., the daughter of Howard C. and Margaret H. (Adams) Adamson, and Margaret traces her family back to John Quincy Adams. We are told she moved with her family to Iowa in 1927. In the 1948 Polk Co. Farm Directory, p. 148, we see Lloyd E. and Neva, living in Ankeny, Ia. It reports he owns 137 acres, general farm, 1937 Buick, John Deere tractor and a corn picker. Neva has a great talent for playing the organ and had been for many years the church organist. Lloyd died of a heart ailment, 19 Oct 1982[SS] in Ankeny, Polk Co., Ia., and was buried in Rittgers Cem, Johnston, Ia. They had no children. They lived in Ankeny, where he was remembered for his efforts to conserve the soil and pioneered crop rotation and contouring. In a memorial to him in a 1985 issue of Wallace's Farmer, it expounds on his ability to farm, and his conservation efforts. In his obituary, we see that he was a member of Ankeny Golden Kiwanis Club. [Photocopy of obituary, bound in "OBITUARIES OF FORMER ANKENY, IA, RESIDENTS AND RELATIVES; Ankeny Gen. Chapter of Iowa Gen. Soc. A copy is in the Iowa Historical Soc., Des Moines.; Also Tombstone, Rittgers Cem.]
+ .1628.4   Lester Findley RITTGERS, born 12 Sep 1912.
+ .1628.5   Frederick Henry RITTGERS, born 24 Oct 1914, died 31 Oct 1950.
+ .1628.6   Margaret Elizabeth RITTGERS, born 19 Jun 1917.

162.A Vivian Adelaid[4] RITTGERS (Reuben[3], Daniel[2], John[1]) was born 25 Jul 1880[Family records written in her own hand] in Valley Twp., Polk Co., Ia., the daughter of Reuben R. RITTGERS and Abigail Ann FINDLEY. The family story tells us that because Vivian wanted to go to high school, arrangements were made for her to work for her room and board with a family in the neighborhood of West High, Des Moines. Laura Emmert tells us that when her mother's sister, Maude Trissel, first saw this girl from out in the country she decided she would not try to be friends with her. But when Maude observed how intelligent Vivian was, and that she got some of the classes highest grades, she changed her mind and wanted to become Vivian's friend. They became chums and remained so the rest of their lives. The 1900 census found Vivian, age 19, living in the home of her Aunt, Elizabeth J. (Findley) Jennings, spouse of Nathan Brownfield Jennings. He was 55, and a farmer in McPherson, McPherson Co., Ks. Elizabeth, 53, was caring for the home. It is noted that Vivian, niece, 19, was "at school."[ED 143, p 4A, fam #68/68] In Oct, 1902, we find Vivian's signature on the Declaration for Widow's Pension, as a witness for her mother's signature, signed "Vivian Rittgers".

She married **William Ellsworth RORABAUGH** 21 Jun 1906,[PVRM, Bk 12, p. 229] on the porch of her parents' home, "Appledoor." At the occasion of their fiftieth wedding anniversary, granddaughter Mary Lou Rorabaugh modeled her wedding gown. It is amazing to see the resemblance of Mary Lou to Vivian in her wedding picture.

William was born 19 Dec 1876 in Mound Prairie, Jasper Co., Ia., the son of Garret Ressler and Sarah Jane (Lysle, or Lisle) Rorabaugh. On the 1880 census, Mound Prairie Twp., Jasper Co., Ia., we see Garret, 28, farmer, b. Pa. Wife Sarah, 21, b. Ia., is caring for their 2 children.[p. 13, fam #123/127] His father had left the home during William's childhood, and his mother supported the family by running a boarding house in Des Moines. He studied Homeopathic medicine, but was unable to establish a practice. At this time, the M.D.'s were organizing and doing their best to discredit Homeopaths, who based their medical philosophy on the natural forms of healing. This is a philosophy that is making a comeback today. We see William, 23, as head of household on the 1900 census, Des Moines, Lee Twp., Polk Co., Ia. He is listed as "Physician", living at 1624 Grand Ave. Mother, Sarah, 41, is listed as "packer, spice mill." She declares she has been married 24 years, and has born 3 children, 2 alive at this time. Also in the home is William's sister, Mary E., 21.[Ed 101, fam #573]

After William and Vivian had two children, he tried to gain entry into a seminary school in Chicago. The admissions officer was aghast that a man of his age with a wife and children would want to go to school and go into missionary work. He didn't gain admittance. William decided to try farming. Vivian's Aunt Ella (Findley) Ford and her husband, Rev Asa Ford, had moved to Altamonte Springs, Seminole Co., Florida, and encouraged them to come to Florida, at that time still more wild than tame, and open for development, and William felt that he could make a new life for his family there. They came by train in 1911. Even the trip turned into an adventure. Vivian didn't like the taste of the barreled water on the train, so at every stop William would get out and get fresh water in a milk-glass pitcher. At one stop, he checked with the conductor about how long they would be in the station, and was assured he had fifteen minutes or more. He took his pitcher and went into the depot. There was no water there, but at a business across the street he could get some. As he was filling the pitcher, William heard the whistle! Vivian had seen him go across the street, and when the train started to pull out she started hollering and pleading with the conductor to stop the train. The train kept on. She was in a panic. Besides being fearful for him, she knew he had their money and tickets in his pocket. She didn't have a dime on her. About the time she was trying to figure out how to get off the train, William walked into the car. When he heard the whistle, he took off running - pitcher and all. Unaware of how upset she was, he presented her the pitcher, full to the brim with fresh water.

In the family is a lovingly written memoir done by daughter Josephine, with contributions from her brothers and sister, that chronicles their early years in Florida. Times were hard. William tried farming, but the crops he knew how to grow didn't grow in Florida sand! He worked in construction, and eventually moved to Clermont, Lake Co., Fla. In 1913 he started the first newspaper in Clermont. Vivian wrote a local gossip column for her husband's paper. She would walk through town, dropping in on ladies to inquire about social events, parties, and family news. The ladies would plan their entire week's schedule around her visits, so as to have an item for her column. Later the Orlando newspaper would pay her ten cents an inch of news that THEY chose from her column.

On 6 Jan 1914, W.E. Rorabaugh, 38, publisher, registered to vote as a member of the Prohibitionist party. The main platform for this party was to outlaw liquor. The party never gained a lot of support and soon faded away, and we later see him as a Democrat. We see that in Oct. 1914 they bought a house lot in Clermont. Money was tight as they had invested in the newspaper equipment, but William's construction boss promised to build them a house at cost. More people were coming into the area and construction was booming, leaving little time to do a friend a favor. Finally, William got a platform built on the site and erected a large tent. The family moved into the tent for almost a year. They had a stove that heated it in winter, and we are told if it got too cold, they just went to bed. The winter days were cozy, as the sun on the canvas warmed the tent well. In warmer weather, they opened the flaps and a nice breeze blew through. Water came from a hose run up the hill to a neighbor's pump. On "water day" William would go up the hill and started to pump water into a funnel in the end of the hose. Vivian held the other end of the hose over a barrel until it was full. We are told by son John that after about a year the tent was deteriorating and one day during a thunderstorm, it ripped wide open. By the time William got home, Vivian had moved the children out. She informed him it was time to build a real house!! She was soon living in her own home.

Vivian Rorabaugh, 42, housewife, first appears on the Lake Co., Fla., voters list in 1918.

On the 1920 census, we see our little family in Clermont, Lake Co., Fla., William, age 43, gives his occupation as "Printer, newspaper". Vivian, 39, is taking care of their five children.[fam # 89/96] Shortly after this, a business group came into town and informed him they were starting a paper, he could sell out or face the competition. He sold the subscription list to the newcomers, and the machinery to a man who was starting a paper in a nearby town. The family reports they don't believe he was ever paid in full for the equipment. He worked for the paper in the nearby town until the paper was moved to a town about 30 miles away. This was before there were many paved roads, and he had an old car, so he decided to go back into construction.

Florida did state census' in 1935 and 1945. In 1935, we see William, "Dairy man," 58. Vivian, 54, is a housewife in Clermont, Lake Co, Fla. All five children are listed in the home in Clermont. Among his many ways to supplement his income, William had several milk cows, and we see him listed as "dairy man."[Reel 17, precinct 15, p. 1] The 1945 state census shows William, 69, retired. "Mrs. W.E.", 65, is still a housewife.[Reel 27, precinct 15] Son John, 37, is shown as head of house, even though the notation "Army" is in his occupation. It is not known if he was actually in the home at this time, as he had been in the National Guard on active duty during the war. William was very religious and lived his life as such. Vivian was a lady of few needs and much religious conviction, and raised her family accordingly. We are told that they were teaching Sunday School in two different churches for a while, and were active in both.

There are now grand children and great-grand children who are in missionary fields. In his obituary, we find that William suffered a hip injury in 1946. We are told that he missed his step on a roof and fell off. It drove the ball of his femur through the hip socket. It was many months healing, and never healed properly. This didn't slow him down, according to family stories. He did construction and was on a ladder or roof much of the time right up to his last illness. William died of a heart attack 30 Mar 1957 in Clermont, Lake Co., Fla. Vivian died 12 Mar 1959 in Clermont, Lake Co., Fla. In her obituary, we are told that Vivian was a member of the Methodist Church in Clermont, and of the Christian Missionary Alliance Church in Minneola, Lake Co. They are buried in Minneola Cemetery, Minneola, Lake Co., Fla. Their little home was left to daughter Josephine, who sold it to son Philip and his wife, Marion. Philip and Marion still live in this home.

ISSUE:

+ .162A.1   John Rittgers RORABAUGH, born 12 Jan 1908, died 30 Jun 1993.

  .162A.2   Sarah Josephine RORABAUGH, born 14 Sep 1909[Family in Des Moines, Polk Co., Ia., died 6 Sep 1993 in Clermont, Lake, Fla., and was buried in Oak Hill Cemetery, Clermont, Fla.[Funeral memorial card]   On the 1920 census, age 10, with parents in Clermont, Lake Co., Fla.[p 555, fam #89/96] Josephine had the religious calling that so many of this line had, and served her entire adult life in the Grace Hope Mission in various cities. A broken leg forced her retirement, and she lived her last few years in Clermont, Florida, near her family.   It is this lady's collection of childhood memories that preserved the warmth and love that made this family a huge success, even though it has never had a large amount of material wealth.   Aunt Jo was a woman of firm conviction in her beliefs.   This writer was moved almost to tears at her bedside following a broken hip and the complications following it.   It was obvious that Aunt Jo was in a great deal of pain and she called on me to help make her comfortable.   As we tried to shift her position, she would merely say, "Praise God" or "It is His Will."   Her expression was one of total serenity and acceptance, even through the pain.   It was as if she felt this trial was a brief inconvenience and she was already looking beyond it to what was to come, and was happy with what she saw.

+ .162A.3   William Lysle RORABAUGH, Sr., born 24 Apr 1912.
+ .162A.4   Philip Findley RORABAUGH, born 11 Jun 1913.
+ .162A.5   Vivian Abigail RORABAUGH, born 12 Sep 1917.

162.B Carrie Mabel[4] RITTGERS (Reuben[3], Daniel[2], John[1]) was born 5 Apr 1882 in Valley Twp., Polk Co., Ia., the daughter of Reuben R. RITTGERS and Abigail Ann FINDLEY. She is on the 1900 census, age 18, with widowed mother in Grimes, Webster Twp., Polk Co., Ia. [ED 112, p 8B, fam #152/159] The family story tells us Mabel attended high school in Des Moines and Moody Bible Institute in Chicago, Ill., where she prepared for the Mission Field Service. As she sailed to Korea from the U.S.A., she met a male missionary who would later become the Presbyterian Mission Treasurer in Korea. We are told his first impression was that Mabel and the young ladies she was traveling with were much to frivolous to survive the hardships of missionary life. She must have shown him she was from tough pioneer stock, as he was soon quite taken with her. **John F. GENSO** and Mabel were married shortly after they arrived in Korea in 1909. Josephine Rorabaugh, daughter of Mabel's sister, Vivian, (#162.A) remembers in her journal a visit from "Uncle John and Aunt Mabel".

"Our Grandma Rittgers (Abigail) spent the winter with us (in Clermont, Fla.) several times. The first winter we were in the (new) house was the first time I remember very much about her being there. And because she (Abigail) was there, Aunt Mabel and Uncle John came to us first when they came from Korea, where they were missionaries. Their Abigail was a little more than a year old and Anna Barbara was a tiny baby. She had a basket bed that was her trunk when not a bed. The rest of us did not have a great deal of furniture to use. Many times a box served as a chair. But soon after the folks came we had furniture sent to us from Grandma Rorabaugh's home in Iowa. The first night when the family came, after a little while Aunt Mabel called Abigail (her daughter) over to her and said, "Now here is Josephine." They had told her about me and she had been interested in seeing me. That year a holly tree added to our Christmas decorations. It was beautiful and was the first tree we ever had. There were Korean costumes for Abigail and me and special baskets to hold the goodies. Mama (Vivian) put in her bid for the basket bed and before their return to Korea, it came our way. It was put away carefully that it might be in readiness for a future need."

Our family story continues, "John and Mabel were in Korea for nearly 40 years when they were hurriedly evacuated to Japan when China invaded Korea. John died of a heart attack shortly thereafter in 1950. We are told that "he died of a broken heart at having to leave his ministry." Mabel returned to the U.S. to live with her daughters, but missed Korea. She became interested in Rev. Lauback's 'Each One Teach One' literacy program and returned to Korea to teach that program for several years. She served a total of 44 years in Korea. When she died in Falls Church, Va., 27 June 1957, her ashes were returned to Korea to be scattered. Her daughters set up a memorial scholarship fund for a deserving Korean girl to be educated at the high school they attended in Seoul, Korea in John and Mabel's names."

ISSUE:

.162B.1   John F. "Jack" GENSO, born in Seoul, Korea, died young in Seoul, Korea.

.162B.2   Abigail Findley GENSO, born 1913 in Seoul, Korea. She married Robert KINNEY. Spent most of her childhood in Korea with missionary parents.

.162B.3   Anna Barbara GENSO, born 23 Sept 1915[SS] in Seoul, Korea, and spent most of her childhood there with missionary parents. Emmert's Journal tell us she attended High School in Seoul, Korea, but came to U.S. to college and medical school in Wooster and Madison, Wisconson. Here she met Dr. Benedict GISLA, born 10 May 1915[SS] He was an Italian Catholic, and she became Catholic before they were married. They lived in San Jose, Calif, where they reared their six children. They each had their own medical practice. Barbara had poor eyesight and became blind before her family was grown. She managed her household with help and had a practice in Psychiatry. Ben died Dec 1981[SS], soon after they retired, and Barbara went to live with a daughter near Fresno. Barbara used to walk everywhere with her seeing eye dog. She was struck and killed by a hit and run driver on 15 May 1988[SS]. The family never received a satisfactory explanation about how the dog let her be in the street with traffic coming. We do not have the names of their children.

162.C Chester Daniel[4] RITTGERS (Reuben[3], Daniel[2], John[1]) was born 7 Jun 1883 in Valley Twp., Polk Co., Ia., the son of Reuben R. RITTGERS and Abigail Ann FINDLEY. He is on the 1900 census, age 17, with widowed mother in Grimes, Polk Co.,Ia.[ED 112, p 8B, fam #152/159] He married **Mary RANDOLPH** 28 Sep 1906 in Polk Co., Ia.[PVRM, book 12, p 225 (p 43 of transcript)] She was born 1886 in Neb. We are told he went to Texas for his health. We see him on the 1920 census, Corpus Christi, Nueces Co., Tx., Chester D., 36, is a mechanic, auto shop. Mary, 34, is caring for their seven children.[ED 180, p 8B, fam 168/169] They lived their adult life in Corpus Christi, Texas and are buried there.

ISSUE:

.162C.1   Dorotha Lea RITTGERS, born about 1907 in Okla. On 1920 census, age 12, with parents in Corpus Christi, Nueces Co., Tx.[ED 180, p 8B, fam #168/169]

.162C.2   Elbert RITTGERS, born 10 Jul 1908[SS] in Okla. On 1920 census, age 11, with parents in Corpus Christi, Nueces Co., Tx.[ED 180, p 8B, fam #168/169] He married Myrtle____. Elbert died Sep 1982 in Tx.[SS]

.162C.3   Daisy May RITTGERS, born 1912 in Texas. On 1920 census, age 8, with parents in Corpus Christi, Nueces Co., Tx. [ED 180, p 8B, fam #168/169] She married _____ JONES; they divorced.

.162C.4   Ethylin RITTGERS, born 1913 in Corpus Christi, Nueces, Tx.On 1920 census, age 7, with parents in Corpus Christi, Nueces Co., Tx. [ED 180, p 8B, fam #168/169] She married _____ HEINZE.

.162C.5   Elsie RITTGERS, born 1914 in Corpus Christi, Nueces, Tx. On 1920 census, age 6, with parents in Corpus Christi, Nueces Co., Tx. [ED 180, p 8B, fam #168/169] She married _____ THEEM.

+ .162C.6   Robert Chester RITTGERS, born 2 May 1916, died 29 Mar 1989.

.162C.7   Jessie Mae RITTGERS, born Mar 1919 in Corpus Christi, Nueces, Tx. On 1920 census, age 10/12, with parents in Corpus Christi, Nueces Co., Tx. [ED 180, p 8B, fam #168/169] She married _____ WRIGHT.

+ .162C.8   David Earl RITTGERS, born 18 Dec, died May 1986.

.162C.9   Clebert RITTGERS, born in Corpus Christi, Texas. He married Betty ___.

.162C.A   Delbert RITTGERS, born in Corpus Christi, Texas. He married Nellie ____.

.162C.B   Colbert RITTGERS, born 14 May 1928[SS] in Corpus Christi, Nueces, Tx. He married Maxine. Colbert died 15 Feb 1992. [SS]

162.D John Henry[4] RITTGERS (Reuben[3], Daniel[2], John[1]) was born 14 Nov 1884 in Valley Twp., Polk Co., Ia., the son of Reuben R. RITTGERS and Abigail Ann FINDLEY. He is on the 1900 census, age 15, with widowed mother in Grimes, Webster Twp., Polk Co., Ia.[ED 112, p 8B, fam #152/159] He married **Gretchen Ima TRISSEL** 5 Nov 1908.[PVRM, book 13, p 225. (p 46 of transcript)] She was born 3 Jan 1888[SS] in Union City, Tenn. In 1910 we find John, age 25, with wife Gretchen, age 22, in Precinct #1, Webster Twp., Polk Co., Ia. He is a farmer. They have been married one year and have no children. With them is Forest S., age 7, nephew (son of Max #127.6 and his deceased second wife, Effie Helms.)[ED 184, p 8A, fam #89/89] In 1920, John, now 35, and Gretchen, now 32, are in Walnut Twp., Dallas Co., Ia. His mother, Abigail, is still with him, and we see their daughter, Laura Ann, age 7.[ED 21, p 8A, fam #192/194] We are told in family story that he was in the grocery business with brother Abel F. and is the "J.H.Rittgers" on the ad we have seen, photocopied from a Farmer's Almanac without date, for the store in Havelock,(now Camp Dodge), Ia. In 1938, he deeded over 80 acres of his land to Jasper. It appears that he held on to 120 acres, Polk Co., Ia.[Abst. 76811, p 42] John died 8 Sep 1957 in Polk Co., Ia. Gretchen died 15 Jun 1972[SS] in Des Moines, Polk, Ia. John and Gretchen are buried in Ridgedale Cemetery, Polk Co.,Ia., along with baby daughter Eleanor; sect S, row 5.[RidgeCem, p 8.]

ISSUE:

+ .162D.1   Laura RITTGERS, born 16 Jun 1912.

.162D.2   Eleanor Josephine RITTGERS, born 18 Nov 1914 in Johnston, Polk, Ia., died there
           14 Dec 1916, and was buried in Ridgedale Cem., Polk Co., Ia.
+ .162D.3   John Henry RITTGERS, Jr., born 1 Aug 1920, died 22 Dec 1992.
+ .162D.4   Thomas Eugene RITTGERS, born 11 Dec 1923.

162.E Mary Eve[4] RITTGERS (Reuben[3], Daniel[2], John[1]) was born 2 Sep 1886 in Grimes, Polk
Co., Ia., the daughter of Reuben R. RITTGERS and Abigail Ann FINDLEY. She is on the 1900
census, age 14, with widowed mother there.[ED 112, p 8B, fam #152/159] She married **Henry
HARDIE** 8 Nov 1911 in Polk Co., Ia.[PVRM Book 15, p. 106. (p 56 of transcript)] He was
born 2 Nov 1886 in Ia. Mary lived in Boone and Fort Dodge, Ia. She was a registered nurse.
Henry was a motorman on an inter-urban run between Des Moines and "their city." They retired
to Garden Grove, Calif. Mary died 16 Dec 1974 in Westminster, Calif., and was buried in
Westminster, Calif.

ISSUE:
.162E.1   Philip Rittgers HARDIE, born 10 Dec 1913 in Boone Co., Ia. He married Florence
           ____. Philip died 26 Nov 1983 in San Francisco, Ca.. We are told that Philip and
           Florence lived near San Francisco, Calif. He had been hospitalized for something.
           Shortly after returning home, his house caught fire and he suffered extensive burns.
           Florence managed to drag him out of the burning house, but the burns were too
           severe. He lived three months before succumbing. It is thought that the original
           discharge certificate of Reuben Rittgers' Civil War Service was lost in the fire.
           Widow Florence has moved to Westminster, California. They had no children.
+ .162E.2   Ruth Ellen HARDIE, born 13 Jan 1914.

164.1 John Timothy[4] DENNEY (Sarah[3], Daniel[2], John[1]) was born 14 Aug 1860[DDBible] in
Polk Co., Ia., the son of James DENNY and Sarah RITTGERS. We find John, age 9, on the
1870 census with his parents in Walnut Twp., Polk Co., Ia.[p 421, fam #163/112] On 1880
census, he is age 19, with parents, Grimes, Polk Co., Ia.[ED 175, p 586C, fam 219/223] He
married **Nettie DUNN** 26 Mar 1890.[DDBible] She was born Jul 1863 in Ill.[DDBible] On the
1900 census, Thompson Twp., Guthrie Co., Ia., we see John, 39, a farmer. Wife Nettie, 36,
declares they have been married 9 years and she has born 4 children, all alive at this time, and
in the home. She declares that her father was born in Ind., and her mother born in Ill.[Ed 65, p
13A, fam #281/281] In 1910, they are in Waukee, Walnut Twp.,Dallas Co., Ia. John, 48, is
farming. Nettie, 46, declares they have been married 20 years and she has born 4 children, all
alive at this time and listed with their parents.[ED 20, p 10A, fam #181/185] They continue here
on the 1920 census, we find John, 59, managing a general farm. With him is wife Nettie, "58",
and still caring for adult children in the home, as well as his mother, Sarah, 76, a widow.[ED 21,
p 8, fam 187/189]

ISSUE:
.1641.1   Myrtle Vey DENNEY, born 14 Jan 1891[DDBible] in Ia., died 7 Jan 1976 in
           Grimes, Polk, Ia., and was buried 9 Jan 1976 in Highland Mem. Garden, Polk Co.,
           Ia. On 1900 census, age 9, with parents in Thompson Twp., Guthrie Co., Ia.[ED 65,
           p 13A, fam #281/281] In 1910 she is age 19, with her parents in Waukee, Dallas
           Co., Ia.[ED 20, p 10A, fam #181/185] On 1920 census, age 29, with parents there.
           No occupation listed.[ED 21, p 8, fam #187/189]
.1641.2   Raymond DENNEY, born 20 Mar 1894[DDBible] in Ia. On 1900 census, age 6,
           with parents in Thompson Twp., Guthrie Co., Ia.[ED 65, p 13A, fam #281/281]

In 1910 he is age 16, with his parents in Waukee, Dallas Co., Ia.[ED 20, p 10A, fam #181/185] On 1920 census, age 26, with parents in Waukee, Dallas Co., Ia., farm laborer.[ED 21, p 8, fam #187/189] He married Bessie ENGLISH. Died before 1976, as in sister Myrtle's obituary, 1976, it states she only has brother, Harold, and sister Edith.

.1641.3   Edith DENNEY, born Aug 1896 in Thompson Twp., Guthrie Co., Ia.. On 1900 census, age 4, with parents there.[ED 65, p 13A, fam #281/281] In 1910 she is age 13, with her parents in Waukee, Dallas Co., Ia.[ED 20, p 10A, fam #181/185] On 1920 census, age 22, with parents in Waukee, Dallas Co., Ia., school teacher.[ED 21, p 8, fam #187/189] In sister Myrtle's obituary, "sister, Edith, of Denver, Colo." 1976.

.1641.4   Harold DENNEY, born May 1900 in Thompson Twp., Guthrie Co., Ia.. On 1900 census, age 1 mo., with parents there.[ED 65, p 13A, fam #281/281] In 1910 he is age 9, with his parents in Waukee, Dallas Co., Ia.[ED 20, p 10A, fam #181/185] On 1920 census, age 19, with parents in Waukee, Dallas Co., Ia., laborer.[ED 21, p 8, fam #187/189] Called "Mr. and Mrs Harold Denney of Portland, Ore." in sister Myrtle's obituary, 1976.

164.3 Ida[4] DENNEY (Sarah[3], Daniel[2], John[1]) was born 23 Jun 1867 [DDBible] in Grimes, Polk Co., Ia., the daughter of James DENNY and Sarah RITTGERS. We find Ida, age 3, on the 1870 census with her parents in Walnut Twp., Polk Co., Ia.[p 421, fam #163/112] On 1880 census, she is age 13, with parents, Grimes, Polk Co., Ia.[ED 175, p 586C, fam 219/22] She married **James F. HUGHES** 30 Nov 1898.[DDBible] He was born Mar 1867 in Pa. On the 1900 census, James, age 33, is a farmer in Powhatan Twp., Pocahontas Co., Ia. With him is wife Ida J., age 32. She declares they have been married 1 year and she has born no children. James declares his parents also born in Pa.[ED 167, p.9A, fam 3162/165] By the 1920 census, James, age 52, is a farm laborer, general farm, in Des Moines, Polk Co., Ia. Ida, 52, is caring for the two children.[ED 85, p 16B, fam # 352/413] They resided there at 2932 Rutland Ave.

ISSUE:

.1643.1   Alice Bell HUGHES, born 2 Apr 1902 in Polk Co., Ia. On the 1920 census, age 17, with parents in Des Moines, Polk Co., Ia.[ED 85, p 16B, fam #352/413]

.1643.2   Herschel HUGHES, born 1 Dec 1904. On the 1920 census, age 15, with parents in Des Moines, Polk Co., Ia.[ED 85, p 16B, fam #352/413]

164.4 Albert R.[4] DENNEY (Sarah[3], Daniel[2], John[1]) was born 31 Mar 1871[DDBible] in Grimes, Polk Co., Ia., the son of James DENNY and Sarah RITTGERS. He is on the 1880 census, age 9, with parents in Grimes, Polk Co., Ia.[ED 175, p 586C, fam #219/223] In 1900, "A.R.", 29, is with his parents in Bloomfield, Polk Co., Ia.[ED 61, p 5A, fam #58/59] He married **Bertha Bell HUGHES**.[DDBible] On the 1910 census, Albert, 39, is a "farmer, home." He is listed next door to his parents, so has probably built a house on the home farm. Wife Bertha, 27, declares they have been married 7 years and she has born one child. That child is with them.[ED 21, p.8A, fam #107/107]

ISSUE:

.1644.1   Helen Bell DENNEY, born 31 May 1905. On the 1910 census, age 5, with parents in Grimes, Polk Co., Ia.[ED 184, p 8A, fam #107/107]

167.1 Harry[4] RITTGERS (George[3], Daniel[2], John[1]) was born about 1874 in Valley Twp., Polk Co., Ia., the son of George RITTGERS and Mary Alice RHOADS. He is on the 1880 census, age 6, listed with parents in Valley Twp, Polk Co., Ia.[p 546, fam #215/220] Not shown with parents on the 1900 census. He married (1) **Irena FRAME** 23 Aug 1900 in Polk County, Ia.[PVRM, Book 9, p. 225. (p 40 of transcription)] Harry married (2) **Maude____** about 1916 in Ia. She was born about 1888 in Ia. The 1920 census shows Harry, 45, with wife Maude, 32, in Otter Twp., Warren Co., Ia. With them is daughter Margaret, age 2 7/12. He is a farmer on a "general farm."[ED 219, p 3B, fam #67/69] Harry died 1945, and was buried in Sunny Hill Cem., Grimes, Ia.. Harry is interred with his parents, Sec. 2, Lot 221, Row 2. No wife is with him, but at the time the transcription was made by the historical society it is noted that there is a space next to him.[GPCem., p 13]

ISSUE:

.1671.1   Margaret RITTGERS, born 1893 in Ia. On 1920 census, age 2yrs, 7 mo., with parents in Otter Creek, Warren Co., Ia.[ED 219, p 3B, fam #67/69]

167.2 Grace[4] RITTGERS (George[3], Daniel[2], John[1]) was born 20 Feb 1877 in Valley Twp., Polk Co., Ia., the daughter of George RITTGERS and Mary Alice RHOAD. She is on the 1880 census, age 4, with her parents in Valley, Polk Co. Ia.[p 546, fam #215/220] She married **Dr. Abraham Leo PEACOCK** 2 Jun 1899 in Polk Co., Ia. He was born 27 Nov 1854 in Howard Co., Ind., the son of Elwood Peacock (1823-1897) and Naomi Jones (1827-1901) He married (1) Louvina Elvira Ford, who bore him a daughter, Carrie Mae, b. Aug 1878, Putnam Co., Mo. Louvina died 23 Nov 1884. Abraham, born to the Quaker faith, was a Medical Doctor and an avid gardner, we are told. His journals, still in the care of family members we are told, chronicle the births of several Rittgers. On the 1900 census, we see Abraham, 46, physician. Wife "Daisy", age 24, declares they have been married one year and she has born no children. In 1910, Grimes, Polk Co., Ia., we see Abraham, 54, doctor, b. Ind. Grace, 34, declares they have been married 11 years and she has born 2 children, one alive at this time. Charlotte, 4, is with them. Abraham died 20 Oct 1927 in Grimes, Polk Co., Ia. Grace died 15 May 1948 in Des Moines, Polk Co., Ia. They are buried in Sunny Hill Cemetery, Grimes, Ia. [*From a documented family group sheet, submitted by grand-daughter Lorene Alice Wineland.(#16722.1)*]

ISSUE:

+ .1672.1   Charlotte Alice PEACOCK, born 20 Jul 1905, died 18 Jan 1987.

168.1 Charles R.[4] RITTGERS (Michael[3], Daniel[2], John[1]) was born 26 Dec 1872 in Polk Co., Ia., the adopted son of Michael RITTGERS and Mary Ellen "Nell" BARTON. We are told he was the son of Francis (Frank) and Addie (Whipps) Rittenour. Addie's oldest sister married Jacob Rittgers (#12.7) It appears that Addie died, but we don't know what happened to Frank. We see Charles on the 1880 census, age 7, with Michael in Webster Twp., Polk Co., Ia.[ED 175, p 587A, fam #282/236] He married **Mary Elizabeth KAVANAUGH** 22 Sep 1898 in Polk Co., Ia. She was born Sep 1875 in Oh. In 1900, we found Charles in Brooklyn, Kings Co., NY. Here he was 27 and a "machinist". Wife Mary, 25, declares they have been married 1 year and she has born one child, seen with them on the census. Also in the home at 87 Vanderbuilt Ave., is Mary's mother, Annie, b. Aug 1846 in NY. Annie is 53, a widow, and declares she has born 3 children, 2 alive at this time. She also states her father was born in Ireland and her mother born in NY. She and her husband lived in Ohio for some time, as both Mary and Joseph were born there. Also in the home is Joseph Kavanaugh, brother, age 20, b. Aug 1879, a "machine operator." [ED 309, p. 10B, fam#114/228] At the time of his sister, Gretchen's, death in 1917, her obit states he was living in Brooklyn, New York. We are told that Charles heard about the opportunities on the Brooklyn Ship Yard and went there to seek his fortune. Mary died in childbirth, 13 Mar 1918. We have no record of her being buried in the Rittgers Cemetery, and assume she is buried in Brooklyn, NY. On the 1920 census, Charles, now a widower, age 41, has come home to Webster, Polk Co., Ia., with his children. He is a farmer on a "general farm." Besides his children, we see living with him his mother, Mary E. Rittgers, age 73. He is probably running his father's farm as it states he is renting.[ED 187, p 12B, fam #125/126] In the 1948 Polk Co., Ia., Farm Directory, we see that Charles lives in Grimes, owns 41/2 acres, and drives a 1942 Ford car. Charles died 5 Dec 1957 in Grimes, Polk, Ia., and was buried in Rittgers Cemetery, Johnston, Ia.[RitCem]

ISSUE:

+ .1681.1   Harry Washburn RITTGERS, born 9 Jul, died Dec 1975.
  .1681.2   Dorothy May RITTGERS, born 1 Dec 1900[SS] in Brooklyn, Kings, NY, On 1920 census, age 19, with widowed father, siblings, and widowed grandmother in Webster, Polk Co., Ia.[ED 187, p 12B, fam #125/136] Dorothy never married. We see her listed in the 1948 Polk Co., Ia., Farm Directory as keeping house for her father. She retired from the Pioneer Hi-Bred International, Inc. and was a member of Eastern Star. She died of a stroke 8 Jun 1976[SS] in Des Moines, Polk Co., Ia., and was buried in Rittgers Cemetery, Polk Co., Ia.
+ .1681.3   Charles Barton RITTGERS, born 15 Oct 1903, died 17 Jan 1996.
+ .1681.4   Grace Ann RITTGERS, born 27 Mar 1905, died 30 Jan 1977.
+ .1681.5   Walter J. RITTGERS, 15 Aug 1907, died 1996.
+ .1681.6   Herbert D. RITTGERS, born 25 Sep 1909, died 2 Oct 1993.
  .1681.7   Elizabeth E. RITTGERS, born 24 Feb 1913 in Brooklyn, Kings Co., NY. On 1920 census, age 6, with widowed father Charles and Grandmother, Mary E (Barton) Rittgers, a widow.[ED 187, p 12B, fam #125/126] She died of Bronchial Pneumonia, 15 Mar 1922 in Webster, Polk Co., Ia., and was buried in Rittgers Cemetery, Polk Co., Ia. [RitCem]
  .1681.7   Unnamed Infant, born and died 13 Mar 1918.

168.4 Anson[4] RITTGERS (Michael[3], Daniel[2], John[1]) was born 22 Sep 1885 in Webster Twp, Polk Co., Ia., the son of Michael RITTGERS and Mary Ellen "Nell" BARTON. He is on the 1900 census, age 14, with parents in Grimes, Webster Twp., Polk Co., Ia. Also in the home is "Lizzie Close, boarder, age 10.[ED 112, p 290B, fam #154/162] Family story tells us that Anson married a girl named Florence, who had been raised by his family. The only one "being raised" in the family is Lizzie. In 1910 she is called "servant", age 20.[ED 84, p 7B, fam #77/77] He married **Florence Eliza CLOSE** 9 Nov 1910 in Polk County, Ia.[PVRM, Book 14, p.225.(p 50 of transcript)] She was born Jul 1889[SS] in Ia. In his sister, Gretchen's obituary, 1917, he was living in Ankeny, Polk Co., Ia. In 1920 we find Anson, 34, farming in Crocker, Polk Co., Ia. With him is wife Florence, age 30, caring for their three children.[ED 232, p 2A, fam #36/37] Anson died 30 Mar 1950, and was buried in Rittgers Cemetery, Johnston, Ia. From his obituary, we learn of his life. He worked on the farm while attending school, then attended the CCC college in Des Moines, where he completed a commercial course. The family record tells us, "Later he attended Drake University two years, pursuing medical studies. Due to illness he went to the state of Washington, working as a surveyor and joined the national guard of that state. (It is believed that he had asthma)" It continues that when he recovered his health, he returned to Polk Co., married Florence, and it continues "He was a good neighbor, always willing to help those in need. He took a great deal of pride in his sales work which he pursued because he enjoyed meeting and talking with people." He is called a "prominent Polk City man....has always had a deep interest in school and civic affairs in the community." It also mentions that he farmed. Florence died 14 Mar 1968[SS] in Des Moines, Polk Co., Ia. From her obituary, we find that Florence had three sisters still living in 1968: Lucille Wackerbarth of Dundee, Ore.; Mrs Eva Willock of San Jose, Calif.; and Mrs Dolly Thorp of Ventura, Calif. She died at "Des Moines General Hospital after an illness of five years." It states she was born in Des Moines and lived in Polk City 54 years. She was a member of the First Evangelical United Brethren Church of Des Moines.

ISSUE:

.1684.1   Brenda Byrl RITTGERS, born 7 Sep 1911 in Webster Twp., Polk, Ia.[PVRB, book 6, p 97 of transcript.] Seen with parents in Crocker Twp., Polk Co., Ia., at age 8 on 1920 census.[ED 232, p 2A, fam #36/37] She married ___ HUTCHISON. Brenda died 1937 in Polk Co., Ia., and was buried in Rittgers Cem., Johnston, Ia.[RitCem]

+ .1684.2   Barton RITTGERS, born 5 Feb 1914, died 30 Dec 1985.

.1684.3   Michael Daniel "Dan" RITTGERS, born 7 Mar 1917 in Polk Co., Ia. Seen on the 1920 census 5, with parents in Crocker Twp., Polk Co., Ia.[ED 232, p 2A, fam #36/37] We are told he never married. He was a farmer in Polk City, Ia. He died 23 Apr 1959 in the Veteran's Hospital, and was buried in Rittgers Cemetery, Johnston, Ia. His stone tells us he P.F.C., Marine Corps Res., WW II.[RitCem]

.1684.4   Doris RITTGERS, born after 1920 in Polk Co., Ia. She married Norman LANDRESS.   In her father's obituary, 1986, she is called "Doris Landess of California."

169.1 Nellie Josephine[4] McDOWELL (Caroline[3], Daniel[2], John[1]) was born 24 Feb 1872, the daughter of Palmer McDOWELL and Caroline "Nina" RITTGERS. She married **Robert K. PURVIANCE** 21 May 1894. He was born 1 Jan 1870. On the 1900 Census, Robert is 30 and a farmer in Washington Twp, Dallas Co., Ia. Nellie, 28 is caring for their two children. She declares they have been married 6 years and she has born 2 children, both alive at this time.[ED 20, p 9A, fam #109/109] On the 1910 census, age 40, farming a general farm that he owns with a mortgage. Wife Nellie, 38, declares they have been married 15 years and she has born 4 children, seen with them. Also in home is "Lorence", brother, 29, farm laborer, odd jobs. Since no last name given, we suppose this is Robert's brother.([D 21; p. 7A; fam #93/96] On the 1920 census, Robert, 50, is still farming in Wash Twp., Dallas Co., Ia. Nellie is 48 and caring for the three youngest children, still in the home. The three sons are all listed as "labor, home farm." Robert died 9 Mar 1933. Nellie died 22 Jan 1966.

ISSUE:

+ .1691.1   Floyd Sidney PURVIANCE, born 13 Jul 1895, died 19 Jul 1972.
+ .1691.2   Rex PURVIANCE, born 11 Jul 1898, died 19 Jul 1972.
+ .1691.3   Keith PURVIANCE, born about 1904.
+ .1691.4   Paul PURVIANCE, born about 1906.

169.3 Jennie[4] McDOWELL (Caroline[3], Daniel[2], John[1]) was born 13 Aug 1877., the daughter of Palmer McDOWELL and Caroline "Nina" RITTGERS. She married **Elmer THOMPSON** about 1900 in Ia. He was born about 1878 in Ia. On the 1920 census, Davenport, Scott Co., Ia., Elmer, 42, is a laborer, "coal hauling". He reports his father was born in Ireland and his mother born in Pa. Jennie, 45, is caring for their 3 children.[ED 162, p 3B, fam #64/89]

ISSUE:
.1693.1   Alvin THOMPSON, born about 1901 in Ia. 1920 census, age 19, a truck driver,
            "grocery store," with parents in Davenport, Scott Co., Ia.[ED 162, p 3B, fam
            #64/89]
.16932   Zola THOMPSON, born about 1908 in Ia. 1920 census, age 12, with parents in
            Davenport, Scott Co., Ia.[ED 162, p 3B, fam #64/89]
.1693.3   Lester THOMPSON, born about 1909 in Ia. On 1920 census, age 11, with parents
            in Davenport, Scott Co., Ia.[(ED 162, p 3B, fam #64/89]

16A.1 George Abel[4] FINDLEY (Rosannah[3], Daniel[2], John[1]) was born 24 Jan 1877 in Grimes,
Polk Co., Ia., the son of Ulcestes S. FINDLEY and Rosannah RITTGERS. We see George on
the 1880 census, age 3 with his parents in Walnut, Dallas Co., Ia.[p 38, 311/313] On the 1900
census, age 23, with parents.[ED 19, p 8B, fam #158/161] He married **Maybelle PRESSLEY**
1 Dec 1902. She was born 4 Dec 1877. After their marriage, they lived at "Hoff Settlement,"
Waukee, Dallas Co., Ia., then "moved to the Pressley Farm, 2 miles west of Johnston, Ia.," after
1903. By 1910 George, 33, is farming in Webster Twp., Polk Co., Ia. Wife Mabelle, 32,
declares they have been married 7 years and she has born 2 children, both shown with them.[ED
189, p 6B, fam #55/55] In 1920, George, 43, continues farming in Webster Twp. Wife "Mary
B.", 42, is caring for their three children as well as boarder John O'Brian, 54.[ED187, p 10A,
fam #62/62] George died 13 Feb 1961. Maybelle died 30 Jan 1966.
ISSUE:
+ .16A1.1   Sidney George FINDLEY, born 13 Nov 1903, died 14 Aug 1982.
.16A1.2   Virginia Elizabeth FINDLEY, born 2 Mar 1910. We see her on the 1910 census,
            age 2/12, with parents in Webster Twp., Polk Co., Ia.[ED 184, p 63B, fam #55/55]
            On 1920 census, age 9, with parents, Webster, Polk Co., Ia.[ED 187, p 10A, fam
            #62/62] She married Paul WEFELMEYER 30 Apr 1967. He was born 18 Nov
            1917. Paul died 5 Oct 1978, Virginia died 1992 in Polk Co., Ia. They are buried in
            Hillcrest Cemetery, Omaha, Neb.
+ .16A1.3   Craig Wallace FINDLEY, born 30 Apr 1915.

16A.3 Ray Ulcestes[4] FINDLEY (Rosannah[3], Daniel[2], John[1]) was born 13 May 1880 in Grimes,
Polk Co., Ia., the son of Ulcestes S. FINDLEY and Rosannah RITTGERS. He is on the 1900
census, age 20, with parents.[ED 19, p. 8B, fam #158/161] In 1910, he is in Walnut, Dallas Co.,
Ia., 29, single, renting a farm.[ED 20, p 9B, fam #172/176] He married **Effa May WOOD** 8 Jun
1910. She was born 29 Apr 1880. We see them in Walnut on the 1920 census. Ray, 39, is
"managing farm." Effie, 39, is caring for their children.[ED 21, p 8B, fam #193/195] Effa died
7 Apr 1949, Ray died 1956. They are buried in Sec. G., lot 51, Brethren Cem., Sugar Grove
Twp., Dallas Co., Ia.[DalCem, p 14]
ISSUE:
+ .16A3.1   Helen Faye FINDLEY, born 21 Apr 1911, died 19 Aug 1989.
+ .16A3.2   Paul Ashley FINDLEY, born 14 Jan 1915, died 28 Jul 1985.
+ .16A3.3   Wandah Marguerite FINDLEY, born 1920, died 1990.

16A.4 Charles Daniel[4] FINDLEY (Rosannah[3], Daniel[2], John[1]) was born 13 Jan 1883 in Grimes,
Polk Co., Ia., the son of Ulcestes S. FINDLEY and Rosannah RITTGERS. He is on the 1900
census, age 17, with parents in Walnut Twp., Dallas Co., Ia.[ED 19, p. 8B, fam #158/161] He
married **Ida GROSSMAN** 14 Feb 1907. She was born 1884. On the 1910 census, age 27, he

is farming his own general farm in Granger, Dallas Co., Ia. Wife "Oda", 25, declares they have been married 3 years and she has born 2 children, both alive at this time. She reports her father b. Pa., and mother b. Ill. [ED 9, p 6A, fam #114/115] On 1920 census, age 37, farming in Grant Twp., "outside Granger City Limits", Dallas co., Ia. Wife Ida, 35, is caring for four children in the home located on the "Panora Speedway".[Ed 10, p. 7B, fam #157/162] Charles died 1950, and was buried in Colfax Cemetery. Ida died 1977.

ISSUE:

+ .16A4.1   Hildred Lurene FINDLEY, born 12 Dec 1907.
  .16A4.2   Mary Christine FINDLEY, born 24 Oct 1909 in Polk Co., Ia. On the 1910 census, age 6/12, with her parents in Grant Twp., Dallas Co., Ia.[ED 9, p 6A, fam #114/115] In 1920, age 10, she remains in parents home there.[ED 10, p. 7B, fam #157/163]She married Al MILLER.
+ .16A4.3   Charles Herbert FINDLEY, born 4 Nov 1913.
+ .16A4.4   Vinson Grossman FINDLEY, born 3 Sep 1919.

16A.5 Wendell Ivan[4] FINDLEY (Rosannah[3], Daniel[2], John[1]) was born 9 Oct 1885 in Grimes, Polk Co., Ia., the son of Ulcestes S. FINDLEY and Rosannah RITTGERS. He is on the 1900 census, age 14 with parents, Walnut Twp., Dallas Co., Ia. [ED 19, p. 8B, fam #158/161] He married **Sophia MOSER**. She was born 26 Jun 1887 in Ia., to parents b. in Germany. On the 1920 census, age 34, Wendell is a farm manager, in Waukee, Dallas Co., Ia. Sophia, 32, is caring for their three children.[ED 21, p. 8A, fam 3183/185] Sophia died 1 Nov 1972, and Wendell died 1975. They are in Brethren Cemetery, Dallas Co., Ia., Sect G, lot 47.[DalCem, p 14]

ISSUE:

  .16A5.1   Donald Wendell FINDLEY, born 4 Sep 1914 in Waukee, Dallas Co., Ia. On the 1920 census, age 5, with parents there.[ED 21, p 8A, fam #183/185] He married Hazel MASH. Donald died 9 Apr 1986 in DeQueen, Ark., and was buried in Brethren Cem., Dallas Center, Ia.
  .16A5.2   Rose Arlene FINDLEY, born 1 Feb 1917 in Waukee, Dallas Co., Ia. On the 1920 census, age 2 11/12, with parents there. [ED 21, p 8A, fam #183/185] She married George DOUGLAS.
+ .16A5.3   Esther Fern FINDLEY, born 31 Mar 1919.
  .16A5.4   Keith Moser FINDLEY, born 3 Apr 1923. Family story states he lost in South Pacific in W.W.II
  .16A5.5   Wayne Iven FINDLEY, born 28 Apr 1928.

16B.1 Clarence[4] PICKENBROCK (Nancy[3], Daniel[2], John[1]) was born about 1878 in Iowa. He was the son of William PICKENBROCK and Nancy Jane RITTGERS. He is on the 1880 census with parents in Valley Twp, Polk Co., Ia., age 2.[ED 3, p 545, fam #212/217] He married about 1901, **Emily L.** ____. She was born about 1880 in Ia. In 1910 we find him, age 31, a farmer in Precinct #1, Webster Twp., Polk Co., Ia. With him wife Emily L., age 30, who declares they have been married nine years. She has born three children, one is still alive. We see with them Louise V., age 4.[ED 184, p 9B, fam #126/126] On the 1920 census, age 41, he is a farmer on a "general farm" he owns free & clear in Webster, Polk Co., Ia. Wife Emily L. is 40, and caring for their children.[ED 187, p 9B, fam #68/68] We are told he committed suicide in 1952.

ISSUE:

  .16B1.1   Louise V. PICKENBROCK, born about 1906 in Polk Co., Ia. On 1910 census, age 4, with parents in Webster Twp., Polk Co., Ia.[ED 184, p 9B, fam #126/126]

On 1920 census, age 14, with parents there.[ED 187, p 9B, fam #68/68]   She
married Allen THOMPSON.
.16B1.2   Viola Marie PICKENBROCK, born about 1915 in Webster, Polk Co., Ia. On 1920
census, age 5, with parents in Webster, Polk Co., Ia.[ED 187, p 9B, fam # 68/68]

173.3 Solomon F.[4] UNKLE (Caroline[3], Elizabeth[2], John[1]) was born Oct 1861 in Hocking Co.,
Oh., the son of David UNKLE and Caroline H. STROHL. The 1870 census shows us Solomon,
age 9, with his parents in Laurel Twp., Hocking Co., Oh.[p 490, fam #232/232] and there with
them in 1880, age 19, working on his father's farm.[p 95B, fam #233/244] He married **Sarah
E. McCOWEN** 4 Sep 1884 in Hocking Co., Oh.[HVRM, Bk E, p. 261] She was born Jul 1867
in Oh. On the 1900 census, Solomon F., 38 is farming in Laurel Twp. Wife Sarah, 32, states
they have been married 16 years and she has born 5 children, listed with parents.[ED 31, p 102A,
fam #98/100] On the 1910 census, now in Logan, Falls Twp., Hocking Co., Oh., Solomon is
51, and a "laborer, odd jobs." Sarah is 42. They have been married 25 years and she has born
8 children, six still alive. Four are in the home at 341 E. Diamond St.[ED 84, p 16A, fam
#368/369] On the 1920 census, Solomon is age 59, with no income, in Logan, Falls Twp.,
Hocking Co., Oh. Wife Sarah, 52, continues keeping the home. Son Truman, 15, is with them.
Also in home is Harriett McCowen, 84, Mother-in-law.; and son-in-law William Griner, 39,
divorced, an "air inspector, rail road", and two grandchildren. These are most probably children
by Florence, as she is not on the 1910 census with parents.[ED 40, p 8B, fam #160/199]
Harriett declares she is a widow and was born in Oh. Her father was born in Pa. and her mother
in Md. Sarah declares her father was born in Pa.
ISSUE:
.1733.1   Charles W. UNKLE, born Dec 1885 in Laurel Twp., Hocking Co., Oh. On 1900
census, in Laurel, Hocking Co., Oh., age 14, with parents. Listed as a laborer.[ED
31, p 102A, fam #98/100]
.1733.2   Ada E. UNKLE, born Nov 1888 in Laurel Twp., Hocking Co., Oh. On 1900
census, in Laurel, Hocking Co., Oh., age 11, with parents.[ED 31, p 102A, fam
#98/100] On 1910 census, age 21, with parents, Falls Twp., Hocking Co., Oh.[ED
84, p 16A, fam #368/369]
+ .1733.3   Flossie A. UNKLE, born Sep 1889.
.1733.4   Merl D. UNKLE, born 29 Jun 1892[SS] in Laurel Twp., Hocking Co., Oh. On 1900
census, in Laurel, Hocking Co., Oh., age 7, with parents.[ED 31, p 102A, fam
#98/100] On 1910 census, age 16, with parents, Falls Twp., Hocking Co., Oh.[ED
84, p 16A, fam #368/369] He had a rail road retirement, and died July 1966,
Toldedo , Lucas Co., Oh.[SS]
.1733.5   James G. UNKLE, born Mar 1896 in Laurel Twp., Hocking Co., Oh. On 1900
census, in Laurel, Hocking Co., Oh., age 4, with parents.[ED 31, p 102A, fam
#98/100] On 1910 census, age 15, with parents, Falls Twp., Hocking Co., Oh.[ED
84, p 16A, fam #368/369]
.1733.6   Truman UNKLE, born 9 Aug1904[SS] in Hocking Co., Oh. On 1910 census, age
5, with parents in Falls Twp., Hocking Co., Oh.[ED 84, p 16A, Fam #368/369] On
1920 census, age 15, with parents in 3rd Ward, Logan, Falls Twp., Hocking Co.,
Oh. Listed as "bootblack, barber shop."[ED 40, p 55B, fam #160/199] He died Mar
1965.[SS]

173.4 John J.[4] UNKLE (Caroline[3], Elizabeth[2], John[1]) was born Sep 1862 in Laurel, Hocking Co., Oh., the son of David UNKLE and Caroline H. STROHL. The 1870 census shows John J., age 8, with parents there, [p 490 fam #232/232] and continues there on the 1880 census, age 17, with parents, listed as farmer.[p 95B, fam #233/244] He married **Ida WATTS** 6 Aug 1885 in Hocking County, Oh.[HVRM, Bk E, p.312] On the 1900 census, Laurel, Hocking Co., Oh., John, age 37, is a farmer. Wife Ida A., 35, is caring for their children. They have been married 14 years and have had 3 children, shown with them on census. Also shown is Vernon Watts, 18, hired hand.[ED 31, p 101B, fam #31]

ISSUE:

.1734.1   Edna A. UNKLE, born Dec 1887 in Laurel Twp., Hocking Co., Oh. On 1900 census, age 12, there with parents.[ED 31, p 101B, fam #92/94]

.1734.2   Lottie M. UNKLE, born Aug 1891 in Laurel Twp., Hocking Co., Oh. On 1900 census, age 8, there with parents.[ED 31, p 101B, fam #92/94]

.1734.3   William R. UNKLE, born Feb 1896 in Laurel Twp., Hocking Co., Oh. On 1900 census, age 4, there with parents.[ED 31, p 101B, fam #92/94]

173.7 Daniel[4] UNKLE (Caroline[3], Elizabeth[2], John[1]) was born about 1869 in Hocking Co., Oh., the son of David UNKLE and Caroline H. STROHL. He is on the 1870 census, age 1, with parents there [p 490, fam #232/232], and on the 1880 census there, age 11, with his parents.[p 95B, fam #233/244] He married **Agnes R. Shick**, 12 May 1889 in Hocking Co., Oh.[HVRM, Bk E, p.564] She was born Aug 1875 in Oh. In 1900 we see Daniel, age 28, in Perry Twp., Hocking Co., Oh. It states he was born Sept 1871, but we found him on the 1870 census - this was a common mistake. Wife Agnes R., 24, is caring for their children. She declares they have been married 9 years and she has born 2 children, both alive at that time.[ED 33, p 8A, fam #154/154]

ISSUE:

.1737.1   LeRoy UNKLE, born May 1892 in Hocking Co., Oh. On 1900 census, age 8, with parents in Perry Twp., Hocking Co., Oh.[ED 33, p 8A, fam #154/154]

.1737.2   Grace UNKLE, born June 1896 in Hocking Co., Oh. On 1900 census, age 4, with parents in Perry Twp., Hocking Co., Oh.[ED 33, p 8A, fam #154/154]

194.1 John[3] RUFF (Elizabeth[2], Susanna[1]) was born Dec 1859 in Marion Twp., Hocking Co., Oh., the son of Daniel Friedrich RUFF and Elizabeth DAUBENMIRE. He is on the 1860 census, age 1, with parents there.[p 152, fam #958/946], and on the 1870, age 12, with parents.[p 506, fam #216/217] On 1880 census, age 21, still with parents Marion Twp, listed as "laborer".[ED 63, p 101D, fam #106/107] He married **Nancy M.____** about 1884. She was born Oct 1861 in Oh. On 1900 census, age 41, a farmer in Greenfield Twp., Fairfield Co., Oh. With him is wife Nancy M., age 38. She declares they have been married 16 years and she has born 6 children, five alive at this time. These 5 are with them, as well as one Bessie Miller, niece, b. Aug 1891, age 8.[ED 7, p 7A, fam #71/73]

ISSUE:

.1941.1   William A. RUFF, born Feb 1887 in Fairfield Co., Oh. On 1900 census, age 13 with parents, Greenfield Twp., Fairfield Co., Oh.[ED 7, p 7A, fam #71/73]

.1941.2   Ada E. RUFF, born Feb 1890 in Fairfield Co., Oh. On 1900 census, age 10 with parents, Greenfield Twp., Fairfield Co., Oh.[ED 7, p 7A, fam #71/73]

.1941.3   Leola E. RUFF, born Jun 1891 in Fairfield Co., Oh. On 1900 census, age 8 with parents, Greenfield Twp., Fairfield Co., Oh.[ED 7, p 7A, fam #71/73]

.1941.4 Lewis R. RUFF, born Mar 1895 in Fairfield Co., Oh. On 1900 census, age 5 with parents, Greenfield Twp., Fairfield Co., Oh.[ED 7, p 7A, fam #71/73]

.1941.5 Jessie M. RUFF, born Apr 1899 in Fairfield Co., Oh. On 1900 census, age 1 with parents, Greenfield Twp., Fairfield Co., Oh.[ED 7, p 7A, fam #71/73]

194.3 William[3] RUFF (Elizabeth[2], Susanna[1]) was born Jun 1863 in Marion Twp., Hocking Co., Oh., the son of Daniel Friedrich RUFF and Elizabeth DAUBENMIRE. The 1870 census shows William, age 8, with parents there [p506, fam #216/219], and continues there on the 1880 census, age 17, with parents, listed as "laborer".[ED 63, p 101D, fam #106/107] He married **Catherine E.____** about 1889. She was born Mar 1866 in Oh. In 1900, William, age 36 is in Greenfield Twp., Fairfield Co., Oh., with wife Catherine E., age 34. She declares they have been married 11 years. They have 3 children with them.[ED 8, p 2B, fam #41/41]

ISSUE:

.1943.1 Elmer RUFF, born Nov 1890 in Fairfield Co., Oh. On 1900 census, age 9 with parents, Greenfield Twp., Fairfield Co., Oh.[ED 8, p 2B, fam #41/41]

.1943.2 Clara RUFF, born Apr 1894 in Fairfield Co., Oh. On 1900 census, age 6 with parents, Greenfield Twp., Fairfield Co., Oh.[ED 8, p 2B, fam #41/41]

.1943.3 Rose RUFF, born Apr 1897 in Fairfield Co., Oh. On 1900 census, age 3 with parents, Greenfield Twp., Fairfield Co., Oh.[ED 8, p 2B, fam #41/41]

194.4 Frederic[3] RUFF (Elizabeth[2], Susanna[1]) was born Jun 1864 in Marion Twp., Hocking Co., Oh., the son of Daniel Friedrich RUFF and Elizabeth DAUBENMIRE. The 1870 census shows William, age 6, with parents there [p506, fam #216/219] and continues there on the 1880 census, age 16, with parents, listed as "farm laborer".[ED 63, p 101D, fam #106/107] He married **Malinda____** about 1893. She was born Apr 1874 in Oh. On 1900 census, age 35, a farmer in Rush Creek Twp., Fairfield Co., Oh. With him is wife "Malina", age 26, who declares they have been married 7 years and she has born 4 children, all living at this time.[ED 21, p 17, fam #401/401] In 1910, Fredrick, 46, is still farming in Rush Creek Twp. Malinda, 36, declares they have been married 17 years. She has born 9 children, all alive at this time. We see them all listed.[ED 76, p 12B, fam #267/283] On 1920 census, age 55, "Fred" continues to farm in Rush Creek. Wife Malinda B., 45, is caring for the house full of children. They live on Boyce Road.[ED 30, p 1A, fam #4/4]

ISSUE:

.1944.1 Robert R. RUFF, born 27 Dec 1893[SS] in Rush Creek Twp., Fairfield Co., Oh. On 1900 census, age 6, with parents there[ED 21, p 17, fam #401/401], and there, age 16, with them in 1910.[ED 76, p 12B, fam #267/283] Robert died Feb 1967, Amanda, Fairfield Co., Oh.[SS]

.1944.2 Franklin A. RUFF, born Nov 1895 in Rush Creek Twp., Fairfield Co., Oh. On 1900 census, age 4, with parents there [ED 21, p 17, fam #401/401], and there, age 14, with them in 1910.[ED 76, p 12B, fam #267/283]

.1944.3 Clarence F. RUFF, born 22 Oct 1897[SS] in Rush Creek Twp., Fairfield Co., Oh. On 1900 census, age 2, with parents there [ED 21, p 17, fam #401/401], and there, age 12, with them in 1910.[ED 76, p 12B, fam #267/283] In 1920, he continues in the home, age 22, with the occupation, "teacher, common school."[ED 30, p 1A, fam #4/4] He died Sept 1981, Amanda, Fairfield Co., Oh.[SS]

.1944.4   Edith M. RUFF, born Oct 1899 in Rush Creek Twp., Fairfield Co., Oh. On 1900
            census, age 7/12, with parents there [ED 21, p 17, fam #401/401] and there, age 10,
            with them in 1910.[ED 76, p 12B, fam #267/283]
.1944.5   Fanny RUFF, born 1902 in Rush Creek Twp., Fairfield Co., Oh. On the 1910
            census, age 8, with parents there [ED 76, p 12B, fam #267/283], and in 1920, age
            18, with parents there.[ED 30, p 1A, fam #4/4]
.1944.6   Della RUFF, born 1903 in Rush Creek Twp., Fairfield Co., Oh. On the 1910 census,
            age 7, with parents there [ED 76, p 12B, fam #267/283] and in 1920, age 16, with
            parents there.[ED 30, p 1A, fam #4/4]
.1944.7   Jennie RUFF, born 1905 in Rush Creek Twp., Fairfield Co., Oh. On the 1910
            census, age 5, with parents there [ED 76, p 12B, fam #267/283], and in 1920, age
            14, with parents there.[ED 30, p 1A, fam #4/4]
.1944.8   Mary RUFF, born 1907 in Rush Creek Twp., Fairfield Co., Oh. On the 1910 census,
            age 3, with parents there [ED 76, p 12B, fam #267/283], and in 1920, age 12, with
            parents there.[ED 30, p 1A, fam #4/4]
.1944.9   Nellie RUFF, born Mar 1910 in Rush Creek Twp., Fairfield Co., Oh. On the 1910
            census, age 3/12, with parents there [ED 76, p 12B, fam #267/283] and in 1920, age
            9, with parents there.[ED 30, p 1A, fam #4/4]
.1944.A   Ruth M. RUFF, born about 1913 in Rush Creek Twp., Fairfield Co., Oh. On 1920
            census, age 7 with parents there. [ED 7, p 7A, fam #71/73]
.1944.B   Lucy L. RUFF, born about 1915 in Rush Creek Twp., Fairfield Co., Oh. On 1920
            census, age 5 with parents there.[ED 7, p 7A, fam #71/73]
.1944.C   Beulah M. RUFF, born Aug 1917 in Rush Creek Twp., Fairfield Co., Oh. On 1920
            census, age 2 5/12 with parents there.[ED 30, p 1A, fam #4/4]

194.7 Jacob[3] RUFF (Elizabeth[2], Susanna[1]) was born 18 Jun 1873 in Marion Twp., Hocking,
Oh., the son of Daniel Friedrich RUFF and Elizabeth DAUBENMIRE. On the 1880 census, age
6, with his parents there.[ED 63, p 101D, fam #106/107] He married **Nancy** about 1899. She
was born Jul 1876 in Oh. On 1900 census, Marion Twp., Jacob, a farmer, age 26, married one
year to Nancy, b. July 1876, age 23. No children yet. He is a farmer.[ED 32, p 115B, fam
#169/169] On 1920 census, age 45, a farmer in Marion Twp. Wife "Nannie" 43, is caring for
their son, and his parents. Their address is given as #4 Ridge Road.[ED 45, p 10A, fam
#182/182]
ISSUE:
.1947.1   Homer RUFF, born 18 Mar 1907 in Hocking Co., Oh. On 1920 census, age 12,
            with parents in Marion, Hocking Co., Oh.[ED 45, p 10A, fam #182/182] He died
            Oct 1976, Amanda, Fairfield Co., Oh.[SS]

19B.3 Charles[3] ELLINGER (Sarah[2], Susanna[1]) was born Sep 1877 in Fairfield Co., Oh., the
son of John Philip ELLINGER and Sarah Elizabeth DAUBENMIRE. On 1880 census, age 3,
with parents in Walnut Twp., Fairfield Co., Oh.[p 259B, fam #255/270] "Charley" is still in his
parent's home in Walnut Twp. on the 1900 census. At age 22, he is most probably working on
the farm.[ED 24, p. 351A, fam #117/121] He married **Emma E.** about 1906 in Oh.. She was
born about 1878 in Oh. In 1910, we see Charles, 31, farming his own farm in Berne, Sugar
Grove Twp., Fairfield Co., Oh. Wife Emma E., 32, declares they have been married 4 years and
she has born 2 children, both alive at that time. She declares her parents born in Ohio.[ED 50,
p. 8A, fam #102/104]

ISSUE:
.19B3.1   Teresa M. ELLINGER, born about 1907 in Bern Twp. Fairfield Co., Oh. On 1910
           census, age 3, with parents there.[ED 50, p 8A, fam #102/104]
.19B3.2   John R. ELLINGER, born Jul 1908 in Bern Twp., Fairfield Co., Oh. On 1910
           census, age 1 11/12, with parents there.[ED 50, p 8A, fam #102/104]

19B.7 Bertha³ ELLINGER (Sarah², Susanna¹) was born 23 Sep 1887 in Fairfield Co., Oh., the
daughter of John Philip ELLINGER and Sarah Elizabeth DAUBENMIRE. On 1900 census, age
12, with parents in Walnut Twp., Fairfield Co., Oh.[ED 24, p 35A, fam #117/121] There is a
"Tina, dau, 24," in the home on the 1910 census. It is not known if this is her. Dorothy not
listed.[ED 80, p 1A, fam #4/4] She married **Edward Andrew KLUMP** in Oh. He was born
26 Nov 1884 in Marion Twp., Hocking Co., Oh. Edward died 27 Mar 1958 in Granville,
Licking, Oh. Bertha died 30 Mar 1975 in Licking County, Oh. [Family group sheet submitted
to Fairfield Chapter of the Oh. Gen. Soc.]
ISSUE:
.19B7.1   Dorothy Evaline KLUMP, born 9 May 1909 in Fairfield Co., Oh.

19C.7 Frank³ ELLINGER (Caroline², Susanna¹) was born Aug 1882 in Marion Twp., Hocking
Co., Oh., the son of Jacob ELLINGER and Caroline DAUBENMIRE. He is age 17 with
parents on 1900 census there.[ED 32, p 113A, fam #114/114] He married **Clara M.____** abt.
1906. She was born 1888 in Oh. On the 1910 census there, Frank, 29, is a "laborer". Clara,
22, states they have been married 4 years she has born 2 children, both shown with them.[ED
83, fam #36/36]
ISSUE:
.19C7.1   Geraldine M. ELLINGER, born about 1907 in Hocking Co., Oh.. On 1910 census,
           age 3, with parents in Marion Twp., Hocking Co., Oh.[ED 83, fam #36/36]
.19C7.2   _____ ELLINGER, born Mar 1910 in Hocking Co., Oh. On 1910 census as
           "unnamed son", age 3/12, with parents in Marion Twp., Hocking Co., Oh.[ED 83,
           fam #36/36]

19C.8 Frederic³ ELLINGER (Caroline², Susanna¹) was born Mar 1884 in Marion Twp.,
Hocking Co., Oh., the son of Jacob ELLINGER and Caroline DAUBENMIRE. He is age 16
with parents on 1900 census there.[ED 32, p 113A, fam #114/114] He married **Bertha S.____**
before 1905. She was born 1881 in Oh. On the 1910 census, "Fredrick," 26, is farming in Marion
Twp. Bertha, 29, states they have been married 6 years, she has born 2 children, both shown
with them.[ED 88, p8A, fam #163/164] In 1920, "C.F.", 36, is a "steal" worker, car shop. Wife
Bertha S, 39, is caring for their four children, and four more people living in the home; Will
Kornmiller, nephew, 20, a laborer in a tile plant (probably kin to Bertha, as we haven't found any
Kornmillers in our lines), 3 boarders, and Frederic's brother, "Samuel," 28. This is most probably
brother Solomon.[ED 41, p 5B, fam #101/124]
ISSUE:
.19C8.1   Agnes M. ELLINGER, born about 1905 in Hocking Co., Oh. On 1910 census, age
           5, with parents in Marion, Hocking Co., Oh.[ED 88, p 8A, fam #163/164] On 1920
           census, age 15, with parents in Logan, Ward 4, Hocking Co., Oh.[ED 41, p 5B, fam
           # 104/124]
.19C8.2   Marie R. ELLINGER, born Sep 1908 in Hocking Co., Oh. On 1910 census, age 1
           9/12, with parents in Marion, Hocking Co., Oh.[ED 88, p 8A, fam #163/164] On

1920 census, age 11, with parents in Logan, Ward 4, Hocking Co., Oh. Name written "Mary".[ED 41, p 5B, fam # 104/124]

.19C8.3   Fannie ELLINGER, born about 1911 in Hocking Co., Oh. On 1920 census, age 9, with parents in Logan, Ward 4, Hocking Co., Oh.[ED 41, p 5B, fam # 104/124]

.19C8.4   Caroline ELLINGER, born Feb 1919 in Hocking Co., Oh. On 1920 census, age 10/12, with parents in Logan, Ward 4, Hocking Co., Oh.[ED 41, p 5B, fam # 104/124]

CHAPTER 5

GENERATION NO. 5

1121.1 Virginia⁵ RITTGERS (Daniel⁴, Abraham³, Joseph², John¹) was born 30 Jun 1879 in Brown Twp, Darke Co., Oh., the daughter of Daniel RITTGERS and Mary Ann WAGNER. She is on the 1880 census, age 1, with parents there.[ED 56, p 46D, fam #70/75]. She married (1) **David Otho PORTER** 15 May 1898 in Darke County, Oh.[DkCoM-1, p. 224] He is the son of Steven and Susan (__) Porter. Continues in parents' home in Brown Twp. on the 1900 census, age 22. It indicates she is married, but no last name (other than Rittgers) is given. At the end of the family is listed "Beatrice J. Porter, grand-daughter" (of Daniel and Mary), age 1.[ED 50, p 57B, fam #193/196] She married (1) **David Otho PORTER** 15 May 1898 in Darke County, Oh.[DkCoM-1, p. 224] He is the son of Steven and Susan (__) Porter. Virginia married (2) **Isaac BUTT** 5 Apr 1902 in Greenville, Darke Co., Oh.[DkCoM-2, p. 39(it is noted here she is listed under "Rittgers."] He was born 20 Sep 1876 in Darke Co., Oh., the son of John and Nancy (Coddle) Butt. He may have had a step-mother, as on the 1920 census, we see one "Mary A., 74, mother" listed. This is not Virginia's mother, as we see her in her own home on this census. We see on 1910 census, Isaac Butt, 33, b. in Oh. and a farmer, with wife "Jennie," 31, in Brown Twp., Darke Co., Oh. It is interesting to note on this record it has "M2" next to both names, indicating second marriage for both. This is not often noted. They have been married 9 years and she states she has born 4 children, all alive at this time. The question arises - where is Beatrice? The four Butts children are seen in the home.[ED 76, p 1B, fam #15/15] On 1920 census, we see Isaac, now 43, and "Jennie" 41, have in home all the children, including 20 year old Irene Porter, "step-daughter".[ED 108, p 5B, fam #111/111] Isaac died 9 Jun 1938 in Union City, Darke Co, Oh, and was buried 11 Jun 1935 in Teegarden Cem, Darke Co., Oh. Virginia died 9 Jan 1963 in Darke Co., Oh, and was buried beside Isaac.[Family group sheet submitted by grand-daughter Vera (Walters) Boolman.]

ISSUE of Otho and Virginia:

+ .11211.1   Beatrice J. PORTER, born 23 Feb 1899.

ISSUE of Isaac and Virginia:

+ .11211.2   Erma Othello BUTT, born 28 Sep 1902.
+ .11211.3   Herbert Otto BUTT, born 28 Dec 1904.
+ .11211.4   Charles Leo BUTT, born 28 Mar 1908.
+ .11211.5   Hazel Fern BUTT, born 16 Mar 1910.
+ .11211.6   Evelyn Pauline BUTT, born 3 Oct 1912, died 22 Feb 1972.
  .11211.7   Thelma BUTT, born 26 Jan 1915 in Darke Co., Oh., died 15 Mar 1915 in Darke County, Oh., and was buried in Teegarden Cem., Ansonia, Oh.

1121.2 Ira⁵ RITTGERS (Daniel⁴, Abraham³, Joseph², John¹) was born 18 Dec 1880[SS] in Brown Twp., Darke Co., Oh., the son of Daniel RITTGERS and Mary Ann WAGNER. On 1900 census, age 19, with parents there.[ED 50, p 57B, fam #193/196] He married **Cora Blanche HUFFORD** 6 Apr 1904 in Darke Co., Oh.[DkCoM-2; p 210] She was born about 1880 in Oh., the daughter of Daniel and Matilda (Troxell) Hufford, both born in Ohio. We see Ira, 29 and farming a rented farm in 1910, Brown Twp. With him is wife Cora B., 30, born in Ohio. She declares they have been married 6 years and she has born 2 children, one living at this time, daughter Echo R., 1 3\12.[ED 76, p 1B, fam #14/14] Cora died between 1914 when the youngest child was born, and 1920, where her husband is listed as a widower. The 1920 census gives us Ira, 39, living with his parents in Darke Co., Oh., where he is listed as being a "Carpenter, house carpenter." Also listed is one "Evert A., grandson, 6". We also find a Daniel Rittgers, 6, living with his uncle, Charles Hufford in Darke Co., Oh.[ED 93, p 1B, fam #24/24] Daughter Echo is with her maternal grandmother, Matilda Hufford. Ira died 15 Sep 1963[SS] in Darke County, Oh., and was buried in Teegarden Cem., Ansonia, Oh.

ISSUE:
.1121.1   Virgil RITTGERS, born 1904 in Darke County, Oh., died 1906.
+ .1121.2   Echo RITTGERS, born 10 Feb 1909.
.1121.3   Everett RITTGERS, born 16 Mar 1911 in Darke County, Oh. He married Barbalou
            HOLDEN.
+ .1121.4   Daniel RITTGERS, born 28 Sep 1913.

1121.3 Minnie[5] RITTGERS (Daniel[4], Abraham[3], Joseph[2], John[1]) was born 20 Sep 1883 in Darke Co., Oh., the daughter of Daniel RITTGERS and Mary Ann WAGNER. Minnie is seen on the 1900 census, age 16, with her parents there in Brown Twp. She married (1) **William LIVINGSTON** 1904. Minnie married (2) **Willard HART** 5 Dec 1914 in Darke County, Oh. He was born 1878, and died in 1954. Minnie died 28 May 1955. They are buried in Teegarden, Darke Co., Oh.

ISSUE of Minnie and William:
+ .11213.1   Helen LIVINGSTON, born 28 Jun 1906.
ISSUE of Minnie and Willard:
+ .11213.2   Willis Paul HART, born 17 Dec 1916.
+ .11213.3   Violet Marcella HART, born 15 May 1920.
+ .11213.4   Betty HART, born 12 Jun 1922.
+ .11213.5   Wilma Wavelene HART, born 11 Sep 1925.

1123.2 Vernon[5] RITTGERS (Samuel[4], Abraham[3], Joseph[2], John[1]) was born 21 Oct 1901[SS] in Darke Co., Oh., the son of Samuel RITTGERS and Hulda Catherine STONEROCK. On the 1910 census, age 8, with parents there.[ED 76, p 8A, fam #173/177] In 1920, age 18, he is still with them, listed as a house carpenter.(ED 93, p 2] He married **Edith C. JOHNSON** 5 Apr 1924. She was born 11 Apr 1904 in Johnson's Crossing, Darke Co., Oh.,s the daughter of Paul and Margaret (Andrews) Johnson. Vernon died 15 Mar 1986. Edith died 26 Dec 1987, and was buried in Pleasant Hill Ce, Darke Co., Oh.

ISSUE:
+ .11232.1   Joe Franklin RITTGERS, born 13 May 1926.
+ .11232.2   Roberta Ruth RITTGERS, born 19 Aug 1928.

1123.3 Elva Stanton[5] RITTGERS (Samuel[4], Abraham[3], Joseph[2], John[1]) was born 1904 in Darke County, Oh. He was the son of Samuel RITTGERS and Hulda Catherine STONEROCK. On the 1910 census, age 5, with parents there.[ED 76, p 8A, fam #173/177] In 1920, age 15, she is still in the home.[ED 93, p 2] He married **Ruby ERVIN**. She was born Aug 1904. Elva died 1956, and was buried in Teegarden Cem., Darke Co., Oh. Ruby died 1982.

ISSUE:
.11233.1   Wilma RITTGERS
.11233.2   Linda RITTGERS.

1121.4 Perry⁵ J. RITTGERS (Daniel⁴, Abraham³, Joseph², John¹) was born 30 Jan 1887 in Brown Twp., Darke Co., Oh., the son of Daniel RITTGERS and Mary Ann WAGNER. On the 1900 census, age 13, with parents there.[ED 50, p 57B, fam #193/196] In 1910 we see him still with parents, age 21, listed as "fireman, R.R." [ED 76, p 1A, fam #13/13] He married **Clara SMITH** 6 Jun 1913 in Oh. She was born about 1890 in Oh. Perry died 22 Oct 1918 in Brown Twp., Darke Co., Oh.,[FOFH, p 91.] and was buried 25 Oct 1918 in Teegarden Cemetery, Ansonia, Oh. Clara is living with her parents on the 1920 census. Father, Jerry Smith, 58, born in Oh., is a farmer. He declares his father born in Oh., but his mother born in Pa. Her mother, Elizabeth, 52, states she was born in Ill, but her parents were born in Oh. Clara has with her two children labeled "grand-son"(to Jerry), Perry Rittgers, Jr., 5; and James Rittgers, 2 7/12.[ED 108, p 4, fam #82/82] Clara died in 1957. [*Family group sheet submitted by Vera (Walters) Boolman.*]

ISSUE:

+ .1124.1   Perry J. RITTGERS, Jr., born 17 Sep 1914.
+ .1124.2   James RITTGERS, born 1917, died 1966.

1121.5 Eli (Pete)⁵ RITTGERS (Daniel⁴, Abraham³, Joseph², John¹) was born 3 Mar 1893 in Brown Twp., Darke Co., Oh., the son of Daniel RITTGERS and Mary Ann WAGNER. On 1900 census, age 7, with parents there.[ED 50, p 57B, fam #193/196] He continues in the home, age 17, where he is listed as a farm laborer, home farm.[ED 76m, 1A, fam #13/13] He married **Kathryn WARE** 7 Aug 1917 in Oh. She was born about 1898 in Ohio, the daughter of Patrick Ware. Eli continues to live in Brown Twp., where, on the 1920 census we find him, age 26, as a laborer, steam railroad. Wife Kathryn, 24, is caring for daughter Glendora, 1 10/12.[ED 93, p 4A, fam #77/77] Eli died 28 Oct 1968, and was buried in Teegarden Cem., Darke Co., Oh. Kathryn died 15 Jan 1969.[*Family group sheet submitted by Vera (Walters) Boolman.*]

ISSUE:

+ .11215.1   Glendora RITTGERS, born 23 Feb 1918.

1123.4 Velda E.⁵ RITTGERS,(Samuel⁴, Abraham³, Joseph², John¹) born 7 Sep 1921 in Darke Co., Oh., to Samuel RITTGERS and Hulda STONEROCK. She married **Francis Raymond GIBBONS** 30 June 1951. He was born 2 Dec 1922 in Hooker, Okla.

ISSUE:

+ .11234.1   Pamela Joy GIBBONS, born 4 June 1953.
  .11234.2   Craig Philip GIBBONS, born 1 Mar 1955.

1134.1 Ray Benson⁵ CONRAD (Lafayette⁴, Lucinda³, Joseph², John¹) was born 30 Sep 1895 in Darke Co., Oh., the son of Lafayette Fountaine CONRAD and Laura Ellen SULLENBARGER. On the 1900 census, age 4, with parents in Union, Jackson Twp., Darke Co., Oh.[ED 59, p 1B, fam #14/14] On 1910 census, age 13, with parents there.[ED 92, p 9A] Not with parents on 1920 census. He married **Ethel Grace HAINES** 19 Jul 1930. She was born 12 Nov 1903 in Armstrong Co., Pa. Ethel is the daughter of John C. (b. 1874, Pa. d. 1949, Rosscommon Co., Mich.) and Maude S. (Shelly)(b. 1879, Pa., d. 1951, Rosscommon Co., Mich.) Haines. Ethel died 17 May 1972[SS] in Randolph Co., Ind. Ray died 7 May 1984[SS says March 1984] in Darke Co., Oh. [*Family group sheet submitted by Kevin Marshall to the Fairfield Co. Gen. Soc.*]

ISSUE:

+ .11341.1   Virginia Lois CONRAD, born 16 Dec 1932.

1141.3 William[5] HUFFORD (Theodore[4], Catherine[3], Joseph[2], John[1]) was born Oct 1887 in Brown Twp., Darke Co., Oh., the son of Theodore HUFFORD and Amanda. On 1900 census, age 12, with parents there.[ED 50, p 57B, fam #196/199] He married **Ada** _____ about 1908. She was born about 1892 in Oh. In 1920 they are seen in Jackson Twp., Darke Co., Oh., age 33. He is a farmer. Wife Ada, 28, is caring for the home, their four children, and a boarder, 17 year old Nellie Collins, "student, high school."[ED 108, p. 1B, fam #21/21]

ISSUE:

.11413.1   Blanche HUFFORD, born about 1909 in Darke Co., Oh. On 1920 census, age 11, with parents in there in Jackson Twp.[ED 108, p. 1B, fam #21/21]
.11413.2   Marion HUFFORD, born about 1914 in Darke Co., Oh. On 1920 census, age 6, with parents there in Jackson Twp.[ED 108, p. 1B, fam #21/21]
.11413.3   Omer HUFFORD, born Oct 1915 in Darke Co., Oh. On 1920 census, age 4 4/12, with parents there in Jackson Twp..[ED 108, p. 1B, fam #21/21]
.11413.4   Noel HUFFORD, born Jun 1919 in Darke Co., Oh. On 1920 census, age 7/12, with parents there in Jackson Twp.[ED 108, p. 1B, fam #21/21]

1144.1 Lawrence R.[5] HUFFORD (Abraham[4], Catherine[3], Joseph[2], John[1]) was born Aug 1891 in Union, Darke Co., Oh., the son of Abraham HUFFORD and Della M._____. On 1900 census, age 8, with parents there.[ED 59, p 5B, fam #107/107] On 1910 census, age 18, with parents in Brown Twp., Darke Co., Oh. He is listed as "laborer, auto factory."[ED 75, p 5A, fam #140/140] He married **Iva L.**_____ about 1912 in Oh. She was born about 1895 in Oh. On the 1920 census, age 28, with wife Iva L., age 25, b. abt 1895, Oh., two children, Mother and sister Onda, in Piqua, Washington Twp., Miami Co., Oh. He is a "machinist, oil machinery company".[ED 190, p 8B, fam #211/199]

ISSUE:

.11441.1   Harold HUFFORD, born about 1913 in Oh. On 1920 census, age 7, with parents in Piqua, Miami Co., Oh.[ED 190, p. 8B, fam #211/199]
.11441.2   Archibald HUFFORD, born about 1915 in Oh. On 1920 census, age 5, with parents in Piqua, Miami Co., Oh.[ED 190, p. 8B, fam #211/199]

1151.1 William Arthur[5] LEFLER (Malinda[4], Mary[3], Joseph[2], John[1]) was born 7 May 1889 in Canton, Mcpherson Co., Ks., the son of Malinda LEFLER. [Found on the LDS-GedCom Ancestry File, Ver. 1.0, 1993 CD.(He #JXVG-3L-3)] He married **Carrol L. MIDDLESWART** 14 Feb 1912 in Mcpherson Co., Ks. She was born 8 Jan 1895 in Newkirk, Ok Terr., the daughter of J.D.S. and Wilma E. (White) Middleswart. Carrol is found on the LDS-GedCom Ancestry File, Ver. 1.0, 1993 CD.(She #JXVG-9M) Carrol died 23 Oct 1918 in Canton, Marion Co., Ks. William died 14 Jun 1962 in Goessel, Marion Co., Ks. They are buried in Canton Cemetery, Canton, Ks.

ISSUE:

.11511.1   _____ LEFLER. Found on the LDS-GedCom Ancestry File, Ver. 1.0, 1993 CD.(He #JXVG-VK) Married Della Christine Barb. At the time of submission, this man was still alive, and so the information withheld.
.11511.2   Edna Arlene LEFLER, born 23 Aug 1916 in Canton, Mcpherson Co., Ks., died 7 Jan 1950 in Kansas City, Wyandotte Co., Ks., and was buried Jan 1950 in Canton

Cem., Mcpherson Co., Ks.. Found on the LDS-GedCom Ancestry File, Ver. 1.0, 1993 CD.(She #JXVG-3Q)

1161.3 Willard Elsworth[5] GROVE (George[4], Anna[3], Joseph[2], John[1]) was born 17 Jun 1891 in Rockbridge, Hocking Co., Oh., the son of George GROVE and Lavina "Vine" HAMPTON. Willard was one when his father died. We are told his step-father wasn't very nice to he and his 2 sisters. Willard loved to fish and hunt squirrel, rabbit, coon, etc., and we are told he was a good marksman. He also gathered mushrooms and ginsing. He always enjoyed a good card game. He married **Ethel Alberta MURPHY** 12 Jun 1913 in Newport, Ky. She was born 11 Dec 1895 in Carroll, Fairfield Co., Oh., the daughter of Albert B. and Lydia J. (White) Murphy. Her mother died about 1900 and her father died about 1911, leaving her orphaned at 16. She worked at the "Joe Huls home" in Rockbridge until she and Willard married. They lived in Rockbridge, Oh., in a home they bought from her uncle, Clinton White. While Willard worked at Anchor Hocking Glass plant #2, Ethel did washing and ironing for others, cut hair and sold milk and butter to make extra money. Ethel died 1 Jan 1967 in Hocking Co., Oh. In the last few months of his life, Willard went to daughter Stella's to live, then into a nursing home in Sugar Grove, Oh. Willard died 19 Aug 1967 in Fairfield Co., Oh. They are buried in Fairview Cem., Hocking Co., Oh. [Bigham]

ISSUE:
+ .11613.1   Ruth Marie GROVE, born 25 Mar 1914, died 1 Sep 1982.
+ .11613.2   Purl Frederick GROVE, born 27 Aug 1916, died 4 Sep 1979.
+ .11613.3   George Albert GROVE, born 10 Jun 1918, died 8 Oct 1971.
+ .11613.4   Stella Mae GROVE, born 11 Sep 1921.
+ .11613.5   Harry Willard GROVE, born 17 Nov 1923, died 12 Oct 1977.

1169.2 Helen Leone[5] RITCHEY (Rosetta[4], Anna[3], Joseph[2], John[1]) was born 13 Dec 1901 in Lancaster, Fairfield Co., Oh., the daughter of Edward Allison RITCHEY and Rosetta GROVE. She married **Edward Charles COURNOYER** before 1922 in Orange County, Ca. He was born 25 Dec 1896 in Lake Linden, Houghton Co., Mi., the son of Charles and Mary (Mercier) Cournoyer. Edward died 17 Mar 1968 in Tustin, Orange Co., Ca. Helen died 13 Aug 1984 in Tustin, Orange Co., Ca. They buried in Fairhaven Cemetery, Santa Ana, Ca. [Bigham/Berens]

ISSUE:
+ .11692.1   Robert Mercier COURNOYER, born 19 Jul 1922.
+ .11692.2   Rosemary Jean COURNOYER, born 28 Mar 1929.

1212.1 Effie A.[5] WOODS (Martha[4], Samuel[3], Jacob[2], John[1]) was born 1876 in Mercer Co., Mo., the daughter of William F. "Willie" WOODS and Martha "Elly" RITTGERS. She married **W. D. SMITH**. He was born 1873. W. D. died 1964, and Effie died 1960. They are buried in Goshen Cem., Mercer Co., Mo.

ISSUE:
.12121.1   Dewey SMITH. We are told he worked for Guarantee Trust Co., in NY and he also worked for them in Hong Kong.

1212.2 Lulu Belle[5] WOODS (Martha[4], Samuel[3], Jacob[2], John[1]) was born 24 Jun 1886 in Mercer Co., Mo., the daughter of William F. "Willie" WOODS and Martha "Elly" RITTGERS. On 1900 census, age 14, with widowed mother.[ED 122, p. 15A, fam # 305/305] She married

Charles Albert RENFRO. He was born 6 Jan 1883, and died 8 Dec 1964[SS]. Lulu died 11 Sep 1980[SS]. They are buried in Princeton Cemetery, Mercer Co., Mo.

ISSUE:

.12122.1   Eldon RENFRO. He married Audrey.

1212.3 Eldon D.[5] **WOODS** (Martha[4], Samuel[3], Jacob[2], John[1]) was born 9 Jan 1889[SS] in Mercer Co., Mo., the son of William F. "Willie" WOODS and Martha "Elly" RITTGERS. On 1900 census, age 11, with widowed mother.[ED 122, p. 15A, fam # 305/305] He married (1) **Lulu F.____**. She was born 1888. Lulu died 1918 in Mercer County, Mo., and was buried in Princeton Cemetery, Mercer, Mo. Eldon married (2) **Marie___**. Eldon died Aug 1974. Stone in Princeton Cemetery, Mercer Co., Mo. No death date for Eldon entered at time of transcription, but social security death index gives us Aug 1974, with his last residence in Kansas City, Clay Co., Mo.

ISSUE:

.12123.1   William WOODS. A question in the family record as to which wife of father is his mother. We are told he lived in Houston, Texas.

1217.1 Nellie Avis[5] **VIRDEN** (Sarah[4], Samuel[3], Jacob[2], John[1]) was born 10 Aug 1889 in Princeton, Mercer Co., Mo., the daughter of Andrew Jackson "Jack" VIRDEN and Sarah Isabel RITTGERS. On 1900 census, age 10, with parents in Harrison, Mercer Co., Mo.[ED 113, p 3B, fam #58/60] She married **William Adair FINNEY** 22 Jan 1910 in Mercer Co., Mo. He was born 14 Apr 1889. On 1910 census, Mercer Co., Mo., William, 21, and Nellie, 21, are in home with her sister and father. William died 6 Aug 1960 in Princeton, Mercer Co., Mo. Nellie died there Oct 1961. They are buried in Goshen Cemetery, Mercer Co., Mo.[*Family group sheet submitted by daughter Margaret (Finney) Thomas*]

ISSUE:

.12171.1   Catherine Isabel FINNEY, born 30 Dec 1910 in Princeton, Mercer Co., Mo.. She married Charles Wesley CAMPBELL.
+ .12171.2   Glen Jackson FINNEY, born 30 Aug 1914.
+ .12171.3   John Virden FINNEY, born 2 Dec 1920.
+ .12171.4   Jennie Margaret FINNEY, born 27 Feb 1923.
+ .12171.5   Mary Frances FINNEY, born 20 Jan 1927.

1217.2 Agnes Elizabeth[5] **VIRDEN** (Sarah[4], Samuel[3], Jacob[2], John[1]) was born Dec 1889 in Mercer Co., Mo., the daughter of Andrew Jackson "Jack" VIRDEN and Sarah Isabel RITTGERS. On 1900 census, age 4, with parents in Harrison, Mercer Co., Mo.[ED 113, p 3B, fam #58/60] She married **John William PEACOCK** 25 Mar 1922 in Lake Co., Ill.. He was born 14 Nov 1896 in Winchester, Ind., the son of Charlton Alva Peacock (b. 15 Dec 1862, Randolph Co. Ind.-d.1 May 1955, Randolph Co., Ind.) and Phoebe Jane Marquis (b. 19 Mar 1870, Darke Co., Oh.-d.28 Apr 1947, Winchester, Ind.) who were married 11 Oct 1890, Randolph Co., Ind. John served in the U.S. Army during WWI. He died 18 Oct 1956 in Chicago, Cook Co., Ill., and was buried in Fountain Park Cemetery, Ill. In Dec 1992, Agnes was in a congregate living home at age 97.[*Family group sheet submitted to the Ohio Gen. Soc. by daughter Anna Lou (Peacock) Arnett.*]

ISSUE:

.12172.1   Jackson PEACOCK.
+ .12172.2   Anna Lou PEACOCK, born 22 Jul 1924.

+ .12172.3   Robert Alva PEACOCK.

1219.1 Freda[5] RITTGERS (Sanford[4], Samuel[3], Jacob[2], John[1]) was born 18 Mar 1904 in Mo., the daughter of Sanford S. RITTGERS and Etta GAY. On 1920 census, age 15, with parents in Roxbury, McPherson Co., Ks.[D 67, p 6A, fam #76/76] She married **Charles LeRoy SMITH** about 1928 in Ks.
ISSUE:
.12191.1   Harold LeRoy SMITH, born 4 Nov 1930.
.12191.2   Shirley Marie SMITH, born 25 Feb 1934.
.12191.3   Charles Keith SMITH, born 25 Aug 1937.

121A.1 Hollie[5] HERIFORD (Margaret[4], Samuel[3], Jacob[2], John[1]) was born in Mercer Co., Mo., the daughter of Joe HERIFORD and Margaret RITTGERS. She married **Keith BOWERS** in Mercer Co., Mo. Hollie died and is buried in Union Cem., Mercer Co., Mo. At her death, she left her money to city of Princeton, Mo., in memory of her parents. The city built a new swimming pool with it.
ISSUE:
.121A1.1   Peggy BOWERS.

1281.1 Ronald Wade[5] CAYWOOD (Edith[4], Eli[3], Jacob[2], John[1]) was born 24 Jun 1916 in Salina, Saline Co., Ks., the son of Roland Blanchard CAYWOOD and Edith Helen RITTGERS. He married **Marietta BURTCH** 30 Dec 1939. She was born 25 Aug 1915, died Jun 1993.[SS] Her last address was given as Reading, Middlesex Co., Mass.
ISSUE:
.12811.1   James Ronald CAYWOOD, born 2 Jan 1941. He married Ann DeLING 7 Jun 1963.
.12811.2   Donna Mae CAYWOOD, born 23 Nov 1946. She married James SERGENT 22 Jun 1968.
.12811.3   Jane Edith CAYWOOD, born 24 Mar 1948.
.12811.4   Julie Ann CAYWOOD, born 14 Jul 1950.

1281.2 Frank Rittgers[5] CAYWOOD (Edith[4], Eli[3], Jacob[2], John[1]) was born 28 Jun 1920., the son of Roland Blanchard CAYWOOD and Edith Helen RITTGERS. He married **Sheri____**.
We are told he married a second time and had two more children. Frank died 31 Dec 1992.[SS]
ISSUE:
.12812.1   Kim CAYWOOD. Family record states "adopted by Frank."

1292.1 Myra A.[5] PATTEE (Esther[4], Perry[3], Jacob[2], John[1]) was born Jan 1895 in Mcpherson County, Ks., the daughter of Erma F. PATTEE and Esther RITTGERS. Seen on the 1900 census, age 5, with parents in Battle Hill Twp., McPherson Co., Ks.[ED 127, p 2B, fam #35/35] She married **John DUHR**. He was born 27 Feb1892, died Aug 1977, Portland, Ore.[SS] Myra also possibly m. ____ Holman as second husband.
ISSUE:
.12921.1   Barbara DUHR, born 1913.

1292.2 Perry B.[5] PATTEE (Esther[4], Perry[3], Jacob[2], John[1]) was born 26 Nov 1896[SS] in McPherson Co., Ks., the son of Erma F. PATTEE and Esther RITTGERS. Seen on the 1900

census, age 3, with parents in Battle Hill Twp., McPherson Co., Ks.[ED 127, p 2B, fam #35/35]
He married **Freida** ____. Perry died July 1965.[SS]
						ISSUE:
+ .12922.1		Harold PATTEE, born 1934.

1292.3 Peter F.[5] PATTEE (Esther[4], Perry[3], Jacob[2], John[1]) was born Aug 1897 in McPherson
Co., Ks. He was the son of Erma F. PATTEE and Esther RITTGERS. Seen on the 1900
census, age 2, with parents in Battle Hill Twp., McPherson Co., Ks.[ED 127, p 2B, fam #35/35]
He married **Mary KOPLIN**.
						ISSUE:
+ .12923.1		Erma PATTEE, born 1922.
.12923.2		Melvin PATTEE. He married Janet____. We are told they have three daughters.

1292.4 Maude[5] PATTEE (Esther[4], Perry[3], Jacob[2], John[1]) was born Jan 1900 in McPherson Co.,
Ks., the daughter of Erma F. PATTEE and Esther RITTGERS. Listed as "unnamed" daughter,
age 4 mo., on 1900 census, with parents, Battle Hill Twp., Mcpherson Co., Ks.[ED 127, p 2B,
fam #35/35] She married **Joe HALLMEYER**.
						ISSUE:
.12924.1		Ester HALLMEYER, born 1923.
.12924.2		Dorothy HALLMEYER, born 1926.
.12924.3		Kenneth HALLMEYER.

1292.5 Patrick[5] PATTEE (Esther[4], Perry[3], Jacob[2], John[1]) was born 4 Sept 1914[SS] in Ks., the
son of Erma F. PATTEE and Esther RITTGERS. He married **Della**___. Patrick died 9 Apr
1989, Santa Ana, Orange Co., Ca.[SS]
						ISSUE:
.12925.1		Francis PATTEE.
.12925.2		Ruth PATTEE, born 1926. She married Robert HUBER.

1294.1 Roy[5] DARLING (Evelyn[4], Perry[3], Jacob[2], John[1]) was born 1901., the son of Frank
DARLING and Evelyn RITTGERS. He married (1) **Thelma**____. Roy married (2) **Ruth**___.
					ISSUE of Roy and Thelma:
.12941.1		Leslie DARLING, born 1926.
.12941.2		Arthur DARLING, born 1927.
					ISSUE of Roy and Ruth:
.12941.3		Flora DARLING, born 1934.
.12941.4		Karen DARLING, born 1941.
.12941.5		Kathy DARLING, born 1941.

1296.1 Lester[5] KOPLIN (Daisy[4], Perry[3], Jacob[2], John[1]) was born Mar 1898 in Ks., the son of
Archie KOPLIN and Daisy RITTGERS. Seen on the 1900 census, age 2, "Lester E.," with his
parents in the home of his maternal grandfather, Perry Rittgers.[ED 118, p 75B, fam # 32/33]
He married **Lilly**____. She was born 1902 in Wash. In 1920 we find "Callwood L.", 21, in
Vancouver, Clark Co., Wash. Wife Lillis J., 18, is caring for their child. Their address is given
as "River Road to crossing ferry."[ED 7, p 7A, fam #116/116]
						ISSUE:

.12961.1 Wilma L. KOPLIN, born Nov 1919 in Clark County, Wash.. On 1920 census, age 2 mo., with parents in Vancouver, Clark Co., Wash.(ED 7, p 7A, fam # 116/116)

1296.2 Artie⁵ KOPLIN (Daisy⁴, Perry³, Jacob², John¹) was born Sep 1899 in Liberty, Saline Co., Ks., the son of Archie KOPLIN and Daisy RITTGERS. Seen on the 1900 census, age 9/12, "Lester E.," with his parents in the home of his maternal grandfather, Perry Rittgers.[ED 118, p 75B, fam # 32/33]He married **Mary____**. Artie died 1918.
ISSUE:
.12962.1 Lillian KOPLIN.

1296.3 Elmer Charles⁵ KOPLIN (Daisy⁴, Perry³, Jacob², John¹) was born 1901 in Ore., the son of Archie KOPLIN and Daisy RITTGERS. On the 1920 census, age 18, with his parents in Vancouver, Clark Co., Wash., "Charles" is listed as a "riggon rassler-logging camp."[ED 7, p, 7A, p 115/115] He married **Elsie____**.
ISSUE:
.12963.1 Sonnie Lee KOPLIN.

1296.7 Lois⁵ KOPLIN (Daisy⁴, Perry³, Jacob², John¹) was born 1921., the daughter of Archie KOPLIN and Daisy RITTGERS. She married **Joe VAUGHN**.
ISSUE:
.12967.1 JoAnn VAUGHN.
.12967.2 Jerry VAUGHN.

1298.1 Dorothy Evelyn⁵ RITTGERS (John⁴, Perry³, Jacob², John¹) was born 4 Dec 1907 in Salina, Saline Co., Ks., the daughter of John Andrew RITTGERS and Lula Maude MONTGOMERY. She is age 2, on the 1910 census with her parents in Walnut Twp., Saline Co., Ks.[ED 124, p 61, fam #158/163] In 1920, she is 12 and in Salina, Saline Co., Ks. with her parents.[ED 148, p. 7B, fam #163/191] She married **Thomas Ray "Ray T" JONES** 31 Oct 1935 in Kansas City, Jackson Co., Ks. He was born 27 Dec 1904 in LaCygne, Linn Co., Ks., the son of Leonard Lee and Emma Grace (Taylor) Jones. He was a salesman for Adams Hats. In her father's obituary, Sept., 1945, it names daughter, Mrs. Ray T. Jones of Hutchinson, Ks. Thomas died, 21 Apr 1961 in York, York Co., Neb. Dorothy died 15 Dec 1985 in Hutchinson, Reno Co., Ks. They are buried 21 Dec 1985 in Gypsum Cem., Salina, Saline Co., Ks. [*Family record submitted by Anna C. (Attwater) Jones*]
ISSUE:
+ .12981.1 Larry Lee JONES, born 11 Jan 1937, died 15 Feb 1991.
.12981.2 Jerry Joe JONES, born 21 May 1938 in Hutchinson, Reno Co., Ks. He married Connie MERRITT 30 Jul 1960 in Haven, Reno Co., Ks. She was born 11 Jan 1938, the daughter of John and Mildred Merritt. Connie is an R.N. Jerry received a BS in Electrical Engineering from Kansas State University in June, 1961. Three days laterhe was killed in an accident where a piece of equipment broke and struck him in the chest while he was watching them repair an oil rig. Jerry died, and was buried in Gypsum Cemetery, Salina, Ks. Jerry and Connie had no children.
+ .12981.3 Sharon Rae JONES, born 27 Dec 1939.

1298.2 William Dale Arlington⁵ RITTGERS (John⁴, Perry³, Jacob², John¹) was born 14 Apr 1909 in Salina, Saline Co., Ks., the son of John Andrew RITTGERS and Lula Maude MONTGOMERY. He is age 1, on the 1910 census with his parents in Walnut Twp., Saline Co., Ks.[ED 124, p 61, fam #158/163] In 1920, he is 10 and in Salina, Saline Co., Ks. with his parents.[ED 148, p. 7B, fam #163/191] He married **Thelma Marie ELLSWORTH** 1 Jun 1937 in Ks. She was born 11 Apr 1908 in Hutchinson, Reno, Ks., the daughter of William Ralph and Lulu Rose (Peck) Ellsworth. She was living in Hutchinson, Ks., in 1992. We are told he was a Kansas Highway Patrolman. In his father's obituary, Sept., 1945, it states that he lives in Hutchinson, Ks. William died 13 Jun 1950 in Hutchinson, Reno Co., Ks, and was buried in Gypsum Hills Cemetery, Salina Co., Ks. [*Family record submitted by Anna C. (Attwater) Jones*]

ISSUE:

+ .12982.1   Barbara Dale "Bobbie" RITTGERS, born 9 Mar 1937.

129B.1 Ruth⁵ RITTGERS (Jacob⁴, Perry³, Jacob², John¹) was born 27 Feb 1911 in Mcpherson Co., Ks., the daughter of Jacob RITTGERS and Nina SURAN. In 1920, she is age 9 on census with her parents in Glendale, Saline Co., Ks.[ED 138, p 8A, fam #49/31] She married **Fred BERKLEY**. He was born 14 Jul 1906. In her father's obituary in 1954, we learn that "Mrs. Ruth Berkely" and her family were in Tescott, Ks. at that time. Ruth died 18 Jul 1975.

ISSUE:

+ .129B1.1   Vernon BERKLEY, born 22 May 1930.

129B.2 Vernon LeRoy⁵ RITTGERS (Jacob⁴, Perry³, Jacob², John¹) was born 29 Oct 1912 in Saline Co., Ks., the son of Jacob RITTGERS and Nina SURAN. In 1920, he is age 7 on census with his parents in Glendale, Saline Co., Ks.[ED 138, p 8A, fam #49/31] In his father's obituary in 1954, we learn that he was living in North Liberty, Iowa. He married **Mildred LEBERT**. She was born 31 Jan 1914.

ISSUE:

+ .129B2.1   Melvin RITTGERS, born 15 Nov 1934.
.129B2.2   Gary RITTGERS, born 27 Jun 1942.
.129B2.3   Rita RITTGERS, born 24 Sep 1946. She married Robert KAUFFMAN 30 Jan 1970.

129B.3 Frances⁵ RITTGERS (Jacob⁴, Perry³, Jacob², John¹) was born 16 Jan 1915 in Saline Co., Ks., the daughter of Jacob RITTGERS and Nina SURAN. In 1920, she is age 5 on census with her parents in Glendale, Saline Co., Ks.[ED 138, p 8A, fam #49/31] In her father's obituary in 1954, we learn that "Mrs. Frances Martin" was living in Abilene, Ks. She married **Carl MARTIN**. He was born 20 Jan 1907. Frances died 23 Dec___.

ISSUE:

+ .129B3.1   Sandra MARTIN, born 3 Apr 1938.
+ .129B3.2   Carl Martin, JR., born May 1942.

129B.4 Maxine⁵ RITTGERS (Jacob⁴, Perry³, Jacob², John¹) was born 12 Feb 1920 in Saline Co., Ks., the daughter of Jacob RITTGERS and Nina SURAN. We learn from her father's obituary that "Mrs. Maxine Hawk" was living in Abilene in 1954. She married **Harry HAWK**. He was born 14 Oct 1905.

ISSUE:

.129B4.1   Linda HAWK, born 9 Oct 1942.

+ .129B4.2   Paul HAWK, born 25 May 1949.

129B.5 Arletta⁵ RITTGERS (Jacob⁴, Perry³, Jacob², John¹) was born 11 Nov 1922 in Saline Co., Ks., the daughter of Jacob RITTGERS and Nina SURAN. We learn from her father's obituary that "Mrs. Arletta Wilmore" was living in Wichita, Ks., in 1954. She married **Robert WILMORE**. He was born 27 Sep 1916. Robert died 21 Aug 1976.

ISSUE:
+ .129B5.1   Arletta Kaye WILMORE, born 2 Mar 1942.
.129B5.2   Robert Dale WILMORE, born 11 Jul 1946.
.129B5.3   Benjamin Carter WILMORE, born 12 Oct 1950.
.129B5.4   DeWitte Hudson WILMORE, born 18 Feb 1960.

129B.6 Kathryn Jean⁵ RITTGERS (Jacob⁴, Perry³, Jacob², John¹) was born 6 Jul 1924 in Saline Co., Ks. She was the daughter of Jacob RITTGERS and Nina SURAN. She married **Charles KOHRS**. He was born 31 Mar 1923. We learn from her father's obituary that "Mrs. Kathryn Kohrs" was living in Manhattan, Ks., in 1954.

ISSUE:
+ .129B6.1   Nina Irene KOHRS, born 17 Jan 1946.
.129B6.2   Sheryl Rae KOHRS, born 11 Jul 1947. She married Robert THILLER 26 Aug 1967.
.129B6.3   Jeanette KOHRS, born 8 Nov 1959.

129B.7 Jacob B.⁵ Rittgers, JR. (Jacob⁴, Perry³, Jacob², John¹) was born 30 Jul 1927[SS] in Saline Co., Ks., the son of Jacob RITTGERS and Nina SURAN. He married **Gladys GRUBB**. She was born 28 Mar 1928. We learn from his father's obituary that he was living in Abilene, Ks., in 1954. Gladys died 22 Aug 1964. We are told Jacob died 16 Dec 1974, but SS reports Nov 1974.

ISSUE:
.129B7.1   Vicki Elaine RITTGERS, born 31 Aug 1948. She married Tom FAULKNER.
+ .129B7.2   Darrell Vincent RITTGERS, born 26 Jan 1950.
+ .129B7.3   Jacque Berniece RITTGERS, born 29 Dec 1951.
.129B7.4   James Lee RITTGERS, born 9 Feb 1953.
.129B7.5   Emma Jean RITTGERS, born 4 Oct 1959.

129B.8 Darrell⁵ RITTGERS (Jacob⁴, Perry³, Jacob², John¹) was born 28 Feb 1929, the son of Jacob RITTGERS and Nina SURAN. He married **Jeanette LATSHAW**. She was born 24 Apr 1933. We learn from his father's obituary that he was living in Junction City, Ks., in 1954.

ISSUE:
.129B8.1   James Ray RITTGERS, born 18 Feb 1959.

129C.1 Kenneth Arthur⁵ RITTGERS (Perry⁴, Perry³, Jacob², John¹) was born 28 Aug 1916 [SS] in Salina, Saline Co., Ks., the son of Perry Arthur RITTGERS and Anna REINBOLD. The 1920 census finds Kenneth, age 3, with his parents in Greely, Saline Co., Ks.[ED 139, p 2D, fam #46/47] He married **Barbara ELDER** 15 Dec 1945 in San Francisco, Calif. She was born 24 Aug 1918. After retirement, he and his wife made their home in San Francisco, Calif. Kenneth died 30 Apr 1966[SS] in San Francisco, Calif., and was buried in San Francisco, Calif. From his obituary, we learn that Kenneth was a Chief Petty officer, in the Navy for 22 years.[obituary - photocopy furnished with no newspaper banner.] Barbara died 26 Feb 1988.[SS]

ISSUE:

+ .129C1.1   Troy Kenneth RITTGERS, born 11 Jan 1950.

129C.2 Bernard Edward[5] RITTGERS (Perry[4], Perry[3], Jacob[2], John[1]) was born 12 Jan 1921 in Salina, Saline Co., Ks., the son of Perry Arthur RITTGERS and Anna REINBOLD. He married **Dorothy ANDREWS** 6 Nov 1944 in Salina, Saline Co., Ks. She was born 3 Apr 1923. He served in the Navy during WWII, on board the U.S.S. Cleveland in the South Pacific. Bernard, an optician, and Dorothy live in Salina, Ks.

ISSUE:

+ .129C2.1   Jerry Lee RITTGERS, born 15 Jun 1947.
+ .129C2.2   Jolene Kay RITTGERS, born 21 Nov 1949.
+ .129C2.3   Lynette Jean RITTGERS, born 19 Jun 1956.

129C.3 Robert Dean[5] RITTGERS (Perry[4], Perry[3], Jacob[2], John[1]) was born 9 Jul 1924 in Saline Co., Ks., the son of Perry Arthur RITTGERS and Anna REINBOLD. Robert is listed as being in the Navy in his father's obituary in 1947. He married **Lee Ann RALSTON** 12 Mar 1950 in Salina, Saline Co., Ks. She was born 29 Apr 1929. In his brother, Kenneth's, obituary in 1966, it is noted he is living in Salina, Ks.

ISSUE:

+ .129C3.1   Michael Dean RITTGERS, born 16 May 1951.
+ .129C3.2   Mary Patricia RITTGERS, born 16 Jun 1954.
  .129C3.3   Sue Ellen RITTGERS, born 27 Jan 1957 in Salina, Saline Co., Ks. She married Thomas STEGER 15 Jul 1983.

129C.4 Anna Lee[5] RITTGERS (Perry[4], Perry[3], Jacob[2], John[1]) was born 26 Sep 1932 in Salina, Saline Co., Ks., the daughter of Perry Arthur RITTGERS and Anna REINBOLD. She married **James GRIDER** 3 Jan 1954 in Salina, Saline Co., Ks. He was born 13 Aug 1930. In her brother, Kenneth's, obituary in 1966, it is noted she was living in San Francisco, Calif.

ISSUE:

  .129C4.1   Anna Jane GRIDER, born 1 Apr 1956.
  .129C4.2   Steven James GRIDER, born 30 Mar 1959. He married Joan DWIGHT 17 Dec 1977.
  .129C4.3   Ronald Jay GRIDER, born 31 Dec 1960, died 6 Jan 1974.

129C.5 Marlene Rose[5] RITTGERS (Perry[4], Perry[3], Jacob[2], John[1]) was born 24 Oct 1935 in Salina, Saline Co., Ks., the daughter of Perry Arthur RITTGERS and Anna REINBOLD. She married **Marvin DAWDY** 20 Dec 1953 in Salina, Saline Co., Ks. In her brother, Kenneth's, obituary in 1966, it is noted that she is living in Wichita, Ks.

ISSUE:

+ .129C5.1   Cynthia Ann DAWDY, born 29 May 1957.
  .129C5.2   Linda Kay DAWDY, born 6 Jul 1961.

129D.1 William Glea[5] RITTGERS (William[4], Perry[3], Jacob[2], John[1]) was born 7 Sep 1917[SS] in Salina, Saline Co., Ks., the son of William Henry RITTGERS and Frances UNDERWOOD. We find him on the 1920 census, at age 2 with his parents in Salina, Saline Co., Ks.[ED 149, p.

1A, fam #4/4) He married **Margaret____**, born 8 Feb 1917.[SS] In father's obituary, Nov 1962, it states William lived at 9719 Hardtner, Wichita Co., Ks. Further states father survived by three grandchildren. William died 19 May 1989[SS] in Wichita, Ks. At the time he died, he was living in Sedgwick Co., Ks. Margaret died Wichita, Sedgwick Co., Ks., 13 Feb 1995.[SS]

ISSUE:

+ .129D1.1   Harlan RITTGERS, born 10 Jan 1938.
+ .129D1.2   Susan RITTGERS.
+ .129D1.3   Ann RITTGERS.

12C1.2 Arthur Morrison[5] NOSLER (Alva[4], Esther[3], Jacob[2], John[1]) was born Oct 1892[1900 census] in San Diego, San Diego Co., Calif., the son of Alva Asbury NOSLER and Alice E. COLTON. [LDS-IGI; Calif, 1992, fiche #0067, page #3,650 gives a birth date of 8 Nov 1893], Seen on the 1900 census, age 7, with parents in San Diego, San Diego Co., Calif.[ED 196, p 11A, fam #160/229]   On 1910 census, age 16, with parents there.[ED 159, p 236, fam #196/236] He married **Thelma____** about 1918 in San Diego, San Diego Co., Calif. She was born about 1900 in Canada to parents born in Canada. She reports she came into this country in 1908, and naturalized in 1918. On the 1920 census, age 26, Arthur is a "chauffeur, transfer co." in home with parents, San Diego. Also in home is wife Thelma, 20, and their daughter.[ED 336, p 8B, fam #186/252]

ISSUE:

.12C12.1   Betty NOSLER, born Jun 1918 in San Diego, San Diego, Calif.. On 1920 census, age 1 6/12, with parents and grand-parents, San Diego, San Diego Co., Calif.[ED 336, p 8B, fam #186/252]

12D1.3 Odessa Fern[5] RITTGERS(William[4], Henry[3] , Jacob[2], John[1]) was born 26 June 1904 in Glenwood, Pope Co,, Minn.., to William Henry RITTGERS and Melissa Mae MERRIAM. She is on the 1910 census, age 5, with parents in Glenwood, Pope Co., Minn.[ED 99, p 7B, fam #91/106] She married **Dorf JONES**. He was born9 May 1900 in Wells, Minn. We are told he was a taxidermist. Among his other interests, he made telescopes which were of such high precision that "We were able to see the moons of Jupiter and the rivet holes in a water tank a couple of miles away." Dorf also enjoyed carving and photography, which he won awards for. The family moved to Pasadena, Ca., in 1927, and Kelso, Wa., in 1929, where he lived until about 1953. He next moved to Olympia and finally Valley, Wa. Odessa died in Kelso, Wash., June 1942. Dorf died Sept 1965 in Deer Park, Wa.

ISSUE:

.12D13.1   Clarence W. JONES, born 2 Nov 1926, Minn. We are told he is a retired Orthopaedic surgeon, now living in Aberdeen, Wa. Five children.
.12D13.2   David JONES, born 31 Mar 1928, died by drowning 1935.
+ .12D13.3   Ralph H. Jones, born 21 Mar 1929.

12D1.4 Lester Norman[5] RITTGERS (William[4], Henry[3], Jacob[2], John[1]) was born 22 Jul 1907 in Glenwood, Pope Co., Minn., the son of William Henry RITTGERS and Melissa May MERRIAN. On 1910 census, age 2, with parents in Glenwood, Pope Co., Minn.[ED 99, p 7B, fam #91/106] He married **Emma____**. Lester died 17 Nov 1966.

ISSUE:

.12D14.1   Mary RITTGERS. She married Thomas KEES.

12D1.5 Eula Mae⁵ RITTGERS (William⁴, Henry³, Jacob², John¹) was born in Minn., the daughter of William Henry RITTGERS and Melissa May MERRIAN. She married _____ **CARLSON**.

ISSUE:

.12D15.1   Norman CARLSON.
.12D15.2   Suzie CARLSON.
.12D15.3   Mary Ann CARLSON.
.12D15.4   Bobbie CARLSON.

12D1.6 Kenneth Herbert⁵ RITTGERS (William⁴, Henry³, Jacob², John¹) was born 15 Aug 1913 in Thief River Fall, Minn., the son of William Henry RITTGERS and Melissa May MERRIAN. He married (1) **Verna LaVonne HENSLIN** 26 May 1947 in Tijuana, Mexico; they divorced. She was born 18 Nov 1919 in Dodge Center, Minn., the daughter of Walter and Ruth Eliza (Kent) Hinslin. Kenneth married (2) **Sandra Lynn PRUITT**. In the family record, she is called "of Florida."[Family group sheet by Kenneth Rittgers.]

ISSUE of Kenneth and Verna:

.12D16.1   Darrell Evan RITTGERS, born 19 Jan 1948 in Altadena, Calif.
.12D16.2   Ruth Ann RITTGERS, born 31 Mar 1949 in Monrovia, Calif. She married
               _____ BERNSTEIN.
+ .12D16.3   Roberta Kay RITTGERS, born 31 May 1950.
.12D16.4   Barbara Jean RITTGERS, born 19 Apr 1960 in Covina, Calif.

12D8.4 Orville Thomas⁵ RITTGERS (Joe⁴, Henry³, Jacob², John¹) was born 7 Oct 1930 in Glenwood, Minn., the son of Joe Ross RITTGERS and Georgia Anna DOBBINS. He married **Marlene Vay JOHNSON** 17 Aug 1952 in Glenwood, Minn. She was born 23 Nov 1933, the daughter of Myrl Joseph and Gladys (Hansen) Johnson.. *[Family group sheet, submitted by Orvill T. Rittgers]*

ISSUE:

.12D84.1   Jeffrey Allen RITTGERS, born 5 Aug 1954 in Fort Smith, Ark. He married Gina
           GRILLO in Hibbing, Minn.
.12D84.2   Debra Lynn RITTGERS, born 12 Jan 1956 in Hibbing, Minn.
.12D84.3   Kevin Bruce RITTGERS, born 10 Feb 1957 in Hibbing, Minn.

12E1.3 Bryan O.⁵ YOUNG (Almeda⁴, Daniel³, Jacob², John¹) was born 10 Sep 1919 in Washington Twp., Greene Co., Ia., the son of Orsanus W. YOUNG and Almeda Catharine RITTGERS. Seen on 1920 census, age 3 months, with parents in Washington Twp., Greene Co., Ia.[ED 118, p 3B, fam #66/66] He married **Mavis Grade SHORTS** 16 Jun 1943.

ISSUE:

.12E13.1   Bryan Terry YOUNG, born 14 May 1944 in Rockland, Me.
.12E13.2   Stephen Douglas YOUNG, born 2 Jan 1947 in Jefferson, Polk Co., Ia.
.12E13.3   Sterling Craig YOUNG, born 9 Sep 1948 in Jefferson, Polk Co., Ia.
.12E13.4   Mark Allen YOUNG, born 29 Aug 1952 in Jefferson, Polk Co., Ia.
.12E13.5   Lynn Ann YOUNG, born 18 Oct 1954 in Jefferson, Polk Co., Ia.

12E1.4 Wallace⁵ YOUNG (Almeda⁴, Daniel³, Jacob², John¹) was born 4 Mar 1922 in Washington Twp., Greene Co., Ia., the son of Orsanus W. YOUNG and Almeda Catharine RITTGERS. He married **Ruth JOHNSON** 24 Jun 1951. Wallace died Feb 1987.[SS]

ISSUE:
.12E14.1   Roger Wallace YOUNG, born 9 Jan 1953 in Perry, Ia..

12E1.5 Mary Ella⁵ YOUNG (Almeda⁴, Daniel³, Jacob², John¹) was born 6 May 1925 in Washington Twp., Greene Co., Ia., the daughter of Orsanus W. YOUNG and Almeda Catharine RITTGERS. She married **Lawrence HUBER** 22 Jun 1948 in Rippey, Greene Co., Ia.
ISSUE:
.12E15.1   Robert Lawrence HUBER, born 9 Dec 1950 in Jefferson, Polk Co., Ia.
.12E15.2   Ruth Marie HUBER, born 6 May 1954 in Jefferson, Polk Co., Ia.

12E2.1 Alice Almeda⁵ RITTGERS (Burton⁴, Daniel³, Jacob², John¹) was born 21 Dec 1911 in Paton, Greene Co., Ia., the daughter of Burton A. RITTGERS and Effie Mae FORD. Seen on the 1920 census, age 8, with parents in Paton, Greene Co., Ia.[ED 116, p 4A, fam #114/119] She married **Owen LAPE**.
ISSUE:
.12E21.1   Albert LAPE.

12E3.1 Mary Zetta⁵ RITTGERS (Grover⁴, Daniel³, Jacob², John¹) was born 1 Oct 1914 in Washington Twp., Greene Co., Ia., the daughter of Grover C. RITTGERS and Nellie GROVES. On 1920 census, age 5, with parents in Washington Twp., Greene Co., Ia.[ED 118, p 4B, fam #94/94] She married **Marvin LIND** in Rippey, Greene Co., Ia. Her engagement announcement in the newspaper reports she to be married on 23 Dec., but gives no year. No banner or date with photocopy of announcement.
ISSUE:
.12E31.1   Marvin Grover LIND, born 1945.

12H1.1 Benjamin Joseph⁵ RITTGERS (Horace⁴, Benjamin³, Jacob², John¹) was born 3 Apr 1933 in Pocahontas Co., Ia., the son of Horace B. RITTGERS and Phyllis Mildred TURNER. He married **JoAnn COOPER**. She was born 1935.
ISSUE:
+ .12H11.1   Minyon Rose RITTGERS, born 1958.
.12H11.2   Rochel Rae RITTGERS, born 1959. She married Glen SEEMAYER.
+ .12H11.3   Dana Rene RITTGERS, born 1961.

12H2.1 Arlene LaVonne⁵ ALBERTS (Clara⁴, Benjamin³, Jacob², John¹) was born 16 Feb 1925 in Pocahontas Co., Ia., the daughter of Ora P. ALBERTS and Clara Catherine RITTGERS. She married **Clinton Arthur FODGE**. He was born He was born 12 Feb 1925 in Richmond Hights, St. Louis, Mo., the son of Arthur C. FOGDE and Bernice HOLLAND. He served in the Air Force, and made a career in petrolium sales. Arlene was a graduate of Iowa State Teachers College, Cedar Fals, Ia., and was an elementary school teacher.
ISSUE:
+ .12H21.1   Christina Catherine FODGE, born 29 Nov 1947.
+ .12H21.2   Linda LaVonne FODGE, born 20 Mar 1955.

22H3.1 Richard Allen⁵ NAEVE (Hattie⁴, Benjamin³, Jacob², John¹) was born 24 Oct 1930 in Humbolt, Humbolt Co., Ia., the son of Otto John NAEVE and Hattie Lovina RITTGERS. He married (1) **LaVonne Adela KREUTZKAMPF** 10 Nov 1957 in Jewell, Ia. She was born

29 May 1935, the daughter of Albert and Pearl (__) Kreutzkampf. LaVonne died 24 Dec 1980 in Humbolt, Ia. Richard married (2) **Elaine (LeBrun) TOW**. In mother's obituary, 1995, he was reported living in Humbolt, Humbolt Co. Ia.

ISSUE of Richard and LaVonne:

+ .12H31.1   Brent Loren NAEVE, born 4 Dec 1958.
  .12H31.2   Valerie Lynn NAEVE, born 1960. She married Gregory Keith HAINES.
+ .12H31.3   Thad Lowell NAEVE, born 1960.

12H3.2 Philip Frederick[5] NAEVE (Hattie[4], Benjamin[3], Jacob[2], John[1]) was born 12 Oct 1932 in Humbolt, Humbolt Co., Ia., the son of Otto John NAEVE and Hattie Lovina RITTGERS. He married **Marilynne Joyce SYKES**. In mother's obituary, 1995, he was reported living in Humbolt, Humbolt Co. Ia.

ISSUE:

+ .12H32.1   Kyndra Suzanne NAEVE, born 1962.
  .12H32.2   Camille NAEVE, born 1964.

12H3.3 Keith Lowell[5] NAEVE (Hattie[4], Benjamin[3], Jacob[2], John[1]) was born 28 May 1938 in Humbolt, Humbolt Co., Ia., the son of Otto John NAEVE and Hattie Lovina RITTGERS. He married **Diane HOFFMAN**. In mother's obituary, 1995, he was reported living in Racine, Wis.

ISSUE:

+ .12H33.1   Todd Allen NAEVE, born 1967.
  .12H33.2   Nichole Marie NAEVE, born 1970.

12H4.1 Delores Marie[5] BREIHOLZ (Coral[4], Benjamin[3], Jacob[2], John[1]) was born 12 Jul 1926 in Ia., the daughter of Alfred J. BREIHOLZ and Coral Martha RITTGERS.She married **Robert STROUP**. He was born 1922. We are told they lived in Mallard, Ia. Robert died 1995.

ISSUE:

+ .12H41.1   Joan Suzanne STROUP, born 1951.

12H4.2 Robert Alfred[5] BREIHOLZ (Coral[4], Benjamin[3], Jacob[2], John[1]) was born 19 Apr 1931 in Ia., the son of Alfred J. BREIHOLZ and Coral Martha RITTGERS. He married **Doris MARESH**.

ISSUE:

+ .12H42.1   Scott Robert BREIHOLZ, born 1960.
  .12H42.2   Todd Alfred BREIHOLZ, born 1961. He married Cheryl.

12H5.1 Laura Jean[5] RITTGERS (Frank[4], Benjamin[3], Jacob[2], John[1]) was born 11 Oct 1933 in Ft. Dodge, Webster Co., Ia., the daughter of Frank Elmer RITTGERS and Lucy Reyburn HARTLEY. Laura is a teacher. She married **Edwin Lloyd JOHNSON, Jr.**. He was born 18 Mar 1930., the son of Edwin Lloyd and Vivian (__) Johnson. He is an executive and a Methodist. They live in Seattle, Wash. Lloyd is an avid photographer and documented the 1997 Rittgers Reunion in Branson, Mo., for which we extend our thanks for the wonderful job.[*Family group sheet submitted by Darlene (Hartley) Hudek.*]

ISSUE:

+ .12H51.1   Pamela Lynne JOHNSON, born 16 Jul 1961.
  .12H51.2   Derek Todd JOHNSON, born 7 Nov 1962 in Seattle, King Co., Wash. He married Diane Marie NOTTINGHAM 11 Aug 1994.

.12H51.3   Cameron Brett JOHNSON, born 27 Jul 1967 in Seattle, King Co., Wash.

12H5.2 Iora Kay[5] RITTGERS (Frank[4], Benjamin[3], Jacob[2], John[1]) was born 2 Oct 1942 in Pocahontis Co., Ia., the daughter of Frank Elmer RITTGERS and Lucy Reyburn HARTLEY. Iora married (1) Bill Blomker. She married **Joel DOP** 24 Jan 1976. He was born 17 Jul 1947, the son of Howard and Betty (Holland) Dop. She is a teacher. They are Methodists and live in Santa Fe., N.M.[Family group sheet submitted by Darlene (Hartley) Hudek.]

ISSUE of Joel and Iora:

.12H52.1   Monte DOP, born 13 Jun 1979 in Des Moines, Polk Co., Ia.

12H5.3 Mary Ann[5] RITTGERS (Frank[4], Benjamin[3], Jacob[2], John[1]) was born 1 Sep 1944 in Ft. Dodge, Webster Co., Ia., the daughter of Frank Elmer RITTGERS and Lucy Reyburn HARTLEY. She is a therapist, and lives in Tarpon Springs, Fla. She married (1) **Howard L. WILLIAMS** 1970; they divorced. He was born 28 Oct 1945 in Webster City, Hamilton, Ia., the son of John and Francis (___) Williams. He is an electrical engineer. She married (2) John _____. Mary married (3) _____ **JARVIS**.

ISSUE of Howard and Mary:

.12H53.1   Travis John WILLIAMS, born 18 Aug 1972 in Arlington Height, Ill..

12H6.1 Roland Dale[5] RITTGERS (Ernest[4], Benjamin[3], Jacob[2], John[1]) was born 26 Dec 1926 in Plover, Pocahontas Co., Ia., the son of Ernest J. RITTGERS and Leila Alice GILLELAND. He married **Mary Bell MARCUM** 17 July 1946 in Humbolt, Ia. She was born 31 Jan 1925 in Kansas City, Mo., the daughter of Ed MARCUM and Dorothy DeVault. Roland served in the U.S. Army 1945-46. He is a retired farmer.

ISSUE:

+ .12H61.1   Roxana Dale RITTGERS, born 27 Oct 1948.
+ .12H61.2   George Ernest RITTGERS, born 7 Oct 1950.
+ .12H61.3   Bryan Anthony RITTGERS, born 15 Sept 1952.

12H6.2 Wanda Lucerne[5] RITTGERS (Ernest[4], Benjamin[3], Jacob[2], John[1]) was born 22 Jul 1928 in Ia., the daughter of Ernest J. RITTGERS and Leila Alice GILLELAND. She married **Robert Edward IVERSON** 2 Jun 1951 in Nashua, Ia. He was born 21 Jun 1924 in Waterloo, Ia., the son of Clarence Leroy and Hattied Mae (Tuman) Iverson. She is a teacher and housewife, and husband Robert was a tool & dye maker. He served in WWII. They lived in Waterloo, Black Hawk Co., Ia. Robert died 13 Feb 1991 in Rochester, Olmsted Co., Minn., and was buried 16 Jan 1991 in Memorial Park Cemetery., Waterloo, Ia. [*Family group sheet submitted by Wanda Iverson.*]

ISSUE:

+ .12H62.1   Debra Sue IVERSON, born 30 Jun 1953.
+ .12H62.2   Donald James IVERSON, born 30 Jun 1953.
+ .12H62.3   Rebecca Kay IVERSON, born 8 Apr 1961.
+ .12H62.4   Timothy John IVERSON, born 13 Aug 1962.

12H8.1 Larry Lee[5] COOKSEY (Ruth[4], Benjamin[3], Jacob[2], John[1]) was born 18 Jul 1940 in Pocahontas, Pocahontas Co., Ia., the son of Earl Jones COOKSEY and Ruth Iora RITTGERS. He married (1) **Jane Garnet MADDOX**. Larry married (2) **Sandra WEBER**.

ISSUE of Larry and Jane:

.12H81.1   Neal Alan COOKSEY, born 1960.
+ .12H81.2   Natalie Ann COOKSEY, born 1962.
                    ISSUE of Larry and Sandra:
+ .12H81.3   Annette Ann COOKSEY.
.12H81.4   Suzette Lynn COOKSEY, born 1972.

12HA.1 Donald Eugene[5] RITTGERS (Jacob[4], Benjamin[3], Jacob[2], John[1]) was born 29 May 1936 in Rolphe, Pocahontas Co., Ia., the son of Jacob B. RITTGERS and Jeane SCHEFFERS. He married **Beatrice Anne HAYNES**. She was born 1942.
                    ISSUE:
+ .12HA1.1   David Edward RITTGERS, born 1961.
+ .12HA1.2   Rhonda Renee RITTGERS, born 1962.
+ .12HA1.3   Brenda Kaye RITTGERS, born 1963.
+ .12HA1.4   Donna Jeane RITTGERS, born 1970.

12HA.2 Joan Kay[5] RITTGERS (Jacob[4], Benjamin[3], Jacob[2], John[1]) was born 5 Jun 1938 in Rolphe, Pocahontas Co., Ia., the daughter of Jacob B. RITTGERS and Jeane SCHEFFERS. She married **Larry BURNS** 7 Aug 1960, Rolfe, Pocahontas Co., Ia. We are told in her wedding announcement (submitted with no banner, but 1960 written on it) that she graduated from Morningside College, Sioux City, Ia., and has been teaching in Rolfe, Ia. They were to make their home in Humbolt, Ia.
                    ISSUE:
+ .12HA2.1   Jane Louise BURNS, born 1961.
+ .12HA2.2   Janet BURNS, born 1964.
+ .12HA2.3   Judy BURNS, born 1966.
+ .12HA2.4   James BURNS, born 1967.

12HA.3 Allen Lee[5] RITTGERS (Jacob[4], Benjamin[3], Jacob[2], John[1]) was born 20 Feb 1940 in Rolfe, Pocahontas Co., Ia., the son of Jacob B. RITTGERS and Jeane SCHEFFERS. He married **Diana KAELMA**.
                    ISSUE:
.12HA3.1   Tanya Rene RITTGERS, born 1971. She married Michael BURNS.
.12HA3.2   Mark RITTGERS, born 1972. He married Robin____.
.12HA3.3   Tiffiny RITTGERS.
.12HA3.4   Amanda RITTGERS.
.12HA3.5   Stephanie RITTGERS.

12HB.1 Janet Katherine[5] RITTGERS (Robert[4], Benjamin[3], Jacob[2], John[1]) was born 19 Dec 1934 in Rolfe, Pocahontas Co., Ia., the daughter of Robert Woodrow RITTGERS and Beulah Maureen CHRISTENSEN. She married **Gordon POTTER**. In a letter about family, Jan shares her history. She has been married and divorced; she is a lab technologist and lives in Cincinatti, Oh.
                    ISSUE:
.12HB11   Diane POTTER, born 1957.
.12HB12   Karen POTTER, born 1959. She married Patrick SWEENEY.
.12HB13   Barbara POTTER, born 1961.
.12HB14   Jennifer POTTER, born 1968.

12HB.2 Barbara Joan⁵ RITTGERS (Robert⁴, Benjamin³, Jacob², John¹) was born 9 Dec 1936 in Rolfe, Pocahontas Co., Ia., the daughter of Robert Woodrow RITTGERS and Beulah Maureen CHRISTENSEN. She married **Peter J. CLASSEN**.

ISSUE:

+ .12HB2.1   Daniel Robert CLASSEN.
+ .12HB2.2   Ann Elizabeth CLASSEN, born 1961.
+ .12HB2.3   Martha Joan CLASSEN, born 1965.

12HB.3 Jon Curtis⁵ RITTGERS (Robert⁴, Benjamin³, Jacob², John¹) was born 9 May 1940 in Rolfe, Pocahontas Co., Ia., the son of Robert Woodrow RITTGERS and Beulah Maureen CHRISTENSEN. He married (1) **Flora TUBALDOS** 1 May 1965. She was born 9 May 1940, died 29 Apr 1974.[SS] Jon married (2) **Ellen Victoria BRADLEY** 14 Dec 1974 in Sharon, Mass. She was born 26 Jun 1952, the daughter of Chester Josiah and Gladys Mae (Miller) Bradley.

ISSUE of Jon and Flora:

.12HB3.1   Robert James RITTGERS, born 15 Aug 1967 in Fort Collins, Colo.
.12HB3.2   Karla Marie RITTGERS, born 23 Jul 1969 in Wakefield, R.I.

ISSUE of Jon and Ellen:

.12HB3.3   Katherine Nile RITTGERS, born 3 Jan 1977 in West Newbury, Mass.
.12HB3.4   Justin Bradley RITTGERS, born 28 Mar 1979 in West Newbury, Mass.

12J1.2 Maynard LeRoy⁵ RITTGERS (Glen⁴, George³, Jacob², John¹) was born 5 Feb 1918 in Paton, Greene Co., Ia., the son of Glen Edwin RITTGERS and Laura N. SEXTON. On 1920 census, age 1 10/12, with parents in Paton, Greene Co., Ia.[ED 116, p 7A, fam #50/50] He married **Bertie Frances KINSLEY** 1 Sep 1934 in Crocker, Pulaski Co., Mo. She was born 25 Jan 1915 in Iberia, Miller Co., Mo. Maynard was in the Army during WW II.

ISSUE:

+ .12J12.1   Naomi Ruth RITTGERS, born 23 Jul 1935.
+ .12J12.2   Laura Marie RITTGERS, born 4 Aug 1939.
+ .12J12.3   George Earl RITTGERS, born 27 May 1942.
+ .12J12.4   Nettie Edith RITTGERS, born 11 May 1944.
+ .12J12.5   LeRoy Edwin RITTGERS, born 27 Nov 1946.
  .12J12.6   Darlene Sue RITTGERS, born 31 Jan 1951 in Highland, Madison Co., Ill. She married Richard Boyett HODGE 15 May 1982 in Cadiz, Ky. He was born 12 Jul 1946.
+ .12J12.7   Connie Mae RITTGERS, born 9 Jan 1955.
+ .12J12.8   Bonnie Rae RITTGERS, born 9 Jan 1955.
+ .12J12.9   Joyce Kay RITTGERS, born 8 Feb 1959.

12J3.1 Joyce Georgette⁵ GAYLORD (Bessie⁴, George³, Jacob², John¹) was born 3 Jan 1922 in Ia., the daughter of Roy Dennison GAYLORD and Bessie Elizabeth RITTGERS. She married **Alfred Bacon HOBBS** 7 Jan 1944. He was born 4 Dec 1920 in Bushee, Ariz.

ISSUE:

.12J31.1   Robert Roy HOBBS, born 16 Jul 1946 in Tucson, Ariz..
.12J31.2   Richard Dennison HOBBS, born 11 Jul 1950 in Tucson, Ariz., died 16 Sep 1950 in Tucson, Ariz.
.12J31.3   Karlene Georgette HOBBS, born 11 Sep 1953 in Tucson, Ariz.

12J3.2 Roy Dennison[5] GAYLORD, Jr. (Bessie[4], George[3], Jacob[2], John[1]) was born 3 May 1924 in Des Moines, Polk Co., Ia., the son of Roy Dennison GAYLORD and Bessie Elizabeth RITTGERS. He married **Dorothy BROOKSHIER** Nov 1947.
ISSUE:
.12J32.1   Ronald Roy GAYLORD, born 24 May 1950 in Roswell, N.M..

12J6.1 Dick Duane[5] RITTGERS (Lloyd[4], George[3], Jacob[2], John[1]) was born 15 Jul 1933 in Grand Junction, Greene Co., Ia., the son of Lloyd Ellison RITTGERS and Margaret Ann TUCKER. He married **Maureen Joan CANAVAN** 5 Nov 1955 in Grand Junction, Greene Co., Ia. She was born 21 Nov 1936 in Ft. Dodge, Webster Co., Ia., the daughter of Patrick J. and Geraldine (Jack) Canavan. They live in Gowrie, Ia., where he is a farmer. [Family group sheet submitted by Maureen (Canavan) Rittgers]
ISSUE:
+ .12J61.1   Brian Richard RITTGERS, born 5 Jul 1957.
+ .12J61.2   Veronica Ann RITTGERS, born 4 May 1960.
.12J61.3   Mark David RITTGERS, born 20 Sep 1961 in Ft. Dodge, Webster Co., Ia. He married Lynn____ 25 Jun 1988 in Vail, Audobon Co., Ia. Lives in Paton, Ia.
.12J61.4   Richard Lloyd RITTGERS, born 20 Feb 1963 in Ft. Dodge, Webster Co., Ia. Lives in Gowrie, Ia.
.12J61.5   Christopher Patrick RITTGERS, born 26 May 1964 in Ft. Dodge, Webster Co., Ia. Lives in Arlington, Va.

12K2.2 Anthony Johnson[5] RITTGERS (Anthony[4], Andrew[3], Jacob[2], John[1]) was born 2 Feb 1945, the son of Anthony Theodore RITTGERS and Florence THOMPSON. He married (1) **Mary____**. Anthony married (2) **Kaye____**.
ISSUE of Anthony and Mary:
.12K22.1   Andrew RITTGERS.

12K3.1 Mary Ann[5] RITTGERS (Robert[4], Andrew[3], Jacob[2], John[1]) was born 8 Feb 1932 in Johnston, Polk Co., Ia., the daughter of Robert Johnson RITTGERS and Cecil "Marjorie" SNYDER. She married (1) **Donald "Dean" BOWEN**. He was born 1930. Donald died 1950, and was buried in Rittgers Cemetery, Johnston, Ia. Mary married (2) **Charles Lowell ROBERTS** 23 Feb 1952. He was born 30 Jan 1928 in Martinsdale, Ia. Charles was an attorney in Des Moines. One of his prime family concerns was the Rittgers Cemetery on part of the original land of Jacob (#1.2) Rittgers. He wanted to make sure that it would be available to descendants of the Rittgers family. Mary Ann is involved with the family association, and has been secretary of the reunion several times. She lives in the house her father built on the property of Jacob Rittgers, #1.2. In an attempt to level the driveway, she and Charles started digging around some stone. They discovered that the stone near the back door were rutted and had a pattern etched into them. In researching, they discovered that the stagecoach once forded the Des Moines River near their home, and stopped at Jacob's house. The driveway was once part of the stage route, with groves cut by the wheels of the many coaches that passed through. Charles died 11 Sep 1996 in Des Moines, Polk Co., Ia., and is buried in the Rittgers Cemetery. [*Interview with Mary Ann (Rittgers) Roberts.*]
ISSUE of Donald and Mary Ann:
.12K31.1   Rebecca Susan (Bowen) ROBERTS, born 8 Sep 1949. She married John BECKER.

ISSUE of Charles and Mary Ann:
+ .12K31.2   Deborah Ann ROBERTS, born 15 Jan 1956.
+ .12K31.3   Marjorie Diane ROBERTS.
+ .12K31.4   Julia Anne ROBERTS.
  .12K31.5   Charles Beaumont ROBERTS, born 20 Jul 1960 in Polk Co., Ia. He married Melissa ALBRIGHT. Divorced.

12K3.2 Carol Virginia⁵ RITTGERS, (Robert⁴, Andrew³, Jacob², John¹) was born 16 Apr 1933 in Johnston, Polk Co., Ia., to Robert Johnson RITTGERS and Marjorie SNIDER. She married Donald I. DICKINSON 6 June 1959. He was born 21 Oct 1927 in Ft. Collins, Larimer Co., Co., the son of I.E. DICKINSON and Lucy BEEBE. We are told he is of the fifth generation of Colorado Dickinsons. He is a college professor and has taught in Hawaii and Saudi Arabia. Donald is currently with the Colorado School of Mines, Golden, Co., as an assistant director of Liberal Arts and International Studies. He enjoys reading, travel, and classic cars - especially Buicks. Carol received her masters degree from the University of Hawaii in 1964. She reports that her career has had three tracks. She taught at several universities, including U. of Hawaii, and was the first female college teacher in Saudi Arabai, teaching at the University of Dhahran, 1969-70. She writes for several arts publications, and is currently Executive Director of Foothills Art Center, Golden, Co. She has received many Press Woman's Awards. For all her worldly travels and experiences, Carol tells us she most loves the memories of her childhood on the family farm. The yearly "Rittgers Picnics" and family activities are sorely missed. She remembers putting flowers on all the graves in the Rittgers Cemetery every Memorial Day.
ISSUE:
.12K32.1   Lauren Lucy DICKINSON, b. 8 Oct 1967 in Saudi Arabia. She attended Adams State College, Alamosa, Co., and is interested in creative writing, psychology, and early childhood education. Lauren currently works at a children's early learning center in Golden., Co.

12K3.4 Rex Van⁵ RITTGERS (Robert⁴, Andrew³, Jacob², John¹) was born in Johnston, Polk Co., Ia., the son of Robert Johnson RITTGERS and Florence BANNING. His spouse has not been identified.
ISSUE:
.12K34.1   Ross Van RITTGERS, born 17 May 1990.
.12K34.2   Morgan Lane RITTGERS, born 25 Oct 1991.

12K4.1 Barry Clifford⁵ BLOOM (Pauline⁴, Andrew³, Jacob², John¹) was born 2 Nov 1942 in Bell Fourche, Butte Co., SD., the son of Clifford Donald BLOOM and Pauline Elfreda RITTGERS. He married **Julie Ann ROSENTHAL** 1974. She was born 3 Mar 1946. He is a teacher.
ISSUE:
.12K41.1   Jacob Barry BLOOM, born 19 Apr 1978.
.12K41.2   Benjamin Henry BLOOM, born 23 Aug 1980.

12K4.2 Robert Jay⁵ BLOOM (Pauline⁴, Andrew³, Jacob², John¹) was born 17 Apr 1946 in Denison, Crawford Co., Ia., the son of Clifford Donald BLOOM and Pauline Elfreda RITTGERS. He is a dentist. His spouse has not been identified.
ISSUE:

.12K42.1   Clifford Robert BLOOM.
.12K42.2   Corey Jay BLOOM, born 5 Dec 1987.

1342.1 Emma⁵ RITTGERS (William⁴, Tobias³, John, Jr.², John¹) was born May 1878 in Monday Creek, Perry Co., Oh. She was the daughter of William Franklin RITTGERS and Melissa STIMMEL. Seen on the 1880 census, age 2, with her parents in Monday Creek, Perry Co., Ia.[ED 212, p 207A, fam #233/233] She married **Charles LANNING** about 1898 in Hocking County, Oh. He was born about 1874 in Oh. The 1900 census gives Charles, 27, and a "blast furnace cager" in Falls Twp., Hocking Co., Oh. Wife Emma, 22, is caring for their son. She declares they have been married one year and she has born one child, alive at that time. They are next door to her parents.[ED 26, p 1B, fam #11/11] In 1910, Charles, 36, and Emma, 31, are still in Falls Twp. Son Franklin L., 10., is with them and they appear to be in her parents' home. Charles is a "shot blast tender, iron furnace".[ED 82, p 17A, fam #364/36_] On the 1920 census, they continue to live with her parents. Charles, 46, is now a "miner, coal" in Falls Twp. Emma, 41, is caring for the family.[ED 37, p 16B, fam #364/367]
ISSUE:
.13421.1   Franklin L. LANNING, born Sep 1899 in Hocking Co., Oh. On 1900 census, age 8 months, with parents in Falls Twp., Hocking Co., Oh.[ED 26, p 1B, fam #11/11] He continued there in parents home in 1910, age 10[ED 82, p 17A, fam #364/365] and in 1920, age 20.[ED 37, p 16B, fam #364/36_]

1344.5 Connel E.⁵ RITTGERS (Isaac⁴, Tobias³, John, Jr.², John¹) was born 16 Dec 1899[SS] in Rush Creek Twp., Fairfield Co., Oh., the son of Isaac W. RITTGERS and Nancy Alice POLING. On 1900 census, age 4/12, with parents in Rush Creek Twp., Fairfield Co., Oh.[ED 12, p 308B, fam #256/257] and 1910 census, age 10, with parents there.[ED 76, p 3B, fam #68/69] In 1920, he is 20 and continues on the home farm.[ED 30, p 10B, fam #245/247] He married **Erma____**. Connel died Jul 1970[SS] in Columbus, Franklin Co., Oh., and was buried there.[*family group sheet submitted by Richard C. Rittgers (#1344A.1)*]
ISSUE:
.13445.1   Wilma RITTGERS. She married Charles JACOBY.
.13445.2   Merle RITTGERS. Works in Florida in Construction.

1344.A Walter Reed⁵ RITTGERS (Isaac⁴, Tobias³, John, Jr.², John¹) was born 17 May 1909 [SS] in Rush Creek Twp., Fairfield Co., Oh., the son of Isaac W. RITTGERS and Nancy Alice POLING. On 1910 census, age 1, with his parents [ED 76, p 3B, fam #68/69], and there with them on 1920 census, age 10.[ED 30, p 10B, fam #245/247] He married **Sarah Elizabeth FOERST**. She was born 23 Sep 1908 in Columbus, Franklin Co., Oh. Walter and Sarah are members of Glenwood United Meth. Church in Columbus. He retired from Abbott Labs. Walter died 1 Jun 1993[SS] in Franklin Co., Oh.[*We thank their son Richard for the information on this line.*]
ISSUE:
+ .1344A.1   Richard Charles RITTGERS, born 15 Feb 1934.
.1344A.2   Ruth Ann RITTGERS. She married Stewart W. CHAPMAN 6 Feb 1955 in Columbus, Franklin Co., Oh.
+ .1344A.3   James Arthur RITTGERS, born 29 Feb 1940.
+ .1344A.4   Mary Virginia RITTGERS, born 5 Jun 1943.

.1344A.5   Thomas Lincoln RITTGERS, born 10 May 1946 in Columbus, Franklin Co., Oh.
He married Madonna 21 Feb 1971 in Columbus, Franklin Co., Oh..

1345.1 Minnie B.⁵ RITTGERS (John⁴, Tobias³, John, Jr.², John¹) She was the daughter of
John B. RITTGERS and Zeuriah Edith DAVIS. Her spouse has not been identified.*[Family
group sheet on grandfather Tobias, submitted to Ohio Gen. Soc. unsigned.]*
ISSUE:
.13451.1   Howard, died before 1949.

1347.1 Virginia Grace⁵ RITTGERS (Albert⁴, Tobias³, John², John¹) was born Apr 1889 in
Hocking County, Oh., the daughter of Albert J. RITTGERS and Mary L. MCLIN. She is on
the 1900 census, age 11, with parents in Marion Twp., Hocking Co., Oh.[ED 32,p.110A, fam
#43/43]   She married **Ernest Dwight COHAGAN** 28 Nov 1909 in Hocking County,
Oh.[HVRM Bk K,p.570] He was born 19 Jan 1909 in Perry County, Oh. Ernest was a laborer
in a brick yard, and age 18, at the time of their marriage.   Family record tells us Virginia had 8
children, but only one, Mildred Cohagan, mentioned in father's estate.[Hocking Probate est.
#3706]
ISSUE:
.13471.1   Mildred COHAGAN.   She was listed in her grandfather's estate as living in New
Straitsville, Oh., in 1934.

1347.2 Herbert McCullough⁵ RITTGERS (Albert⁴, Tobias³, John, Jr.², John¹) was born Apr
1893[SS] in Marion Twp., Hocking Co., Oh., the son of Albert J. RITTGERS and Mary
McLIN. On 1900 census, age 7, with parents there.[ED 32, p 110A, fam #43/43] He continues
in parents home in 1910, age 17, Falls Twp., Hocking Co., Oh. Listed on census as a "laborer
in brick factory".[ED 82, p 16A, fam #338/342] He married **Inez E. WILEY** before 1917 in Oh.
She was born 19 Apr 1898 in Oh. On daughter Helen's birth record, we find Inez "Hillery", age
19. Herbert was 25 on this record, and declares they living in Falls Twp., Hocking Co. On the
1920 census, "Cull" age 25, is an oil worker in the oil fields. With him in Falls Twp. is wife Inez,
21, who is caring for their children. They live on the Logan Straitsville Rd.[ED 37, p 16B, fam
#365/368] Herbert died Aug 1949. Inez died Jan 1976[SS] in Perry Co., Oh.*[Family group sheet
on grandfather Tobias, submitted by James Rittgers, #1347.3]*
ISSUE:
.13472.1   Helen RITTGERS, born Apr 1917 in Hocking Co., Oh.[HVRB, Bk 14] On 1920
census, age 2 10/12, with parents in Falls Twp., Hocking Co., Oh.[ED 37, p 16B,
fam #365/368]
.13472.2   Leona RITTGERS, born Jun 1918 in Hocking Co., Oh. On 1920 census, age 1
8/12, with parents in Falls Twp., Hocking Co., Oh.[ED 37, p 16B, fam #365/368]
.13472.3   Bernard RITTGERS, born 5 June 1930, died Dec 1986.[SS]
.13472.4   Chester Lincoln RITTGERS, born 11 Jan 1936 in Hocking Co., Oh. He married
Mary Louise SMITH 18 May 1957 in Hocking Co., Oh. She was born 26 Dec 1934,
the daughter of William Franklin and Thelma (Davis) Smith. Her father deceased at
time of her marriage.   Chester was an oil field pumper at the time of his
marriage.[HVRM, book "AA", p 332.Record lists birth, parents and occupation.]
"Linc" died 27 Sept 1991.[SS]

1347.3 James F.[5] **RITTGERS** (Albert[4], Tobias[3], John[2], John[1]) was born 24 Mar 1896 in Hocking County, Oh., the son of Albert J. RITTGERS and Mary L. MCLIN. He is seen on the 1900 census, age 4, with parents in Marion Twp., Hocking Co., Oh.[ED 32, p.110A, fam #43/43] He continues in parent's home on the 1910 census, age 14.[ED 82, p.16A, fam #338/342] He married **Frances FICKLE** [Wife's maiden name listed on daughter's birth record] about 1919. She was born about 1896. On the 1920 census, age 23, he is a "teacher, school", in Logan, Falls Twp., Hocking Co., Oh. Wife Frances is caring for their home, and boarder Henry Ruble, 55. Their address is given as 406 Church St.[ED 89, p.6A, fam#137/138]James died Dec 1980 in Hocking County, Oh.[SS] We are told that one Loda Rittgers found on the Social Security death index, b. 2 Mar 1896, d. Apr 1977, was the "wife of James, son of Albert."

ISSUE:

.13473.1   Mary Ellen RITTGERS, born 27 Aug 1920.[HVRB Bk 16, p.80]

1347.5 Hugh William[5] **RITTGERS** (Albert[4], Tobias[3], John[2], John[1]) born 8 Mar 1901 in Hocking Co., Oh., the son of Albert RITTGERS and Mary L. MCLIN. [HVRB-bk C, p. 165] He is on 1910 census, age 9, with parents in Falls Twp., Hocking Co., Oh.[ED 82, p 16A, fam #338/342] In 1920 we see him, age 18, a farm laborer on the home farm, with parents in Marion Twp., Hocking Co., Oh.[ED 45, p. 3A, fam #47/47] He married Edna M. KIENZLE 17 Nov 1921 in Hocking Co., Oh. [HVRM, book P, p 20] She was born 7 May 1902 in Fairfield Co., Oh., the daughter of William and Sarah (Seifort) Kienzle. We find in HVRB Bk 1, p.7, that "Hugh William Rittgers, 21 and a farmer, and Edna May Kienzle, 19, had their first child, Harley Maywood Rittgers, 7 Apr 1922, Hocking Co., Oh. We find no other reference to this child, and he may have died young. Reported in father's estate, 1934, to be living in Logan, Oh. Marriage Book "U", p. 92, tells us that Edna, "widow of Hugh Rittgers," married on 17 Oct 1938, John G. Byerly of Logan, Hocking Co., Oh. John is a "Clerk". This led us to believe Hugh died before Oct 1938, yet on the social security death record we find one Hugh Rittgers with the same birth date, but a death date of Aug 1975. It is possible that he hadn't died when his wife remarried, but that they divorced. His spouse has not been identified.

ISSUE:

+ .131141   Harley Maywood RITTGERS.

134B.1 Elmer[5] **RITTGERS** (James[4], Tobias[3], John, Jr.[2], John[1]) was born Jan 1885 in Oh., the son of James R. RITTGERS and Laura ALLEN. On the 1900 census, age 15, a servant in home of Ray Musser, Walnut Twp., Fairfield Co., Oh.[ED 23, p 4A, fam #73/76] He married **Sylvia M.____** about 1906 in Oh. She was born about 1885 in Oh. He on 1920 census, Hamilton Co., age 34, and a brakeman on the railroad. With him is wife Sylvia M., 35, and five children.[ED 517, fam #53/55] There is some question as to where Elmer's father, James, belongs in the family. Thus we will place Elmer here, as this is where the family placed James. When more information clarifies this line, the numbering may change.

ISSUE:

.134B1.1   Edith RITTGERS, born about 1907 in Oh. On 1920 census, Hamilton Co., Oh, age 13, with parents.[ED 517, fam #53/55]

.134B1.2   Carl M. RITTGERS, born about 1908 in Oh. On 1920 census, Hamilton Co., Oh, age 12, with parents.[ED 517, fam #53/55]

.134B1.3   Harry H. RITTGERS, born 10 Aug 1909[SS] in Oh, died Jun 1972[SS] in Delaware Co., Ind. On 1920 census, Hamilton Co., Oh, age 10, with parents. His death date is not an absolute match with the family record.[ED 517, fam #53/55]

.134B1.4   Merle N. RITTGERS, born about 1912. On 1920 census, Hamilton Co., Oh, age 8, with parents. Here it reports he born in Colo., but sibling before and after b. Oh. [ED 517, fam #53/55]

.134B1.5   Herman N. RITTGERS, born May 1915 in Oh. On 1920 census, Hamilton Co., Oh, age 4 8/12, with parents.[ED 517, fam #53/55]

1381.1 Isaac Rolland[5] BRIGHT (Mary[4], Anna[3], John[2], John[1]) was born 31 Aug 1881 in Hocking County, Oh., the son of Peter Whitehead BRIGHT and Mary WOLF. We see his on the 1900 census, age 18, with his parents in Falls Twp., Hocking Co., Oh.[ED 26, p 8A, fam #150/155] He married **Gertrude MARTIN**. She was born 20 Dec 1882 in Hocking County, Oh., the daughter of William H. & Minerva (McKin) Martin. Called "Roland", he was a school teacher, clerk of courts of Hocking Co., served on school board, representative from Hocking Co., to State of Oh., Banker of Citizens Bank of Logan, Oh., and Auditor of the United Rubber Worker's Union of Akron, Oh. Gertrude died 15 Jun 1966 in Hocking Co., Oh. and Isaac died 17 Jan 1969 in Logan, Hocking Co., Oh.[Bright, p.58]

ISSUE:

+ .13811.1   Blanche Marguerita BRIGHT, born 21 Jun 1906.
.13811.2   Harmond D. BRIGHT, born 4 Sep 1908 in Hocking County, Oh., died 14 Mar 1909 in Hocking County, Oh., and was buried in Oak Grove Cemetery, Hocking Co., Oh.
+ .13811.3   Glendon Rolland BRIGHT, born 4 Mar 1914.

1381.2 Samuel Hamilton[5] BRIGHT (Mary[4], Anna[3], John, Jr.[2], John[1]) was born 13 Apr 1883 in Hocking Co., Oh., the son of Peter Whitehead BRIGHT and Mary WOLF. On 1900 census, age 17, with parents in Falls Twp., Hocking Co., Oh.[ED 26, p 8A, fam #150/155] He married **Jennie A. MCKIN** 18 Apr 1908 in Hocking Co., Oh. She was born 21 Jan 1882 in Oh., the daughter of A.M. & Sarah E. (Nott) McKin. In 1910 the census shows him in Logan, Hocking Co., Oh., a "moulder, pottery", with wife Jennie A., 28, and daughter. Jennie declares they have been married 3 years and she has born one child, seen with them.[ED 84, p 3A, fam #63/63] On 1920 census, age 36, a "molder, pottery." Wife Jennie A., 37, is caring for their home at 177 Maple St.[ED 40, p 16A, fam #108/115] Samuel died 9 Sep 1963 and Jennie died 13 Jul 1967 in Logan, Hocking Co., Oh. They are buried in Oak Grove Cemetery, Logan, Oh. [Bright, p.59]

ISSUE:

.13812.1   Hilda E. BRIGHT, born Apr 1909 in Hocking Co., Oh. On 1910 census, age 1yr., 2 mo., with parents, Logan, Hocking Co., Oh.[ED 84, p 3A, fam #63/63] On 1920 census, age 10, with parents Logan, Falls Twp., Hocking Co., Oh.[ED 40, p 16A, fam #108/115]

1381.3 James Henry[5] BRIGHT (Mary[4], Anna[3], John[2], John[1]) was born 29 Dec 1884 in Hocking Co., Oh., the son of Peter Whitehead BRIGHT and Mary WOLF. He is not in his father's home on the 1900 census. He married **Augusta DISBENNET** 2 Oct 1907 in Hocking County, Oh.; they divorced. Augusta was the daughter of Isaac & Mary (Blosser) Disbennet. She m. (2) F. Miller. James never remarried. He was a moulder for Logan Pottery Co. James died 11 Mar 1968 in Logan, Hocking Co., Oh., and was buried in Oak Grove Cemetery, Logan, Oh. We are told Augusta is also in that cemetery.[Bright, p.59]

ISSUE:

.13813.1   Edward J. BRIGHT. Married Geraldine Holshoe, lives Columbus, Oh.[Bright, p.59]
.13813.2   Mary Jane BRIGHT. Married a _____ Miller.[Bright, p.58]

1381.4 Bertha May[5] **BRIGHT** (Mary[4], Anna[3], John, Jr.[2], John[1]) was born 28 Apr 1887 in Hocking County, Oh., the daughter of Peter Whitehead BRIGHT and Mary WOLF. We see her on the 1900 census, age 13, with her parents in Falls Twp., Hocking Co., Oh.[ED26, p.6, fam#150/155] She married **David Littler RUTTER** 27 May 1905. He was born 28 Aug 1879, the son of Jacob and Elizabeth (Poling) Rutter.[Bright, p. 59] David died 1 Feb 1960, and was buried in Oak Grove Cemetery, Logan, Oh..

ISSUE:

.13814.1   Mary RUTTER, born 7 Dec 1905. [Bright, p.5, appendix]
.13814.2   Kenneth RUTTER, born 2 Feb 1907. [Bright, p.5, appendix]
+ .13814.3   Walter Edward RUTTER, born 8 Aug 1915.
+ .13814.4   Ernest Euna RUTTER, born 16 Jun 1914.
+ .13814.5   Charles RUTTER, born 29 Oct 1915.
+ .13814.6   Pearl Lester RUTTER, born 7 Oct 1924.
+ .13814.7   Robert David RUTTER, born 5 Mar 1931.

1381.5 Charles Marion[5] **BRIGHT** (Mary[4], Anna[3], John, Jr.[2], John[1]) was born 2 Mar 1890[SS] (Bright tells us 21 Mar) in Hocking Co., Oh., the son of Peter BRIGHT and Mary WOLF. On the 1900 census, age 10, with parents in Falls Twp., Hocking Co., Oh.[ED 26, p 8A, fam #150/155] He continues with his parents on the 1910 census, age 20, where he is a "Laborer, Pottery."[ED82, p.5B, fam#107/107] He married **Marie STRUBLE** 26 Apr 1913 in Oh. She was born 8 Sep 1895, the daughter of Daniel and Isabel (Weedy) Struble. On the 1920 census, age 29, a "moulder, pottery," in Falls Twp. Wife Marie, 24, is caring for their two children in their home at 583 E. 2nd St.[ED 40, p 7A, fam #164/204] Marie died 1970, and was buried in Oak Grove Cemetery, Logan, Oh.. He died Jan 1971, Columbus, Franklin Co., Oh.[SS] [Bright, p. 60]

ISSUE:

.13814.1   Lois Juanita BRIGHT, born about 1914 in Hocking Co., Oh. On 1920 census, age 6, with parents in Falls Twp., Hocking Co., Oh.[ED 40, p 7A, fam # 164/204] She married John E. GOTHAN. In 1978 she was living in Clearwater, Fla.[Bright,p.60]
.13814.2   Helen O. BRIGHT, born about 1915 in Hocking Co., Oh. On 1920 census, age 5, with parents in Falls Twp., Hocking Co., Oh.[ED 40, p 7A, fam # 164/204] She married M.W.Kraft and in 1978 was living in Wooster, Oh. We are told Charles lived with her in 1978.[Bright,p60]

1381.6 Lillie Maude[5] **BRIGHT** (Mary[4], Anna[3], John, Jr.[2], John[1]) was born 28 Jan 1892 in Hocking County, Oh., the daughter of Peter Whitehead BRIGHT and Mary WOLF. She is seen on the 1900 census, age 8, with her parents in Falls Twp., Hocking Co., Oh. [ED36, p.8A, fam150/155] and "Mabel" is on the 1910 census there, age 18.[ED82, p.5B,fam#107/107] She married **George Elmer HITE** 4 Jul 1914. He was born 11 Jun 1889 in Maxville, Oh., the son of Thomas and Emma (Walters) Hite.[Bright, p.60] George died 1 Jul 1954 in Logan, Oh., and was buried in Oak Grove Cemetery, Logan, Oh.

ISSUE:

.13816.1   Ralph HITE. Killed in WWII.[Bright, p.60]
+ .13816.2   Edna HITE.

1382.1 Charles A.[5] **WOLF** (Isaac[4], Anna[3], John, Jr.[2], John[1]) was born Aug 1887 in Rush Creek Twp., Fairfield Co., Oh., the son of Isaac WOLF and Chloe____. He is on the 1900 census, age

12, with parents there.[ED 21, p 13B, fam #276/276] He married **Sarah**____ abt 1908. She was born about 1887 in Oh. On 1910 census, age 22, is farming. Sarah, 23, states they have been married 2 years and she has born one child. This child alive, and shown with them on census.[ED 76, p 9A, fam #195/204]

ISSUE:

.13821.1   Dortha May WOLF, born Feb 1910 in Fairfield Co., Oh. On 1910 census, age 4 mo., with parents in Rush Creek, Fairfield Co., OH.[ED 76, p 9A, fam #195/204]

1385.2 Earl⁵ HOCKMAN (Sylvester⁴, Anna³, John², John¹) was born Nov 1897 in Marion Twp., Hocking Co., Oh., the son of Sylvester HOCKMAN and Mary E. SHOLL. He is on the 1900 census, age 2, with parents in Marion Twp., Hocking Co., Oh. [ED 32, p.111B, fam #80/80] and there with parents on the 1910 census, age 12.[ED 88,p.4A, fam#58/58] He married **Ruth V.**___. She was born 1901. Ruth died 1945, and was buried in Grandview Cem., Hocking Co., Oh.

ISSUE:

.13852.1   Vera R. HOCKMAN, born 12 Oct 1927, died 18 Oct 1927, and was buried in Grandview Cemetery, Hocking Co., Oh.[HockCem]

1441.3 Charles Vincent⁵ SHORT (Sarah⁴, Daniel³, Magdalene², John¹) was born 22 Aug 1880 in Ia., the son of Benjamin F. SHORT and Sarah ROOT. He is seen on the 1885 Iowa State census, age 4, with his parents in Webster Twp., Polk Co., Ia.[1885,#7] He married **Judith MULLENEAUX** 5 Nov 1902.

ISSUE:

.14413.1   Margaret Easter SHORT, born 1 Oct 1905.
.14413.2   Katherine Ellen SHORT, born 6 Sep 1909.

1531.1 Eva Susanna⁵ RAAB (Susan⁴, Susan³, Katherine², John¹) was born 23 Jul 1884 in Fairfield Co., Oh., the daughter of John Casper RAAB and Susan BODAMER. She married **Arthur Dwight HUFFORD** 12 Oct 1910. He was born 12 Oct 1880 in Perry Co., Oh. Eva died 15 Oct 1910 in Akron, Summit Co., Oh. Arthur died 25 Jul 1943 in Columbus, Oh.

ISSUE:

.15311.1   Beatrice Juanita HUFFORD, born 20 Dec 1913 in Bremen, Fairfield Co., Oh. She married Clifton HALL. He was born 12 Sep 1911 in Creston, Oh.

1542.7 James⁵ AMSPAUGH (John⁴, Jonas³, Katherine², John¹) was born Mar 1893 in Oh., the son of John D. AMSPAUGH and Mary Jane VOUGHT. On the 1900 census, age 7, with parents in Greenfield Twp., Fairfield Co., Oh.[ED 7, p 4A, fam #76/79] He married **Eva**____ about 1914. She was born about 1895 in Oh. In 1920, age 27, renting a farm in Greenfield Twp., on Campground Rd. Wife Eva, 25, is caring for their children.[ED 10, p. 8B, fam #197/200]

ISSUE:

.15427.1   Gladys AMSPAUGH, born about 1915 in Oh.
.15427.2   Marybelle AMSPAUGH, born about Sep 1916 in Oh.
.15427.3   Dewey AMSPAUGH, born 12 Aug 1918,died 8 June 1992. Last lived in Reinersville, Morgan Co., Oh.[SS]

1561.5 Alta L.[5] AMSPAUGH (John[4], Daniel[3], Katherine[2], John[1]) was born Oct 1891 in Fairfield Co,, Oh., son of John AMSPAUGH and Mary E.____. On 1900 census, age 8, with parents in Rush Creek, Fairfield Co., Oh.[ED 21, p 6A, fam #127/127] He married **Louretta** ____ about 1913. She was born about 1897 in Oh. In 1920, age 28, farm manager, general farm, he is in Rush Creek Twp. Wife Louretta, 23, is caring for their children. They live on Oak Hill Rd. [ED 30, p. 9A, fam #200/200]

ISSUE:
.15615.1   Raymond C. AMSPAUGH, born 27 Dec 1913[SS] in Oh. In 1920, age 6, with parents in Rush Creek Twp., Fairfield Co., Oh.[ED 30, p. 9A, fam #200/200] He died 24 Apr 1993, Bellefontaine, Logan Co., Oh.[SS]
.15615.2   Lauren A. AMSPAUGH, born Nov 1917 in Oh. In 1920, age 3 2/12, with parents in Rush Creek Twp., Fairfield Co., Oh.[ED 30, p. 9A, fam #200/200]
.15615.3   Alva C. AMSPAUGH, born Feb 1919 in Oh. In 1920, age 11/12, with parents in Rush Creek Twp., Fairfield Co., Oh.[ED 30, p. 9A, fam #200/200]

1614.2 Francis "Frank"[5] RITTGERS (Timothy[4], David[3], Daniel[2], John[1]) was born 24 Jun 1899[SS] in Grimes, Polk Co., Ia., the son of Timothy Denny RITTGERS and Agnus WILSON. [PVRB, book 6, p 93 of transcript; photocopy of orig. birth record.] On the 1900 census, age 11 mo., with parents Grant Twp., Dallas Co., Ia.[ED 9, p 5, fam #86/87] On 1910 census, age 11, with parents in Granger, Dallas Co.[ED 9, p 4B, fam #76/77] On 1920 census, age 20, with parents in Granger.[ED 10, p 7A, fam #138/143] He married **Lois Esther WILSON** 8 Mar 1936[Funeral memorial card] in Dallas County, Ia. She was born 18 Mar 1914[Funeral memorial card] in Cambridge, Story Co., Ia., the daughter of William Guy and Almina Esther (Nelson) Wilson. Frank and Lois lived at Dallas Center, Ia. Frank was a farmer and a handyman. He enjoyed being out doors and always took jobs that kept him out, mowing lawns, shoveling snow, and working on farms. They adopted their two children. She was a member of the Sunbeam Rebekah Lodge #73 of Dallas Center for 50 years. Francis died 26 Sep 1976[SS] in Dallas Co., Ia., and Lois died 21 Mar 1995 in Perry, Dallas Co., Ia. They are buried in Sec. H, lot 10 of Brethren Cemetery, Dallas, Ia.[DalCCm, p 31]

ISSUE:
+ .16142.1   Stephen Ray RITTGERS, born 30 Jan 1950.

1614.3 Elizabeth A.[5] RITTGERS (Timothy[4], David[3], Daniel[2], John[1]) was born about 1904 in Dallas Co., Ia., the daughter of Timothy Denny RITTGERS and Agnus WILSON. On 1910 census, age 7, with parents in Granger, Dallas Co., Ia.[ED 9, p 4B, fam #76/77] On 1920 census, age 16, with parents there.[ED 10, p 7A, fam #138/143] She married **Burton OLSEN 31 May 1929**.[Dallas Co. Newspaper] We are told Burton and Elizabeth lived in Dallas Center, Dallas Co., Ia.

ISSUE:
.16143.1   Carol OLSEN.
.16143.2   Jean OLSEN.
.16143.3   David OLSEN.

1614.4 Robert[5] RITTGERS (Timothy[4], David[3], Daniel[2], John[1]) was born 5 Aug 1907[SS] in Dallas Co., Ia., the son of Timothy Denny RITTGERS and Agnus WILSON. On 1910 census, age 3, with parents in Granger, Dallas Co., Ia.[ED 9, p 4B, fam #76/77[On 1920 census, age

13, with parents there.[ED 10, p 7A, fam #138/143] He married **Florence STERZETECKI**. We are told he and Florence lived in Chicago, Ill. Robert died Nov 1983 in Dallas Co., Ia.[SS]
ISSUE:
.16144.1   Robert Rittgers, Jr.

1616.1 Carl "Glenn"⁵ GARTEN (Kitty⁴, David³, Daniel², John¹) was born 5 Feb 1897 in Boone, Boone Co., Ia., the son of William "Carl" GARTEN and Kitty Klyde RITTGERS. On 1900 census, age 3, with parents in Webster, Polk Co., Ia.[ED 112, p 8B, fam #160/167] On 1920 census, age 23, in home with parents in Boone. He was a lawyer in Des Moines. He married **Elizabeth "Beth" HARRINGTON** 29 Aug 1927. Carl died 12 Feb 1976 in Ia.
ISSUE:
.16161.1   Betty GARTEN.
.16161.2   William Burton GARTEN.

1616.2 Pearl Elizabeth⁵ GARTEN (Kitty⁴, David³, Daniel², John¹) was born 29 Dec 1900 in Boone, Boone Co., Ia., the daughter of William "Carl" GARTEN and Kitty Klyde RITTGERS. On the 1920 census, age 19, with parents there.[ED 112, p 8B, fam #160/167] She married **Mason UTTERBACH** 4 Apr 1931. We are told they lived in Cedar Falls, Black Hawk Co., Ia. Mason died 28 Oct 1950.
ISSUE:
.16162.1   Joyce Garten UTTERBACH, born 13 Sep 1943.

1617.1 Harold David⁵ RITTGERS (George⁴, David³, Daniel², John¹) was born 24 Jul 1898[SS] in Grimes, Polk Co., Ia., the son of George Eugene "Gene" RITTGERS and Margaret "Maggie" CHRISPIN. On 1900 census, age 1, with parents there [ED 112, p 290A, fam #145/151], and continued in 1910, age 11, with parents there. [ED 184, p 6b, fam #49/48)] In 1920, age 21, laborer on father's farm in Indian Creek Twp., Story Co., Ia.[ED 193, p 10A, fam #13/13] His spouse has not been identified. Harold died Apr 1978[SS] in Story Co., Ia.
ISSUE:
.16171.1   Harold D. Rittgers, JR., born 1924.

1617.2 Dale Eugene⁵ RITTGERS (George⁴, David³, Daniel², John¹) was born 15 Mar 1903 in Grimes, Polk Co., Ia., the son of George Eugene "Gene" RITTGERS and Margaret "Maggie" CHRISPIN.[PVRB, book 6, (p 70 of transcript] In 1910, age 7, with parents there.[ED 184, p 6b, fam #49/48] In 1920, age 17, laborer on father's farm in Indian Creek Twp., Story Co., Ia.[ED 193, p 10A, fam #13/13] His first spouse has not been identified. He married second, Sylvia _____.
ISSUE:
.16172.1   Janice RITTGERS.
.16172.2   Rose RITTGERS.
.16172.3   George RITTGERS.
.16172.4   James RITTGERS.
.16172.5   Al RITTGERS.

1618.1 Mina May⁵ WILSON (Flora⁴, David³, Daniel², John¹) was born 15 Dec 1895, the daughter of Alexander "Alec" WILSON and Flora May RITTGERS. Mother died when she was 2 yrs. old. Raised by her Grandmother, Sarah (Denny) Rittgers until her father married again in 1901. We see her age 4 in her grandparents' home on the 1900 census. On 1910 census, age 14, with father and step-mother in Webster Twp., Polk Co., Ia.[ED 184, p 6B, fam #59/59] She married **Merle Robert ALLEN** 22 Jan 1916. On the 1920 census, we see Robert is 25, b. Ia., but his parents b. Ire., a farmer. Wife Mina, 24, is keeping house in Gravity, Washington Twp., Taylor Co., Ia. [ED 154, p 5B, fam #14/14] Merle died 29 Aug 1977. Mina died 19 Jul 1979.[Pledge]

ISSUE:

+ .16181.1   Dean Calvin ALLEN, born 26 Dec 1923.

161A.2 Gertrude Isabel[5] RITTGERS (James[4], David[3], Daniel[2], John[1]) was born 1 Mar 1912 in Webster, Polk Co., Ia. the daughter of James Albert "Jim" RITTGERS and Daisy Porter BISHOP.[PVRB, book 7, p 127 of transcript] On 1920 census, age 7, with parents in Webster, Polk Co., Oh.[ED 187, p 12B, fam #200/202] She married **Carroll E. STONE** 7 Mar 1936. Gertrude died 14 Mar 1991 in Ia.

ISSUE:

.161A2.1   Elden LeRoy STONE, born 26 Mar 1938.
.161A2.2   Twin Infant STONE, born 26 Mar 1938, died young.
.161A2.3   Janet Daisy STONE, born 6 Oct 1941.
.161A2.4   James Emerson STONE, born 18 Sep 1944.

161A.3 William James[5] RITTGERS (James[4], David[3], Daniel[2], John[1]) was born 4 Oct 1914 in Webster Twp., Polk Co., Ia., the son of James Albert "Jim" RITTGERS and Daisy Porter BISHOP.[PVRB, book 7, p 127 of transcript] On 1920 census, age 5, with parents in Webster, Polk Co., Oh.[ED 187, p 12B, fam #200/202] He married **Annette Sylvia LEE** 29 Apr 1939. He and wife Annette lived in Litchfield, Minn. William died 9 Mar 1993 in Litchfield, Meeker Co., Minn.[SS]

ISSUE:

.161A3.1   Darline Ann RITTGERS, born 20 Feb 1941.
.161A3.2   Shirley M. RITTGERS, born 19 Nov 1943.
.161A3.3   David Lee RITTGERS, born 9 Dec 1947.

161B.4 Hazel Pearl[5] WILSON (Cora[4], David[3], Daniel[2], John[1]) was born 4 Aug 1913 in Grimes, Polk Co., Ia., the daughter of William James "Will" WILSON and Cora Nina RITTGERS. She is seen with her parents in People's Twp., Boone Co., Ia., in 1920, age 6.[ED 24, p 4B, fam #88/88] She married **Robert Miller SCOTT** 6 Apr 1935. He was born 21 Feb 1910 in Mitchellville, Jasper Co., Ia. We are told Robert was a farmer. They lived near Colfax, then moved near Moravia, Ia. Hazel now lives in Newton, Ia. Robert died 8 Dec 1986, and was buried in Mitchellville, Jasper Co., Ia.

ISSUE:

+ .161B4.1   David Iri SCOTT, born 18 May 1937.
+ .161B4.2   Herbert Elwin SCOTT, born 31 Aug 1939.
+ .161B4.3   Fred Verald SCOTT, born 2 Apr 1948.

161B.5 Charles Woodrow[5] WILSON (Cora[4], David[3], Daniel[2], John[1]) was born 16 Mar 1915 in Woodward, Dallas Co., Ia., the son of William James "Will" WILSON and Cora Nina RITTGERS. He is seen with his parents in People's Twp., Boone Co., Ia., in 1920, age 5.[ED

24, p 4B, fam #88/88] He married **Dorothy "Kathryn" DRAKE** 10 Oct 1945 in Nashua, Ia. She was born 29 Dec 1919 in Quincy, Ia.

ISSUE:
+ .161B5.1   Wayne William WILSON, born 4 Jul 1946.
+ .161B5.2   Jane Kathryn WILSON, born 20 Dec 1947.

161B.6 Cora Beth[5] WILSON (Cora[4], David[3], Daniel[2], John[1]) was born 6 Jan 1917 in Woodward, Dallas Co., Ia., the daughter of William James "Will" WILSON and Cora Nina RITTGERS. "Beth" is seen with her parents in People's Twp., Boone Co., Ia., in 1920, age 3 yr, 6 mo.[ED 24, p 4B, fam #88/88] She married **Clarence Arthur WILSON** 6 Nov 1948 in Denver, Colo. He was born 12 Jan 1907 in Grimes, Ia., the son of Thomas and Marcella (McHarge) Wilson. They are first cousins, their father's being brothers. This family is outlined in a Wilson-Fryer family history that circulates in the family.

ISSUE:
+ .161B6.1   Connie Beth WILSON, born 12 Jun 1954.
.161B6.2   Tammy Pearl WILSON, born 8 Oct 1957 in Denver, Colo. She married Thomas OLSON.

161B.7 William George[5] WILSON (Cora[4], David[3], Daniel[2], John[1]) was born 24 Oct 1920 in Woodward, Dallas Co., Ia., the son of William James "Will" WILSON and Cora Nina RITTGERS. He married **Helen Juanita DIETZ** 1 Nov 1941 in Camp Robinson, Little Rock, Ark.. She was born 4 Sep 1918. They live in Boone Co., Ia.

ISSUE:
+ .161B7.1   Helen "Marie" WILSON, born 18 Jan 1943.
+ .161B7.2   Dale Everett WILSON, born 20 Sep 1945.
+ .161B7.3   Sharon Elaine WILSON, born 27 Oct 1947.
.161B7.4   Lloyd LeRoy WILSON, born 6 Sep 1954 in Boone, Ia.
.161B7.5   Cynthia Kim WILSON, born 15 Oct 1955 in Webster City, Ia.
+ .161B7.6   Wayde Matthew WILSON, born 17 May 1959.

1621.1 Mary Alice[5] RITTGERS (Ambrose[4], Reuben[3], Daniel[2], John[1]) was born 30 Oct 1891 in, Kiowa Co., Colo., the daughter of Ambrose Robert RITTGERS and Verta Alice SNIDER. On the 1900 census, age 8, with parents in Waltentown, Kiowa Co., Colo.,[ED 43, p 3A, fam #44/46] and on the 1910 census, age 18, with parents in "Precinct 5",Kiowa Co., Colo.[ED 88, p 5A, fam #106/108] She married **Willard Kent FRANCE** 15 Sept 1913 in Kiowa County, Co. He was born 30 Nov 1879. Their wedding caused a bit of a stir. In a newspaper article shared with us by Barbara Abrams we see that "On the fifteenth day of Sept Miss Mary Rittgers left here via Pueblo for Denver presumably to visit friends and Kent France left at the same time for the same destination via Kit Carson in this way they eluded the vigilance of their friends and surprised them completely. As prearranged they met at Denver and were married that day. After a few days visit with Denver friends they quietly hied back to the Chivington ranch where they remained a week or so before their existence in Kiowa County became known. Well, they are excellent young people and even at this late date we are pleased to join their host of friends in wishing them a long and happy wedded life and remember we'll keep agitating a buge serenade for them first time they come to town if not for six months." [no date or banner submitted with copy] In her father's obituary, 1936, she is "of Chivington, Co." Mary died 21 Sep 1945 in Eads, Kiowa Co., Colo. Willard died 20 Jun 1958 in Eads.

ISSUE:
+ .16211.1   Ruth FRANCE, born 13 Apr 1915.
+ .16211.2   Lois FRANCE, born 26 May 1917.
+ .16211.3   LaVerne Mildred FRANCE, born 25 Jun 1925.

1621.2 Reuben Burn[5] RITTGERS (Ambrose[4], Reuben[3], Daniel[2], John[1]) was born 21 Sep 1893
[SS] in Kiowa Co., Colo., the son of Ambrose Robert RITTGERS and Verta Alice SNIDER.
On the 1900 census, age 6, with parents in Waltentown, Kiowa Co., Colo.,[ED 43, p 3A, fam
#44/46] and on the 1910 census, age 16, with parents in "Precinct 5",Kiowa Co., Colo.[ED 88,
p 5A, fam #106/108] He was reported to be living in Eads, Co., in his father's obituary, 1936.
He married **Jane (Koepsel) WILLIAMS** 29 Oct 1943 in Aurora County, Colo. She was born
17 May 1918 in Woodbine, Dickenson Co., Colo. He was a Veteran of WW I, and they lived
in Eads, Colo.   Reuben died 11 Jan 1974 in Kiowa Co., and was buried in Eads Cemetery,
Kiowa Co., Colo.[*Family group sheet submitted by wife Jane (Koepsel)(Williams) Rittgers.*]
ISSUE:
+ .16212.1   Leslie Milton RITTGERS, born 17 Jun 1945.

1621.3 Luetta Blanche[5] RITTGERS (Ambrose[4], Reuben[3], Daniel[2], John[1]) was born 27 Dec
1896 in Eads, Kiowa Co., Colo., the daughter of Ambrose Robert RITTGERS and Verta Alice
SNIDER. On the 1900 census, age 4, with parents in Waltentown, Kiowa Co., Colo.,[ED 43,
p 3A, fam #44/46] and on the 1910 census, age 14, with parents in "Precinct 5",Kiowa Co.,
Colo.[ED 88, p 5A, fam #106/108] She married **Daniel FAINE** 14 Sep 1914 in Eads, Kiowa
Co., Colo. Killed by husband in a murder-suicide on 6 Apr 1920.   They are buried in Eads
Cemetery.   Son Robert adopted by her parents, Ambrose (#172.1) and Verta (Snider) Rittgers,
and went by name of Rittgers.
ISSUE:
+ .16213.1   Robert Lewis Faine RITTGERS, born 15 May 1915.

1621.4 Edith Pearl[5] RITTGERS (Ambrose[4], Reuben[3], Daniel[2], John[1]) was born 25 Jan 1898
in Eads, Kiowa Co., Colo., the daughter of Ambrose Robert RITTGERS and Verta Alice
SNIDER. On the 1900 census, age 2, with parents in Waltentown, Kiowa Co., Colo.,[ED 43,
p 3A, fam #44/46] and on the 1910 census, age 12, with parents in "Precinct 5",Kiowa Co.,
Colo.[ED 88, p 5A, fam #106/108] Pearl left Colo. so she could go to high school as none in
Eads then. She lived in Johnston, Iowa, with her Uncle Findley and Aunt Mabel (Rittgers,
#172.7) and helped them with housework and child care while in High School. Began Nurses
Training in I.L.H. in Des Moines. We are told her health was poor -pernicious anemia. Worked
as an office nurse for dentist, Dr. Fike, while single. She married **James Edmund BLOOMER**
5 Jul 1924.[PVRM, book 24, p 26.(p 34 of transcript)] In her father's obituary, 1936, she is
reported as living in Des Moines, Ia. He was born 9 Mar 1898. James died 1 Feb 1942, we are
told, of meningitis. Edith died 2 Sep 1947.
ISSUE:
+ .16214.1   Verta Marie BLOOMER, born 17 Jun 1927.
  .16214.2   Coleen Ann BLOOMER, born 21 Jun 1932. Emmert's Journal - after her mother's
              death, she went to Ill. to make her home with J.A. and Helen (Rittgers) (#1727.2)
              Baker.   Attended Downers Grove High School. Has worked in Wheaton area since.
              Lived in Carol Stream, Ill.

1621.5 Sylvia Ann⁵ RITTGERS (Ambrose⁴, Reuben³, Daniel², John¹) was born 6 Jul 1900 in Sheridan Lake, Colo., the daughter of Ambrose Robert RITTGERS and Verta Alice SNIDER. In her obituary, we are told the family moved to Eads "the next year." On the 1910 census, age 10, with parents in "Precinct 5",Kiowa Co., Colo.[ED 88, p 5A, fam #106/108] She married (1) **John Ward CLEMENTS** 4 Sep 1918; they divorced. He was born 19 Sep 1898, and died 3 Sep 1963. The 1920 census, Eads, shows John, 25, farming. Sylvia, 19, is caring for Alice, age 6 mo.[ED 108, p 9A, fam #94/96] " Mrs. John Clements of Chivington, Co.," is listed in her father's obituary, 1936. Her obituary reports she moved to "the Gunnison area in 1939" Sylvia married (2) **Raymond PRALL** 30 June 1942 at Montrose, Colo. Sylvia died 14 Aug 1955 in Gunnison, Gunnison Co., Colo. "Unexpectedly..after being hospitalized just a few days."[Obituary submitted with no date or banner.]

ISSUE of John and Sylvia:
+ .16215.1   Alice Blanche CLEMENTS, born 19 Jun 1919.
  .16215.2   John Ward CLEMENTS, Jr., born 4 Jan 1921. Called "of Ouray" in mother's obituary, 1955.He married Eva ZELLER 14 Aug 1956. She was born 14 Mar 1915.
  .16215.3   Kenneth George CLEMENTS, born 23 Feb 1936. Called "of the U.S.Marine Corps form California" in mother's obituary, 1955. He married Carolyn Jo BURNHAM 24 Nov 1956.

ISSUE of Raymond and Sylvia:
  .16215.4   Donna Rae PRALL, born 21 Feb 1943. In mother's obituary, reported she age 11, 1955.

1621.6 Archibald Maurice⁵ RITTGERS (Ambrose⁴, Reuben³, Daniel², John¹) was born 8 Jul 1902[SS] in Eads, Kiowa Co., Colo., the son of Ambrose Robert RITTGERS and Verta Alice SNIDER. On the 1910 census, age 8, with parents in "Precinct 5",Kiowa Co., Colo.[ED 88, p 5A, fam #106/108], and age 17, in Eads, with them on the 1920 census.[ED 109, p 4A, fam #81/87] Seen as "Archie M." on several family reports. Archie came to Johnston, Ia. to pursue High School and made his home with Uncle Fin (#172.7) and Aunt Mabel (Rittgers). He helped by clerking in their general merchandise & grocery store. A family story tells us he was caught sleeping overnight in the schoolhouse with a girl and expelled.   We are told he lived in Healey, Lane Co., Kansas "many years." He married (1) **Florence Elizabeth LEAZER** 6 Jun 1926. She died 7 Oct 1935, Ordway, Colo. Her obituary, submitted without date or banner, gives us a glimpse of her life. She was born 21 Oct 1899, Lake Benton, Minn. Her father, an ordained minister(name not given)of the Methodist Church gave 33 years of service in that relationship. One brother entered the ministry of the church at the age of 17 years. Two sisters, after graduating from Morningside College, became missionaries to South America. At an early age Mrs. Rittgers consciously dedicated her life to God, and united with the Methodist Church." Here it gives a long religious dissertation. It reports that she leaves "in the shadow of bereavement," her husband and two little girls, five sisters and three brothers. In his father's obituary, 1936, it reports he is living in Chivington, Co. Archibald married (2) **Gladys Cecelia DANIELS** 24 Dec 1937. She was born 12 Apr 1903. In a note sent by son Barton, we are told he "worked for the Missouri Pacific R.R. until the 1940's, then ran his own business until 1950, then worked on the State Highway for the state of Kansas. Archibald died 9 Sep 1989 in Eads, Kiowa Co., Colo.

ISSUE of Archibald and Florence:

.16216.1   Betty Lucille RITTGERS, born 6 Aug 1927. She married Leslie GOODPASTOR 22 Dec 1946. He was born 1920.   She lives in Wichita, Ks.

.16216.2   Aloha Lee RITTGERS, born 29 Jan 1930, died 24 Jan 1931. Her death is told in a newspaper account. "Special to The News; Eads, Jan 24; The baby of Mr. and mrs. Archie Rittgers, who live on a farm about two miles east of Eads, was drown in the tank this morning at about 9:30 o'clock.   The little girl, Lola Lee, was one year old this month. She was playing in the yard while her mother was hanging up clothes. The mother missed the child and found her body in the tank.   The child's grandmother, Mrs. A. R. Rittgers, is critically ill at her home in Eads suffering from pneumonia."

.16216.3   Jewel Eva RITTGERS, born 10 Jan 1932. She married Robert McNANLEY 7 Jan 1954.

.16216.4   Donald Eugene RITTGERS, born 7 Oct 1933, died 7 Oct 1933.

ISSUE of Archibald and Gladys:

.16216.5   Barton Verlane RITTGERS, born 29 Oct 1940 in Ransom, Ks. He married Visitation COMARYS 20 Dec 1963.   He went to High school at St. Joseph's Military Academy, then enlisted in the Air Force in 1959.   He retired in 1985, and now lives in Sacramento, Ca., and works as a security guard. [Letter sent by Bart Rittgers in answer to family query, 1995.]

1621.7 Abigail Violet[5] RITTGERS (Ambrose[4], Reuben[3], Daniel[2], John[1]) was born 24 Aug 1905 in Eads, Kiowa Co., Colo., the daughter of Ambrose Robert RITTGERS and Verta Alice SNIDER. On the 1910 census, age 5, with parents in "Precinct 5",Kiowa Co., Colo.[ED 88, p 5A, fam #106/108], and age 15, in Eads, with them on the 1920 census.[ED 109, p 4A, fam #81/87]She married (1) **William Wilson WALKER** 12 Sep 1923. He was born 1892. In her father's obituary, April 1936, she is living in Seneca, Nebraska. William died 27 Nov 1936. Abigail married (2) **William SCHOOLER** after 1936.   Abigail died 10 Aug 1947 in Neb.

ISSUE:

.16217.1   William Wilson WALKER, Jr., born 23 Sep 1925. He married Dorothy FINNEY 19 Jul 1947. She was born 1927.   We are told they had four children.

.16217.2   Robert Lee WALKER, born 7 Oct 1926. He married Mabel MILLER Apr 1948.

.16217.3   Bernard Eugene WALKER, born 30 Jul 1930. He married Lois MEIERS 27 Nov 1952. She was born 1929.   We are told they had 4 children and live in California.

1621.8 Clara Sunshine[5] RITTGERS (Ambrose[4], Reuben[3], Daniel[2], John[1]) was born 16 Nov 1907 in Eads, Kiowa Co., Colo. She was the daughter of Ambrose Robert RITTGERS and Verta Alice SNIDER. On the 1910 census, age 3, with parents in "Precinct 5",Kiowa Co., Colo.[ED 88, p 5A, fam #106/108], and age 11, in Eads, with them on the 1920 census.[ED 109, p 4A, fam #81/87] She married **Bernard KOCH** 28 Oct 1931 He was born 2 Feb 1908. She lived her entire life in Eads, Colo, and this is where she was listed as living in her father's obituary, 1936.   Clara died 12 Jul 1985 in Eads, Kiowa Co., Colo., and was buried in Eads Cemetery.

ISSUE:

.16218.1   Verta Billi KOCH, born 12 Jan 1934 in Eads, Kiowa, Colo. She married K. A. SIMPSON 17 Jun 1956 in Longmont, Colo.   We are told they had four children.

.16218.2   Rita Kary KOCH, born 11 Mar 1938 in Eads, Kiowa, Co.. She married James Gregory MUDGE 15 Sep 1961 in Longmont, Colo.   We are told they had one son.

1621.9 Donald Howard[5] RITTGERS (Ambrose[4], Reuben[3], Daniel[2], John[1]) was born 25 Feb 1910[SS] in Eads, Kiowa Co., Colo., the son of Ambrose Robert RITTGERS and Verta Alice SNIDER. He is seen, age 9, listed as "John", in Eads, Kiowa Co., Colo., with his parents on the 1920 census.[ED 109, p 4A, fam #81/87] He married (1) **Mary Iva BLOODING** 25 Apr 1936 in Garden City, Ks.[Obit] She was born 10 Jan 1912, and died 14 Oct 1962 in Eads. She is buried in Eads Cemetery, Eads, Colo. In his father's obituary, 1936, he is reported living in Eads, Co. Donald married (2) **Roberta THEESEN** 24 Apr 1965. She was born 1916. Roberta is not mentioned at all in his obituary. Donald died 10 Nov 1991.[SS] His obituary, submitted with no date or banner, reports much about his life. As a young man he was a butcher, but he became part owner, along with brother Reuben and brother-in-law Bernard Koch, in a local John Deere Implement Dealership. He retired from this in 1972. He served in the U.S.Army 18 Feb 1942 to 12 Oct 1945. Don was a longtime member of the Eads Masonic Lodge, Unity Lodge #142 A.F.&A.M., and a member of the Kit Carson VFW Post #3411.

ISSUE of Donald and Mary:

.16219.1   Diana Jeanette RITTGERS, born 8 Feb 1946. We are told she was adopted and married Dale Seeger, of Pueblo, Co.

+ .16219.2   Donald LeRoy RITTGERS, born 1 Jun 1947.

1621.A Verta Faye[5] RITTGERS (Ambrose[4], Reuben[3], Daniel[2], John[1]) was born 8 Mar 1912 in Eads, Kiowa Co., Colo. She was the daughter of Ambrose Robert RITTGERS and Verta Alice SNIDER. She is seen, age 8, in Eads, with her parents, on the 1920 census.[ED 109, p 4A, fam #81/87] We are told she was a twin, but the other twin only lived a few days. In her father's obituary, she is listed as "Miss Faye Rittgers, Denver, Co." She married **Fredrick H. GUTIERREZ** 15 Aug 1938. He was born 16 May 1916. She and Fred lived in Denver, Colo.

ISSUE:

.1621A.1   Patricia Ann GUTIERREZ, born 31 Jul 1945. She married Spencer MEIR.

.1621A.2   Fredrick Jerald GUTIERREZ, born 4 Dec 1948.

1621.C Roy Verlaine[5] RITTGERS (Ambrose[4], Reuben[3], Daniel[2], John[1]) was born 2 Feb 1914 in Eads, Kiowa Co., Colo., the son of Ambrose Robert RITTGERS and Verta Alice SNIDER. He is seen, age 6, in Eads, Kiowa Co., Colo., with his parents on the 1920 census.[ED 109, p 4A, fam #81/87] In his father's obituary, he is listed as living in Seneca, Neb. He married **Jessie NICHOLSON** 17 June 1941, Rockport, Tx.[Obit] She was born 2 Nov 1913. Roy died 7 Oct 1958, Omaha, Neb. His obituary, submitted without banner or date, gives us a picture of his life. He "lived in Freemont (Neb.) most of his life." It reports he "was appointed to Freemont Police force in June, 1952. Prior to that he was employed by Fremont Foundry for several years. He was a member of the Fremont Congregational Church, the Fraternal Order of Eagles, and the Nebraska Police Officers Assn. He had been ill about one month, but doesn't report what was wrong. It notes that there is no pension established for widows of policemen who are not killed in the line of duty.

ISSUE:

.1621C.1   Wanda Lee RITTGERS, born 6 Dec 1942. Reported to be age 15 in father's obituary, 1958. She married David G. KELLOGG. He was born 29 May 1940.

.1621C.2   Alice Mae RITTGERS, born 2 Feb 1946. Reported to be age 12 in father's obituary, 1958. She married Robert E. ROLIK 4 Sep 1965. He was born 5 Feb 1945.

1624.1 Lloyd Rittgers⁵ WILSON (Daisy⁴, Reuben³, Daniel², John¹) was born 16 Sep 1895 in Grimes, Polk Co., Ia., the son of Robert A. WILSON and Daisy Marie RITTGERS.[Pledge] On 1900 census, age 4, with parents there.[ED 112, p 10, fam #201/208] and on the 1910 census, age 14, with father and step-mother in Webster Twp., Polk Co., Ia.[ED 184, p 7B, fam #73/73]   Mentioned several times over the years between 1906 and 1913 in the estate of his grandfather, Reuben Rittgers. Since Lloyd's mother died, her share was to be divided between her surviving heirs. Eventually the property was sold by their father with permission from the estate. He married **Allie REED**.[Abst. #76811] She was born 20 Jul 1894. In 1938, Lloyd R. and Allie B., his wife., "conveys an undivided 1/75 interest" in an 80 acre plot that was part of his grandfather's estate. Lloyd died 28 Apr 1984, and Allie died 1987. They are buried in Ridgedale Cemetery, Sec. S., lot 5. Behind his stone is a military marker, "Pvt. US Army, WWI Vet."[RPCem, p 10] Allie died Mar 1987, Independence, Jackson Co., Mo.[SS]

ISSUE:
+ .16241.1   Frieda Madeleine WILSON, born 20 Feb 1921.
+ .16241.2   Glen Reed WILSON, born 3 Feb 1926.
+ .16241.3   Gilbert Rittgers WILSON, born 12 Aug 1928, died 1975.
  .16241.4   Virginia WILSON, died young.
+ .16241.5   Daisy Marie WILSON, born 15 Jan 1930.
+ .16241.6   Herbert Edward WILSON, born 21 Jun 1934.
  .16241.7   Robert WILSON, died in infancy.
  .16241.8   Virginia WILSON, died in infancy.

1624.3 Paul James⁵ WILSON (Daisy⁴, Reuben³, Daniel², John¹) was born 16 Jul 1898 in Grimes, Polk Co., Ia., the son of Robert A. WILSON and Daisy Marie RITTGERS.[Pledge] On 1900 census, age 2, with parents in Grimes, Polk Co., Ia.[ED 112, p 10, fam #201/208] On 1910 census, age 11, with father and step-mother in Webster Twp., Polk Co., Ia.[ED 184, p 7B, fam #73/73] Paul went to live for some time with his great-aunt, Mrs. L.J. (Lizzie Findley) Jennings in McPherson Co., Ks., where we see him at the time he was served with papers to show his father was selling the property the children inherited from their Grandfather, Reuben Rittgers. He married **Edith SHIFFER** 1 Jun 1921.[Abst. 76811] She was born 11 Dec 1901 In June, 1921, he and wife Edith signed off all "rights and title" to the estate of grandparents, to Able Findley Rittgers. We are told they lived in California. Edith died in Calif., May 1972, and Paul died there Oct 1980.[SS] In the Ridgedale Cemetery, there is a stone in sec. S, row 4, with their names and years of birth on it. At the time the transcription was compiled, there were no death dates on the stones.[RPCem, p 10]

ISSUE:
  .16243.1   Carroll Robert WILSON, born 20 May 1922 in Polk Co., Ia., died 4 Jan 1928 in
              Polk Co., Ia.
+ .16243.2   Eugene Clark WILSON, born 11 Feb 1924.
+ .16243.3   Lowell Allen WILSON, born 13 Jan 1931.
  .16243.4   Laurel Philip WILSON, born 18 Dec 1932 in Polk County, Ia., died 8 Jan 1933 in
              Polk County, Ia.

1624.5 Daisy⁵ WILSON (Daisy⁴, Reuben³, Daniel², John¹) was born 8 Dec 1900 in Grimes, Polk Co., Ia., the daughter of Robert A. WILSON and Daisy Marie RITTGERS.[Pledge] Twin to Marie, #1724.6. One record gives her name as "Daisy Evadna". She frequently left out of early estate papers of her late grandfather, Reuben Rittgers, and later written in, as she was apparently confused with her deceased mother. On 1910 census, age 9, with father and step-mother in Webster Twp., Polk Co., Ia.[ED 184, p 7B, fam #73/73] She married **Roscoe Ward WELLS** before 1929. He was born 27 Jan 1890. She is called Daisy Wilson Wells in 1929 in a property tax search regarding her grandparents' estate. She is again called Daisy Wells in 1938 when she and Ward signed off rights to the estate. They lived in Kerrville, Texas.[Abst. #76811] Roscoe died 21 Apr 1962 in Texas. Daisy died 31 Oct 1988, Ingram, Kerr Co., Tx.[SS]

ISSUE:

+ .16245.1   Roberta WELLS, born 13 Feb 1937.

1624.6 Marie⁵ WILSON (Daisy⁴, Reuben³, Daniel², John¹) was born 8 Dec 1900 in Grimes, Polk Co., Ia., the daughter of Robert A. WILSON and Daisy Marie RITTGERS.[Pledge] Twin to Daisy, # 1724.5. On the 1910 census, age 9, with father and step-mother in Webster Twp., Polk Co., Ia.[ED 184, p 7B, fam #73/73] Mentioned in estate papers of Grandfather, Reuben Rittgers.She married **Rev. William Marion GRIFFIN** 15 May 1926. He was born 10 Sep 1897. She is called Marie Griffin in a 1929 property tax search regarding her grandparents' estate. In 1938, she deeded over her property claim to Jasper Rittgers. The Griffins lived in Kerrville, Texas [Abst. #76811] William died 17 Oct 1956.

ISSUE:

.16246.1   Warren GRIFFIN, born 29 Jan 1929, died 20 May 1986. Lived in Kerrville, Tx.
+ .16246.2   Martin GRIFFIN, born 15 Oct 1933.
.16246.3   Mary GRIFFIN.
.16246.4   Betha GRIFFIN.

1626.1 Thomas Park Findley⁵ RITTGERS (Maxwell⁴, Reuben³, Daniel², John¹) was born 20 Jan 1896 in Grimes, Polk Co., Ia., the son of Maxwell M. RITTGERS and Rebecca WILSON. We first see Park as "Park S.", 4, on the 1900 census for Grimes, Polk, Ia. with his maternal grandparents, Thomas and Jane Wilson.[ED 112, p 5B, fam # 97/102] In 1920, at age 24, he is a boarder with uncle, Fred Wilson in Grimes, Polk Co., Ia. He is "foreman, Bridge Building."[ED 187, p 10A, fam #61/61] Thomas was a WW I vet., serving in 135th Aero Squadron, France. After the war he moved to Wisconsin to work in the lumber camps. We are told he was a bit of a loner and lived in a small cabin. He read everything he could get his hands on, and at some point, he felt the calling to minister. He attended the Bible Training School, Madison, Wisc., where he met Elsie. He married **Elsie Anna Wilhelmine SIMON** 28 Oct 1927 in St. Paul, Ramsey Co., Minn.. She was born 20 Apr 1899 in Altura, Minn. She grew up in the Menomonie, Wisc., area., and attended Bible Training School in St. Paul, Minn. He was a self-employed minister in Christian Missionary Alliance Church. Early in their ministry, Thomas and Elsie took a pastorate at Tadisson, Wisc. Later they served on the Lac Courte Oreilles Indian Reservation at New Post, Wisc. Son Clarence, in a tribute read at Thomas' funeral, shared some experiences as a child - among them the story that one Christmas Eve, Thomas was caught in a blizzard trying to get home, where he was expected to lead a service for "people from the reservation." His car stalled out and he had to struggle six miles home - we are told he admitted he never thought he would make it home. When he finally did arrive, the house was so packed that he barely get in the door. The Bible was passed over every ones heads so that he could read the Christmas Story, then he gave each person a small gift. They were in Superior, Wisc., in Oct 1940, when it is reported in his father's obituary, that Max died in their home. They moved to Cedar Rapids, S.D. in 1948, then on to Madison, S.D., where they affiliated with the Church of the Nazarine. Besides raising their 8 children, Elsie was always engaged in church and mission

work. In her funeral memorial card, it is noted that she had 30 grandchildren and 17 great-grandchildren. Elsie died 28 Sep 1984 in Howard, Miner, S.D., and was buried 1 Oct 1984 in Graceland Cemetery, Madison, S.D. Thomas died 11 Mar 1986 when hit by a car while visiting daughter Lois Baggetto in Long Beach, Ca., and was buried in Rittgers Cemetery, Johnston, Ia. In his obituary, it is reported that Thomas also owned and operated "Cedar Tin Shop" and "Lennox Furnace and Air Conditioning" business in Madison, S.D. In 1985, Thomas went to Alaska with son Clarence, and it is noted that few could keep up with Thomas. He was self-educated in many areas, among them being geology. He spent the entire trip up a mountain and back, identifying rocks and lichens. We are told he studied Spanish so that he could read to the Spanish people in the church he attended while wintering in Calif. Thomas was involved in the Prairie Village, near Madison, a type of living farm museum. He had display of rocks there, and attended to this display every day during the summer months when the museum was open. In a newspaper article published in the Madison, S.D. Daily Leader, 15 Apr 1986, Marlene Shurz, manager of the Village, commented in her column about the rock collection and how much Thomas would be missed by those at the Village. A fitting epitaph for him would be the phrase from a card he had clipped to the sun visor of his car for years. Son Clarence remembers it as: Only one life,
                    `Twill soon be past
                    Only what's done,
                    For Christ will last.
                                ISSUE:
+ .16261.1   Thomas Wilson RITTGERS, born 27 Sep 1928.
+ .16261.2   Clarence John RITTGERS, born 23 Nov 1929.
+ .16261.3   Philip Bruce RITTGERS, born 12 Dec 1930.
+ .16261.4   Ruth "Carolyn" RITTGERS, born 21 Jul 1933.
+ .16261.5   William Henry "David" RITTGERS, born 14 Jun 1934.
+ .16261.6   Lois Elinor RITTGERS, born 15 Nov 1935.
+ .16261.7   Bessie Louise RITTGERS, born 25 Mar 1937.
+ .16261.8   Maxwell Benjamin RITTGERS, born 25 Apr 1938.

1626.2 Lt. Col. Forest Sheldon[5] RITTGERS (Maxwell[4], Reuben[3], Daniel[2], John[1]) was born 2 Jul 1902 in Waldron, Harper Co., Ks. (Okla.Terr). He was the son of Maxwell M. RITTGERS and Effie HELMS. On the 1910 census in home of Uncle, John H. Rittgers (#16.2), in Webster, Polk Co., Ia., age 7.[D 184, p 8A, fam #89/89] On 1920 census, age 17, with father and his wife, Katheryn, in Boone City Greene Co., Ia. He is a student.[ED 12, p 1A, fam #5/5] He married **Gail COURTNEY**. She was born 30 Jul 1902 in Clarksville, Butler Co., Ia., the daughter of Samuel G. and Myrtie (Sumner) Courtney. We see in his father's obituary, 1940, he is called Major Forest S. Rittgers, of fort McClellan, Ala. Gail is an author of children's books - and, we are told, a staunch Republican. We thank her for her contribution to the family history. She donated a copy of his obituary and information on her family. She is now 90 years old (1992) and reports that she is quite active in the current Republican presidential re-election, as well as many other activities. Her handwriting is as clear as one half her age. We learn from his obituary, that Forest graduated from Coe College in Cedar Rapids, Ia., and had a masters in physical education from Stanford U. He was a reserve officer and was an assistant professor of military science at Coe College. During WW II he was involved in troop training in Ft. McLellan and then in Birmingham, Ala. After the war, he was one of the oldest infantry officers to be taken into the regular Army, where he served as a military government officer in Kyoto,

Japan 1945-1949. He returned to this country and became professor of military science at Syracuse University. In 1952 he attended the Army Language School in Monterey, Calif., where he studied Chinese and Cantonese. At the conclusion of his studies, he was the U.S. Army liaison officer to the British Crown Colony of Hong Kong. He retired in 1957 and worked seven years as an administrative engineer. Among his other accolades he won a Legion of Merit Award and an honorary doctorate of Sinology (the study of Chinese, their language, literature and culture.) from the Defense Language School. He was named to the Coe College Athletic Hall of Fame. Gail shared that they had 15 WONDERFUL years after he retired in 1964, traveling and "enjoying life" before he succumbed to emphysema at Walter Reed Hosp., Washington, D.C. 21 Mar 1980. He was buried 26 Mar 1980 in Arlington National Cemetery, Arlington, Va.

ISSUE:

+ .16262.1   Forest Sheldon RITTGERS, Jr., born 27 Aug 1931.
+ .16262.2   Courtney RITTGERS, born 7 Dec 1937.

1627.2 Helen Lucille[5] **RITTGERS** (Abel[4], Reuben[3], Daniel[2], John[1]) was born 22 Mar 1909 in Johnston, Polk Co., Ia., the daughter of Abel Findley RITTGERS and Mabel McCREIGHT. We see her on the 1910 census, age 1 1/12, with her parents in Webster, Polk Co., Ia.[ED 184, p 9A, fam #119/119] On 1920 census, age 10, with family in Webster.[ED 187, p 11B, fam #106/106] Listed in papers filed in the property abstract of Rittgers Acres, we see widowed mother filing for administration of her father's estate. Helen is listed as age 12 in July 1922.[Abst 76811, p 35] Laura (Rittgers) Emmert shares with us that Helen remembered playing with her as a baby "at Herrold, Ia., where our fathers had a grocery business. Helen was Laura's bridesmaid when she married Earl Peitzman. There appears to be a warm and close bond between Helen and Laura that has grown over the years. We are told that when Helen finished high school her uncle, George McCreight helped her get a teaching certificate from Drake University. Her first teaching position was at Grimes High School and later taught at Orient, Ia. She married **Jesse Ardon BAKER** 31 Dec 1938. He was born 27 Mar 1913. They lived in Downers Grove, Ill. Mother Mabel lived with them in the summers. Helen died 4 Feb 1985 in Downers Grove, Cook Co., Ill.

ISSUE:

+ .16272.1   Dorothy Ruth BAKER, born 8 Mar 1941.
+ .16272.2   Marie Louise BAKER, born 19 Nov 1943.
+ .16272.3   George Samuel BAKER, born 14 Sep 1945.
+ .16272.4   Donald Bertram BAKER, born 3 Mar 1950.

1627.4 Dorothy Marguerite[5] **RITTGERS** (Abel[4], Reuben[3], Daniel[2], John[1]) was born 12 Dec 1915 in Johnston, Polk Co., Ia., the daughter of Abel Findley RITTGERS and Mabel McCREIGHT. On 1920 census, age 4, with parents, Webster, Polk Co., Ia.[ED 187, p 11B, fam #106/106] Age 6, in estate administration papers filed by her mother, 1922, after her father's death.[Abst 76811, p. 35] She married **Kenneth WEBSTER** 3 Apr 1945. He was born 27 Aug 1915. Family history reports she worked in an office in Des Moines after High School but, after marriage to Kenneth, whom she met at church, they left the Johnston area. Kenneth had worked for the Pioneer Co. in Johnston but desired more education. He doggedly pursued this ambition until he received his master's degree. Dorothy typed papers for him and cared for their little children in small living quarters. "It was not an easy life and both Kenneth and Dorothy should always be honored for this accomplishment. Kenneth built a home for them in Downers Grove,

Ill., where he taught school until retirement age." Laura Emmert speaks very warmly of the friendship with Kenneth and Dorothy. Dorothy died 8 Mar 1995, Downers Grove, Ill.[SS]

ISSUE:

+ .16274.1   Helen "Maurine" WEBSTER, born 22 Oct 1947.
.16274.2   Mildred Louise "Millie" WEBSTER, born 27 Apr 1949. An RN with a B.S. degree, she is a missionary in Africa.
+ .16274.3   Phyllis WEBSTER, born 9 Dec 1950.
+ .16274.4   Laura Marguerite WEBSTER, born 1 Jul 1952.
+ .16274.5   Kenneth Robert "Ken" WEBSTER, born 12 Jan 1957.

1628.1 Lawrence W.[5] RITTGERS (Jasper[4], Reuben[3], Daniel[2], John[1]) was born 13 Jun 1904 in Johnston, Polk Co., Ia., the son of Jasper C. "Jass" RITTGERS and Margaret "Maggie" WILSON.[PVRB, book 6, p 70 of transcript.] Seen on the 1910 census, age 7, with parents in Webster Twp., Polk Co., Ia.[ED 184, p7B, fam #80/80] 1920 census, age 16, with parents in Crocker, Polk Co., Ia.[ED 232, p 2A, fam #32/32] He married **Esther A. BALLHEAGAN** 10 Mar 1926. She was born 25 Dec 1907 in Black Hawk County, Ia., the daughter of Leon and Pearl (___) Ballheagen. He and Esther made their home near Harford, Ia. In his mother's obituary, Aug 1958, he is called "of New Hartford.." Esther died 22 Jun 1954 in New Hartford, Butler Co., Ia., and was buried in Oak Hill Cemetery, New Hartford, Ia.[obit. with no newsbanner] Lawrence died 11 Jun 1990[SS] in New Hartford, Butler Co., Ia., and was buried in Oak Hill Cemetery, New Hartford, Ia.

ISSUE:

+ .16281.1   Gladys June RITTGERS, born 30 Apr 1927.
+ .16281.2   Eugene Merlen RITTGERS, born 10 Sep 1928.
.16281.3   Charlotte Anne RITTGERS, born 2 Feb 1930 in New Hartford, Butler Co., Ia.
+ .16281.4   Merle Edwin RITTGERS, born 27 Dec 1932.
+ .16281.5   Ralph Alden RITTGERS, born 13 Jan 1934.
.16281.6   Donald LeRoy RITTGERS, born 10 Feb 1935 in New Hartford, Butler Co., Ia. He served in the Army.
.16281.7   Elizabeth Allene RITTGERS, born 16 Jul 1936 in New Hartford, Butler Co., Ia.
.16281.8   Ardith Jane RITTGERS, born 29 Jul 1937 in New Hartford, Butler Co., Ia.

1628.2 Ruth Evelyn[5] RITTGERS (Jasper[4], Reuben[3], Daniel[2], John[1]) was born 19 Aug 1905. She was the daughter of Jasper C. "Jass" RITTGERS and Margaret "Maggie" WILSON. Seen on the 1910 census, age 4, with parents in Webster, Polk Co., Ia.[ED 184, p7B, fam #80/80], and on the 1920 census, age 14, with parents in Crocker, Polk Co., Ia.[ED 232, p 2A, fam #32/32] Attended Teacher's College in Cedar Falls, Black Hawk Co., Ia., and here was introduced to the brother of college chum Clara Mast. She married (1) **Harry MAST** 26 Jun 1926.[PVRM, book 26, p 186; p 31 of transcript.] He was born 1896. He served in the army during WW I. Harry was a farmer, and Ruth worked hard on their farm tending the field and the livestock. We are told she canned large amounts of all sorts of food-stuffs grown on the farm, tended the animals, and raised the children while Harry traveled in his business. She also found time to be active in her church, Women's Farm Bureau, and the Black Hawk Women's Republican's Committee. Harry also had a business hauling coal, lime and gravel. He was killed when his truck was hit by a train 29 Jun 1945 in Cedar Falls, Black Hawk Co., Ia. Harry was buried in Fairview Cem., Cedar Falls, Ia. Ruth married (2) **Ralph SUNDERLIN** 14 Mar 1953. He was born 1906. In mother's obituary, Aug 1958, she is called "Mrs. Ralph Sunderlin of

Cedar Falls." She cared for Ralph's father in their home for many years and also cared for her own father during his "declining years." Ralph died 19 Oct 1961.[Interview with Margaret (Rittgers) McBride, 1994]

ISSUE Of Harry and Ruth:

.16282.1   Richard E. MAST, born and died 30 May 1927 in Cedar Falls, Black Hawk Co., Ia.,
+ .16282.3   Clarence Eugene MAST, born 23 Feb 1933.
+ .16282.4   Wayne Eldon MAST, born 4 Apr 1936.
.16282.5   Noel Eldon MAST, born 25 Dec 1938 in Cedar Falls, Black Hawk Co., Ia. He married Carol Ann MAXWELL 30 Jul 1966.
.16282.6   Harold Edward MAST, born 14 Jan 1942, died 16 Mar 1942 in Cedar Falls, Black Hawk Co., Ia., and was buried in Fairview Cemetery, Cedar Falls, Ia.
+ .16282.7   Harriet Esther MAST, born 26 Jan 1943.
+ .16282.8   David Elgin MAST, born 16 Aug 1945.

1628.4 Lester Findley[5] RITTGERS (Jasper[4], Reuben[3], Daniel[2], John[1]) was born 12 Sep 1912 in Webster Twp., Polk Co., Ia., the son of Jasper C. "Jass" RITTGERS and Margaret "Maggie" WILSON.[PVRB, book 7, p 127 of transcript] On the 1920 census, age 7, with parents in Crocker Twp., Polk Co., Ia.[ED 232, p 2A, fam #32/32] Family story tells us how he and his siblings worked on the home farm while growing up. He went to Iowa State College for one year, but the depression was on. He worked for Poineer Seed Co. during and after college. He married **Alice RASSMANSEN** 6 Sep 1941. She was born 8 Aug 1914 in Grundy Co., Ia., the daughter of Niels and Anna Marie (Hansen) Radmussen. They moved to near Cedar Falls, Ia. in 1948, and there have remained. He won several awards for his corn and received recognition for his dairy herd. He and Alice have been active in the First Baptist Church, he a deacon and Alice taught Sunday School for many years.

ISSUE:

+ .16284.1   Lois Frances RITTGERS, born 15 Oct 1942.
+ .16284.2   Lee Francis RITTGERS, born 8 Jul 1944.
.16284.3   Mary Ellen RITTGERS, born 17 Dec 1947 in Cedar Falls, Ia. She married Thomas Lynn KEIS 10 Jun 1970 in Independence, Ia. He was born 16 Oct 1949.
+ .16284.4   Larry Lester RITTGERS, born 3 Apr 1952.
+ .16284.5   Alice Lynn RITTGERS, born 2 Jul 1955.

1628.5 Frederick Henry[5] RITTGERS (Jasper[4], Reuben[3], Daniel[2], John[1]) was born 24 Oct 1914 in Ankeny, Polk Co., Ia., the son of Jasper C. "Jass" RITTGERS and Margaret "Maggie" WILSON. On 1920 census, age 5, with parents in Crocker, Polk Co., Ia.[ED 232, p 2A, fam #32/32] Graduated 1939 from Wheaton College with a B.A. in Geology and Geography. He married **Joyce Winifred DAVIS** 24 Oct 1940. She was born 26 Jan 1918 in McPherson, Mcpherson Co., Ks., the daughter of Verne Arthur and Joan (Hargraves) Davis. They moved to Knoxville, Tenn., where he graduated from University of Tenn. with a masters in geography and geology. In 1941, was a civil engineer on the June Hales bar dam project. He served as a Lt. in U.S. Navy, WW II., seeing service in the South Pacific and the invasion of Borneo. Promoted to Captain before discharge in 1946. He returned home to farm in Ankeny. In the 1948 Polk Co. Farm Directory, p. 148, we see Fred H. and Joyce in Ankeny, owning 137 acres, general farming. He owns a 1935 Ford car and a John Deere Tractor. A member of the Gospel Missionary Church, he was church clerk and a teacher of young adults. He also "filled the pulpit" several times during the minister's absences. Frederick was killed 31 Oct 1950[SS] in Des

Moines, Polk Co., Ia., when the tractor he was riding down the highway on tipped over into a ditch, pinning him beneath it. He was buried in Union Cemetery, Polk Co., Ia. [UPCem, p 3] Joyce now lives in New York City.[Obituary & news stories regarding accident, copy submitted with no newspaper banner]

ISSUE:

.16285.1   Winifred Faye RITTGERS, born 18 May 1944 in Des Moines, Polk Co., Ia. She married Norman Howard CHRIST 6 Jun 1964. He was born 22 Dec 1943. They live in Irvington, N.Y.

+ .16285.2   Stanley Earle RITTGERS, born 24 Jan 1947.

.16285.3   Jean Ellen RITTGERS, born 24 May 1949 in Des Moines, Polk Co., Ia. She married Richard ROSENBLATT 30 Dec 1972. He was born 4 Jan 1944.

.16285.4   Ann Elaine RITTGERS, born 24 Jul 1950 in Des Moines, Polk Co., Ia. She married Allen BUCHANAN 30 Dec 1972. He was born 7 Apr 1948.

1628.6 Margaret Elizabeth[5] RITTGERS (Jasper[4], Reuben[3], Daniel[2], John[1]) was born 19 Jun 1917 in Johnston, Polk Co., Ia., the daughter of Jasper C. "Jass" RITTGERS and Margaret "Maggie" WILSON. On the 1920 census, age 2 7\12, with parents in Crocker Twp., Polk Co., Ia. [ED 232, p 2A, fam 32/32] She graduated from Iowa State College, Mar 1941, with a degree in Dietetics and Home Economics. She married **John Adolph McBRIDE** 21 Jun 1941. He was born 31 Oct 1913. John graduated from Wheaton College with a degree in business in 1940. At the time of their marriage, he was working for DuPont Paint Co., Columbus, Oh. They were transferred to Indianapolis, and then to Des Moines in 1943. In 1952, they purchased the farm that was the 1868 homestead of John's great grandfather, John McBride. John died 21 Jan 1971, and was buried in Union Cemetery, Polk Co., Ia. Margaret lives near Polk City, Ia. Called "of Polk City," in Mother's obituary, Aug 1958.[Interview with Margaret (Rittgers) McBride, 1994]

ISSUE:

+ .16286.1   John Ade McBRIDE, born 7 Jan 1943.

+ .16286.2   David Evan McBRIDE, born 16 Jan 1945.

.16286.3   Richard James McBRIDE, born 31 Jan 1949 in Polk City, Polk, Ia.

+ .16286.4   Barbara Ann McBRIDE, born 18 Jun 1952.

162A.1 John Rittgers[5] RORABAUGH (Vivian[4], Reuben[3], Daniel[2], John[1]) was born 12 Jan 1908 in Des Moines, Polk Co., Ia., the son of William Ellsworth RORABAUGH and Vivian Adelaid RITTGERS. He moved to Montverde, Lake Co., Florida in 1911 with parents. On the 1920 census, age 11, with parents in Clermont, Lake Co., Fla.[p 555, fam #89/96] We see him on the 1935 Florida state census, age 27, listed with his parents in precinct 15, Clermont, Fla, but it is noted his occupation is "C.C. camp."[reel 17, precinct 15] He married **Palma FOUNTAIN** 26 Dec 1943 in Clermont, Lake Co., Fla. She was born 25 Nov 1914 in Harvy, Ill., the daughter of Philip and Suretta (Burton) Fountain. On the 1945 state census, he is listed as head of house with his parents in Precinct 15, Clermont, but the notation "Army" is in the occupation column so we don't know if he was actually there. Wife, Palma, not listed. [Reel 27, precinct 15] Made a career out of The National Guard, his unit being mobilized by Army during World War II. After the war he served in Europe, taking advantage of the travel opportunities. Retired to Clermont, Fla., where he resided until his death. [Interview with John R. Rorabaugh in Sept 1992] Palma died 15 May 1991 in Clermont, Lake, Fla. John died of heart failure 30 Jun 1993 in Clermont, Lake, Fla. They are buried 3 Jul 1993 in Oak Hill Cem., Clermont, Fla.[funeral memorial card]

ISSUE:
+ .162A1.1   Richard John RORABAUGH, born 22 Mar 1950.

162A.3 William Lysle[5] RORABAUGH, Sr. (Vivian[4], Reuben[3], Daniel[2], John[1]) was born 24 Apr 1912 in Montverde, Lake Co., Fla., the son of William Ellsworth RORABAUGH and Vivian Adelaid RITTGERS. On the 1920 census, age 7, with parents in Clermont, Lake Co., Fla.[p 555, fam #89/96] We see him in his parents home, age 22, in Precinct 15, Clermont, Fla., on the 1935 Florida state census, where he is listed as "C.C. camp."[reel 17] He married **Myrtle Ruth QUIGLEY** 1 Jul 1938 in Winter Garden, Orange Co., Fla. She was born 31 Mar 1921 in Luthersville, Meriwether Co., Ga., the daughter of James Taylor and MaryLou (Davis) Quigley. She moved from Luthersville to Winter Garden, Orange Co., Fla. with her widowed mother, and siblings, about 1926. On the 1945 state census there, he is 33 and a mechanic. With him is wife Myrtle and two children. Also in the home are her mother, 2 sisters, a brother and a nephew.[reel 27, precinct 15] William held several agricultural jobs as a very young man, and then drove an ice truck (in Florida!) Became an electrician and retired from that career. Currently resides in Ocoee, Fla. Enjoys grand-children and great-grand-children, as well as fishing.

ISSUE:
+ .162A3.1   William Lysle RORABAUGH, Jr., born 5 Jan 1938.
+ .162A3.2   Sarah Ruth RORABAUGH, born 20 Dec 1941.
+ .162A3.3   Donna Josephine RORABAUGH, born 19 Oct 1947.

162A.4 Philip Findley[5] RORABAUGH (Vivian[4], Reuben[3], Daniel[2], John[1]) was born 11 Jun 1913 in Clermont, Lake Co., Fla., the son of William Ellsworth RORABAUGH and Vivian Adelaid RITTGERS. On the 1920 census, age 6, with parents in Clermont, Lake Co., Fla.[p 555, fam #89/96] He married **Marian HARDY** 12 Sep 1935. Worked in agriculture, and owned a filling station in Clermont, Fla. Later worked in dairy and in meat packing. Now retired and living in Clermont, Fla., in his parents original home.[Interview with Philip F. Rorabaugh in 1992]

ISSUE:
+ .162A4.1   Philip Arthur RORABAUGH, born 4 Jun 1936.
.162A4.2   Mary Louise RORABAUGH, born 11 Jan 1938 in Clermont, Lake Co., Fla. Mary Lou has degrees in Christian Education as well as her Masters in both Pediatric Nursing and Public Health Nursing. In 1990 she received her doctorate in Public Health Nursing and was an assistant professor of Pediatric Nursing at Emery University in Atlanta, Ga. In her early career, Mary Lou took her nursing skills into the Missionary field to Laos and Cambodia from 1969-1975 through the Christian and Missionary Alliance Church. She has recently returned to Cambodia and is working to rebuild the hospital she was involved with there. [Interview with Philip Rorabaugh, 1992]
.162A4.3   Paul Ellsworth RORABAUGH, born and died 17 Jun 1942 in Clermont, Fla.
+ .162A4.4   Anna Marie RORABAUGH, born 12 Aug 1943.
+ .162A4.5   Esther Judith RORABAUGH, born 16 Oct 1946.

162A.5 Vivian Abigail[5] RORABAUGH (Vivian[4], Reuben[3], Daniel[2], John[1]) was born 12 Sep 1917 in Clermont, Lake Co., Fla., the daughter of William Ellsworth RORABAUGH and Vivian Adelaid RITTGERS. On 1920 census, age 2 3/12, with parents in Clermont, Lake Co., Fla.[p

555, fam #89/96]   She married **Herman COX** 27 May 1937 in Clermont, Lake, Fl. He was born 4 Mar 1914 in Montverde, Lake Co., Fla., the son of James and Nellie G. (__) Cox of Montverde, Lake Co., Fla. Gail always loved the story of her mother and father marrying on the porch of her mother's home, Appledoor, so chose to be married on the porch of her parent's home in Clermont. Money was scarce, so their honeymoon was financed by driving a carload of wealthy Cuban schoolboys from a private boarding school in Mont Verde, Lake Co., Fla., to Miami to catch the boat home for summer break. They were thrilled to get $5 per boy! Herman worked in agriculture. After retirement, they bought a mini-motor home, named it "The Toy" and enjoyed traveling and going to camp-outs. Herman died 5 May 1995[funeral card] in Mount Dora, Lake Co., Fla., and was buried there.[Interview with Gail (Rorabaugh) Cox, 1992]

ISSUE:

+ .162A5.1   Herman "Kenneth" COX, born 29 Apr 1938.
+ .162A5.2   Carolyn Abigail COX, born 16 Jul 1940.
+ .162A5.3   Randall William COX, born 15 Dec 1944.
+ .162A5.4   Marilyn Louise COX, born 14 Oct 1952.

162C.6 Robert Chester[5] RITTGERS (Chester[4], Reuben[3], Daniel[2], John[1]) was born 2 May 1916[SS] in Corpus Christi, Nueces Co., Texas., the son of Chester Daniel RITTGERS and Mary RANDOLPH. On the 1920 census, age 3 8/12, with parents there.[ED 180, p 8B, fam #168/169]He married **Kathleen L. EMMERT**. Robert died 29 March 1989.[SS]

ISSUE:

+ .162C6.1   Albert Joe RITTGERS, born 20 Apr 1937.

162C.8 David Earl[5] RITTGERS (Chester[4], Reuben[3], Daniel[2], John[1]) was born 18 Dec 1920 in Corpus Christi, Nueces Co., Tx., the son of Chester RITTGERS and Mary RANDOLPH. David was in the Army during WWII and saw combat in Luzon, the Philippines. David married **Christine Mary VAJDOS**. She was born 22 Aug 1932 in Karnes City, Karnes Co., Tx. He worked at Columbia Southern Industries. David died May 1986[SS says Dec 1986] in Corpus Christi, Nueces Co., Tx. They were Catholics.

ISSUE:

+ .162C8.1   Daniel William RITTGERS, born 1 Apr 1952.
 .162C8.2   David Earl RITTGERS, II, born 19 Jul 1953 in Corpus Christi, Nueces, Tx.
 .162C8.3   Donald DeWitt RITTGERS, born 15 Apr 1955 in Corpus Christi, Nueces, Tx, died 1980.

162D.1 Laura[5] RITTGERS (John[4], Reuben[3], Daniel[2], John[1]) was born 16 Jun 1912 in Johnston, Polk Co., Ia., the daughter of John Henry RITTGERS and Gretchen Ima TRISSEL. [PVRB, book 7, p 127 of transcript] On the 1920 census, age 7, with parents in Walnut, Polk Co., Ia.[ED 21, p 8A, fam #192/194] She married (1) **Earl L. PEITZMAN** 14 Feb 1936 in Grimes, Polk Co., Ia. He was born 2 Nov 1899 in Dallas Center, Dallas Co., Ia., the son of John H. and Clara Elizabeth (Foltz) Peitzman. We find Earl on the 1920 census as 20, living with his widowed mother, Clara, three sisters and a brother in Jefferson Twp., Polk Co., Ia. This is the author of Emmert's Journal. It is due to her insertion into family records some of her childhood memories that we have a colorful picture of some of the family members. Earl died 19 Feb 1978 in Dallas Center, Polk Co., Ia., and was buried in Sunny Hill Cemetery, Grimes, Ia. Laura married (2) **L. Dale EMMERT** 2 Jan 1979. He was born 9 Feb 1909. He was a farmer. He married (1) _____ and had two sons. Dale died 6 Apr 1995 in Dallas Center, Dallas Co., Ia., and

was buried in Panther Creek Ch, Adel, Ia. [Interview with Laura (Rittgers)(Peitzman) Emmert, 1992, 1994]
ISSUE:
+ .162D11   Lloyd John PEITZMAN, born 18 Feb 1937.

162D.3 John Henry[5] RITTGERS, Jr. (John[4], Reuben[3], Daniel[2], John[1]) was born 1 Aug 1920 in Des Moines, Polk Co., Ia., the son of John Henry RITTGERS and Gretchen Ima TRISSEL. [PVRB, book 10, p 105 of transcript] During WWII, John served in the South Pacific with the U.S. Army 1943-1946. He married **Elsie Arlene WISE** 10 Jul 1946. She was born 14 Jan 1922. John died 22 Dec 1992 in Des Moines, Polk, Ia., following a long battle with kidney disease and five years of renal dialysis.[Interview with Laura (Rittgers) (Peitzman) Emmert, 1992]
ISSUE:
+ .162D3.1   Sharon Kay RITTGERS, born 25 Nov 1949.
+ .162D3.2   Gary John RITTGERS, born 21 Mar 1953.
  .162D3.3   Karen Sue RITTGERS, born 12 Jun 1955. Laura Emmert tells us that Karen works as a nurses aide at Adel Acres Nursing Home. "Is competent and caring and dependable."

162D.4 Thomas Eugene[5] RITTGERS (John[4], Reuben[3], Daniel[2], John[1]) was born 11 Dec 1923 in Des Moines, Polk Co., Ia., the son of John Henry RITTGERS and Gretchen Ima TRISSEL. He married **Phyllis G. CLIPSON** 27 Mar 1948. She was born 23 Aug 1928., the daughter of Hugh William and Gertrude Evelyn (Falwell) Clipson. Phyllis was raised in Lenox, Ia. Thomas is a professional farm manager and Phyllis an elementary school teacher. They are Presbyterians, and reside in Grimes, Ia., wintering in Florida.[*Interview with Thomas Rittgers, 1993*]
ISSUE:
+ .162D4.1   Mark Thomas RITTGERS, born 10 Feb 1949.
+ .162D4.2   Hugh John RITTGERS, born 30 Dec 1950.

162E.2 Ruth Ellen[5] HARDIE (Mary[4], Reuben[3], Daniel[2], John[1]) was born 13 Jan 1914., the daughter of Henry HARDIE and Mary Eve RITTGERS. She married (1) **Eddie DePEW**. Ruth married (2) **Ed BOMAN**. He was born 3 Apr 1906. She lived in Westminster, Ca., in her later years.
ISSUE of Eddie and Ruth:
  .162E2.1   Jack DePEW. They lived in Mahtomedi, Minn.
+ .162E2.2   Deanna DePEW, born 11 Aug 1940.
+ .162E2.3   Frances "Cookie" DePEW.
ISSUE of Ed and Ruth:
  .162E2.4   David BOMAN.
  .162E2.5   Robin BOMAN, born 7 May 1955.

1672.1 Charlotte Alice[5] PEACOCK (Grace[4], George[3], Daniel[2], John[1]) was born 20 Jul 1905 in Grimes, Polk Co., Ia., the daughter of Dr. Abraham Leo PEACOCK and Grace RITTGERS. We see her on the 1910 census, age 4, with her parents in Grimes, Jefferson Twp., Polk Co., Ia.[ED106, p.54, fam#108/109] She married **Eugene Charles WINELAND** 30 Apr 1927 in Grimes, Polk Co., Ia. He was born 27 Feb 1893 in Kansas City, Jackson Co., Mo., the son of Charles E. and Anna Ellen (Beck) Wineland. He was a printing pressman. Eugene died 21 Jan 1952 in Kansas City, Jackson, Mo. Charlotte died 18 Jan 1987 in Raytown, Jackson Co., Mo.

Charlotte and Eugene are buried in Block 6, Lot 37, of Elmwood Cem. [Family Group sheet submitted by Lorene A. (Wineland) Summerskill]

ISSUE:

+ .16721.1   Lorene Alice WINELAND, born 20 Sep 1927.
+ .16721.2   Delores Ella WINELAND, born 27 Aug 1929, died 30 Aug 1993.

1681.1 Harry Washburn^5 RITTGERS (Charles^4, Michael^3, Daniel^2, John^1) was born 9 Jul 1899, the son of Charles R. RITTGERS and Mary Elizabeth KAVANAUGH. We see him on the 1900 census, age 10 mo., with his parents in Brooklyn, Kings Co., NY. [ED309, p.68, fam #114/228] On the 1920 census, Harry, 20, is listed with his widower father in Webster Twp., Polk Co., Ia. He is listed as a "ships waiter (or writer, hard to read)He married (1) **Happy** ____; married (2) Louise____. Harry died 28 Dec 1975, and was buried in Rittgers Cemetery, Johnston, Ia.

ISSUE:

.16811.1   Carol RITTGERS, born Aug 1927.

1681.3 Charles Barton^5 RITTGERS (Charles^4, Michael^3, Daniel^2, John^1) was born 15 Oct 1903 in Brooklyn, Kings Co., NY., the son of Charles R. RITTGERS and Mary Elizabeth KAVANAUGH. On the 1920 census, age 16, with widowed father, siblings, and widowed grandmother in Webster, Polk Co., Ia.[ED 187, p 12B, fam #125/136] He married **Mary C. FISHER** 21 Sep 1927 in Johnston, Polk Co., Ia.[PVRM, book 27, p 256; p 27 of transcript] She was born 23 Oct 1903, Ogden, Ia., the daughter of Charles Christian FISHER and Minerva Ellen Dunkle. In his sister Dorothy's obituary, it states he living in Maxwell, Ia., June 1976. Charles died 17 Jan 1996 in Winterset, Madison Co., Ia.,of complications of Alzheimer's. In his obituary it reports he had lost two daughters prior to his death. He had 3 grand children and 10 great grandchildren.[obit with no newspaper banner] He is buried in the Rittgers Cemetery, Johnton, Ia. Mary is currently in a nursing home in Nevada, Ia.(1997)

ISSUE:

+ .16813.1   Marion Irene RITTGERS, born 11 Aug 1928.
+ .16813.2   Harold Charles RITTGERS, born 29 Dec 1929.
.16813.3   Ruth Mae RITTGERS, born 16 Dec 1933, died 17 Dec 1933, and was buried in Rittgers Cemetery, Johnston, Ia. We are told she died of RH factor in her blood.
.16813.4   Shirley Rose RITTGERS, born 20 Feb 1937, died 20 Feb 1937, and was buried in the Rittgers Cemetery, Johnston, Ia. We are told she died of the RH factor in her blood.

1681.4 Grace Ann^5 RITTGERS (Charles^4, Michael^3, Daniel^2, John^1) was born 27 Mar 1905. She was the daughter of Charles R. RITTGERS and Mary Elizabeth KAVANAUGH. She married **Herbert Herman KUEFNER** 10 Sept 1927, Polk Co., Ia.[PVRM, Bk 27, p169]. He was born 27 Mar 1905. Grace died 30 Jan 1977, and was buried in Grimes, Ia. We are told Herbert remarried.

ISSUE:

+ .16814.1   Barbara Jean KUEFNER, born 23 Dec 1928.
+ .16814.2   Robert KUEFNER, born 4 Jul 1940.

1681.5 Walter Joseph^5 RITTGERS (Charles^4, Michael^3, Daniel^2, John^1) was born about 1908 in NY., the son of Charles R. RITTGERS and Mary Elizabeth KAVANAUGH. On 1920 census, age 12, with widowed father, siblings, and widowed grandmother in Webster, Polk Co., Ia.[ED 187, p 12B, fam #125/136] He married **Lillie QUICK**. In the 1948 Polk Co. Farm Directory, p. 148, we see that Walter and Lillie live in Grimes. "Owns home," works pioneer Hi-Bred Corn Co. Ford 1940 car. In sister Dorothy's obituary, it states he living in Johnston, Ia., June 1976. Walter died in 1996.

ISSUE:
+ .16815.1   Kenneth RITTGERS, born abt. 1942.
+ .16815.2   James "Jim" RITTGERS, born abt. 1946.
+ .16815.3   Janet RITTGERS, born abt. 1946.
+ .16815.4   Donald RITTGERS, born abt. 1947.

1681.6 Herbert Daniel[5] RITTGERS (Charles[4], Michael[3], Daniel[2], John[1]) was born 25 Sep 1909, Kings Co., NY., the son of Charles R. RITTGERS and Mary Elizabeth KAVANAUGH. We see him on the 1920 census, age 10, with his widower father, Webster Twp., Polk Co., Ia. He married **Marjorie THORNTON** 3 Jun 1939. Marjorie was born 5 Nov 1908, died 17 Aug 1988 in Maricopa Co., Az.[SS] Herbert died 2 Oct 1993 in Sun City, Maricopa Co., Az. They are buried in Rittgers Cemetery, Johnston, Ia.

ISSUE:
.16816.1   Alan RITTGERS, born Mar 1942.

1684.2 Barton[5] RITTGERS (Anson[4], Michael[3], Daniel[2], John[1]) was born 5 Feb 1914[SS] in Johnston, Polk Co., Ia., the son of Anson RITTGERS and Florence Eliza CLOSE. Seen on the 1920 census 5, with parents in Crocker Twp., Polk Co., Ia.[ED 232, p 2A, fam #36/37] He married **Jeanette M. HAYES**. In the 1948 Polk Co. Farm Directory, p.148, we see Barton in Polk City, owns 240 acres of general farming. He owns a 1937 Chevrolet, John Deere Tractor, combine, and a corn picker. Barton died 30 Dec 1985, from cancer, and was buried in Rittgers Cemetery, Johnston, Ia. In his obituary, we see that he was a retired farmer at the time of his death. He had been a chairman of the Polk Co. Extension service, a charter member of the Farm Bureau, and a member of the Sheridan Park United Methodist Church. She is called "M. Jean" in husband's obituary. The obituary also reports a step-daughter, Phyllis Bagg of Charleston, SC; and a stepson, Randall Deremiah of Aurora, Colo.

ISSUE:
.16842.1   Janice RITTGERS, born abt. 1944 in Polk County, Ia. She married _____
            LaCOUR. In father's obituary, 1986, is said to be "Janice LaCour of Hazelwood,
            Mo.,"
.16842.2   Barbara RITTGERS, born abt. 1946 in Polk County, Ia. She married _____
            LEONARD. In father's obituary, 1986, is said to be "Barbara Leonard of Ankeny,"
            Polk, Ia.
.16842.3   Ronald B. RITTGERS, born abt. 1947 in Polk Co., Ia. In father's obituary, 1986,
            is said to be of West Des Moines, Polk Co., Ia.

1691.1 Floyd Sidney[5] PURVIANCE (Nellie[4], Caroline[3], Daniel[2], John[1]) was born 13 Jul 1895., the son of Robert K. PURVIANCE and Nellie Josephine McDOWELL. On 1900 census, age 4, with parents, Washington Twp., Dallas Co., Ia.[ED 20, p 9A, fam #109/109] On 1910 census, age 14, with parents there.[ED 21, p. 7A, fam 393/96] Listed as farm laborer, home farm. He married **Lola Marie REPP** 24 Jul 1918. Floyd died 19 Jul 1972 in Perry, Dallas Co., Ia.[SS]
ISSUE:

+ .16911.1   Edith LaVonne PURVIANCE, born 19 Apr 1920.

1691.2 Rex⁵ PURVIANCE (Nellie⁴, Caroline³, Daniel², John¹) was born 11 Jul 1898., the son
of Robert K. PURVIANCE and Nellie Josephine McDOWELL. On 1900 census, age 1, with
parents, Washington Twp., Dallas Co., Ia.[ED 20, p 9A, fam #109/109], on 1910 census, age
11 with parents [ED 21; p. 7A; fam #93/96] and there with them, age 21, on the 1920 census.
He is listed as a "laborer, home farm."[ED 22, p 2A, fam #27/27] He married **Hazel REPP**.
Rex died Jul 1972.[SS] His last residence listed as Ames, Story Co., Ia.

ISSUE:

.16912.1   Rita Ray PURVIANCE.
.16912.2   Donald Dale PURVIANCE.
.16912.3   Carol Jean PURVIANCE. She married William S. ELLIOT.

1691.3 Keith⁵ PURVIANCE (Nellie⁴, Caroline³, Daniel², John¹) was born about 1904 in
Washington Twp., Dallas Co., Ia., the son of Robert K. PURVIANCE and Nellie Josephine
McDOWELL. On 1910 census, age 6 with parents in Washington Twp., Dallas Co., Ia.[ED 21;
p. 7A; fam #93/96]and on 1920 census, age 16, with parents there, "laborer, home farm."[ED
22, p 2A, fam #27/27] He married **Lucille KIMBALL**.

ISSUE:

.16913.1   Lois Jean PURVIANCE.

1691.4 Paul⁵ PURVIANCE (Nellie⁴, Caroline³, Daniel², John¹) was born about 1906 in
Washington Twp., Dallas Co., Ia., the son of Robert K. PURVIANCE and Nellie Josephine
McDOWELL. On 1910 census, age 4 with parents in Washington Twp., Dallas Co., Ia.[ED 21;
p. 7A; fam #93/96] and on 1920 census, age 14, with parents there, "laborer, home farm."[ED
22, p 2A, fam #27/27] He married **Hazel McCLELAND**.

ISSUE:

.16914.1   Roderick PURVIANCE, born 18 Feb 1929.
+ .16914.2   Nadine PURVIANCE, born 4 Aug 1934.

16A1.1 Sidney George⁵ FINDLEY (George⁴, Rosannah³, Daniel², John¹) was born 13 Nov
1903., the son of George Abel FINDLEY and Maybelle PRESSLEY. We see him on the 1910
census, age 6, with his parents in Webster Twp., Polk Co., Ia.,[ED184, p.63B, fam#55/55] and
on the 1920 census there with parents, age 16, with parents.[ED 184, p 63B, fam #55/55] He
married (1) **Martharine HANSEN** 1928; they divorced. Sidney married (2) **Grace Ella
ARMSTRONG** 12 Apr 1935. She was born 25 May 1910 in Omaha, Neb.[obit] We are told
that Sidney, and then brother Craig, raised sheep and seed corn on the Pressley farm until into
the 1950's. Sidney died 14 Aug 1982. Grace died 22 Jun 1995 in Des Moines, Polk, Ia., and was
buried in Sunny Hill Cem., Grimes, Ia. We are told in her obituary that she was the daughter of
a postal worker. She grew up on a farm in Granger, Ia., the youngest of three children. Ella
graduated from Parsons College in Fairfield, Ia., with a Bachelor of Fine Arts degree, graduating
Cum Laude in 1932. They lived on the family farm. Besides raising her family, Ella was a
newspaper correspondent and, later, a secretary.

ISSUE of Sidney and Ella:

.16A11.1   Eleanor Elizabeth FINDLEY, born 9 Jan 1937. She married Howard SULLIVAN
               13 Oct 1975. Eleanor died 26 Sep 1984.
+ .16A11.2   Jon Dennis FINDLEY, born 13 Jul 1940.

16A1.3 Craig Wallace[5] FINDLEY (George[4], Rosannah[3], Daniel[2], John[1]) was born 30 Apr 1915., the son of George Abel FINDLEY and Maybelle PRESSLEY. On the 1920 census, age 4, with parents, Webster, Polk Co., Ia.[ED 187, p 10A, fam #62/62] He married **Marian SMITH** 9 Oct 1942. They farmed near Johnston, Ia., on the Pressley farm where he grew up. They are members of the Johnston Federated Church. Craig died 2 Dec 1997, in Des Moines, Ia., and was buried 5 Dec 1997 in Sunny Hill Cemetery, Grimes, Ia.

ISSUE:
+ .16A13.1   Marcia Mae FINDLEY, born 3 May 1945.
  .16A13.2   Stephen Craig FINDLEY, born in Des Moines, Polk Co., Ia.

16A3.1 Helen Faye[5] FINDLEY (Ray[4], Rosannah[3], Daniel[2], John[1]) was born 21 Apr 1911., the daughter of Ray Ulcestes FINDLEY and Effa May WOOD. Seen on the 1920 census, age 9, with parents in Waukee, Walnut Twp., Dallas Co., Ia.[ED 21, p 8B, fam #193/195] She married (1) **Rev. A. Douglas STEFFENSON**. He was born 24 Apr 1908. She owned the original Findley family farm outside of Grimes, Ia. Fern Findley, (#16A.6), had owned it and Helen purchased it from her estate. She willed it to her three children. A. Douglas died 10 Apr 1968. Helen married (2) **John Ellsworth KING** 1973. He was born 5 Sep 1900. Helen died 19 Aug 1989 in Tucson, Ariz.. John died 2 Jan 1993.

ISSUE:
  .16A31.1   Michael R. STEFFENSON. He married Jean.
+ .16A31.2   Norman Douglas STEFFENSON, born 9 May 1943.
+ .16A31.3   Mary Karen STEFFENSON, born 20 Jan 1946.

16A3.2 Paul Ashley[5] FINDLEY (Ray[4], Rosannah[3], Daniel[2], John[1]) was born 14 Jan 1915., the son of Ray Ulcestes FINDLEY and Effa May WOOD. Seen on the 1920 census, age 5, with parents in Waukee, Walnut Twp., Dallas Co., Ia.[ED 21, p 8B, fam #193/195] He married **Gertrude MELOS** 1 Sep 1942. She was born 4 Nov 1920. Paul died 28 Jul 1985.

ISSUE:
+ .16A32.1   Jean Pauline FINDLEY, born 21 Jul 1947.

16A3.3 Wandah Marguerite[5] FINDLEY (Ray[4], Rosannah[3], Daniel[2], John[1]) was born 1920., the daughter of Ray Ulcestes FINDLEY and Effa May WOOD. She married **William DIEHL** 26 Jun 1943. Wandah died 1990.

ISSUE:
+ .16A33.1   Paul DIEHL.
+ .16A33.2   Mark DIEHL.
+ .16A33.3   Philip DIEHL.

16A4.1 Hildred Lurene[5] FINDLEY (Charles[4], Rosannah[3], Daniel[2], John[1]) was born 12 Dec 1907 in Polk Co., Ia., the daughter of Charles Daniel FINDLEY and Ida GROSSMAN. On the 1910 census, age 2, with her parents in Grant Twp., Dallas Co., Ia. [ED 9, p 6A, fam #114/115] In 1920, age 12, she remains in parents home there. [ED 10, p. 7B, fam #157/163] She married **John T. KINSEY**. He was born 1908. John died 17 Sep 1976, and was buried in Grimes, Polk Co., Ia.

ISSUE:
+ .16A41.1   Anne KINSEY, born 3 Sep 1934.
+ .16A41.2   Ruth KINSEY, born 10 Feb 1936.

16A4.3 Charles Herbert[5] FINDLEY (Charles[4], Rosannah[3], Daniel[2], John[1]) was born 4 Nov 1913 in Polk Co., Ia., the son of Charles Daniel FINDLEY and Ida GROSSMAN. In 1920, age 6, he is in parents home in Grant Twp., "outside Granger," Dallas Co., Ia.[ED 10, p. 7B, fam #157/163] He married **Beulah ARMBRUSTER**. Charles died June 1985.

ISSUE:
.16A43.1 Gary FINDLEY. He married Diana.
.16A43.2 Patricia FINDLEY. She married Steve UNDERWOOD.
.16A43.3 Grant FINDLEY. He married Patti.

16A4.4 Vinson Grossman[5] FINDLEY (Charles[4], Rosannah[3], Daniel[2], John[1]) was born 3 Sep 1919., the son of Charles Daniel FINDLEY and Ida GROSSMAN. In 1920, age 4 3/12, he is in parents home in Grant Twp., "outside Granger," Dallas Co., Ia. [ED 10, p. 7B, fam #157/163] He married **Edith BURTON**.

ISSUE:
.16A441 Susan FINDLEY.
.16A442 Ray FINDLEY.
.16A443 Randi FINDLEY.

16A5.3 Esther Fern[5] FINDLEY (Wendell[4], Rosannah[3], Daniel[2], John[1]) was born 31 Mar 1919 in Waukee, Dallas Co., Ia., the daughter of Wendell Ivan FINDLEY and Sophia MOSER. On the 1920 census, age 10/12, with parents in Waukee, Dallas Co., Ia.[ED 21, p 8A, fam #183/185] She married _____ **ALEXANDER**

ISSUE:
.16A53.1 Jean ALEXANDER.

1733.3 Flossie A.[5] UNKLE (Solomon[4], Caroline[3], Elizabeth[2], John[1]) was born Sep 1889 in Laurel Twp., Hocking Co., Oh., the daughter of Solomon F. UNKLE and Sarah E. McCOWEN. On 1900 census, age 10, with parents there.[D 31, p 102A, fam #98/100] Not on 1910 with parents. Believe that she married **William GRINER** about 1908 in Oh. He was born about 1881 in Oh. In 1920 we see in Solomon's home, William Griner, son-in-law, 39, divorced, "air inspector, R.R." With him are two children, grand-children of Solomon. The other daughters are accounted for.

ISSUE:
.17333.1 Florence GRINER, born about 1909 in Oh. On the 1920 census, age 11, with father in home of her grandfather, Solomon Unkle, in Logan, 3rd Ward, Falls Twp., Hocking Co., Oh.[ED 40, p 55B, fam #160/199]
.17333.2 Fredrick J. GRINER, born about 1914 in Oh. On the 1920 census, age 6, with father in home of his grandfather, Solomon Unkle, in Logan, 3rd Ward, Falls Twp., Hocking Co., Oh.[ED 40, p 55B, fam #160/199]

CHAPTER 6

GENERATION NO. 6

11211.1 Beatrice J.[6] PORTER (Virginia[5], Daniel[4], Abraham[3], Joseph[2], John[1]) was born 23 Feb 1899 in Brown Twp., Darke Co., Oh., the daughter of David Otho PORTER and Virginia RITTGERS. On 1900 census, age 1, as "grand-daughter" of Daniel and Mary L. Rittgers there. [ED 50, p 57B, fam #193/196] Not found to date on 1910 census. On the 1920 census, age 20, with mother and step-father in Greenville, Darke Co., Oh.[ED 108, p 5B, fam#111/111] She married **Lewis Kenneth WALTERS** 11 Mar 1920 in Darke Co., Oh. He was born 23 Dec 1897 in Brown Twp., Darke Co., Oh. Lewis died 29 Apr 1985 in Darke Co., Oh., and was buried in Teegarden Cem, Ansonia, Oh. Beatrice was still living in Darke Co., Oh., and being cared for by her daughter, Vera (Walters) Boolman - Jan 1993.[Family group sheet submitted by daughter, Vera (Walters) Boolman]
ISSUE:
+ .112111.1   Vera Belle WALTERS, born 29 Sep 1920.
+ .112111.2   Ruby Jeanine WALTERS, born 29 May 1930

11211.2 Erma Othello[6] BUTT (Virginia[5], Daniel[4], Abraham[3], Joseph[2], John[1]) was born 28 Sep 1902., the daughter of Virginia RITTGERS. She married **Harold WASSON** 16 Sep 1926. He was born 15 Jul 1905 in Darke County, Oh. We were told his mother's name was Laura Bickel.
ISSUE:
+ .112112.1   Janice WASSON, born 25 Oct 1932.

11211.3 Herbert Otto[6] BUTT (Virginia[5], Daniel[4], Abraham[3], Joseph[2], John[1]) was born 28 Dec 1904 in Darke County, Oh., the son of Virginia RITTGERS. He married (1) **Hazel BILLHEIMER**; they divorced. Herbert married (2) **Blanche HARTER** 24 Dec 1952. She was born 15 Feb 1903, died 14 Feb 1981. Herbert died 23 Mar 1991.[SS] They are buried in the Teegarden Cemetery, Darke Co., Oh.
ISSUE:
+ .112113.1   Herbert Owen BUTT, born 12 Feb 1928.
+ .112113.2   Phyllis Fern BUTT, born 6 Nov 1929.

11211.4 Charles Leo[6] BUTT (Virginia[5], Daniel[4], Abraham[3], Joseph[2], John[1]) was born 28 Mar 1908 in Darke Co County, Oh., the son of Virginia RITTGERS. He married **Bernice D. TIPPLE** 20 Jul 1929. She was born 23 Dec 1910, died 26 Mar 1989. [SS]
ISSUE:
+ .112114.1   Wendell Leo BUTT, born 5 Jul 1932.
+ .112114.2   Neil Mitchell BUTT, born 27 Aug 1935.
+ .112114.3   Ardith Ann BUTT, born 27 Feb 1937.
+ .112114.4   Myron Lowell BUTT, born 20 Mar 1940.
+ .112114.5   Karen Janice BUTT, born 16 Jul 1943.

11211.5 Hazel Fern[6] BUTT (Virginia[5], Daniel[4], Abraham[3], Joseph[2], John[1]) was born 16 Mar 1910 in Darke County, Oh., the daughter of Virginia RITTGERS. She married **Walter STIVER**

12 Jun 1926. He was born 12 Dec 1906, the son of Earl Stiver and Osa Wilkerson. Walter died 1 Nov 1983.

ISSUE:

+ .112115.1   Doyle Freymoth STIVER, born 22 Dec 1926.
+ .112115.2   Jeanette Frances STIVER, born 5 May 1933.
+ .112115.3   Ronald Farrell STIVER, born 21 Oct 1938.
+ .112115.4   Tony Faye STIVER, born 15 Sep 1947.

11211.6 Evelyn Pauline[6] BUTT (Virginia[5], Daniel[4], Abraham[3], Joseph[2], John[1]) was born 3 Oct 1912 in Darke County, Oh., the daughter of Virginia RITTGERS. She married (1) **George ROSE** 11 Jun 1930. He was born 5 Jun 1902, died 22 Feb 1972, and was buried in Teegarden Cemetery, Darke Co., Oh. Evelyn married (2) **Delbert SANDERS** 8 Jul 1974. He was born 9 Jan 1902, died 20 May 1976.

ISSUE:

+ .112116.1   Veo ROSE, born 20 Sep 1932.
+ .112116.2   Gene ROSE, born 27 Aug 1942.
  .112116.3   Eric ROSE, born 7 Dec 1964 in Union City, Oh.

11212.2 Echo[6] RITTGERS (Ira[5], Daniel[4], Abraham[3], Joseph[2], John[1]) was born 10 Feb 1909 in Darke County, Oh., the daughter of Ira RITTGERS and Cora HUFFORD. We see her on the 1910 census, age 1 yr., 3 mo., with her parents in Brown Twp., Darke Co., Oh. She married **Forest STRAIT** Nov 1934.

ISSUE:

+ .112122.1   Ted STRAIT, born 18 Jun 1937.

11212.4 Daniel[6] RITTGERS (Ira[5], Daniel[4], Abraham[3], Joseph[2], John[1]) was born 28 Sep 1913, the son of Ira RITTGERS and Cora HUFFORD. He married **Pauline MILLER** 8 Nov 1934. She was born 1919.

ISSUE:

+ .112124.1   Sharon RITTGERS, born 24 May 1935.
+ .112124.2   Shelia RITTGERS, born 24 Jun 1937.

11213.1 Helen[6] LIVINGSTON (Minnie[5], Daniel[4], Abraham[3], Joseph[2], John[1]) was born 28 Jun 1906 in Darke County, Oh., the daughter of William LIVINGSTON and Minnie RITTGERS. She married **Everett DANCER**. He was born 25 Jun 1903. Everett died 16 Oct 1985, and was buried in Greenville, Oh.

ISSUE:

+ .112131.1   Buddy DANCER.

11213.2 Willis Paul[6] HART (Minnie[5], Daniel[4], Abraham[3], Joseph[2], John[1]) was born 17 Dec 1916 in Darke County, Oh., the son of Willard HART and Minnie RITTGERS. He married **Betty Eileen ROGERS** 20 Jun 1942. She was born 30 Nov 1923.

ISSUE:

+ .112132.1   Sandre Lee HART, born 31 Oct 1944.
+ .112132.2   Jerlyne Kay HART, born 18 Dec 1942.

11213.3 Violet Marcella⁶ HART (Minnie⁵, Daniel⁴, Abraham³, Joseph², John¹) was born 15 May 1920 in Darke County, Oh., the daughter of Willard HART and Minnie RITTGERS. She married **Gerald Eugene MENDENHALL** 9 Dec 1939. He was born 5 Jul 1917.

ISSUE:

.112133.1 Larry Eugene MENDENHALL, born 23 Apr 1940 in Union City, Randolph Co., Ind, died 9 Apr 1949.

+ .112133.2 Terry Duane MENDENHALL, born 29 Aug 1941.

.112133.3 Marla Sue MENDENHALL, born 10 Jul 1956 in Union City, Randolph Co., Ind. She married Todd G. COPPEDGE 2 Jun 1979. He was born 20 Jan 1956.

11213.4 Betty⁶ HART (Minnie⁵, Daniel⁴, Abraham³, Joseph², John¹) was born 13 Jun 1922 in Darke County, Oh., the daughter of Willard HART and Minnie RITTGERS. She married **Franklin WILCOX** 21 Sep 1974.

ISSUE:

+ .112134.1 Connie WILCOX, born 28 Jun 1947.

+ .112134.2 Steven WILCOX, born 23 Mar 1950.

11213.5 Wilma Wavelene⁶ HART (Minnie⁵, Daniel⁴, Abraham³, Joseph², John¹) was born 11 Sep 1925 in Darke County, Oh., the daughter of Willard HART and Minnie RITTGERS. She married **Glenn Eugene WENGER** 17 Oct 1942. He was born 21 Jun 1922, the son of Harry Wenger.

ISSUE:

+ .112135.1 Karen Sue WENGER, born 5 Oct 1946.

+ .112135.2 Randy Gene WENGER, born 19 Sep 1950.

+ .112135.3 Denise Ann WENGER, born 5 Nov 1955.

11214.1 Perry J.⁶ RITTGERS (Perry⁵, Daniel⁴, Abraham³, Joseph², John¹) was born 17 Sep 1914 in Darke Co., Oh., the son of Perry RITTGERS and Clara SMITH. We see Perry, Jr., age 5, on the 1920 census with his widowed mother on the farm of his maternal grandparents, Jerry and Elizabeth Smith, in Jackson Twp., Darke Co., Oh. [ED108, p.4, fam#82/82] He married **Ilse LEOPOLD**. She was born 10 Mar 1912.

ISSUE:

+ .112141.1 Charles Henry RITTGERS, born 26 Feb 1951.

11214.2 James⁶ RITTGERS (Perry⁵, Daniel⁴, Abraham³, Joseph², John¹) was born 1917 in Darke Co., Oh., the son of Perry RITTGERS and Clara SMITH. We see James, age 2yrs, 7mo., on the 1920 census with his widowed mother on the farm of his maternal grandparents, Jerry and Elizabeth Smith, in Jackson Twp., Darke Co., Oh. [ED108, p.4, fam#82/82] He married **Geraldine ZERRING**. She was born 1917, and died 1976. James died 1966.

ISSUE:

+ .112142.1 Meta Sue RITTGERS.

+ .112142.2 Bonnie RITTGERS.

11215.1 Glendora⁶ RITTGERS (Eli⁵, Daniel⁴, Abraham³, Joseph², John¹) was born 23 Feb 1918 in Darke County, Oh., the daughter of Eli RITTGERS and Kathryn WARE. We see her on the 1920 census, age 1yr, 10 mo., with her parents in Brown Twp., Darke Co., Oh. She married **Howard Woodrow HIGGINS** 24 Oct 1936.

ISSUE:

.112151.1 Byron Patrick HIGGINS, born 6 Aug 1937, died 20 Jun 1959.
.112151.2 Charles Richard HIGGINS, born 24 Nov 1940. He married Anne Puanami MEDERIO 4 Jul 1970. She was born 19 Oct 1940.

11232.1 Joe Franklin[6] **RITTGERS** (Vernon[5], Samuel[4], Abraham[3], Joseph[2], John[1]) was born 13 May 1926 in Franklin County, Oh., the son of Vernon RITTGERS and Edith C. JOHNSON. He married **Jenny Louise HRENCHE** 6 Jun 1953.

ISSUE:

+ .112321.1 Stephen Vernon RITTGERS, born 17 Nov 1955.
  .112321.2 Venita Marie RITTGERS, born 15 Feb 1959.
  .112321.3 Timothy Vincent RITTGERS, born 15 Sep 1961.

11232.2 Roberta Ruth[6] **RITTGERS** (Vernon[5], Samuel[4], Abraham[3], Joseph[2], John[1]) was born 19 Aug 1928, the daughter of Vernon RITTGERS and Edith C. JOHNSON. She married **Charles McGRIFF** 22 Oct 1949. He was born 14 Sep 1985, the son of Michael David McGRIFF and Debra Lynn EDWARDS.

ISSUE:

+ .112322.1 Michael David McGRIFF, born 28 Jul 1950.
+ .112322.2 Melissa Ann McGRIFF, born 22 Feb 1961.

11234.2 Pamela Joy[6] **GIBBONS** (Velda[5], Samuel[4], Abraham[3], Joseph[2], John[1]) was born 4 Jun 1953, the daughter of Francis Raymond GIBBONS and Velda E. RITTGERS. She married **Thomas M. METZGER** 3 Feb 1973. He was born 28 Jun 1953.

ISSUE:

.112342.1 Christopher Sean METZGER, born 14 Apr 1975.
.112342.2 January Michelle METZGER, born 3 Mar 1977.

11341.1 Virginia Lois[6] **CONRAD** (Ray[5], Lafayette[4], Lucinda[3], Joseph[2], John[1]) was born 16 Dec 1932 in Wayne Co., Mich., the daughter of Ray Benson CONRAD and Ethel Grace HAINES. She married **Lloyd Kenneth MARSHALL** 18 Aug 1962. He was born 24 Feb 1930 in LaGrange County, Ind., the son of Harry S. and Mayretta L. (Browand) Marshall. *[Family group sheet submitted by Kevin Marshall to the Fairfield Co. Gen. Soc.]*

ISSUE:

.113411.1 Kevin Lee MARSHALL, born 6 Aug 1963 in St. Joseph Co., Mich.. Information on this line taken from Ancestor Chart submitted by him 16 Aug 1984 to Fairfield Co. Historical Soc., Fairfield Co., Oh.

11613.1 Ruth Marie[6] **GROVE** (Willard[5], George[4], Anna[3], Joseph[2], John[1]) was born 25 Mar 1914 in Rockbridge, Hocking Co., Oh., the daughter of Willard Elsworth GROVE and Ethel Alberta MURPHY. She married **Pearl Donald BIGHAM** 6 May 1935 in Logan, Hocking Co., Oh. He was born 8 Aug 1912 in Lancaster, Fairfield Co., Oh. Pearl started working at Alten Foundry and Machine Works in Lancaster, Fairfield Co., Oh., at a young age and remained there his entire working life. He held position of Laborer, Machine operator, painter and Blacksmith Shop Foreman. For some reason, Pearl and Ruth left oldest son Bob with her parents to raise, but they raised the other children. Pearl died 15 Mar 1977 in Fairfield Co., Oh. Ruth died 1 Sep 1982 in Fairfield County, Oh. They are buried in Fairview Cemetery, Hocking Co., Oh.[Bigham]

ISSUE:
+ .116131.1   Robert Eugene BIGHAM, born 18 Sep 1935.
+ .116131.2   Ronald Lee BIGHAM, born 4 May 1937.
  .116131.3   Gary Thomas BIGHAM, born 19 Aug 1939 in Fairfield Co., Oh.
+ .116131.4   Larry George BIGHAM, born 14 Aug 1943, died Aug 1981.
  .116131.5   Linda Kay BIGHAM, born 24 May 1947 in Fairfield Co., Oh. She married Herbert Leo SMITH.
  .116131.6   Charles Edward BIGHAM, born 29 Apr 1949 in Fairfield Co., Oh. He married Darlene Ann RIFE.
  .116131.7   Richard Keith BIGHAM, born 5 Apr 1950 in Fairfield Co., Oh.
  .116131.8   Peggy Alberta BIGHAM, born 6 Feb 1952 in Fairfield Co., Oh.

11613.2 Purl Fredrick[6] **GROVE** (Willard[5], George[4], Anna[3], Joseph[2], John[1]) was born 27 Aug 1916 in Rockbridge, Hocking Co., Oh., the son of Willard Elsworth GROVE and Ethel Alberta MURPHY. He married **Barbara Joann____**. Purl died 4 Sep 1979 in Bogalusa, La. [Bigham]
ISSUE:
  .116132.1   Pamela GROVE.
  .116132.2   Theresa GROVE, born 1954.

11613.3 George Albert[6] **GROVE** (Willard[5], George[4], Anna[3], Joseph[2], John[1]) was born 10 Jun 1918 in Rockbridge, Hocking Co., Oh., the son of Willard Elsworth GROVE and Ethel Alberta MURPHY. He married **Bernadine Marie FRANKLIN** 15 May 1944 in Fairfield Co., Oh. She was born 16 May 1918 in Fairfield Co., Oh., to Thomas and Marie K. (Raybourne) Franklin. Bernadine died 1966 in Hocking Co., Oh. George died 8 Oct 1971 in Fairfield Co., Oh. [Bigham]
ISSUE:
  .116133.1   Rose Mary GROVE, born 18 May 1946 in Fairfield Co., Oh.
  .116133.2   George Thomas GROVE, born 12 Nov 1947 in Fairfield Co., Oh. He married Donna Kay MILLER. [Bigham]
  .116133.3   Timothy Willard GROVE, born 8 May 1950 in Fairfield Co., Oh.

11613.4 Stella Mae[6] **GROVE** (Willard[5], George[4], Anna[3], Joseph[2], John[1]) was born 11 Sep 1921 in Rockbridge, Hocking Co., Oh., the daughter of Willard Elsworth GROVE and Ethel Alberta MURPHY. She married **Harold Russel GLENN** 1939 in Hocking Co., Oh. He was born 19 Sep 1919 in Fairfield Co., Oh., to Russsell L. and Minnie (Harvey) Glenn. Harold died Sep 1977 in Columbus, Franklin Co., Oh.[Bigham]
ISSUE:
+ .116134.1   Roderick Elsworth GLENN.
  .116134.2   George GLENN. He married Nancy MOLER.
  .116134.3   Harold Russel GLENN, Jr., born 23 Sep 1946 in Fairfield Co., Oh. He married Charlene Adele KING. She was born 1950.
+ .116134.4   Vicki Jean GLENN, born 31 May 1946.
  .116134.5   Debra Sue GLENN, born 29 Sep 1953 in Fairfield Co., Oh. She married James William KING 13 Oct 1970 in Fairfield Co., Oh.

11613.5 Harry Willard[6] **GROVE** (Willard[5], George[4], Anna[3], Joseph[2], John[1]), was born 17 Nov 1923 in Rockbridge, Hocking Co., Oh., the son of Willard Elsworth GROVE and Ethel Alberta

MURPHY. He married **Betty Mae GRAHAM** in Fairfield Co., Oh. She was born 12 Aug 1923 in Columbus, Franklin Co., Oh. Harry died 12 Oct 1977 in Fairfield Co., Oh. Betty died 30 Nov 1995 in Fairfield Co., Oh.[Bigham]

ISSUE:

.116135.1 Kenny GROVE.
.116135.2 Roger William GROVE, born 14 Feb 1947 in Fairfield Co., Oh.
.116135.3 Jeffery Lynn GROVE, born 31 Mar 1949 in Fairfield Co., Oh. He married Deborah Lynn UHL 12 Apr 1969 in Fairfield Co., Oh.
.116135.4 James Harry GROVE, born 31 Mar 1949 in Fairfield Co., Oh. He married Rowena Christine COX 2 Jun 1973 in Fairfield Co., Oh.

11692.1 Robert Mercier[6]COURNOYER (Helen[5], Rosetta[4], Anna[3], Joseph[2], John[1]) was born 19 Jul 1922 in Anaheim, Orange Co., Ca. He was the son of Edward Charles COURNOYER and Helen Leone RITCHEY. He married **Janeave Edna WRIGHT** 7 Jun 1946 in Columbia, Lexington Co., SC. She was born 16 May 1927 in Columbia, Lexington Co., SC.[Bigham/Berens]

ISSUE:

.116921.1 Robert Mercier COURNOYER, Jr., born 31 Aug 1947 in Long Beach, Los Angeles Co., Ca. [Bigham/Berens]
+ .116921.2 Jennifer Lee COURNOYER, born 1 Jul 1958.

11692.2 Rosemary Jean[6] COURNOYER (Helen[5], Rosetta[4], Anna[3], Joseph[2], John[1]) was born 28 Mar 1929 in Santa Ana, Orange Co., Ca. She was the daughter of Edward Charles COURNOYER and Helen Leone RITCHEY. She married **Philip S. POULEN** 17 Aug 1950 in Long Beach, Los Angeles Co., Ca. He was born 6 Aug 1927 in Burlington, Chittenden Co., Vt. [Berens]

ISSUE:

+ .116922.1 Gregory Philip POULEN, born 5 Aug 1952.
+ .116922.2 Lisa Leone POULEN, born 5 Apr 1956.

12171.2 Glen Jackson[6] FINNEY (Nellie[5], Sarah[4], Samuel[3], Jacob[2], John[1]) was born 30 Aug 1914 in Princeton, Mercer Co., Mo., the son of William Adair FINNEY and Nellie Avis VIRDEN. He served in the U.S. Navy during WWII. We are told they lived in California. He married **Marjorie HART**.

ISSUE:

+ .121712.1 Susan FINNEY.

12171.3 John Virden[6] FINNEY (Nellie[5], Sarah[4], Samuel[3], Jacob[2], John[1]) was born 2 Dec 1920 in Princeton, Mercer Co., Mo., the son of William Adair FINNEY and Nellie Avis VIRDEN. We are told he served in the Second World War, but don't know what branch of service. He married **Charlene HART**. She was born 26 Aug 1923.

ISSUE:

.121713.1 Sharon FINNEY. She married _____ FREEMAN.

12171.4 Jennie Margaret[6] FINNEY (Nellie[5], Sarah[4], Samuel[3], Jacob[2], John[1]) was born 27 Feb 1923 in Princeton, Mercer Co., Mo., the daughter of William Adair FINNEY and Nellie Avis VIRDEN. She married **Stanley Argus THOMAS** 6 Feb 1948 in Mo. He was born 17 Oct 1923

in Liberty, Clay Co., Mo. He served in the U.S. Navy during WWII. They live in Liberty Mo., and are Methodists.[*Family record submitted by Margaret (Finney) Thomas in 1994*]
ISSUE:
+ .121714.1   Stanley Michael THOMAS, born 6 Nov 1950.
+ .121714.2   Patrick Alan THOMAS, born 18 Dec 1952.
+ .121714.3   Brian Virden THOMAS, born 16 Jan 1962.

12171.5 Mary Frances⁶ FINNEY (Nellie⁵, Sarah⁴, Samuel³, Jacob², John¹) was born 20 Jan 1927 in Princeton, Mercer Co., Mo., the daughter of William Adair FINNEY and Nellie Avis VIRDEN. She married **Melvin Don ROGERS** 20 Nov 1943 in Princeton, Mercer Co., Mo. He was born 6 Apr 1923 in Trenton, Grundy Co., Mo. H served in the U.S. Navy during WWII. [*Family record submitted by Mary (Finney) Rogers in 1994*]
ISSUE:
+ .121715.1   Melvin Jack ROGERS, born 9 Sep 1944.
 .121715.2   Marvin Gene ROGERS, born 7 Dec 1946 in Yakima, Yakima Co., Wash. He married Marica Lynn SANDBROOK 23 Oct 1987 in Kansas City, Jackson Co., Mo. She was born 10 Feb 1951 in Kansas City, Jackson Co.,
+ .121715.3   Gary Lynn ROGERS, born 16 Dec 1952.

12172.2 Anna Lou⁶ PEACOCK (Agnes⁵, Sarah⁴, Samuel³, Jacob², John¹) was born 22 Jul 1924 in Chicago, Cook Co., Ill., the daughter of John William PEACOCK and Agnes Elizabeth VIRDEN. She married **Raymond Allen ARNETT** 28 Jul 1945 in Winchester, Ill. He was born 30 Mar 1923. Raymond was in the U.S. Army Air Corps during WWII. We thank Anna for all the material she has submitted.[*Family group sheet submitted to the Ohio Gen. Soc., Mansfield, Oh. by Anna L. (Peacock) Arnett.*]
ISSUE:
+ .121722.1   Marjorie ARNETT, born 30 Apr 1946.
 .121722.2   Peggy ARNETT. She married Jesus E. PACHECO. Peggy works for Suntrust Mortgage, where she has the honor of being the top sales agent for 1992. She lives in Huntington Beach, Ca.
+ .121722.3   Dale ARNETT.
+ .121722.4   John ARNETT.

12172.3 Robert Alva⁶ PEACOCK (Agnes⁵, Sarah⁴, Samuel³, Jacob², John¹). He was the son of John William PEACOCK and Agnes Elizabeth VIRDEN. Robert served in the U.S. Army during the Korean War. He married **Elizabeth Lee "Betty" WARD**. Lived in Park Ridge, Ill.
ISSUE:
+ .121723.1   Karen PEACOCK.
 .121723.2   Robert Alva Peacock, JR.. Lived in Illinois.
 .121723.3   Kathy PEACOCK. Lived in Illinois.

12922.1 Harold⁶ PATTEE (Perry⁵, Esther⁴, Perry³, Jacob², John¹) was born 1934. He was the son of Perry B. PATTEE and Freida. He married **Betsy_____**. She was born 1937.
ISSUE:
 .129221.1   Scott PATTEE, born 1961.
 .129221.2   Amy PATTEE, born 1964.

12923.1 Erma⁶ PATTEE (Peter⁵, Esther⁴, Perry³, Jacob², John¹) was born 1922. He was the son of Peter F. PATTEE and Mary KOPLIN. He married **Jessie____**.
ISSUE:
.129231.1   Neil PATTEE.
.129231.2   Douglas PATTEE.

12981.1 Larry Lee⁶ JONES (Dorothy⁵, John⁴, Perry³, Jacob², John¹) was born 11 Jan 1937 in Hutchinson, Reno Co., Ks. He was the son of Thomas Ray "Ray T" JONES and Dorothy Evelyn RITTGERS. Received a BS in Electrical Engineering from Kansas State University, was in the U.S. Army 2 years and then was an Engineering Supervisor at AT&T Technologies for 28 years. He married **Anna Corrinne ATTWATER** 6 Feb 1960 in Wichita, Sedgwick Co., Ks. She was born 1 Jan 1938 in Wichita, Sedgewick, Ks., the daughter of Paul Russell and Anna Lue (Jones) Attwater. Anna received her B.A. in Art in 1972 and her M.A. in counseling in 1981 from the University of Missouri, Kansas City, Mo. She has taught art for 19 years. Larry died of pancreatic cancer 15 Feb 1991 in Lee's Summit, Jackson, Mo, and was buried 23 Feb 1991 in Sunset Cemetery, Manhattan, Ks.[*Family record submitted by Anna C. (Attwater) Jones*]
ISSUE:
+ .129811.1   Warren Thomas JONES, born 30 Nov 1961.
.129811.2   Michael Andrew JONES, born 24 Dec 1962 in Kansas City, Jackson Co., Ks. He married Heidi Jo TIDBALL 19 Jul 1986 in Manhattan, Riley Co., Ks; they divorced. Received a BS in Mechanical Engineering from Kansas State University, 1986. Served four years in the U.S. Army Corps of Eng. and was in Panama 3 years. Works for Burns and McDonald, an Engineering Firm in Kansas City, Mo. He lives in Lee's Summit.
.129811.3   Stephen Matthew JONES, born 12 Oct 1970 in Kansas City, Jackson, Mo. Married Angela Lynn HOCH 10 Aug 1996, Springfield, Mo. She was born Dec 1975, the daughter of Robert HOCH and Vickie Lynn____. Stephen is an insurance claims representative.

12981.3 Sharon Rae⁶ JONES (Dorothy⁵, John⁴, Perry³, Jacob², John¹) was born 27 Dec 1939 in Hutchinson, Reno Co., Ks., the daughter of Thomas Ray "Ray T" JONES and Dorothy Evelyn RITTGERS. She married **Bob Dean DeVAULT** 10 Jun 1961 in Hutchinson, Ks. He was born 11 Apr 1937 in Hutchinson, Ks., the son of Leland Tasway & Ona Me (Waird) DeVault. They live in Hutchinson, Kansas, where he is an accountant and Sharon a substitute teacher.[Family record supplied by Anna C. (Attwater) Jones.]
ISSUE:
+ .129813.1   Jerry Ray DeVAULT, born 20 Jul 1962.
+ .129813.2   Edie Beth DeVAULT, born 28 Aug 1965.
+ .129813.3   Larry Dean DeVAULT, born 25 Sep 1968 in Hutchinson, Ks. He married Jennifer PENINGER 18 Jul 1992 in Hutchinson, Ks. She is the daughter of Millard E. and Linda Kay (Reaves) Peninger. He is a graduate of Kansas State University, 1992.

12982.1 Barbara Dale "Bobbie"⁶ RITTGERS (William⁵, John⁴, Perry³, Jacob², John¹) was born 9 Mar 1937 in Hutchinson, Ks., the daughter of William Dale Arlington RITTGERS and Thelma Marie ELLSWORTH. She married **James Melvah LONKER** 27 Dec 1961 in Hutchinson, Ks. He was born 7 Mar 1938 in Wichita, Sedgewick Co., Ks. , the son of Melvah Ernest and Mildred Carolina (Nelson) Lonker. James was a graduate of Kansas State Univ. and was a rancher in Medicine Lodge, Ks. He served in the U.S. Air Force. They lived in Hutchinson, Ks. He died 10 Jul 1988 in Medicine Lodge, Barber Co., Ks., and was buried in Medicine Lodge. Barbara is currently house mother at Beta Theta Pi House in Manhattan, Ks.[*Family record supplied by Anna C. (Attwater) Jones.*]

ISSUE:

.129821.1   James Dale LONKER, born 26 May 1964 in Medicine Lodge, Barber Co., Ks. He married Jodi McCULLOUGH 17 Jun 1989 in Medicine Lodge, Barber Co., Ks. She was born 18 Mar 1968. James graduated from Kansas State U. and lives at the ranch in Medicine Lodge, Ks.

.129821.2   Jamie Lee LONKER, born 8 Aug 1966 in Medicine Lodge, Barber Co., Ks. She lives in Manhattan, Ks.

.129821.3   John Andrew LONKER, born 31 Mar 1970 in Medicine Lodge, Barber Co., Ks. He married Mary Theresa OSTMEYER 12 Jun 1993 in Manhattan, Riley Co., Ks. She is the daughter of Dale and Jean Ostmeyer, and works in education. John attended Kansas State U. and works in Manhattan, Ks., as a plumber.

129B1.1 Vernon[6] BERKLEY (Ruth[5], Jacob[4], Perry[3], Jacob[2], John[1]) was born 22 May 1930, the son of Fred BERKLEY and Ruth RITTGERS. He married **Shirley WERRIES**. She was born 6 Aug 1932.

ISSUE:

.129B11.1   Ronald Dean BERKLEY, born 6 May 1952. He married Debra WAUGH 9 Nov 1974.

.129B11.2   Royce William BERKLEY, born 1 Sep 1953. He married Dianna____.

.129B11.3   Renee Lynn BERKLEY, born 1 Jul 1963.

129B2.1 Melvin[6] RITTGERS (Vernon[5], Jacob[4], Perry[3], Jacob[2], John[1]) was born 15 Nov 1934, the son of Vernon LeRoy RITTGERS and Mildred LEBERT. He married **Edith RANSHAW**. She was born 12 Dec 1933.

ISSUE:

.129B21.1   Kevin RITTGERS, born 3 Apr 1955.

.129B21.2   Kristie RITTGERS, born 5 May 1957.

.129B21.3   Kerrie RITTGERS, born 31 Mar 1962.

.129B21.4   Kletes Royce RITTGERS, born 20 Apr 1965.

129B3.1 Sandra[6] MARTIN (Frances[5], Jacob[4], Perry[3], Jacob[2], John[1]) was born 3 Apr 1938, the daughter of Carl MARTIN and Frances RITTGERS. She married **Charles BRANDT** 18 Nov 1967.

ISSUE:

.129B31.1   Chris BRANDT, born 25 May 1968.

.129B31.2   Tracy BRANDT, born 6 Mar 1970.

129B3.2 Carl[6] Martin, JR. (Frances[5], Jacob[4], Perry[3], Jacob[2], John[1]) was born May 1942, the son of Carl MARTIN and Frances RITTGERS. He married **Sandra SWANSON** 21 Feb 1969.

ISSUE:

.129B32.1   Mike MARTIN, born 15 Apr 1974.

.129B32.2   Mark MARTIN, born 15 Apr 1974.

129B4.2 Paul[6] HAWK (Maxine[5], Jacob[4], Perry[3], Jacob[2], John[1]) was born 25 May 1949, the son of Harry HAWK and Maxine RITTGERS. He married **Deborah FRENCH**. She was born 18 Dec 1951.

ISSUE:

.129B42.1 Joseph Henry HAWK.

129B5.1 Arletta Kaye[6] WILMORE (Arletta[5], Jacob[4], Perry[3], Jacob[2], John[1]) was born 2 Mar 1942, the daughter of Robert WILMORE and Arletta RITTGERS. She married **James LOVE**.

ISSUE:

.129B51.1 Arletta Jane LOVE, born 24 Jun 1963.
.129B51.2 Georgia LOVE, born 22 Jun 1964, died Nov 1971.

129B6.1 Nina Irene[6] KOHRS (Kathryn[5], Jacob[4], Perry[3], Jacob[2], John[1]) was born 17 Jan 1946, the daughter of Charles KOHRS and Kathryn Jean RITTGERS. She married (1) **John THOMAS**. He was born 7 Jul 1933. Nina married (2) **Greg YARDLEY**.

ISSUE:

.129B61.1 John THOMAS.

129B7.2 Darrell Vincent[6] RITTGERS (Jacob[5], Jacob[4], Perry[3], Jacob[2], John[1]) was born 26 Jan 1950, the son of Jacob B. Rittgers, JR. and Gladys GRUBB. He married **Martha WICK**.

ISSUE:

.129B72.1 Bryan RITTGERS, born 1970.

129B73 Jacque Berniece[6] RITTGERS (Jacob[5], Jacob[4], Perry[3], Jacob[2], John[1]) was born 29 Dec 1951, the daughter of Jacob B. Rittgers, JR. and Gladys GRUBB. She married **Steve MEULI**.

ISSUE:

.129B73.1 Mike MEULI, born 1973.
.129B73.2 Jennifer MEULI, born 1976.

129C1.1 Troy Kenneth[6] RITTGERS (Kenneth[5], Perry[4], Perry[3], Jacob[2], John[1]) was born 11 Jan 1950, the son of Kenneth Arthur RITTGERS and Barbara ELDER. At the time of his father's death in 1966, he was with his mother in San Francisco. He married **Ellen Doreen CRAWFORD** 23 Jan 1971.

ISSUE:

.129C11.1 Christopher RITTGERS, born 12 Oct 1976.
.129C11.2 Alisa Marie RITTGERS, born 28 Feb 1979.

129C2.1 Jerry Lee[6] RITTGERS (Bernard[5], Perry[4], Perry[3], Jacob[2], John[1]) was born 15 Jun 1947 in Salina, Saline Co., Ks., the son of Bernard Edward RITTGERS and Dorothy ANDREWS. He married **Sharyn LONGHOFER** 23 Aug 1969 in Salina, Saline Co., Ks. She was born 17 Apr 1947, the daughter of Lloyd and Lelia (Leive) Longhofer. Sharyn is an elementary teacher. Jerry is a computer programmer and they are members of the Lutheran Church.

ISSUE:

.129C21.1 Jennifer Sue RITTGERS, born 16 Apr 1971 in Emporia, Lyon Co., Ks. She is an accountant, and attends the Lutheran Church.

.129C21.2 Sarah Lee RITTGERS, born 18 Feb 1974 in Kansas City, Jackson Co., Ks. She married David William Chellberg7 June 1997. He was born 18 Aug 1972, Topeka, Shawnee Co., Ks., the son of Lowell and Lorraine (Larson) Chellberg.

129C2.2 Jolene Kay[6] RITTGERS (Bernard[5], Perry[4], Perry[3], Jacob[2], John[1]) was born 21 Nov 1949 in Salina, Saline Co., Ks., the daughter of Bernard Edward RITTGERS and Dorothy ANDREWS. She married (1) **Robert REYNOLDS** 18 Apr 1970 in Salina, Saline Co., Ks. He was born 14 Jan 1950, the son of Paul and Delma (Meier) Reynolds. He is an accountant. Jolene married (2) **Larry TRAVIS** May 1989 in Las Vegas, Clark Co., Nev. Larry is the son of John E. and Evellyn W. (Hall) Travis. He is a computer analyst. She works in Mortgage Banking, and lives in Newbury Park, Calif.
ISSUE of Robert and Jolene:
.129C22.1 Mark REYNOLDS, born 19 Dec 1972 in Salina, Saline Co., Ks.
.129C22.2 Lori REYNOLDS, born 11 Mar 1975 in Salina, Saline Co., Ks.

129C2.3 Lynette Jean[6] RITTGERS (Bernard[5], Perry[4], Perry[3], Jacob[2], John[1]) was born 19 Jun 1956 in Salina, Saline Co., Ks., the daughter of Bernard Edward RITTGERS and Dorothy ANDREWS. She married **Jeff WEIL** 21 Aug 1982 in Salina, Saline Co., Ks. He was born 5 Mar 1956, the son of Harry L. and Opal J. (Campbell) Weil. Lynette is a pharmacist. Jeff is with the Kansas Highway Patrol in Communications.
ISSUE:
.129C23.1 Megan Elizabeth WEIL, born 31 Mar 1984 in Salina, Saline Co., Ks.
.129C23.2 Bryan Edward WEIL, born 31 May 1985 in Salina, Saline Co., Ks.

129C3.1 Michael Dean[6] RITTGERS (Robert[5], Perry[4], Perry[3], Jacob[2], John[1]) was born 16 May 1951 in Salina, Saline Co., Ks., the son of Robert Dean RITTGERS and Lee Ann RALSTON. He married **Jayne ALEXANDER** 12 Sep 1971.
ISSUE:
.129C31.1 Krosby RITTGERS, born 24 Apr 1972.

129C3.2 Mary Patricia[6] RITTGERS (Robert[5], Perry[4], Perry[3], Jacob[2], John[1]) was born 16 Jun 1954 in Salina, Saline Co., Ks., the daughter of Robert Dean RITTGERS and Lee Ann RALSTON. She married **Charles WRIGHT** 10 Dec 1977.
ISSUE:
.129C32.1 Amy Michelle WRIGHT, born 19 Jun 1981.
.129C32.2 Kyle William WRIGHT, born 28 Sep 1983.

129C5.1 Cynthia Ann[6] DAWDY (Marlene[5], Perry[4], Perry[3], Jacob[2], John[1]) was born 29 May 1957, the daughter of Marvin DAWDY and Marlene Rose RITTGERS. She married **Tom MILTNER** 20 Sep 1975.
ISSUE:
.129C51.1 Shawn MILTNER, born 28 Jul 1976 in Witchita, Ks..

129D1.1 Harlan[6] RITTGERS (William[5], William[4], Perry[3], Jacob[2], John[1]) was born 10 Jan 1938, the son of William Glea RITTGERS and Margaret. He married (1) **Farida**. She was born in Aparri, Burma. Farida died 8 Aug 1974. Harlan married (2) **Judy ARPIN**.
ISSUE of Harlan and Farida:

.129D11.1 Suzanna RITTGERS.
.129D11.2 Alan RITTGERS.
.129D11.3 John RITTGERS.

129D1.2 Susan⁶ RITTGERS (William⁵, William⁴, Perry³, Jacob², John¹). She Is the daughter of William Glea RITTGERS and Margaret. She married **Louis GAYNOR** 19 Sep 1973.
                                     ISSUE:
.129D12.1 Amanda GAYNOR.
.129D12.2 Chancey GAYNOR.

129D1.3 Ann⁶ RITTGERS (William⁵, William⁴, Perry³, Jacob², John¹). She was the daughter of William Glea RITTGERS and Margaret. She married (1) **Kenny JOY**; they divorced. Ann married (2) **Eric KAWAHARA** 7 Oct 1973.
                              ISSUE of Kenny and Ann:
.129D13.1 Sheri JOY.
.129D13.2 Kim JOY.
                              ISSUE of Eric and Ann:
.129D13.3 Mark KAWAHARA, born about 1976.

12D13.3 Ralph H.⁶ JONES (Odessa⁵, William⁴, Henry³, Jacob², John¹) was born 21 Mar 1929, Pasadena, Ca., the son of Dorf JONES and Odessa Fern RITTGERS. He married Viola M. ____, born 29 June 1934. Ralph is a retired pastor, teacher, and educational administrator. After graduate school he taught for 4 years in the U.S. They went to India as missionaries and as principal of an Indian High School. He served in three different high schools, was a college professor, chaplain, and dean of education and Academic Dean. Viola was also a teacher and besides being Ralph's helpmate, she taught classes in Home Science and Health Education. They spent a total of 25 years in India and 6 in Singapore before retiring.
                                     ISSUE:
.12D133.1 Randall B. JONES, born 6 Aug 1957, Longview, Wa. He is now CEO of a firm working in computer technology. He has seven children and lives in McHenry, Ill.
.12D133.2 Wesley E. JONES, born 22 Apr 1959, Longview, Wa., He is an accountant for the U.S. Govt. He has 2 children and lives in Md.
.12D133.3 Kent L. JONES, born 4 Nov 1964, Nuzvid, Kt.Dt. India. He is a college instructor in Spokane, Wa. He has one child.
.12D133.4 Juanita R. JONES, married ____ Jenson. Has six children, including four adopted Korean children.
.12D133.5 Dale N. JONES, he has three children.
.12D133.6 Ernest A. JONES, he is a nurse. Four children.

12D16.3 Roberta Kay⁶ RITTGERS (Kenneth⁵, William⁴, Henry³, Jacob², John¹) was born 31 May 1950 in Monrovia, Calif., the daughter of Kenneth Herbert RITTGERS and Verna LaVonne HENSLIN. She married **Larry RODMAN**.[Family group sheet prepared by father, Kenneth Rittgers.]
                                     ISSUE:
.12D163.1 Jeffrey RODMAN.

12H11.1 Minyon Rose⁶ RITTGERS (Benjamin⁵, Horace⁴, Benjamin³, Jacob², John¹) was born 1958, the daughter of Benjamin Joseph RITTGERS and JoAnn She married **Ron EASTON**. She is an M.D.
ISSUE:
.12H111.1 Garrett EASTON.
.12H111.2 Mikala Minyon EASTON.

12H11.3 Dana Rene⁶ RITTGERS (Benjamin⁵, Horace⁴, Benjamin³, Jacob², John¹) was born 1961, the daughter of Benjamin Joseph RITTGERS and JoAnn COOPER. She married **Thomas RIES**.
ISSUE:
.12H113.1 Thomas RIES.
.12H1132 Kathryn RIES.
.12H1133. John RIES.

12H21.1 Christina Catherine⁶ FODGE (Arlene⁵, Clara⁴, Benjamin³, Jacob², John¹) was born 29 Nov 1947 in Iowa City, Ia., the daughter of Clinton Arthur FODGE and Arlene LaVonne ALBERTS. She married **Richard Leonard BROWN** before 1969. She is a teacher and he is a salesman.
ISSUE:
.12H211.1 Shannon Elizabeth BROWN, born 6 Sept 1969, Corvalis, Ore..
.12H211.2 Joshua Peter Leonard BROWN, born 1974.

12H21.2 Linda LaVonne⁶ FODGE (Arlene⁵, Clara⁴, Benjamin³, Jacob², John¹) was born 20 Mar 1955. in Kankakee, Ill., the daughter of Clinton Arthur FODGE and Arlene LaVonne ALBERTS. She married **Richard Dean "Rick" BENDER**. He is a church organist. Linda is a teacher.
ISSUE:
.12H212.1 Katherine Ada BENDER, born 10 Feb 1981.

12H31.1 Brent Loren⁶ NAEVE (Richard⁵, Hattie⁴, Benjamin³, Jacob², John¹) was born 4 Dec 1958 in Fort Dodge, Ia., the son of Richard Allen NAEVE and LaVonne Adela KREUTZKAMPF. He married **Denise Renee STAPLES** 30 May 1981 in Jewell, Ia. She was born 29 Nov 1959, the daughter of Russel LeRoy and Donna May (Essing) Staples.
ISSUE:
.12H311.1 Nashay Lynn NAEVE, born 10 Aug 1984 in Ft. Dodge, Ia..
.12H311.2 Brennon Royce NAEVE, born 8 Jun 1988 in Ft. Dodge, Ia..

12H31.3 Thad Lowell⁶ NAEVE (Richard⁵, Hattie⁴, Benjamin³, Jacob², John¹) was born 1960., the son of Richard Allen NAEVE and LaVonne Adelia KREUTZKAMPF. He married **Nancye REMPERT**.
ISSUE:
.12H3131 Joshua Benjamin NAEVE, born 1992.
.12H313.2 Abigail LaVonne NAEVE, born 1996.

12H32.1 Kyndra Suzanne[6] NAEVE (Philip[5], Hattie[4], Benjamin[3], Jacob[2], John[1]) was born 1962., the daughter of Philip Frederick NAEVE and Marilynne Joyce SYKES. She married **Randy WALTON**.

ISSUE:

.12H321.1 Brianna WALTON.

12H33.1 Todd Allen[6] NAEVE (Keith[5], Hattie[4], Benjamin[3], Jacob[2], John[1]) was born 1967, the son of Keith Lowell NAEVE and Diane HOFFMAN. He married **Cindi_____**.

ISSUE:

.12H331.1 Connor NAEVE.

12H41.1 Joan Suzanne[6] STROUP (Delores[5], Coral[4], Benjamin[3], Jacob[2], John[1]) was born 1951., the daughter of Robert STROUP and Delores Marie BREIHOLZ. She married (1) **Eric HOCKERT**. Joan married (2) **Sid CORNELIUS**.

ISSUE of Eric and Joan:

.12H4111   Neil Robert HOCKERT, born 1982.
.12H4112   Joy Marie HOCKERT, born 1984.

12H42.1 Scott Robert[6] BREIHOLZ (Robert[5], Coral[4], Benjamin[3], Jacob[2], John[1]) was born 1960, the son of Robert Alfred BREIHOLZ and Doris MARESH. He married **Margaret___**.

ISSUE:

.12H421.1 Chelsea BREIHOLZ.
.12H421.2 Jacob BREIHOLZ.

12H51.1 Pamela Lynne[6] JOHNSON (Laura[5], Frank[4], Benjamin[3], Jacob[2], John[1]) was born 16 Jul 1961 in Seattle, King Co., Wash., the daughter of Edwin Lloyd JOHNSON, Jr. and Laura Jean RITTGERS. She married **Thomas ORR** 2 Jun 1984.[Family group sheet submitted by Darlene (Hartley) Hudek.]

ISSUE:

.12H511.1 Thomas Anthony ORR, born 1987.

12H61.1 Roxana Dale[6] RITTGERS (Roland[5], Ernest[4], Benjamin[3], Jacob[2], John[1]) was born 27 Oct 1948 in Ft. Dodge, Ia., the daughter of Roland Dale RITTGERS and Mary Bell MARCUM. She married **Eugene Lee KERNS, M.D.** 8 Sep 1970 in Havelock, Ia. He was born 10 Oct 1948 in Emmetsburg, Ia.

ISSUE:

.12H611.1 Justin Eugene KERNS, born 23 Jul 1974 in Iowa City, Ia.
.12H611.2 Brandon Isaac KERNS, born 31 May 1976 in Iowa City, Ia.
.12H611.3 Austin Giles KERNS, born 25 Jun 1978 in Davenport, Ia.
.12H611.4 Ethan Earl KERNS, born 27 Dec 1980 in Davenport, Ia.
.12H611.5 Nathan Roland KERNS, born 27 Dec 1980 in Davenport, Ia.

12H61.2 George Ernest[6] RITTGERS (Roland[5], Ernest[4], Benjamin[3], Jacob[2], John[1]) was born 7 Oct 1950 in Emmetsburg, Ia., the son of Roland Dale RITTGERS and Mary Bell MARCUM. He married **Diane Marie LUEDTKE** 24 Jul 1970 in Fenton, Ia. She was born 1953, the daughter of Ervin and Clarice (Strayer) Leudtke. George is a computer technician.

ISSUE:

+ .12H612.1 Robin Dawn RITTGERS, born 1972 in Emmetsburg, Ia..
.12H612.2 Eric Steven RITTGERS, born 1976 in Bartlesville, Ok.

12H61.3 Bryan Anthony⁶ RITTGERS (Roland⁵, Ernest⁴, Benjamin³, Jacob², John¹) was born 15 Sept 1952, in Ft. Dodge, Ia., the son of Roland Dale RITTGERS and Mary Bell MARCUM. He married **Wanda Sue SHIMON**. She was born 1959.
ISSUE:
.12H613.1 Rachel Marie RITTGERS, born 1987.
.12H613.2 Christina Kay RITTGERS, born 1989.
.12H613.3 Ryan Daniel RITTGERS, born 1992.

12H62.1 Debra Sue⁶ IVERSON (Wanda⁵, Ernest⁴, Benjamin³, Jacob², John¹) was born 30 Jun 1953 in Waterloo, Black Hawk Co., Ia., the daughter of Robert Edward IVERSON and Wanda Lucerne RITTGERS. She married **Duane Robert BENEDICT** 16 Jul 1977. [*Family group sheet submitted by Wanda Iverson.*]
ISSUE:
.12H621.1 Bethany Lisa BENEDICT, born 17 Sep 1978.
.12H621.2 Reilly Robert BENEDICT, born 6 Apr 1982.

12H62.2 Donald James⁶ IVERSON (Wanda⁵, Ernest⁴, Benjamin³, Jacob², John¹) was born 30 Jun 1953 in Waterloo, Ia., the son of Robert Edward IVERSON and Wanda Lucerne RITTGERS. He married **Marie Regine REYES** 1 Aug 1993.[*Family group sheet submitted by Wanda Iverson.*]
ISSUE:
.12H622.1 Gabriella Julianna IVERSON, born 13 Apr 1995.

12H62.3 Rebecca Kay⁶ IVERSON (Wanda⁵, Ernest⁴, Benjamin³, Jacob², John¹) was born 8 Apr 1961 in Waterloo, Ia., the daughter of Robert Edward IVERSON and Wanda Lucerne RITTGERS. She married **James CURRAN** 14 Jul 1984.[*Family group sheet submitted by Wanda Iverson.*]
ISSUE:
.12H623.1 Jenna Kay CURRAN, born 25 Apr 1986.
.12H623.2 Jake Dalton CURRAN, born 18 Jun 1995.

12H62.4 Timothy John⁶ IVERSON (Wanda⁵, Ernest⁴, Benjamin³, Jacob², John¹) was born 13 Aug 1962 in Waterloo, Black Hawk Co., Ia., the son of Robert Edward IVERSON and Wanda Lucerne RITTGERS. His spouse has not been identified. [*Family group sheet submitted by Wanda Iverson.*]
ISSUE:
.12H624.1 Chad William CURRY, born 1 Dec 1987.

12H81.2 Natalie Ann⁶ COOKSEY (Larry⁵, Ruth⁴, Benjamin³, Jacob², John¹) was born 1962., the daughter of Larry Lee COOKSEY and Jane Garnet MADDOX. She married **Dan DUBERT**.
ISSUE:
.12H812.1 Heather Marie DUBERT.
.12H812.2 Brooke DUBERT.

.12H812.3 Bret DUBERT.

12H81.3 Annette Ann⁶ COOKSEY (Larry⁵, Ruth⁴, Benjamin³, Jacob², John¹). She was the daughter of Larry Lee COOKSEY and Sandra WEBER. She married (1) **Roger MONSON**. Annette married (2) **Joe GAGEN**.

> ISSUE of Roger and Annette:

.12H813.1 Tara MONSON.

> ISSUE of Joe and Annette:

.12H813.2 Matthew GAGEN.
.12H813.3 Sara GAGEN.

12HA1.1 David Edward⁶ RITTGERS (Donald⁵, Jacob⁴, Benjamin³, Jacob², John¹) was born 1961, the son of Donald Eugene RITTGERS and Beatrice Anne HAYNES. He married **Janelle Lynne NAEVE**.

> ISSUE:

.12HA11.1	Jacob RITTGERS.
.12HA11.2	Jonathan RITTGERS.
.12HA11.3	Mackencie Lynn RITTGERS.

12HA1.2 Rhonda Renee⁶ RITTGERS (Donald⁵, Jacob⁴, Benjamin³, Jacob², John¹) was born 1962, the daughter of Donald Eugene RITTGERS and Beatrice Anne HAYNES. She married **Steve GUSTAFSON**.

> ISSUE:

.12HA12.1 Bryce GUSTAFSON.

12HA1.3 Brenda Kaye⁶ RITTGERS (Donald⁵, Jacob⁴, Benjamin³, Jacob², John¹) was born 1963, the daughter of Donald Eugene RITTGERS and Beatrice Anne HAYNES. She married **Alan DUDLEY**.

> ISSUE:

.12HA13.1	Jeffery DUDLEY, born 1992.
.12HA13.2	Gregory DUDLEY, born 1992.
.22HA13.3	Grant DUDLEY.

12HA1.4 Donna Jeane⁶ RITTGERS (Donald⁵, Jacob⁴, Benjamin³, Jacob², John¹) was born 1970. She was the daughter of Donald Eugene RITTGERS and Beatrice Anne HAYNES. She married **Steve TISUE**.

> ISSUE:

.12HA14.1 Megan Elizabeth TISUE.

12HA2.1 Jane Louise⁶ BURNS (Joan⁵, Jacob⁴, Benjamin³, Jacob², John¹) was born 1961, the daughter of Larry BURNS and Joan Kay RITTGERS. She married **Larry NELSON**.

> ISSUE:

| .12HA21.1 | Dillon NELSON. |
| .12HA21.2 | Dalton NELSON. |

12HA2.2 Janet⁶ BURNS (Joan⁵, Jacob⁴, Benjamin³, Jacob², John¹) was born 1964. She was the daughter of Larry BURNS and Joan Kay RITTGERS. She married **David MIDDLETON**.

ISSUE:
.12HA22.1   Jessica MIDDLETON.
.12HA22.2   Lisa MIDDLETON.
.12HA22.3   Robert Joe MIDDLETON.

12HA2.3 Judy[6] **BURNS** (Joan[5], Jacob[4], Benjamin[3], Jacob[2], John[1]) was born 1966., the daughter of Larry BURNS and Joan Kay RITTGERS. She married **Dennis REISING**.
ISSUE:
.12HA23.1   Lindsey REISING.
.12HA23.2   Sandra REISING.
.12HA23.3   Nathan REISING.

12HA2.4 James[6] **BURNS** (Joan[5], Jacob[4], Benjamin[3], Jacob[2], John[1]) was born 1967. He was the son of Larry BURNS and Joan Kay RITTGERS. He married **Chris____**.
ISSUE:
.12HA24.1   Jennie BURNS.

12HB2.1 Daniel Robert[6] **CLASSEN** (Barbara[5], Robert[4], Benjamin[3], Jacob[2], John[1]). He was the son of Peter J. CLASSEN and Barbara Jean RITTGERS. He married **Amy McCARTHY**. Daniel is now farming the farm his grandfather had near West Bend, Ia.[Family information submitted by Jan Rittgers(#12HB.1)]
ISSUE:
.12HB21.1   Zachary James CLASSEN.
.12HB21.2   Allison Brooke CLASSEN.

12HB2.2 Ann Elizabeth[6] **CLASSEN** (Barbara[5], Robert[4], Benjamin[3], Jacob[2], John[1]) was born 1961, the daughter of Peter J. CLASSEN and Barbara Jean RITTGERS. She married **Jeff BERNER**.
ISSUE:
.12HB22.1   Christina Jean BERNER.
.12HB22.2   Katheryn Helen BERNER.

12HB2.3 Martha Joan[6] **CLASSEN** (Barbara[5], Robert[4], Benjamin[3], Jacob[2], John[1]) was born 1965, the daughter of Peter J. CLASSEN and Barbara Jean RITTGERS. She married **William JOHNSON**.
ISSUE:
.12HB23.1   Samuel Ray JOHNSON.
.12HB23.2   Hannah Sue JOHNSON.

12J12.1 Naomi Ruth[6] **RITTGERS** (Maynard[5], Glen[4], George[3], Jacob[2], John[1]) was born 23 Jul 1935 in Crocker, Pulaski Co., Mo., the daughter of Maynard LeRoy RITTGERS and Bertie Frances KINSLEY. She married **James MYRICK** 19 Apr 1956. He was born 22 May 1925.
ISSUE:
+ .12J121.1   Vicky Lynn MYRICK, born 4 May 1957.
+ .12J121.2   James Max MYRICK, Jr., born 26 Jul 1964.
+ .12J121.3   Lana Yvette MYRICK, born 24 Mar 1964.

12J12.2 Laura Marie[6] RITTGERS (Maynard[5], Glen[4], George[3], Jacob[2], John[1]) was born 4 Aug 1939 in Crocker, Pulaski Co., Mo., the daughter of Maynard LeRoy RITTGERS and Bertie Frances KINSLEY. She married **Donald Adolph BRUNE** 6 Jun 1964 in Troy, Madison Co., Ill. He was born 2 Feb 1935 in Washington, Mo..

ISSUE:

.12J122.1   Denise Kay BRUNE, born 17 Jun 1966.
.12J122.2   Daryl Arthur BRUNE, born 6 Sep 1967.
.12J122.3   Donald "Shane" BRUNE, born 21 Oct 1971.

12J12.3 George Earl[6] RITTGERS (Maynard[5], Glen[4], George[3], Jacob[2], John[1]) was born 27 May 1942 in Crocker, Pulaski Co., Mo., the son of Maynard LeRoy RITTGERS and Bertie Frances KINSLEY. He married (1) **Maridell___**; they divorced. George married (2) **Virginia Lee (__) GORACZKOWSKI**. She was born 17 Apr 1945. Virginia has a son, Lonnie.

ISSUE of George and Maridell:

.12J123.1   George Laurence RITTGERS, born 30 Aug 1968. He married Patricia_____.
.12J123.2   Kristan RITTGERS, born 5 Jan 1972. She married Allen PAYNE.

12J12.4 Nettie Edith[6] RITTGERS (Maynard[5], Glen[4], George[3], Jacob[2], John[1]) was born 11 May 1944 in Highland, Madison Co., Ill., the daughter of Maynard LeRoy RITTGERS and Bertie Frances KINSLEY. She married **John Marshall CLINE, Sr.** 24 Jun 1961 in Troy, Madison Co., Ill. He was born 7 Aug 1927 in Troy, Ill..

ISSUE:

+ .12J124.1   Marsha Ann CLINE, born 13 Sep 1962.
+ .12J124.2   John Marshall CLINE, Jr., born 27 Mar 1964.
+ .12J124.3   Mark Allen CLINE, born 20 Jun 1966.
+ .12J124.4   Susan Rene CLINE, born 3 Sep 1968.
  .12J124.5   Sarah Amanda CLINE, born 4 Jan 1977.
  .12J124.6   Adam Christopher CLINE, born 29 Jan 1981.

12J12.5 LeRoy Edwin[6] RITTGERS (Maynard[5], Glen[4], George[3], Jacob[2], John[1]) was born 27 Nov 1946 in Highland, Madison Co., Ill., the son of Maynard LeRoy RITTGERS and Bertie Frances KINSLEY. He married **Joan Marie BEHRENS** 16 Dec 1967 in Fairmont, Minn.. She was born 20 Nov 1948 in Fairmont, Minn.

ISSUE:

.12J125.1   Gregory Lee RITTGERS, born 21 May 1970.
.12J125.2   Andrew Peter RITTGERS, born 30 Aug 1972.
.12J125.3   Emily Brooke RITTGERS, born 8 Sep 1978.

12J12.7 Connie Mae[6] RITTGERS (Maynard[5], Glen[4], George[3], Jacob[2], John[1]) was born 9 Jan 1955 in Highland, Madison Co., Ill., the daughter of Maynard LeRoy RITTGERS and Bertie Frances KINSLEY. She married **Larry Harvey WRIGHT** 15 Jun 1973 in Troy, Madison Co., Ill. He was born 8 Dec 1949 in Pana, Christian Co., Ill.

ISSUE:

.12J127.1   Michael Lloyd WRIGHT, born 13 Apr 1974.
.12J127.2   Bruce Aaron WRIGHT, born 29 Oct 1975.

12J12.8 Bonnie Rae⁶ RITTGERS (Maynard⁵, Glen⁴, George³, Jacob², John¹) was born 9 Jan 1955 in Highland, Madison Co., Ill., the daughter of Maynard LeRoy RITTGERS and Bertie Frances KINSLEY. She married (1) **Kenneth Ray OBERKFELL** 30 Jan 1976 in Troy, Madison, Ill.; they divorced. He was born 4 May 1956. Bonnie married (2) **Terrance Gene HARRIS** 20 Sep 1985 in Edwardsville, Ill.

ISSUE of Kenneth and Bonnie:

.12J128.1   Tami Rae OBERKFELL, born 22 May 1981.
.12J128.2   Elizabeth Rae OBERKFELL, born 8 Sep 1982.
.12J128.3   Joseph Ray OBERKFELL, born 8 Sep 1982.

12J12.9 Joyce Kay⁶ RITTGERS (Maynard⁵, Glen⁴, George³, Jacob², John¹) was born 8 Feb 1959 in Staunton, Madison Co., Ill., the daughter of Maynard LeRoy RITTGERS and Bertie Frances KINSLEY. She married **James Howard BLAIR** 21 Apr 1979 in Maryville, Ill. He was born 27 Jun 1959 in Ill.

ISSUE:

.12J129.1   Jennifer Kylene BLAIR, born 27 Dec 1978.
.12J129.2   Timothy James BLAIR, born 16 Nov 1985.

12J61.1 Brian Richard⁶ RITTGERS (Dick⁵, Lloyd⁴, George³, Jacob², John¹) was born 5 Jul 1957 in Ft. Dodge, Webster Co., Ia., the son of Dick Duane RITTGERS and Maureen Joan CANAVAN. He married **Patricia Ann VOPAT** 9 Aug 1980 in Grand Junction, Greene Co., Ia. She was born 4 Dec 1956 in Aurora, Kane Co., Ill. Brian is a marketing manager. They currently (1994) reside in Carmel, Ind.[Family group sheet submitted by Maureen (Canavan) Rittgers]

ISSUE:

.12J611.1   Christopher Vopat RITTGERS, born 16 Mar 1983.
.12J611.2   Paige Canavan RITTGERS, born 24 Nov 1987.

12J61.2 Veronica Ann⁶ RITTGERS (Dick⁵, Lloyd⁴, George³, Jacob², John¹) was born 4 May 1960 in Ft. Dodge, Webster Co., Ia., the daughter of Dick Duane RITTGERS and Maureen Joan CANAVAN. She married **Scott J. MORTON** 16 Jan 1982 in Grand Junction, Greene Co., Ia. They live in Appleton, Wisc.[Family group sheet submitted by Maureen (Canavan) Rittgers]

ISSUE:

.12J612.1   Cara Marie MORTON, born 20 May 1985 in Houston, Harris Co., Tx.
.12J612.2   Jessica Lynn MORTON, born 16 Feb 1987 in Katy, Harris Co., Tx.
.12J612.3   Jonathan Scott MORTON, born 10 Apr 1989 in Katy, Harris Co., Tx.
.12J612.4   Cayla Maureen MORTON, born 10 May 1993 in Appleton, Outagamie Co., Wisc.

12K31.2 Deborah Ann⁶ ROBERTS (Mary⁵, Robert⁴, Andrew³, Jacob², John¹) was born 15 Jan 1956., the daughter of Charles Lowell ROBERTS and Mary Ann RITTGERS. She married **Milton VAUGHAN**.

ISSUE:

.12K312.1   Dylan Thomas VAUGHAN, born 1991.

12K31.3 Marjorie Diane⁶ ROBERTS (Mary⁵, Robert⁴, Andrew³, Jacob², John¹). She was the daughter of Charles Lowell ROBERTS and Mary Ann RITTGERS. She married **Clyde William FICKES**. He was born 1957.

ISSUE:

.12K313.1 Robert Charles FICKES.

.12K313.2 William Clyde FICKES, born 1992.

12K31.4 Julia Anne[6] ROBERTS (Mary[5], Robert[4], Andrew[3], Jacob[2], John[1]). She was the daughter of Charles Lowell ROBERTS and Mary Ann RITTGERS. She married **Ronald Dean BALES**.

ISSUE:

.12K314.1 Tiffany Marie BALES, born 1980.

.12K314.2 Deanne Daisy BALES, born 1982.

1344A.1 Richard Charles[6] RITTGERS (Walter[5], Isaac[4], Tobias[3], John, Jr.[2], John[1]) was born 15 Feb 1934 in Columbus, Franklin Co., Oh., the son of Walter Reed RITTGERS and Sarah Elizabeth FOERST. He married **Della Marie DUFFY** 14 Jun 1959 in Columbus, Franklin Co., Oh. She was born 5 Jan 1939 in Columbus, Franklin Co., Oh., the daughter of Thomas Walter and Vera Iola (Smith) Duffy. Richard shared with us that he had polio as a child. It didn't slow him down any and he worked for the State of Ohio for many years, the last position held was that of Administrative Storekeeper for the State. He was forced to retire as he acquired "Post Polio Syndrome", an early deterioration in the nerves that is recently being seen in those who appeared to recover from polio acquired in childhood. When not working and raising his family, Richard made time to do a lot of community service and church work. He was 1968 recipient of the Man and Boy Award for outstanding service to youth of the inner city. Jan 1985, he received the Elizabeth Blackwell Award for outstanding leadership in the community for his work with youth. Not one to sit home, Della has also left her mark on the community through her work in the Methodist Church, being involved in Methodist Women, worked with groups on Evangelism and education, and on the Board of Council Ministries.[Family Group Sheet by Richard Rittgers]

ISSUE:

.1344A1.1 Nancy Alice RITTGERS, born 3 Sep 1960 in Columbus, Franklin Co., Oh. She served nine years in the Air Force 1977-1985, as an aircraft mechanic. In 1983 & 1984 she served in Korea. For health reasons, Nancy has to live in a dry climate, so settled in Las Vegas, Nev. She is currently employed grinding lenses for glasses, and puts her mechanical training to use doing maintenance on the machines involved.

+ .1344A1.2 Lynn Marie RITTGERS, born 16 Jun 1962.

.1344A1.3 Todd Richard RITTGERS, born 9 Feb 1970 in Columbus, Franklin Co., Oh. Todd is currently employed by Hoy Surveying, surveying lands being subdivided for development.

1344A.3 James Arthur[6] RITTGERS (Walter[5], Isaac[4], Tobias[3], John, Jr.[2], John[1]) was born 29 Feb 1940 in Columbus, Franklin Co., Oh., the son of Walter Reed RITTGERS and Sarah Elizabeth FOERST. He married **Elaine____** 18 Jul 1959 in Columbus, Franklin Co., Oh.

ISSUE:

.1344A3.1 James Rittgers, JR..

.1344A3.2 daughter RITTGERS. Drill Sgt. in Army in Germany

.1344A3.3 John RITTGERS, born 23 Mar 1962[SS] in Oh, died 15 Mar 1985[SS] in Oh. Family record tells us he was killed by backhoe.

1344A.4 Mary Virginia⁶ RITTGERS (Walter⁵, Isaac⁴, Tobias³, John, Jr.², John¹) was born 5 Jun 1943 in Lancaster, Fairfield Co., Oh., the daughter of Walter Reed RITTGERS and Sarah Elizabeth FOERST. She married **William F. BUGH.**
ISSUE:
.1344A4.1   Jason BUGH.

13475.1 Harley Maywood⁶ RITTGERS (hugh⁵, albert⁴, tobias³, John², John¹). He was the son of Hugh RITTGERS. He married Mary Lee Applegate.
ISSUE:
+ .134751.1   Lawrence Russell RITTGERS, born 17 Jul 1948.

13811.1 Blanche Marguerita⁶ BRIGHT (Isaac⁵, Mary⁴, Anna³, John², John¹) was born 21 Jun 1906 in Hocking County, Oh., the daughter of Isaac Rolland BRIGHT and Gertrude MARTIN. She married **Dr. James Donald FRANCIS** 16 Sep 1928. He was born 4 Mar 1907. They lived in Columbus, Oh.[Bright,p.88]
ISSUE:
+ .138111.1   Joan Francis BRIGHT.
+ .138111.2   Barbara FRANCIS.
+ .138111.3   James D. FRANCIS, Jr..

13811.3 Glendon Rolland⁶ BRIGHT (Isaac⁵, Mary⁴, Anna³, John², John¹) was born 4 Mar 1914 in Hocking County, Oh., the son of Isaac Rolland BRIGHT and Gertrude MARTIN. He married **Maggie TERRELL**; they divorced. He married **(2)Mrs. Harriet (_) HERMAN** 3 Aug 1946. They live in Florida.
ISSUE:
+ .138113.1   Terry BRIGHT.
+ .138113.2   Sherry BRIGHT.

13814.3 Walter Edward⁶ RUTTER (Bertha⁵, Mary⁴, Anna³, John², John¹) was born 8 Aug 1915. He was the son of David Littler RUTTER and Bertha May BRIGHT. He married **Mildred STOVER** 26 Aug 1933. She was born 8 Aug 1915. [Bright, p.5, appendix]
ISSUE:
.138143.1   Edward Lee RUTTER, born 11 Jan 1938.
.138143.2   James Lester RUTTER, born 2 Jul 1939.
.138143.3   Thomas Lowell RUTTER, born 10 Feb 1942.

138144 Ernest Euna⁶ RUTTER (Bertha⁵, Mary⁴, Anna³, John², John¹) was born 16 Jun 1914. He was the son of David Littler RUTTER and Bertha May BRIGHT. He married (1) **Margaret SPENCER** 17 May 1937. She was born 8 Oct 1919. Ernest married (2) **Leona BLACKSTONE**. [Bright, p.5, appendix]
ISSUE:
.1381441   Charles Eugene RUTTER, born 11 Jan 1938.

13814.5 Charles⁶ RUTTER (Bertha⁵, Mary⁴, Anna³, John², John¹) was born 29 Oct 1915. He was the son of David Littler RUTTER and Bertha May BRIGHT. He married **Dorothy HYSELL** 2 Jul 1939. She was born 30 Jun 1918.[Bright, p.5, appendix]
ISSUE:

.138145.1	Mickey Elwyn RUTTER, born 15 Mar 1941.
.138145.2	Karolyn Ruth RUTTER, born 4 May 1945.

13814.6 Pearl Lester⁶ RUTTER (Bertha⁵, Mary⁴, Anna³, John², John¹) was born 7 Oct 1924. He was the son of David Littler RUTTER and Bertha May BRIGHT. He married **Helen FARLEY** 15 Sep 1945.[Bright, p.5, appendix]
ISSUE:
.138146.1	William Edward RUTTER, born 5 May 1946. [Bright, p.5, appendix]
.138146.2	Ronald David RUTTER, born 29 Dec 1950. [Bright, p.5, appendix]

138147 Robert David⁶ RUTTER (Bertha⁵, Mary⁴, Anna³, John², John¹) was born 5 Mar 1931. He was the son of David Littler RUTTER and Bertha May BRIGHT. He married **Mary CLARK** 15 Jul 1950.[Bright, p.5, appendix]
ISSUE:
.138147.1	Jane Ann RUTTER, born 3 Jul 1961, died 3 Jul 1961, and was buried in Oak Grove Cem., Logan, Oh.

13816.2 Edna⁶ HITE (Lillie⁵, Mary⁴, Anna³, John², John¹). She was the daughter of George Elmer HITE and Lillie Maude BRIGHT. She married **Chester LACKEY**. Edna served for 7 years as Chief Deputy in County Auditor's Office, and was a member of Trinity Methodist Church.[Bright, p.88]
ISSUE:
.138162.1	George LACKEY.
.138162.2	Ruth LACKEY. She married Robert TOBIAS. Lived in Dayton, Oh.

16142.1 Stephen Ray⁶ RITTGERS (Francis⁵, Timothy⁴, David³, Daniel², John¹) was born 30 Jan 1950 in Perry, Dallas Co., Ia., to Fred & Dnela Howe. He was adopted by Frank and Lois (Wilson) Rittgers. He married (1) **Carol WAGNER** 17 Jun 1970 in Neb.; they divorced. She was born 5 Jan 1950 in Evanston, Ill. Stephen married (2) **Angel GRAHAM** in Las Vegas, Nev. Stephen married (3) **Lorraine Kaymay CASSELE** 27 Sep 1994 in Las Vegas, Clark Co., Nev. She was born 12 Dec 1970 in Las Vegas.[Ancestry chart submitted by Lorraine Summy] In his mother's obituary, 1995, he is listed as living in Las Vegas.
ISSUE of Stephen and Carol:
+ .161421.1	Stephen Ray RITTGERS, Jr., born 14 Apr 1971.
ISSUE of Stephen and Angel:
.161421.2	Misty Marie RITTGERS, born 22 Jun 1984 in Las Vegas, Nev.

16181.1 Dean Calvin⁶ ALLEN (Mina⁵, Flora⁴, David³, Daniel², John¹) was born 26 Dec 1923, the adopted son of Merle Robert ALLEN and Mina May WILSON. He married **Mary Margaret MOORE**.
ISSUE:
.161811.1	John Dean ALLEN, died age seven.

161B4.1 David Iri⁶ SCOTT (Hazel⁵, Cora⁴, David³, Daniel², John¹) was born 18 May 1937 in Newton, Ia., the son of Robert Miller SCOTT and Hazel Pearl WILSON. He married **Carolyn Ann CORDS**. She was born 14 May 1937. We are told they live in New Orleans.
ISSUE:

+ .161B41.1 Jean Marie SCOTT, born 15 Jun 1960.
.161B41.2 Deborah Sue SCOTT, born 14 Sep 1961 in Okla.
.161B41.3 Matthew John SCOTT, born 2 Dec 1970 in Ketchikan, Alaska.

161B4.2 Herbert Elwin[6] **SCOTT** (Hazel[5], Cora[4], David[3], Daniel[2], John[1]) was born 31 Aug 1939 in Newton, Ia., the son of Robert Miller SCOTT and Hazel Pearl WILSON. He married **Sybel Jean TIGGES** 3 Mar 1963 in Peterson, Ia. She was born 26 Feb 1941 in Cherokee, Ia.
ISSUE:
.161B42.1 Paul Kylan SCOTT, born 29 Jun 1965 in Cleveland, Oh.
.161B42.2 Susanne Elaine SCOTT, born 8 Nov 1968 in Newton, Ia.

161B4.3 Fred Verald[6] **SCOTT** (Hazel[5], Cora[4], David[3], Daniel[2], John[1]) was born 2 Apr 1948 in Newton, Ia., the son of Robert Miller SCOTT and Hazel Pearl WILSON. He married **Susan Jane "Sue" GLECKLER**. She was born 10 Sep 1949.
ISSUE:
.161B43.1 William Theophilus SCOTT, born 20 Feb 1973 in Bloomfield, Ia.
.161B43.2 Kathryn Elizabeth SCOTT, born 27 Jan 1975 in Bloomfield, Ia.
.161B43.3 Naomi Lois SCOTT, born 14 Jun 1976 in Muscatine, Ia.
.161B43.4 Tabitha Jane SCOTT, born 22 Apr 1978 in Iowa City, Ia.
.161B43.5 Andrew Benjamin SCOTT, born 1 Nov 1981 in Iowa City, Ia.

161B5.1 Wayne William[6] **WILSON** (Charles[5], Cora[4], David[3], Daniel[2], John[1]) was born 4 Jul 1946 in Denver, Colo., the son of Charles Woodrow WILSON and Dorothy "Kathryn" DRAKE. He is a physician. He married **Karen Lea ROGERS** 27 Apr 1974 in Colusa, Calif.
ISSUE:
.161B51.1 Amy Marie WILSON, born 27 Aug 1976.
.161B51.2 Andrew William WILSON, born 1 May 1981.

161B5.2 Jane Kathryn[6] **WILSON** (Charles[5], Cora[4], David[3], Daniel[2], John[1]) was born 20 Dec 1947 in Denver, Colo., the daughter of Charles Woodrow WILSON and Dorothy "Kathryn" DRAKE. She married **Norman Harold FLICKINGER** 21 Dec 1968 in Palo Alto, Calif. He was born 18 Apr 1947.
ISSUE:
.161B52.1 Emily Kathryn FLICKINGER, born 22 Jul 1972.
.161B52.2 Eric James FLICKINGER, born 5 Sep 197.

161B6.1 Connie Beth[6] **WILSON** (Cora[5], Cora[4], David[3], Daniel[2], John[1]) was born 12 Jun 1954 in Denver, Colo., the daughter of Clarence Arthur WILSON and Cora Beth WILSON. She married **Edwin Carl "Ed" CROSS** 9 Jun 1973.
ISSUE:
.161B61.1 Angela Elizabeth CROSS, born 3 Jul 1974.
.161B61.2 Andrea Marie CROSS, born 26 May 1977.
.161B61.3 Adam David CROSS, born 20 Dec 1979.

161B7.1 Helen "Marie"[6] **WILSON** (William[5], Cora[4], David[3], Daniel[2], John[1]) was born 18 Jan 1943 in Perry, Ia., the daughter of William George WILSON and Helen Juanita DIETZ. She married (1) **Jon W. ABRAHAMSON** Jun 1963 in Boone, Boone, Ia.; they divorced. Helen married (2) **Sidney CROOKSHANK**.

ISSUE of Jon and Helen:

.161B71.1 Michelle Marie ABRAHAMSON, born 5 Feb 1967 in Tucson, Ariz..

161B7.2 Dale Everett⁶ WILSON (William⁵, Cora⁴, David³, Daniel², John¹) was born 20 Sep 1945 in Newton, Ia., the son of William George WILSON and Helen Juanita DIETZ. He married **Mary LAMPING** 22 Dec 1966 in Boone, Boone Co., Ia. She was born 20 Aug 1946.

ISSUE:

.161B72.1 Greg Scott WILSON, born 10 Feb 196.
.161B72.2 Daniel Everett WILSON, born 26 Oct 1969.
.161B72.3 Matthew John WILSON, born 28 Apr 1971.
.161B72.4 Melissa Ann WILSON, born 13 Jul 1976.

161B7.3 Sharon Elaine⁶ WILSON (William⁵, Cora⁴, David³, Daniel², John¹) was born 27 Oct 1947 in Boone, Ia., the daughter of William George WILSON and Helen Juanita DIETZ. She married **Harvey B. ROBERTSON** Mar 1968.

ISSUE:

.161B73.1 George Irving ROBERTSON, born 20 Nov 1968.
.161B73.2 Guy William ROBERTSON, born 29 Nov 1969. He married Stephanie Arlene HARRIS 24 Jul 1987 in Kingman, Ariz.

161B7.6 Wayde Matthew⁶ WILSON (William⁵, Cora⁴, David³, Daniel², John¹) was born 17 May 1959 in Webster City, Ia., the son of William George WILSON and Helen Juanita DIETZ. He married **Sylvia Ann LOWE** 7 Jul 1979. She was born 13 Aug 1961.

ISSUE:

.161B76.1 Luke Matthew Henry WILSON, born 6 Jan 1980.
.161B76.2 Juanita Ann WILSON, born Mar 1982.
.161B76.3 Joshua Adam WILSON, born 9 May 1984.

16211.1 Ruth⁶ FRANCE (Mary⁵, Ambrose⁴, Reuben³, Daniel², John¹) was born 13 Apr 1915., the daughter of Willard Kent FRANCE and Mary Alice RITTGERS. She married **Joseph William DAWSON** 24 Jul 1938. He was born 1 Apr 1913. They lived in Brandon, Colo. Joseph died in Brandon, Colo.

ISSUE:

.162111.1 William France DAWSON, born 3 Jul 1940. He married Judy HANSON 24 Jul 1959. They have 2 children, we are told.
.162111.2 Mary Lou DAWSON, born 6 Feb 1944. She married Arthur WAITMAN 21 Sep 1962. We are told they had three children.
.162111.3 Lee DAWSON. We are told he had four children.
.162111.4 Cathy DAWSON. She married Tom DAVIS. We are told they had two children.

16211.2 Lois⁶ FRANCE (Mary⁵, Ambrose⁴, Reuben³, Daniel², John¹) was born 26 May 1917. She was the daughter of Willard Kent FRANCE and Mary Alice RITTGERS. She married **Clarence Gordon FINNEY** 29 May 1938. He was born 2 Nov 1915. They live in Lamar, Colo.

ISSUE:

.162112.1 Gary Manly FINNEY, born 1 Jan 1948.

.162112.2 Darrel Mitchell FINNEY, born 8 Jun 1950.
.1621123 Penny Ray FINNEY, born 22 Mar 1952. She married Homer ROBERTS. We are told they have four children.

162113. LaVerne Mildred[6] FRANCE (Mary[5], Ambrose[4], Reuben[3], Daniel[2], John[1]) was born 25 Jun 1925, the daughter of Willard Kent FRANCE and Mary Alice RITTGERS. She married **Benny W. FISHER** 24 Dec 1944. He was born 9 Apr 1921. They lived in Eads, Colo.
ISSUE:
.162113.1 Richard Douglas FISHER, born 1 Apr 1946, died 1946.
.162113.2 David Kent FISHER, born 14 Aug 1950.
.162113.3 Sharon Bonnell FISHER, born 5 Dec 1951. She married Charles BOWEN.
.162113.4 Barbara Ann FISHER, born 1 Jul 1953. She married Ted ABRAMS.

16212.1 Leslie Milton[6] RITTGERS (Reuben[5], Ambrose[4], Reuben[3], Daniel[2], John[1]) was born 17 Jun 1945, the son of Reuben Burn RITTGERS and Jane (Koepsel) WILLIAMS. He married **Kathryn WILCOX** 24 May 1969. She is the daughter of Leroy and June (Wirrich) Wilcox. Kathryn is a nurse. Leslie and Kathryn live in the country outside Eads, Colo.
ISSUE:
.162121.1 Jennifer Lea RITTGERS, born 3 Oct 1970 in Lamar, Kiowa Co., Colo.
.162121.2 Lisa Marie RITTGERS, born 25 Jul 1972 in Lamar, Colo, died 27 Jul 1972.
+ .162121.3 Becky Lynette RITTGERS, born 17 Sep 1973.
.162121.4 Robert Allen RITTGERS, born 18 Jun 1976 in Lamar, Kiowa Co., Co.
.162121.5 LeRoy Burn RITTGERS, born 18 Jun 1977 in Lamar, Kiowa Co., Co.

16213.1 Robert Lewis Faine[6] RITTGERS (Luetta[5], Ambrose[4], Reuben[3], Daniel[2], John[1]) was born 15 May 1915 in Eads, Kiowa Co., Colo., the son of Daniel FAINE and Luetta Blanche RITTGERS. Laura Emmert's Journal reports that after his father killed his mother and then committed suicide, Robert adopted by grandparents, Ambrose (#172.1) and Verta Rittgers. He is reported in Ambrose Rittgers obituary to be "adopted son, Robert L. Rittgers, Estes Park, Co." He married **Helen (Hossman) BROOKS** 1941. She was born Oct 1915. He lived in Texas 1981 and last know to be living in California.
ISSUE:
+ .162131.1 Charlene (Brooks) RITTGERS, born 28 Oct 1936.
+ .162131.2 Charles (Brooks) RITTGERS.

16214.1 Verta Marie[6] BLOOMER (Edith[5], Ambrose[4], Reuben[3], Daniel[2], John[1]) was born 17 Jun 1927, the daughter of James Edmund BLOOMER and Edith Pearl RITTGERS. She married **Rev. William H. MOON** Dec 1947. He was born 14 Aug 1924.
ISSUE:
.162141.1 Beth Ann MOON, born 11 Jun 1949.
.162141.2 William MOON, Jr., born 11 Sep 1951.
.162141.3 Mary Louise MOON, born 25 Dec 1957.
.162141.4 Daniel MOON.

16215.1 Alice Blanche[6] CLEMENTS (Sylvia[5] Ambrose[4], Reuben[3], Daniel[2], John[1]), born 19 Jun 1919, the daughter of John W. CLEMENTS and Sylvia Ann RITTGERS. She is on the 1920 census, age 6 mo., with parents, Eads, Kiowa Co. Colo.[ED 108, p 9A, fam #94/96] She

married (1) Marion James BUCK 1940. Alice married (2) Joseph REED, in 1948 according to family record. In mother's obituary, 1955, we see Mr. and Mrs. Harrison (Alice Blanche) Buck of Arlington, Ks. and daughter Judy" attended the funeral.
ISSUE:
.162151.1   Judy BUCK, named in grandmother's obituary.

16219.2 Donald LeRoy[6] **RITTGERS** (Donald[5], Ambrose[4], Reuben[3], Daniel[2], John[1]) was born 1 Jun 1947 in Eads, Kiowa Co., Co., the son of Donald Howard RITTGERS. He is a business executive in Syracuse, NY., and enjoys building stereo components as a past time. He married **Sheila Ann O'DEA** 7 Oct 1967; they divorced.
ISSUE:
.162192.1   David Howard RITTGERS, born 30 Jul 1975 in York, York Co., Pa. David is a 2nd Lt., U.S. Army, and plans to go to the Army Ranger School.
.162192.2   Andrew Robert RITTGERS, born 10 Mar 1978 in York, York Co., Pa.
.162192.3   Mary Caroline RITTGERS, born 14 Jun 1980 in York, York Co., Pa.

16241.1 Frieda Madeleine[6] **WILSON** (Lloyd[5], Daisy[4], Reuben[3], Daniel[2], John[1]) was born 20 Feb 1921, the daughter of Lloyd Rittgers WILSON and Allie REED. She married **John DENNIS** 29 Jun 1945. Married second, _____Wickwire. Lives in Greenville, Ill.
ISSUE:
.162411.1   John Lloyd DENNIS, born 22 Jul 1946. He married Nina Gayle TURNER 28 Nov 1965. She was born 30 Oct 1946.
.162411.2   Richard Steven DENNIS, born 13 Jun 1949.
.162411.3   Lloyd Robert DENNIS, born 6 Jul 1952, died 6 Aug 1953.

16241.2 Glen Reed[6] **WILSON** (Lloyd[5], Daisy[4], Reuben[3], Daniel[2], John[1]) was born 3 Feb 1926, the son of Lloyd Rittgers WILSON and Allie REED. He married **Wanda Elaine SNYDER** 17 Nov 1948 in Independence, Mo. She was born 28 Feb 1926.
ISSUE:
.162412.1   Linda Louise WILSON, born 1 Aug 1951, died 1 Aug 1951.
.162412.2   Douglas Allen WILSON, born 16 Feb 1953.
.162412.3   James WILSON, born 21 Jan 1956, died 21 Jan 1956.
.162412.4   Kenneth Dale WILSON, born 15 Aug 1958.
.162412.5   Diana WILSON.

16241.3 Gilbert Rittgers[6] **WILSON** (Lloyd[5], Daisy[4], Reuben[3], Daniel[2], John[1]) was born 12 Aug 1928, the son of Lloyd Rittgers WILSON and Allie REED. He married **Betty Arlene PLUMB**. She was born 7 Jan 1932. Gilbert died 1975.
ISSUE:
.162413.1   David Gilbert WILSON, born 1 Feb 1955.
.162413.2   Darrell Rittgers WILSON, born 23 Aug 1956.
.162413.3   Dennis Harry WILSON, born 10 Feb 1964.

16241.5 Daisy Marie[6] **WILSON** (Lloyd[5], Daisy[4], Reuben[3], Daniel[2], John[1]) was born 15 Jan 1930, the daughter of Lloyd Rittgers WILSON and Allie REED. She married **Milton Lynn PEITZMAN**. He was born 30 Jan 1927. Milton died Jun 1979, and was buried in Sunny Hill Cemetery, Grimes, Ia.

ISSUE:
.162415.1 Lyle Edward PEITZMAN, born 9 Jan 1951.
.162415.2 William Robert PEITZMAN, born 4 Jan 1952.
.162415.3 Joyce Elaine PEITZMAN, born 7 Mar 1956.

16241.6 Herbert Edward⁶ WILSON (Lloyd⁵, Daisy⁴, Reuben³, Daniel², John¹) was born 21 Jun 1934., the son of Lloyd Rittgers WILSON and Allie REED. He married **Mary Lou SCOTT** 17 Aug 1955. She was born 28 Aug 1934. We are told he works on space ships at Cape Kennedy.
ISSUE:
.162416.1 Steven Scott WILSON, born 29 May 1959.
.162416.2 Roger Alan WILSON, born 29 Oct 1961.
.162416.3 Susan Kay WILSON, born 10 Aug 1963.

16243.2 Eugene Clark⁶ WILSON (Paul⁵, Daisy⁴, Reuben³, Daniel², John¹) was born 11 Feb 1924, the son of Paul James WILSON and Edith SHIFFER. He married **Ruby Virginia___**.
ISSUE:
.162432.1 Dennis Eugene WILSON, born 3 Sep 1947.
.162432.2 Steve Allen WILSON, born 28 Nov 1948.
.162432.3 Patricia Annette WILSON, born 15 Jun 1950.
.162432.4 Janet Elaine WILSON, born 28 Aug 1951.
.162432.5 Mary Louise WILSON, born 21 Apr 1954.

16243.3 Lowell Allen⁶ WILSON (Paul⁵, Daisy⁴, Reuben³, Daniel², John¹) was born 13 Jan 1931 in Polk County, Ia., the son of Paul James WILSON and Edith SHIFFER. He married **Karen NYGREN** 28 Dec 1957; they divorced.
ISSUE:
.162433.1 James Clifford (Nygren) WILSON, born 28 May 1957. Adopted by Lowell.
.162433.2 MiAnn Sue WILSON, born 31 Dec 1958.
.162433.3 Jeffrey Allen WILSON, born 1 Aug 1960.

16245.1 Roberta⁶ WELLS (Daisy⁵, Daisy⁴, Reuben³, Daniel², John¹) was born 13 Feb 1937., the daughter of Roscoe Ward WELLS and Daisy WILSON. She married (1) **Alan LANE** 1959; they divorced. Roberta married (2) **Daniel F. WAGNER** 1969.
ISSUE of Alan and Roberta:
.162451.1 Roberta Ellen LANE, born 15 Oct 1964.

16246.2 Martin⁶ GRIFFIN (Marie⁵, Daisy⁴, Reuben³, Daniel², John¹) was born 15 Oct 1933., the son of Rev. William Marion GRIFFIN and Marie WILSON. He married **Nell COX** about 1957. She was born 27 Sep 1933. Another family sheet gives name as "Lester". Do we have the right son?
ISSUE:
.162462.1 Lyn Ann GRIFFIN, born 22 Jan 1958.
.162462.2 Melissa Marie GRIFFIN, born 12 Oct 1960.
.162462.3 Wayne Martin GRIFFIN, born 9 Jul 1962.

16261.1 Thomas Wilson[6] RITTGERS (Thomas[5], Maxwell[4], Reuben[3], Daniel[2], John[1]) was born 27 Sep 1928, the son of Thomas Park Findley RITTGERS and Elsie Anna Wilhelmine SIMON. He married **Zelda Rose HAWBAKER** 6 Jun 1946. She was born 13 Apr 1924.

ISSUE:

- .162611.1 Fredrick Aaron RITTGERS, born 13 Oct 1946, died young.
- + .162611.2 Keith LaVerne RITTGERS, born 25 Nov 1947.
- .162611.3 Rosalie Ruth RITTGERS, born 15 Jan 1949. She married John Willis DOWNING. We are told they live in Sandy, Utah.
- .162611.4 Bruce Park RITTGERS, born 14 Mar 1950. Lives in Grimes, Ia.
- + .162611.5 Alice Juanita RITTGERS, born 2 Jul 1951.

16261.2 Clarence John[6] RITTGERS (Thomas[5], Maxwell[4], Reuben[3], Daniel[2], John[1]) was born 23 Nov 1929 in Raddison, Sawyer Co., Wisc., the son of Thomas Park Findley RITTGERS and Elsie Anna Wilhelmine SIMON. He married **Mary Elizabeth NOONAN** 25 Jan 1951 in Dallas Center, Dallas Co., Ia. She was born 24 Jul 1924 in Galesburg, Knox Co., Ill. Clarence is a retired teacher and enjoys farming. He and his family live on a small portion of what was Daniel Rittgers' original land in Johnston, Ia. Wife Mary and daughter Mary Esther are Rittgers Super Sleuths, having tracked down a lot of information on our Comer ancestry. Clarence has cared for the Rittgers Cemetery for many years.

ISSUE:

- + .162612.1 John Parker RITTGERS, born 28 Nov 1952.
- .162612.2 Mary Esther RITTGERS, born 20 Jul 1954 in Des Moines, Polk Co., Ia. She works for a temporary office service as a clerk. "Missy" has been secretary of the Rittgers family association, and has helped this author immeasurably in the Iowa research.
- .162612.3 Stanley Forest RITTGERS, born 24 Dec 1956.

16261.3 Philip Bruce[6] RITTGERS (Thomas[5], Maxwell[4], Reuben[3], Daniel[2], John[1]) was born 12 Dec 1930 in Sawyer Co., Wisc., the son of Thomas Park Findley RITTGERS and Elsie Anna Wilhelmine SIMON. He married **Ruth LEDERACH** 31 Aug 1957. They live in Goshen, Ind. and winter in Homossassa, Fla. He is a retired principal in a school for special ed.

ISSUE:

- + .162613.1 Philip Bruce RITTGERS, Jr., born 22 May 1960.
- .162613.2 Rebecca Ruth RITTGERS, born 19 Nov 1961 in Lapeer, Lapeer Co., Mi.. Works for Rockerfeller Foundation in NY, supervising and awarding grants.
- .162613.3 Timothy Willis RITTGERS, born 4 Oct 1964 in Lansdale, Montgomery Co., Pa. Pilot with American Airlines and flies 757's and 767's., based in Chicago.

16261.4 Ruth "Carolyn"[6] RITTGERS (Thomas[5], Maxwell[4], Reuben[3], Daniel[2], John[1]) was born 21 Jul 1933 in Sawyer Co., Wisc., the daughter of Thomas Park Findley RITTGERS and Elsie Anna Wilhelmine SIMON. She married **Franklin Lanier "Frank" CLARK** 12 Apr 1953. He was born 20 Feb 1932. In her mother's obituary, 1984, it was reported that she lived in Fair Oaks, Ca. In 1986, in her father's obit, it was reported they live in Sacramento, Calif.

ISSUE:

- .162614.1 Cecelia Marie CLARK, born 1 Jul 1954. She married Dennis HUITING.
- .162614.2 Timothy Dwaine CLARK, born 4 Feb 1956.
- .162614.3 Larry Lanier CLARK, born 8 Jan 1958.
- .162614.4 Leonard Ray CLARK, born 9 Jan 1964.

.162614.5   Leland Bert CLARK, born 9 Jan 1964.

16261.5 William Henry "David"[6] **RITTGERS** (Thomas[5], Maxwell[4], Reuben[3], Daniel[2], John[1]) was born 14 Jun 1934 in Sawyer Co., Wisc., the son of Thomas Park Findley RITTGERS and Elsie Anna Wilhelmine SIMON. He married **Shirley Jean ARNOLD**. She was born 7 Feb 1934. Changed his name to David William Rittgers. In his parents obituaries, 1984 & 1986, it is reported that he lives in Cedar Rapids, Ia.
ISSUE:
.162615.1   Cynthia Lou RITTGERS, born 3 Jun 1954, died 1996.
.162615.2   Phyllis Jean RITTGERS, born 3 Jun 1956.

16261.6 Lois Elinor[6] **RITTGERS** (Thomas[5], Maxwell[4], Reuben[3], Daniel[2], John[1]) was born 15 Nov 1935 in Sawyer Co., Wisc., the daughter of Thomas Park Findley RITTGERS and Elsie Anna Wilhelmine SIMON. She married (1) **Delbert OVERTON**. Lois married (2) **Darrell SHY**. Lois married (3) **Elmo BAGGETTO** before 1984. In her mother's obituary, in 1984, she is called Mrs. Elmo (Lois) Bogetto of Long Beach, Ca.
ISSUE of Delbert and Lois:
+ .162616.1   Rebecca Lynn OVERTON, born 11 Jun 1953.
+ .162616.2   Deborah Kay OVERTON, born 19 Dec 1954.
ISSUE of Darrell and Lois:
.162616.3   Karen Marie SHY. She married Dr. John HUNSINGER.   John is a dentist.
.162616.4   Kevin David SHY, born 1 Feb 1959.

16261.7 Bessie Louise[6] **RITTGERS** (Thomas[5], Maxwell[4], Reuben[3], Daniel[2], John[1]) was born 25 Mar 1937, the daughter of Thomas Park Findley RITTGERS and Elsie Anna Wilhelmine SIMON. She married **Robert "Bob" BLACK** 14 Aug 1953. In her mother's obituary, 1984, she is said to live in Olatha, Ks. In her father's obituary, 1986, she is of Papua, New Guinea.
ISSUE:
+ .162617.1   Carl Robert BLACK, born 2 Jan 1955.
+ .162617.2   Wayne Albert BLACK, born 29 Jun 1956.
+ .162617.3   Laurie Ann BLACK, born 23 Dec 1964.
.162617.4   Paul Wilson BLACK, born 30 Dec 1966. Lives in Olanthe, Kansas.

16261.8 Maxwell Benjamin[6] **RITTGERS** (Thomas[5], Maxwell[4], Reuben[3], Daniel[2], John[1]) was born 25 Apr 1938, the son of Thomas Park Findley RITTGERS and Elsie Anna Wilhelmine SIMON. He married (1) **Rita Rae MUNDT**. She was born 5 Mar 1941. Maxwell married (2) **Irene B._____** .
ISSUE:
.162618.1   Daniel Paul RITTGERS, born 13 Dec 1959, died 24 Oct 1991[SS].
.162618.2   Robert Michael RITTGERS, born 15 Jun 1965.
.162618.3   Leicha Rae RITTGERS, born 11 May 1963. She married _____ San MIGUEL.

16262.1 Forest Sheldon[6] **RITTGERS, Jr.** (Forest[5], Maxwell[4], Reuben[3], Daniel[2], John[1]) was born 27 Aug 1931 in Cedar Rapids, Linn Co., Ia., the son of Lt. Col. Forest Sheldon RITTGERS and Gail COURTNEY. He married **Sally Preston POSTHILL** 20 Jun 1953 in Syracuse, Onondaga Co., NY. She was born 16 Mar 1930 in Syracuse, Onondaga Co., NY.

In his father's obituary in 1980, he is referred to as "Col. Forest S. Rittgers, Jr., of Albany, NY." He retired from the army in 1983 and worked as an electrical manufacturer's representative. He is currently (1995) a real estate appraiser. In his spare time, he enjoys working on the family camp on a lake in New York.

ISSUE:

+ .162621.1   Terry Preston Wilcox-RITTGERS, born 3 Jul 1954.
+ .162621.2   Scott Courtney RITTGERS, born 7 Dec 1956.
+ .162621.3   Karen Sumner RITTGERS.

16262.2 Courtney[6] RITTGERS (Forest[5], Maxwell[4], Reuben[3], Daniel[2], John[1]) was born 7 Dec 1937 in Cedar Rapids, Linn Co., Ia., the son of Lt. Col. Forest Sheldon RITTGERS and Gail COURTNEY. He married **Mateele Louise BLESSING** 12 Feb 1962 in Ocean Park, Ks. She was born 22 Jun 1940. He is called "Lt. Col. Courtney M. Rittgers of El Paso, Tx." in his father's obituary of 1980. Lives in Calif.

ISSUE:

.162622.1   Trenton Maxwell RITTGERS, born 17 Mar 1964 in Ft. Bragg, NC.
.162622.2   Rana Louise RITTGERS, born 25 Oct 1966 in Ft. Leavenworth, Ks.

16272.1 Dorothy Ruth[6] BAKER (Helen[5], Abel[4], Reuben[3], Daniel[2], John[1]) was born 8 Mar 1941, the daughter of Jesse Ardon BAKER and Helen Lucille RITTGERS. She married **David MOORMAN** 27 Jun 1964. He was born 14 May 1943.

ISSUE:

.162721.1   Donald Thomas MOORMAN, born 14 Sep 1972.
.162721.2   Richard Ardon MOORMAN, born 24 Oct 1975.

16272.2 Marie Louise[6] BAKER (Helen[5], Abel[4], Reuben[3], Daniel[2], John[1]) was born 19 Nov 1943, the daughter of Jesse Ardon BAKER and Helen Lucille RITTGERS. She married (1) **Walter SUBLETT**; they divorced. Marie married (2) **David JAMESON**. He was born 16 May 1950.

ISSUE of Marie and David:

.162722.1   Sarah JAMESON, born 5 Mar 1979.
.162722.2   Rebecca JAMESON, born Apr 1984.

16272.3 George Samuel[6] BAKER (Helen[5], Abel[4], Reuben[3], Daniel[2], John[1]) was born 14 Sep 1945, the son of Jesse Ardon BAKER and Helen Lucille RITTGERS. He married **Elizabeth "Betsy" REYES** 28 Dec 1968. She was born 22 Oct 1946.

ISSUE:

.162723.1   Joshua BAKER, born 1 Feb 1976.
.162723.2   Katherine BAKER, born 12 Sep 1978.
.162723.3   Jesse BAKER, born 17 Feb 1985.

16272.4 Donald Bertram[6] BAKER (Helen[5], Abel[4], Reuben[3], Daniel[2], John[1]) was born 3 Mar 1950, the son of Jesse Ardon BAKER and Helen Lucille RITTGERS. He married **Sharon GREGERSEN** 15 Aug 1970. She was born 19 Jul 1951.

ISSUE:

.162724.1   Heather BAKER, born 5 Sep 1971.
.162724.2   Paul BAKER, born 27 Jul 1983.

16274.1 Helen "Maurine"[6] **WEBSTER** (Dorothy[5], Abel[4], Reuben[3], Daniel[2], John[1]) was born 22 Oct 1947, the daughter of Kenneth WEBSTER and Dorothy Marguerite RITTGERS. She married **Eduardo MEJIAS**. She is an R.N. with a B.S. degree, and is a missionary in Costa Rica
ISSUE:
.162741.1   Roy MEJIAS, born 6 Nov 1983.

16274.3 Phyllis[6] **WEBSTER** (Dorothy[5], Abel[4], Reuben[3], Daniel[2], John[1]) was born 9 Dec 1950., the daughter of Kenneth WEBSTER and Dorothy Marguerite RITTGERS. She married **Paul ERICKSON** 1 Dec 1979.
ISSUE:
.162743.1   Stephen Isaac ERICKSON, born 4 Jul 1981.

16274.4 Laura Marguerite[6] **WEBSTER** (Dorothy[5], Abel[4], Reuben[3], Daniel[2], John[1]) was born 1 Jul 1952, the daughter of Kenneth WEBSTER and Dorothy Marguerite RITTGERS. She married **Donald KRUPA** 22 May 1976.
ISSUE:
.162744.1   Christopher Luke KRUPA, born 28 Jun 1979.
.162744.2   Peter Joseph KRUPA, born 2 Jan 1981.
.162744.3   Toby Daniel KRUPA, born 9 May 1982.

16274.5 Kenneth Robert "Ken"[6] **WEBSTER** (Dorothy[5], Abel[4], Reuben[3], Daniel[2], John[1]) was born 12 Jan 1957, the son of Kenneth WEBSTER and Dorothy Marguerite RITTGERS. He married **Patti MERRILL** 12 Jun 198__.
ISSUE:
.162745.1   Timothy Clayton WEBSTER, born 1986.

16281.1 Gladys June[6] **RITTGERS** (Lawrence[5], Jasper[4], Reuben[3], Daniel[2], John[1]) was born 30 Apr 1927 in New Hartford, Butler Co., Ia., the daughter of Lawrence RITTGERS and Esther A. BALLHEAGAN. She married **Calvin Kay ELLIOTT** 5 Jul 1948 in Aplington, Butler Co., Ia.. He was born 15 Oct 1924 in Aplington. the son of Alton and Myrtle (Whitney) Elliott.
ISSUE:
.162811.1   Barton Michael ELLIOTT, born 2 Jun 1949 in New Hartford, Butler Co., Ia. He married Barbara JUNKER 1 Oct 1968.
.162811.2   Andrea June ELLIOTT, born 26 Apr 1950 in New Hartford, Butler Co., Ia. She. married Dean MOELLER 6 Jun 1969.
.162811.3   Brenda Kay ELLIOTT, born 11 Jun 1954 in New Hartford, Butler Co., Ia. She married Michael UNDERWOOD 29 May 1976. He was born 23 Oct 1953.

16281.2 Eugene Merlen[6] **RITTGERS** (Lawrence[5], Jasper[4], Reuben[3], Daniel[2], John[1]) was born 10 Sep 1928 in New Hartford, Butler Co., Ia., the son of Lawrence RITTGERS and Esther A. BALLHEAGAN. He married **Marvel COFFIN** 29 Jun 1953. She was born 26 Aug 1935.
ISSUE:
.162812.1   Darwin Eugene RITTGERS, born 24 Aug 1957. He married Carolyn PFEISLE 4 Sep 1976. She was born 13 Dec 1955.
.162812.2   Delaine Marie RITTGERS, born 9 Oct 1958.
.162812.3   Delbert Lawrence RITTGERS, born 6 Feb 1965.

16281.4 Merle Edwin⁶ RITTGERS (Lawrence⁵, Jasper⁴, Reuben³, Daniel², John¹) was born 27 Dec 1932 in New Hartford, Butler Co., Ia., the son of Lawrence RITTGERS and Esther A. BALLHEAGAN. He married **Rose Ella FINK** 26 Feb 1955. She was born 19 May 1936. We are told they lived in Lincoln, Ia.

ISSUE:
+ .162814.1   Lori Lee RITTGERS, born 23 Apr 1956.
+ .162814.2   Karla Rae RITTGERS, born 29 May 1957.
  .162814.3   Laine Allen RITTGERS, born 1 Aug 1960.
  .162814.4   Karen Sue RITTGERS, born 29 Jul 1961.
  .162814.5   Marla Kae RITTGERS, born 15 Jan 1963.
  .162814.6   Judith Faye RITTGERS, born 2 Dec 1964.

162815 Ralph Alden⁶ RITTGERS (Lawrence⁵, Jasper⁴, Reuben³, Daniel², John¹) was born 13 Jan 1934 in New Hartford, Butler Co., Ia., the son of Lawrence RITTGERS and Esther A. BALLHEAGAN. He married **Arlene NELSON** 3 Oct 1953 in Cedar Falls, Ia.. She was born 1937. They moved to Nevis, Minn. We are told he is a "line-man, heavy equipment."

ISSUE:
.162815.1   Maurine Arlene RITTGERS, born 13 Apr 1954 in Cedar Falls, Ia.
.162815.2   Dennis Allen RITTGERS, born 1955, died 1955 in New Hartford, Butler Co., Ia., and was buried in Oak Hill Cem., New Hartford.
.162815.3   Kelly Michael RITTGERS, born 10 Jun 1956.
.162815.4   Denise Renae RITTGERS, born 22 Jun 1957.
.162815.5   Lynda Ellen RITTGERS, born 4 Jan 1959.
.162815.6   Perry Alan RITTGERS, born 31 Dec 1959.
.162815.7   LuAnn Joyce RITTGERS, born 27 Dec 1960.
.162815.8   Craig Ralph RITTGERS, born 27 Mar 1962.

16282.2 Roger Ellsworth⁶ MAST (Ruth⁵, Jasper⁴, Reuben³, Daniel², John¹) was born 23 Jul 1931 in Ia., the son of Harry MAST and Ruth Evelyn RITTGERS. He married **Donna Mae COOK** 19 Dec 1954. She was born 26 May 1931, the daughter of Arthur L. Cook.

ISSUE:
.162822.1   Marilyn Ruth MAST, born 20 Jun 1960.
.162822.2   Marlene Joy MAST, born 4 May 1963.
.162822.3   Myron Paul MAST, born 4 Oct 1966.

16282.3 Clarence Eugene⁶ MAST (Ruth⁵, Jasper⁴, Reuben³, Daniel², John¹) was born 23 Feb 1933, the son of Harry MAST and Ruth Evelyn RITTGERS. He married **Martha ELLIS** 1 Aug 1970. She was born 9 May 1940.

ISSUE:
.162823.1   Jennifer Elaine MAST, born 20 Jan 1972.
.162823.2   Katherine Elizabeth MAST, born 2 Jul 1974.

16282.4 Wayne Eldon⁶ MAST (Ruth⁵, Jasper⁴, Reuben³, Daniel², John¹) was born 4 Apr 1936., the son of Harry MAST and Ruth Evelyn RITTGERS. He married **Delores Jean PORTER** 9 Dec 1956. She was born 14 May 1937.

ISSUE:
.162824.1   Jonathan Wayne MAST, born 8 Sep 1957.

.162824.2 Donald William MAST, born 18 Jul 1959.
.162824.3 Diane Wynne MAST, born 4 Sep 1961.
.162824.4 Adam Lee MAST, born 15 Nov 1964.
.162824.5 David Everett MAST, born 18 Aug 1967.

16282.7 Harriet Esther[6] **MAST** (Ruth[5], Jasper[4], Reuben[3], Daniel[2], John[1]) was born 26 Jan 1943, the daughter of Harry MAST and Ruth Evelyn RITTGERS. She married **Douglas C. SHARP** 12 Jun 1964. He was born 30 Sep 1941, the son of William Sharp. Douglas and Harriet live in Cedar Falls, Ia., where they are members of the First Baptist Church. They are both teachers.
ISSUE:
.162827.1 Mindy Sheree SHARP, born 11 Aug 1967.
.162827.2 Michelle Lauree SHARP, born 23 May 1970.
.162827.3 Donovan Douglas SHARP, born 29 Mar 1976.

16282.8 David Elgin[6] **MAST** (Ruth[5], Jasper[4], Reuben[3], Daniel[2], John[1]) was born 16 Aug 1945, the son of Harry MAST and Ruth Evelyn RITTGERS. He married **Lois Lynette ZHORNE** 8 Aug 1970. She was born 30 Sep 1952.
ISSUE:
.162828.1 Ian Christopher MAST, born 22 Sep 1972.

16284.1 Lois Frances[6] **RITTGERS** (Lester[5], Jasper[4], Reuben[3], Daniel[2], John[1]) was born 15 Oct 1942 in Des Moines, Polk Co., Ia., the daughter of Lester Findley RITTGERS and Alice RASSMANSEN. She married **Robert Dale STORK** 7 Apr 1961 in Cedar Falls, Black Hawk Co., Ia. He was born 2 Feb 1942. He is a farmer south of New Hartford, Butler Co., Ia., and they are members of the Lutheran Church, Cedar Falls, Ia.
ISSUE:
.162841.1 Brian Robert STORK, born 5 Jan 1969.
.162841.2 Lori Jean STORK, born 12 Jan 1976.
.162841.3 Sarah Jean STORK, born 5 Dec 1981.

16284.2 Lee Francis[6] **RITTGERS** (Lester[5], Jasper[4], Reuben[3], Daniel[2], John[1]) was born 8 Jul 1944 in Des Moines, Polk Co., Ia., the son of Lester Findley RITTGERS and Alice RASSMANSEN. He married **Mary Bernhard JACOBSON** 5 Jun 1945. She is the daughter of Bernhard and Mary (Campbell) Jacobson. He is a teacher and a farmer. They attend the First Baptist Church, Cedar Falls, Ia.
ISSUE:
.162842.1 Mark Charles RITTGERS, born 10 Sep 1964 in Sioux Falls, Minnehaha Co., S.D.

16284.4 Larry Lester[6] **RITTGERS** (Lester[5], Jasper[4], Reuben[3], Daniel[2], John[1]) was born 3 Apr 1952 in Cedar Falls, Butler Co., Ia., the son of Lester Findley RITTGERS and Alice RASSMANSEN. He married **Susan Ellen VISLISEL** 26 May 1973 in Cedar Falls, Black Hawk Co., Ia. She was born 4 Jun 1951, the daughter of George and Lottie (__) Vislisel. They are teachers, and live in Dike, Ia. They attend the First Baptist Church, Cedar Falls., Ia.
ISSUE:
.162844.1 Amy Sue RITTGERS, born 16 Oct 1976 in Cedar Falls, Black Hawk Co., Ia.
.162844.2 Daniel Lawrence RITTGERS, born 15 Jul 1979.

.162844.3   Timothy Martin RITTGERS, born 20 May 1981.
.162844.4   Matthew RITTGERS.

16284.5 Alice Lynn[6] RITTGERS (Lester[5], Jasper[4], Reuben[3], Daniel[2], John[1]) was born 2 Jul 1955 in Cedar Falls, Butler Co., Ia., the daughter of Lester Findley RITTGERS and Alice RASSMANSEN. She married **John Steven KORECKI** 23 May 1987 in Perris, Riverside Co., Ca. He was born 9 Jun 1956 in El Paso, El Paso Co., Tx.

ISSUE:

.162845.1   Steven Robert KORECKI, born 2 Nov 1988 in Novato, Marin Co., Ca.
.162845.2   Jethna Susan KORECKI, born 21 May 1994 in Oakland, Almeda Co., Ca.

16285.2 Stanley Earle[6] RITTGERS (Frederick[5], Jasper[4], Reuben[3], Daniel[2], John[1]) was born 24 Jan 1947 in Des Moines, Polk Co., Ia., the son of Frederick Henry RITTGERS and Joyce Winifred DAVIS. He married **Eva Mae COTY** 1971. She was born 15 Sep 1948 in Jasper Co., Ind., the daughter of Lional and Cecelia (Pilotte) Coty.

ISSUE:

.162852.1   David Thomas RITTGERS, born 2 Sep 1973 in Troy, Miami Co., Oh.
.162852.2   Andrew Michael RITTGERS, born 13 Jul 1976 in Columbus, Franklin Co., Oh.

16286.1 John Ade[6] McBRIDE (Margaret[5], Jasper[4], Reuben[3], Daniel[2], John[1]) was born 7 Jan 1943, the son of John Adolph McBRIDE and Margaret Elizabeth RITTGERS. He married (1) **Judith Eileen DICKERSON** 15 May 1965. John married (2) **Janet (__) BROCKETT.** He is a trucker and a farmer.[Interview with Margaret (Rittgers) McBride, 1994]

ISSUE of John and Judith:

.162861.1   Monica Jean McBRIDE, born 20 May 1968.

16286.2 David Evan[6] McBRIDE (Margaret[5], Jasper[4], Reuben[3], Daniel[2], John[1]) was born 16 Jan 1945 in Polk City, Polk Co., Ia., the son of John Adolph McBRIDE and Margaret Elizabeth RITTGERS. He married **Barbara Sue HEFFERN** 5 Jun 1967. She was born 20 Oct 1944. He is a minister and resided for a time in Vermont. Of Wenham, Mass. in father's obituary, 1971.[*Interview with Margaret (Rittgers) McBride, 1994*]

ISSUE:

.162862.1   Jane Elizabeth McBRIDE, born 21 Aug 1975.
.162682.2   John Evan McBRIDE, born 10 Dec 1978.
.162862.3   James Elliott McBRIDE, born 7 Mar 1984.

16286.4 Barbara[6] McBRIDE (margaret[5], Jasper[4], Reuben[3], Daniel[2], John[1]) was born 18 Jun 1952 in Des Moines, Polk Co., Ia., the daughter of John Adolph McBRIDE and Margaret Elizabeth RITTGERS. She married **Steven W. FELDMAN** 17 Sep 1976. He was born 25 May 1952 in Des Moines, Polk Co., Ia., the son of Delbert Leroy FELDMAN and Virginia M. WALDO. Steve and Barbara attended school together from first grade. After graduation, they became sweethearts. He joined the army (1972-1977). After his service, they returned to Ankeny, where he worked at the John Deere plant in Ankeny, until making a career change to medical records. Barbara is a registered nurse.

ISSUE:

.162864.1   Rebecca Elizabeth FELDMAN, born 2 Sep 1978 in Des Moines, Polk Co., Ia.
.162864.2   David Aaron FELDMAN, born 8 Feb 1980 in Des Moines, Polk Co., Ia.

.162864.3 Sarah Ann FELDMAN, born 19 Oct 1981 in Des Moines, Polk Co., Ia.

162A1.1 Richard John[6] RORABAUGH (John[5], Vivian[4], Reuben[3], Daniel[2], John[1]) was born 22 Mar 1950 in Rutland, Rutland Co., Vt., the son of John Rittgers RORABAUGH and Palma FOUNTAIN. He married **Suzanne Mary GOMEZ** 23 Feb 1974 in Kenner, Jefferson Par., La.; they divorced in 1993. She was born 11 Dec 1955 in New Orleans, Orleans Par., La., the daughter of Donald Raymond and Joyce Mary (Toups) Gomez. Rick and Sue were clogging instructors for several years, until their children's various activities took precedence.[*Interview with John R. Rorabaugh, 1992.*]

ISSUE:

.162A11.1 Richard John Rorabaugh, JR., born 15 Mar 1974.

.162A11.2 Christine Marie RORABAUGH, born 16 Jun 1975.

162A3.1 William Lysle[6] RORABAUGH, Jr. (William, Sr.[5], Vivian[4], Reuben[3], Daniel[2], John[1]) was born 5 Jan 1938 in St. Augustine, Fl., the son of William Lysle RORABAUGH, Sr. and Myrtle Ruth QUIGLEY. He graduated from Clermont (Florida) High School. Served two years active duty in U.S. Navy, Atlantic Fleet, in Mediterranean, and 21 years in the reserves.   Since 1961, he has been a letter carried, U.S. Postal Service, Tavares, Fla. He married (1) **Norma Jean WISE** 29 Sep 1962 in Mount Dora, Lake, Fl; they divorced. She was born 22 Jul 1939 in Eustis, Lake, Fl., died Jan 1985 in Eustis, Lake, Fl. She was the daughter of Curtis and Norma (__) Wise. Bill married (2) **Joyce (Tarling) HORD** 15 Aug 1981 in Clermont, Lake Co., Fl. She was born 5 Jul 1943 in Portsmouth, Rockingham Co., NH., the daughter of Ernest Richard and Marian (Sanborn) Tarling. Bill and Joyce had been childhood sweethearts, but went their separate ways until 1980. Joyce, an R.N., has three children. They enjoy traveling now that they are semi-retired. Many trips involve the grandchildren they share. Joyce loves genealogy and crafts, and is the author of this history. Bill is polishing up his golf game and enjoys bowling.

ISSUE of William and Norma:

+ .162A31.1 William Jeffrey RORABAUGH, born 15 Jul 1965.

162A3.2 Sarah Ruth[6] RORABAUGH (William, Sr.[5], Vivian[4], Reuben[3], Daniel[2], John[1]) was born 20 Dec 1941 in Clermont, Lake Co., Fl., the daughter of William Lysle RORABAUGH, Sr. and Myrtle Ruth QUIGLEY. Seen on the 1945 Florida state census, age 3, with parents in Precinct 15, Clermont, Fla.[reel 27] She married **Dean RICHARDS** 3 Oct 1958 in Clermont, Lake Co., Fl. He was born 15 Oct 1938. Dean worked for Continental Can Co., Winter Garden, Fla., until retirement. She worked as a bank teller.[Interview with Myrtle (Quigley) Rorabaugh]

ISSUE:

+ .162A32.1 Cheryl Denise RICHARDS, born 3 Mar 1961 in Orlando, Orange Co., Fl.

+ .162A32.2 Brenda Diane RICHARDS, born 12 May 1962 in Orlando, Orange Co., Fl.

+ .162A32.3 Sarah Elizabeth RICHARDS, born 8 Apr 1968 in Orlando, Orange Co., Fla.

.162A32.4 Curtis Dean RICHARDS, born 5 Mar 1971 in Orlando, Orange Co., Fla. He is currently going to Florida State Univ.

162A3.3 Donna Josephine[6] RORABAUGH (William, Sr.[5], Vivian[4], Reuben[3], Daniel[2], John[1]) was born 19 Oct 1947 in Clermont, Lake Co., Fl., the daughter of William Lysle RORABAUGH, Sr. and Myrtle Ruth QUIGLEY. She graduated from Florida State University with a degree in Social Work. She married **Gale MATTISON** 24 Mar 1973 in Tallahassee, Fl. Currently, Donna is a social worker in a large nursing home in West Hartford, Conn. Gale is

Chief Fiscal Officer for the Department of Corrections, and was active in the Youth Ice Hockey League, when their son, Josh, was a member. They reside in West Hartford, Conn. They are active in their church and have a wide range of social interests.
ISSUE:
.162A33.1 Joshua David MATTISON, born 22 Sep 1976. Currently attending college at Gettysburg, Pa.

162A4.1 Philip Arthur[6] RORABAUGH (Philip[5], Vivian[4], Reuben[3], Daniel[2], John[1]) was born 4 Jun 1936 in Union Park, Orange Co., Fla., the son of Philip Findley RORABAUGH and Marian HARDY. He married **Donna Marion KING** 3 Aug 1956 in Orlando, Orange Co., Fla. She was born 26 Mar 1937 in Binghamton, Browne Co., N.Y. Philip is a pastor of Fairview Southern Methodist Church, West Union, South Carolina.[*Interview with Philip Rorabaugh, 1992.*]
ISSUE:
+ .162A41.1 Deborah Elaine RORABAUGH, born 18 Jun 1957.
.162A41.2 Diane Esther RORABAUGH, born 15 Dec 1959 in Nyack, Rockland Co., N.Y.
.162A41.3 Philip Daniel RORABAUGH, born 6 Apr 1961 in Nyack, Rockland Co., N.Y. He married Robyn GARCIA 21 Jul 1990. She was born 21 Jul 1956 in San Diego, Calif. He and Robyn have both been in the Navy.
.162A41.4 Donald Paul RORABAUGH, born 6 Apr 1961 in Nyack, Rockland Co., N.Y. He married Mary Diane HURLEY 19 Apr 1986.

162A4.4 Anna Marie[6] RORABAUGH (Philip[5], Vivian[4], Reuben[3], Daniel[2], John[1]) was born 12 Aug 1943 in Clermont, Lake Co., Fla., the daughter of Philip Findley RORABAUGH and Marian HARDY. A registered nurse, Ann worked in Korea 1970-1972 with Compassion, Inc., as a public health nurse in their orphanages. While there, she adopted Becky, who was found abandoned. Ann has had a wide variety of nursing experiences, many in pediatrics.[*Interview with Philip Rorabaugh, 1992.*]
ISSUE:
.162A44.1 Rebecca Joy RORABAUGH, born 5 May 1970 in Pusan, Korea, Adopted. She married Robert Lee STOVALL 8 Aug 1992 in Clermont, Lake Co., Fla.

162A4.5 Esther Judith[6] RORABAUGH (Philip[5], Vivian[4], Reuben[3], Daniel[2], John[1]) was born 16 Oct 1946 in St. Petersburg, Pinellas Co., Fla., the daughter of Philip Findley RORABAUGH and Marian HARDY. She married **Tedman Earl HEGLUND** 12 Jun 1970. He was born 8 Mar 1946., the son of Carl Richard and Katherine (Hendry) Heglund. Judy is a Registered Nurse. She and husband are missionaries in Indonesia. Among their many interests is translating the Bible into the local Indonesian languages.[Interview with Philip Rorabaugh, 1992.]
ISSUE:
.162A45.1 Scott Tedman HEGLUND, born 13 Nov 1972 in Pit River, IrianJaya, Indonesia. He went to high school in Indonesia. He is now going to college in the United States. [Interview with Judith (Rorabaugh) Heglund, 1992.]
.162A45.2 Darrel Richard HEGLUND, born 26 Aug 1974 in Pit River, IrianJaya, Indonesia, died there 20 Sep 1974.
.162A45.3 Denise Kay HEGLUND, born 11 Dec 1975 in Palm Beach Gdns., Palm Beach Co., Fla. Raised in Pit River, IrianJaya, Indonesia., where she attends High School. [Interview with Judith (Rorabaugh) Heglund, 1992.]

162A5.1 Herman "Kenneth"[6] COX (Vivian[5], Vivian[4], Reuben[3], Daniel[2], John[1]) was born 29 Apr 1938 in Clermont, Lake Co., Fla., the son of Herman COX and Vivian Abigail RORABAUGH. He married **Linda Sue FRISBY** 15 May 1959. She was born 6 Feb 1941. He is retired Fire Chief of Mount Dora (Fla.) Fire Dept.[Interview with Abigail (Rorabaugh) Cox, 1992]

ISSUE:

.162A51.1 Brian Kenneth COX, born 7 Apr 1969 in Eustis, Lake, Fla.

162A5.2 Carolyn Abigail[6] COX (Vivian[5], Vivian[4], Reuben[3], Daniel[2], John[1]) was born 16 Jul 1940 in Astatula, Lake Co., Fla., the daughter of Herman COX and Vivian Abigail RORABAUGH. She married **Charles Ellis HUNTER** 18 Jul 1958.[Interview with Abigail (Rorabaugh) Cox, 1992]

ISSUE:

+ .162A52.1 Charles Daniel HUNTER, born 11 Nov 1959.
.162A52.2 Daryl Ellis HUNTER, born 16 Feb 1962 in Eustis, Lake Co., Fla. He married Carolina Haydee MERIDA. She was born 19 Jul 1971 in Guatemala City, Guatemala, Central America.[Interview with Abigail (Rorabaugh) Cox, 1992]
.162A52.3 Kathryn Maria HUNTER, born 27 Jan 1978 in Winter Park, Orange, Fla.

162A5.3 Randall William[6] COX (Vivian[5], Vivian[4], Reuben[3], Daniel[2], John[1]) was born 15 Dec 1944 in Eustis, Lake Co., Fla., the son of Herman COX and Vivian Abigail RORABAUGH. He married **Carolyn Sue SPADAFORA** 21 Jan 1967. She was born 29 Sep 1946.[Interview with Abigail (Rorabaugh) Cox, 1992]

ISSUE:

.162A53.1 Randi Sue COX, born 30 Jun 1970. She married Richard HUTCHINGSON 11 Aug 1990 in Tavares, Lake, Fla..
.162A53.2 Roger William COX, born 15 Apr 1972.
.162A53.3 John Randall COX, born 16 Jul 1979.
.162A53.4 Anthony James COX, born 29 Sep 1981.

162A5.4 Marilyn Louise[6] COX (Vivian[5], Vivian[4], Reuben[3], Daniel[2], John[1]) was born 14 Oct 1952 in Eustis, Lake Co., Fla., the daughter of Herman COX and Vivian Abigail RORABAUGH. Her spouse has not been identified

ISSUE:

.162A54.1 Abigail Joy COX, born 14 May 1984 in Colorado Springs, El Paso, Colo..
.162A54.2 Samuel Broderick COX, born 11 Jul 1990 in Eustis, Lake, Fla.

162C6.1 Albert Joe[6] RITTGERS (Robert[5], Chester[4], Reuben[3], Daniel[2], John[1]) was born 20 Apr 1937 in Corpus Christi, Nueces Co., Tx., the son of Robert Chester RITTGERS and Kathleen L. EMMERT. He married (1) **Sharon Lee GILL** 18 Jun 1960. She was born 10 Sep 1942 in Hot Springs, Ark., the daughter of Robert and Georgia (___) Gill. Albert married (2) **Sharon Leigh WEISS**. She was born 26 Oct 1942 in Denver, Colo., the daughter of Harry and Jocine (Heffner) Weiss. They own Wesco Fabrics and reside in Littleton, Colo.

ISSUE of Albert and Sharon:

.162C61.1 Laura Renee RITTGERS, born 18 Feb 1962 in Corpus Christi, Nueces Co., Tx.

162C8.1 Daniel William⁶ RITTGERS (David⁵, Chester⁴, Reuben³, Daniel², John¹) was born 1 Apr 1952 in Houston, Harris Co., Tx., the son of David Earl RITTGERS and Christine Mary VAJDOS. He married **Consetta Jo DuBOSE** 4 Oct 1980. She was born 20 Dec 1957 in Galveston, Galveston Co., Tx., the daughter of Charles Ray DuBOSE and Josephine IMBROGUGLIO.   Dan has his masters degree in Business Accounting and does Tax accounting. They attend the Catholic Church and met at the church they still attend. "C.J.", who works as an Ad Assistant in an office, has always enjoyed working with children. She and Dan take pregnant teens into their home and cares for them until they are back on their feet after having their babies. She also does volunteer work and enjoys crafts and music. Dan and C.J. are active in their church.

ISSUE:

.162C81.1 Amber RITTGERS, born 24 Sep 1984 in Houston, Ft. Bend Co., Tx.

162D1.1 Lloyd John⁶ PEITZMAN (Laura⁵, John⁴, Reuben³, Daniel², John¹) was born 18 Feb 1937. He was the son of Earl L. PEITZMAN and Laura RITTGERS. He married **Carol Elizabeth HOLMQUIST** 29 Mar 1958. She was born 8 Feb 1937.[Interview with Laura (Rittgers)(Peitzman) Emmert, 1992, 1994]

ISSUE:

+ .162D11.1 Linda Ruth PEITZMAN, born 21 Feb 1959.
.162D11.2 Baby Boy PEITZMAN, born 19 Mar 1961, died 19 Mar 1961.
+ .162D11.3 Robert John PEITZMAN, born 10 Mar 1960.
.162D11.4 James Lloyd PEITZMAN, born 9 Feb 1964.
.162D11.5 John Richard PEITZMAN, born 15 Apr 1968.

162D3.1 Sharon Kay⁶ RITTGERS (John, Jr.⁵, John⁴, Reuben³, Daniel², John¹) was born 25 Nov 1949, the daughter of John Henry RITTGERS, Jr. and Elsie Arlene WISE.Sharon married (1) **Randy Van METER** 28 Aug 1970, Dallas Co., Ia. He is the son of Dr. & Mrs. Kenneth Van Meter. They divorced. She married (2) **Charles HALL**. In her father's obituary, 1992, it reports "Sharon Kay Hall of Scranton, Pa."

ISSUE of Charles and Sharon:

.162D31.1 Nikol Van METER, born 11 Jun 1978.

162D3.2 Gary John⁶ RITTGERS (John, Jr.⁵, John⁴, Reuben³, Daniel², John¹) was born 21 Mar 1953, the son of John Henry RITTGERS, Jr. and Elsie Arlene WISE. He married **Sally BOWMAN**. We find in the Dallas Co. News, 19 Nov 1980 an article reporting that Gary and Sally Rittgers of fifty Lakes, Minn, are proud parents of Rachelle Marie.

ISSUE:

.162D32.1 Audrey Ann RITTGERS, born 17 Dec 1976.
.162D32.2 Jasmine Lea RITTGERS, born 1 Aug 1978.
.162D32.3 Rachel Marie RITTGERS, born 15 Nov 1980.

162D4.1 Mark Thomas⁶ RITTGERS (Thomas⁵, John⁴, Reuben³, Daniel², John¹) was born 10 Feb 1949 in Des Moines, Polk Co., Ia., the son of Thomas Eugene RITTGERS and Phyllis G. CLIPSON. He married **Cheryl GELATT** 10 Jun 1971 in New Berlin, N.Y.. She was born 8 Dec 1950 in Binghamton, NY., the daughter of Charles and Ginny (Silvers) Gelatt. Mark is comptroller for a chain of insurance agencies and Cheryl does sign language for the deaf. They are affiliated with the Baptist Church. In a letter in response to a query, he reports he lives in West Winfield, Ia.[*Family group sheet submitted by Thomas Rittgers*]

ISSUE:

.162D41.1 Aaron William RITTGERS, born 23 Oct 1974 in Roanoke, Va.. He married Sabra ___. He is in the US Air Force in Valdosta, Ga., where he is a security officer.

.162D41.2 Rebekah Joy RITTGERS, born 15 Dec 1977 in Culpepper, Va.. She is attending (1995) Grove City College, Pa.

.162D41.3 Daniel Mark RITTGERS, born 21 Jan 1981 in Ames, Story Co., Ia.

.162D41.4 Sarah Michelle RITTGERS, born 1 Feb 1983 in Longmont, Co.

162D42 Hugh John[6] RITTGERS (Thomas[5], John[4], Reuben[3], Daniel[2], John[1]) was born 30 Dec 1950 in Des Moines, Polk Co., Ia., the son of Thomas Eugene RITTGERS and Phyllis G. CLIPSON. He married (1) **Diana MEYERS** 10 Jul 1971 in McCallsburg, Story Co., Ia.; they divorced. She is the daughter of Gerald and Nedra (Toot) Myers. Hugh married (2) **Judy CANTONWINE** 22 Nov 1980; they divorced. He married (3) **Debbie** ___ 31 Dec 1986. Debbie had Tanya, b. Jan 1974; and Nikki, b. Mar. 1977.[*Family group sheet submitted by Thomas Rittgers*]

ISSUE of Hugh and Diana:

.162D42.1 Chad Jason RITTGERS, born 6 Jul 1972 in Nevada, Story Co., Ia.

162E2.2 Deanna[6] DePEW (Ruth[5], Mary[4], Reuben[3], Daniel[2], John[1]) was born 11 Aug 1940, the daughter of Eddie DePEW and Ruth Ellen HARDIE. She married _____ **DUNLAP**; they divorced.

ISSUE:

.162E22.1 Kelly DUNLAP.

162E2.3 Frances "Cookie"[6] DePEW (Ruth[5], Mary[4], Reuben[3], Daniel[2], John[1]). She was the daughter of Eddie DePEW and Ruth Ellen HARDIE. She married _____, they divorced.

ISSUE:

.162E23.1 Traci.

16721.1 Lorene Alice[6] WINELAND (Charlotte[5], Grace[4], George[3], Daniel[2], John[1]) was born 20 Sep 1927 in Grimes, Polk Co., Ia., the daughter of Eugene Charles WINELAND and Charlotte Alice PEACOCK. She married (1) **William Frederick MEEK** 18 Sep 1948 in Kansas City, Jackson Co., Mo.; they divorced. He was born 25 Jun 1925 in Kansas City, Jackson Co., Mo., the son of John and Constance (Frederick) Meek. Lorene married (2) **Gordon Eugene SUMMERSKILL** 8 Apr 1961. He was born 9 May 1930 in Kansas City, Mo., the son of Waldo Tally and Mattie May (McClelland) Summerskill. He adopted Lorene's 2 children. William died 1983 in Burbank, Calif, and was buried in Forest Lawn, Burbank, Calif.[Family group sheet submitted by Lorene (Wineland)(Meek) Summerskill]

ISSUE of William and Lorene:

+ .167211.1 Janene Alice (Meek) SUMMERSKILL, born 22 Jan 1955.

+ .167211.2 Melissa Dee (Meek) SUMMERSKILL, born 25 Feb 1959.

16721.2 Delores Ella[6] WINELAND (Charlotte[5], Grace[4], George[3], Daniel[2], John[1]) was born 27 Aug 1929 in Des Moines, Polk Co., Ia., the daughter of Eugene Charles WINELAND and Charlotte Alice PEACOCK. She married **Clare Vincent CARR, Jr.** 5 Oct 1951 in Kansas City, Jackson Co., Mo. He was born 5 Oct 1928 in Ponca City, Okla., the son of Clare V. and Mary

F. (Cowen) Carr. Delores died 30 Aug 1993 in Highland Park, Cook, Ill., and was buried in Vernon Twp. Cemetery, Half Day, Cook Co., Ill.
ISSUE:
.167212.1   Vincent Gene CARR, born 18 Jul 1954 in Kansas City, Jackson Co., Mo.
.167212.2   David Andrew CARR, born 7 Nov 1958 in Kansas City, Jackson Co., Mo.
.167212.3   Heather Jo CARR, born 18 Aug 1966 in Kansas City, Jackson Co., Mo.

16813.1 Marion Irene[6] **RITTGERS** (Charles[5], Charles[4], Michael[3], Daniel[2], John[1]) was born 11 Aug 1928, the daughter of Charles Barton RITTGERS and Mary Catherine FISHER. She married **Mervin Deitrich KUEFNER** 3 Sep 1960. He was born 13 May 1932.
ISSUE:
+ .168131.1   Jeanie Marie KUEFNER, born 21 Sep 1963.

16813.2 Harold Charles[6] **RITTGERS** (Charles[5], Charles[4], Michael[3], Daniel[2], John[1]) was born 29 Dec 1929 in Des Moines, Polk, Ia., the son of Charles Barton RITTGERS and Mary Catherine FISHER. He married **Delores Elaine SHELDAHL** 14 Jun 1952 in Huxley, Ia. She was born 13 Apr 1929 in Huxley, Ia., the daughter of Silas Benjamin and Elizabeth Emayjulen (Saveraid) Sheldahl. Delores is a retired Junion High teacher.
ISSUE:
+ .168132.1   Roger Harold RITTGERS, born 18 Nov 1956.
+ .168132.2   Mark Alan RITTGERS, born 22 Aug 1959.

16814.1 Barbara Jean[6] **KUEFNER** (Grace[5], Charles[4], Michael[3], Daniel[2], John[1]) was born 23 Dec 1928., the daughter of Herbert Herman KUEFNER and Grace Ann RITTGERS. She married (1) **William GRAVES**. William died 1993. Barbara married (2) **George KAY**. He was born 17 Jun 1924.
ISSUE:
+ .168141.1   Gary GRAVES, born 27 May 1954.
+ .168141.2   Brian Kent GRAVES, born 6 May 1959.

16814.2 Robert[6] **KUEFNER** (Grace[5], Charles[4], Michael[3], Daniel[2], John[1]) was born 4 Jul 1940, the son of Herbert Herman KUEFNER and Grace Ann RITTGERS. He married (1) **Joleen___**. Robert married (2) **Mary DILLER**. She was born 26 Apr 1944.
ISSUE:
.168142.1   Scott Leonard KUEFNER, born 7 Jan 1963. He married Tracey. She was born 20 Jan 1961.
+ .168142.2   Barbara KUEFNER, born 20 Jan 1966.
+ .168142.3   Robert KUEFNER, born 13 Oct 1967.

16815.1 Kenneth Wayne[6] **RITTGERS** (Walter[5], Charles[4], Michael[3], Daniel[2], John[1]) was born 15 Aug 1942, the son of Walter Joseph RITTGERS and Lillie Mathilda QUICK. He married **Nancy HENDRICKS** 22 Dec 1969. She was born 8 Mar 1945.
ISSUE:
.168151.1   Lisa Ann RITTGERS, born 17 Apr 1971.
.168151.2   Julie Ann RITTGERS, born 19 Dec 1972.

.16815.2 Janet Carol⁶ RITTGERS (Walter⁵, Charles⁴, Michael³, Daniel², John¹) was born 23 May 1945, the daughter of Walter Joseph RITTGERS and Lillie Mathilda QUICK. She married **Laurin Jay COLE** 25 Nov 1978. He was born 25 Feb 1948.
ISSUE:
.168152.1 Corinne Renee COLE, born 5 Oct 1979.
.168152.2 Christi Lynn COLE, born 19 Mar 1982.
.168152.3 Rhonda Suzanne COLE, born 9 Jun 1984.
.168152.4 Ryan Samuel COLE, born 9 Jun 1984.

16815.3 James Gareld⁶ RITTGERS (Walter⁵, Charles⁴, Michael³, Daniel², John¹) was born 23 May 1945, the son of Walter Joseph RITTGERS and Lillie Mathilda QUICK. He married **Judy ALMS** 27 Dec 1969. She was born 6 Feb 1946. Judy died 1991, and was buried in Rittgers Cemetery, Johnston, Ia.
ISSUE:
.168153.1 Stephen RITTGERS, born 1 Jun 1973.
.168153.2 David RITTGERS, born 15 May 1976.

16815.4 Donald Walter⁶ RITTGERS (Walter⁵, Charles⁴, Michael³, Daniel², John¹) was born 10 Jun 1946., the son of Walter Joseph RITTGERS and Lillie Mathilda QUICK. He married **Marcia VARNEY** 7 Aug 1968. She was born 3 Jul 1947.
ISSUE:
.168154.1 Infant RITTGERS, died in infancy.
.168154.2 Angelia RITTGERS, born 31 Jul 1977.
.168154.3 Joseph RITTGERS, born 10 Feb 1981.

16911.1 Edith LaVonne⁶ PURVIANCE (Floyd⁵, Nellie⁴, Caroline³, Daniel², John¹) was born 19 Apr 1920, the daughter of Floyd Sidney PURVIANCE and Lola Marie REPP. She married **Carroll Raymond CROUSE** 28 Dec 1941. He was born 12 Sep 1914.
ISSUE:
+ .169111.1 Carolyn Ruth CROUSE, born 3 Nov 1944.
.169111.2 Kenneth Ray CROUSE, born 14 Jul 1947.

16914.2 Nadine⁶ PURVIANCE (Paul⁵, Nellie⁴, Caroline³, Daniel², John¹) was born 4 Aug 1934, the daughter of Paul PURVIANCE and Hazel McCLELAND. She married **Stanley Paul WEISER** 24 Feb 1952.
ISSUE:
+ .169142.1 David Paul WEISER, born 29 Apr 1953.
+ .169142.2 Dennis Paul WEISER, born 14 Sep 1954.
+ .169142.3 Joy Lynn WEISER, born 30 Sep 1955.

16A11.2 Jon Dennis⁶ FINDLEY (Sidney⁵, George⁴, Rosannah³, Daniel², John¹) was born 13 Jul 1940, the son of Sidney George FINDLEY and Grace Ella ARMSTRONG. He married **Janelle WARREN** 24 May 1971. She was born 15 Mar 1945. Jon has been a school teacher and an editor. Currently he works for the EPA. Jon and Jannelle live in Tempe, Ariz. He has submitted a lot of Findley information, and we thank him for sharing the old family stories. [*Family group sheet submitted by Jon Findley*]
ISSUE:

.16A112.1 Benjamin FINDLEY, born 16 Oct 1988.

16A13.1 Marcia Mae[6] FINDLEY (Craig[5], George[4], Rosannah[3], Daniel[2], John[1]) was born 3 May 1945, the daughter of Craig Wallace FINDLEY and Marian SMITH. She married (1) **Donald WEBER** 17 Dec 1966; they divorced. Marcia married (2) **Richard WICKS**.

ISSUE of Donald and Marcia:
.16A131.1 Christopher Greg WEBER, born 9 Apr 1969.
.16A131.2 Andrea Paige WEBER, born 5 Oct 1970.

16A31.2 Norman Douglas[6] STEFFENSON (Helen[5], Ray[4], Rosannah[3], Daniel[2], John[1]) was born 9 May 1943. He was the son of Rev. A. Douglas STEFFENSON and Helen Faye FINDLEY. He married (1) **Mary Lynn FALKENBERG**. Norman married (2) _____ .

ISSUE of Norman and Mary:
.16A312.1 Rachel STEFFENSON.
ISSUE of Norman and _____:
.16A312.2 Gretchen STEFFENSON.
.16A312.3 Tyler STEFFENSON.

16A31.3 Mary Karen[6] STEFFENSON (Helen[5], Ray[4], Rosannah[3], Daniel[2], John[1]) was born 20 Jan 1946, the daughter of Rev. A. Douglas STEFFENSON and Helen Faye FINDLEY. She married **Craig DENNIS**.

ISSUE:
.16A313.1 Aaron DENNIS.
.16A313.2 Andrew DENNIS.
.16A313.3 Lauren DENNIS.

16A32.1 Jean Pauline[6] FINDLEY (Paul[5], Ray[4], Rosannah[3], Daniel[2], John[1]) was born 21 Jul 1947, the daughter of Paul Ashley FINDLEY and Gertrude MELOS. She married (1) **Robert McCOY** 8 Aug 1970. He was born 3 Jul 1944. Jean married (2) **James F. PILLING** 27 Jul 1991.

ISSUE of Robert and Jean:
.16A321.1 Michael Patrick McCOY, born 7 Nov 1973.
.16A321.2 Timothy Paul McCOY, born 13 Oct 1976.

16A33.1 Paul[6] DIEHL (Wandah[5], Ray[4], Rosannah[3], Daniel[2], John[1]). He was the son of William DIEHL and Wandah Marguerite FINDLEY. He married **Dedra____**.

ISSUE:
.16A331.1 Ethan DIEHL.
.16A331.2 Amy DIEHL.

16A33.2 Mark[6] DIEHL (Wandah[5], Ray[4], Rosannah[3], Daniel[2], John[1]). He was the son of William DIEHL and Wandah Marguerite FINDLEY. He married **Mary BROWN**.

ISSUE:
.16A332.1 Rebekah DIEHL.
.16A332.2 Will DIEHL.

16A33.3 Philip⁶ DIEHL (Wandah⁵, Ray⁴, Rosannah³, Daniel², John¹). He was the son of William DIEHL and Wandah Marguerite FINDLEY. He married **Jacquita** ____.

ISSUE:

.16A333.1 Michael DIEHL.
.16A333.2 Alex DIEHL.

16A41.1 Anne⁶ KINSEY (Hildred⁵, Charles⁴, Rosannah³, Daniel², John¹) was born 3 Sep 1934, the daughter of John T. KINSEY and Hildred Lurene FINDLEY. She married **Floyd WILLIAMS** 20 Dec 1958. He was born 27 Apr 1931.

ISSUE:

.16A411.1 Thomas David WILLIAMS, born 12 Nov 1959.
.16A411.2 John Alfred WILLIAMS, born 31 Jul 1961.
.16A411.3 Kristy Anne WILLIAMS, born 2 Apr 1963.
.16A411.4 Katherine Lynn WILLIAMS, born 17 Sep 1965.

16A41.2 Ruth⁶ KINSEY (Hildred⁵, Charles⁴, Rosannah³, Daniel², John¹) was born 10 Feb 1936, the daughter of John T. KINSEY and Hildred Lurene FINDLEY. She married **Ronald CLINTON** 14 Jun 1958. He was born 4 Apr 1936.

ISSUE:

.16A412.1 Debra Lynn CLINTON, born 5 Apr 1959.
.16A412.2 Carole Anne CLINTON, born 6 Aug 1960.

CHAPTER 7

112111.1 Vera Belle⁷ WALTERS (Beatrice⁶, Virginia⁵, Daniel⁴, Abraham³, Joseph², John¹) was born 29 Sep 1920 in Brown, Darke Co., Oh., the daughter of Lewis Kenneth WALTERS and Beatrice J. PORTER. She married **Ralph William BOOLMAN** 18 Oct 1941 in Union City, Ind.. He was born 20 Jul 1918 in Brown, Darke Co., Oh., the son of Leroy Oscar and Esther (Stump) Boolman. Ralph died 21 Jun 1990 in Dayton, Oh., and was buried 23 Jun 1990 in Teegarden Cemetery, Darke Co., Oh.[*Family group sheet submitted by Vera (Walters) Boolman*]

ISSUE:
+ .1121111.1 Gary K. BOOLMAN, born 6 Aug 1942.
+ .1121111.2 Ronnie E. BOOLMAN, born 28 Jul 1945.

112111.2 Ruby Jeannine⁷ WALTERS (Beatrice⁶, Virginia⁵, Daniel⁴, Abraham³, Joseph², John¹) was born 29 May 1930 in Darke County, Oh., the daughter of Beatrice PORTER. She married (1) **Robert Eugene WALLS** 26 Aug 1950 in Union City, Ind. He was born 16 Jun 1930 in Brown Twp., Darke Co., Oh., the son of Richard WALLS and Molly _____. We are told they have two daughters and one grandchild. Robert died 29 Mar 1975 in Darke County, Oh.

ISSUE:
+ .1121112.1 Penny Ann WALLS, born 6 Nov 1957.
  .1121112.2 Amy Jo WALLS, born 19 Jun 1959 in Darke County, Oh..
  .1121112.3 Todd David WALLS, born 21 Feb 1963 in Darke County, Oh..

112112.1 Janice⁷ WASSON (Erma⁶, Virginia⁵, Daniel⁴, Abraham³, Joseph², John¹) was born 25 Oct 1932 in Darke County, Oh., the daughter of Harold WASSON and Erma Othello BUTT. She married **Joe DWYER**.

ISSUE:
  .1121121.1 Mike DWYER, born 3 Sep 1930.
+ .1121121.2 Jeffrey DWYER, born 18 Aug 1931.

112113.1 Herbert Owen⁷ BUTT (Herbert⁶, Virginia⁵, Daniel⁴, Abraham³, Joseph², John¹) was born 12 Feb 1928 in Darke County, Oh., the son of Herbert Otto BUTT and Hazel BILLHEIMER. He married **Helen Louise SPHAR** 8 Mar 1947. She was born 20 Jun 1930.

ISSUE:
+ .1121131.1 Linda Louise BUTT, born 11 Nov 1947.
+ .1121131.2 Rex Wayne BUTT, born 21 Mar 1950.
  .1121131.3 Pamela BUTT, born 15 Nov 1953 in Troy, Oh. She married Mark Leonard FAVOR 12 Aug 1976. He was born 6 Jan 1954.
+ .1121131.4 Kevin Owen BUTT, born 31 Oct 1956.

112113.2 Phyllis Fern⁷ BUTT (Herbert⁶, Virginia⁵, Daniel⁴, Abraham³, Joseph², John¹) was born 6 Nov 1929 in Troy, Oh., the daughter of Herbert Otto BUTT and Hazel BILLHEIMER. She married **James ANDERSON** 30 Jun 1950.

ISSUE:
.1121132.1 Deborah ANDERSON, born 17 Mar 1958 in Troy, Oh.
+ .1121132.2 Mary ANDERSON, born 7 Oct 1960.
.1121132.3 James ANDERSON, born 14 Sep 1962 in Troy, Oh. He married Karen Drake 1 Sept 1984. She was born 3 May 1962.

112114.1 Wendall Leo[7] **BUTT** (Charles[6], Virginia[5], Daniel[4], Abraham[3], Joseph[2], John[1]) was born 5 Jul 1932 in Union City, Darke Co., Ind., the son of Charles Leo BUTT and Bernice D. TIPPLE. He married **Patty Lori PIERSON** 18 Feb 1931. She was born 23 Dec 1931.
ISSUE:
+ .1121141.1 Errol Dean BUTT, born 8 Oct 1955.
+ .1121141.2 Kevin Myron BUTT, born 28 May 1959.

112114.2 Neil Mitchell[7] **BUTT** (Charles[6], Virginia[5], Daniel[4], Abraham[3], Joseph[2], John[1]) was born 27 Aug 1935 in Union City, Darke Co., Ind., the son of Charles Leo BUTT and Bernice D. TIPPLE. He married **Kay Frances GIRTON** 1 Feb 1955. She was born 11 Mar 1937. Kay died 28 Aug 1980.
ISSUE:
+ .1121142.1 Gregory Scott BUTT, born 6 Aug 1955.
.1121142.2 Brian Neil BUTT, born 12 Jun 1957 in Union City, Ind.

112114.3 Ardith Ann[7] **BUTT** (Charles[6], Virginia[5], Daniel[4], Abraham[3], Joseph[2], John[1]) was born 27 Feb 1937 in Union City, Darke Co., Ind., the daughter of Charles Leo BUTT and Bernice D. TIPPLE. She married **Glenn William DAY** 24 Jul 1955. He was born 10 May 1934.
ISSUE:
+ .1121143.1 Glenna Janice DAY, born 30 Aug 1958.
.1121143.2 Craig Allen DAY, born 26 Sep 1960.
.1121143.3 Kim Jeffrey DAY, born 6 Apr 1962. He married Elaine PEARSON 1 Oct 1988. She was born 2 Jul 1967.

112114.4 Myron Lowell[7] **BUTT** (Charles[6], Virginia[5], Daniel[4], Abraham[3], Joseph[2], John[1]) was born 20 Mar 1940 in Union City, Darke Co., Ind., the son of Charles Leo BUTT and Bernice D. TIPPLE. He married **Sharon Abbott O'DELL** 4 Nov 1975; they divorced. She was born 7 Nov 1946.
ISSUE:
.1121144.1 John Wendell BUTT, born 28 Dec 1976 in Union City, Ind.
.1121144.2 Nathan Brian BUTT, born 30 Jun 1978 in Union City, Ind.

112114.5 Karen Janice[7] **BUTT** (Charles[6], Virginia[5], Daniel[4], Abraham[3], Joseph[2], John[1]) was born 16 Jul 1943 in Union City, Darke Co., Ind., the daughter of Charles Leo BUTT and Bernice D. TIPPLE. She married **James Edward HUMMEL** 16 Jul 1940. He was born 28 Sep 1940.
ISSUE:
.1121145.1 Michael Edward HUMMEL, born 21 Nov 1962 in Union City, Ind.
.1121145.2 Michele Ann HUMMEL, born 9 Feb 1965 in Union City, Ind.
+ .1121145.3 Mark Douglas HUMMEL, born 26 May 1967.
.1121145.4 Mitchell Ray HUMMEL, born 10 Apr 1973 in Union City, Ind.

.1121145.5 Matthew Lee HUMMEL, born 11 Aug 1982 in Union City, Ind.

112115.1 Doyle Freymoth[7] STIVER (Hazel[6], Virginia[5], Daniel[4], Abraham[3], Joseph[2], John[1]) was born 22 Dec 1926 in Darke County, Oh., the son of Walter STIVER and Hazel Fern BUTT. He married **Zelma SMITH**. We are told she died and is buried in the Greenville Cemetery, no other location indicated. He married (2) Jewell_____.

ISSUE:

+ .1121151.1 Wavelyn Evelyn STIVER, born 20 Oct 1951.
+ .1121151.2 Hazel Jeanette STIVER, born 30 Dec 1952.
+ .1121151.3 Linda Kay STIVER, born 7 Oct 1954.
  .1121151.4 Doyle Freymoth STIVER, Jr., born in Darke County, Oh.

112115.2 Jeanette Frances[7] STIVER (Hazel[6], Virginia[5], Daniel[4], Abraham[3], Joseph[2], John[1]) was born 5 May 1933 in Darke County, Oh. She was the daughter of Walter STIVER and Hazel Fern BUTT. She married **Billy MIKESELL**.

ISSUE:

+ .1121152.1 Bruce MIKESELL, born 2 Aug 1951.
+ .1121152.2 Brice MIKESELL, born 28 Jul 1954.
+ .1121152.3 Jodena MIKESELL, born 14 Nov 1956.

112115.3 Ronald Farrell[7] STIVER (Hazel[6], Virginia[5], Daniel[4], Abraham[3], Joseph[2], John[1]) was born 21 Oct 1938 in Darke County, Oh., the son of Walter STIVER and Hazel Fern BUTT. He married **Carolyn WYMER** 7 Jun 1959.

ISSUE:

.1121153.1 Jason Lee STIVER, born 12 Aug 1973 in Darke County, Oh.

112115.4 Tony Faye[7] STIVER (Hazel[6], Virginia[5], Daniel[4], Abraham[3], Joseph[2], John[1]) was born 15 Sep 1947 in Darke County, Oh., the son of Walter STIVER and Hazel Fern BUTT. He married (1) **Gwen WARREN**; they divorced. Tony married (2) **Kay____**.

ISSUE of Tony and Gwen:

.1121154.1 Jeffery Scott STIVER, born 21 Jun 1969 in Darke County, Oh.
.1121154.2 Gregory STIVER, born 28 Jul 1971 in Greenville, Oh.

ISSUE of Tony and Kay:

.1121154.3 Trinity Faye STIVER, born 7 Nov 1975 in Greenville, Oh.
.1121154.4 Toni Frances STIVER, born 7 Jul 1877 in Mi.

112116.1 Veo[7] ROSE (Evelyn[6], Virginia[5], Daniel[4], Abraham[3], Joseph[2], John[1]) was born 20 Sep 1932 in Union City, Oh., the daughter of George ROSE and Evelyn Pauline BUTT. She married **Carl HENRY** 19 Dec 1952.

ISSUE:

.1121161.1 Gary HENRY, born 27 Aug 1953 in Union City, Ind.
.1111161.2 Tony HENRY, born 14 Nov 1971 in Union City, Ind.

112116.2 Gene[7] ROSE (Evelyn[6], Virginia[5], Daniel[4], Abraham[3], Joseph[2], John[1]) was born 27 Aug 1942 in Union City, Oh., the son of George ROSE and Evelyn Pauline BUTT. He married **Janet PINGRY** 8 Oct 1960.

ISSUE:

+ .1121162.1 Tina ROSE, born 17 Apr 1962.
.1221162.2 Eric ROSE, born 7 Dec 1964, Union City, Ind.

112122.1 Ted⁷ STRAIT (Echo⁶, Ira⁵, Daniel⁴, Abraham³, Joseph², John¹) was born 18 Jun 1937 in Darke County, Oh., the son of Forest STRAIT and Echo RITTGERS. He married **Wilma RAPP** 23 Feb 1958.

ISSUE:
+ .1121221.1 Scott STRAIT, born 14 Aug 1960.
.1121221.2 David STRAIT, born 2 Dec 1961 in Darke County, Oh.

112124.1 Sharon⁷ RITTGERS (Daniel⁶, Ira⁵, Daniel⁴, Abraham³, Joseph², John¹) was born 24 May 1935, the daughter of Daniel RITTGERS and Pauline MILLER. She married **Bob DWYER** 26 Nov 1955.

ISSUE:
.1121241.1 Bruce DWYER, born 9 Aug 1958. He married Katy ULE.
.1121241.2 Ryan Michel DWYER, born 27 Mar 1987.
.1121241.3 Lisa Michelle DWYER, born 22 Apr 1960. She married Dick SNODGRASS May 1988.

1121124.2 Shelia⁷ RITTGERS (Daniel⁶, Ira⁵, Daniel⁴, Abraham³, Joseph², John¹) was born 24 Jun 1937, the daughter of Daniel RITTGERS and Pauline MILLER. She married (1) _____ **ELLIOT**; they divorced. Shelia married (2) **Larry WILSON**. She married (3) **Rick HOCKER** 11 Oct 1986.

ISSUE:
.1121242.1 Larry Craig ELLIOT, born 21 Jun 1960.
.1121242.2 Sandra Renee ELLIOT, born 31 Jul 1965.

112131.1 Buddy⁷ DANCER (Helen⁶, Minnie⁵, Daniel⁴, Abraham³, Joseph², John¹). He was the son of Everett DANCER and Helen LIVINGSTON. He married **Barbara MARKWITH** 17 Jan 1965. She was born 3 Dec 1945.

ISSUE:
.1121311.1 Duane DANCER, born 16 Jan 1966 in Darke County, Oh.
.1121311.2 Dina DANCER, born 24 Apr 1968, died 3 Aug 1970.
+ .1121311.3 Diane DANCER, born 7 Jul 1974.

112132.1 Sandre Lee⁷ HART (Willis⁶, Minnie⁵, Daniel⁴, Abraham³, Joseph², John¹) was born 31 Oct 1944 in Darke Co County, Oh. She was the daughter of Willis Paul HART and Betty Eileen ROGERS. She married **Ivan John BALTES**; they divorced.

ISSUE:
.1121321.1 Alyssa Ann BALTES, born 5 Oct 1963. She married Jerry BLINN 21 Jun 1986.
.1121321.2 John Robert BALTES, born 11 Feb 1966. He married Angela Marie____.

.112132.2 Jerlyne Kay⁷ HART (Willis⁶, Minnie⁵, Daniel⁴, Abraham³, Joseph², John¹) was born 18 Dec 1942 in Darke Co County, Oh., the daughter of Willis Paul HART and Betty Eileen ROGERS. She married **Jerome Paul MONNIN** 21 Sep 1963.

ISSUE:
.1121322.1 Jerome Paul MONNIN, Jr., born 22 Dec 1963, died 12 Apr 1980.

.1121322.2 Mark Andrew MONNIN, born 11 Jan 1965.
.1121322.3 Edward Joseph MONNIN, born 1 Nov 1968.
.1121322.4 Jeffrey Lee MONNIN, born 12 Apr 1970.

112133.2 Terry Duane[7] **MENDENHALL** (Violet[6], Minnie[5], Daniel[4], Abraham[3], Joseph[2], John[1]) was born 29 Aug 1941 in Union City, Randolph Co., Ind., the son of Gerald Eugene MENDENHALL and Violet Marcella HART. He married **Sherry Lynn DICKEY** 29 Jul 1988. She was born 22 Aug 1944.

ISSUE:
.1121332.1 Larry Eugene MENDENHALL, born 7 Jun 1963. He married Kimberly Lynn POAD 25 Jun 1988. She was born 2 Nov 1965.
.1121332.2 Lori Ann MENDENHALL, born 5 Jul 1966. She married Dale Eugene BREYMIER 20 Jun 1987. He was born 2 Jun 1964.

112134.1 Connie[7] **WILCOX** (Betty[6], Minnie[5], Daniel[4], Abraham[3], Joseph[2], John[1]) was born 28 Jun 1947 in Union City, Randolph Co., Ind., the daughter of Franklin WILCOX and Betty HART. She married **James DUNN**. He was born 30 Sep 1955.

ISSUE:
.1121341.1 Jacquelin Renee DUNN, born 28 Feb 1983.
.1121341.2 Jameson Bradley DUNN, born 25 May 1987.

112134.2 Steven[7] **WILCOX** (Betty[6], Minnie[5], Daniel[4], Abraham[3], Joseph[2], John[1]) was born 23 Mar 1950 in Union City, Randolph Co., Ind., the son of Franklin WILCOX and Betty HART. He married **Linda COTTER** 21 Sep 1974. She was born 14 Nov 1951.

ISSUE:
.1121342.1 Brett Steven WILCOX, born 2 Sep 1976.
.1121342.2 Keith Andrew WILCOX, born 26 Jan 1979.
.1121342.3 Amy Marie WILCOX, born 11 Jun 1983.

112135.1 Karen Sue[7] **WENGER** (Wilma[6], Minnie[5], Daniel[4], Abraham[3], Joseph[2], John[1]) was born 5 Oct 1946 in Union City, Randolph Co., Ind., the daughter of Glenn Eugene WENGER and Wilma Wavelene HART. She married **Dennis Martin TIPPLE** 26 Feb 1965. He was born 13 Nov 1945.

ISSUE:
.1121351.1 Kirby Gene TIPPLE, born 8 Nov 1965. He married Marjorie Low OREN 21 Aug 1987. She was born 21 Jan 1965.

112135.2 Randy Gene[7] **WENGER** (Wilma[6], Minnie[5], Daniel[4], Abraham[3], Joseph[2], John[1]) was born 19 Sep 1950 in Union City, Randolph Co., Ind., the son of Glenn Eugene WENGER and Wilma Wavelene HART. He married (1) **Joyce Elaine ADDINGTON** 19 Oct 1968; they divorced. Randy married (2) **Roberta LaVonne** 22 Jun 1974. She was born 5 Feb 1955.

ISSUE of Randy and Joyce:
.1121352.1 Amy Jo WENGER, born 2 May 1969.
.1121352.2 Jennifer Elaine WENGER, born 26 Feb 1971.

ISSUE of Randy and Roberta:
.1121352.3 Rachel Nicole WENGER, born 4 Feb 1977.
.1121352.4 Robert Eugene WENGER, born 26 Feb 1980.

112135.3 Denise Ann[7] WENGER (Wilma[6], Minnie[5], Daniel[4], Abraham[3], Joseph[2], John[1]) was born 5 Nov 1955 in Union City, Randolph Co., Ind., the daughter of Glenn Eugene WENGER and Wilma Wavelene HART. She married (1) **Robert Alan ENICKS** 14 Feb 1975; they divorced. He was born 24 Dec 1947. Denise married (2) **Raymond Dee RUDY** 31 May 1986. He was born 24 Feb 1939.

ISSUE:
.1121353.1 Cary Robert ENICKS, born 23 Aug 1975.

112141.1 Charles Henry[7] RITTGERS (Perry[6], Perry[5], Daniel[4], Abraham[3], Joseph[2], John[1]) was born 26 Feb 1951, the son of Perry J. RITTGERS and Ilse LEOPOLD. He married **Ellen BISCOTTI**. She was born 9 Aug 1953.

ISSUE:
.1121411.1 Charles Matthew RITTGERS, born 31 May 1983.
.1121411.2 Anne Claire Elizabeth RITTGERS, born 13 May 1983.

112142.1 Meta Sue[7] RITTGERS (James[6], Perry[5], Daniel[4], Abraham[3], Joseph[2], John[1]). She was the daughter of James RITTGERS and Geraldine ZERRING. She married (1) _____ **HIATT**. Meta married (2) **Jerry LIVINGSTON**.

ISSUE of ___ and Meta:
.1121421.1 Eric HIATT.

ISSUE:
.1121421.2 Jamie LIVINGSTON.
.1121421.3 Shane LIVINGSTON.

112142.2 Bonnie[7] RITTGERS (James[6], Perry[5], Daniel[4], Abraham[3], Joseph[2], John[1]). She was the daughter of James RITTGERS and Geraldine ZERRING. She married **Paul BLANKENBAKER**.

ISSUE:
.1121422.1 Michelle BLANKENBAKER.
.1121422.2 Heidi BLANKENBAKER.

112321.1 Stephen Vernon[7] RITTGERS (Joe[6], Vernon[5], Samuel[4], Abraham[3], Joseph[2], John[1]) was born 17 Nov 1955. He was the son of Joe Franklin RITTGERS and Jenny Louise HRENCHE. He married **Tamara FRAZIER** 4 Mar 1981. She was born 8 Mar 1958.

ISSUE:
.1123211.1 Christina Renee RITTGERS, born 30 Aug 1981.

112322.1 Michael David[7] McGRIFF (Roberta[6], Vernon[5], Samuel[4], Abraham[3], Joseph[2], John[1]) was born 28 Jul 1950. He was the son of Charles Edward McGRIFF and Roberta Ruth RITTGERS. He married **Debra Lynn EDWARDS** 25 Jun 1977. She was born 21 Aug 1956.

ISSUE:
.1123221.1 Charles Edward McGRIFF, born 14 Sep 1985.
.1123221.2 Chelsie Lynn McGRIFF, born 3 Jan 1988.

112322.2 Melissa Ann[7] McGRIFF (Roberta[6], Vernon[5], Samuel[4], Abraham[3], Joseph[2], John[1]) was born 22 Feb 1961. She was the daughter of Charles Edward McGRIFF and Roberta Ruth RITTGERS. She married ___ OLAYA.

ISSUE:

.1123222.1 James Joham OLAYA, born 5 Apr 1988.

116131.1 Robert Eugene[7] BIGHAM (Ruth[6], Willard[5], George[4], Anna[3], Joseph[2], John[1]) was born 18 Sep 1935 in Rockbridge, Hocking Co., Oh., the son of Pearl Donald BIGHAM and Ruth Marie GROVE. He married **Mary Kathleen McDANIEL** 21 Feb 1958 in Maysville, Ky. She was born 20 Apr 1938 in Circleville, Pickaway Co., Oh. We thank Robert for the information on this line.[Bigham]

ISSUE:

+ .1161311.1 Robert Willard BIGHAM, born 2 Feb 1960.
+ .1161311.2 Randy Lee BIGHAM, born 29 Aug 1961.
+ .1161311.3 Beth Renee BIGHAM, born 2 Sep 1963.

116131.2 Ronald Lee[7] BIGHAM (Ruth[6], Willard[5], George[4], Anna[3], Joseph[2], John[1]) was born 4 May 1937 in Fairfield County, Oh., the son of Pearl Donald BIGHAM and Ruth Marie GROVE. He married **Mary Louise WILLIAMS**. She was born 1938. [Bigham]

ISSUE:

.1161312.1 Jan BIGHAM, born 1959.
+ .1161312.2 Kathy Lee BIGHAM, born 1960.
.1161312.3 Carla Louise BIGHAM. She married Graig Eugene POSTON. He was born 1959.
.1161312.4 Doug BIGHAM, born 1962.
.1161312.5 Darla BIGHAM, born 1963.

116131.4 Larry George[7] BIGHAM (Ruth[6], Willard[5], George[4], Anna[3], Joseph[2], John[1]) was born 14 Aug 1943 in Fairfield Co., Oh., the son of Pearl Donald BIGHAM and Ruth Marie GROVE. He married **Dixie Lee DeLONG**. She was born 1947. Larry died Aug 1981 in Fairfield County, Oh, and was buried in Fairview Cem., Hocking Co., Oh. [Bigham]

ISSUE:

.1161314.1 Georgie BIGHAM.
.1161314.2 Larry BIGHAM.

116134.1 Roderick Elsworth[7] GLENN (Stella[6], Willard[5], George[4], Anna[3], Joseph[2], John[1]) . He is the son of Harold Russell GLENN and Stella Mae GROVE. He married **Joyce KARSHNER**. [Bigham]

ISSUE:

.1161341.1 Rory Ann GLENN.
.1161341.2 Blaine GLENN.

116134.4 Vicki Jean[7] GLENN (Stella[6], Willard[5], George[4], Anna[3], Joseph[2], John[1]) was born 31 May 1946 in Fairfield Co., Oh., the daughter of Harold Russel GLENN and Stella Mae GROVE. He married **Joyce KARSHNER**. [Bigham]

ISSUE:

.1161344.1 Kelly LINEHAN.

116921.2 Jennifer Lee⁷ COURNOYER (Robert⁶, Helen⁵, Rosetta⁴, Anna³ , Joseph², John¹) was born 1 Jul 1958 in Dallas, Dallas Co., Tx., the daughter of Robert Mercier COURNOYER and Janeave Edna WRIGHT. She married **Gary Louis SIEB** 9 Dec 1988 in Dallas, Dallas Co., Tx. He was born about 1947 in Mi. [Bigham/Berens]

ISSUE:

.1169212.1 Robert Warren SIEB, born 17 Nov 1990 in Dallas, Dallas Co., Tx. [Bigham/Berens]

116922.1 Gregory Philip⁷ POULEN (Rosemary⁶, Helen⁵, Rosetta⁴, Anna³ , Joseph², John¹) was born 5 Aug 1952 in Long Beach, Los Angeles Co., Ca., the son of Philip S. POULEN and Rosemary Jean COURNOYER. He married **Nanci Ann LUDOVISE** 20 Jan 1979 in Tustin, Orange Co., Ca. She was born 21 Oct 1957 in Burbank, Los Angeles Co., Ca. [Berens]

ISSUE:

.1169221.1 Shawn Samuel POULEN, born 16 Nov 1980 in S. Lake Tahoe, El Dorado Co, Ca.
.1169221.2 Corey James POULEN, born 3 Nov 1982 in S. Lake Tahoe, El Dorado Co., Ca.

116922.2 Lisa Leone⁷ POULEN (Rosemary⁶, Helen⁵, Rosetta⁴, Anna³ , Joseph², John¹) was born 5 Apr 1956 in Long Beach, Los Angeles Co., Ca., the daughter of Philip S. POULEN and Rosemary Jean COURNOYER. She married **Michael Leigh McKINNON** 26 Mar 1983 in Tustin, Orange Co., Ca. He was born 4 Apr 1955 in Riverside, Riverside Co., Ca. [Berens]

ISSUE:

.1169222.1 Marcus Leigh McKINNON, born 6 Feb 1986 in S. Lake Tahoe, El Dorado Co., Ca.
.1169222.2 Britanny Rose McKINNON, born 1 Aug 1989 in S. Lake Tahoe, El Dorado Co., Ca.

121712.1 Susan⁷ FINNEY (Glen⁶, Nellie⁵, Sarah⁴, Samuel³, Jacob², John¹). She was the daughter of Glen Jackson FINNEY and Marjorie HART. She married **Tim WHERRY**.

ISSUE:

.1217121.1 Patrick WHERRY.
.1217121.2 Kevin Glen WHERRY.

121714.1 Stanley Michael⁷ THOMAS (Jennie⁶, Nellie⁵, Sarah⁴, Samuel³, Jacob², John¹) was born 6 Nov 1950 in Kansas City, Jackson Co., Mo., the son of Stanley Argus THOMAS and Jennie Margaret FINNEY. He married **Martha Jane HOLLISTER** 20 May 1979; they divorced. Family record submitted by Margaret (Finney) Thomas in 1994. MARRIAGE: Ibid

ISSUE:

.1217141.1 Eric Michael THOMAS, born 17 Oct 1986.
.1217141.2 Bradley Scott THOMAS, born 20 Jul 1987.

121714.2 Patrick Alan⁷ THOMAS (Jennie⁶, Nellie⁵, Sarah⁴, Samuel³, Jacob², John¹) was born 18 Dec 1952 in Kansas City, Jackson Co., Mo., the son of Stanley Argus THOMAS and Jennie Margaret FINNEY. He married **Marianna BREDWELL** 4 Sep 1976. [*Family record submitted by Margaret (Finney) Thomas in 1994*]

ISSUE:

.1217142.1 Adam Patrick THOMAS, born 1 May 1985.
.1217142.2 Alan Christopher THOMAS, born 1 Dec 1986.

121714.3 Brian Virden[7] THOMAS (Jennie[6], Nellie[5], Sarah[4], Samuel[3], Jacob[2], John[1]) was born 16 Jan 1962 in Independence, Jackson Co., Mo., the son of Stanley Argus THOMAS and Jennie Margaret FINNEY. He married **Lisa Jo Van DIVER** 24 Oct 1987.*[Family record submitted by Margaret (Finney) Thomas in 1994]*
ISSUE:
.1217143.1 Blake Andrew THOMAS, born 15 Aug 1989.
.1217143.2 Austin Jentry THOMAS, born 20 May 1992.

121715.1 Melvin Jack[7] ROGERS (Mary[6], Nellie[5], Sarah[4], Samuel[3], Jacob[2], John[1]) was born 9 Sep 1944 in Trenton, Grundy Co., Mo., the son of Melvin Don ROGERS and Mary Frances FINNEY. He married **Carolyn Sue WHITEHEAD** 20 Jul 1967 in Colorado Springs, El Paso, Co.; they divorced. She was born 13 Jan 1946 in Ore. We are told he lives Pleasant Hill, Cass Co., Mo.*[Family record submitted by Mary (Finney) Rogers in 1994]*
ISSUE:
.1217151.1 Samantha Kay Ferroire ROGERS, born 26 Oct 1966 in Colorado Springs, El Paso Co., Colo.
+ .1217151.2 Jacquelyn Suzanne ROGERS, born 31 Mar 1968.
.1217151.3 Jessica Renee ROGERS, born 9 Jul 1976 in Kansas City, Jackson Co., Mo.
.1217151.4 Richard Donald ROGERS, born 10 Jul 1978 in Independence, Jackson Co., Mo.
.1217151.5 Sadie Elizabeth ROGERS, born 19 Apr 1983 in Harrison, Cass Co., Mo.

121715.3 Gary Lynn[7] ROGERS (Mary[6], Nellie[5], Sarah[4], Samuel[3], Jacob[2], John[1]) was born 16 Dec 1952 in Yakima, Yakima Co., Wash., the son of Melvin Don ROGERS and Mary Frances FINNEY. He married (1) **Pam WINGATE** 20 Jan 1973; they divorced. Gary married (2) **Belinda KICK** 18 May 1979 in Independence, Jackson Co., Mo. He lives in Independence, Mo. *[Family record submitted by Mary (Finney) Rogers in 1994]*
ISSUE of Gary and Pam:
.1217153.1 Melissa Lynn ROGERS, born 12 Jul 1976.

121722.1 Marjorie[7] ARNETT (Anna[6], Agnes[5], Sarah[4], Samuel[3], Jacob[2], John[1]) was born 30 Apr 1946, the daughter of Raymond Allen ARNETT and Anna Lou PEACOCK. She married (1) **Carl Clifton WILSON**; they divorced. Marjorie married (2) **William POWELL**. Marjorie received her PhD. in Urban Education in Nov. of 1992, from University of Wisconsin-Milwaukee. She currently lives in Redlands, Wisc.
ISSUE of Carl and Marjorie:
.1217221.1 Ronald Roy WILSON, born 1966, died 1989. He was killed in an auto accident.
ISSUE of William and Marjorie:
.1217221.2 Chad William POWELL.

121722.3 Dale[7] ARNETT (Anna[6], Agnes[5], Sarah[4], Samuel[3], Jacob[2], John[1]). He was the son of Raymond Allen ARNETT and Anna Lou PEACOCK. He married (1) **Dawn Elaine HOBBS**; they divorced. Dale married (2) **Linda M. "Joy" BARTON**. Dale is an attorney. Wife Joy works for him. Dale and Joy also raise Suffolk Sheep.
ISSUE of Dale:
.1217223.1 Abbie Michelle LOUGH, born 22 May 1982.
ISSUE of Dale and Dawn:
.1217223.2 Joy Kathleen ARNETT.

ISSUE of Dale and Linda:
.1217223.3 Justin James ARNETT, died in infancy.
.1217223.4 Brandon Ray ARNETT, born 24 Oct 1991.

121722.4 John[7] **ARNETT** (Anna[6], Agnes[5], Sarah[4], Samuel[3], Jacob[2], John[1]). He was the son of
Raymond Allen ARNETT and Anna Lou PEACOCK. He married **Susan CRISAN**. They live
in Minn, where he is a vice-president of Serving Software.
ISSUE:
.1217224.1 Clay Parker ARNETT.

121723.1 Karen[7] **PEACOCK** (Robert[6], Agnes[5], Sarah[4], Samuel[3], Jacob[2], John[1]). She is the
daughter of Robert Alva PEACOCK and Elizabeth Lee WARD. She married **Karl HARTMAN**.
Karen lives in Illinois.[Hartman, p. 626]
ISSUE:
.1217231.1 Erich Robert HARTMAN, born 13 May 1991.

129811.1 Warren Thomas[7] **JONES** (Larry[6], Dorothy[5], John[4], Perry[3], Jacob[2], John[1]) was born
30 Nov 1961 in Ft. Riley, Geary Co., Ks., the son of Larry Lee JONES and Anna Corrinne
ATTWATER. He married **Barbara Ann YOHN** 1 Aug 1987 in Prairie Village, Johnson, Ks.
She was born 19 Feb 1965 in Prairie Village, Johnson Co., Ks., the daughter of Billy S. and
Sharon R. (Keif) Yohn. Barbara is a Registered Nurse. Warren received his degree in DVM
from the University of Missouri, 1988. Served as Captain in the U.S. Army, Hanau, Germany.
He continues in the Army and is serving at Fort Leavenwork, Ks.(1993)[*Family record supplied
by Anna C. (Attwater) Jones*]
ISSUE:
.1298111.1 Matthew Ryan JONES, born 16 Nov 1991 in Frankfurt, Germany.
.1298111.2 Nicholas Austin JONES, born 6 Feb 1995, Kansas City, Jackson Co., Mo.

129813.1 Jerry Ray[7] **DeVAULT** (Sharon[6], Dorothy[5], John[4], Perry[3], Jacob[2], John[1]) was born
20 Jul 1962 in Hutchinson, Reno Co., Ks., the son of Bob Dean DeVAULT and Sharon Rae
JONES. He married **Karyn Elizabeth SWANSON** 27 May 1989 in Kansas City, Jackson, Mo..
She was born 15 Nov 1961 in New York, Richman Co., NY., the daughter of Harold and Sara
J. (Blakmen) Swanson. Jerry is a CPA and Karyn is an R.N. They live in Kansas City, Mo.
[*Family record supplied by Anna C. (Attwater) Jones*]
ISSUE:
.1298131.1 James Ross DeVAULT, born 23 May 1992 in Kansas City, Jackson Co. Mo.
.1298131.2 John Arthur DeVAULT, born 5 Aug 1995.
.1298131.3 Corinne Elizabeth DeVAULT, born 5 Aug 1995.

129813.2 Edie Beth[7] **DeVAULT** (Sharon[6], Dorothy[5], John[4], Perry[3], Jacob[2], John[1]) was born
28 Aug 1965 in Hutchinson, Ks., the daughter of Bob Dean DeVAULT and Sharon Rae JONES.
She married **Mark Andrew LARSON** 5 Aug 1989 in Hutchinson, Ks. He was born 31 Oct
1965 in Riley, Riley Co., Ks., the son of Verlin and Paula (Phillips) Larson. Edie is a teacher
of learning disabled children, receiving her Masters Degree in May, 1992. Mark is a
veterinarian.[*Family record supplied by Anna C. (Attwater) Jones*]
ISSUE:
.1298132.1 James Michael LARSON, born 13 Sep 1992 in Peoria, Ill.

.1298132.2 Sarah Marie LARSON, born 30 Aug 1994, Peoria, Ill.

129813.3 Larry Dean DeVAULT (Sharon[6], Dorothy[5], John[4], Perry[3], Jacob[2], John[1]) , born 25 Sep 1968 in Hutchinson, Ks., the son of Bob Dean DeVAULT and Sharon Rae JONES. He married Jennifer PENINGER 18 Jul 1992 in Hutchinson, Ks. She was born 30 Oct 1969 in Levelland, Hockley Co., Tx., the daughter of Millard E. and Linda Kay (Reaves) Peninger. He is a graduate of Kansas State University, 1992, and works in sales. Jenniger is a speech pathologist.

ISSUE:

.1298133.1 Renee Elizabeth DeVAULT, born 10 Sept 1996, Hutchinson, Reno Co., Ks.

12H612.1 Robin Dawn[7] RITTGERS (George[6], Roland[5], Ernest[4], Benjamin[3], Jacob[2], John[1]) was born 1972, the daughter of George Ernest RITTGERS and Diane Marie LUEDTKE. She married **Randall Bryan YARDLEY**.

ISSUE:

.12H6121.1   Tyler Bryan YARDLEY, born 1996.

12J121.1 Vicky Lynn[7] MYRICK (Naomi[6], Maynard[5], Glen[4], George[3], Jacob[2], John[1]) was born 4 May 1957, the daughter of James MYRICK and Naomi Ruth RITTGERS. She married **Carl "David" WALTERS** 2 Apr 1983. He was born 12 Sep 1954.

ISSUE:

.12J1211.1 Jenna Lynn WALTERS, born 15 Jul 1985.
.12J1211.2 Craig David WALTERS, born 16 Mar 1987.

12J121.2 James Max[7] MYRICK, Jr. (Naomi[6], Maynard[5], Glen[4], George[3], Jacob[2], John[1]) was born 26 Jul 1964, the son of James MYRICK and Naomi Ruth RITTGERS. He married **Natalie WILLIAMS** 29 Jul 1981. She was born 21 Oct 1961.

ISSUE:

.12J1212.1 Katie Elizabeth MYRICK, born 19 Mar 1984.
.12J1212.2 Jamie Nicholl MYRICK, born 22 Jun 1988.

12J121.3 Lana Yvette[7] MYRICK (Naomi[6], Maynard[5], Glen[4], George[3], Jacob[2], John[1]) was born 24 Mar 1964, the daughter of James MYRICK and Naomi Ruth RITTGERS. She married **Finley MASQUAT** 30 Jan 1985. He was born 6 Sep 1959.

ISSUE:

.12J1213.1 Lindsey Marie MASQUAT, born 31 Aug 1987.

12J124.1 Marsha Ann[7] CLINE (Nettie[6], Maynard[5], Glen[4], George[3], Jacob[2], John[1]) was born 13 Sep 1962, the daughter of John Marshall CLINE, Sr. and Nettie Edith RITTGERS. She married **Clayton Lee HALL**. He was born 14 Jun 1953.

ISSUE:

.12J1241.1 Daniel Wayne HALL, born 24 Jul 1982.
.12J1241.2 Wayne Andrew HALL, born 15 Mar 1984.
.12J1241.3 Matthew Clayton HALL, born 17 Sep 1987.

12J124.2 John Marshall[7] CLINE, Jr. (Nettie[6], Maynard[5], Glen[4], George[3], Jacob[2], John[1]) was born 27 Mar 1964, the son of John Marshall CLINE, Sr. and Nettie Edith RITTGERS. He married **Carolyn Kay BULLARD**. She was born 14 Nov 1965.

ISSUE:

.12J1242.1 Rebecca Lynn CLINE, born 25 Apr 1986.

.12J1242.2 Benjamin Marshal CLINE, born 19 Sep 1988.

12J124.3 Mark Allen[7] CLINE (Nettie[6], Maynard[5], Glen[4], George[3], Jacob[2], John[1]) was born 20 Jun 1966, the son of John Marshall CLINE, Sr. and Nettie Edith RITTGERS. He married **Christina Marie (Burcham) ROTENEK**. She was born 15 Nov 1966.

ISSUE:

.12J1243.1 Nicholas Allen CLINE, born 21 Sep 1989.

12J124.4 Susan Rene[7] CLINE (Nettie[6], Maynard[5], Glen[4], George[3], Jacob[2], John[1]) was born 3 Sep 1968, the daughter of John Marshall CLINE, Sr. and Nettie Edith RITTGERS. She married **Larry Dale AMIS**. He was born 3 Feb 1964.

ISSUE:

.12J1244.1 Sarah Amanda AMIS.

.12J1244.2 Zachariah Thomas AMIS, born 18 Mar 1989.

1344A1.2 Lynn Marie[7] RITTGERS (Richard[6], Walter[5], Isaac[4], Tobias[3], John, Jr.[2], John[1]) was born 16 Jun 1962 in Columbus, Franklin Co., Oh., the daughter of Richard Charles RITTGERS and Della Marie DUFFY. Lynn graduated from junior college and is currently employed as Supervising Storekeeper for a large insurance company in Columbus, Oh. She married **Jeffrey Lewis THOMAS** 4 Aug 1985 in Columbus, Franklin, Oh. He was born 31 May 1957 in Lancaster, Fairfield Co., Oh.[Family Group Sheet submitted by father, Richard Rittgers]

ISSUE:

.1344A12.1 Jessica Marie THOMAS, born 13 Aug 1986 in Columbus, Franklin, Oh.

.1344A12.2 Bradley Matthew THOMAS, born 21 Apr 1990 in Columbus, Franklin, Oh.

134751.1 Lawrence Russell[7] RITTGERS (Harley[6], hugh[5], albert[4], tobias[3], John[2], John[1]) was born 17 Jul 1948 in Bremerton, Kitsap, Wa.. He was the son of Harley Maywood RITTGERS and Mary Lee Applegate. "Russ" graduated from Ohio State with a B.A. in Slavic languages (Russian) and an MBA in Finance. He recently retired with 25 years in the U.S. Navy Reserve. Russ has traveled through the Soviet Union in 1970, and has been just about all over the world. Even though he isn't a Catholic, he accepted the opportunity to attend a Papal audience with Pope John Paul II at the Vatican. When he got there the huge Chapel was filled and, he found himself pressed against the back wall. As he was thinking he would only see a small figure in the far distance, the door next to him opened and the Pope was escorted in! Russ was one of the first he touched and Blessed. He participated in a project to update Navy telecommunication manuals prior to the Persian Gulf War 1990-1991. Russ is a CPA, and lives in Hilliard, Oh. He married **Rita Gene CONARD** 21 May 1983 in Columbus, Franklin Co., Oh. She was born 26 Nov 1948 in Columbus, Oh., the daughter of John Calvin and Ruby Elizabeth (Smith) Conrad. She comes from very early German pioneer stock, being a descendant of Thones Cunraed, who came from Kreutzfeld, Ger. in 1683. Rita is a bookkeeper and enjoys singing in the Methodist Church Choir.

ISSUE:
.1347511.1 James Russell RITTGERS, born 1 Apr 1986 in Columbus, Franklin Co., Oh. "Jimmy" enjoys computer games, and science fiction. He was able to discuss his Rittgers lineage at great length at the 1997 Rittgers Reunion in Branson, Mo.
.1347511.2 Amanda Elizabeth RITTGERS, born 4 Jun 1991 in Columbus, Franklin Co., Oh.

138111.1 Joan Francis[7] **BRIGHT** (Blanche[6], Isaac[5], Mary[4], Anna[3], John[2], John[1]). She was the daughter of Dr. James Donald FRANCIS and Blanche Marguerita BRIGHT.She married **Robert LEALRY**.[Bright, p. 88]

ISSUE:
.13811111 Michael LEALRY.
.13811112 Katherine LEALRY.
.13811113 Ellen LEALRY.
.13811114 Carol LEALRY.
.13811115 Timothy LEALRY.
.13811116 Mary Elizabeth LEALRY.

138111.2 Barbara[7] **FRANCIS** (Blanche[6], Isaac[5], Mary[4], Anna[3], John[2], John[1]). She was the daughter of Dr. James Donald FRANCIS and Blanche Marguerita BRIGHT.She married **Dr. Ernesto J. MORALES**.[Bright, p. 88]

ISSUE:
.1381112.1 Vincent MORALES.
.1381112.2 John MORALES.
.1381112.3 Edesto J. MORALES, Jr.
.1381112.4 Thomas MORALES.

138111.3 James D.[7] **FRANCIS, Jr.** (Blanche[6], Isaac[5], Mary[4], Anna[3], John[2], John[1]). He was the son of Dr. James Donald FRANCIS and Blanche Marguerita BRIGHT.He married **Patience SANGER**; they divorced.[Bright, p. 88]

ISSUE:
.1381113.1 David Christopher FRANCIS.
.1381113.2 Sarah FRANCIS.

138113.1 Terry[7] **BRIGHT** (Glendon[6], Isaac[5], Mary[4], Anna[3], John[2], John[1]). He was the son of Glendon Rolland BRIGHT and Maggie TERRELL. He married **Dorothy Karyl OLSON**.[Bright, p. 88]

ISSUE:
.1381131.1 Adam Scott BRIGHT.
.1381131.2 Andrea Jo BRIGHT.

138113.2 Sherry[7] **BRIGHT** (Glendon[6], Isaac[5], Mary[4], Anna[3], John[2], John[1]). She was the daughter of Glendon Rolland BRIGHT and Maggie TERRELL. She married **Richard KORN, D.D.S.**[Bright, p. 88]

ISSUE:
.1381132.1 Larry KORN.
.1381132.2 Terri KORN.
.1381132.3 Scott KORN.

.1381132.4 Todd KORN.

161421.1 Stephen Ray[7] RITTGERS, Jr. (Stephen[6], Francis[5], Timothy[4], David[3], Daniel[2], John[1]) was born 14 Apr 1971 in Iowa City, Ia., the son of Stephen Ray RITTGERS and Carol WAGNER. He married **Wednesday FISHER**.
ISSUE:
.1614211.1 Christian Wilson RITTGERS, born 7 Apr 1993 in Las Vegas, Clark Co., Nev.

161B41.1 Jean Marie[7] SCOTT (David[6], Hazel[5], Cora[4], David[3], Daniel[2], John[1]) was born 15 Jun 1960 in Newton, Ia., the daughter of David Iri SCOTT and Carolyn Ann CORDS. She married **William Desmond "Billy" SEKEL**.
ISSUE:
.161B411.1 Jeremy Scott SEKEL, born 12 Dec 1982.
.161B411.2 Adam William SEKEL, born 12 Sep 1984 in New Orleans, La.

162121.3 Becky Lynette[7] RITTGERS (Leslie[6], Reuben[5], Ambrose[4], Reuben[3], Daniel[2], John[1]) was born 17 Sep 1973 in Lamar, Kiowa Co., Colo., the daughter of Leslie Milton RITTGERS and Kathryn WILCOX.
ISSUE:
.1621213.1 Matthew Wade RITTGERS, born 5 Mar 1992.

162131.1 Charlene (Brooks)[7] RITTGERS (Robert[6], Luetta[5], Ambrose[4], Reuben[3], Daniel[2], John[1]) was born 28 Oct 1936. She was the daughter of Helen (Hossman) BROOKS and adopted by Robert RITTGERS after their marriage. She married **Devon R. SHIMEK**. He was born 1935.
ISSUE:
.1621311.1 Valerie D. SHIMEK, born 4 Jul 1957.
.1621311.2 Peggy Ann SHIMEK, born 27 Apr 1959.
.1621311.3 Christopher Anthony SHIMEK, born 25 Sep 1960.

162131.2 Charles (Brooks)[7] RITTGERS (Robert[6], Luetta[5], Ambrose[4], Reuben[3], Daniel[2], John[1]). He was the son of Helen (Hossman) BROOKS, and adopted by Robert RITTGERS after their marriage. He married **Gayle BINGHAM** 26 Sep 1959. She was born 21 Dec 1941.
ISSUE:
.1621312.1 Robert Keith RITTGERS, born 18 Jul 1965.

162611.2 Keith LaVerne[7] RITTGERS (Thomas[6], Thomas[5], Maxwell[4], Reuben[3], Daniel[2], John[1]) was born 25 Nov 1947, the son of Thomas Wilson RITTGERS and Zelda Rose HAWBAKER. He married **Ruth Ann RITCHEY**. She was born 3 Nov 1948. They live in San Antonio, Texas.
ISSUE:
.1626112.1 Benjamin Thomas RITTGERS, born 22 Apr 1977. He served in the U.S. Navy.
.1626112.2 Sarah RITTGERS, she is a nursing student.

162611.5 Alice Juanita[7] RITTGERS (Thomas[6], Thomas[5], Maxwell[4], Reuben[3], Daniel[2], John[1]) was born 2 Jul 1951, the daughter of Thomas Wilson RITTGERS and Zelda Rose HAWBAKER. She married **Garron CROSS**. We are told they live in Huston, Texas.

ISSUE:
.1626115.1 Mike CROSS, born 1980.
.1626115.2 Emily CROSS, born 1983.
.1626115.3 Laura CROSS, born 1985.

162612.1 John Parker[7] RITTGERS (Clarence[6], Thomas[5], Maxwell[4], Reuben[3], Daniel[2], John[1]) was born 28 Nov 1952, the son of Clarence John RITTGERS and Mary Elizabeth NOONAN. He married **Catherine Amy MOODY** 3 Feb 1979. Parker is editor of the Rittgers Family Newsletter. He and "Kit" live in Sunnyvale, Ca.
ISSUE:
.1626121.1 Kelly Grace RITTGERS, born 26 Nov 1988.
.1626121.2 Katelyn Gail RITTGERS, born 26 Nov 1988.

162613.1 Philip Bruce[7] RITTGERS, Jr. (Philip[6], Thomas[5], Maxwell[4], Reuben[3], Daniel[2], John[1]) was born 22 May 1960 in Lapeer, Lapeer Co., Mi., the son of Philip Bruce RITTGERS and Ruth LEDERACH. He married **Merti DJELANTIK** 28 Dec 1984 in Mass.. She was born 16 Dec 1962 in Bali, Indonesia. Philip is a metallurgical engineer and is currently in charge of repair parts for jet engines in south-east Asia.[*Family group sheet by Ruth Lederach Rittgers*]
ISSUE:
.1626131.1 Shanti Hope RITTGERS, born 16 Sep 1990 in Bandung, Java.
.1626131.2 Tobias RITTGERS, born 28 Nov 1991 in Bandung, Java.

162616.1 Rebecca Lynn[7] OVERTON (Lois[6], Thomas[5], Maxwell[4], Reuben[3], Daniel[2], John[1]) was born 11 Jun 1953, the daughter of Delbert OVERTON and Lois Elinor RITTGERS. She married _____ **RITTER**.
ISSUE:
.1626161.1 Ronald RITTER.
.1626161.2 James RITTER.

162616.2 Deborah Kay[7] OVERTON (Lois[6], Thomas[5], Maxwell[4], Reuben[3], Daniel[2], John[1]) was born 19 Dec 1954, the daughter of Delbert OVERTON and Lois Elinor RITTGERS. She married _____ **JONES**.
ISSUE:
.1626162.1 Robert JONES.
.1626162.2 Alisha JONES.

162617.1 Carl Robert[7] BLACK (Bessie[6], Thomas[5], Maxwell[4], Reuben[3], Daniel[2], John[1]) was born 2 Jan 1955, the son of Robert "Bob" BLACK and Bessie Louise RITTGERS. He married **Karen** _____. We are told they live in South Dakota and that he is a Chiropractor.
ISSUE:
.1626171.1 Rainy Kay BLACK, born 23 Mar 1982.
.1626171.2 Joby Franklin BLACK, born 28 Aug 1984.

162617.2 Wayne Albert[7] BLACK (Bessie[6], Thomas[5], Maxwell[4], Reuben[3], Daniel[2], John[1]) was born 29 Jun 1956, the son of Robert "Bob" BLACK and Bessie Louise RITTGERS. He married **Dawn**____. We are told they live in South Dakota.
ISSUE:

.1626172.1 Adrienne BLACK.
.1626172.2 Alexandria BLACK.

162617.3 Laurie Ann[7] BLACK (Bessie[6], Thomas[5], Maxwell[4], Reuben[3], Daniel[2], John[1]) was born 23 Dec 1964, the daughter of Robert "Bob" BLACK and Bessie Louise RITTGERS. She married **Robert KARIE**. We are told they live in South Dakota.
ISSUE:
.1626173.1 Robert Alexander KARIE.
.1626173.2 Sam KARIE.

162621.1 Terry Preston[7] Wilcox-RITTGERS (Forest, Jr.[6], Forest[5], Maxwell[4], Reuben[3], Daniel[2], John[1]) was born 3 Jul 1954, the son of Forest Sheldon RITTGERS, Jr. and Sally Preston POSTHILL. He married **Cynthia WILCOX**. He is a psychologist in San Mateo, Ca. Cynthia is finishing up her doctorate in clinical psychology.
ISSUE:
.1626211.1 Nicholas Forest Wilcox-RITTGERS, born about 1989.

162621.2 Scott Courtney[7] RITTGERS (Forest, Jr.[6], Forest[5], Maxwell[4], Reuben[3], Daniel[2], John[1]) was born 7 Dec 1956, the son of Forest Sheldon RITTGERS, Jr. and Sally Preston POSTHILL. He married **Judy _____**. She was born 5 Jan 1957. He is a carpenter and lives in Townsend, Mass.
ISSUE:
.1626212.1 Chad RITTGERS, born 13 Mar 1978.
.1626212.2 Amie RITTGERS, born 30 May 1980. She enjoys playing softball.
.1626212.3 Bryan Courtney RITTGERS, born 11 Dec 1988.

162621.3 Karen Sumner[7] RITTGERS (Forest, Jr.[6], Forest[5], Maxwell[4], Reuben[3], Daniel[2], John[1]). She was the daughter of Forest Sheldon RITTGERS, Jr. and Sally Preston POSTHILL. She married **Marc D. POWELL**. Karen is a teacher. Marc is an engineering designer/ technician. They live in Georgetown, Tx.
ISSUE:
.1626213.1 Daniel Justin POWELL.
.1626213.2 Kathryn Marie POWELL.

162814.1 Lori Lee[7] RITTGERS (Merle[6], Lawrence[5], Jasper[4], Reuben[3], Daniel[2], John[1]) was born 23 Apr 1956, the daughter of Merle Edwin RITTGERS and Rose Ella FINK. She married **William MARTIN** 1976.
ISSUE:
.1628141.1 Angela Michelle MARTIN, born 18 Oct 1976.

162814.2 Karla Rae[7] RITTGERS (Merle[6], Lawrence[5], Jasper[4], Reuben[3], Daniel[2], John[1]) was born 29 May 1957, the daughter of Merle Edwin RITTGERS and Rose Ella FINK. She married **Kenneth Roy SMITH** 24 Sep 1975. He was born 3 Nov 1954.
ISSUE:
.1628142.1 Jennifer Lynn SMITH, born 10 Mar 1976.

162A31.1 William Jeffrey[7] RORABAUGH (William, Jr.[6], William, Sr.[5], Vivian[4], Reuben[3], Daniel[2], John[1]) was born 15 Jul 1965 in Eustis, Lake Co., Fl., the son of William Lysle RORABAUGH, Jr. and Norma Jean WISE. He married **Jennifer VAUGHAN** 30 Sep 1989 in Decatur, Ga. She was born 7 Nov 1962 in Atlanta, Ga., the daughter of Rex and Sacra (Faull) Vaughan. Jeff graduated from U. of Ga. with B.S. in Chemistry, and has his Masters in Operations Production Management. Works for Coca Cola Co., Atlanta, Ga. They currently reside in Lawrenceville, Ga. Jennifer has a degree in education and taught high school.

ISSUE:
.162A311.1   Samantha Joy RORABAUGH, born 28 Jul 1993 in Atlanta, Fulton Co., Ga.
.162A311.2   Nicholas Jeffrey RORABAUGH, born 15 Feb 1996 in Atlanta, Fulton Co., Ga.

162A32.1 Cheryl Denise[7] RICHARDS (Sarah[6], William, Sr.[5], Vivian[4], Reuben[3], Daniel[2], John[1]) was born 3 Mar 1961 in Orlando, Orange Co., Fla., the daughter of Dean RICHARDS and Sarah Ruth RORABAUGH. She married **Joseph Edward DAVIDSON** 11 Apr 1981 in Ocoee, Orange Co., Fla. They currently reside in Clermont, Lake Co., Fla. Ed works in maintenance for a large grocery chain.
•   ISSUE:
.162A321.1   Joseph Edward DAVIDSON, born 15 Aug 1983.
.162A321.2   Keli Rene DAVIDSON, born 19 Jul 1986.

162A32.2 Brenda Diane[7] RICHARDS (Sarah[6], William, Sr.[5], Vivian[4], Reuben[3], Daniel[2], John[1]) was born 12 May 1962 in Orlando, Orange Co., Fla., the daughter of Dean RICHARDS and Sarah Ruth RORABAUGH. She married **Michael Eugene BASS** 24 Jul 1982 in Ocoee, Orange Co., Fla.; divorced. He works in maintenance at Disney's Epcot Center. They live in Ocoee, Fla.
ISSUE:
.162A322.1   Brittney DeAnn BASS, born 2 Feb 1984.
.162A322.2   Megan Elizabeth BASS, born 6 May 1988.
.162A322.3   Justin Michael BASS, born 10 May 1991 in Orlando, Orange Co., Fla.

162A32.3 Sarah Elizabeth[7] RICHARDS (Sarah[6], William, Sr.[5], Vivian[4], Reuben[3], Daniel[2], John[1]) was born 8 Apr 1968 in Orlando, Orange Co., Fla., the daughter of Dean RICHARDS and Sarah Ruth RORABAUGH. She has worked in banking. She married Terran Roy "Terry" FREEMAN 1 June 1996.
ISSUE:
.162A323.1   Blain Allen FREEMAN, born 8 July 1997.

162A41.1 Deborah Elaine[7] RORABAUGH (Philip[6], Philip[5], Vivian[4], Reuben[3], Daniel[2], John[1]) was born 18 Jun 1957 in Nyack, Rockland Co., N.Y., the daughter of Philip Arthur RORABAUGH and Donna Marion KING. She married **Lynn Alan ECKLEBARGER** 7 May 1976 in New Paris, Elkhart Co., Ind. He was born 7 Sep 1954 in Goshen, Elkhart Co., Ind. Lynn is in construction and Debbie is an office secretary.[Interview with Philip Rorabaugh 1992]
ISSUE:
.162A411.1   Eric Lee ECKLEBARGER, born 29 Nov 1978 in Goshen, Elkhart Co., Ind.
.162A411.2   Dustin Alan ECKLEBARGER, born 27 Mar 1981 in Goshen, Elkhart Co., Ind.
.162A411.3   Delania Lynn ECKLEBARGER, born 20 Feb 1984 in Goshen, Elkhart Co., Ind.

162A52.1 Charles Daniel[7] HUNTER (Carolyn[6], Vivian[5], Vivian[4], Reuben[3], Daniel[2], John[1]) was born 11 Nov 1959 in Eustis, Lake Co., Fla., the son of Charles Ellis HUNTER and Carolyn Abigail COX. He married **Cindi Ann WEST** 28 Feb 1981 in Casselberry, Orange Co., Fla.

ISSUE:

.162A521.1   Charles Joseph HUNTER, born 9 Feb 1986 in Winter Park, Orange Co., Fla.
.162A521.2   Daniel Zackery HUNTER, born 26 Mar 1987 in Winter Park, Orange Co., Fla.
.162A521.3   Andrew Xavier HUNTER, born 31 Oct 1990 in Winter Park, Orange Co., Fla.
.162A521.4   Chelsea Amanda HUNTER, born 31 Oct 1990 in Winter Park, Orange Co., Fla.

162D11.1 Linda Ruth[7] PEITZMAN (Lloyd[6], Laura[5], John[4], Reuben[3], Daniel[2], John[1]) was born 21 Feb 1959, the daughter of Lloyd John PEITZMAN and Carol Elizabeth HOLMQUIST. Linda is an M.D. - graduate of U. of Minn. She married (1) **Steven JANOUSEK** 8 May 1983. Linda married (2) **Paul KUNKEL** 19 Oct 1985. He was born 7 Jul 1953. [*Interview with Laura (Rittgers)(Peitzman) Emmert, 1994*]

ISSUE:

.162D111.1   Cassandra Grace KUNKEL, born 1 Oct 1986.
.162D111.2   Alexander James KUNKEL, born 18 Nov 1989.

162D11.3 Robert John[7] PEITZMAN (Lloyd[6], Laura[5], John[4], Reuben[3], Daniel[2], John[1]) was born 10 Mar 1960, the son of Lloyd John PEITZMAN and Carol Elizabeth HOLMQUIST. He married **Carol Joan JOHNSON** 11 Feb 1984.*[Interview with Laura (Rittgers)(Peitzman) Emmert, 1994]*

ISSUE:

.162D113.1   Emily Myrtice PEITZMAN, born 20 Apr 1985.
.162D113.2   Elizabeth Ruth PEITZMAN, born 15 Dec 1987.
.162D113.3   Elysia Charlotte PEITZMAN, born 14 Aug 1990.

167211.1 Janene Alice (Meek)[7] SUMMERSKILL (Lorene[6], Charlotte[5], Grace[4], George[3], Daniel[2], John[1]) was born 22 Jan 1955 in Kansas City, Jackson Co., Mo., the daughter of William Frederick MEEK and Lorene Alice WINELAND. Adopted by step-father, Gordon Summerskill, Sept 1972. She married (1) **Ronald Wayne JAKOBE** 16 Nov 1973 in Raytown, Jackson Co., Mo. He was born 2 Aug 1952, died 4 Aug 1981. Janene married (2) **Lloyd CHANDLER** 6 Feb 1990. He was born 19 May 1945.

ISSUE of Ronald and Janene:

.1672111.1 Rachel Alice JAKOBE, born 20 Oct 1979.
.1672111.2 Natalie Jo JAKOBE, born 27 Feb 1981.

167211.2 Melissa Dee (Meek)[7] SUMMERSKILL (Lorene[6], Charlotte[5], Grace[4], George[3], Daniel[2], John[1]) was born 25 Feb 1959 in Kansas City, Jackson Co., Mo., the daughter of William Frederick MEEK and Lorene Alice WINELAND. Adopted by step-father, Gordon Summerskill, Sept 1972. She married **Anthony FAUCETT** 1 Jun 1984 in Kansas City, Jackson Co., Mo.; they divorced.

ISSUE:

.1672112.1 Jamie Lynn FAUCETT, born 27 Oct 1986.

168131.1 Jeanie Marie[7] **KUEFNER** (Marion[6], Charles[5], Charles[4], Michael[3], Daniel[2], John[1]) was born 21 Sep 1963. She was the daughter of Mervin Deitrich KUEFNER and Marion Irene RITTGERS. She married **David Wayne CALVIN**. He was born 17 Jul 1961.

ISSUE:

.1681311.1 Patrick Alan CALVIN, born 17 Mar 1988.

.1681311.2 Kaitlyn Marie CALVIN, born 22 Jun 1992.

168132.1 Roger Harold[7] **RITTGERS** (Harold[6], Charles[5], Charles[4], Michael[3], Daniel[2], John[1]) was born 18 Nov 1956 in Ames, Ia., the son of Harold Charles RITTGERS and Delores Elaine SHELDAHL. He married (1) **Linda Marie HANSEN** 6 Jun 1981 in Story, Ia. She was born 18 Aug 1959. Lorraine brought four children to this union, Monica, James, Sarah, and Kara Sorenson. Roger married (2) **Lorraine (Fagenbush) SORENSON** 10 Aug 1995. She was born 24 Oct 1954.

ISSUE:

.1681321.1 Nicole Marie RITTGERS, born 27 Oct 1982 in Ames, Ia.

.1681321.2 Brandon James RITTGERS, born 9 Dec 1987 in Ames, Ia.

168132.2 Mark Alan[7] **RITTGERS** (Harold[6], Charles[5], Charles[4], Michael[3], Daniel[2], John[1]) was born 22 Aug 1959 in Ames, Ia., the son of Harold Charles RITTGERS and Delores Elaine SHELDAHL. He married **Mary Ellen JAVORKA** 5 Sep 1986 in South Holland, Ill. She was born 7 Dec 1959 in Chicago, Cook Co., Ill., the daughter of Martin Robert and Irene Wyonne (Gjovig) Javorka.

ISSUE:

.16813221 Melissa Catherine RITTGERS, born 19 Jul 1991 in Munster, Ind.

.16813222 Megan Elizabeth RITTGERS, born 4 Nov 1993 in Munster, Ind, died 4 Dec 1993 in Munster, Ind, and was buried 6 Dec 1993 in Concordia Cem., Hammond, Ind.

.16813223 Madeline Elaine RITTGERS, born 15 Jun 1995 in Munster, Ind.

168141.1 Gary[7] **GRAVES** (Barbara[6], Grace[5], Charles[4], Michael[3], Daniel[2], John[1]) was born 27 May 1954, the son of William GRAVES and Barbara Jean KUEFNER. He married **Kathy___**. She was born 3 Feb 1955.

ISSUE:

.1681411.1 Emily GRAVES, born 18 Jul 1983.

.1681411.2 Sarah GRAVES, born 19 Jun 1986.

.1681411.3 Hannah GRAVES, born 9 Jul 1987.

168141.2 Brian Kent[7] **GRAVES** (Barbara[6], Grace[5], Charles[4], Michael[3], Daniel[2], John[1]) was born 6 May 1959, the son of William GRAVES and Barbara Jean KUEFNER. He married **Jane____**. She was born 8 Mar 1958.

ISSUE:

.1681412.1 Charlotte GRAVES, born 11 Mar 1984.

.168142.2 Barbara[7] **KUEFNER** (Robert[6], Grace[5], Charles[4], Michael[3], Daniel[2], John[1]) was born 20 Jan 1966, the daughter of Robert KUEFNER and Joleen_____. She married **Tom THOMPSON**.

ISSUE:

.1681422.1 Allison Nicole THOMPSON, born 20 Dec 1995.

168142.3 Robert[7] KUEFNER (Robert[6], Grace[5], Charles[4], Michael[3], Daniel[2], John[1]) was born 13 Oct 1967, the son of Robert KUEFNER and Joleen_____. He married **Amy KUEFNER**.

ISSUE:

.1681423.1 Alexander Nicholas KUEFNER, born 21 Mar 1996.

169111.1 Carolyn Ruth[7] CROUSE (Edith[6], Floyd[5], Nellie[4], Caroline[3], Daniel[2], John[1]) was born 3 Nov 1944, the daughter of Carroll Raymond CROUSE and Edith LaVonne PURVIANCE. She married **Tom HRADEK** Jul 1980.

ISSUE:

.1691111.1 Sarah Marie HRADEK, born 28 Dec 1980.

169142.1 David Paul[7] WEISER (Nadine[6], Paul[5], Nellie[4], Caroline[3], Daniel[2], John[1]) was born 29 Apr 1953, the son of Stanley Paul WEISER and Nadine PURVIANCE. He married **Sheryl Lynn SIGLON** 9 Sep 1972.

ISSUE:

.1691421.1 Kevin Paul WEISER, born 1 Mar 1979.
.1691421.2 Janae Marie WEISER, born 1 May 1981.

169142.2 Dennis Paul[7] WEISER (Nadine[6], Paul[5], Nellie[4], Caroline[3], Daniel[2], John[1]) was born 14 Sep 1954, the son of Stanley Paul WEISER and Nadine PURVIANCE. He married **Kathryn STANLEY** 20 May 1978.

ISSUE:

.1691422.1 Jay Dennis WEISER, born 2 May 1981.
.1691422.2 Joel Craig WEISER, born 8 Mar 1983.

169142.3 Joy Lynn[7] WEISER (Nadine[6], Paul[5], Nellie[4], Caroline[3], Daniel[2], John[1]) was born 30 Sep 1955, the daughter of Stanley Paul WEISER and Nadine PURVIANCE. She married **John SCHNEIDER** 17 Sep 1981.

ISSUE:

.1691423.1 Jenny Lynn SCHNEIDER, born 10 Sep 1978.
.1691423.2 Jonna Joy SCHNEIDER, born 19 Apr 1982.

CHAPTER 8

1121111.1 Gary Keith[8] BOOLMAN (Vera[7], Beatrice[6], Virginia[5], Daniel[4], Abraham[3], Joseph[2], John[1]) was born 6 Aug 1942 in Greenville, Darke Co., Oh., the son of Ralph William BOOLMAN and Vera Belle WALTERS. He married (1) **Sharon SUBLER** 10 Aug 1961. Gary married (2) **Pamela HUFF**; they divorced. He married (3) **Nina WISE** 15 Aug 1985.

ISSUE of Gary and Sharon:
+ .11211111.1   Teri R. BOOLMAN, born 22 Mar 1962.
  .11211111.2   Tonya N. BOOLMAN, born 15 Nov 1963 in Columbus, Ga. She married Thomas WOODRUFF 10 Nov 1990.

ISSUE of Gary and Nina:
  .11211111.3   Kenneth LeRoy BOOLMAN, born 20 Dec 1986 in Houston, Tx.

1121111.2 Ronnie E.[8] BOOLMAN (Vera[7], Beatrice[6], Virginia[5], Daniel[4], Abraham[3], Joseph[2], John[1]) was born 28 Jul 1945 in Greenville, Oh., the son of Ralph William BOOLMAN and Vera Belle WALTERS. He married **Diane MOORMAN** 29 Aug 1965.

ISSUE:
  .11211112.1   Tamara A. BOOLMAN, born 30 Mar 1967.
  .11211112.2   Christal H. BOOLMAN, born 25 May 1969 in Greenville, Darke Co., Oh.
  .11211112.3   Gina L. BOOLMAN, born 20 Mar 1972 in Greenville, Darke Co., Oh.

1121112.1 Penny Ann[8] WALLS (Ruby[7], Beatrice[6], Virginia[5], Daniel[4], Abraham[3], Joseph[2], John[1]) was born 6 Nov 1957 in Columbus, Oh. She was the daughter of Robert Eugene WALLS and Ruby Jeannine WALTERS. She married **Dan LEES** 1 Jun 1980; they divorced.

ISSUE:
  .11211121.1   Logan LEES, born 16 Feb 1982 in Ft. Wayne, Ind.

1121121.2 Jeffrey[8] DWYER (Janice[7], Erma[6], Virginia[5], Daniel[4], Abraham[3], Joseph[2], John[1]) was born 18 Aug 1931. He was the son of Joe DWYER and Janice WASSON. His spouse has not been identified. They are divorced.

ISSUE:
  .11211212.1   Justin DWYER, born Apr 1985.

1121131.1 Linda Louise[8] BUTT (Herbert[7], Herbert[6], Virginia[5], Daniel[4], Abraham[3], Joseph[2], John[1]) was born 11 Nov 1947 in Troy, Oh., the daughter of Herbert Owen BUTT and Helen Louise SPHAR. She married **Donald Lee BUIRLEY** 17 Dec 1966. He was born 24 Jun 1945.

ISSUE:
  .11211311.1   Juli Anne BUIRLEY, born 10 Jan 1970.
  .11211311.2   Aaron Michael BUIRLEY, born 14 May 1973.
  .11211311.3   Christopher Lee BUIRLEY, born 16 Oct 1981.

1121131.2 Rex Wayne[8] **BUTT** (Herbert[7], Herbert[6], Virginia[5], Daniel[4], Abraham[3], Joseph[2], John[1]) was born 21 Mar 1950 in Troy, Oh., the son of Herbert Owen BUTT and Helen Louise SPHAR. He married **Karen Lee DANKE** 3 May 1975. She was born 15 Apr 1950.

ISSUE:

.11211312.1   Jared August BUTT, born 13 Aug 1978.

.11211312.2   Chad Ian BUTT, born 6 Apr 1982.

1121131.4 Kevin Owen[8] **BUTT** (Herbert[7], Herbert[6], Virginia[5], Daniel[4], Abraham[3], Joseph[2], John[1]) was born 31 Oct 1956 in Troy, Oh., the son of Herbert Owen BUTT and Helen Louise SPHAR. He married **Nancy Lee DAWSON** 25 Jun 1976. She was born 1 Sep 1955.

ISSUE:

.11211314.1   Jason Owen BUTT, born 14 Jan 1978.

.11211314.2   Andrew Lee BUTT, born 1 May 1980.

.11211314.3   Steven Adam BUTT, born 5 Jun 1982.

1121132.2 Mary[8] **ANDERSON** (Phyllis[7], Herbert[6], Virginia[5], Daniel[4], Abraham[3], Joseph[2], John[1]) was born 7 Oct 1960 in Troy, Oh., the daughter of James ANDERSON and Phyllis Fern BUTT. She married **Michael PORAZZO** 1 May 1981.

ISSUE:

.11211322.1   Daniel Michael PORAZZO, born 14 Feb 1982 in Troy, Oh.

.11211322.2   Melissa Megan PORAZZO, born 24 Jan 1986 in Troy, Oh.

1121141.1 Errol Dean[8] **BUTT** (Wendall[7], Charles[6], Virginia[5], Daniel[4], Abraham[3], Joseph[2], John[1]) was born 8 Oct 1955 in Union City, Ind., the son of Wendall Leo BUTT and Patty Lori PIERSON. He married (1) **Barbara SCOTT** 6 Dec 1974; they divorced. She was born 4 Nov 1955. Errol married (2) **W. Beverly DAY** 24 Oct 1980. She was born 7 Mar 1949.

ISSUE of Errol and Barbara:

.11211411.1   Shaun Nickolus BUTT, born 17 Dec 1974.

1121141.2 Kevin Myron[8] **BUTT** (Wendall[7], Charles[6], Virginia[5], Daniel[4], Abraham[3], Joseph[2], John[1]) was born 28 May 1959, the son of Wendall Leo BUTT and Patty Lori PIERSON. He married **Claudia SCOTT** 8 Nov 1979. She was born 2 Dec 1959.

ISSUE:

.11211412.1   Seth Kevin BUTT, born 9 May 1983.

.11211412.2   Alexander Ryon BUTT, born 20 Mar 1987.

1121142.1 Gregory Scott[8] **BUTT** (Neil[7], Charles[6], Virginia[5], Daniel[4], Abraham[3], Joseph[2], John[1]) was born 6 Aug 1955 in Union City, Ind. He was the son of Neil Mitchell BUTT and Kay Frances GIRTON. He married **Dana Darlene MAY** 14 Dec 1975. She was born 19 Mar 1959.

ISSUE:

.11211421.1   Alyssa Renee BUTT, born 20 Jun 1976 in Union City, Ind.

.11211421.2   Curtis Heath BUTT, born 7 Jun 1980.

1121143.1 Glenna Janice[8] **DAY** (Ardith[7], Charles[6], Virginia[5], Daniel[4], Abraham[3], Joseph[2], John[1]) was born 30 Aug 1958. She was the daughter of Glenn William DAY and Ardith Ann

BUTT. She married (1) **David NEARON** 15 Feb 1975; they divorced.   Glenna married (2) **Terry HALL** 31 Dec 1986. He was born 11 Sep 1956.
ISSUE of David and Glenna:
.11211431.1   Christopher David NEARON, born 9 Sep 1976.
.11211431.2   Joy Ann NEARON, born 11 Jul 1981.
ISSUE of Terry and Glenna:
.11211431.3   Zachary Lee HALL, born 12 Aug 1987.

1121145.3 Mark Douglas[8] HUMMEL (Karen[7], Charles[6], Virginia[5], Daniel[4], Abraham[3], Joseph[2], John[1]) was born 26 May 1967 in Union City, Ind., the son of James Edward HUMMEL and Karen Janice BUTT. He married (1) **Lisa Marie LAWRENCE** 6 Sep 1986. She was born 29 Apr 1967.
ISSUE:
.11211453.1   Courtney Lynn HUMMEL.

1121151.1 Wavelyn Evelyn[8] STIVER (Doyle[7], Hazel[6], Virginia[5], Daniel[4], Abraham[3], Joseph[2], John[1]) was born 20 Oct 1951 in Darke County, Oh., the daughter of Doyle Freymoth STIVER and Zelma SMITH. She married (1) **Douglas HEWITT**. Wavelyn married (2) **Michael JOHN**.

ISSUE of Douglas and Wavelyn:
.11211511.1   Brandy Lynn HEWETT, born 5 Aug 1974 in Sidney, Oh.
.11211511.2   Douglas HEWETT, Jr., born Nov 1976 in Sidney, Oh.
ISSUE of Michael and Wavelyn:
.11211511.3   Michael JOHN, Jr., born 30 May 1969 in Sidney, Oh.
.11211511.4   Robert Anthony JOHN, born 5 Nov 1970 in Sidney, Oh.

1121151.2 Hazel Jeanette[8] STIVER (Doyle[7], Hazel[6], Virginia[5], Daniel[4], Abraham[3], Joseph[2], John[1]) was born 30 Dec 1952 in Darke Co., Oh., the daughter of Doyle Freymoth STIVER and Zelma SMITH. She married **Jessie COFFEY**.
ISSUE:
.11211512.1   Bobbie Joe COFFEY, born 27 Dec 1969 in Sidney, Oh.
.11211512.2   Jessie William COFFEY, Jr., born 2 Mar 1972 in Sidney, Oh.
.11211512.3   Amanda Lynn COFFEY, born Oct 1973 in Sidney, Oh.

1121151.3 Linda Kay[8] STIVER (Doyle[7], Hazel[6], Virginia[5], Daniel[4], Abraham[3], Joseph[2], John[1]) was born 7 Oct 1954 in Darke Co., Oh., the daughter of Doyle Freymoth STIVER and Zelma SMITH. She married _____ **WICAL**. They divorced.
ISSUE:
.11211513.1   Cherrie Michelle WICAL, born 5 Oct 1973 in Sidney, Oh.
.11211513.2   Eric WICAL, born 13 Jul 1976.

1121152.1 Bruce[8] MIKESELL (Jeanette[7], Hazel[6], Virginia[5], Daniel[4], Abraham[3], Joseph[2], John[1]) was born 2 Aug 1951 in Darke Co., Oh., the son of Billy MIKESELL and Jeanette Frances STIVER. He married **Gail STILLWELL**.
ISSUE:
.11211521.1   Benjamin Lee MIKESELL, born 4 Oct 1975 in Ill.
.11211521.2   Bradley Lucas MIKESELL, born 19 Jul 1982 in Ill.

1121152.2 Brice⁸ MIKESELL (Jeanette⁷, Hazel⁶, Virginia⁵, Daniel⁴, Abraham³, Joseph², John¹) was born 28 Jul 1954 in Darke Co., Oh., the son of Billy MIKESELL and Jeanette Frances STIVER. He married **Cherie JONES**.
ISSUE:
.11211522.1   Shawna MIKESELL, born 3 Oct 1980 in Darke Co., Oh.
.11211522.2   Jenny Mae MIKESELL, born 7 Jun 1982 in Darke Co., Oh.

1121152.3 Jodena⁸ MIKESELL (Jeanette⁷, Hazel⁶, Virginia⁵, Daniel⁴, Abraham³, Joseph², John¹) was born 14 Nov 1956 in Darke Co., Oh. She was the daughter of Billy MIKESELL and Jeanette Frances STIVER. She married _____ **RABY**; they divorced.
ISSUE:
.11211523.1   Charles Jedediah RABY, born 14 Feb 1976 in N.D..

1121162.1 Tina⁸ ROSE (Gene⁷, Evelyn⁶, Virginia⁵, Daniel⁴, Abraham³, Joseph², John¹) was born 17 Apr 1962 in Union City, Ind., the daughter of Gene ROSE and Janet PINGRY. She married **Dennis AUSTERMAN** 31 Jan 1980.
ISSUE:
.11211621.1   Chrystal Marie AUSTERMAN, born 22 May 1982 in Union City, Ind.

1121221.1 Scott⁸ STRAIT (Ted⁷, Echo⁶, Ira⁵, Daniel⁴, Abraham³, Joseph², John¹) was born 14 Aug 1960 in Darke Co., Oh., the son of Ted STRAIT and Wilma RAPP. He married **Pamela KELL**.
ISSUE:
.11212211.1   Shantelle STRAIT, born 2 Feb 1984.
.11212211.2   Victoria STRAIT, born Oct 1986.

1121311.3 Diane⁸ DANCER (Buddy⁷, Helen⁶, Minnie⁵, Daniel⁴, Abraham³, Joseph², John¹) was born 7 Jul 1974 in Darke County, Oh., the daughter of Buddy DANCER and Barbara MARKWITH.
ISSUE:
.11213113.1   Justin DANCER, born 1 Jul 1986 in Darke Co., Oh.

1161311.1 Robert Willard⁸ BIGHAM (Robert⁷, Ruth⁶, Willard⁵, George⁴, Anna³, Joseph², John¹) was born 2 Feb 1960 in Lancaster, Fairfield Co., Oh., the son of Robert Eugene BIGHAM and Mary Kathleen McDANIEL. He married (1) **Mary Kay ANDERSON** 1 Mar 1980 in Crocker, Mo. She was born 1953.[Bigham] Robert's spouse (2) has not been identified.
ISSUE of Robert and Mary:
.11613111.1   Brock Michael BIGHAM, born 1980.
.11613111.2   Brandon J. BIGHAM.
ISSUE of Robert and ____:
.11613111.3   Patrick Lane BIGHAM, born 1986.
.11613111.4   Steven Allen ROE, born 1989.

1161311.2 Randy Lee⁸ BIGHAM (Robert⁷, Ruth⁶, Willard⁵, George⁴, Anna³, Joseph², John¹) was born 29 Aug 1961 in Lancaster, Fairfield Co., Oh. He was the son of Robert Eugene BIGHAM and Mary Kathleen McDANIEL. He married **Pamela Joan METZGER** 17 Oct 1981 in Somerset, Perry Co., Oh.[Bigham]

ISSUE:

.11613112.1   Stacy Ann BIGHAM, born 1984.
.11613112.2   Brad Westley BIGHAM, born 1987.

1161311.3 Beth Renee[8] BIGHAM (Robert[7], Ruth[6], Willard[5], George[4], Anna[3], Joseph[2], John[1]) was born 2 Sep 1963 in Fairfield Co., Oh., the daughter of Robert Eugene BIGHAM and Mary Kathleen McDANIEL. She married (1) **Randy Dee SHUMAKER** 2 Sep 1983 in Lancaster, Fairfield Co., Oh. Beth married (2) **Curt Douglas McCUNE**. [Bigham]

ISSUE:

.11613113.1   Randy Allen McCUNE, born 1980.
.11613113.2   Douglas Allen McCUNE, born 1984.

1161312.2 Kathy Lee[8] BIGHAM (Ronald[7], Ruth[6], Willard[5], George[4], Anna[3], Joseph[2], John[1]) was born 1960. She was the daughter of Ronald Lee BIGHAM and Mary Louise WILLIAMS. She married **Robert Lewis BAER, Jr.**. He was born 1957.[Bigham]

ISSUE:

.11613122.1   Brock BAER, born 1981.
.11613122.2   Seth BAER, born 1982.

1217151.2 Jacquelyn Suzanne[8] ROGERS (Melvin[7], Mary[6], Nellie[5], Sarah[4], Samuel[3], Jacob[2], John[1]) was born 31 Mar 1968 in Independence, Jackson Co., Mo., the daughter of Melvin Jack ROGERS and Carolyn Sue WHITEHEAD. She married **Amos Clint SPRINGER** 31 Mar 1990 in Pleasant Hill, Cass Co., Mo. He was born 15 Apr 1969 in Harrisonville, Cass Co., Mo. [Family record submitted by Mary (Finney) Rogers in 1994]

ISSUE:

.12171512.1   Tyler Cole SPRINGER, born 15 Jan 1990 in Independence, Jackson Co., Mo.
.12171512.2   Katherine Mari SPRINGER, born 20 Dec 1991 in Harrisonville, Cass Co., Mo.

CHAPTER 9

GENERATION NO. 9

11211111.1 Teri Ranea[9] **BOOLMAN** (Gary[8], Vera[7], Beatrice[6], Virginia[5], Daniel[4], Abraham[3], Joseph[2], John[1]) was born 22 Mar 1962 in Columbus, Ga.. She was the daughter of Gary Keith BOOLMAN and Sharon SUBLER. She married **Steve WILSON** 1 Jun 1983.

ISSUE:

.112111111.1   Stuart Craig WILSON, born 13 Jan 1985 in Dayton, Oh.
.112111111.2   Chelsea Jordan WILSON, born 25 Jan 1988 in Dayton, Oh.

11211112.1 Tamara Ann[9] **BOOLMAN** (Ronnie[8], Vera[7], Beatrice[6], Virginia[5], Daniel[4], Abraham[3], Joseph[2], John[1]) was born 30 Mar 1967 in Darke County, Oh. She was the daughter of Ronnie Eugene BOOLMAN and Diane MOORMAN. She married **Polo SAMANIEGO** 17 Jan 1987.

ISSUE:

.112111121.1   Amanda Beth SAMANIEGO, born 14 Aug 1987 in Naples, Fla..

CHAPTER   10

RITTGERS WHO ARE STILL ROVING

In our pursuit of all with the surname of Rittgers we have located several who aren't connected to the family as yet. That they belong in our fold is a foregone conclusion, as we have yet to find any indication that there is another Rittgers line in this country. The closest we have found is RITGER, a family with roots in Wisconsin. In reviewing their family genealogy, it appears to be a separate family all together. It is our hope that all of the following folks can be placed in their correct lineage. Many of the females are probably spouses of family members we have already identified.

Rittgers, Ann - b. 6 oct 1883, s.s. card issued Okla., died Mar 1969, with the last res. Teaneck, Bergen Co., NJ.

Rittgers, Bennie - born 5 Feb 1925, s.s. card issued Mo., d. 7 Feb 1988, last res. Los Angeles, Ca.

Rittgers, Bernean- b. 15 Apr 1904, s.s. card issued Ill., d. 12 Feb 1995, last res. Dorchester, Macoupin Co., Ill.

Rittgers, Betty - b. 10 Feb 1921, s.s. card issued Ind., d. May 1978, last res. Hamilton Co., Oh.

Rittgers, Carl - b. 2 Jan 1906, s.s. card issued Ill., d. 17 Jan 1992, lasr res. Shelby Co., Ill.

Rittgers, Charles, b. 16 Apr 1902, s.s. card issued Oh., d. June 1979, last res., Amanda, Fairfield   Co., Oh.

Rittgers, Clara - b. 12 June 1903, s.s. card issued Oh., d. 12 Jan 1992.

Rittgers, Cleo - b. 8 Oct 1902, s.s. card issued NJ, d. 8 Oct1993,

Rittgers, Don - b. 15 Apr 1956, s.s. card issued Tx., d. May 1980.

Rittgers, Edna - b. 20 July 1906, s.s. card issued Calif., d. Oct 1983.

Rittgers, Elva - b. 17 Aug 1904, s.s. card issued in Oh., d. Oct 1956.

Rittgers, Fern - b. 5 June 1917, s.s. card issued Ia., d. Nov 1986, last res. Perry, Dallas Co., Ia.

Rittgers, Flora - b. 9 May 1940, s.s. card issued Ia., d. 21 Mar 1995, last res. Ankeny, Polk Co., Ia.

Rittgers, Florence - b.20 July 1889, s.s. issued Ia., d.Mar 1968, last res Polk City, Polk Co., Ia.

Rittgers, George - b. 23 June 1907, s.s. card issued Mo., d. June 1985, last res., Kansas City, Mo. In a letter from wife Gwen, we learn that he had a varied and active life. We are told that he was   in the navy "during peace time," but lost his sight in a boiler explosion in the China Sea. He lived   at the military home at Wadsworth, [nearest thing to this I can find is Wardsville in Mo.] for a   number of years. He married about 38 or 39 and moved to the Ozarks, where he ran a cattle farm. He was divorced in 1945 and came to Kansas City in 1950, where he worked at the main Post   Office until he was hit by a car in 1965. He operated a beauty salon for about 12 years and had   three operators. In 1977 he suffered a stroke.." He later had another stroke and remained an   invalid until his death on 5 June 1985. Gwen reports in the letter he was very active in the National Federation of the Blind and the VFW, Disabled American Veterans, and Blinded Veterans. She   tells us that she, too, is blind. They had been married for 22 years and in her letter she tells us "He was a good man, a loyal friend, and generous in spirit." He was cremated and his ashes sprinkled at sea.

Rittgers, Glen - b. 13 Nov 1908, s.s. card issued Ill., d. Dec 1955.

Rittgers, Gwendolyn, b. 3 Feb 1914, s.s. issued Mo., d.May 1994, last res Kansas City, Clay Co., Mo. Strongly suspect this is spouse of George.

Rittgers, Harold - b. 27 June 1910, s.s. card issued Ill., d. 26 apr 1993, last res., Shelby Co., Ill.

Rittgers, Helen - b. 9 Dec 1906, s.s. card issued Colo., d. Nov 1988, last res Oklahoma City, Ok.

Rittgers, Ida - b. abt 1873, on 1920 census, age 47, widow, b. Oh., of father b. Pa., mother b. Oh., a "chambermaid, hotel" living at 260 Wood St., Logan, Hocking Co., Oh. In her home is her mother, Margaret Liff, 77, widow, "housekeeper, pvt. Home".[ED39, p. 6B, fam 132/143]

Rittgers, Irene - b. 16 Jan 1919, s.s. card issued Ks.,d. Feb 1987, last res. Wichita, Sedgwick Co., Ks.

Rittgers, Jacob - b. 30 Jul 1927, s.s. card issued Ks., d.Nov 1974.

Rittgers, John - b. 16 Aug 1898, s.s. card issued Oh., d.June 1959.

Rittgers, Leslie - b. 10 Oct 1954, s.s. card issued Tx., d. Aug 1977.

Rittgers, Louise - b. 29 July 1897, s.s. card issued Oh., d. Apr 1973, last res. Mount Vernon, Knox Co., Oh.

Rittgers, M. - b. 23 Nov 1933, s.s. card issued Minn., d. Mar 1992.

Rittgers, Margaret - b. 7 Aug 1890, s.s. card issued NY, d. mar 1966, last res Syracuse, Onondaga Co., NY.

Rittgers, Marjorie - b. 7 Sept 1954, s.s. card issued Minn., d. June 1981.

Rittgers, Megan - b. and d.4 Dec 1993, s.s. card issued Ind.

Rittgers, Minnie - b. 23 Jan 1890, s.s. card issued NJ., d. Dec 1980, last res. Ocean Grove, Monomouth Co., NJ.

Rittgers, Minnie - b. 10 Feb 1886, s.s. card issued Ill., d. Mar 1973, last res Shelby Co., Ill.

Rittgers, Nellie - b. 26 Oct 1891, s.s. card issued Ia., d. 19 Jan 1991, last res Perry, Dallas Co., Ia.

Rittgers, Nonnie - b. 17 July 1904, s.s. issued Ill, d. 12 Feb 1995,last res Dorchester, Macoupin Co., Ill.

Rittgers, Robert - b. 22 July 1929, s.s. card issued ND., d. Mar 1978.

Rittgers, Robert - b. 22 Jan 1924, s.s. card issued Pa., d. 28 Oct 1989.

Rittgers, Ruby - b. 1 Aug 1903, s.s. card issued Oh., d. may 1982, last res. Preble Co., Oh.

Rittgers, Russell - , b. 8 Dec 1906, s.s. card issued Fla., d. Mar 1969.

Rittgers, Ruth - b. 9 Aug 1894, s.s. card issued Ill., d. Mar 1980.

Rittgers, Ruthann - d. 14 Jan 1939, s.s. card issued Mich., d. Sept 1984, last res., Grand Rapids, Kent Co., Ill.

Rittgers, William - d. 29 Oct 1898, s.s. card issued Ill., d. Apr 1965.

Rittgers, Zelda - b. 17may 1897, s.s. card issued Ia., d. may 1976, Story Co., Ia.

CHAPTER 11

INTRODUCTION

In reading THOSE ROVING RITTGERS, you have been reading from 1795 forward to the present. The COMER APPENDIX starts with Catharine Comer and reads back in time. We will look at her parents and the line that has been constructed as hers. In pointing out that this is a constructed line, I caution family historians to realize that much of this has been put together with few records and a lot of faith! We use as our basis for this work a lineage that was done for admission to DAR. This author was unable to contact the author of the work to request more information on her sources. Since she was admitted to DAR we feel that the records up to her ancestor, Michael Comer, Jr., Captain in the Revolution, were well documented. This Michael is son of Michael, Sr. and uncle to our Catharine, being her father's brother. [DAR-Huffman, Beulah Comer; THE GOMER (COMER) FAMILY HISTORY; Luray, Va.] The early records in this area are scant and scattered. What started out as part of Orange Co., Va., became Augusta Co., part of which became Shenandoah Co., until today the very same land is in Page Co., Va.

Our family members are identified by the "ahnentafel" numbering system. Our first person, Catharine, is #1. We double her number to get her father's number, 2. Add one for the mother's number. The father's number is doubled to get his father and the mother's number doubled to get her father. Add one to each man's number to get his wife's number, and so on. We won't distract ourselves in this appendix with following the descendants of the other children in the family. They will be listed so that anyone interested in pursuing this family will have other names with which to identify the family.

SHENANDOAH VALLEY, VA.

From the Blue Ridge Parkway along the spine of the Blue Ridge Mountains one can look out over the Shenandoah Valley and across to the Massanutten Mountains. The valley floor gently rolls and is a mosaic of shades of green - cultivated fields, wild meadows, and woodlands. This pattern is broken into irregular pieces by silver threads of streams and creeks flowing down off the mountains on both sides to join and form the Shenandoah River. Wild deer still wander the hills, and often obstruct traffic on the Parkway. Black bear, wildcat, fox and beaver are just a few of the hundreds of species of animal making their home in the area. Appalachian crafters, outdoor recreation, and historical sites attract many visitors. Luray Caverns is one of the most spectacular and unique caves in the U.S., bragging the only underground organ. Music is created when the organ keys are struck, triggering a soft mallet to strike one of the stalagmites or stalactites, each chosen for its tone. Whether you want to walk the paths of your ancestors or just visit a beautiful part of this country, it is hard to top this garden spot. Our ancestors owned land on the Hawksbill Creek between Stony Man and Luray, Va. We are told that a direct descendant still lives on the land. Near the town of Shenandoah is a small community called "Comertown." There are streets and avenues in the area named after the family, and a "Gomer" church is just outside of Stony Man.

EARLY HISTORY

The first German wave of immigrants started in 1683. By 1710 there were over 3,000 Germans in this country. They first landed in New York, then began arriving in Philadelphia and settling in Berks and Bucks Co., Pa. As the numbers continued to increase, good farmland became harder to obtain. In 1716, Governor Alexander Spotswood of Va., led an exploration across the mountains and into the Shenandoah Valley. Fearful that the French would find the area first and settle it under the French flag, he made generous land grants to encourage settlement. Large numbers of Germans were wooed to come to this area from Pa. There were also large numbers of English and Scotch-Irish from the Virginia Tidewater area that settled in the valley. They apparently each settled in their respective areas, as we see German still being spoken fluently four generations later. Many of these early Germans were displaced from the Rhine Valley Palatinates. When these early travelers first sighted the Shenandoah Valley, they must have felt as if they were home - minus the constant warfare so prevalent in Germany at that time. Today the history of these hearty pioneers can be experienced first hand at the Museum of American Frontier Culture in Staunton, Va. Here there are four working farms, German, Scotch, English, and, where the three cultures blend, an Appalachian ("American") Farm. It is a chance to see how our ancestors lived, worked, and played.

OUR COMER ANCESTRY

Listing 7 ancestors for 5 generations.

GENERATION NO. 1

1. **Catharine**[1] **COMER** was born 29 Apr 1775 in Shenandoah Co., Va., the daughter of **2.John COMER** and **3.Mary Ann KIBLER**. Catharine died 9 May 1834 in Fairfield, Oh. She married **John Augustin RITTGERS** 9 May 1797 in Shenandoah Co., Va. He was born 2 Dec 1767 in Prussia, Germany. John died 27 Feb 1848 in Fairfield, Oh., and was buried in North Berne, Hocking, Oh.

GENERATION NO. 2

2. **John**[2] **COMER** (1.Catharine[1]) was born 1755 or 1756 in Shenandoah Co., Va.[LDS-IGI, 1992, Va, fiche #1612, p.1779.] He was the son of **4.Michael COMER** and **5.Catharine____**. John died Nov 1804 in Shenandoah Co., Va. He married **3.Mary Ann KIBLER** 1775 in Shenandoah Co., Va.[Vogt, John; SHENANDOAH COUNTY MARRIAGE BONDS, 1772-1850; Iberian Publishing Co., Athens, Ga., p.73] We first see John "Comber" in a deed from Michael Comber and Catherine his wife to John Comber son of said Michael...part of a tract of land lying on the Hawksbill Creek....received from Adam Comber...23 April 1763... containing 135 acres... and part of another tract of 194 acres...by deed from proprietors office 15 Oct 1763...containing 57 acres...13 June 1783, recorded 28 Aug 1783. This was one of three almost identical deeds made that day. The other two were to John's brothers Michael, Jr., and Christopher. It was witnessed by Augustine Comber.[Shenandoah Co. Deed book, p.287] On a local 1783 census listing we see seven Comers, but no John. He may have been living on a relative's farm and so enumerated with that family. On the 1785 census list, he is given with 5 people in his home. He also has one "dwelling" and one "other building."[Wayland, John W.; A HISTORY OF SHENANDOAH COUNTY, VA.; Regional Publishing Co., Baltimore, 2nd edition, p.225] John is shown in the Shenandoah County Personal Property Tax 1787 - list "B"

as being taxed on 2 horses and 6 cattle.[Shreiner-Yantis, Netti; THE 1787 CENSUS OF VIRGINIA, Vol I; Genealogical Books in Print; Springfield, Va.; p.607. Copy in the Staunton Public Library.] Just how he came to buy the bond of John Rittgers is not known. It was such a common practice, that there were probably "bond brokers" that made the connections and transported the immigrant to the purchaser. Our GUESS is that John Rittgers came in through Philadelphia. Having had time to only make a brief stop in the area, we have uncovered no deeds or tax records as yet in the name of John Rittgers (or Richards, as we found him on the Marriage and Bond record). It is probable that he remained on the Comer farm until migrating to Ohio, but a more in depth study of local records might give us other information. We find John listed as the third son in his father's will, 1799. John's Will was made 6 Oct 1804 and proven Dec 1804. In it he gives one third of everything to "Mary Ann my dearly beloved wife during her life", and this is to be divided between the children at her death. His other bequests are shown with the children in the following list.[Shenandoah Co. Will Book F, p. 268]

3. Mary Ann² KIBLER (1.Catharine¹). We haven't determine her parentage, but she may have been somewhat younger than her husband, as we see she was left with minor children at her husband's death. On the 1810 census of Shenandoah Co., Va., we see one Mary Comer with one female over 45(probably herself) one female 26-45, two males 16-26, and one male 10-16. This is probably sons and a daughter living with her. Mary made out her will 5 Mar 1825. In it she wills "unto my grand daughter Mary Ann Campbell, daughter of Robert Campbell", several household items such as "two feather beads beadsteads with sufficient bedclothing boalsters & pillows, pewter plates, spinning flax, one shelf or cupboard, one table one chest." It is noted that if she died before she married or turned 21 the above property is to go to her two brothers, James and Robert Campbell, Jr. If they, too, die without issue, then the items revert back to my children Daniel Jonas John Molly Caly Lizzy & Sally. "I further loan to her all the within property so long as she may live but that my executor shall keep an eye over the said property so that it shall not be sold or squandered to deprive the heirs of their right, this all being property that I have accumulated since the death of my husband John Comer which has nothing to do with his will now of record in the County Coarts of Shenandoah......" She signed it with her mark. Mary died 1825/1830 in Shenandoah Co., Va. On the outside of the will is written "1830 July proved by the oath of Reuben Miller a wit.. Thereto. Jo. Evans Exec therein named refused to qualify [more but unable to read] granted David Blosser bond given and sworn." This was found a few years ago in a desk or file drawer in the Shenandoah County Courthouse. We were told that there were several "unrecorded" wills found in various places when the courthouse was cleaned out for renovation. These wills are now photocopied and in a book called "Unrecorded Will's Book", p. 14A. What did get recorded was her estate sale. Her list of appraised items included 1 bed and bedstead, 1 spinning wheel, 1 pewter dish and 7 plates, and some pots, for a total value of $14.75. It reports that this was the "property willed to her grand daughter, Mary Ann Campbell. On 7 Aug 1830 these items were sold. Robert Campbell bought the pots and another man who's name hasn't shown up in any family record bought the beds and flax. The sale price total was $9.99 1/4 (they had fractions of pennies.) We don't know if Mary Ann died or if she married the person who bought the other items. And if that was the case, why did they have to buy what she was given. Unfortunately, the record doesn't give us the family news, just the court facts. The estate was finalized on 11 Oct 1831.

ISSUE based on bequests in will:
  i. Daniel, born before 1783 as appears to be adult in father's will, first son listed, bequeathed 30 acres and one horse.

ii. Jonas, born after 1783, second son listed in will, receives 30 acres and one horse "at the age of twenty-one."

iii. John, born after 1783, third son listed in will, receives 30 acres and one horse "at the age of twenty-one."

1. iv. Catherine COMER, born 29 Apr 1775, died 9 May 1834. First daughter listed in father's will, called Catharine "Richards." She received "six pounds in addition to what she has received." This probably reflects the fact that her father "forgave" the bond to husband John Rittgers. Probably the daughter called "Caly" in mother's will.

v. Elizabeth, second daughter listed in father's will, called "Elizabeth Nail", given 18 pounds. She is seen with husband Peter as witnesses to the baptism of nephew Jacob Rittgers (#1.2)Probably daughter called "Lizzy" in mother's will.

vi. Mary, called "Mary Wimer" in father's will, third daughter named, receives 18 pounds. Probably daughter called "Molly" in Mother's will.

vii. Sarah, probably over 21 and unmarried at time of father's will, as he leaves her 18 pounds with no age stipulation. She later married Robert Campbell and had (1)James; (2) Robert, Jr.; and (3) Mary Ann. This Mary Ann is grand daughter that was mentioned in her grand mother's will

GENERATION NO. 3

4. Michael³ COMER (2.John², 1.Catharine¹). He was the son of **8.Johans Adam COMER.** Michael died 1799 in Shenandoah Co., Va.. He married **5.Catharine____** before 1755. On 13 June 1783, he sells to three sons each approx. 50 acres of land "in consideration of thirty pounds."[Shenandoah Co. Deeds, p.284, 287, 290] Michael Comer, Sr., is listed on the 1783 state census Shenandoah Co., with 7 people in his home, and it is either he or son Michael, Jr., not specified which, on the 1785 census with 6 people in the home, 1 dwelling and 2 other buildings.[Wayland, p.225] On the 1787 personal property tax list Michael, Sr., is listed as being taxed for 4 horses and 6 cattle.[Schriener-Yantis, p.607] On 1 Apr 1797, we see Michael and Catharine, along with John and Elizabeth Miller selling land ... "lying and being on the Hawksbill Creek it being part of a tract of 206 acres which was formerly granted by deed from the late proprietors office the 1ˢᵗ of July 1777 to Daniel Parker who conveyed same to Christopher Comer by his deed the 24ᵗʰ and 25ᵗʰ Nov 1778...Christopher Comer and Eve his wife conveyed part thereof to Augustine Comer the 25ᵗʰ Aug 1783..Augustine Comer and Catharine his wife conveyed the same to said John Miller by deed 29 Sept 1790..also part of Michael Comers tract of 135 acres which was conveyed to him by Adam Comber and Margaret his wife by deed 23 April 1763..containing 50 acres.." Michael Comer, Jr. witnessed it with a signature, but Michael and Catharine made their marks.[Shenandoah Co., Bk K of Deeds, p.526. His will was made 25 Sept 1799, and wife Catharine not mentioned in it, so probably deceased. The will was proven 7 June 1802. [Gilreath, Amelia C.; SHENANDOAH COUNTY VIRGINIA ABSTRACT OF WILLS 1772-1850; Manuscript found in Luray Public Library]

5. Catharine³ _____(2.John², 1.Catharine¹). Most probably died before husband made out his will 25 Sept 1799, as she not listed. On the LDS-IGI record of 1992, fiche 1612, Va., pages 6,675-6,688, we find two listings that appear to be the same couple, but with wide discrepancies in the ages of the children. It is believed to be the same family, as the children are in similar birth order and same names with one exception and that name is very similar. It is possible that these were christening dates and submitted as birth dates to LDS. We will give the first date with the second following in parenthesis.

ISSUE:

    i.   Philip, b. 1743 (1770), named first in father's will.

    ii. Elizabeth, b. 1745 (1764), named as first daughter in will.

    iii. Catharine, b. 2748 (1765), named as second daughter in will.

    iv. Judith, b. 1750. Julian_(this how name recorded on LDS) 1772 and named as third daughter in father's will. (This combination conjecture)

    v. Christopher, b. 1752 (1755) second son listed in father's will.

2. vi. John COMER, b. 1755 or 1756, died Nov 1804.

    vii. Michael, b. 1758, named as executor of father's will, 1799, but not given any bequest. It is possible that he received lands from father earlier. Seen in deed of 1783 when deeded 57 acres for 30 pounds. He was Capt. in Rev. war. 12 children. The first birth date given for Michael is 1741, but DAR accepted a birth date of "about 1760" so we will place him here.

    viii. Augustine, fourth son named in father's will.

    ix. Samuel, b. 1762 (1768) fifth son named in will.

    x. William, b. 1762 (1765) not named in father's will.

GENERATION NO. 4

8. Johans Adam[4] COMER (4.Michael[3], 2.John[2], 1.Catharine[1]) was born before 1700 in Palatinate, Ger. He was the son of **16.Christopher COMER**. We find a file on the LDS-IGI "Gedcom" CD that gives us Johan Adam(#G45G-GL) as a son of Christopher. It reports his spouse is **9. Margaret____**.(G45H-41) His spot in this line is based on the fact that Adam Comber and wife Margaret conveyed to Michael Comer 135 acres in a deed dated 23 Apr 1763. We see one "Hans Gomer" listed after "Christiper Gomer" on "a list of ye men that are Pallatine Passengers from sixteen years and upwards on board the Snow Molly, John Howell, Master, from Dover. [Qualified Sept 10, 1737]" The next list is "Palatines imported in the Snow Molly, John Howell, Master. Qualified the 10th day of Sept 1737." Here "Christofel Gomer" is immediately followed by "Johans Adam Gomer." The third list given is "At the Courthouse of Philad[ia,] Sept 10th 1737. The Palatines whose Names are underwritten, imported in the Snow Molly, John Howell, Master, from Amsterdam, but last from Dover, [Eng.] did this day take & subscribe the Oaths to the Governement." Here "Christstofel Gomer" is immediately followed by Johans Adam Gomer. It is unfortunate for us that the person compiling the list didn't see fit to put ages down![Strassburger, Ralph Beaver; PENNSYLVANIA GERMAN PIONEERS; Genealogical Pub. Co.; Baltimore; 1980. P. 173] There was speculation in the Comer DAR booklet that Christopher and Adam might have been brothers. Based on the fact that we see Michael's first child born in either 1741 or 1743, we believe him to have been born by 1721 at the latest, and so was born in Germany. It is possible that he and Adam were brothers, as the deed quoted only reported Michael received the land from Adam - it did not specify relationship. Since the deed was published in the abstracted form, we might find out more when we locate the original. It will take some searching through the Augusta Co. and Shenandoah Co. records to see if we can find out more about Adam Comer. That he was over 16 at the time he arrived has been shown, and so we base his birth on that. We have seen that he deeded property to Michael Comer in 1763. On 25 July 1779, "Adam Comber & Margarett his wife of County of

Shanandoah & Colony of Virginia" to Martin Comber of County & Colony aforesaid... part of the "tract Peter Rufner conveyed 271 acres thereof to Christopher Comber who by his last will and Testament did bequeath same to said Adam Comber..."[Shenandoah Co. Deed book B, p. 358, Deed book series, Vol 1, p.133 abstracted by Amelia C. Gilreath.]

9. Margaret _____. We believe that not all children have been found.

ISSUE as found in the DAR booklet:

4.   i.   Michael COMER, before 1721, died 1799.
     ii. Martin COMER, married Molly.

GENERATION NO. 5

16. Christopher⁵ COMER (8.Johans⁴, 4.Michael³, 2.John², 1.Catharine¹) was born before 1716 in Ger. Christopher died in Va. His spouse has not been identified. We have seen in the sketch of Adam Comer, that he and Christopher came into this country together. We have no record to date of their stay in Pa., but he purchased 271 acres "on the Hawksbill" in Augusta Co., (that part that is today Page Co.,) Va., from Peter Ruffner on Apr 10 and 11, 1746. We are told that this property was "271 acres of the south end of the Hawksbill Patent, at Stony Man."[Strickler, Harry M.; SHORT HISTORY OF PAGE CO., VA.; Diety Press, Richmond, Va.; 1952, p. 113] It is unfortunate that the deeds all give clumps of trees as landmarks to the location of the property, thus we have not been able to determine it's exact location.

ISSUE:

8.   i.   Johans Adam COMER, born most prob. before 1700, in Germany

INDEX OF NAMES

BLINN Alyssa Ann (Baltes) 234 Jerry 234
BLOODING Mary Iva 171
BLOOM Barry Clifford 96 157 Benjamin
Henry 157 Clifford Donald 96 15 Clifford
Robert 158 Corey Jay 158 Jacob Barry
157 Julie Ann (Rosenthal) 157 Pauline
Elfreda (Rittgers) 96 157 Robert Jay 6
157
BLOOMER Coleen Ann 168 Edith Pearl
(Rittgers)168 211 James Edmund168 211
Verta Marie 168 211
BODAMER Catherine 51 Daniel 50
Demarius (--) 50 Elizabeth 50 Gertrude
(--) 50 Jacob 50 Jacob Frederick 50 106
John 50 Lanie 51 Lavina 51 Matilda51
Noah 50 Phebe A.(--)50 Susan 51 106
163 Susan (Amspaugh) 50 106
BOLTON George 33 Salena Sara (Rittgers)
33
BOMAN David 181 Ed 181 Robin 181
Ruth Ellen (Hardie) 181
BOOLMAN Christal H. 251 Diane
(Moorman)251 257Gary K. 231 251 Gary
Keith 257 Gina L. 251 Kenneth LeRoy
251 Nina (Wise) 251 Pamela (Huff) 251
Ralph William 231 251 Ronnie E. 231
251 Ronnie Eugene 257 Sharon (Subler)
251 257 Tamara A. 251 Tamara Ann 257
Teri R. 251 Teri Ranea 257 Tonya N.
251 Vera Belle (Walters) 231 251
BOWEN Charles 211 Donald "Dean" 156
Mary Ann (Rittgers) 156 Sharon Bonnell
(Fisher) 211
BOWERS Hollie (Heriford) 143 John D. 22
Keith 143 Lucinda (Strohl) 22 Peggy 143
BOWMAN Sally 224
BRADLEY Ellen Victoria 155
BRANDT Charles195 Chris195 Sandra
(Martin)195 Tracy195
BREDWELL Marianna 238
BREIHOLZ Alfred J. 92 152 Chelsea 200
Cheryl (--) 152 Coral Martha (Rittgers)
92 152 Delores Marie92 152 200 Doris
(Maresh) 152 200 Jacob 200 Margaret (--
) 200 Robert Alfred 92 152 200 Scott
Robert 152 200 Todd Alfred 152
BREYMIER Dale Eugene 235 Lori Ann

(Mendenhall) 235
BRIGHT Adam Scott 243 Andrea Jo 243
Augusta (Disbennet) 161 Bertha May 101
162 207 208 Blanche Marguerita 161 207
243 Charles M. 102 162 Dorothy Karyl
(Olson) 243 Edward J. 161 Gertrude
(Martin) 161 207Glendon Rolland 161
207 243 Harmond D. 161 Helen O. 162
Hilda E. 161 Iola (Nowbray) 102 Isaac
Rolland 101, 161, 207 James Henry 101,
161 Jennie A. (--) 161 Joan Francis 207
243 Joseph Elburn 102 Lillie Maude 102
162 208 Lois Juanita 162 Maggie
(Terrell) 207 243 Marie (Struble) 162
Mary (Wolf) 161 162 Mary Jane 161
Peter 101 161 162 Peter Whitehead 161
162 Samuel H. 161 Samuel Hamilton 101
Sherry 207 243 Terry 207 243
BROCKETT Janet (__) 220
BROOKS Helen (Hossman) 211 244
BROOKSHIER Dorothy 156
BROWN Christina Catherine (Fodge) 199
Isaac 48 John 48 Joshua Peter Leonard
199 Mary 48 228 Richard Leonard 199
Sarah (Root) 48 Shannon Elizabeth 199
BROWNING Loretta (Simpson) 34
BRUNE Daryl Arthur 204 Denise Kay 204
Donald "Shane" 204 Donald Adolph 204
Laura Marie (Rittgers) 204
BUCHANAN Allen 178 Ann Elaine
(Rittgers) 178
BUCHOLZ Clarice Louise (Rittgers) 90
Russell 90
BUCK Alice Blanche (Clements) 211
Marion James 212
BUGH Jason 207 Mary Virginia (Rittgers)
207 William F. 207
BUIRLEY Aaron Michael 251Christopher
Lee 251 Donald Lee 251 Juli Anne 251
Linda Louise (Butt) 251
BULLARD Carolyn Kay 242
BURNHAM Carolyn Jo 169
BURNS Chris (--) 203 James 154 203 Jane
Louise 154 202 Janet 154 202 Jennie 203
Joan Kay (Rittgers) 154 202 203 Judy
154 203 Larry 154 202 203 Michael 154
Tanya Rene (Rittgers) 154

COLE Christi Lynn 227 Corinne Renee 227
Janet Carol (Rittgers) 227 Laurin Jay 227
Rhonda Suzanne 227 Ryan Samuel 227
COLTON Alice E. 86 149
COMARYS Visitation 170
COMER Catharine 3 9 14 16-18 21 22 262
264 Catharine (--) 262 264 Christopher
265 266 Johans Adam 264-266 John 3
262 265 Mary Ann (Kibler) 3 262
Michael 262 264 266
CONARD Rita Gene 242
CONRAD David C. 26 75 76 Effie A. 26
Emanuel J. 26 75 Emma 26 75 Ethel
Grace (Haines) 139 190 Florence (Hart)
27 George 76 Goldie I. 75 Jesse 26 76
Julia A. (Kerns) 75 Lafayette Fountaine
26 76 139 Laura Ellen (Sullenbarger) 76
139 LaVernon H. 77 Lucinda (Rittgers)
26 75 76 Margaret (Phillipps) 75 Martha
(Zeek) 76 Mary E. 26 Mimi 75 Opal 77
Ray Benson 76 139 190 Russell Dewey
77 Ruth76 Sylvia B. 75 Virginia Lois 140
190 William 26
COOK Amanda A. 50 Daniel 50 Donna
Mae 218 John 50 Malinda 50 Samuel 50
COOKSEY Annette Ann 154 202 Earl
Jones 93 153 Jane Garnet (Maddox) 153
201 Larry Lee 93 153 201 202 Natalie
Ann 154 201 Neal Alan 154 Ruth Iora
(Rittgers) 93 153 Sandra (Weber) 153
202 Suzette Lynn 154
COOPER JoAnn 151 199
COPPEDGE Marla Sue (Mendenhall) 189
Todd G. 189
CORDS Carolyn Ann 208 244
CORNELIUS Joan Suzanne (Stroup) 200
Sid 200
COTTER Linda 235
COTY Eva Mae 220
COURNOYER Edward Charles 141 192
Helen Leone (Ritchey) 141 192 Janeave
Edna (Wright) 192 238 Jennifer Lee 192
238 Robert Mercier 141 192 238 Robert
Mercier, Jr. 192 238 Rosemary Jean 141 192
238
COURTNEY Gail 174 215 216
COX Abigail Joy 223 Anthony James 223

Brian Kenneth 223 Carolyn Abigail 180
223 248 Carolyn Sue (Spadafora) 223
Herman 180 223 Herman "Kenneth" 180
223 John Randall 223 Linda Sue (Frisby)
223 Marilyn Louise 180 223 Nell 213
Randall William 180, 223 Randi Sue 223
Roger William 223 Rowena Christine 192
Samuel Broderick 223 Vivian Abigail
(Rorabaugh) 180 223
CRAWFORD Ellen Doreen 196
CRISAN Susan 240
CROOKSHANK Helen "Marie" (Wilson)
210 Sidney 210
CROSS Adam David 209 Alice Juanita
(Rittgers) 245 Andrea Marie 209 Angela
Elizabeth 209 Connie Beth (Wilson)209
Edwin Carl "Ed"209 Emily 245 Garron
244 Laura 245 Mike 245
CROUSE Carolyn Ruth 227 250 Carroll
Raymond 227 250 Edith LaVonne
(Purviance) 227 250 Kenneth Ray 227
CURRAN Jake Dalton 201 James 201
Jenna Kay 201 Rebecca Kay (Iverson)
201
CURRY Chad William 201
DAHN Cytella 90
DANCER Barbara (Markwith)234 254
Buddy188 234 254 Diane 234 254 Dina
234 Duane 234 Everett 188 234 Helen
(Livingston) 188 234 Justin 254
DANIELS Gladys Cecelia 169
DANKE Karen Lee 252
DARLING Arthur 144 Evelyn (Rittgers) 83
144 Flora 144 Frank 83 144 Karen 144
Kathy 144 Leslie 144 Roy 83 144 Ruth (-
-) 144 Thelma (--) 144
DAUBENMIRE Anna Mary (Ellinger) 67
Anna S. 71 Barbara 23 Caroline 23 69
135 Catherine 23 Christina 23 68 Cora
Helena 71 Dora Carolina 72 Elizabeth 23
66 132-134 Eva 23 Eve 23 George 23 71
Homer E. 71 Jacob A. 23 70 Jacob W.
68 Johann Eduard 72 Levi A. 71 Loda
M. 71 Magdalene 68 Maria Magdalena 23
Miene Katharine 71 Peter 22 66-71 Peter
B. 23 67 Renetta 72 Rosana 23 66 Sarah
Elizabeth 23 68 134, 135 Sophia

GOODPASTOR Betty Lucille (Rittgers) 170 Leslie 170

GORACZKOWSKI Virginia Lee (__) 204

GRAHAM Angel 208 Betty Mae 192

GRAVES Barbara Jean (Kuefner) 226 249 Brian Kent 226 249 Charlotte 249 Emily 249 Gary 226 249 Hannah 249 Jane (--) 249 Kathy (--) 249 Sarah 249William 226 249

GREGERSEN Sharon 216

GRIDER Anna Jane 148 Anna Lee (Rittgers) 148 James 148 Joan (Dwight) 148 Ronald Jay 148 Steven James 148

GRIFFIN Betha 173 Lyn Ann 213 Marie (Wilson) 173 213 Martin 173 213 Mary 173 Melissa Marie 213 Nell (Cox) 213 Warren 173 Wayne Martin 213 William Marion, Rev. 173 213

GRILLO Gina 150

GRINER Florence 186 Flossie A. (Unkle) 186 Fredrick J. 186 William 186

GROSSMAN Ida 129 185 186

GROVE Anna (Rittgers)28 78 Barbara Joann (--) 91 Bernadine Marie (Franklin) 191 Bertha Viola78 Betty Mae (Graham) 192 Deborah Lynn (Uhl) 192 Donna Kay (Miller) 191Effie Jane 28 Ethel Alberta (Murphy) 190-192 Francis 28 George Albert 141 191 George Thomas 191 Harry Willard 141 191 James Harry 192 Jeffery Lynn 192 Kenny 192 Lavina "Vine" (Hampton) 78 Pamela 191 Purl Fredrick 141, 191 Rexie Freddonia 78 Roger William 192 Rose Mary 191 Rowena Christine (Cox) 192 Ruth Marie 141 190 237 Samuel 27 78 Stella Mae 141 191 237 Theresa 191 Timothy Willard 191 Willard Elsworth 78 141 190 191William 28

GROVES Ada (--) 28 Edward Theodore 28 Elizabeth 28 Ethel Alberta (Murphy) 141 George 28 78 141 James 28 Joseph Ellsworth 28 Lavina "Vine" (Hampton) 141 Mary 28 Nellie 91 151 Rosetta 28 78 141

GRUBB Gladys 147 196

GUISER Abraham 25 Ann 25 George 25 Joseph 25 Julia A. (Rittgers) 25 Louisa 25

GUSTAFSON Bryce 202 Rhonda Renee (Rittgers) 202 Steve 202

GUTIERREZ Fredrick H. 171 Fredrick Jerald 171 Patricia Ann 171 Verta Faye (Rittgers) 171

GUY Bertha (Rittgers) 85 George 85

HAINES Ethel Grace 139 190 Gregory Keith 152 Valerie Lynn (Naeve) 152

HALL Beatrice Juanita (Hufford) 163 Charles 224 Clayton Lee 241 Clifton 163 Daniel Wayne 241 Glenna Janice (Day) 253 Marsha Ann (Cline) 241 Matthew Clayton 241 Sharon Kay (Rittgers) 224 Terry 253 Wayne Andrew 241 Zachary Lee 253

HALLMEYER Dorothy 144 Ester 144 Joe 144 Kenneth 144 Maude (Pattee) 144

HAMILTON Catherine 31 Jacob 31 Joseph H. 30 Margaret (Rittgers) 30 Reuben 31

HAMPTON Lavina "Vine" 78 141

HANSEN Leuthon 34 Linda Marie 249 Mabel (Rittgers) 34 Martharine 184

HANSON Blanche Alta (Rittgers) 39 Elwyn 39 Judy 210

HARDIE Florence (--) 124 Henry 124 181 Mary Eve (Rittgers) 124 181 Philip Rittgers 124 Ruth Ellen 124 181 225

HARDY Marian 179 222

HARPER Bertha Viola (Grove) 78 Fred 78

HARRINGTON Elizabeth "Beth" 165

HARRIS Bonnie Rae (Rittgers) 205 Stephanie Arlene 210 Terrance Gene 205

HART Archie R. 77 Betty 138 189 235 Betty Eileen (Rogers) 188 234 Charlene 192 Ernest R. 77 Florence 27 Ida (Hufford) 77 Jerlyne Kay 188 234 Marjorie 192 238 Minnie (Rittgers) 138 188 189 Sandre Lee 188 234 Thomas L. 77 Violet Marcella 138 189 235 Willard 138 188 189 Willis Paul 138 188 234 Wilma Wavelene 138 189 235 236

HARTER Blanche 187

HARTLEY Lucy Reyburn 92 152 153

HARTMAN Erich Robert 240 Karen (Peacock) 240 Karl 240

HARVEY A. M., Lt. 96 Hoover Revere 96

Vicky Lynn 203 241

NAEVE Abigail LaVonne 199 Brennon Royce 199 Brent Loren 152, 199 Camille 152 Cindi (--) 200 Connor 200 Denise Renee (Staples) 199 Diane (Hoffman) 152 200 Elaine (LeBrun) (Tow) 152 Hattie Lovina (Rittgers) 92 151 152 Janelle Lynne 202 Joshua Benjamin199 Keith Lowell 92 152 200 Kyndra Suzanne1 52 200 LaVonne Adela (Kreutzkampf) 151 199 Marilynne Joyce (Sykes) 152 200 Nancye (Rempert) 199 Nashay Lynn 199 Nichole Marie 152 Otto John 92 151 152 Philip Frederick 92 152 200 Richard Allen 92 151 199 Thad Lowell 152 199 Todd Allen 152 200 Valerie Lynn 152

NEARON Christopher David 253 David 253 Glenna Janice (Day) 253 Joy Ann 253

NELSON Arlene 218 Dalton 202 Dillon 202 Jane Louise (Burns) 202 Larry 202

NIBLING Adam 22 Rosanna (Strohl) 22

NICHOLSON Jessie 171

NIHISER Susan 22

NOONAN Mary Elizabeth 214 245

NOSLER Alberta Evalene 36 87 Alice E. (Colton) 86 149Alice N. (--) 36Alva Asbury 35 86 149Alva Asbury, Jr. 87 Arthur Morrison 87 149Betty 149Birdie (--) 35 Elwyn 88 Esther May (Rittgers) 86 87 Eugene Elmer 36 87 Harry W. 87 Israel Rittgers 36 Lula M. (Moulton) 35 Mary 36 Minnie Etta 36 Nina C. (--) 87 Oscar Laurance 35 Osha (--) 87 Samuel Manford 35 Sarah A. 35 Thelma (--) 149 William Henry Harrison 34 86 87

NOTTINGHAM Diane Marie 152

NOWBRAY Iola 102

NYGREN Karen 213

O'DEA Sheila Ann 212

O'DELL Sharon Abbott 232

OBERKFELL Bonnie Rae (Rittgers) 205 Elizabeth Rae 205 Joseph Ray 205 Kenneth Ray 205 Tami Rae 205

OLAYA James Joham 237

OLSEN Burton 164 Carol 164 David 164 Elizabeth A. (Rittgers) 164 Jean 164

OLSON Dorothy Karyl 243 Tammy Pearl (Wilson) 167 Thomas 167

OREN Marjorie Low 235

ORR Pamela Lynne (Johnson) 200 Thomas 200 Thomas Anthony 200

OSTMEYER Mary Theresa 195

OVERTON Deborah Kay 215 245 Delbert 215 245 Lois Elinor (Rittgers) 215 245 Rebecca Lynn 215 245

OWEN Hazel 94

PACHACE Peggy (Arnett) 193

PACHECO Jesus E. 193

PATTEE Amy193 Betsy (--) 193 Della (--) 144 Douglas 194 Erma 144 194 Erma F. 83 143 144 Esther (Rittgers) 83 143 144 Francis 144 Freida (--) 144 193 Harold 144 193 Janet (--) 144 Jessie (--) 194 Mabel 83 Mary (Koplin) 144 194 Maude 83 144 Melvin 144 Myra A. 83 143 Neil 194 Patrick 83 144 Perry B. 83 143 193 Peter F. 83 144 194 Ruth 144 Scott 193

PATTERSON Hester 9 28-32 34 36 Louise 98

PAYNE Allen 204 Kristan (Rittgers) 204

PEACOCK Abraham Leo, Dr. 126 181 Agnes Elizabeth (Virden) 142 193 Anna Lou 142 193 239 240 Charlotte Alice 126 181 225 Elizabeth Lee (Ward) 193 240 Grace (Rittgers) 126 181 Jackson 142 John William 142, 193 Karen 193 240 Kathy 193 Robert Alva 143 193 240 Peacock, JR. Robert Alva 193

PEARSON Elaine 232

PEASE Agnes 85 Grover 84 Mary Etta 85 Orrin G. 85

PEITZMAN Baby Boy 224 Carol Elizabeth (Holmquist) 224 248 Carol Joan (Johnson) 248 Daisy Marie (Wilson) 212

Vander LINDEN _____ 110 Edna Mae
(Rittgers) 110
VARNEY Marcia 227
VAUGHAN Deborah Ann (Roberts) 205
Dylan Thomas 205 Jennifer 247 Milton
205
VAUGHN Jerry 145 JoAnn 145 Joe 145
Lois (Koplin) 145
VIRDEN Agnes Elizabeth 81 142 193
Andrew Jackson, "Jack" 80 142 Nellie
Avis 81 142 192 193 Sarah Isabel
(Rittgers) 81 142
VISLISEL Susan Ellen 219
VOPAT Patricia Ann 205
VOUGHT Mary Jane 106 163
WAGNER Carol 208 244 Daniel F. 213
Mary Ann 73 137 139 Roberta (Wells)
213
WAGONER Elizabeth (Rittgers) 46 Jacob
46 Peter 45
Wagoner, SR. Katherine (Rittgers) 17
Peter 17
WAITMAN Arthur 210 Mary Lou
(Dawson) 210
WALKER Abigail Violet (Rittgers) 170
Bernard Eugene 170 Dorothy (Finney)
170 Lois (Meiers) 170 Mabel (Miller) 170
Robert Lee 170 William Wilson 170
William Wilson, Jr. 170
WALLS Amy Jo 231 Penny Ann 231 251
Robert Eugene 231 251 Ruby Jeannine
(Walters) 231 251 Todd David 231
WALTERS Beatrice J. (Porter) 187 231
Carl "David" 241 Craig David 241 Jenna
Lynn 241 Lewis Kenneth 187 231 Ruby
Jeanine 187 Ruby Jeannine 231 251 Vera
Belle 187 231 251 Vicky Lynn (Myrick)
241
WALTON Brianna 200 Kyndra Suzanne
(Naeve) 200 Randy 200
WARD Elizabeth Lee 193 240
WARE Kathryn 139 189
WARREN Gwen 233 Janelle 227
WASSON Erma Othello (Butts) 187 231
Harold 187 231 Janice 187, 231, 251
WATTS Ida 132
WAUGH Debra 195

WEBER Andrea Paige 228 Christopher
Greg 228 Donald 228 Marcia Mae
(Findley) 228 Sandra 153 202
WEBSTER Dorothy Marguerite (Rittgers)
176 217 Helen "Maurine" 176 217
Kenneth 175 217 Kenneth Robert "Ken"
176 217 Laura Marguerite 176 217
Mildred Louise "Millie" 176 Patti (Merrill)
217 Phyllis 176 217 Timothy Clayton 217
WEFELMEYER Paul 129 Virginia
Elizabeth (Findley) 129
WEIL Bryan Edward 197 Jeff 197 Lynette
Jean (Rittgers) 197 Megan Elizabeth 197
WEISER David Paul 227 250 Dennis Paul
227 250 Janae Marie 250 Jay Dennis 250
Joel Craig 250 Joy Lynn 227 250 Kathryn
(Stanley) 250 Kevin Paul 250 Nadine
(Purviance) 227 250 Sheryl Lynn (Siglon)
250 Stanley Paul 227 250
WEISS Alva H. 108 Carl R. 108 George 107
Pauline 108 Sarah Katherina (Amspaugh)
108 Sharon Leigh 223
WELLS Daisy (Wilson) 173 213 Roberta
173 213 Roscoe Ward 173 213
WELLWOOD_____ 107 Barbarey Ellen
(Amspaugh) 107 Clarence 107
WENGER Amy Jo 235 Denise Ann 189 236
Glenn Eugene 189 235 236 Jennifer Elaine
235 Joyce Elaine (Addington) 235 Karen
Sue 189 235 Rachel Nicole 235 Randy
Gene 189 235 Robert Eugene 235 Roberta
LaVonne (--) 235 Wilma Wavelene (Hart)
189 235 236
WERRIES Shirley 195
WEST Cindi Ann 248
WHELCHEL Cyrus Clinton 83 Etta
(Rittgers) 83 LaVera 83
WHERRY Kevin Glen 238 Patrick 238
Susan (Finney) 238 Tim 238
WHIPPS Mary F. 31, 82
WHITEHEAD Carolyn Sue 239 255
WICAL _____ 253 Cherrie Michelle 253
Eric 253 Linda Kay (Stiver) 253
WICK Martha 196
WICKS Marcia Mae (Findley) 228 Richard
228
WILBUR Marvel Margaret (Rittgers) 41

Roy 41

WILCOX Amy Marie 235 Betty (Hart) 189
235 Brett Steven 235 Connie 189 235
Cynthia 246 Franklin 189 235 Kathryn
211 244 Keith Andrew 235 Linda
(Cotter) 235 Steven 189 235

Wilcox-RITTGERS Nicholas Forest 246
Terry Preston 216 246

WILEY Inez E. 159

WILLIAMS Anne (Kinsey) 229 Floyd 229
Howard L. 153 Jane (Koepsel) 168 211
John Alfred 229 Katherine Lynn 229
Kristy Anne 229 Lydia 47 104 Mary Ann
(Rittgers) 153 Mary Louise 237 255
Natalie 241 Phebe 43 96 97 99 101
Thomas David 229 Travis John 153

WILMORE Arletta (Rittgers) 147 196
Arletta Kaye 147 196 Benjamin Carter
147 DeWitte Hudson 147 Robert 147
196 Robert Dale 147

WILSON_____ 112 Agnus 109 164
Alexander "Alec" 111 165 Allie (Reed)
172 212 213 Amy Marie 209 Andrew
William 209 Bethia 114 Betty Arlene
(Plumb) 212 Carl C. 239 Carroll Robert
172 Charles Woodrow 112 166 209
Chelsea Jordan 257 Clarence Arthur 167
209 Connie Beth 167 209 Cora Beth 112
167 209 Cora Beth (Wilson) 167 209
Cora Nina (Rittgers) 166 167 Cynthia
Kim 167 Daisy 114 172 213 Daisy Marie
172 212 Daisy Marie (Rittgers) 114 172
173 Dale Everett 167 210 Daniel Everett
210 Darrell Rittgers 212 David Gilbert
212 Dennis Eugene 213 Dennis Harry 212
Diana 212 Dorothy "Kathryn" (Drake)
167 209 Dorothy Jane 112 Douglas Allen
212 Edith (Shiffer) 172 213 Edna Minnie
112 Elizabeth (Jennings) 114 Eugene
Clark 172 213 Flora May (Rittgers) 111
165 Frieda Madeleine 172 212 Gilbert
Rittgers 172 212 Glen Reed 172 212
Greg Scott 210 Hazel Pearl 112 166 208
209 Helen "Marie" 167 209 Helen Juanita
(Dietz) 167 209 210 Herbert Edward 172
213 James 212 James Clifford (Nygren)
213 Jane B. (Fryer) 109 111 112 114 117

Jane Kathryn 167 209 Janet Elaine 213
Jeffrey Allen 213 John 51 Joshua Adam
210 Juanita Ann 210 Karen (Nygren) 213
Karen Lea (Rogers) 209 Kenneth Dale
212 Larry 234 Laurel Philip 172 Lester
114 Linda Louise 212 Lloyd LeRoy 167
Lloyd Rittgers 114, 172, 212, 213 Lois
Esther 164 Lowell Allen 172, 213 Luke
Matthew Henry 210 Margaret "Maggie"
117 176-178 Marie 114 173 213 Marjorie
(Arnett) 239 Mary (Lamping) 210 Mary
Lou (Scott) 213 Mary Louise 213 Mary
M. (Amspaugh) 51 Matthew John 210
Melissa Ann 210 MiAnn Sue 213 Mildred
Elizabeth 112 Mina May 111 165 208
Patricia Annette 213 Paul James 114 172
213 Rebecca 114 173 Robert A. 114 172
173 Roger Alan 213 Ronald Roy 239
Ruby Virginia (--) 213 Sharon Elaine 167
210 Shelia (Rittgers) 234 Steve 257 Steve
Allen 213 Steven Scott 213 Stuart Craig
257 Susan Kay 213 Sylvia Ann (Lowe)
210 Tammy Pearl 167 Teri Ranea
(Boolman) 257 Thomas 109 111 112 114
115 117 Virginia 172) Wanda Elaine
(Snyder 212 Wayde Matthew 167 210
Wayne William 167 209 William George
112 167 209 210 William James "Will" 112
166 167

WINELAND Charlotte Alice (Peacock) 182
225 Delores Ella 182 225 Eugene Charles
181 225 Lorene Alice 182 225 248

WINGATE Pam 239

WISE Elsie Arlene 181 224 Nina 251 Norm
Jean 221 247

WOLF Addie E. 102 Anna (Rittgers) 45 101-
103 Anna I. 103 Carol A. 103 Charles A.
102 162 Charles D. 103 Chloe (--) 102
162 Clara E. 102 Clarence H. 103 Dortha
May 163 Elizabeth (Fickle) 103 Homer
102 Isaac 45 102 162 Laura 102 Levi C.
102 Louis 102 Mary 45 101 161 162
Mary J. 102 Roy 103 Sarah (--) 163
William 45 101-103

WOLFE Anna "Jane" (Rittgers) 97 Cora B.
97 Myrtle 97 Noah 96 Oscar D. 97 Rosa
97

www.ingramcontent.com/pod-product-compliance
Lightning Source LLC
Chambersburg PA
CBHW061716270326
41928CB00011B/2008